CHANGING TIMES
CHANGING MINDS

CHANGING TIMES CHANGING MINDS

100 Years of Psychiatry

at the

University of Maryland School of Medicine

by Pat McNees

with a foreword by Anthony F. Lehman

DEPARTMENT OF PSYCHIATRY
UNIVERSITY OF MARYLAND
SCHOOL OF MEDICINE

Changing Times, Changing Minds:
100 Years of Psychiatry at the University of Maryland School of Medicine

by Pat McNees
with a foreword by Anthony F. Lehman

Published in the United States by
The Department of Psychiatry
University of Maryland School of Medicine
110 Paca Street, 4th Floor
Baltimore, MD 21201
(410) 328-0932

ISBN: 978-0-9828431-0-9 (softcover)
 978-0-9828431-1-6 (hardcover)

Library of Congress Control Number: 2010931962

Design and composition: www.dmargulis.com

First printing

MANUFACTURED IN THE REPUBLIC OF KOREA

Contents

Foreword

Not long after becoming the fifth chair of the department of psychiatry, I sat down with a group of our residents to discuss a patient. In passing I mentioned an illustrious faculty member who had recently died. I had been on the faculty for fifteen years and assumed these young trainees would all know about him, but I got blank stares. This stunned me and, looking at the walls as I walked back to my office, I realized they bore few reminders of our past. The department had recently undergone a series of relocations, and we were neglecting to maintain a sense of our history. This bothered me. As psychiatrists we pride ourselves on taking careful histories of patients as the key to understanding them and their experiences. We know that helping people understand where they have been helps them figure out where they want to go. We were losing our own narrative and, I thought, were at risk of losing our direction.

Shortly after that, I had several wonderful conversations with Gerry Klee, a former member of the faculty, who urged me to undertake a project to excavate our history. From the beginning I knew that we needed a narrative, not simply a catalogue with photos and listings of who was here when. This eventually led me to our gifted author, Pat McNees, who also values personal narrative. Her preface captures the process that ensued: we opened up a fascinating stream of rich stories, capturing the century-long evolution of psychiatry at the University of Maryland School of Medicine and more broadly of psychiatry in Maryland and the nation.

We know that history offers essential perspectives, providing context for the present and yielding critical lessons for the future. I hope this history helps future generations of our department, instilling pride in who we are and where we have been and excitement about where we are going.

To all those who shared their memories, stories, and pictures for this history project we are deeply grateful. I especially want to thank our author, Pat McNees, and my invaluable staff, especially Vee Porter-Brown and Tony Bibbo, without whom this project would not have been possible.

—Anthony F. Lehman, MD, MSPH
Professor and Chairman, Department of Psychiatry
University of Maryland School of Medicine

Preface
and Acknowledgments

The Department of Psychiatry at the University of Maryland School of Medicine was founded in 1950, after a newspaper exposé brought to public attention the appalling conditions in many of Maryland's state mental hospitals. Jacob Finesinger, a noted psychiatrist and educator from Harvard, was recruited to oversee construction of the Psychiatric Institute, a state-of-the-art psychiatric hospital and clinic that would serve the public sector (especially Baltimore's poor), would support research into mental illness, and would serve as a training facility for psychiatrists and other mental health care workers.

Tony Lehman, the department's current chair, commissioned this history to celebrate the sixtieth anniversary of the department's official founding. I began by mailing several hundred letters inviting memories of and stories about the department, and I heard right away from Virginia Truitt Sherr (medical school class of 1956). Ginny's uncle, Ralph P.

Truitt, before he died, bequeathed her his unpublished manuscript about his fifty years in psychiatry—starting in 1910, at the University of Maryland—and she offered it for our use. Truitt had become a psychiatrist in 1910 and, toward the end of his career, had been on the search committee that selected Jake Finesinger as the first official department chair. Truitt was one of several psychiatrists who had taught psychiatry at the medical school before there was an official department. With selections from his manuscript and memories from alumni from the 1940s, the scope of the project grew. The sixty-year history of the department became a hundred-year history of psychiatry at the university. In a sense it became a history of psychiatry in America, wrapped around the story of a sizable department that consistently focused, in interesting ways, on serving people who cannot afford to pay for their own mental health care.

In brief, what had started as a decentralized apprenticeship model of training in community-based clinics evolved into a formal system of training as part of mainstream American medical education. Psychiatric training, which had initially been community-based (especially in child psychiatry), moved to academic medical centers—except for psychoanalytical training, which maintained an arm's-length relationship with, and a steady distrust of, the academy. There was a shift from psychodynamic and psychoanalytic preeminence in the 1950s and 1960s to evidence-based medicine in the 1980s; from almost exclusively psychotherapeutic interventions to a major emphasis on psychopharmacology combined with psychosocial approaches; from psychotherapy provided chiefly by psychiatrists to a multidisciplinary approach, including psychosocial and vocational rehabilitation, provided by various kinds of health care workers; from a hospital-based system, emphasizing maintenance and containment of individuals with chronic and persistent mental illness, to a patient-centered model for mental health, with an emphasis on hope and recovery. Patients for whom even professionals early in the twentieth century had used such terms as *idiot, feeble-minded, lunatic,* and *insane,* had by the end of the century become first *patients*, then *clients*, and finally *consumers* of mental health care—individuals who were dealing with a mental illness or disorder, but were not defined by it.

Psychiatry, which in the early years was practiced mostly by men of European descent (if not directly from Europe), has become more diverse: 64 percent of the department's seventy-seven residents and fellows in 2009 were women, 23 percent were African American, 13 percent were of Asian or Pacific Island descent, and 5 percent were Hispanic. The department currently offers one of the largest psychiatry programs in the country—with, at any given time, about eighty psychiatric trainees, not all of them full time at the University of Maryland. The department currently has a full-time, steady-state faculty of about one hundred, with another hundred volunteer faculty. Maryland's chief local rival is Johns Hopkins, across town. Hopkins has a much smaller program, tending toward people more interested in academic psychiatry. Most of the people who come to Maryland come to train to become practitioners.

What I thought would be a loosely organized and lightly edited oral history morphed into something more like an analytic narrative, and even then it got a lot longer than we expected, because there were so many interesting facets to this department's story. I planned at first to interview a couple dozen past and present members of the department, transcribe the interviews, and weave them into a loose narrative about what had gone on and how psychiatry had changed. Inevitably it became more than that, including to some extent how society and the economy had changed. And what we'd envisioned as a slim volume grew fatter and fatter. Narrative lies at the heart of psychiatry—and this particular department is full of good storytellers. Each interview led to five more ("You must speak with X") so in no time I had interviewed nearly a hundred people—some in person and some by phone—and got a lot more material through correspondence and e-mail. (E-mail also facilitated the digital transmission of most of the photographs.)

Many of the people I interviewed mentioned the newspaper series, "Maryland's Shame," which ran in the *Baltimore Sun* in 1949 and was instrumental in getting the state to kick in enough money to launch the department and build the Psychiatric Institute, the department's first real home. Almost no one remembered what the series actually reported, except that the state hospitals were overcrowded and understaffed, with patients warehoused rather than treated. It took me a while to get my hands on a copy of the series. You may be surprised to read what the *Sun* reporter felt the state hospitals should be doing for the indigent patients who spent whole lifetimes in those state hospitals.

Part of what made the department an exciting place to work in its official first thirty years, when psychiatry itself was still in its infancy and early adolescence, was the many new approaches to mental health care the department was exploring. Maryland delivered solid psychiatric training and development, sending practitioners into the community with sophisticated therapeutic skills. The department developed strength in research, yet never lost its focus on providing solid training in psychiatry and services to the community.

My assignment from Tony Lehman was to write something people would actually read, not an academic treatise. In that spirit, and to reduce verbiage, I took shortcuts. Most of the people mentioned have an MD, and relatively few a PhD, so on first reference it's Jacob Finesinger, not Jacob Finesinger, MD, and on second reference Finesinger (not "Jake," which everyone called him at the time). Most abbreviations are stripped of periods (MD, not M.D.) and most often-capitalized words (such as Department, Dean, Chair) are lowercase. The "department" is the Department of Psychiatry; "the medical school," the University of Maryland School of Medicine; and Maryland, when not the state, is the University of Maryland. Reprivatized in 1984, University Hospital became the University of Maryland Medical Center, but is still often referred to here as University Hospital. Few and brief citations appear in the notes at the end of the book, with just enough information to guide you to the full citation in the bibliography.

My task was to provide as coherent, accurate, and interesting a narrative as possible. I based that narrative largely on the stories, impressions, insights, and language shared so generously by the people I interviewed. I hope this comes close to conveying what actually happened and how people experienced change, over the years. Luckily, this is a field that values narrative, there were plenty of good storytellers and intelligent observers, quite a few interesting characters, and many interesting and important advances—and side trips—in mental health care and research to write about. Most of the stories you'll read here I heard in interviews conducted between 2007 and 2010, supplemented by many letters and e-mail messages. (The digital age was especially helpful for sharing old photographs and getting people to identify who was in them.)

I don't provide citations for who told me what, or when, mostly because I was asked to produce not a scholarly document but a collective piece of storytelling, and partly because I ran out of time. I speak in present tense for quotations from those interviews, writing "Brody says," not "Brody said," in quoting from an interview with Gene Brody in 2007, even though he died while the manuscript was being edited. This history was based heavily on interviews and correspondence with people who have worked in the Department of Psychiatry of the University of Maryland School of Medicine, the Psychiatric Institute (later known as the Institute for Psychiatry and Human Behavior), and various mental health care facilities associated with the department.

Acknowledgments

This was a highly collaborative project kicked off by Gerry Klee, whose dogged insistence that Jake Finesinger not be forgotten led us all on this adventurous quest to discover and relate the department's full history. Virginia Truitt Sherr graciously shared the memoirs her uncle, Ralph P. Truitt, bequeathed her, which gave us a look at psychiatry at the university from 1910 to 1949, the year Jake Finesinger came to Baltimore. Richard J. Behles, the historical librarian and preservation officer in the university's Health Sciences & Human Services Library, provided documents from the early years, including letters Riva Novey had written about the mental health faculty in the 1940s. He also helped track down and scan some documents and photographs we wouldn't otherwise have had access to. But of the many people who helped us gather photographs in the race toward production, surely Vertell "Vee" Porter-Brown, Tony Lehman's assistant, was most effective. Without saying much, she gets people to produce!

Gerry Klee provided many documents and photos from the 1950s and shared tapes of his interviews with Bill Fitzpatrick, Bob Grenell, and Jerome Styrt, who died before I became involved in the history project. Instead of interviewing a couple dozen people, I ended up interviewing eighty or so, some of them several times, and one of them (Jon Book) for eleven hours. I thank here, in alphabetical order, the many people who helped make this history come to life by speaking to me and my digital recorder, often following up with additional e-mails: Barbara Baumgardner, Alan Bellack (through a presentation on cognitive remediation in schizophrenia), Joseph Bierman, Jon Book, Gene Brody, Jessica Brown, Frank Calia (not a member of the department, but a great observer and storyteller), Will Carpenter Jr., Louis Guy Chelton, Elliot S. Cohen, Bob Derbyshire (who helped recreate the sixties), Lisa Dixon, Bernadine Faw (Arnold), Marianne Felice, Lois Flaherty, Stephen Fleishman, Stanford B. Friedman, George Gallahorn, Brian Grady, Nelson Goldberg (a plastic surgeon but an interesting rabble-rouser), Samuel T. Goldberg, Howard Goldman, Herb Gross, Henry Harbin, Eileen Hastings, Elizabeth Robin Hatcher, John P. Haws, Alice Heisler, Brian Hepburn, Marcela Horvitz-Lennon, Jerry Hunt, Jerald "Jerry" Kay, Stuart Keill, Ted Knowles, Tom Krajewski, Tony Lehman, Steve Levy, Joseph Liberto, Robert Ludicke, James Lynch, Bishop Denis Madden, Dave Mallott, Tom Milroy, Thurman Mott, Arthur Z. Mutter, Carole Norris-Shortle, Gary Nyman, Gerald Perman, Jay Phillips, Marguerite Pinard, Michael Plaut, David Pruitt, Jill RachBeisel, Jonas Rappeport, Victor Reus, Paul Ruskin, Richard Sarles, Nate Schnaper, Robert "Robbie" Schwarcz, Virginia Truitt Sherr, Kenneth Stern (the patient on the psychosomatic ward, who went on to become a psychiatrist), John Talbott, Carol Tamminga, Irving Taylor, Ronald Taylor, Stuart Tiegel, Jerome Tilles, Alma Troccoli, Jonathan Tuerk (Isadore's son), Ulku Ulgur, Barbara Wahl, Stanley Weinstein,

Daniel Weintraub, Eric Weintraub, Walter Weintraub (a central character in many stories), Chris Welsh, Aron Wolf, and Léon Wurmser.

The following people provided stories, information, and observations through letters and e-mails: David Barrett, Gary Bawtinhimer, James C. Bozzuto, Roderick Charles, Joseph Robert Cowen, Mark Ehrenreich, James G. Gamble, David Geddes, Angela Guarda, Peter Hartman, Dave Helsel, John Hensala, Leonard Hertzberg, C. William Hicks III, Manfred K. Joares, Violet Samorodin Kron, Dennis Kutzer, Sally Kutzer, Arthur Clifton "Clif" Lamb, Leandra Prosen Lamberton, Margo Leahy, Lila Nappi, Marcio V. Pinheiro, Warren Poland (who walked me through the history of psychoanalysis), Lewis Richmond, Gavin Rose, David Rosen, Bruce Rounsaville, Andrew Rudo, Jonathan Scher, Bernard Shochet, Basri Sila, Jeff Snow, Joseph Stapen, Donald Thompson, Arthur Wolpert, Y. Pritham Raj, and Theodore Zanker. I apologize for any names I've failed to list, in the haste of getting this book to press.

Many people in the department, now or earlier, read drafts, checked facts or spelling, and responded to my frequent queries. I am especially grateful to Gene Brody, Bob Derbyshire, Will Carpenter Jr., Bernadine Faw, Lois Flaherty, Henry Harbin, Tony Lehman, Bishop Denis Madden, Carole Norris-Shortle, Gary Nyman, Marcio V. Pinheiro, David Pruitt, Jonas Rappeport, Robbie Schwarcz, Ginny Sherr, John Talbott, and Stan Weinstein. Two outside readers, my friends Kristie Miller and Judy Sklar Rasminsky, also read and commented on early drafts of many chapters. Others who helped finding facts and photos include Sue Jaeger at Springfield Hospital Center and Patty Greenberg at the Maryland Psychiatric Research Center.

Dick Margulis, who both copyedited the manuscript and designed the book, coped with a manuscript that was still being written as he began trying to produce a book worthy of the department. I am grateful to Dick for elegantly designing and project managing a book under more time pressure than is comfortable and for the good-natured teamwork of Gregory W. Zelchenko (who proofed the pages) and Tia Leschke (who created the index). Lynne Lamberg, who has written about the department and the medical school for *JAMA* and other publications, was asked to write this history but felt that doing so would involve a journalistic conflict of interest for future assignments. I am so glad she recommended me instead (telling me it was an interesting and worthwhile subject—she was right!). Above all, many thanks to Tony Lehman and Tony Bibbo, the department's senior administrator, for remaining apparently calm in the face of a writing schedule that lasted about eight months longer than projected. If they were anxious about getting this book ready in time for the sixtieth anniversary, they concealed it beautifully.

When Tony Lehman sent me on this adventure of discovering the department's story, I asked him what the main story line would probably be. "If there is a consistent theme," he told me, "from the founding of the department and especially in the last thirty years, it is probably this central partnership between academia and the public health system to help the people who are the most disadvantaged and the most severely ill. The research, the training programs, and the clinical programs have all been focused on that. It's both a blessing and a curse because, depending on the era, it hasn't been the sexiest thing you can do. But it is really one of the most enduring and important. And I don't think that even people currently in the university appreciate that story."

—Pat McNees

Bethesda, Maryland
July 2010

Major Events
in the
Department's
History

1872	The Maryland Hospital for the Insane is officially relocated from Baltimore to Spring Grove.
1896	

	Construction begins on second Maryland hospital for the insane: Springfield State Hospital.
1901	School for practical nurses is initiated at Springfield Hospital (one of first training programs).
1910	Hospital for the Negro Insane of Maryland is built in Crownsville (Crownsville State Hospital closed 2004).
1915	Eastern Shore State Hospital opens.
1918	Women are admitted to the medical school on equal terms with men.
	Whit Newell organizes training in child psychiatry for third year medical students (**p. 16**).
1946	Child guidance clinic becomes training center for schools of social work (**p. 17**).
1949	January: *Baltimore Sun* runs Howard M. Norton's series, "Maryland's Shame" (**pp. 22–32**).

	May: Department of psychiatry is established, acknowledging state's responsibility for training programs.
1950	January: Jacob Finesinger, department's first full-time chairman, starts full time (profile, **p. 72**).

	Finesinger hires first residents and instructors (**p. 46**).
1952	Free-standing Psychiatric Institute opens November 17 at 645 West Redwood Street (**p. 51**).
1953	Psychiatric Institute accepts first patients (**p. 49**).
1959	Jacob Finesinger dies; second department chairman is Eugene Brody (profile, **p. 104**).
1960	Neurobiology laboratories organized (**p. 44**).

Chairmen of the department

Jacob E. Finesinger	1949–59
Eugene B. Brody	1959–76
Russell R. Monroe	1976–85
John A. Talbott	1985–99
Anthony Lehman	1999–

Directors, child (and adolescent) psychiatry division

Child Guidance Clinic

H. Whitman Newell	?–1956
Charles Bagley	1956
Marvin Jaffe	1956–57
Joseph S. Bierman, acting	1957–59

Division of Child (and, later, Adolescent) Psychiatry

Frank Rafferty	1961–71
Taghi Modarressi, acting	1971–73
Stan Friedman	1973–83
Lois Flaherty, acting, then director	1983–92
Dick Sarles, acting, then director	1992–99
Hari Ghuman, acting	1999–2000
David Pruitt	2000–

Director, Maryland's Mental Hygiene Administration

Gary Nyman	1976–81
Alp Karahasan	1981–85
Henry T. Harbin	1985–88
Stuart B. Silver	1988–97
Oscar Morgan	1997–2002
Brian Hepburn	2002–

Russell Monroe is hired to study brain's electrical activity as it relates to human behavior.

Open Clinic, launched in early sixties, will close in 1977, as Carter Center gets going (**pp. 243–45**).

1961 Frank Rafferty directs strengthened child psychiatry division (**p. 114**).

1963 President Kennedy signs Community Mental Health Act, framework for department's future focus (**p. 138**).

Division of community psychiatry is established (**p. 140**).

Psychiatry and the Law program begins (see Jonas Rappeport and forensic psychiatry, **p. 147**).

New experiences include sensitivity training sessions, T-groups, experiential weekends at Donaldson Brown (**p. 160 ff.**).

1967 University closes during riots; racial issues lead to demands for community control (**p. 83**).

1968 The world's first shock–trauma center opens in University Hospital; in time, a building will follow (**p. 263**).

1970 Combined Accelerated Program in Psychiatry (CAPP) is launched as psychiatry track for medical students (**pp. 180–192**).

1970 Al Kurland establishes Maryland Psychiatric Research Center at Spring Grove, leads controlled studies on therapeutic effects of LSD.

1971 The Psychiatric Institute is renamed the Institute of Psychiatry and Human Behavior (IPHB; **p. 193**).

Family therapy begins shifting the focus of therapy from the patient to the patient in social context (**p. 228**).

New briefer approaches to therapy flourish, including hypnosis, behavioral modification, cognitive therapy (**p. 223 ff.**).

Alcohol and drug abuse division is moved to the dean's office (**p. 196**).

VA psychiatry department at Loch Raven is launched to treat substance abuse (**p. 501**).

1972 Forces conspire to speed up deinstitutionalization of patients with mental illness.

1973 Behavioral pediatrician Stanford Friedman directs child psychiatry for ten years (**p. 202**).

1974	Medicare reimbursement changes medical economics; department establishes faculty practice plan (**p. 255**).
	National Research Act requires institutional review board for all research.
	Regulation D reduces involuntary admissions; number of psychotic, out-of-control patients increases (**p. 244**).
1975	Flood in the basement of IPHB displaces some faculty, many records.
1976	Russell Monroe becomes department's third chair (profile, **p. 224**).
	Walter P. Carter Center (comprehensive community mental health center) opens.
	Negotiations between department and state begin for the Maryland Plan (**chapter 6**).
1977	Maryland Psychiatric Research Center (MPRC) transferred from state to department.
	Will Carpenter Jr. creates major center for schizophrenia research at MPRC (**chapter 7**).
	Human Dimensions in Medical Education retreats open to students (**p. 236 ff**).
1978	Department of psychiatry put in charge of psychiatric care in Carter Center.

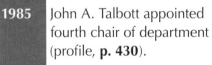

	Under the Maryland Plan (**chapter 6**), Krajewski and Book launch university training at Springfield Hospital.
1980s	DSM-III puts psychiatry back squarely in the culture of medical school (**p. 234**).
	Insurers no longer reimburse for long psychiatric stays and staff-intensive therapy.
1982	The Center for Infant Study launched by Taghi Modarressi (**pp. 208–13**).
1983	Congress introduces prospective payment system and diagnosis-related groups, or DRGs, to control escalating Medicare costs (**p. 448**).
1984–85	University Hospital becomes private not-for-profit hospital complex, the University of Maryland Medical System (UMMS; **pp. 261–62**).
1985	John A. Talbott appointed fourth chair of department (profile, **p. 430**). 
1986	MPRC becomes NIMH-funded Clinical Research Center for study of schizophrenia (**pp. 355–57**).
	Carpenter will become principal investigator for five NIMH centers.
	Division of alcohol and drug abuse services returns to the department (**p. 374**n).

Goldman and Lehman participate in RWJ Foundation nine-city demonstration study (**pp. 380–83**).

1987 MPRC launches Maryland Brain Collection (**pp. 343–44**).

MPRC becomes founding institution for International Congress on Schizophrenia Research (**p. 357**).

Johns Hopkins University–University of Maryland Center for Research on Services for Severe Mental Illness is established (**p. 393**).

1989 Shock Trauma Center begins replacing the IPHB, bit by bit (**pp. 263–70**).

Psychiatric rehabilitation is introduced as part of community psychiatry (**p. 423**).

1990 Center for Mental Health Services Research is established in department (**p. 393**).

1991 Mental Health Services Training Center is established (**p. 397**).

Lehman introduces Program for Assertive Community Treatment (PACT) as demonstration project (**p. 385**).

Geriatric psychiatry becomes first of several official new psychiatric subspecialties (**p. 485–86**).

1992 Child psychiatry division leads the move to renovated building at 701 West Pratt Street.

1993 Baltimore VA Medical Center (VAMC) opens across from UMMS (**p. 503**).

Department initiates a psychiatric service in the new VA facility.

Community psychiatry launches Community Support Program and SSI Outreach (**pp. 436–39**).

HIV psychiatry outpatient clinic, co-located with infectious disease, is first of several new consultation liaison (CL) programs (**p. 486**).

1994 The School of Medicine rolls out overhauled curriculum (**p. 482**).

1995 Center for School Mental Health is awarded first grant (**p. 471**).

Consultation liaison division launches CL fellowship (**p. 487**).

1996 The medical school's first predominantly female class graduates.

1997 The move from the IPHB to 701 West Pratt Street is completed.

Department and Sheppard Pratt merge their psychiatric residency training programs (**p. 493**).

1998 Lehman announces results of AHCPR's Patient Outcomes Research Team (PORT) on evidence-based practices for schizophrenia (**pp. 389–92**).

1999. Swiss firm Novartis Pharma AG awards MPRC $24 million grant to discover new treatments for schizophrenia (**p. 357**).

2000 Anthony F. Lehman, acting chair, becomes fifth chair of department (profile, **p. 518**).

VA awards MIRECC, directed by Alan Bellack, to improve care of veterans with schizophrenia and other serious mental illnesses (**pp. 508–9**).

2001 Evidence-Based Practice Center and Systems Evaluation Center are created.

EBPC, SEC, and Mental Health Services Training Center form Mental Health Services Improvement Collaborative (**p. 398**).

2004 MPRC and Oxford University Press jointly assume ownership and responsibility for publishing *Schizophrenia Bulletin*—the only jointly owned Oxford journal (**p. 364**).

2005 MPRC starts $25 million contractual collaboration with NIDA to study co-occurring disorders (**p. 360**).

Child psychiatry launches Innovations Institute to develop model of care called wraparound services, for families of children with intensive needs (**pp. 479–81**).

2007 Department and VA hire Brian Grady to run telemental health care program (**pp. 504–05**).

2010 MPRC sets up major neuroimaging center with funding from NIMH (**p. 348**).

CHANGING TIMES
CHANGING MINDS

Psychopathic Ward, Fort Riley, 1918. Ralph P. Truitt in front row; third from left.

1

The First Round of Biological Psychiatry

1910–1940

The psychiatry staff at the University of Maryland in the years before there was an official department of psychiatry was part-time and fairly low in the medical school's pecking order. We know something about psychiatric training, practices, and trends in the forty years before 1950 from an unpublished manuscript left with his niece by Ralph Truitt, who graduated from the medical school in 1910 and was acting director of psychiatry before Jacob "Jake" Finesinger became the department's first official chair.

In the University of Maryland medical school in 1909–10, wrote Truitt, only a few hours (no more than twelve sessions) were offered on "nervous and mental diseases," the professor was an "alienist," and he was more proficient in neurology than in "insanity." The psychiatric phase of Truitt's medical training was provided mainly at Bay View Asylum in Baltimore. "This consisted of displaying patients before the students at that institution. Only a few sessions were scheduled and I attended only two or three of these 'side show' trips because of the horribleness of it all. The place reeked with terrible odors, the patients yelling, soiling, untidy, locked in 'strong rooms,' tied up or down with restraint of various kinds, herded together in wards and under the domination of guards who were untrained for the job. This was my introduction to the field of public care of the insane and it was not unusual elsewhere. . . ."

At this time, wrote Truitt, "the organized movement for mental hygiene was getting under way, the Binet–Simon Intelligence Test was just in use, Freudianism was being whispered about, syphilis was found to be the cause of paresis, many new concepts regarding mental disorders were being announced, and Kraepelin was hailed as the great leader of psychiatry."[1] For much of the time Truitt practiced,

Fifty Years of Psychiatry, by Ralph P. Truitt, unpublished manuscript, courtesy of Truitt's niece, Virginia Truitt Sherr, a fourth-generation medical student at the University, starting in 1952. Ralph Truitt was a third-generation graduate of the medical school and the first psychiatrist in the family. You'll find Sherr's story at the end of this chapter. All of the quotations from Truitt are drawn from that manuscript. Truitt was the sole psychiatrist on the committee that selected Finesinger to be the new chair.

The Bay View Asylum began life in 1773 as the Baltimore City and County Alms House. It became known as the Bay View Asylum in 1866, when it housed the poor and the insane. Baltimore mothers disciplining their children would say, "If you don't behave, you're going to end up at Bay View!" It was renamed Baltimore City Hospitals in 1925 (plural because there was one hospital for acute care, one for chronic care, and one for tuberculosis patients). Psychiatric patients were admitted at City Hospitals through the 1930s. Anne Bennett Swingle and Neil A. Grauer tell the story of Bay View in the Johns Hopkins publication Dome, www.hopkinsmedicine.org/dome/0404/centerpiece.cfm. Today the Bayview Medical Center is a 700-bed community teaching hospital with many important research and service programs.

Mental illness caused by late-stage syphilis, known as general paresis of the insane, was at the time a common form of dementia.

custodial care and the asylum were the only alternatives for the mentally ill. But reform was in the air, and Truitt was a reformer. "Lunatic asylums" were being recast as "hospitals"; mentally ill patients ("the insane") were being moved out of poorhouses and jails and into hospitals; patients were being freed from restraints; "strong rooms" (cells with strong doors) were being converted into patient dormitories; Southard was "opening out the shut-in personality"; research was being done in eugenics and in aphasia; and paresis was being treated by the Swift–Ellis method, and later by intraventricular puncture.

Captain Ralph P. Truitt, U.S. Army, at Fort Riley, Kansas (1917–19). After an ear infection he lost hearing in one ear.

For several years, wrote Truitt, most of the leaders in psychiatry came up from laboratories in hospitals in Danvers and Worcester, Massachusetts, and Kankakee, Illinois, where many trained in bacteriology, pathology, and so forth. In the years before psychoanalysis came to dominate psychiatric education, the psychological and bio-

The Swift–Ellis method for treating paresis was to introduce the blood serum of syphilitics treated with Salvarsan (an arsenical drug) into the central nervous system. Introducing Salvarsan alone was not as effective. Penicillin was discovered in 1928 but was not successfully used to treat infections until World War II. For a brief time syphilitic patients were given "malarial treatment."

logical aspects of illness were viewed as more integrated. So, for example, many of the mentally ill patients who were hospitalized were, for a brief period, subjected to tooth extractions and tonsillectomies because Henry A. Cotton, a psychiatrist with whom Truitt worked (not at Maryland), believed "focal infections" were responsible for mental illness and delinquency. Cotton claimed to have produced cures by removing the infected body parts and was very persuasive—until Kopeloff and Cheney (1922) reported no discernible improvement after such surgeries, when they compared results from a study group of 58 and a control group of 64 patients.

After a brief sojourn in a New Jersey facility, Truitt returned to Baltimore in the spring of 1912 as psychiatrist-in-chief of the Bay View Asylum, where he had attended clinics as a medical student. As a general hospital, Bay View

Dossie, Liberated

"'Dossie,' a small Negro woman" about 40 years old, had a record of bad behavior dating back to her admission to Bay View roughly 20 years earlier. No one knew her real name or background, because "she arrived at the city hospital when either no records were kept or they had been lost. … She was minus one ear, which was said to have been bitten off by a fellow patient. For several years she had been secluded in a 'strong room' and in a 'strait jacket.' I believe her diagnosis had been 'chronic mania.'" For years her main line of communication with a limited outside world was through a small peephole in the door to her strong room, through which a tin plate and cup with her food were passed.

Because of her reputation as being destructive and combative, Dossie was to be the last patient relieved of restraints. "My reputation was at stake. It took considerable planning and maneuvering before acting. She had unusual facility in the use of her mouth and teeth and lower extremities." It was decided to free her on a day when a three-piece Italian band came to play for the patients in the yard. "The big question was how to get her in the yard once her jacket was off and she was dressed. Fortunately there was a fire escape with a spiral inside running from the fourth floor to the yard. This was to be her conveyance to the dance." Dossie put up a bit of a fight about having her jacket removed and about dressing, and after she rejected the idea of leaving her room she was carried to the fire escape.

"Down the fire escape Dossie traveled and she landed on her feet in the yard. The little band was playing and at once she began to dance, and dance she did until the musical program was over. By then she was about exhausted. The most pathetic thing about her 'launching' was [that] when she started to dance she attempted to hold up her skirts but was unable to do so because of the weakness and wasting of her arms." That night Dossie returned with the other patients to her ward "and in her room she found a bed. She ate the evening meal with the other patients in the dining hall. The patients tended to avoid her at first. She was never again in trouble. Generally [when I entered] her ward she joined me on rounds. Subsequently with the use of massage and other treatments she regained the use of her arms and held a job in the laundry. When transferred to the state hospital I understand she became the cook in the superintendent's home, where she presided for several years. I always considered her my most grateful patient."

Source: *Fifty Years of Psychiatry*, unpublished manuscript copyright © 1960 Ralph P. Truitt

provided medical and surgical services, a department for tuberculosis, and an almshouse, which housed many chronic patients. As the receiving department for Baltimore City, Bay View averaged about 300 new patients a year. Truitt's department for the insane averaged about 400 patients, most of whom were brought there by the police department. ("Most patients from the better families went directly to the state hospitals.") There was room for more "but the buildings had been condemned and the upper floors were not used." His salary was $1,500 a year.

Truitt was intent on reforming the department, which meant, among other things, removing patients from restraints, as the great reformer Phillipe Pinel had done at Bicêtre, in France. Bay View's lay superintendent, a Confederate veteran from a distinguished Maryland family, whom everyone called "Captain," informed Truitt that he would not be responsible for anything that might happen because of the remaining dangerous patients being removed from strong rooms and restraints. Many of the male and female attendants were leaving or threatening to leave because of the violence that was predicted to ensue when restraints were removed. "Needless to say many weird and even homicidal stories had been woven around some of the 'dangerous' patients," wrote Truitt. "Some of the attendants had been there for thirty or forty years and were rather close to the superintendent. A small raise in salaries, better classification in their jobs, and selecting applicants for brains rather than brawn was of great assistance in making personnel replacements. It was a rather embarrassing situation but a reformer once under way rarely gives up and I felt certain of my calling." Dossie (see sidebar) was the last patient to be liberated from restraints.

Truitt enjoyed his work at Bay View, because this was "a virgin field" and he could make over much of what he had experienced there as a medical student. "After all, I had had less than two years in psychiatry and perhaps

Dr. G. Stanley Hall had been in charge of the department at one time. This was "perhaps the only instance in this country where a psychologist was the head of a department for the insane. Later, as President of Clark University, Dr. Hall brought Freud to this country for his only visit in 1909," wrote Truitt.

"In 1909–10 only a few hours were offered on 'nervous and mental diseases.'"

Ralph P. Truitt in Illinois during his time as medical director for the Illinois Society of Mental Hygiene from 1919 to 1923.

only a smattering of knowledge about psychiatry and institutional administration." He was one of the first of a series of young reformers in Maryland.

Soon after arriving at the City Hospital, Truitt was visited by Adolf Meyer and his associates from Johns Hopkins Hospital and Medical School. Meyer, a psychobiologist, is sometimes referred to as the father of American psychiatry; he certainly left his imprint on psychiatry, particularly in Baltimore. A kindly man, Meyer was a poor lecturer, Truitt wrote, clearly more intelligent than most but not always adept at conveying his thoughts clearly. Colleagues who sat with Meyer on a board of examiners wrote afterward, "He sat for hours on end, turning gravely toward one speaker and then another. When he had something to say he would make a little rumble in his throat as a preliminary and then in a very low voice express an idea that often had so much cogency that it took the Board a moment or two to comprehend it. Often he proceeded to qualify it and after a while the qualifications began to reverberate among each other and the skein of thought became untangled."

Meyer and his colleagues were opening the Phipps Psychiatric Clinic and invited Truitt to join them in their outpatient work at Hopkins. He accepted a position there as first assistant resident in psychiatry even though his salary was to be less than $34 a month—"quite a step down from the $2,000 offered me to remain at the City Hospital." He never regretted accepting the position as the clinic was "perhaps the latest word not only in its construction and the facilities, but in its setting, personnel, and opportunities. The formal opening occurred in the spring of 1913. It was celebrated by the attendance of many distinguished guests from this country and abroad."

At this period in psychiatry, "Kraepelinism was diminishing, psychobiology was most highly respected, and

Freudianism was on the upgrade. One evening a rather heated discussion revolved about whether the patients thus far treated had been more helped by the orthodox or Freudian methods used in treatment. To settle the debate the admission book was scanned by the assembled residents," with the associate professor to pass on the outcome. The results were about fifty–fifty.

Some consider Emil Kraepelin to be the founder of modern scientific or biological psychiatry. Kraepelin posited that biological and genetic malfunction are the chief cause of psychiatric disease and classified the main types of psychiatric illness as dementia praecox (renamed schizophrenia by Eugen Bleuler) and manic-depressive psychosis. Kraepelin suspected that a specific brain or other biological pathology underlay each major psychiatric disorder. It was in Kraepelin's laboratory that his colleague, Alois Alzheimer, discovered the pathologic basis of the disease that took his name: Alzheimer's disease.

Another time an excited intern rushed up to Truitt on the wards "and shouted, 'I have a transference!' It seemed that his scullery maid patient had dreamed about him the previous night."

A report circulated that when the Queen of Romania was visiting this country she came to see the Johns Hopkins Hospital. It was suggested that she also visit the Phipps. Meyer's male secretary gave word to Dr. Meyer "that the Queen of Romania wished to speak with him. The professor asked, 'How long has she believed that?'"

After two and a half years at the Phipps clinic, Truitt began the peripatetic part of his career. In 1914, he was clinical director in a state hospital in Louisiana. In 1916 he was in Trenton and Princeton, New Jersey, preparing for military service in World War II, when he learned he was color blind, which prevented his serving overseas. He served in the Medical Corps until 1919, providing training and other services at Fort Snelling, Camp Funston, Fort Riley, and the army prison at Fort Leavenworth. After leaving the military, he worked for the Society for Mental Hygiene in Los Angeles, before becoming involved with the Commonwealth Fund, helping them set up child guidance clinics in Los Angeles and Philadelphia and doing other work for them in New York City. Worsening problems with his hearing led him to give up that work. After seventeen years of sailing the professional "seas of psychiatry," Truitt spent four months traveling in France and England. He visited such stations of the psychiatric cross as the Bicêtre, Pinel's old asylum in Paris, "Old Bedlam" (Bethlem Royal Hospital) in London, and the Tavistock Clinic.

Then, in 1927, he returned to Baltimore and arranged to set up a clinic at the University of Maryland, to function under the auspices of the Mental Health Society of Maryland, which had long been dissatisfied with available services in Baltimore.

"No doubt sentiment played a big part in my desiring to take part in the work at the University," wrote Truitt on returning to his home port medical school. His desire to reform psychiatry had begun soon after he entered medical school and "realized the terrible status of the teaching of psychiatry"; it was strengthened during his stay at Bay View. Before starting the clinic, he consulted with Drs. Adolf Meyer of Johns Hopkins, Ross Chapman (superintendent of Sheppard and Enoch Pratt Hospital—commonly shortened to Sheppard Pratt—and professor of psychiatry at the University of Maryland), and Maurice C. Pincoffs (later to become chief of medicine at Maryland's medical school and a vital force behind establishing an official department of psychiatry there).

"Our principal aim was to establish a real psychiatric department"

The Commonwealth Fund of New York City and the Community Fund of Baltimore each granted $50,000 to support the clinic's work for five years. The University of Maryland furnished quarters, supplies, and services, including those of two psychiatrists, one psychologist, three psychiatric social workers, and two clinical workers. Their priorities were to serve, first, local social and other community agencies, then University Hospital and the outpatient department, and finally, mental health activities in the community as a whole, including seminars and discussion groups. One priority above all was work with children.

The Mental Health Society of Maryland existed only on paper, its last budget from the Community Fund down to $3000 a year. Clinic quarters at University Hospital were in a deserted, dilapidated old house with broken windowpanes, through which tom cats entered at night, but strong community protest quickly brought them better quarters. Several workers from social and community agencies spent time getting training in the clinic and attending staff conferences held to discuss their clinic patients. Student social workers from such schools as Smith College and Catholic University came to the clinic for field training, as did school workers and Commonwealth Fund fellows in psychiatric training. The university resisted the clinic's early efforts to encourage the establishment of a school of social work in Baltimore.

"On at least a couple of occasions the Community Fund officials questioned our budget and wished to cut or do away with it since we were located at and gave service to a state institution (University of Maryland Hospital), which in turn made no considerable cash contribution to our work. On each occasion the Agencies and other groups arose in our defense, and in one protest instance our budget was increased." Many psychiatry advances would be made only with strong community support.

As chief of the university's adult outpatient department, doing ward consultations and some teaching of nurses and medical students, Truitt did what he could to improve the psychiatric part of medical school. "During the course of our years there the hours of teaching psychiatry were considerably increased, the department of psychiatry was separated from the department of medicine and became an independent unit, and psychology and psychiatric social work were introduced in the curriculum of the nurses and medical students. Our principal aim at the University was to establish a real psychiatric department through providing beds for adult and child patients." Truitt and his colleagues wanted a department independent of the asylum superintendent, with a full-time director and enough personnel to undertake research and teaching as well as the diagnosis and treatment of patients. They wanted the department to serve as a training center for state hospital personnel and to cooperate in community health efforts. "There were too many inherent handicaps in the situation to do a decent job of medical teaching, especially when the medical faculty itself tended to 'pooh pooh' anything psychiatric."

Psychiatric help was needed at the most basic levels, judging from the following letter, which Truitt quotes in his brief history. It came from one of the orphanages surveyed by the clinic, which had the services of a leading psychiatrist for several years:

The Lyme Wars

In 1910, when Ralph "Chess" Purnell Truitt began practicing psychiatry, many of the long-term patients in state hospitals had diagnoses as much biological as psychological: epilepsy, age-related dementia, and "general paresis of the insane"—a severe manifestation of untreated or inadequately treated neurosyphilis. Before the advent of penicillin, this spirochetal brain infection was responsible for a huge epidemic of chronic and ultimately fatal dementias. They often were first manifested by personality changes, memory losses, and poor judgment, but not uncommonly they presented also as depression, psychosis, or mania. Little was known about how to treat most of these diseases at the time, but Ralph Truitt figured there were more humane ways to treat the patients. He helped call a halt to icewater baths, unnecessary shock treatment, and relentless restraints on mental patients. He cleaned up unsanitary conditions in the psychiatric hospitals where he worked.

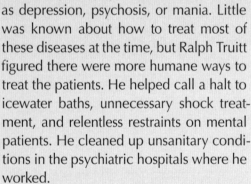

Virginia Truitt Sherr

Truitt's niece, psychiatrist Virginia Truitt Sherr, remembers experiencing an epiphany while spending a day at Spring Grove hospital as a University of Maryland medical student (class of 1956). "I had known that I was going to be a psychiatrist but I had seen psychiatry as the 'fifty-minute hour.' I was going to sit in an office and listen to folks talk, and analyze, as Ralph did in his later years." Then, as she observed patients milling around in an open ward, one of the women started flapping her arms while running around the room proclaiming, "I'm an eagle! I'm an eagle!" Transfixed, Sherr thought, *this doesn't fit the fifty-minute paradigm*. It appeared to be mania, but her instructor explained that it was syphilis of the brain. Sherr thought, *an infection can cause that?*

That memory came back when she had her own prolonged encounter with tick-borne diseases. She has spent many years campaigning for the humane treatment of oft-misunderstood Lyme complex sufferers, working to educate those doctors and the public who have not learned first-hand of the psychiatric and encephalopathic similarities between those two spirochetal illnesses: syphilis and Lyme disease. Pamela Weintraub, senior editor at *Discover* magazine and author of *Cure Unknown: Inside the Lyme Epidemic*, told Sherr's story in a three-part series on *Psychology Today's* Emerging Diseases blog.[2] While Sherr still suffers relapsing and remitting bouts of chronic tick-borne diseases, she continues to medically guide patients "whose health has been wrecked by neuroborreliosis (neurological Lyme disease)." Sherr is co-founder of a medical association, the International Lyme and Associated Diseases Society. She and her colleagues dispute the validity of currently extant but, by their experience, outmoded "treatment guidelines" that many doctors still go by. Sir William Osler called syphilis "the great imitator" because in its late stages it simulates almost every disease known to man. Some say the great imitator today is chronic Lyme disease. Sherr believes Ralph Truitt would have joined her in today's Lyme Wars.

I am one of the housemothers in a home for boys from four to sixteen years of age. I have found one boy who wants information on sex, probably there are others too, and he thinks no one would answer his questions. I do not know whether there is a reason for this or not as I have not been here as long as the others. He wants to get it in the right way. I found him reading a book which does not seem to be the kind he needs and wondered if I could get something better for him. He is nearly fifteen years old. He told me that only one housemother had ever told them anything and she did not [tell them] very much, but perhaps she would now as she has been gone three years or more. I have some material for myself but nothing to give the boys and would like some advice as to what is best. This boy has no father or mother and it is a difficult thing to do but I would like to help him if I can. The superintendent does not feel that he can but might if he had some help. Any advice you can give will be greatly appreciated.

Freud had not yet become the household word it soon would be. The letter from the orphanage came at "about the same time that this story was making the rounds," writes Truitt:

Psychoanalysis was popular in the community and a group of social workers were taking a course in this subject. One of the young and enthusiastic members of the group discussed her course with the psychobiologist in an outpatient department. The psychiatrist asked the worker what she had learned that was so interesting, and the worker said, "He teaches us about the stages of infancy and what happens if we get fixated at a stage. The first stage is the sucking phase. If a person is fixated there he goes through life as a colorless, weak, 'taking it,' grasping individual."

"That's interesting—what's the next stage?"

"Next is the biting stage. If a person is fixated there he is punishing and always hurting people."

"That's interesting—what's the next stage?"

"I don't know. We're going to take that up next time."

"Well, I'll tell you the next stage—it's the swallowing stage. And if a person is fixated there he goes through life believing everything anyone tells him."

"So," wrote Truitt, "in Baltimore, the battle wages between the psychobiologist and the psychoanalyst. It was my feeling that perhaps we needed a bit more sex in the psychobiological school and a bit more biology other than sex in the analytic group."

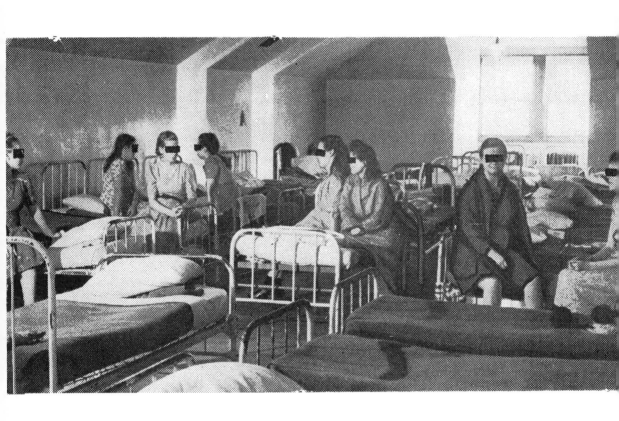

2

Child Guidance and Maryland's Shame

The 1940s

Before 1950, when the department of psychiatry was officially established, the University of Maryland's medical school had no full-time psychiatry faculty. Psychiatrists from the community—especially from Sheppard and Enoch Pratt Hospital—occasionally gave lectures. A medical student in the early 1930s heard fifteen hours of psychiatry lectures in four years of medical school, plus some clinical demonstrations at the Baltimore City and Spring Grove state hospitals. Occasionally a student elected to go to Spring Grove for a week's exposure to a mental hospital. In 1937, H. Whitman "Whit" Newell, who served as clinical director for psychiatric services from 1933 to 1950, organized training in child psychiatry for third year medical students.

A child guidance clinic supported by the Mental Hygiene Society was well established near the university when Riva Novey joined it as a psychiatric social worker in the fall of 1944, during World War II. "I had done family and children case work in Baltimore for several years," wrote Novey, "and I was proud and happy to be invited to join the staff of this clinic, which case workers regarded as a place where clients could get respectful and thoughtful study and treatment, and where case workers from community agencies felt free to participate actively in staff conferences." At that time Whit Newell was away in the South Pacific, serving with the 142nd University of Maryland Medical Unit. On the staff in his absence were Dr. Ralph Truitt, who had opened the first Commonwealth Fund Clinic in the United States (in Los Angeles); Dr. Hans Loewald, a distinguished psychoanalyst who later joined the Yale faculty; two fellows from the Commonwealth Fund: Dr. Alice Rockwell, "a gifted and inspiring clinical psychologist, who was a fine teacher, diagnostician, and psychotherapist" (Baltimore's Rockwell Center was named after her); Lucia Irons, a

DR. H. WHITMAN NEWELL

Newspaper clipping of H. Whitman "Whit" Newell, who served in the Pacific during World War II. In Maryland he organized training in child psychiatry for medical students.

Psychiatric social worker Riva Novey eventually found herself "looking longingly at the white coats" worn by the female medical students she taught from time to time, applied to medical school, and became a psychiatrist, doing her residency at Sheppard and Enoch Pratt Hospital, but "I remember with great pleasure my days at the University of Maryland Psychiatric Clinic."

psychiatric social worker; Riva Novey; and Rose Fisher, the very competent secretary.[1]

"When I first came to the clinic," wrote Novey, "it was a small, quiet organization and it functioned at a leisurely, yet scholarly pace . . . it was not unusual for Dr. Rockwell, Dr. Loewald, and me to take time to go to Marconi's for lunch. There was plenty of time for thorough discussions of practical and theoretical aspects of cases. During this period the entire staff was united in a desire to raise the standards of the Clinic to a level of some of the finest ones in the country. The entire staff collaborated in developing an 'intake policy,' which . . . was mimeographed and distributed at the Ortho-psychiatric meetings for the benefit of new clinics which were just being established under the auspices of the Association of Psychiatric Clinics for Children.

"In 1946 we began to be a training center for schools of social work. We started with Catholic University and in 1947 we were accepted as a training center for the Smith College School of Social Work. Dr. Whitman Newell returned to the Clinic in 1946, I believe, and it was a great pleasure to work with him. He understood child guidance thoroughly, having been in it for many years. He was a man of many inner resources and an even, steady, temperament, all of which made it possible for him to get along during months of isolation with the University Unit in the South Pacific. His paper, 'Interpretation of Fiji Customs,' was published in the *Journal of Social Psychology* of 1950. . . . By the time he returned to the clinic, his even disposition and his ready supply of corny jokes were all needed; for by then the mounting interest of the post-war public in psychiatry, plus the growing reputation of the Clinic in the community, led to tremendous pressure on our staff. It was then that the era of closed intake and waiting lists began, and there were no more lunches at Marconi's."[2]

Helping in work at the Baltimore clinic, wrote Ralph Truitt, who was chief of the psychiatric clinic and

Both Ralph Truitt and Whit Newell, at different times, were president of the American Orthopsychiatric Association, an interdisciplinary association of mental health professionals concerned with mental health and social justice.

A story about Whit Newell comes down from his tent-mate, Howard Mays (class of 1935), who also served with the University of Maryland Medical Unit in the Fiji Islands. "They didn't believe in mental illness," writes Dennis Kutzer, Mays's son-in-law, so Newell was not allowed to have an office inside the hospital in Fiji. He had to see his patients, suffering from shell shock and other problems, on the steps of the hospital. There was an early bias against psychiatry.

professor of psychiatry in 1949, were Drs. George Preston (later Maryland's Commissioner of Mental Health), Stewart Sniffen (who later accepted a full-time position at the University of Chicago), Manfred Guttmacher (who left to become medical consultant to the Supreme Bench of Baltimore City, a position which was the forerunner of the forensic psychiatrist), Mabel Williams, Elmer Klein, Whit Newell (who directed most of the child guidance and teaching work), and Alice J. Rockwell (the head psychologist for several years). Among Society fellows who became staff after their training was completed: Gordon Stephen, Sidney Berman, Joseph Solomon, and Hans Loewald. Roughly a hundred professionals helped with the work while training in the Baltimore clinic, including local physicians, state hospital psychiatrists, fellows from Dr. Leo Kanner's clinic at Johns Hopkins Hospital, psychologists, and social workers. A few psychiatry courses were offered at the medical school by a part-time but nationally distinguished faculty, including Ross Chapman, a psychoanalyst from Sheppard Pratt who would later achieve national prominence, and Harry Murdock.

"For centuries, psychiatry and neurology were considered a single discipline. It might be time to bring them together again."

For centuries, psychiatry and neurology were considered a single discipline—often called neuropsychiatry—which focused on disorders of the mind and brain. Until shortly after World War II, one was certified in both psychiatry and neurology. In 1948, neuropsychiatry split and became two distinct disciplines: psychiatry and neurology. Psychiatry took on disorders of mood and thought, including depression, schizophrenia, anxiety disorders, and so on. Neurology took on brain disorders that presented with somatic signs, such as stroke, multiple sclerosis, and Parkinson's. There have been many jokes about psychiatry going through its brainless period (with psychoanalysis) and then, after pharmaceuticals began to dominate, its mindless period. With advances in neuroscience, some have suggested that it might be time to bring the disciplines together again.

After World War II, funding to support psychiatric training, staffing, and care increased greatly. Psychiatry was viewed more favorably than it had been, both publicly and in the medical community. Lessons learned in earlier wars had been rediscovered in this one: that combat stress produced disabling psychological symptoms and that prolonged exposure to combat could produce psychological breakdown in anyone. Lessons were learned, too, about the effectiveness of treatment provided rapidly on the front line: Given the right circumstances, all were potentially vulnerable and all were potentially treatable.[3] With the end of the war came the idea that "the mind has the power to liberate itself from illness, the tyranny within."[4]

After the war, psychiatrists were increasingly viewed as important resources who were in short supply, and the federal government provided substantial support for psychiatric education and training, which expanded rapidly. The number of slots for psychiatric residencies expanded from 400 before the war to 1,800 by 1951. From fewer than 200 full-time psychiatric faculty appointments in 1945 the number grew to 2,500 by 1972. In 1935 most psychiatrists had served on the staffs of state mental hospitals. By 1956, only about 17 percent of the 10,000 members of the American Psychiatric Association were employed in state mental hospitals or Veterans Administration facilities.[5]

"Still, psychiatry was not a department but a branch of the department of medicine," says Jonas Rappeport, who started at the medical school in 1948. People just came in and lectured. Rappeport remembers being taught by Harry Tittelbaum, a neurologist and psychiatrist, by a husband and wife team whose names he can't recall, and by George Merrill. "George Merrill was an ordained minister and a farmer. He raised sheep, and we would giggle like hell because he'd come in to lectures sometimes with mud all over his shoes and boots. He had a private office and specialized in electroshock therapy. You did shock in your office then and you had a recovery room and what have you. The two major schools then were the physical, or electroshock, school and the psychoanalytic school. Later, when the psychoanalytic school took over, Merrill was derided."

There was some disillusionment with somatic therapies after the war, and more interest in psychoanalysis, which was often extended even to psychotic patients. "After World War II," said Walter Weintraub, "there was a boom in psychoanalysis. Residents and young practitioners made great sacrifices to undergo psychoanalysis and to obtain psychoanalytic training. . . . The trainees met all the costs out of pocket."[6] Being in analysis became a status symbol and an often unspoken requirement for advancement in academic settings.

It was an exciting time in psychiatry. "Our careers spanned the golden age of medicine, when scientific progress grew rapidly and there was little interference in our relationships with patients by outside agents," wrote Gerald Klee, who joined Maryland's department of psychiatry in 1956 but got his medical training in the 1940s. "We experienced the Great Depression and World War II and entered medical school, where we would get an education that we hoped would help us save the world. Like me, most of my classmates had the benefit of having their tuition paid for by the GI Bill."

The GI Bill (the Servicemen's Readjustment Act of 1944) provided college or vocational education for returning veterans from World War II (commonly called GIs), one year of unemployment compensation, and loans to enable returning vets to buy homes and start businesses.

David Geddes, who graduated from the medical school in 1947, was impressed enough with what he saw to decide on a career in psychiatry. "We were all military students, since it was wartime," said Geddes. "I was in the Navy, and we had to drill every Saturday. We had no vacations because of the war, so in 1945 our school calendar slowed down, with a five-month gap to get back on a normal academic calendar. I spent that summer as an extern at St. Elizabeths Hospital in Washington, D.C., further increasing my fascination with psychiatry. After a rotating internship I went on to residency training at Yale. I am forever indebted to the University of Maryland School of Medicine for exposing me to psychiatric clinical material."

There was no department of psychiatry yet, and the psychiatry that was taught was fairly low key. Basically, there were a couple of outpatient clients—there was no psychiatric treatment in University Hospital—and part-time faculty gave lectures in psychiatry to the medical students. "Our class was a little bit older than most medical school classes," recalls L. Guy Chelton (class of 1950). "We had been in the service, and a lot of us went to medical school on the GI Bill— we probably wouldn't have been able to go if it hadn't been for that. We had come back from the war and we had had some pretty bad experiences. So we were very serious about our studies."

The textbooks in the period 1946–50 were *Principles of Dynamic Psychiatry* by Jules H. Masserman and *The Human Mind* by Karl A. Menninger, says Joseph Robert Cowen (class of 1950). These books and lectures by various practicing psychiatrists described the symptoms of the major psycho-pathological states and concepts of psychosomatic illness. The students were also given directions on how to interview patients to survey for psychiatric symptoms, by such instructors as Ephraim Lisansky, Isadore Tuerk, and Whit Newell. The students received supervised practice in interviewing with outpatients at University Hospital and with inpatients at Spring Grove State Hospital and Sheppard and Enoch Pratt Hospital. At Spring Grove and Sheppard Pratt they also observed patients being given "modern" forms of treatment. "We witnessed what was then termed electroshock treatment," says Chelton, "and believe me, that was without any significant sedation or any medication to prevent seizures; and they certainly did have significant seizures. We were quite shocked when we witnessed that."

Psychiatrist Joseph Robert Cowen (class of 1950) graduated as Jacob Finesinger was refining plans for the Psychiatric Institute.

"Indeed, in those days before muscle relaxants were used with electroshock patients, during shock treatment medical students lay on the patients during grand mal seizures to prevent fracture," says Geddes. "Once a group of ten students watching electroshock were so appalled that one of our members fainted dead away."

The medical students also observed schizophrenia patients undergoing insulin shock treatment. Given insulin, which produced hypoglycemic shock, the patient would become unconscious and have seizures. The students watched them convulse. "It was quite dramatic. We also saw patients who were still in the hospital after having had prefrontal lobotomy some years before," says Chelton. "They were still essentially zombies, which would of course not be a politically correct thing to call them, but that is what they appeared to us to be. I remember them being extremely uncommunicative and walking all over the place. Some of them were very difficult for staff to control, to keep in an orderly fashion. The results of lobotomy were less than what we hoped for.

A psychiatrist named Walter Freeman performed the first-ever transorbital or "ice-pick" lobotomy in his Washington, D.C., office on January 17, 1946. (In the prefrontal lobotomy the doctor drills holes through the top or side of the skull to get access to the patient's brain. Freeman's approach was to go in through the eye sockets.) Freeman became a crusader for the process, performing transorbital lobotomies on some 2,500 patients in twenty-three states, before dying of cancer in 1972. The procedure caught on partly because Freeman was a showman and partly because at the time there were so few options for treatment of serious mental illness.

"Ephraim Lisansky, an internist with a great interest in psychiatry and psychiatric matters, began giving us lectures on psychodynamics—I believe in the third year. Lisansky told us, 'When you see a patient, see the patient as a peer. Don't have a nurse take them into an examining room and take off their clothes, so that the first you see of them is in a one-down position. Meet with them in your office and you learn a lot about them, about how they're dressed, and so on. Take the history yourself, not by having them fill out a form. That's when you make the bond with the patient, the therapeutic alliance, by letting them know you are interested in what they are saying. It's important to look also for the emotional aspects, for how they're feeling about what they're telling you.'

"That was extremely interesting and had a lot of influence on me, certainly, and I think on many others, too," says Chelton. "He was extremely helpful in teaching us interviewing techniques, and I think he stirred our interest in psychiatry. Up to then we were receiving only dry lectures about the major diseases—on what was then called manic–depression, schizophrenia, and so on. But Dr. Lisansky took us in small groups, had us interview patients, and afterwards would meet with us and explain the dynamics. He was excellent—extremely helpful."

"I had an internship at Baltimore City hospitals, the satellite of Johns Hopkins," says Irving Taylor (class of 1943). "As a resident, I was officer of the day at Spring Grove Hospital when Howard Norton of the *Baltimore Sun* was coming to take some pictures. He said, 'Show me your worst cases.'"

Norton was talking about fourteen doctors and one registered nurse for 1,500 patients, so Taylor showed him the worst part of the hospital, "with the urine-soaked floors in an old building built during the Civil War. They published those scenes. The commissioner needed funding to renovate. They had 34 cents a day to spend on food for patients." Isadore Tuerk, superintendent at Spring Grove, was also interested in making conditions public knowledge, hoping that publicity would bring funding to hire more physicians.[8]

In 1949, the Maryland General Assembly voted substantial additional funding for new construction of state mental facilities, capital improvements, better pay, and more staff positions. A significant number of new patient buildings went up at Spring Grove, Springfield, Eastern Shore, and Crownsville state hospitals in the early 1950s. Many existing buildings were renovated to remedy the overcrowding, and Spring Grove built new housing for employees.

The legislature also voted enough funding to build the Psychiatric Institute, the facility that would house the University of Maryland School of Medicine's new department of psychiatry and, as an extension of University Hospital, would provide both inpatient and outpatient psychiatric care. The state authorized funding for the Psychiatric Institute to provide state-of-the-art care, training, and research. So from the beginning, the department of psychiatry was closely linked with public mental health.

Before the series appeared, the state—under Governor William Preston Lane—had taken steps to deal with long-neglected problems within the state, but the newspaper series provided the kind of publicity the hospitals needed to get funding. The legislature allocated $25 million to upgrade the state hospitals, in a package that included $3 million to launch Maryland's department of psychiatry. Partly in response to "Maryland's Shame," the psychiatric community mobilized itself in 1949 and created the Maryland Psychiatric Society, which strongly advocated patients' rights.

For a long time the American Medical Association did not recognize specialties, says Jonas Rappeport. "You were a doctor, period. You might be in the surgical section of AMA but not in a separate society. Then as time went on, in the late 1940s and early 1950s, specialty societies began being organized."

(*main text continues on page 32*)

A historical note

Maryland once depended heavily on a system of "county care," by which various counties provided poor people (including mentally ill poor people) with basic custodial care and shelter in county homes, or almshouses. Between 1908 and 1910, local newspapers ran a series of exposés about the often squalid conditions in those county-run almshouses, illustrated by "candid" photographs taken during unannounced visits.[9]

At the time of that series, a movement called "state care" had taken hold in Maryland, which sought to substantially expand the capacities of the state hospitals so that the responsibility for the care and treatment of mentally ill citizens could be shifted from the nontherapeutic, often substandard environments of the county-run homes to "the pleasant, healthful and therapeutic conditions" at Maryland's two state psychiatric hospitals, Spring Grove and Springfield.

Crownsville State Hospital (for African American patients) and Eastern Shore State Hospital were built early in the twentieth century, at about the same time that bed capacities at Spring Grove and Springfield were expanded. After World War II, labor shortages and low funding levels for Maryland state hospitals, combined with an ever-expanding patient population in all of the state hospitals, led to grossly overcrowded conditions and dangerously low staffing levels.

From January 9 through January 19, 1949, the *Baltimore Morning and Evening Sun* ran Norton's series under the title "Maryland's Shame."

"Maryland's Shame"

Journalist Howard M. Norton, who wrote the heavily illustrated series of stories billed "Maryland's Shame" that ran in the *Baltimore Sun* in early 1949, had been awarded a Pulitzer gold medal in 1947 for disinterested and meritorious public service for his articles on unemployment compensation. Norton now described the deplorable conditions in Maryland's state mental health facilities: the understaffing, dreadful crowding, failure to provide treatment, and poor quality of life and employment in Maryland's public mental health facilities. Highlights from that series are provided below.

The terms used in Norton's stories, written only fifty years ago, may strike readers today as politically incorrect, at a minimum, the understanding of mental illness as limited, by today's standards. Segregation was only beginning to be questioned. Someone reading this history fifty years hence may be equally taken aback at our current state of ignorance, but reading the "Maryland's Shame" series now, one is struck by how much has been learned.

The main problems were crowding and understaffing: too many patients in too little space, with too few doctors, nurses, and good attendants to care for them. Maryland's five tax-supported mental institutions had been built to house 6,000, but "already nearly 9,000 are packed into their gloomy, frequently foul-smelling rooms." Only a few patients were being actively treated. Many of the wards looked like "Bowery flop houses," the battered beds "jammed in side-by-side and head-to-foot, a hundred or more to a room. At one 'hospital' scores of men sleep nude on bare mattresses, even in midwinter, because there are no blankets or sheets to cover them." Staffing was grossly inadequate. "None of Maryland's hospitals has more than half the number of staff members recommended. Two of them have fewer than one third of the standard."

The implications of understaffing might be reported differently today. Having only one nurse for every 750 patients and no student nurses in the system, wrote Norton, "means that such important mental treatment as insulin shock—which requires trained nurse attendance—is all but eliminated from Maryland's mental hospitals. It means that hundreds who might be cured by insulin shock are not going to be cured at all." In another building, only six

Original *Sun* caption: STANDING ROOM ONLY—There are 226 men, but only 126 chairs in this bare, prisonlike "day room" at Springfield State Hospital. Those who have no chairs spend hours sitting or lying on the floor. There is nothing else for them to do.

of 430 "very sick" male mental patients "are getting electric shock treatments, and none is getting insulin shock—the most effective treatment for some of the most prevalent mental ills. Currently only one or two of these men improve sufficiently to leave the hospital in the course of a year."

Norton compared Springfield Hospital, in Maryland, with Worcester State Hospital, in Massachusetts. Worcester had 71 registered nurses (one for every 40 patients); Springfield had one registered nurse for almost 3,000 patients. At Worcester, the 72 registered nurses were aided by 40 to 50 student nurses; not a single nursing school was associated with Maryland's state mental hospitals. "Adequate nursing staff makes most of the difference between a hospital and an asylum," said one Worcester doctor.

Worcester had a large-scale organized program of occupational therapy, with 1,575 of 2,850 patients in a "graduated job program," starting with simple chores and working toward instruction in the trades. Worcester had "curtains on its windows, pictures on its walls. Maryland's hospitals [were] uniformly bare." Worcester had "more than a score of 'continuous tubs' and other apparatus for hydrotherapy (for quieting disturbed patients)"; Maryland had none, in all the state. Worcester was able to perform lobotomy operations in-house; such operations had to be performed in outside hospitals in Maryland.

"Tests have shown," wrote Norton, "that if the most common type of mental patient can get insulin shock within the first year of his illness, the chances are 65 in 100 that he will leave the hospital improved or cured. If he has been ill from one to two years, the chances drop to only 30 in 100 that he can leave the hospital after a course of insulin treatments. After two years, his chances drop to 13 in 100."

Superintendent Robert B. May, at Eastern Shore Hospital, was quoted as saying, "The beauty of deep insulin shock is that it shortens the time of partial recovery even if it does not cure. We only have to keep them weeks, instead of years. Electric shock treatments are being used as a 'poor substitute.' They require less expert handling, but are 'far less effective' for certain patients." Much faith was placed in insulin therapy's ability to cure mental illness—as even better than the other major somatic therapy mentioned, lobotomy. Occupational therapy was viewed as desirable (for taking the patients' minds off their troubles), and there is only one mention of "individual 'psychotherapy,'" at Crownsville. Most of the patients, concluded Norton, "have been neglected so long they are already all but incurable. Other hundreds for whom there is still hope will become hopelessly insane in the next twelve months."

The problems, in brief

The most damaging staff shortage in the hospitals, wrote Norton, was the shortage of skilled nursing help. This shortage was attributable partly to a national shortage of trained nurses, but also to "the low salary ($2,000 a year) offered for the unpleasant work with the insane, and the inadequate living quarters." The state had money budgeted for part-time nurses but this was untapped, because using part-timers created administrative problems for the superintendents. ("The part-timers come in and pick and choose their hours, and get paid almost as much as the ones who work on State schedule.") There was little contact between top management and personnel, and complaints and suggestions went unanswered.

All the hospitals were also "critically—even dangerously—short of attendants," wrote Norton, with similar problems of low pay for "disagreeable work." Thousands of patients "live like animals. Some roll in their own excrement on the floor at night. Others sleep on thin, reeking mattresses on equally reeking floors because there aren't enough beds. ... Thousands of patients have nothing to do but sit. Frequently, there are no chairs for them to sit on. There is no large-scale organized occupational program to keep troubled minds off their troubles. *Patients are often not segregated, except by sex. Sex offenders and small children live together. Violent cases, epileptics, idiots and psychopaths are forced to rub elbows.*"

"Eighty 'working' male patients sleep in one basement storage room. After shoveling all day in the hospital's coal yard, most of them eat their dinners with coal-blackened hands because there are only four wash bowls for the 80 men."

"In one decaying 'day room,' amid falling plaster and rotting floor boards, there are 226 men, but only 126 chairs."

The problems described in the series existed in all of the state hospitals and custodial institutions (such as facilities for the mentally retarded), but the problems seemed to be particularly severe at Spring Grove State Hospital, in Catonsville. About a third of its patient population was being cared for and treated in the aging main building, a structure that in 1948 was nearly 100 years old and a firetrap. Moreover, Spring Grove's staffing levels were somewhat lower than the other Maryland state hospitals, a circumstance perhaps partially attributable to the hospital's decision not to use conscientious objectors as staff members during the labor shortages of World War II. And Maryland, like most states, tended to respond to fiscal crises by reducing mental health budgets.

> *"In one attic room, 60 'disturbed' women fight for the use of two leaky toilets."*

At Spring Grove, only one out of five patients amenable to active treatment was getting it—only 191 out of about 955. The total patient population was 2,359, in facilities designed to hold no more than 1,647, and with fifteen doctors and three registered nurses to treat them. Some employees said the superintendent had "not been seen on some wards for as long as five years."

"On every floor of the prisonlike 'main building,' which houses nearly half the patients, there are dirty, leaking toilets, falling plaster, peeling paint, rotted boards. Tiny, dim light bulbs placed high in the ceiling accentuate the bleakness of the rooms and halls. All of the windows are barred. The atmosphere has more of the prison than the hospital. Through it all there is a heavy composite odor of dirty feet, unwashed bodies, urine-soaked floors, soiled bedding, and much-used toilets. Simple neglect is responsible for some of the decay.

"With a budget that calls for 297 attendants, Spring Grove has only 183. They work 72 hours a week—12 hours a day—and many of them live in dismal attic rooms above the wards, where they can hear the screams and smell the odors

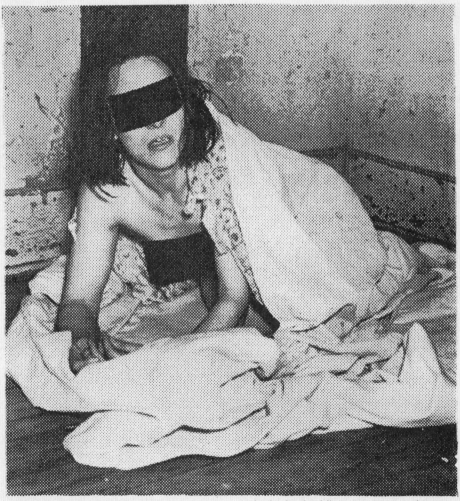

Original *Sun* caption: THIS IS A WOMAN—Naked, she huddles in a coarse sheet on the odorous, filth-stained floor of a battered, run-down seclusion room in Spring Grove Hospital's "main building." The room is dark. She eats on the floor, like an animal. She will probably spend her life this way.

even in the hours off duty. For this, they are paid from $1,380 to $1,725 a year."

Norton told the story of a nineteen-year-old girl—"mildly psychotic but not at all 'crazy'"—who was sent to Spring Grove for treatment to adjust her to normal living. Placed in a "violent" ward with a hundred untidy, screaming women, who regularly soil their own clothing, she fought and was placed in solitary confinement, where she spent much of the time for more than a year. "She spends her days and nights in a tiny, bare room in near-total darkness. The walls are peeling paint and plaster. The floorboards reek with the accumulated odors of the filth of previous inmates. She sleeps on a thin mattress spread on this bare floor. She has had *no treatment at all* since she entered the hospital. Lately, according to attendants, she has grown more bitter and sullen, and has taken to cutting herself on the arms and legs in an attempt to get attention. The only attention she gets is scoldings and bandages."

Springfield State Hospital, in Sykesville, was Maryland's biggest hospital, with problems to match. "It has 49 buildings scattered over 1,400 acres of rolling farm land. It houses more than 3,000 insane men and women. And 'housing' is all that most of them get." With only one registered nurse and one occupational therapist for all 3,000 patients, fewer than 250 patients were getting any active treatment and the patients were "sardined into space meant for only 2,100." There were as few as three toilets for 127 patients, and many patients had little control over their bowels or urine. With enforced idleness

and proximity "the patients grow more disturbed, instead of less."

One female attendant served 110 women in Cottage C, where there was no place for personal possessions, "so they carry toothbrushes in their hair, other personal items wrapped in handkerchiefs. They must carry everything they own everywhere they go."

"Hospital authorities pray nightly that, if there is ever a serious fire, it will not break out in Cottage G." The only fire escape is next to the only stairway and both would be useless for the 76 women crammed into the top floor of this aging structure," wrote Norton. "The patients in this fire trap are among the most 'disturbed' in the hospital. Many have nightmares and seizures. Their beds are so close together that women in seizures frequently pummel the occupants of adjoining beds. And the attendants have to climb over other beds to reach the disturbed ones."

One dingy basement room housed 81 working patients ("borderline" cases do most of the work in the hospital, wrote Norton[*]), their beds six inches apart. They

_____

[*] "In 1949 the word 'borderline' meant one thing," wrote Joe Cowen. "In 2009 it means something else (i.e., it refers to a specific diagnosis in DSM IV, p. 650). In 1949, the patients who did the 'work' in the hospital were patients with chronic schizophrenia who were no longer 'distracted' by their constant auditory hallucinations or interminable conversations with imaginary people so they could function doing repetitive manual tasks or even tasks that required concentration on the job at hand (such as cooking). As many have remarked, the larger psychiatric hospitals in the United States could not function without the labor of some of the chronic patients."

Original *Sun* caption: FIRE TRAP—Forty-one girls sleep in this crowded attic. There is no fire escape and only a single wooden stairway.

shared a dozen chairs. With no place to sit and talk, "the majority go directly to bed after dinner."

There were 1,252 feeble-minded "children" at the Rosewood Training School,* only 156 of whom were attending school. All were white, more than half were over 21, and many were over 70. "Of the 300 children (aged 6 to 16) waiting to get in, most have already waited two or three years—some as long as seven. The buildings are in decay, the floors rotting, beds broken down and crowded, with children sleeping head to foot and side by side, with no privacy or place to keep their belongings." In one cottage 95 boys shared two bathtubs and a shower. However, one jury sent to inspect state facilities found that the "inmates" were all

"humanely and properly treated and cared for."

"Parents of 'low grade' children all over Maryland are being pauperized because the State has allowed Rosewood to get so full that it is 400 over its normal capacity," wrote Norton. "Some are obliged to pay $150 to $200 monthly to keep idiot children in private care because Rosewood can't take them. Others keep defective children at home because they can't afford to pay. ... Mothers become mental cases themselves, normal children are warped, neighbors become hostile, families are broken. One idiot girl on the Baltimore county 'waiting list' for over two years nearly strangled her normal baby brother last month by filling his mouth with dried peas. ... A professional man with two mongolian idiot sons lost his position when one of them became unmanageable. ... Idiots, cripples,

---

* Established in Owings Mills, Maryland, in 1888 as the Asylum and Training School for the Feeble-Minded.

epileptics and 'working children' share crowded sleeping spaces and receive no training in such basic procedures as buttoning clothes, tying shoes, and telling the time of day."

Crownsville State Hospital, near Annapolis, was "the only hope of the insane Negro in Maryland," wrote Norton. But "Crownsville is also the dumping ground for feeble-minded Negro children and epileptics. ... Sex offenders, ex-prostitutes, epileptics and idiots are thrown together with young children who are only feeble-minded or mentally retarded. The younger and more hopeful ones learn bad habits from the older ones. They see epileptics in their 'seizure' struggles. They watch the senseless gesturing of the drooling mongoloids.* ... Girls picked up on the streets by police are dumped into this group indiscriminately, because the State has no other place for them if they are feeble-minded.

"The doctors try to give individual 'psychotherapy' (confidential talks with the patients). But with a ratio of one doctor to 225 patients, they can treat only a few. One hundred and fifteen girls spend most of their days in a single long, bare 'play room' with virtually nothing to play with. There are not even enough chairs for all of them to sit down. Crownsville is supposed to do for Negro children what Rosewood Training School does for feeble-minded white children. But there is no school at Crownsville." None of the

200 children got formal schooling.

"At Eastern Shore State Hospital, more time is spent fighting dirt than insanity. The floors are kept clean, the bed sheets are white and odors are subdued. But the patients get scarcely more attention than they did in the 'insane asylums' of the last century." Eastern Shore was one of the smallest and least crowded of the state mental hospitals, with 500 men and women (in a space built for 334). Many of the women would sit all day in locked chairs because there were too few "girl" attendants. "Because there aren't enough attendants at Eastern Shore Hospital, violent patients often have to be put in cells, locked in their chairs or given sedatives. This irritates them, often worsens their condition and lengthens their stay in the hospital."

Money could solve some of the problems
"Money is the basic need of Maryland's stagnating 'snake pits,'" wrote Norton. One of the less expensive private mental hospitals near Baltimore reported an operating cost of $14.30 a day per patient, which included food, clothing, nursing, doctors' fees, and treatments. Maryland's state-supported mental hospitals spent an average $1.81 per patient (which covered doctors' care, nursing, salaries of all employees, building maintenance, and clothing for patients). New York spent $6.67 per patient; Connecticut, $4.24.

The food served to the [hospital] "inmates in the main looks and smells like garbage, and tastes little better." There was a single dietitian in all the state hospitals—at Springfield.

---

* It is surprising to be reminded how recently the terms "idiot," "imbecile," and "mongoloid" were used to describe people we now commonly describe as having Down syndrome.

The series in the *Baltimore Sun* wasn't the first effort to increase public awareness of treatment of the mentally ill. In 1946 Mary J. Ward's powerful novel, *The Snake Pit*, was widely read.* It was based on her own recovery from a nervous breakdown (with a caring doctor, in an imperfect hospital). Two years later Twentieth Century Fox released the film version, starring Olivia de Havilland, which reached an even wider audience.

In 1948 Albert Deutsch published *The Shame of the States* (with an introduction by Karl Menninger), based on journalistic accounts in local newspapers of overcrowding and understaffing of mental institutions in several states. A national parade of exposés about mental hospitals helped bring about change all over the country, but it was probably the shocking stories in the *Baltimore Sun*, day after day, about conditions in Maryland's state hospitals, that had the greatest effect on the Maryland legislature.

Congress, concerned about conditions in the state hospitals and the incidence of mental illness among soldiers in the military, had passed the National Mental Health Act in 1946. Mental health had traditionally been a state responsibility, but the Mental Health Act authorized creation of the National Institute for Mental Health (NIMH), which was fully funded and established in 1949. Through NIMH, funding became available for training, research, and demonstration projects in mental health care in universities, medical schools, and research institutes. Making federal funds available for such direct support of medicine would have a major impact on American psychiatry.

---

* The idea behind the pejorative term "snake pit" (for a mental asylum) was that if one were lowered into a pit full of snakes one would go crazy, so perhaps lowering someone who was insane into a snake pit would have the opposite effect and shock them back into sanity.

(*continued from page 23*)

"They fired William Preston Lane, a scapegoat," says Irving Taylor, who very soon after owned and ran a local private psychiatric hospital, Taylor Manor Hospital, "and for years afterwards, I had to tell a family when I was transferring patients to the state hospital that it really was okay, that there were lots of wards that were fine—the series had shown only the worst wards. Patients were the work force at Spring Grove; that work was their life and they took that away from them. Now they're sitting around instead of feeling useful."

In May 1949, the Department of Psychiatry was established at the medical school. One of the strongest sources of support for the new department was Maurice C. Pincoffs, a nationally recognized internist and chair of the department of medicine at the University of Maryland School of Medicine (1922–54). With his backing, the state government provided funds; and Jake Finesinger, who had been teaching psychiatry at Harvard Medical School, was invited to create and head the new department. Contracts for a new building to house the department were to be let in the summer.

On June 1, 1949, the Division of Psychiatric Education and Training was established within the Maryland Department of Mental Hygiene and was given responsibility for all of the professional education carried on throughout the department. "For the first time it became possible to coordinate the teaching activities of the various training programs sponsored by the hospitals. Hitherto, the hospitals had always been obliged to limit their training activities to suit the exigencies of the local situation. There was no official recognition of these educational programs as a responsibility of the State. The same situation existed with respect to research. Since this time budgetary allotments have been made in the matter of a sizable sum specifically to implement each program."[10]

The wisdom of this step was subsequently borne out by the resolution adopted by the Governors' Conference on Mental Health (held in Detroit in 1954), which stated: "Training and research in the field of mental health are essential elements of effective mental health programs. The serious accumulation of patients and costs can only be reduced by discovering new knowledge and new methods of treatment and by more adequate training and development of mental health personnel."[11]

There was also a push for outpatient care in mental health clinics. In October 1949, the Council of Psychiatric Societies (a group of Maryland mental health societies) reported that outpatient psychiatric care was provided for only a fraction of the Maryland population. The report opened a drive by the Mental Hygiene Society of Maryland for improved mental health clinics, which it contended were preventive and would save money by cutting down on the number of admissions to mental hospitals. Psychiatric treatment was at that point offered at only two of the state's general hospitals (Johns Hopkins and University Hospital) and at three state clinics: one in Rockville, supported by Montgomery County; a demonstration clinic in College Park, financed by the U.S. Public Health Service; and the Baltimore service, supported until 1949 by the Community Chest, which withdrew its funds in 1949. The report criticized the state legislature, for failing to match federal funds under the National Mental Health Act; the Standard Salary Board, for refusing to recognize the salaries needed to attract competent staff; and so on.

There was a copy of this report, dated October 19, 1949, in the Whit Newell folder in the rare books division of the University of Maryland Health Services Library. The report was signed by Drs. H. Whitman Newell, chair, Manfred S. Guttmacher, Kenneth B. Jones, Paul V. Lemkau, and Theodore Lidz.

In 1950, Jake Finesinger joined Ephraim Lisansky in lecturing to medical students. His influence was felt immediately. "Dr. Finesinger and Ephraim Lisansky really did have a profound influence on my career," says Guy Chelton, who graduated from medical school during Finesinger's first year there. "They said, 'You have to look beyond the symptoms the patients are giving you. Fifteen or twenty years later, I realized that I was actually patterning myself after Ephraim Lisansky. I had always been interested in internal medicine and endocrinology, but during my postgraduate training at the Mayo Clinic, I asked to remain on psychiatry an extra rotation, because I was interested in it. I took a lot of additional work in psychiatry, because of the interest Drs. Finesinger and Lisansky generated. Later in my career, when I became interested in the endocrine aspects of psychosis and certain medical conditions such as hypothyroidism, which produced definite mental effects, I became interested enough in the psychiatric and psychological conditions of these patients that I would fly up to Chicago once a month for four days to take courses at the Chicago Institute for Psychoanalysis. So the onset of the psychiatric department at the University of Maryland was extremely influential in what I did all the way through my career."

Chelton, an internist and endocrinologist, was later CEO and board chairman of an Atlanta hospital. A faculty member at Emory University's medical school, he is also medical director for the state's Medicaid program at Georgia Medical Care Foundation.

Changing times

"It was a different world then," says Jonas Rappeport. "Political correctness wasn't yet a concept. Talking about a case, one of the surgeons told the medical students, 'This big buck nigger came into the office and he had a hernia,' and one of the sensitive students, Phin Cohen, suggested to the professor after class that it was disrespectful to call a patient a 'buck nigger.' After Phin complained to the professor, the dean called him in and told him he would have to apologize. Phin refused to do that and was told if he didn't he would have to leave medical school. Eph Lisansky heard about this and intervened with the dean. Phin never apologized and was allowed to graduate.

Drs. Finesinger and Lisansky taught L. Guy Chelton, an internist and endocrinologist, to "look beyond the symptoms the patients are giving you."

"There were no blacks, of course. Finally in our third or fourth year a black student was admitted. There used to be a little restaurant across from Davidge Hall on Lombard Street called Carl's. We called it Carl's Ptomaine Domain. Different classes would mingle at lunch time and we asked this fellow to come over and have lunch with us, but Carl wouldn't serve him. I said, 'Carl, if he can't eat here, none of us are going to eat here.' Carl was worried about losing his business to truckers and other regulars but finally agreed to serve us all if we sat in the corner."

In 1951, when Roderick E. Charles entered the medical school, he and Donald Stewart were the first black Americans to do so. "I applied there because—having used up my GI Bill money—I felt that being the first black American there would assure me a scholarship from somebody. I also did not feel the state to which I paid taxes could deny me in court despite the frequent objections of the university's president at that time. There was much racial ferment back then and white students were parading in the streets against integration in the public schools. I sought nothing from the institution but a medical degree (which would allow me to study psychiatry).

"Commonly, I saw the lack of respect and disdain with which black patients were often treated and at times spoken of by the faculty," said Charles. "Since I expected it, I was not surprised. I was pleased when I observed the opposite reaction by the psychiatry faculty and staff. Patients were all routinely treated as worthwhile human beings. This extended to the residents under whom I worked as well. This, I felt, came down from Dr. Finesinger, the charismatic chairman of the department. Although his Saturday lectures were not mandated, the amphitheater sessions were highly attended and his charm and wisdom as well as his humanity were always evident. In my third year of residency at the University of Buffalo, I would have accepted his offer to return to Maryland for postgraduate study and teaching. But he told me at that time that he would not be there by the time I came. He had cancer and would not survive. He was as calm as always as he told me this, while introducing me to the chairman-to-be, Dr. [Eugene] Brody. The humaneness of Dr. Finesinger and his department added (for me) much respect for the field of psychiatry and its practitioners."

It was Rappeport's impression that the medical school had a quota of 20 percent on Jews because of the large Jewish community in the state of Maryland. To ensure getting in under that quota, he took an eight-week summer course in organic chemistry in the school of pharmacy, because the organic chemistry test was used to weed out medical school applicants. Acing that, plus getting a recommendation from Eph Lisansky (whose babysitter he was dating), helped him get in.

"There were three women in the medical school then (including Bella Schimmel)," said Rappeport. "Marion Matthews, a lovely, sweet Southern lady, taught in the clinic, talking about psychoanalytical things. Everybody's concept of psychoanalysis was sex, sex, sex. Some of the fellows in my class would interview a patient and ask, 'Tell me about your sex. How did it feel?' There was a great deal of misunderstanding and misconception and joking and abuse, but they were trying. Then Jake arrived and everything changed. Jake built the department and soon people like Maury Greenhill came."

"Jake arrived," said Rappeport, "and he was the epitome of the psychoanalyst, the thinker. Here was somebody new, with new ideas. There were all kinds of upset when Jake came because he was talking about the doctors spending time with their patients, listening to them, and then, worse, he was talking about surgeons telling patients that they had cancer. In those days you didn't tell patients anything and they didn't demand it. Doctors were worshipped then. Jake came, and we started talking about cancer, and psychosomatic medicine, and most important, he with Eph and the others taught interview technique—how all doctors should spend time interviewing patients in a nondirective fashion. You know, 'Hmmmm, what do you mean by that, hmmm?'

Irving J. Taylor

The names of five Taylors in the health care field are listed on the medical school's new freshman lecture hall, the Taylor Lecture Hall: Irving, his son Bruce T. (psychiatry), his daughter-in-law Ellen L. (ob–gyn), his nephews Ronald J. (psychiatry) and Richard L.(neurology). Here's a little of their story.

Irving J. Taylor (class of 1943) was the son of a prominent local merchant, optometrist, jeweler, and watchmaker. As a freshman medical student at Maryland in 1939, he was living above Taylor's Furniture Store (on Main Street, Ellicott City) when Patapsco Manor Sanitarium—a private psychiatric hospital—came up for sale. The hospital had twelve beds and ten patients, most of them chronic; Dr. White, the previous owner, had also treated addictions. "My father said, 'Let's go up and take a look at it,' and the next day we bought it," says Taylor. "He made me an equal partner." They renamed it the Pinel

Clinic, for the French doctor, Philippe Pinel, who had introduced humane treatment for mental patients over a century earlier.

Taylor lived in a patient room in the hospital's main cottage while he finished medical school. He recalls the first clinical director, Dr. Leslie Hohman (from the Phipps Clinic at Johns Hopkins), administering pharmacologic convulsive therapy three times to the wife of a prominent department store owner, using a chemical called Metrazol. She got better (although "of course these patients slip unless you continue the treatments"). Some patients were treated by electroconvulsive therapy, which had been brought over from Italy in 1939. Using a device that looked like a big short-wave apparatus, Hohman administered electric currents across the temples, causing a grand mal convulsion.

Thus, Taylor was exposed to biological therapy as a freshman and

Irving J. Taylor (medical school class of 1943) at the University of
Maryland School of Medicine's Bicentennial Celebration in 2007.

sophomore medical student, "still learning the primary stuff." His father, Isaac,
served as hospital administrator while
Irving completed his medical training and
military service. Toward the end of World
War II, the Army needed psychiatrists,
so Irving volunteered. After a ninety-day
course ("You've heard that term 'ninety-
day wonder'?"), he was made a specialist;
he served two years. After a year at Perry
Point VA Hospital, he completed his residency in psychiatry, working two years at
Spring Grove Hospital (1947–49).

"At that time it was fashionable for

every psychiatrist in training to be on the
analytic bandwagon," says Taylor, "so we
all were in the Baltimore–Washington
Psychoanalytic Institute in the evening.
Five times a week I'd run into Baltimore
to see my analyst for an hour in the afternoon, for personal analysis. After three
years of that I realized, *This is not for me,
and this is not for my patients,* because
the patients in our hospital were all acute
psychotic patients, either schizophrenic
or manic–depressives ('bipolar' didn't
become a fashionable term until later). In
my estimation you don't go digging into a

psychotic's past in psychoanalysis, as this can precipitate an episode. I became an eclectic biological psychiatrist early on, because I saw all of these things before I was in psychoanalysis, so I could take analysis with a grain of salt." In the 1950s, American psychiatry was analytic, even in the treatment of psychosis, so Taylor Manor was different from other private psychiatric hospitals, such as Sheppard Pratt, Chestnut Lodge, and the Institute for Living.

After passing his boards in psychiatry, Taylor became the clinic's medical

director. In December 1952, Frank Ayd, a pioneer in psychopharmacology research, got the first U.S. permit to use Thorazine (chlorpromazine, a phenothiazine), "the granddaddy of all tranquilizers." In January 1953, Taylor got the second permit, and Ayd started sending patients to Taylor, who in 1954 renamed the hospital Taylor Manor Hospital. "I realized this was groundbreaking stuff—nobody else knew about it in the country—so we combined our first thousand patients." Taylor published an article on Thorazine in the medical school *Bulletin* in 1956 and one on the tranquilizer fluphenazine (Prolixin) in the *American Journal of Psychiatry* in 1959.

"The drug saved some from what then seemed to be unavoidable lobo-

The original Patapsco Manor Sanitarium, which burned down in 1923. The replacement building renamed the Pinel Clinic, was Taylor Manor Hospital for many years, before becoming Sheppard Pratt at Ellicott City. The current building, seen below in a photograph taken in about 1970, was built in 1968.

tomies," read Ayd's obituary.* After Taylor's pilot program with Thorazine, the state of Maryland ran a trial for using Thorazine in the state mental hospitals.

"There were a dozen phenothiazines," says Taylor, "and because of my experience with Thorazine, whenever a new phenothiazine came out, the various drug companies (Schering, Squibb, McNeill) looked to me to do the fine clinical work with their drugs before they came on the market. I was not a bold researcher. I took existing drugs, which had been on the market for two years or more, so that we knew that they didn't kill anybody and we knew pretty well what the

rough dosage range was, and I treated the patient's symptoms against the milligrams of the medication to get the maximum therapeutic effect with the minimum of side reactions—which were dramatic." Patients stayed in the hospital at least two to four months. Seven days a week, Taylor saw the patients himself, not depending on a nurse or an attendant to fill out a form, and so he got to know his patients well.

"In the early days, what you learned, you learned by experimenting," says Taylor. "For a while our hospital was the only place within a hundred miles where you could go to get ECT. I gave more than 100,000 ECTs and had no deaths. They didn't teach ECT in medical school until my son Bruce was at Hopkins. In the 1950s they started using anesthesia and muscle relaxants. Later, when we joined the Joint Commission on Hospitals, we had to have a certified anesthesiologist. I had to retrain him. He was trained to anesthetize for a half hour; we only needed two minutes."

In 1968, Taylor's nephew, Ronald J. Taylor—who already had a master's degree in psychology, was a medical student at the University of Maryland, and was already working at Taylor's hospital—persuaded Taylor to start one of the nation's first psychiatric hospital inpatient treatment programs for adolescents. Ron Taylor hired and trained the staff, started an in-hospital school (through the Howard County school system), and developed all the programming. Eventually, two-thirds of their patients were adolescents, many of them with co-morbidities—especially

---

* Ayd graduated from the University of Maryland School of Medicine (1945) and was starting his residency in pediatrics when the Navy called him into active duty at a veterans hospital. His experience there with veterans with psychiatric problems led him to an illustrious career in psychiatry. He established the journal *International Drug Therapy Newsletter* (now *Psychopharm Review*), edited *Ayd's Lexicon of Psychiatry, Neurology, and the Neurosciences*, and helped start the American College of Neuropsychopharmacology and the Collegium Internationale Neuro-Psychopharmacology. "Dr. Ayd worked at a time when there was considerably less government and academic regulation, and when clinicians were able to experiment more freely with emerging drugs to find good uses for them," wrote Douglas Martin in the *New York Times* obituary for Ayd, who died in 2008. "Dr. Ayd never doubted he was treating brain diseases. He tested his patients' psychological, neurological, and behavioral responses to new drugs, then quantified the results. This placed him at odds with the more impressionistic traditions of psychiatry and more in tune with the biological approach favored by many European researchers." In his later years he worked at Taylor Manor Hospital. ("Frank Ayd, 87, Who Advanced Thorazine Use, Is Dead." www.nytimes.com/2008/03/21/health/research/21ayd.html).

Tony Lehman and Irving Taylor presenting the Irving J. Taylor MD Resident Research Paper Award to resident Bernard Fischer in 2006.

addictions—because then, as now, the patients were self-medicating.* After completing medical school at Maryland, Ron went on to a psychiatric residency at Maryland, becoming chief resident from 1975 to 1976.

In 1970, the hospital hosted a three-day symposium, Discoveries in Biological Psychiatry, in which Frank Ayd and seventeen other major researchers highlighted advances in psychopharmacology, including presentations on the serendipity associated with the stories of Dilantin, Librium, LSD, and Valium.

In 1968, the hospital had opened a new Center Building, expanding their capacity to 176 beds. Taylor had six other full-time psychiatrists and one full-time internist on his staff. His son, Bruce Taylor, who trained at Johns Hopkins, joined full time in 1979 and took over as the hospital's medical director. The hospital expanded again into associated treatments such as those for drug and gambling addictions, but the economics of the industry changed. In 2002, Taylor Manor Hospital became part of the Sheppard Pratt Health System: Sheppard Pratt at Ellicott City.

---

* Taylor asked his patients, after they were discharged, what or who was the most important factor in their getting well. Sometimes they would say the doctor or the medical treatment, but generally it was "the person they were closest to in the hospital … just a person that they connected to somehow. It could be a nurse; it could be the maintenance man."

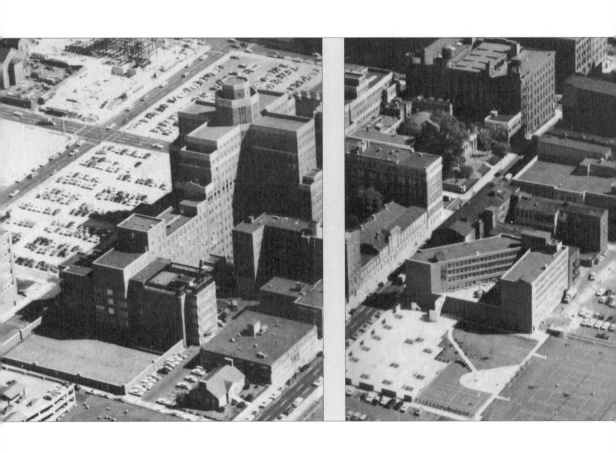

3

The Finesinger Years
The 1950s

Jake Finesinger

Jacob E. Finesinger was appointed in 1949 to organize and head the medical school's first official full-time department of psychiatry. After a few visits to the campus in 1949, Finesinger started full time in January 1950.

He held two titles: chairman of the department of psychiatry in the medical school; and director of the as-yet-unbuilt Psychiatric Institute, a physical extension of University Hospital in which both inpatient and outpatient psychiatric care would be provided.

He immediately began recruiting staff and residents. His first hire was Robert Grenell, a neurophysiologist trained at Yale who had been running his own laboratory at Johns Hopkins School of Medicine. Grenell was hired to direct development of a departmental research plan and would go on to head the neurobiology laboratories. "I had the magnificent salary of $2,000 a year," said Grenell, "which he had to scrape up from someplace, because money wasn't hanging on trees anywhere."

Molly Brazier, a distinguished neuroscientist who had worked closely with Finesinger (publishing several papers when they were both associated with Stanley Cobb), recommended Grenell, and arrangements were made for Finesinger and Grenell to meet in Provincetown. Swimming in the ocean together, they discussed plans for the University of Maryland, and Grenell was hooked.

Much of the material on the Finesinger years was provided by Gerald Klee, a student of Finesinger's at Harvard who was a resident at Johns Hopkins when, in 1956, Finesinger hired him. Toward the end of 2003, he interviewed Bob Grenell, Bill Fitzpatrick, and Jerome Styrt, and was in touch with Enoch Callaway and Jerry Coller, in a then solo effort to preserve memories of Jake Finesinger and the early years of the Psychiatric Institute. All quotations from Grenell, Fitzpatrick, and Styrt are from those interviews. Finesinger told Grenell that the Psychiatric Institute was to be "a department of the university and an institute of the hospital."

This Bressler building, a ramshackle building across from the hospital, also housed the anatomy department. It was eventually torn down. It was not the Bressler Research Building, built later at a slightly different location.

"All we could do initially was to set up a little teaching with the medical students and the one or two residents who came. But nobody had offices," said Grenell. Until the Psychiatric Institute was ready, the whole department was in one room on the ground floor of the old Bressler building, a room formerly used for occasional visits by university officials. Grenell retained the use of the Hopkins lab for a while.

While the Psychiatric Institute was being built, Finesinger's mission was to establish a full-time department of psychiatry. He told Grenell that his responsibility as chair of the department "was directly to the governor. He was not to be held responsible to the dean or the president of the university—only to the governor." While psychiatry was riding high, the Psychiatric Institute would get special treatment.

Finesinger knew that the idea of creating such a department, which the medical school had not had before, had come from Maurice Pincoffs, chief of the medicine department. Part of his strategy was to build bridges to the other departments in the medical school and hospital. Encouraged by Pincoffs, the psychiatry staff provided instruction for the department of medicine's house staff. Fifty years later, internist Jerome Coller said that the "minimal activity" interviewing techniques he learned from Jake Finesinger in the spring of 1950, as he was finishing medical school, were techniques he used for the rest of his career.

"I had the magnificent salary of $2,000 a year."

"When the patient intellectualizes," Finesinger would say, "ask, 'How did you feel?' If the patient experiences an emotion as you talk, you will get further; if it's a pure intellectual exercise, it won't be useful to anyone." In his now-classic paper about minimal activity, Finesinger emphasized that "minimal activity" might not mean "no" activity; you might end up talking the whole session, but you did the minimal amount necessary. Basically, Finesinger showed the medical students how to truly listen to medical patients.

At the same time, Finesinger saw the department as more than medical and hoped to challenge his students' thinking. His most unusual appointment was John Reid, whom he brought in as a visiting professor of philosophy in psychiatry, the first such appointment anywhere. Reid was a brilliant man—one of the few undergraduates ever to get a Guggenheim award (in 1943)—who raised the level of discourse in the department, said Grenell. Reid had been chair of the department of philosophy at Stanford before going to Harvard, where Finesinger met him. Finesinger, Reid, and Grenell would get together in Finesinger's home to "chew the fat" about scientific philosophy.

Reid would come to conferences and talk about things from a philosophical standpoint, says Jonas Rappeport. "Once he was going over to Hopkins Hospital to visit someone. He wanted to get from point A to point B and there was a fence, so he decided to go over it. John was in his 50s, I guess, and he broke his ankle badly."

George Gallahorn remembers being asked by Gene Brody in the 1960s, when he was applying to be a summer fellow, why Reid's first year class in psychiatry wasn't popular among the medical students. Gallahorn responded, "Because it used Freud's *The Ego and the Id* as a textbook, and medical students are too interested in concrete matters and too worried about the physiology and biochemistry exams to learn about abstract concepts in psychoanalysis." Brody seemed pleased with the answer.

Finesinger also started a psychiatry residency program that first year. His first psychiatric residents, Enoch "Noch" Callaway III and William Fitzpatrick, started on the same day in 1950. Both came as instructors but with considerable experience. Noch Callaway would become an eminent figure in the revolution in biological psychiatry that had just begun. "I came here at a house-staff level—with no house," said Fitzpatrick. "We stuck around until we built a house." William Magruder, who had trained at Duke, was hired as chief resident in 1951. Jerome Styrt, who had completed his psychiatric residency at Sheppard Pratt Hospital and Johns Hopkins's Phipps Institute, came on staff as an instructor in 1953.

Fitzpatrick had had a residency in internal medicine and a year in psychosomatic medicine at Duke before coming to Maryland. Noch Callaway had spent some time doing research during his residency at Worcester State Hospital. In 1954, Callaway would receive one of the first NIMH Career Investigator grants ever awarded. "I will be eternally grateful to Jake for getting me that grant," wrote Callaway in an email to Gerry Klee. "Jake had more to do with me getting it than I did." In 1958 Callaway left to become head of research at Langley Porter Neuropsychiatric [later Psychiatric] Institute in California.

Despite their low pay, all of these early psychiatrists underwent psychoanalysis after coming to Baltimore, as that was considered an essential part of psychiatric training in those days. "There was a period of time when if you went into psychiatry you were supposed to get an analysis," said Fitzpatrick. You underwent psychoanalysis on your own to clear your mind of the things that could interfere with your professional work. "That's no longer true, but you were a second-class citizen if you didn't do it in 1950. Everybody talked about it and wanted to be a part of it. I came here because I was accepted at the Baltimore–Washington Institute for Psychoanalysis and I needed a job. I was told that Dr. Finesinger was coming. I decided I would stay in psychiatry after a year's fellowship in psychosomatic medicine."

Styrt was the only one of the four who went on to become a psychoanalyst, and many of the people interviewed for this history remember him as their analyst—one of the best. "Our strong point until we really got the institute running," said Styrt, "was teaching psychiatric concepts to medical people and trying to develop a coordinated concept of a functioning person with psychiatric difficulties, and the way in which that played a part in the development of their illness and their willingness or unwillingness to take part in understanding it. The idea was to develop an awareness in the patient—and I think Finesinger was very important in this—of the contribution of their feelings and their emotional experiences to the kinds of things that were going on in their illness."

Styrt came as an instructor in psychiatry, supervising residents, teaching medical students, and working with small groups. "The organization of physicians sponsored a regular program of teaching psychosomatic medicine to surgeons, medical people, and the like," said Styrt. They came to the University of Maryland for some lectures, but most of the work was done in small groups with instructors such as Callaway, Fitzpatrick, and Kathryn "Katie" Schultz.

"There was a period when if you went into psychiatry you were supposed to get an analysis."

"Everything was outpatient to begin with," said Fitzpatrick. Before the Psychiatric Institute was built, the university had no inpatient care for mental illness, though it had a fairly large outpatient practice in psychiatry. Before Finesinger came, psychiatry had been taught part time in the medical school and residents had rotated through a busy child guidance clinic, which in the 1950s was still run by Whit Newell. Newell stressed to the residents the importance both of empathy and of understanding how patients in our diverse society were affected by culture. Residents met regularly with social workers who were involved in both diagnostic and psychotherapeutic efforts. Old-timers remember in particular Marcella Weisman, MSW, who died young in an automobile accident.

While he was a psychiatric resident at Spring Grove State Hospital (1951–54), Joseph Robert Cowen remembers going to a weekly night psychotherapy clinic at the University of Maryland that Whit Newell had instituted and was in charge of. This volunteer clinic gave residents a chance to interview people "who were attending to their daily chores of working [or] caring for children" but had many symptoms and concerns. They learned how a psychotherapeutic relationship could affect the course of various illnesses, learned in depth about the course of those illnesses, and met regularly with an experienced psychiatrist who supervised them.

"There was a so-called psychiatric clinic across the street," said Fitzpatrick, in a building that offered other services, too. Patients were referred from other inpatient and outpatient services. "There were social workers in the department, so if people wanted to be referred to the psychiatric clinic they could end up with some kind of consultation in those days. I saw outpatients in the psychiatric clinic, and did some lecturing now and then in psychosomatic medicine to medical students and house staff, too. I was one jump ahead of them because I had had a full residency in medicine before I started in with this."

One of Fitzpatrick's jobs was to find a patient in the general hospital for presentation on the psychiatric ward rounds. "This patient has diabetes," he told a medical resident who found Fitzpatrick wandering around one ward, and the medical student said, "What on earth does that have to do with emotions?" Fitzpatrick replied, "Well, we're trying to learn."

Much of the psychiatry staff's clinical work was done as consultations on the general medical and surgical hospital wards and in the medical clinics. Nearly all of the patients had physical problems, but often, with problems such as diabetes, there were also emotional factors. Those could be studied and used as teaching cases for medical students and the new group of psychiatry residents. Finesinger didn't have a huge administrative job at first. "There was a lot of spare time," said Fitzpatrick. "I was mainly gratified by having so much of Dr. Finesinger's time, because he taught me and one or two others interview techniques that have stayed with me ever since. It was a serendipitous moment."

In about 1952 Finesinger brought in Maurice Greenhill, a senior scientist from Duke, to run the training program. Finesinger, Greenhill, and John Romano (who did important work at Rochester) had all trained at Massachusetts General Hospital (which everyone called Mass General) in the 1930s under Stanley Cobb, kept in touch, and saw each other at meetings. When Fitzpatrick was looking for a job,

Greenhill, with whom he had spent a lot of time at Duke, put him in touch with Finesinger; not long after that, Greenhill himself came up from Duke and cast his lot with Finesinger and Maryland. Greenhill was an affable, well-informed fellow, who in ward rounds tried to get across some interviewing techniques that medical students would not necessarily have had training in, said Fitzpatrick. "He was doing the same kind of interviews, but Finesinger really fine-tuned it." Greenhill brought Sidney Easterling, as junior faculty, and Klaus Berblinger.[1]

Klaus Berblinger, who had completed his medical studies in Germany and Switzerland—having been interned briefly in Dachau in the mid-1930s for performing political satire—came to Maryland in 1952 after training in psychiatry at Duke for two years. Berblinger, who "smoked with panache," was in charge of outpatient psychiatry.

Finally, in 1953, the Psychiatric Institute was open to patients. The staff had been scheduling outpatient appointments and interviews in a building across the street, so the transition wasn't that hard to bring about, said Fitzpatrick. "We left the other facility and started working out of the Institute building."

"The P.I. was seen more as a hotel than a psychiatric hospital."

One of the earliest patients, admitted in February 1953, was a 26-year-old public school teacher and night school student working on his master's in sociology. Jerome Styrt diagnosed the patient, Bob Derbyshire, with "depression, suicidal ideation, and psychosomatic angioneurotic edema," as it was called then. Kurt Glaser, a German-born, first year resident with a background in pediatrics, saw Derbyshire for two months inpatient and then two more years outpatient, supervised by Charles Ward. "There is no question the P.I. was seen more as a hotel than a psychiatric hospital," says Derbyshire. "To this day I can vouch for its effectiveness as a healing institution geared to the psychosocial medical needs of patients." Like the other patients, Derbyshire looked forward to Jake Finesinger's daily rounds. "He was patient-

(*main text continues on page 58*)

The Psychiatric Institute

The building

The state had budgeted $2.75 million to build the Psychiatric Institute. Jake Finesinger spent a long time planning the building and went to great lengths to accomplish certain goals, according to Bob Grenell and Bill Fitzpatrick, two of his earliest professional hires.[*] He wanted a psychiatric hospital that looked more like a hotel than a psychiatric hospital, for one thing, so he traveled the country looking at windows everywhere, finally selecting windows that looked like normal hotel windows but were adequate for patient safety—they couldn't be opened wide enough for anyone to jump through them, and they would not be covered by bars or grills.

Other departures from traditional psychiatric institutions were air-conditioning, sound-proofing, standard plumbing fixtures, and treatment rooms with one-way mirrors through which students and supervisors could watch patient interviews or treatment from an adjacent observation room.

Finesinger didn't want the institute to look like a hospital inside, either, so the walls in patient rooms were wallpapered, not painted. Finesinger was personally involved in selecting wallpaper, drapes, rugs, and Scandinavian furniture, with his wife, Grace, helping on color choices.

[*] In addition to material Gerry Klee collected about Finesinger, much of which he made available online, at www.finesinger.com, I also relied on newspaper reports found in the rare books division of the University of Maryland Health Services Library.

Art work was hung throughout the building, and an art exhibit was held when the building opened. Finesinger wanted to create a sense of one big family. "When he got through he had the most beautiful building of its kind in the country," said Grenell.

Each room in the institute was outfitted with a microphone, a speaker, and an input jack for recording equipment. Recordings could be made locally or could be transmitted to a central recording room—and the recording unit could be set to record automatically whenever the noise level reached a pre-determined point. The nurse at each floor station could listen or record from any room or any area. And the whole building was wired to play recordings or transmit announcements or any of four radio programs—channeled to all rooms or to any single room.

Starting in 1952, the building opened one floor at a time, as the department acquired staff. The first piece of equipment moved into the building was the switchboard.

Opening day

The Psychiatric Institute's opening ceremony was held November 17, 1952. Finesinger spoke of the institute's triad of functions: the care and treatment of patients, the teaching of medical students and doctors, and basic research. An extension into community service would be part of the institute's "tentative and flexible" program. The physical plant was to be "the visible symbol of service and research, with unmeasured possibilities."

BALTIMORE, MONDAY, NOVEMBER 17, 1952

New Approach To An Old Problem

New University Hospital Psychiatric Institute To Employ Unique Techniques In Community

"We foresee a chronic interchange of patients between our own service and other services—cutting across departmental lines—the theory being to treat patients wherever they can best be treated," said Finesinger. He announced that the institute was "planning to establish clinics

The Psychiatric Institute, as seen in the 1967 *Terra Mariae Medicus*, outlined here in white. The surrounding neighborhood continued to change. The small building in the foreground (with the gabled roof) was torn down recently to make room for new construction. The arrow points to courtyard side of the Psychiatric Institute.

The Psychiatric Institute was on the western fringe of what in the 1950s was downtown Baltimore. The May Company was one of four big downtown department stores on or near the corner of Howard and Lexington streets, then considered the center of downtown. In the area to the west of the hospital and behind it were row houses in which old Lithuanian families lived. "These very nice Lithuanian families rented out rooms and apartments to medical students and residents," says Bernadine Faw, "but I think no one dared live more than two blocks west, which even then was scary territory." From there west, and spreading out both north and south, was the area depicted in David Simon's book and

documentary, *The Corner*, on which the HBO series *The Wire* was based. *The Wire* was filmed there and in many similar parts of Baltimore, including Brooklyn, the area bounded roughly by Interstate 895 on the north and by the Beltway on the south. Just south of Brooklyn was Cherry Hill, another area one "didn't want to be in at night, even in the late 1950s." There was a small but active police station on Pine Street, just behind the institute.

Early in *The Wire*, the city blows up a high rise and moves people into other neighborhoods. Across Martin Luther King Boulevard, just west of the medical school, there are now new public housing buildings that were part of the change portrayed in the series. The building that would later house the Center for Health Services Research, the Medical School Teaching Facility (MSTF), is a fortress-like structure with only tiny windows on the side facing the projects and no entrance on the ground floor. "They have since built buildings more open to the community," says Howard Goldman.

for the study and treatment of specialized types of mental illness or potential mental distress. These include services looking toward rehabilitation, a clinic for the study of the problems of alcoholics, and a clinic dealing with psychiatric disturbances which lead individuals into courts." The new unit was to provide diagnostic and therapeutic services for patients and educational and training opportunities for physicians, nurses, and auxiliary medical personnel. It was to help patients who had been discharged from mental hospitals and to serve patients who, after short and intensive treatment, would recover enough to go home.

Speakers at the opening ceremony on Monday, November 17, 1952, at 2:30 pm, included former Governor W. Preston Lane, Jr., under whose administration the project had been launched five years earlier, and Ralph P. Truitt, professor of psychiatry emeritus, during whose tenure construction of the institute was conceived. Lane spoke about getting a legislative appropriation of $25 million to alleviate conditions in the state mental hospitals, saying that the nearly $3 million spent on the new institute "would be wholly justified if it contributed to prevention as well as the cure of mental illness."

The scientific program continued on Tuesday morning, November 18. Ralph W. Gerard (from the University of Chicago department of physiology) chaired a program, "Change in Behavior." O. Hobart Mowrer (a research professor of psychology at the University of Illinois) talked about "Learning Theory, Language, and the Problem of Personality Disorder."

A panel discussion followed (Gerard chairing) with these discussants: John von Neumann (a brilliant mathematician, then at the Institute for Advanced Study in Princeton); O. Hobart Mowrer, Raphael Lorente de Nó, J.H. Quastel, Holger Hyden, and Stanley Cobb.

That evening, the famed anthropologist Margaret Mead gave a public

Margaret Mead, Carl Rogers, Stanley Cobb, and Frieda Fromm-Reichmann spoke at the opening of the Psychiatric Institute.

lecture, "The Anthropologist Looks at Contemporary Behavior." John R. Reid (a philosopher and visiting professor at the institute) spoke about "Human Values in Medical Education." Philipp G. Frank, a Harvard philosopher of science, spoke about "Science and Medical Education." A panel discussion on "Methods in Medical Teaching" featured these panelists: George Saslow, an associate professor of psychiatry, Washington University; Thomas Hale Ham, professor of medicine, Western Reserve University; and Jacob Finesinger.

On Wednesday, November 19, in the day room on the fourth floor of the Psychiatric Institute, John C. Whitehorn spoke about "Psychotherapy and Changes in Behavior," Talcott Parsons

Street.[*] Redwood Street ran downhill from Greene so that the institute's entrance on Redwood was a floor below the main hospital building. You entered the institute (typically called the Psych Institute, or the P.I.) on the ground floor. Below that, in the basement, was the child psychiatry division, which opened on a small, attractive outdoor terrace for children. The division had a large playroom, two rooms designed for treatment of children, and space for occupational therapy. As you faced the institute on Redwood, the general hospital was on your left, connected to the institute by a wide corridor one flight up from the street, with psychiatrists' offices along it. Continuing through to the hospital you came to the hospital cafeteria, where the line was so long that residents often ate at neighborhood bars (there was little food service in the P.I.). To the right of the Redwood entrance and on the same level was a walled-in grassy area, so inpatients could go outdoors.

"It was a nice modern building, for then," says Bernadine Faw (Arnold), medical student (1957–61) and resident (1962–64) at the Psych Institute. As you came through the entry alcove, in the middle of the corridor was a stairway. If you went to the right of it, the office doors were all on your right; if you went to the left, they were all on your left. Most of the doors were closed during the day, because many of the psychiatrists and residents

spoke about "Sociological Factors in Changing Behavior: The Therapeutic Process as a Prototype of Social Process," and Anatol Rapoport spoke about "The Role of Symbols in Changing Behavior." A panel discussion followed on "Factors Operating in Psychotherapy," with these discussants: Franz Alexander (director, Chicago Institute of Psychoanalysis); Frieda Fromm-Reichmann (clinical director at Chestnut Lodge); and Carl R. Rogers (professor of psychology at University of Chicago). A powerful group of speakers.

The layout of the building

In 1953, the Psychiatric Institute opened for business at 645 West Redwood Street. It was essentially an extension of University Hospital, one you entered from Redwood

---

[*] This sense of the building is based on the memories of some of those who worked there. Bernadine Faw Arnold, Jon Book, Herb Gross, Gerry Klee, Denis Madden, Michael Plaut, Jonas Rappeport, Ronald Taylor, and Léon Wurmser provided many details.

were seeing patients. "You didn't see a lot of patients in the corridor—one or two at a time, coming in or out," recalls Faw. The waiting room was to the right of the entry, though after 1967, when that became Herb Gross's office, there was no waiting room. (Patients then waited in the hall or went right to the doctors' offices.) To the left of the entryway was the office of Miss Fisher, the department's head secretary, an "older lady," tough but nice.

The six-story institute, a rectangular building, was connected to the University Hospital by a connecting wing. The institute was divided in the middle by a central utility area that opened onto two parallel corridors, giving patients in all of the treatment areas an outside view. This central area contained stairwells. There were elevators near the connecting wing.

This addition to University Hospital held 185 beds, 102 of them psychiatric beds in the Psych Institute* and the rest in the connecting wing. Ultimately the Psychiatric Institute could house 102 patients, including 60 disturbed patients and 14 to 16 children—the rest of the beds being for patients with psychoneurotic or psychosomatic illness. (The psychosomatic wards would disappear in the 1960s.) In full operation, predicted Finesinger in 1952, the institute would require the services of two residents and thirteen assistant residents to handle inpatient care.

The lower three floors were the basement, ground, and first floors, which were given over to outpatient services, psychiatric administration, laboratories, and classrooms. These floors contained attractive offices (admissions and staff) and conference rooms. On the first floor were offices, a completely equipped staff library, and an auditorium that could seat an entire medical school class. One floor below, on the ground floor, was child psychiatry, which opened directly onto a large outdoor recreational area. In the 1960s, there would be an open clinic on the first floor.

On the second floor (connecting with the main floor of the hospital) were Jake Finesinger's office and four units in which observation rooms alternated with treatment rooms. Through the one-way mirror, students in the observation room could watch a master conduct therapy, a supervisor could watch a student or resident interview a patient, or a supervisor and students might watch a student or resident interview a patient, commenting on the process—sometimes phoning comments in to the therapist while the session was going on. Patients couldn't hear sound from the observation room.*

The top three floors contained twelve nursing units for inpatient psychiatric care—four to a floor. These floors, exclusively for inpatient care and treatment, were virtually identical. Each nursing unit had room for fifteen or sixteen patients. Each floor was divided by a central

---

* "Provision has been made for the care of 102 patients within the institute, 18 of them children." *Bulletin,* University of Maryland School of Medicine, Vol. 37, Oct 1952.

* Many nights, one non-psychiatry resident who later became a well-known Baltimore doctor could be seen making out with his girlfriend (a nurse whom he later married), not realizing they were in a room with a one-way mirror.

partition into two main wings, each of which could be isolated by closing the doors in the central service area. One floor, for disturbed patients, was completely soundproofed and air-conditioned.

Bill Fitzpatrick recalled different levels of security, from one completely open ward, which patients walked in and

Through the one-way mirror, students in the observation room could watch a master conduct therapy—or a resident make out with his girlfriend.

out of, to a completely locked ward from which they could not go anywhere without being escorted. This changed over time. "When the Psychiatric Institute got a community psychiatry grant, 2F became a public ward—for indigent patients—which served the catchment area covered by the grant," says Herb Gross. "The catchment area grew with the opening of the Carter Center, and that ward changed function. The wards on the third floor were for more treatable patients. There was a locked ward, 2G, on the second floor." The general adult inpatient psychiatry units were 2G, 3F, and 3G. On the fourth floor were 4G (a fourteen-bed inpatient unit for children) and a gym. On the roof of the building was an attractive recreational area.

The connecting wing, which joined the Psychiatric Institute to the main hospital, held eight floors, including a sub-basement ("terrace") floor. The lower two floors housed laboratories, medical records, plant operations, and auxiliary services. Clinical and research laboratories were located on one floor of the wing. The physiotherapy unit and the electroencephalographic station were housed on the third floor of the wing. Electroshock therapy was also done on the third floor.

As you stepped off the elevator on the fourth floor of the P.I. building, double doors to the right opened into the surgery department's fairly small shock–trauma unit, new in the 1960s. Double doors to the left opened into the general hospital; and as you came through those doors, the women's on-call room was on your right.

Being on call, especially for the non-psychiatric residents, often meant either staying up all night or sleeping in your clothes. There was one large room on the fourth floor of the general hospital building where all the women interns, residents, and medical students who were on call at night on any service could sleep if they could get away from work. Across the hall from it was a place to take showers, although some women took showers in the nursing home building, which had better showers. There weren't many beds for the women, but in the early years there weren't many women, either. The amenities were believed to be nicer in the men's on-call area, says Faw. Sometimes medical students slept overnight in the on-call rooms.

Psychoanalyst Virginia "Ginny" Huffer (shown in 1972), was on the staff longer than most of the early hires.

(continued from page 49)
oriented, personable, and communicative, with both staff and patients." (Derbyshire's story continues on page 96.)

More staff came. Virginia "Ginny" Huffer, a psychoanalytically trained psychiatrist from upstate Maryland, joined the faculty in 1953, working at first under Klaus Berblinger in outpatient psychiatric services. She would remain on the staff longer than many of the others who came in the early days. Bill Magruder, Kent Robinson, and Marion Matthews joined the staff. Nathan "Nate" Schnaper came in 1953, and that year or the next was selected to help strengthen collaboration and rapport with the other disciplines. To some extent, says Schnaper, Finesinger may have felt this was a way for psychiatry to get a foothold, but Finesinger also believed that psychiatry should function with the rest of the hospital and not in an ivory tower.

Finesinger assigned Magruder to working half time with the department of medicine and Robinson to working half time with ob–gyn. Schnaper was to work half time with surgery, to build rapport. This was crazy, Schnaper told Finesinger. Surgery was the department least likely to acknowledge psychiatry even as a low priority. "That's okay," said Finesinger. And at first, surgery's old-boy network simply ignored Schnaper. Around the third year, he was asked for an occasional consult and acknowledged as a psychiatrist. It took about five years for them to treat him as a colleague.

Here was a typical case. One morning at six a surgeon called Schnaper about a little girl who was crossing and uncrossing her knees and throwing utensils at the breakfast table. She had been discharged from University Hospital days before, after being admitted for abdominal pain; and now the surgeon thought she was schizophrenic. Schnaper had a neurologist look at her. She'd had rheumatic fever and, the neurologist said, she had St. Vitus's dance, as it was called then, which often presents with abdominal pain.

Working with surgery got Schnaper involved in working with cancer patients, who needed the kind of help he could provide. "In those days the only treatment for cancer was surgery. If you can take it out, okay, but the only successes of course were breast cancer, and it was massive, mutilating surgery." For anything except breast cancer, the surgeons would "open them up, see metastases, and close them up." Schnaper observed that some of the surgeons tended to become buddies with their patients; they played golf, fished, and socialized with them. But when their buddies were in the hospital with cancer, they avoided them. Schnaper conjectured that with their friends they were dealing not only with their own mortality but also the fact that their omnipotence as surgeons had failed them. He wrote his first paper, "Care of the Dying Patient." Using humor, he helped make the staff more comfortable with death and dying.[2]

Things were so informal that there were no mailboxes for the residents, so in his first year of residency Jonas Rappeport built a box full of slots—a place with everybody's name. "I don't know what kind of psychiatrist you're going to be," said Finesinger, "but you're a good cabinetmaker."

Years after he retired from the faculty, Schnaper kept working as a volunteer, serving as de facto psychiatrist-at-large at the University of Maryland's Greenebaum Cancer Center in Baltimore, counseling patients and families facing cancer. His door is a magnet to which others apply cartoons about doctors, psychiatrists, and psychiatry.

The staff grew quickly, as Finesinger added professional staff in other fields, including psychology, nursing, and social work. Finesinger saw psychiatry as encompassing all of the arts and sciences—and then some. Some medical students complained, resentful that some of their classes were taught by social workers ("even lower on the competitive scale of prestige then than they are now," says Warren Poland, who graduated from the medical school in 1957). "Jake was astonished. His reaction was that he wanted to learn from anybody who could teach him, which led him to talk to the residents about paying respectful attention to hospital workers, specifically workers like the janitors, who often knew things of importance about inpatients that the residents would otherwise never know."

The next wave of residents, says Jonas Rappeport, who was one of them, included a fellow named Tannenbaum; Jordan Scher, who went to Israel; a woman with black hair; and Charles Bagley. "Charlie's father was a neurosurgeon of some repute. Charlie was going to go into surgery, but he couldn't scrub. The soaps gave him all kinds of rashes, so he decided to go into psychiatry."

Nate Schnaper tried to make the medical staff more comfortable with cancer, death, and dying.

Faculty in mid-1950s

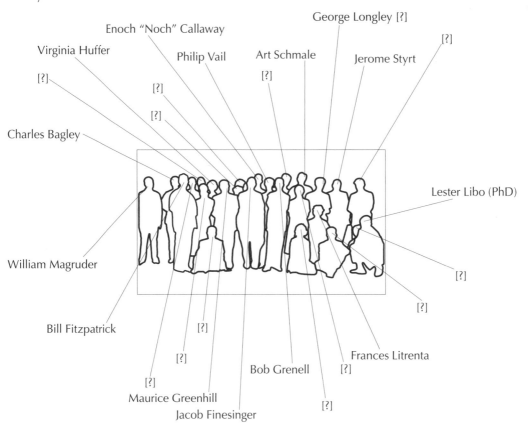

George Longley [?]

Enoch "Noch" Callaway

[?]

Virginia Huffer

Philip Vail   Art Schmale   Jerome Styrt

[?]   [?]   [?]

[?]   [?]

Charles Bagley   [?]

Lester Libo (PhD)

William Magruder

[?]

Bill Fitzpatrick   [?]

[?]

Frances Litrenta

[?]   Bob Grenell   [?]

[?]   Maurice Greenhill   [?]

Jacob Finesinger

Impressed by Enoch Callaway, Jordan Scher (resident 1953–55) decided to try his hand "at reinventing psychiatry. This seemed to me to be a wide open field," says Scher, "since I felt that the then dominant Freudian delusion would soon pass and leave the area available to whatever was to come next." Scher was especially interested in schizophrenia. "Needless to say, I did not crack this code. But I believe that I learned a great deal, and tended to immerse myself in trying to understand and decipher its many manifestations." One day Scher was surprised by the visit of David McKay Rioch, then head of the psychiatry department at Walter Reed Army Institute of Research, who had come to the Psychiatric Institute to accompany home to England one of Scher's schizophrenia patients, a visiting English scientist, "who had apparently been working at a hush-hush Army facility before his schizophrenic breakdown." After returning from England, Rioch again visited the institute, praised Scher for his treatment of this patient, and asked if he would like to join the National Institute of Mental Health, which had just been formed. "Dr Rioch 'hand-carried' me to NIMH, where he introduced me to Dr. Robert Cohen (who lived down the block from him), a transplant from the then much lauded Chestnut Lodge." Cohen invited Scher to join the NIMH staff as a researcher.

Psychiatrists had a big social life then. "Between Thanksgiving and Christmas we'd have sometimes two or three cocktail parties every weekend," says Jonas Rappeport. "After work we'd go have a beer or two in a little tavern around the corner. There was also a psychiatrists' wives club—not just university wives; I guess they were all psychoanalysts."

"While Jake was patient and open to the broad areas of psychiatry and neuroscience," says Poland, "his orientation was profoundly psychoanalytic, his thinking essentially philosophical. The halls of the institute were hung with photographs of Freud and the early group around him; the reading list for medical students in psychiatry was culled from the reading list of the psychoanalytic institute. When in an open class discussion he was attacked for the limitations of psychoanalytic understanding, his response was never defensive. Instead he said 'This is all we know in 1954. Join us in the work and then maybe we'll know more in 1955.' His chief concern—education—was to get physicians to realize the power of unconscious forces and unconscious feelings. The goal of teaching his interviewing technique was to get the interviewer to become alert to and appreciate the presence of concerns in the patient of which the patient himself was not consciously aware."

In 1957, Weldon Wallace wrote in the *Baltimore Sun* of a "new kind of teaching" at the medical school, in which medical students "are free to question the teacher's statements, criticize his methods if they wish, and offer their own suggestions and comments ... "They may even, within certain general limits, study those phases of the subject which they find most interesting or most puzzling." He was describing the psychiatry course John Reid and Jake Finesinger taught to fourth year medical students.

Combining principles of philosophy and psychiatry, the two men were working out new methods in medical instruction, to teach students to become independent thinkers rather than passive recipients of knowledge. In the traditional model, said Reid, "the teacher is an all-knowing person who dictates information and expects acceptance, while the students are limited primarily to taking notes, memorizing material handed them by the teacher, and returning the material to the instructor on examination papers."

Finesinger and Reid, in the new model, discuss the classroom material in an atmosphere of equality, accepting students' opinions and views as important. "The teacher, in this method of instruction, is no longer a dictator who expects uncritical acceptance." This discussion method would not work in fields in which the teacher is supposed to "impart pure facts or train people in mechanical techniques," wrote Wallace, but it is well-suited to psychiatry, which, dealing with "the human personality and its many ramifications and deviations, requires knowledge of many abstract factors such as human motives, goals, and moral issues."

One aim of the course, said Reid, is to ensure that pupil and teacher mean "the same thing by the same words. In psychiatry, as in other fields, people often use terms without a clear idea of their real meaning." Psychiatrists may have sharply different definitions of "psychotherapy" and "psychoneurosis," for example, two terms they use frequently.

Careful choice of words is important for a doctor dealing with patients, because certain words, under certain conditions, may cause intense emotional responses, but actions are important, too. "If the doctor glances at the clock during his examination, if he lets his gaze wander or maintains a careless posture, the patient may readily assume his physician is not interested in his case."[3]

Some of the traditions that started under Finesinger continued and blossomed. One of them was to introduce psychiatry and psychiatric concepts to medical students who did not plan to go into psychiatry. Bernadine Faw remembers one of her medical school classmates seeing a patient for years, starting while he was a first year medical student, with William Holden's encouragement and excellent supervision. Holden, who married Jake Finesinger's secretary, had staying power. He was still a popular lecturer in 1983–87, when Elizabeth "Robin" Hatcher participated in CAPP, an accelerated psychiatry program for medical students. "His theme was: 'You have to know this stuff. You have to be able to talk to patients. That may be life-saving in some circumstances.' He was a great lecturer and a bit of a comic. When he was talking about obsessive–compulsive disorder he would look around the room and find the student who was meticulously taking notes in outline form and underlining and so on. He picked me as a first year student, and then again when I was a fourth year medical student, and went through this whole shebang about OC people and why they do what they do. He stressed the relevance of psychiatry to clinical medicine, which is what he felt his job was, because most of the people in those lectures were not going into psychiatry."

Some of the medical students took advantage of summer fellowships in psychiatry that the NIH offered in the 1950s by way of encouraging an interest in psychiatry. The pay for some was $600, which was more than the women could earn in most summer jobs. Men could earn more doing construction work, working in breweries, operating a bulldozer for Caterpillar in Alaska, working for the U.S. Fish and Wildlife Service, and other jobs to which women didn't have access. The summer fellows would sometimes treat patients, under supervision by Psych Institute staff. During the summers of 1958, 1959, and 1960, Faw was one of several summer fellows who worked at South Baltimore General Hospital, the only hospital in town that was operating in the black.

"They made a point of adding the 'summer,' I suspect because 'fellows' in medicine usually means a fellowship has been granted to a post-residency doctor and we were only lowly medical students," says Bernadine Faw.

(*main text continues on page 68*)

Finesinger's public interviews with patients

Violet Samorodin Kron (then a freshman medical student) was in the anatomy lab in the fall of 1951 when Jake Finesinger came in and announced that "he was willing to meet with students to interview *alive* patients and to teach us more about the practice of medicine and psychiatry." She and about fifteen of her classmates attended these meetings, which took place after the Saturday morning lab dissections. "Dr. Finesinger interviewed patients with medical diseases that were considered to be related to emotional problems— psychosomatic disorders. He discussed the cases with us and would spend two or three hours talking with the first and second year medical students who continued to be interested. This was my introduction to psychiatry. For a young student immersed in basic science courses, it was an extremely valued opportunity to learn about the practice of medicine."[*]

"Every student knew of Jake," says John Hensala (class of 1960), who later took his residency in psychiatry at Langley Porter in San Francisco.

---

[*] During her final three years of medical school, Kron worked with Maurice Greenhill on the psychosomatic inpatient and outpatient service, participating in research under his supervision. Finesinger invited her and other medical students to parties at his home for psychiatric residents. "Thus I rapidly identified with the psychiatric staff and with growing interest, knowledge, and support, I decided to enter the training program at Yale." She practiced psychiatry for fifty years.

"When I entered the medical school," says Robert Ludicke (class of 1961), "my wife asked me did I have any idea what I was planning as far as a career and I guess I really didn't. I just thought it would be good to get into medical school and then see what I was interested in as I progressed." Finesinger was a major factor in his decision to go into psychiatry— something many graduates of the medical school reported. "He used to have live clinical conferences in an auditorium where he would take a patient at random from the outpatient department—not a psychiatric patient, just someone. And he would sit down on a stage and interview this person—often it was a black person— and he would go into his life history and medical history. It was very interesting how he connected the patient's medical problems—which were often hypertension, diabetes, and so on—with their socioeconomic situation, which was often problems with being black in Baltimore at that time.

"He always tied this together. He made psychiatry look not analytically difficult but down to earth. Sometime during medical school I went to Perry Point VA hospital. He used to go up there and do clinical rounds and then have discussions with the psychiatrists about different patients. At that time schizophrenia was the predominant diagnosis for veterans at that VA hospital. I was impressed by how he conducted his rounds, by the way he was with people, how he related to patients, how he made the connections between the medical problems and the psychiatric problems the patient was having, how he approached patients at their level, not with a superior attitude. He had the ability to make everyone feel at ease, whether they were a medical student or a patient. He was a good teacher—a kind, gentle, easy-going man who had a great depth of knowledge about medicine, psychiatry, and people."

Finesinger's public interviews, held in the auditorium, drew a crowd. He could get a patient to give a life history with hundreds of students watching.

Finesinger's public interviews, held in the auditorium of the Psychiatric Institute, were open to anyone and "he always got a good crowd. A lot of people dropped in just because he was having one of his case presentations—whether you were in psychiatry training at the time, or a resident, or a member of the medical school. A lot of medical students, interns, and residents took part in them because he didn't just interview psychiatric patients; he interviewed patients from the outpatient department, at random. Somehow he would sit them down and make them feel comfortable and get their personal life and history in front of an audience of hundreds of people."

Even the students revealed themselves. "During a lecture to the medical students," says Arthur Wolpert (class of 1961), "Dr. Finesinger said that at some time in our lives we may have a homosexual experience, or fantasize about one. One student abruptly stood up and in a shrill voice said, 'Not me!'"

"Their style was not to teach the usual classification of disorders, which puts everyone to sleep except the budding psychiatrists," says Theodore Zanker (class of 1960). "It was amazing how much patients would say, even in front of a hundred students, if they felt someone was really listening and cared. Each of us was then assigned a patient to interview separately on a ward and report back. I still remember mine vividly: a 24-year-old brittle diabetic young woman who kept having crises because she didn't follow the treatment recommendations. That experience firmed up in my mind that to become a 'compleat physician' I needed to understand what made people tick."

Zanker took a psychiatry elective clerkship in his third year. "One day in the clinic I had occasion to do an intake on an anxious (and seemingly paranoid) man who told me he was working on a secret project to send people to the moon (this was pre-Sputnik) and that people were after him and wanted to kidnap him. He didn't show up for his next appointment a few days later, and a few days after that the Secret Service showed up looking for him. They wouldn't tell me why, except that he was working on a sensitive project, became disturbed, and disappeared.

Say as little as possible, said Finesinger, urging "minimal activity"—but his eyebrows spoke louder than words.

A few weeks later (October 4, 1957), Sputnik went up. How's them apples?"

In psychotherapy interviews, Finesinger fostered a concept of minimal activity. "He felt that we should not speak in our interviews and we should use only leading phrases and leading terms but no more than that, reflecting what the patient had said back to him at times," said Jerome Styrt. Nate Schnaper observes, however: "Jake did not believe in much interaction with a patient. The psychiatrist should not ask big questions or use long sentences. But Jake had big black bushy eyebrows and there are videotapes of Jake talking to a patient and he's not saying a lot but his face and his eyebrows were tremendous communicators. I said, 'Your eyebrows speak louder than words. The patient can hear it across the room, when your eyebrows go.'"

"A lot goes on that the doctor doesn't know about," Finesinger explained to a reporter from the *Baltimore*

Sun.[4] Psychiatry was looking for new ways of "finding out what goes on in the mind" of patients and especially in "working out methods of measuring the interaction of patient and doctor," including the silences. Among other things, Finesinger emphasized "the way you get people to talk and how you focus the patient's interest on what you want to find out." In this effort, he told students, it was important that the activity of the doctor be minimal at first, "increasing as needed." Talk less, in other words, and watch and listen more.

"Isn't your technique a kind of Socratic technique, as in Socratic discourse?" Gerry Klee once asked Finesinger, who quickly replied, "No! Socrates made the other guy a stooge. I don't do that."

"In our class," says Bernadine Faw, "more people went into psychiatry than any other field, I think, and everyone says the same thing: It was Jake Finesinger, who had these sessions in the auditorium

"Dr. Finesinger said that at some time in our lives we may have a homosexual experience, or fantasize about one. One student abruptly stood up and in a shrill voice said, 'Not me!'"

in the Psych Institute. Eph Lisansky and Dr. Finesinger ran a clinic that was mandatory for the first year medical students. They would interview a medical patient they had never seen before, taken at random from the medical and surgical wards, and show us how tremendously necessary it was to understand not just the body

"Isn't your technique a kind of Socratic technique?" Gerry Klee once asked Finesinger. "No! Socrates made the other guy a stooge. I don't do that."

but the person's soul. It really was terrific. I don't think I've ever met anybody like Jake Finesinger, who, maybe because he died so young, made you think he was better than he was. But he was very impressive, especially to young people who didn't know anything. He was so soft and nice and kind and able in the gentlest way to interview these people so that they would end up telling him their life stories in front of more than eighty people who, though obviously quite visible, were quiet and respectful. They were not psychiatric patients but they certainly had psychiatric components to their illnesses. Almost everyone in my medical school class made

fun of psychiatry, but they liked him anyway. He got everyone to respect psychiatry in a way that I don't think anyone else was doing in those days."

Finesinger's interviews served as training, recruiting, and role modeling. "I came to medical school from a small town on Long Island, New York," says David Lee Rosen (class of 1961). "We had one doctor in town who seemed to know everyone and take care of everything medical. It was my plan to follow in his footsteps. As I went to lectures on cardiology, neurology, and dermatology I didn't see anyone who reminded me of my family doctor. The first person I saw who did was Dr. Finesinger in psychiatry. I was very naive about the field, but watching Dr. Finesinger I was taken by the way he made eye contact with patients, made them comfortable talking about difficult issues, made them feel that he had all the time in the world to listen to them and, in general was sincerely interested in what brought them to the hospital. Here, I thought, was the physician I knew from my small community."

(*continued from page 63*)

An unstructured approach, with humor

"Jake also put me in charge of setting up a six-week program for the students," wrote Nate Schaper in his book *I Pay You to Listen, Not to Talk*, the story of his fifty-year career told through the stories of his patients. "During the summer, I told him my ideas every week. Repeatedly, and frustratingly for me, he would smile and liltingly chant, 'Good, let it dance around in your head for awhile.' Fall came and the students arrived and I, annoyed by his lack of direction and apprehensive of implementing my ideas, began the program. Jake never did give me the verbal okay, but he was always very supportive."

There was probably method in his madness, but how could one know? "I remember being struck as a medical student by the seeming undirected freedom with which Jake approached each class," says Warren Poland. "It seemed to me that the classes could go in any direction, that material to be transmitted might never be gotten to. Then one day I decided to sit in on the other class section (the class was taught in two separate halves). I was astonished. With the same nondirective method being used, both classes covered the same areas."

Jonas Rappeport admired Finesinger but had trouble with his approach to running the department. "Jake was one hundred percent devoted to the department and he worked like hell but he was not an organizer," says Rappeport. "Jake did not believe in structure, just like he didn't believe in a structured interview. He believed in letting the patient go on. You could direct an interview somewhat, in a matter of time, but not too much. The department was also totally unstructured. There was no such thing as saying, Okay, now we're going to have a lecture about the mental status examination, which is the backbone of psychiatry, where you ask the patient, Do they know who they are and what day it is and repeat ten numbers after me and all that kind of stuff. You had a textbook and he assumed that everybody was mature enough and intellectually aggressive enough to do all this on their own."

"I don't know what kind of psychiatrist you're going to be," Finesinger told Rappeport, "but you're a good cabinetmaker."

"And then there was the supervision," says Rappeport. "Kent [Robinson] was my supervisor and he'd come late and he'd talk about something else. It was a very lackadaisical, relaxed kind of environment. And I went crazy. I'd get anxious. Jake gave people free rein and some people could deal with that and some couldn't. I just couldn't deal with this lack of structure at that point in my life." Rappeport remained associated with the department but finished his residency at Sheppard Pratt.

Finesinger wasn't upset about the same things that bothered others, says Poland. "Jake had arranged for the psychiatry department—unique among all medical school departments—to have its own library and its own librarian, someone who could also help residents develop their knowledge of the literature about any subject they wished to research. Once Jake called us residents together and told us that he had been informed by the librarian that he had to warn us of the consequences of some of our actions. Books were disappearing from the library, at such a rate that the library could not afford to replace them, so the library might end up having to close. Quite earnestly, Jake told us, as the librarian had told him to tell us, that whatever books we had would have to be returned. Then, after a pause, he leaned forward and said, "I want to add, if you are taking books . . . *read them!*"

"I'll tell you the truth, we wanted Anna Freud, but she's busy," said Finesinger, in response to a student's criticism.

Jake was very open, says Rappeport. "He always had a cigarette in his mouth. He had a big, beautiful office, we'd have conferences there, and once in a while Jake would fall asleep." Many of the people interviewed for this history mentioned Jake's frequently falling asleep, especially in small groups, and no two people described or explained it the same way. "He was not asleep," say some; "he closed his eyes to think, but he was not asleep. He was in the revery that comes following 'evenly hovering attention.'" Apparently Jake would nod off during a conference, with a cigarette in his mouth, the ash tumbling off, but then make a comment during the discussion that suggested he didn't miss a thing.

Bob Grenell remembered Finesinger coming into his lab to observe a technically difficult experiment and Grenell having to turn around to catch him two or three times before he fell off the tall stool he was sitting on. Whatever the explanation, fearing he'd nod off at the wheel, nobody enjoyed riding in a car he was driving. Grace Finesinger told Grenell that Jake never slept more than four hours a night his whole life.

Finesinger handled complaints with good humor. In "Struggling to Hear," Poland wrote of something that happened toward the end of Jake's unexpectedly brief life. Poland remembered the first day of his psychiatric residency, in 1958, "when, totally green and feeling lost, I was given the names of a dozen patients for whose therapy I now was responsible. Bewildered, I turned to a new co-resident, an older woman who had left her pediatric practice to learn child therapy and who herself was assigned a dozen child patients.

"She was less confused than outraged. She stormed into the head-of-the-department's office to confront the man at the top. How dare he assign patients the first day, before any of us had any idea of what we were supposed to do? She was willing to work hard, but patients could not be assigned until we had been *taught* how to do therapy. These children were real people, and they could not be treated that way.

"The chief thought for a moment, then leaned forward and answered in a candid tone. 'I'll tell you the truth,' he said. 'We wanted Anna Freud, but she's busy.'"[5]

Three final recruits

Once a week Finesinger commuted to the Veterans Administration hospital in Perry Point, Maryland, an hour's drive from the institute. After World War II, the VA was "undergoing a period of unprecedented expansion," wrote Walter Weintraub.[6] The size of the veteran population after World War II was huge, requiring a great influx of personnel and material. The VA maintained autonomous but affiliated training programs in the various medical disciplines. Dean's committees defined the treatment ideology and strategies taught medical students and residents in the VA hospitals and brought together academic and VA leaders to provide

Standing, left to right: Phil Vail, Ernie Katz, [?], [?], [?],Kurt Glaser, L. Whiting "Whitey" Farinholt, Charles Bagley, [?], Gene Brody, [?], Joe Bierman, [?], Harvey "Corny" Robinson, Bob Grenell, [?], [?], Gerry Klee, Walter Weintraub, Jack Raher, Hector Ramirez, Bill Holden, Dan Johnston, [?]. Seated:, [?] Adoracion "Dorie" Tanego, [?], John Reid, Imogene Young (director, social work), Jake Finesinger, [?], Norman Bocker, Kurt Fiedler, [?].

training. The dean's committee for teaching psychotherapeutic skills at Perry Point, headed by John Whitehorn of Hopkins, brought together an all-star cast of supervisors and consultants who commuted to Perry Point from the Baltimore medical schools and private psychiatric offices. Finesinger was the only one of the all-stars who wasn't from Johns Hopkins.

At Perry Point, Finesinger recruited two key staff members: Gerald "Gerry" Klee and Walter Weintraub. Gerry Klee had left the Public Health Service for Perry Point in 1954 and, he said, "was having weekly sessions, a continuous case seminar, with Jake. By this time we were recording them on an old-fashioned wire recorder; they didn't have tape yet. One of the things he taught me was to always try to think scientifically—even when you are doing individual psychotherapy, you're constantly thinking in hypothesis and always trying to predict what is going to happen next. He encouraged people to do research, but what he said was, 'Whether you are in the laboratory or working with patients, you should always think like a researcher, always as an

(*main text continues on page 74*)

Jacob Ellis Finesinger (1902–59)

Jacob E Finesinger graduated from Johns Hopkins University (BA, 1923; master's in zoology, 1925; medical school, 1929). In 1929 he interned as a neurological house officer at Boston City Hospital, where he became a resident and then a junior visiting physician in neurology, doing investigative work on a minuscule salary. A Commonwealth Fellowship from 1932 to 1935 allowed him (after a seven-year engagement) to marry his wife, Grace Lubin, who had earned a PhD in chemistry from Hopkins in 1925. He trained at the Boston Psychopathic Hospital while a psychiatry fellow at Harvard Medical School. From June 1933 to October 1934, the Finesingers were in Vienna, where he had training analyses with Anna Freud, Helene Deutsch, and Heinz Hartmann. He studied psychoanalysis and neuropathology in Vienna, and conditioned reflexes in Pavlov's laboratory in Leningrad.

On returning from Vienna, Finesinger accepted a position as a psychiatrist at Massachusetts General Hospital, serving also from 1936 to 1949 as an assistant professor of psychiatry at Harvard Medical School. He was an assistant in neuropathology to Professor Stanley Cobb, with whom he did research and training for many years. In 1934 he began psychoanalysis as the first analysand of Hanns Sachs, who had just come from Freud's circle in Vienna to succeed Franz Alexander as the training analyst of the Boston Psychoanalytic Society and Institute. Although trained in psychoanalysis, Finesinger did physiological research, studying cerebral metabolism and anoxia and doing clinical studies of psychiatric factors in atopic dermatitis, essential hypertension, fatigue states, and peptic ulcer.[7]

During World War II, he did research for the National Research Council and conducted studies for the Navy on who would and wouldn't make a good aircraft pilot. He was port executive for the Port of Boston, a consultant in neuropsychiatry for the U.S. Public Health Service, and a member of the medical advisory board of the Selective Service System.

"Jake had worked for twenty years and was still an assistant professor," says Brody. *"At Maryland he would be a full professor, and he would have a chance to build a new center."*

In May 1949, he accepted a position as professor of psychiatry and head of the new department of psychiatry at the University of Maryland medical school and director of the yet-to-be-built Psychiatric Institute. Although he was in line to succeed Cobb, who retired in

1954, Finesinger believed that at Harvard he would not be appointed chair because he was Jewish. "Jake had worked under Stanley Cobb for twenty years and was still an assistant professor," says Brody. "At Maryland he would be a full professor, and, in a town dominated by Johns Hopkins, he would have a chance to build a new center."

Asked in Maryland why he had become a psychiatrist, Finesinger said, "It was difficult to decide. I was interested in the humanities, in English, Latin, Greek, and other things. I began work in biology because I was interested in genetic problems. But I still wanted to work with people. I was interested in trying to figure out how people tick, why they do this or that—what they think about when they sit and twiddle their thumbs. Everybody has one song."[8]

Above all, he was an educator. His forte both at Harvard and at Maryland was the education of medical students. "As his ultimately fatal cancer progressed," says Warren Poland, "he had to drop work functions one by one—remarking that it took too much energy out of him to have to try to make other people comfortable around him in his illness. The very last thing he dropped was teaching the freshman medical students. He was convinced that what was most useful in fostering disciplined open-mindedness was getting in as early as possible, before people's conventional patterns turned rigid." He was a revered leader of the department.

He died of colon cancer in University Hospital on June 19, 1959, at the age of 56.

Dr. Finesinger Dies At 56

6/19/59

Dr. Jacob Ellis Finesinger, 56, professor of psychiatry and head of the department of psychiatry at the University of Maryland Medical School, died today after a long illness.

Born in New Castle, Pa., son of the late Rabbi Hyman J. Finesinger of the Shaarei Zion Congregation, Dr. Finesinger was educated in Baltimore.

He earned his bachelor of arts in 1923, master of arts in 1925 and medical degree in 1929, all at Johns Hopkins University.

In 1932 he married the former Grace Lubin, who received a Ph.D. from Hopkins. They had a son and daughter.

Set Up Institute

Before taking over the helm of the University of Maryland's psychiatric department in January, 1950, Dr. Finesinger was on the staff of the Massachusetts General Hospital. At University Hospital he established the Psychiatric Institute.

In explaining his interest in practicing psychiatry, Dr. Finesinger once said, "I want to work with people . . . to find out how people tick, why they do this or that— what they think about when they sit and twiddle their thumbs."

He belonged to numerous medical societies and groups and was active in civic affairs.

(*continued from page 71*)

investigator, never taking anything for granted. Always be examining, questioning, questioning.' He was the best teacher I ever had."

For months Finesinger tried hiring Klee, who, with a wife and three kids, felt he couldn't afford to take the job. Finally he got money to do research in psychopharmacology and brought Klee to the Psych Institute for "more money than someone at my level would normally get at that time. Left to my own devices I wouldn't have ended up there, but there I was and that was a major assignment. Jake was truly a father figure for me, and treated me like a loved son."

In 1955, Thorazine (chlorpromazine) had been introduced, the first of a series of drugs that would revolutionize psychiatry. Patients with chronic psychotic disorders improved enough on Thorazine that many of them were discharged, ushering in the modern era of psychopharmacology. Other new drugs came in rapid succession: more antipsychotic medications, antidepressants, anti-anxiety medications (the so-called tranquilizers), and more—gradually changing the shape of psychiatric practice. Many of the psychiatrists who had been around for some time were slow to start using the new drugs, and some people went so far as to continue trying to psychoanalyze schizophrenia patients as the sole form of treatment. Others, if they used drugs at all, used them in insufficient doses, says Klee, who in 1961 would help found the American College of Neuropsychopharmacology. Patients at the Psychiatric Institute almost always also got psychotherapy.

Weintraub, had begun his psychiatric residency training at Perry Point in 1956. "Those who are unfamiliar with the post–World War II VA picture will be surprised to learn that many VA centers like Perry Point devoted much of their teaching time to instructing residents in the art of dynamic psychotherapy," writes Weintraub. "Many VA residents were planning careers in psychoanalysis and a number of them were commuting to Baltimore for personal analysis. Pharmacotherapy was in its early stages and thought of as a 'blue collar' form of therapy, not fit for intelligent, nonpsychotic middle-class patients. It is true that Perry Point offered insulin coma therapy and ECT, but these were not considered first line treatments for psychotic patients."

Finesinger, who consulted one afternoon a week at Perry Point, was Weintraub's first psychotherapy supervisor. "'Jake,' as we all called him, was one of the first psychiatrists to use electronically recorded interviews in his supervision," Weintraub wrote in his book *Verbal Behavior*. "He taught his students that syntax and paralanguage were no less important than meaning in the understanding of the psychotherapeutic process. Jake believed that the future of psychotherapy research lay in the microscopic analysis of small samples of recorded speech."

Finesinger liked the way Weintraub treated patients and offered him a job. Weintraub had planned to go into private practice, but Finesinger persuaded him to become an academician, teaching, doing research, and earning half of his income treating patients. Accepting the position of research associate at Maryland allowed him to buy his way out of the VA program. "I gave them several thousand dollars in return for the money they had given me as part of the family plan and I cut myself free from the VA and moved to Baltimore."[9]

In July 1957, Finesinger brought on board another protégé, Eugene Brody, a former student of his from the Harvard Medical School. They'd run into each other at a medical meeting, and Finesinger had offered Brody a job as a professor, with no administrative duties.

Several months after Brody came to Baltimore, it became clear that Finesinger was ill. "He spread it around that he had diverticulitis," says Brody,[10] "but what he really had was a carcinoma of the colon. He said, 'Gene, you're going to have to take over.'" Brody had come to Baltimore to get away from administration, so in 1959 Finesinger appointed him psychiatrist-in-chief. He appointed Walter Weintraub head of inpatient psychiatric services (replacing Raymond Band), Gerry Klee head of outpatient services, and Ginny Huffer head of the new liaison services, doing psychiatric consults with patients in medical and surgical units. Weintraub, Klee, and Huffer, whose offices were near each other, ran both the clinical services and the training programs in their area.

The Journal of Nervous and Mental Disease

In 1958, Jake Finesinger was made editor-in-chief of *The Journal of Nervous and Mental Disease,* the world's oldest independent journal of general psychiatry. Harvey A. "Corny" Robinson, a psychologist who had come down from Yale to join the staff in the early 1950s, was managing editor until his death in 1966. Gene Brody, as consulting editor, and Robinson together oversaw the journal's editing for two years, until Lawrence S. "Larry" Kubie, a prominent psychoanalyst (and one of Brody's psychotherapy supervisors at Yale), retired from his private practice and came to Maryland as director of psychotherapy at Sheppard Pratt Hospital. Kubie, who became a clinical professor in the department and was active in departmental conferences, served as editor-in-chief of the journal from 1961 to 1967. Brody took over as editor-in-chief in 1967 and held that position until 2010. He was assisted in that task in the early years by Jim MacKie and James Lynch. In 1986, when he ended his ties with the university, he took the journal with him to Sheppard Pratt.

Three key people left the department. Enoch Callaway (who had been at Maryland on a career investigator grant) left to become head of research at the Langley Porter Neuropsychiatric Institute in San Francisco; Klaus Berblinger also left for Langley Porter; and Ray Band, who had been head of the inpatient service, left to open a private practice in Washington, D.C.

Finesinger, who had been so good at getting patients to talk frankly about their problems, who had encouraged doctors not to conceal the fact of a patient's cancer, in the end avoided discussing his own. In those days, says Nate Schnaper, "there were big discussions about whether or not to tell the patient he had cancer, and Robert Buxton, the new chief of surgery, said, 'Look, Nate, I know he is going to have cancer, and Jake believes in being told.' After surgery, Jake said, 'Nate, isn't this great? I know, the kids know, Grace knows, so we all know.' And never once after that did Jake use the word 'cancer.' Grace brought him two white pills one day when I was visiting and Jake said, 'I have an infection.' But he didn't have an infection. Those were pain pills."

One morning Bernadine Faw, who had the job of drawing early morning bloods in the hospital, realized that one patient she had to draw blood from was Finesinger. She had gotten pretty good at it—as one does, doing it every day for an hour or two—but when she saw who her patient was she must have "freaked out. His veins weren't so bad considering he must have been stuck a lot by that time. Those were the days before the Hickman catheter so anytime blood was needed the poor patient had to be stuck again. I can still remember clearly his face on the pillow looking up at me with such compassion for *me* and no hint of pain or annoyance. He said something like 'It's hard to stick your old professor.'" She got the vein on the second or third try.

Jake Finesinger died in University Hospital on June 19, 1959, at the age of 56.

Gene Brody had come to Finesinger's bedside every morning at 6 or 6:30 and debriefed him of his nocturnal hallucinations, which had begun two or three months before his death. "Not once did he speak of dying," says Brody, but Jake and his wife, Grace, planned his funeral together, deciding whom to invite as eulogists, what music to play (the second movement from Beethoven's *Eroica* symphony), and so on. This selection of music surprised some, as Finesinger's father was Rabbi Hyman J. Finesinger, and he had come from a long line of cantors. On the way to the funeral Louis Kaplan, head of Baltimore Hebrew College, asked Brody, "How can you participate in such a thing? It's an insult to his relatives."

In December, a search committee headed by Ephraim Lisansky asked Gene Brody to step in as chair. His kids were in school and he felt some obligation to carry on, so the Brodys gave up their dream of joining the rest of their family in San Francisco.

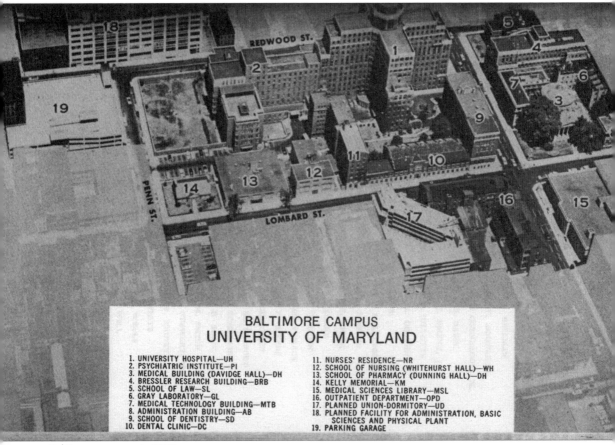

BALTIMORE CAMPUS
UNIVERSITY OF MARYLAND

1. UNIVERSITY HOSPITAL—UH
2. PSYCHIATRIC INSTITUTE—PI
3. MEDICAL BUILDING (DAVIDGE HALL)—DH
4. BRESSLER RESEARCH BUILDING—BRB
5. SCHOOL OF LAW—SL
6. GRAY LABORATORY—GL
7. MEDICAL TECHNOLOGY BUILDING—MTB
8. ADMINISTRATION BUILDING—AB
9. SCHOOL OF DENTISTRY—SD
10. DENTAL CLINIC—DC
11. NURSES' RESIDENCE—NR
12. SCHOOL OF NURSING (WHITEHURST HALL)—WH
13. SCHOOL OF PHARMACY (DUNNING HALL)—DH
14. KELLY MEMORIAL—KM
15. MEDICAL SCIENCES LIBRARY—MSL
16. OUTPATIENT DEPARTMENT—OPD
17. PLANNED UNION-DORMITORY—UD
18. PLANNED FACILITY FOR ADMINISTRATION, BASIC SCIENCES AND PHYSICAL PLANT
19. PARKING GARAGE

Baltimore campus in 1959

Eph Lisansky in action.

A sixties sensitivity training session

In 1959, Berry Gordy founded Motown, G.D. Searle applied to the FDA for approval of the birth control pill, Texas Instruments announced the microchip, the Soviets launched the spacecraft Lunik I, Ford withdrew the Edsel, and the first two American soldiers were killed in South Vietnam. "By the end of 1959, all the elements were in place for the upheavals of the subsequent decades."
—Fred Kaplan, *1959: The Year Everything Changed*

4

The Sixties

The history of the Psychiatric Institute in the 1960s can be understood only in the context of the social liberalism, protest, and youth-based cultural change that made this one of the wilder, more memorable decades of the twentieth century. In 1960, with the election of the vigorous young John F. Kennedy—and the release of the birth control pill—the nation turned its back on the conservatism and social conformity of the 1950s and embraced liberation. Demands for change were constant: for new ways of seeing the world, new ways of learning, of being, of healing, of relating to each other, of fixing the system or getting rid of it altogether. People believed that things could and should be different, and now was the time to make change happen. Kennedy introduced the Peace Corps in 1960 and the Community Mental Health Act in 1963, and he vowed to put a man on the moon by the end of the decade. In 1969 Neil Armstrong fulfilled that promise. Colonialism ended in 32 countries; Catholics could hear the Mass in English, not Latin. In 1963 Betty Friedan published her bestseller, *The Feminine Mystique*, and Kennedy's Presidential Commission on the Status of Women released its report on gender inequality, giving a boost to the women's liberation movement.

Drugs were embraced as a way to liberate the mind. First marijuana use spread from the jazz club subculture to the middle class; then LSD and other psychedelic drugs were popularized through ex-Harvard professor Timothy Leary's exhortation to "turn on, tune in, drop out." Clandestine labs early in the decade began creating methamphetamines, bringing on a speed epidemic that would never quite go away. The counterculture was celebrated most visibly in the Summer of Love in San Francisco's Haight–Ashbury section (1967) and the Woodstock Festival in upstate New York (1969). Influenced by the hippies, young people all over rebelled against dress codes. Sexual liberation in the swinging sixties went way beyond the imagining of those who had enjoyed the innocent fifties world of Doris Day movies.

The civil rights movement and increasing U.S. involvement in Vietnam gave America's youth more serious reasons to protest, and they joined African Americans at sit-ins, freedom rides, voter registration campaigns, and protest marches. A string of murders and assassinations followed: Medgar Evers and John F. Kennedy in 1963, Malcolm X in 1965, Martin Luther King Jr. and Robert F. Kennedy in 1968. After JFK's death, President Lyndon Johnson launched the War on Poverty and succeeded in pushing through the Civil Rights Act in 1964 and Medicare and Medicaid in 1965. But his escalation of an increasingly unpopular war in Vietnam led to protest marches and the election of Richard Nixon as president. Racial issues reached a boiling point. African Americans—no longer "Negroes" and soon to be "blacks"— eventually moved beyond anger, protest, and riots to demands for community control.

Considerable anti-psychiatry sentiment was expressed, in a sense reflecting what Erich Fromm argued in *The Sane Society* (1955): that the culture itself might be unadjusted, not just those individuals so designated by psychiatrists and psychologists. Psychiatrist Thomas Szasz (*The Myth of Mental Illness*, 1960) called psychiatry a pseudoscience that parodies medicine by using medical-sounding words; he challenged the state's right to label people sane or insane or to institutionalize them involuntarily—saying he was not so much anti-psychiatry as anti–coercive psychiatry. R.D. Laing (*The Divided Self*, 1960) offered an existential analysis of alienation, describing how the individual retreats from the world of experience into the fantasy world of psychosis—explaining the dichotomy between false and real selves in terms of the notions of inauthentic and authentic existence. Some felt this fed a tendency to romanticize mental illness. "In the deconstructionist view, mental illness is an arbitrary designation asserted by society for purposes of deviance control that is confirmed by psychiatry (Laing), something perpetuated if not created by mental hospitals (Foucault), or even altogether fictional (Szasz)," wrote Roy W. Menninger.[1]

There had been patient advocacy groups earlier in the century, but they tended to focus on children.

The work of these iconoclastic theorists helped create the climate and space for psychiatric patients to voice their discontent and provided fodder for discussion among emerging patient advocacy organizations representing patients' and families' rights.[2] The civil rights movement also

(*main text continues on page 89*)

Are psychiatrists real doctors?

Ted Woodward, a popular lecturer in the medical school, taught "real medicine."

Eph Lisansky taught medical students to interview patients "above the line and below the line."

Ted Woodward and Eph Lisansky

Of the occasional anti-psychiatry bias in the medical school there was no better-known representative than Theodore "Ted" Woodward, legendary forty-year chair of the department of medicine, and reputedly the most popular teacher in the medical school.* Tom Krajewski could see the disappointment on Woodward's face when he told him he was going into psychiatry. "Tom, my boy," said Woodward to Krajewski, when the time came to match students to the programs they wanted, "I thought you were going to be a real doctor."†

"Dr. Woodward was aghast if one of his bright and promising junior or senior year medical students said they intended to become a psychiatrist," says Joseph Stapen (class of 1967). "He would do everything he could to talk them out of it, which involved no small amount of intimidation. No one stood up to Dr. Woodward."

Woodward taught medical students in their third year, when they began

---

* Jacob Finesinger was said to be second in popularity.
† For this profile I drew on nterviews with Bob Derbyshire, George Gallahorn, Samuel T. Goldberg, Alice Heisler, Tom Krajewski, Tom Milroy, Michael Plaut, Jonas Rappeport, Virginia Truitt Sherr, Walter Weintraub, and Aron Wolf; letters from Joseph Robert Cowen, Robert Ludicke, Gerald Perman, Victor Reus,

and Jerome Tilles; and written tributes by Riva Novey, Bernard R. Shochet, and James W. Thompson. Some alumni saw absolutely no anti-psychiatry bias in Theodore Woodward, and one pointed out that he may have been critical of psychiatry as a department but was himself attentive to patients' personal and emotional needs. When Gene Brody was made chair of the department, however, and paid visits to each department chair in the medical school to ask how he could integrate the teaching of psychiatry with their department, Woodward told Brody he didn't see psychiatry as a real medical specialty.

rotations. "He was dramatic to good effect" in his weekly clinical case conference, discussing a patient's illness, says Samuel T. Goldberg (class of 1978). "He could also be intimidating; he didn't tolerate fools well. But he was fantastic at highlighting the main features of the case. He was both revered and a character. He was already seventyish when I arrived, and he had a role to play, living up to being Ted Woodward." Goldberg remembers his holding up an X-ray, angry that the staff had missed the lung cancer it showed, and saying, "No point in closing the door when the horse is out of the barn."

Woodward "seemed to be present throughout the course of our medical training, a somewhat amazing fact given that he was chairman of medicine," says Victor Reus (class of 1970). "We learned more about tropical diseases than any of us would be able to clinically use. As a class, we were probably more knowledgeable about rickettsial diseases and such things as psittacosis, Q fever, and scrub typhus than any other medical school class in the land. One benefit was that we were all very well prepared to recognize the importance of Lyme disease years later. I do not think that I will ever be able to separate my memories of Dr. Woodward from his ever-present question of us, which must have occurred a thousand times: 'Who of you can tell me what BCG means?'[*] And why is it important?'

"He made sure all students adhered to his standards of personal grooming," says Stapen. "That meant you could not grow your hair so long as to touch the back of your collar. A mustache, if one insisted, was grudgingly accepted; only one student out of the entire class wore one. No beards were allowed. How this changed over the next five years!" A picture of the class of 1972 showed male graduates with hair down to, or below, their shoulders. Woodward also insisted the students refer to men and women as "men and women," not "males and females," to distinguish them from the other animal species, recalls Gerald Perman (class of 1977).

Countering Woodward's message that "psychiatrists aren't real doctors" was the equally popular Ephraim "Eph" (pronounced EEF) Lisansky, a distinguished internist who proudly told everyone he was board certified in both internal medicine and psychiatry. "This was important," says Stapen, "because the field of psychiatry was, and might still be, looked down on by the department of medicine. He wanted students and faculty to know he had the credentials of a 'real' doctor." Part of his agenda was elevating psychiatry relative to other fields of medicine. Lisansky "helped sell the department by making psychiatry seem like an interesting subject to students who might not otherwise have been interested," says Walter Weintraub.

---

[*] Bacillus Calmette-Guérin (or Bacille Calmette-Guérin) is a vaccine against tuberculosis. The medical school has a strong tradition in internal medicine and the treatment of infectious disease. Tom Milroy recalls being strongly influenced by the "stalwarts in American medicine," particularly infectious diseases (Richard Hornick, Elizabeth Jackson, and Theodore Woodward) and neurology (Marshall Rennels)

Lisansky, who also held teaching appointments in the schools of dentistry, law, nursing, and social work, challenged Woodward for longevity and ability to create lasting impressions. He was close to six feet tall, well built, very confident, and showing a depth of knowledge, says Robert Ludicke (class of 1961). He was also "totally charismatic," says Aron Wolf (class of 1963 and chief resident 1967). "His energy level and breadth of training and experience were really significant."

Lisansky, Isadore Tuerk, and Whit Newell were giving medical students instructions on how to interview patients for psychiatric symptoms even before Finesinger arrived, says Joseph Robert Cowen, who started medical school in 1946. After there was an official department, lectures on interviewing and demonstrations of interviews with patients were provided during the first semester of medical students' freshman year, first by Finesinger and after his death by Gene Brody and others. During the second semester, they were provided by Lisansky, who taught interviewing skills mainly by example. Lisansky told medical students to meet patients as peers—to look beyond what they were saying to what they were feeling, to the meaning, or hints of meaning, implicit in what they were talking about. To see him doing a clinical interview with a patient was mesmerizing, says James Bozzuto (class of 1971).

"I have known some remarkable therapists in my life," says Virginia "Ginny" Truitt Sherr (class of 1956), "but this guy was just incredible. He would start talking to a patient and within two or three minutes he could tell you what that patient's history was. He could tell you more about that patient than the patient knew about himself, but factual stuff, not just psychoanalytic stuff—which he was also good at. In those days they would bring patients in and subject them to all

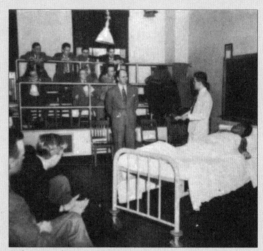

Eph Lisansky in action

these medical students. One day Eph was interviewing a man who was depressed. Eph was asking how his life has changed recently that might account for depression and the man said, 'Absolutely nothing happened. I have absolutely no reason to be depressed, no reason at all.' Eph turned to him and said, 'Tell me about your doctor,' and the guy burst into tears. Everyone wondered, What's going on? and the man finally sobbed and said his family doctor had died. I'm in tears myself remembering. Eph gently drew him out about why that was so important. Turned out the doctor, both a long-term doctor and friend, had saved his life. It was a wonderful snapshot of a moment for a budding psychiatrist—for any physician—to know that a doctor would mean that much to somebody. It had to be respected, not just in terms of transference, that you are going to mean something even if you two don't click, because at least in the patient's mind you stand for a positive force: recovery of health."

"He was an effective teacher, who was able to combine general medicine and psychiatry in a useful way," says Peter Hartmann (class of 1971, resident in family medicine 1972–74, and former faculty). "One of his famous interviewing techniques was what he called 'going above the line and below the line.' This was a strategy to make patients comfortable talking about sensitive topics. He advocated asking questions above the line first (that is, neutral topics, but related to sensitive ones) and then questions below the line (that is, sensitive questions). So, for example, you might ask the patient, 'How well do you sleep?' then 'Do you sleep with anyone?' and, finally, 'Do you experience any sexual difficulties?'"

The point of the class, held on Saturday mornings, was to teach medical students that you could learn about the patient's physical illness by taking a history and understanding their social and economic background, says George Gallahorn, who was a freshman medical student in 1962. "Lab tests and a physical exam are important, but you can often make the diagnosis or come very close to it by taking a careful history. The class was exceedingly popular. Our medical school class had something like 119 men and six women, and many of the guys were either married or seriously dating someone.

They would bring their dates to the class because Eph put on such a good show."

He was not well liked by some of the faculty, and he had quirks that turned some students off, including pride and arrogance, but he was a good teacher, bright and articulate.[*] He included a fair amount of comedy in his presentation and did what it took to get students to come to class on a Saturday. He got their attention and helped them understand that there was more to medicine than simply running tests, doing the numbers, and prescribing off that. "He was a showman in the good sense of the word," says Alice Heisler (fellow 1976–79). "He captivated the medical students."

He also helped recruit some

---

[*] Lisansky, who was well-known in the community, was also in charge of the medical school's continuing medical education department and served as moderator for various presentations. With his wife, Sylvia Lisansky (MSW 1970), he also taught a seminar at the school of social work for five years. After his retirement, the department of family medicine and the school of social work both developed a lectureship named for him. Louis Caplan, Lisansky's nephew, a lecturer in neurology at Harvard University and chief of the cerebrovascular and stroke division at Beth Israel Deaconess Medical Center in Boston, delivered the fourteenth and final Ephraim T. Lisansky lecture (for the school of social work) in May 2008. Caplan noted that the comprehensive interview takes time and much depends on the time available, which is why he believes "managed care is ruining the practice of medicine. The interview is the most powerful, sensitive, and versatile instrument available to the physician and serves many functions. It is in the same genre as social worker interviews with clients. During the interview you find out if the patient can afford to buy the medicine, or has family support for the treatment. Defective interviewing can lead to wrong diagnoses and conclusions." (Rosalia Scalia, "Harvard Doctor Delivers Final Lisansky Lecture," 2008.)

students to the field. "I had no knowledge of psychiatry when I started medical school," says Manfred K. Joeres (class of 1963), who had come to this country from post-war Germany. He'd intended to become a dentist, but switched to pre-med when a college friend suggested he "treat the whole person. My exposure to Dr. Lisansky probably had something to do with my decision to go into psychiatry."

Toward the end Lisansky gave only the very first lecture medical students heard, said James W. Thompson, who heard his last behavioral science lecture in 1991 and wrote about it on the professor's death two years later. "By then he was playing old audiotapes of patient interviews, stopping and starting the tapes and engaging the still-large crowd in a discussion of why and how they could get 'below the line' with a patient and find out what 'really' was going on." Pausing to take nitro for an angina attack, he got across his main point: "Your greatest diagnostic tool is your interaction with the patient."

"Your greatest diagnostic tool is your interaction with the patient," said Eph Lisansky.

Arthur Clifton Lamb came to Baltimore when it was still hard for African Americans to find a place to eat near the medical school.

(*continued from page 83*)
had an impact on patient advocacy. Fights first for racial equality and then for sexual equality had an impact on another disadvantaged minority: people with a mental illness. With hospital care becoming more expensive at a time of social upheaval, the cause of the mentally ill became an extension of the civil rights movement. Eventually the power of psychiatrists to commit people to hospitals involuntarily would be substantially reduced, and the patients and families, for good or for ill, would gain more power to choose or refuse their own treatment.

Beyond complacency

When Arthur Clifton "Clif" Lamb (class of 1963, resident class of 1967) came for his interview to get into the medical school, African American students were still rare enough that the interviewer's secretary could not suggest a place for him to eat. He'd just spent four years at Brown University, in Providence, Rhode Island, where he had no problem being accepted in restaurants. "I walked a few blocks north to a

Clif Lamb and his wife celebrating their forty-eighth wedding anniversary on the Seine, in 2010.

lunch counter, sat down, and was met with hostility from the counter person and consternation from the African American cook, who peeped out from the kitchen. This turned out to be my first and only sit-in." Refused service, Lamb "spread out a paper napkin, poured some peanuts from a dispenser on the counter, and proceeded to eat lunch."

Finding the basic medical science courses interesting and not particularly difficult, but experiencing the clinical years as drudgery and feeling better suited to psychiatry, Lamb began a psychiatric residency at the Psychiatry Institute. There was one other African American in his first year resident group: Walter Shervington, the son of a local surgeon, a friend from high school who had also been in medical school with him.

Junior faculty supervised residents and medical students on the inpatient units. Nathan Davis, a "fledgling analyst who came highly regarded from Chicago," was Lamb's first supervisor. His "persona was that of an aloof scholar who rarely shared his thoughts or feelings," and when he did he would also be puffing on his pipe, says Lamb. Heavy rain would enter through the sliding glass door of his office, on the ground floor, soaking his oriental carpet. His furniture included a huge chair of buttery leather that enveloped you when you sat in it. He was a brilliant, broadly educated man who could talk with you about almost anything, says Faw.

Many of the faculty members were analysts or analytically oriented. "The teaching was eclectic."

Many of the faculty members were analysts or analytically oriented. However, "the teaching, such as it was, was quite eclectic," says Lamb. The inpatient units were organized around "the so-called therapeutic community." Nurses wore street clothes instead of white uniforms (one of many changes that met resistance in the medical school), and the division changed from a closed to essentially an open service. Lamb was assigned to ward 2G, where he worked with Manoel Penna, a resident Brody recruited from Brazil in 1963. Penna would eventually direct the first inpatient unit of the community mental health system.

Unit 3G was supervised by Constantine Sakles, "a muscular Greek with ordinary tastes, who was quite unlike Nathan Davis," says Lamb. Connie Sakles, one of three early residents brought down from Yale, led training in group therapy. "Sakles was a flamboyant character," says Steve Fleishmann, who participated in a weekly seminar with him in the early 1970s. "It was an effusive, animated conference. He was also the psychodrama person. This was very state of the art for the period we're talking about.

"We got a stage for him and he would teach the patients to express themselves," says Walter Weintraub. "I think it helped the residents express themselves. I was never a big one on that, but I always felt that you had to give residents a peek at what was going on in psychiatry, not just show your favorite treatment or diagnosis." Everything has its phases.

The patient on the psychosomatic service
The idea of having a psychiatric ward in a general hospital was still fairly new in the 1950s, when the Psychiatric Institute

(*main text continues on page 93*)

The changing cast of characters (1960–76)

From 1960 to 1976, wrote Gene Brody in a 1976 retrospective on his career in the department, residents who became psychiatrists in charge of inpatient wards included Jose Arana, Carlos Azcarate, Nathan Davis, Clif Lamb, Leon Levin, Manoel Penna, Jack Raher, Constantine Sakles, and Lutz von Muehlen.*

Raymond Band directed resident education until 1960, when Walter Weintraub took over, directing a reorganized division of adult inpatient psychiatry, which provided training for first year residents and third year medical students. In 1970, when Weintraub became director of training, Connie Sakles became director of inpatient care. Sakles also developed the department's first psychodrama program (later led by Dick Schreder).

Part-time faculty who served as ward consultants, supervisors of individual therapy, and seminar and conference leaders included Otto Will and A. Russell Anderson.

Deane Fassett was director of psychiatric nursing, and key nurses, who helped maintain the therapeutic milieu, included Louise Adams, Judy Bankhead, Debbie Clark, Kathy Cole, Kay Cummings, Judy Duvall, Joanne Fike, Nancy Krauss, Ethel Myers, Sarah Perry, Gail Pomerantz, Mary Schenning, Jacqueline Shipley, Phyllis Smelkinson (in Open Clinic), and Greta Warren.

Clinical psychology was established as a separate entity in 1958, under Benjamin Pope. Robert Brown provided leadership and then in 1968 James MacKie became director of clinical psychology. MacKie led a major research effort in child psychiatry, on early enrichment. For several years, the department's clinical psychology internship was a leading national program; it ended in 1974, when federal funds were withdrawn. Clinical psychologists included Leonard Ainsworth, Mary Jo Albright, Harriet Aronson, Thomas Blass, Norman Bradford, Joseph R. Cowen, Lawrence Donner, Alfred Gross, Eleanor Jantz, James MacKie, Ruth Oppenheimer, Benjamin Pope, Morris Roseman, Jacob Schonfield, Winfield Scott, Aron Siegman, and Gerald Whitmarsh. Imogene Young, appointed in 1950, was the first director of psychiatric social work. She was replaced in the mid-1960s by Leonard Press,* who helped move social work into the mainstream of individual and especially family therapy, which was introduced starting in 1961 through such consultants to child psychiatry as Murray Bowen. Press's assistant director and, briefly, his successor was Donald Blumberg, whose chief interest was community mental health. After Blumberg left, Cecelia McCue led the service, until the arrival in 1971 of Joan Scratton, a strong leader from Australia

---

* The lists here, far from complete, are taken from Eugene Brody, "Maryland Psychiatry in the Context of a Personal Career" (1976) and old copies of the Psychiatric Institute *Bulletin*, published every couple of years during Brody's tenure.

* Brody remembers interviewing Press at the now defunct Golden Glow café, observing his horrified attention to the piranha in a tank mutilating a goldfish for lunch.

Leonard Press, pipe in hand, speaks with Phil Vail, Kay Donahoe, and an unidentified woman.

(by way of Smith faculty). The staff in psychiatric social work included Donald Blumberg, Kay Donahoe, Ross Ford, Irving Forster, Rosalind Griffin, George Gutches, Carol Lewis, James Ryan, and Stan Weinstein.

The activities therapy staff, led first by Roman Nagorka and later by Kersley Vauls, included Carl Barnes, Dorothy Forrester, Peggy Ann Jarboe, Charles Kemp, Ben McCoy, Robin Ramsay, Hank Schmuff, and Edythe Wilson.

(continued from page 91)

was built. Also new was the idea of having psychosomatic units in general hospitals—that is, units providing diagnosis and treatment by both psychiatrists and medical specialists. "In those days many illnesses were called psychosomatic that would later be known to have more complex origins," says Guy Chelton. "Peptic ulcers, for example, would be shown to be caused by a bacterium; chronic ulcerative colitis, which might have a psychic aspect, would be classified an autoimmune disorder; there would even appear to be a physiological and organic aspect of irritable bowel syndrome." For much of the time it existed, Jack Raher ran the psychosomatic service in the Psychiatric Institute.

An example of the research: Jack Raher and Angeles M. Flores, "Role of Emotion in the Precipitation and Exacerbation of Symptoms and in the Unexplained Death of an Adolescent with Dermatomyositis: A Case Report." *The Journal of Nervous and Mental Disease* (September 1960) 131: 3, pp. 260–266.

Kenneth Stern (class of 1967) spent the entire year of 1960 in the psychosomatic ward—as a patient. He'd had a minor bout of ulcerative colitis when he was twelve, and then, from the ages of 16 to 23, he'd had serious bouts of bleeding, with subsequent anemia, weight loss, and malnutrition, requiring several hospitalizations. "At the time, Kurt Fiedler was my psychiatrist," says Stern. "He had treated my mother briefly and a year or two later I asked if I could see him. I realized that I was in a lot of trouble psychologically as well as physiologically. Dr. Fiedler proposed that I come into the hospital on the so-called psychosomatic service—having significant illness and obviously emotional problems." Stern wasn't psychotic, wasn't suicidal, wasn't even clinically depressed, but his life "had become a shambles."

Several years before he went into the hospital, doctors had advised that he have a colectomy, but he was reluctant to have his colon removed, put the surgery off, and continued to be rather ill. "If I can be candid, my parents were good people but probably shouldn't have had children. They didn't know how to parent a child. They had had terrible experiences themselves—rather different, but they were deprived physically and moneywise and struggled a great deal. And I didn't have a very good parenting experience." Stern was 23 when he entered the hospital.

"I never felt or was intimidated by the fact that I was a psychiatric patient, however they expressed it at the time of my stay. I had a wonderful full parenting experience at the hospital.

Kenneth Stern, who spent a year on the psychosomatic ward, returned in 1963 as a medical student.

Dr. Fiedler and the inpatient psychiatric service, including Mr. Brown, an African American man, were as wonderful as anyone I have ever known. I was nurtured very well—but not overly so. I felt loved and I healed. They were like aunts and uncles to me. It was tense and difficult; I was struggling a great deal. I probably saw Dr. Fiedler several times a week in his office individually. They had groups. An occupational therapist, a man from Colorado, was superb—we did painting and sculpting and that sort of thing. So I had the opportunity to live with, if you will, and be in contact with some wonderful people who basically gave me in a very generic sense a re-parenting experience that was very meaningful and helpful."

The medical service followed Stern closely the whole time he was in the hospital. Previously he had felt that to have an ileostomy appliance would ruin his life. "By December of 1960 I realized that the only way I was going to have a life was to have the surgery." Frank Ota, chief resident, did the surgery in 1961, and there were complications—there was a second surgery and a third. "I developed fistulas, I became toxic and had septicemia. If I tell you I was near death it is not an exaggeration.

Positive experiences in Baltimore led Stern to become both a psychiatrist and an avid sailor.

At that time they had what they called a cold blanket, where they chilled your body temperature to below normal, and I was on that blanket for twenty days. After I was no longer critically ill, I was told that only one other person had survived those conditions."

When it was clear he would survive, he spent a few more weeks on the inpatient psychiatric service, then saw Dr. Fiedler as a private patient. "I was having a bit of a life. I drove a cab for a while, and finally I got better." Robert Buxton, chief of surgery, diligently handled his postsurgical recovery and saw no reason why Stern could not apply to medical school, which he had decided to do so he could become a psychiatrist.

Stern had started dental school twice, in 1958 and 1959, dropping out because of ill health. Now he applied for and in 1963 was accepted for medical school. He loved it—especially the clinical years, doing rotations on various services, and instruction from Walter Weintraub and Russ Monroe. On the first day of his rotation on the psychiatry service,

Mr. Brown and the other aides on his unit came out and hugged him. It was suggested he keep a low profile about having been a patient there; only two residents from Texas knew.

Influenced by the sailing culture at Maryland, Stern had taught himself to sail in Annapolis and went to Washington partly because there were more sailboats per capita in Seattle than anywhere else. He retired after a 34-year practice in psychiatry, half in Washington state and half in Newport, Rhode Island—two places where he could sail. At Newport, he did both inpatient and outpatient work and became chairman of the department. "I had many years before so-called monitored medicine, when I could spend more time with patients than with paperwork. Unhappily, that changed dramatically and took the joy out of practice. I gave up inpatient when it became much more stressful—because of all the paperwork and all the preauthorization and being told you have to say 'pretty please' and write a long enough justification so you could see your patient in the hospital for four days. It became distasteful and a chore, so my wife and I agreed that it was time for me to get out." Stern and his wife now live on an island in Portsmouth, Rhode Island, where eight months a year, weather permitting, he sails every other day.

Stern was dyslexic but had an excellent memory, so he graduated in 1967 in the middle of his class, receiving the Jacob Finesinger prize for excellence in psychiatry. "My friend Larry Feldman probably should have won the award, but the residents who knew my background probably made a case for my getting it and I was happy to. I took that $100 prize, bought an airline ticket, flew to Seattle, and applied for a residency at the University of Washington."

A strong but unusual hire

Eugene Brody, the new chairman of the department, wanted an academic program that taught general medical students not only about the medical care of psychiatric illness but also how an understanding of human behavior makes it easier to deliver health care services successfully—especially to patients from a different subculture. To that end, one of his first hires was a sociology graduate student named Bob Derbyshire (pronounced DER-bish-er), a broad-shouldered former Marine with a less than sterling record of academic achievement. Derbyshire had failed both first and third grades, despised school as a youth, and dropped out in the tenth grade to join the Marine Corps. At nineteen, he married Joan Love, began raising a family, and set out to get an education. He spent fourteen years in night school, earning a BS in education, working days as a schoolteacher, in a cannery, as a carpenter, and driving cabs.

In 1956, at the age of 27, after two impulsive, hysterical suicide attempts, he was admitted to the Psychiatric Institute with angioneurotic edema: in stressful situations, his tongue,

Bob Derbyshire, seen through a classroom door.

lips, and face swelled up so much he would nearly choke on his tongue. His therapist was a psychiatric resident, Kurt Glaser. "Psychotherapy helped," says Derbyshire. "My last episodes occurred in September 1959. The first Monday of my

Dr. Derbyshire

Dr. Derbyshire Chosen Man of Year

Dr. Robert Derbyshire, associate professor of sociology in psychiatry and director of undergraduate psychiatric education has been selected to receive the seventh annual Student Council faculty man of the year award.

In addition to his many varied teaching activities, Dr. Derbyshire is active in student and community affairs. Most recently he was appointed as member and consultant to the police community relations committee of the mayor's task force for equal rights.

Dr. Derbyshire received the traditional plaque which accompanies the award at the annual student council dinner held on May 14. The dinner was also attended by council members and post recipients of the award.

Last year, the award was presented to Dr. Harlan Firminger. Other winners include: Dr. Mitchell Rosenholtz, Dr. John Wiswell, Dr. Theodore Woodward and Dr. Charles Van Buskirk.

new teaching assignment at Morgan State College, I had an attack. Kurt Glaser had taught me to approach an episode determined not to let it control me. I did just that. Rather than take to my bed and hide as I had done on several previous occasions, I toughed it out and told my class it might be difficult to understand me. They accepted that and after three one-hour classes the edema slowly disappeared. The next morning, Tuesday, I awakened with another severe episode of edema. I returned to my classes at Morgan, made the same announcement, and within two hours all symptoms left, never to return again."

Then began an even busier period, especially for a man with five children. In 1960, when Derbyshire was a graduate student in sociology, Gene Brody invited him to attend medical school conferences and seminars without salary, suggesting he immerse himself in the medical environment. He confessed to Brody that he'd been hospitalized in the P.I. for two months in 1956, fearing that would be held against him. "Bob," said Brody, "most of our staff have had psychotherapy or psychoanalysis at some time, and if they haven't, they should." The staff (to many of whom he was familiar) were warmly accepting.

In 1960–61, while teaching sociology at Morgan State College, Derbyshire spent 20 to 25 hours a week at the medical school, attending the classes first year medical students attended to see what process they went through to become physicians. He spent four years observing the medical environment. In July 1961, Brody hired him as an instructor and researcher, giving him three years to complete his PhD—or "you are out of here." He taught night school three nights a week for three different colleges, while observing the medical students by day, doing the research for his dissertation, and co-teaching an unusual freshman medical class, one semester with Eph Lisansky and the second semester with psychologists and psychiatrist Jean Coyle O'Connor. In January 1964 he was awarded his PhD in sociology and promoted to assistant professor.

"Bob," said Brody, "most of our staff have had psychotherapy or psychoanalysis at some time, and if they haven't, they should."

The medical students Derbyshire was observing and the residents tended to be white, middle-class, and well-educated—not so different from Derbyshire. Many of their patients, on the other hand, were from poor minority families whose attitudes toward health care problems and health care professionals might well be different, in ways that could affect the success of diagnosis and treatment. Brody, who was interested in the social aspects of psychiatry, wondered, given the nature of American culture, why all blacks weren't schizophrenic, considering the racially hostile and often dangerous environment in which many of them lived.

Brody hired Ruth Blumenthal, a graduate student in anthropology, to investigate the childrearing and family patterns of middle-class Negroes. And in 1960 he asked Derbyshire and psychiatrist Carl Schleifer to conduct a study of young adult male patients at Crownsville State Mental Hospital, a hospital for the "Negro mentally ill." (Education had been desegregated in Maryland after the landmark Supreme Court decision in 1954 of *Brown v. Board of Education*, but the hospitals were still segregated. The Psychiatric Institute, which accepted "White and Negro adults as well as children" from the start, was ahead of its time.)

Bob Derbyshire with Rena Victor in Derbyshire's house in 1968. He threw a party for the freshman class and their faculty at the end of the academic year.

In the Crownsville study, first Schleifer, Crownsville's clinical director, interviewed each of one hundred schizophrenia patients; then Derbyshire interviewed them again before going out into the community to interview their families. The team published a number of papers and developed training courses to increase social awareness in medical students.

Among the papers published were Derbyshire, Brody, and Schleifer, "Family Structure of Young Adult Negro Male Mental Patients: Preliminary Observations from Urban Baltimore"; Schleifer, Derbyshire, and Jean Martin, "A Long-Term Follow-Up Study of Neurotic Phobic Patients in a Psychiatric Clinic; and "Clinical Change in Jail-Referred Mental Patients." "Patient access to Maryland State Mental Hospitals from Baltimore is mediated to an unusual degree by the local police," and many of those referred were African American, according to one paper.

"At the hospital, a charity patient tends to say what he thinks the middle-class interrogator wants to hear," Derbyshire told a journalist.[3] "He'll say he's never been in trouble with the police, while at home his mother will reveal a long history of trouble, beginning when he was ten— petty thievery, stealing cars, assault. 'We always worked,' the patient will reply when asked if his family has been on relief. At home, the women of the family speak bitterly of long periods of joblessness when they had nothing to live on *but* relief. A male patient often doesn't know how many brothers and sisters he has or the ages of his parents or where they were born. The aunts, mothers, and grandmothers are the keepers of such information. So home visits clear up many discrepancies in facts but, more importantly, they reveal to the investigator the emotional relationships in the family."

It was unusual to have psychologists and sociologists functioning the way they did at the Psychiatric Institute, says Derbyshire. Traditionally, psychiatrists used psychologists only to conduct psychometric testing—to verify if a diagnosis of schizophrenia was correct, for example. Brody wanted psychologists to study and teach the process of illness: how it starts and what affects it. Psychiatrists might do that today, but they didn't then, says Derbyshire. In those days psychiatrists were more clinically minded, less interested in research.

"Gene decided social science should be an integral part of training," says Derbyshire, who would provide some of that training. Drawing on what he was learning from observing medical students and studying the patients at Crownsville, Derbyshire and a young psychiatrist named Robert Vidaver developed a Huntley–Brinkley approach to helping medical students understand human behavior—a public dialogue supplemented with tapes, live interviews, and film clips showing family dynamics, which the class would discuss. Their goal was "to lure students away from a purely physical view of medicine"—to demonstrate how social class, minority status, and social situation affect both the development of illness and the ability to get well. Most doctors assumed that if they ordered enough lab tests and found the right drug, the patient would do what they say and get better, explained Derbyshire and Vidaver. But when families are barely scraping by, patients often don't have enough money to buy the drugs prescribed, so they often try to do without them, or take only part of what is prescribed, or take the drugs only until they feel better—which can be disastrous for a diabetic patient, for example, for whom getting the proper amount of insulin daily is essential. "Patients who have trouble putting food on the table also tend not to be inquisitive about what's happening to them—and in those days physicians didn't explain much. They said, 'Fill this prescription, go home, take this tablet as directed, and call me in a few days or if it doesn't work.' People had no understanding of what it meant to have a specific illness, what that illness meant for their future, or whether they would pass it on to their children.

Chet Huntley and David Brinkley co-anchored the popular nightly TV news show, the Huntley–Brinkley Report, introducing a relaxed banter to what had previously been a formal and dry format.

"Our job," Derbyshire said, "is to sell them on situation medicine. That means that for every patient there's a social situation that may be making him sicker or helping him get well." Patients Eph Lisansky interviewed in his popular Saturday course in psychiatry had come to the hospital for problems as various as an ulcer, a broken leg, or a psychiatric problem. After Lisansky conducted his interview with a patient, Derbyshire and Vidaver had three or four students visit the patient on his unit and then visit his home to meet the members of his family. Those students then reported back to the class on the physical and

"Gene decided social science should be an integral part of training," says Derbyshire.

emotional atmosphere in the home. Derbyshire and Vidaver tried to convey how living in poverty in an African American community affected health care: whether poor blacks get health care or not, what they do with it, how they treat it after they go home, whether they have anybody at home to help them out—all the social and family issues involved in health care for inner-city people living near or below the poverty line.

"Our job," Derbyshire said, "is to sell them on situation medicine. That means that for every patient there's a social situation that may be making him sicker or helping him get well."

In 1965, Derbyshire left Maryland for a year to do a study at UCLA on Los Angeles schoolchildren's attitudes toward the police. He had seven residents evaluate pictures third grade children drew of police at work before and after "Policeman Bill" came to the school to do a presentation about what a policeman does. The residents tested students in three different schools: one in Watts, one in a Mexican-American area, and one in an upper-middle-class area. Seven residents scored pictures drawn by about sixty students in each school on their levels of hostility vs. passivity and helpfulness vs. aggressiveness. Before Policeman Bill did his talk, the white middle-class children drew the policeman as a nice, helpful guy who directs traffic, helps children cross the street, etc. The children in the Mexican-American area drew them as more aggressive even than the Watts kids did: they were shooting guns, chasing people, beating people, with sirens and red lights running. Both minority groups essentially saw the policeman as someone they can't trust. After the Policeman Bill presentation, the attitude of the students in the Watts school changed the most ("for how long one didn't know"), the students in the white area didn't change one way or the other, and the Mexican-American students changed the least: they didn't buy what Policeman Bill was saying. Conducting a similar study in Baltimore was a step toward what Derbyshire hoped would modify the attitudes inner-city children and police have toward each other. In 1968 Derbyshire led a pilot program designed to reduce the distrust many inner-city children have of policemen. At local schools he conducted an experiment based on his model from the Los Angeles study.

"Under Gene Brody, psychiatry was more geared to psychological and sociological influences on people than to biochemical influences, although after many years Gene finally said to me one day, 'Someday, Bob, it's all going to be biochemical.' Johns Hopkins at that time was biochemically oriented and worked very little on psychodynamic issues. Maryland was psychodynamic and very little biochemical. Bob Grenell was trying to develop a pill that would cure schizophrenia. He had heard that this drug was coming out in Sweden, thought they had stolen his formula, and hadn't tested it yet, so he got Gene Brody to have it tested on about a hundred patients at Crownsville. Gene said the only thing it did was turn their urine blue."

Psychoanalysis: themes and variations

The department in its first two decades was psychoanalytically oriented. Its first three chairs were all fully trained analysts who readily identified themselves as such, which was the norm in academic psychiatry until the 1980s. Psychoanalysis was hot, and, starting in 1938, training in psychoanalysis in the United States had been restricted to psychiatrists—physicians who had completed residencies in a qualified psychiatric hospital. For fifty years, there would be no lay analysts in the United States. The American Psychoanalytic Association had negotiated a special regional status within the International Psychoanalytic Association—a status accorded no other member organization. The APA had an exclusive franchise to psychoanalysis in the United States and "total internal control over training standards and membership criteria, with no accountability to the IPA."[4]

When World War II began, U.S. psychoanalysts—trained in both analysis and medical care—were able to care for soldiers suffering both physically and mentally, which gave psychiatry a boost in the medical hierarchy.[5] So psychoanalysis was an important force at the Psychiatric Institute

(*main text continues on page 109*)

Eugene B. Brody
1921–2010

Chair of the department, 1959–76

Eugene B. Brody served as chair of the department for nearly seventeen years, assuming the position officially after Jake Finesinger's death in December 1959.

Brody was born in Columbia, Missouri, on June 17, 1921, and his mother named him Eugene in honor of Eugene V. Debs, the socialist candidate for president in 1920. His interest in research was fostered by his father, Samuel Brody, a biology professor at the University of Missouri who, as visiting faculty at the Sorbonne, brought young Gene to France for a year and a half. Brody earned bachelor's and master's degrees in experimental psychology at the University of Missouri, expecting to work toward a PhD, but instead decided to become a psychiatrist. In 1944 he got his medical degree from Harvard, where he was the only student in his class to choose a month's elective in psychiatry, directed by Jacob Finesinger (still at Harvard), whom he considered "a very bright man, a hell of a good teacher."

He had two years of psychiatric residency at Yale but disliked psychiatry under the chairmanship of Eugen Kahn. He left before finishing his residency to serve as a psychiatrist in the Army Medical Corps. In mid-1946 he was assigned to evaluate Nazi prisoners at the Nuremberg trials, an experience that heightened his interest in ethical and sociocultural issues.

In January 1948, he returned to Yale, where Fritz Redlich, the new chair of psychiatry, had offered him the chief residency and an eighteen-month instructorship at Yale. He resumed his earlier research in experimental endocrinology and brain function in rats and monkeys (in John Fulton's laboratories) and, from 1949 to 1952, served as chief psychiatrist for the Yale lobotomy project. He grew close to Redlich, whom he credits with much of his interest in social structure and context-driven behavior. He recognized that, with the war, "the internists and neurological psychiatrists had all learned that brief forms of psychoanalytically oriented therapy worked. That was the beginning of the big push toward psychoanalytic training and the centrality of psychoanalysis in this country."

Stimulated in part by concern for his mother's mental illness, he edited (with

Redlich) the book *Psychotherapy with Schizophrenics* (1952), a groundbreaking work in the pre-neuroleptic era. His mother's psychosis had begun when he was six and continued until her death at age ninety-six. "For many years I thought she was schizophrenic, although she never deteriorated and was only hospitalized once, when I was about six months old, after a suicide attempt. Looking back, I decided that she was what they would call bipolar now—but she had a very complex delusional system that never really changed." She was unusually beautiful, outgoing, and very smart—she had majored in philosophy at the University of California at Berkeley in 1910 when few women went to college. "I guess I realized she was psychotic when I was maybe twelve, but everybody else just thought she was eccentric. That was in Columbia, Missouri, a college town, and people were politically liberal and forgiving." Life with his mother conflicted with much of what he was taught about mental illness in medical school. "With patience and love, as well as increasing knowledge, it was possible to learn her language and teach her mine," he wrote. "I learned that no one is unreachable or incomprehensible 24 hours a day, or 60 minutes an hour."

Redlich told Brody that his chances of promotion beyond assistant professor were slim if he didn't become a psychoanalyst. Despite disliking the idea, he entered the New York Psychoanalytic Institute, the oldest and most rigidly Freudian in the country, commuting there for classes. Not long after, Alfred Gross, a refugee from Hitler, moved to New Haven

as a training analyst, and after five years of five sessions weekly, Brody completed his training analysis. "After about eight months I was speaking with a German accent, so I knew it was taking."

About halfway through this period, Redlich offered to recommend Brody for the rank of associate professor if Brody

would develop the psychiatric service at the new Veterans Administration hospital, still under construction. This was to be the major teaching facility for Yale's first year residents and third year medical students, so Brody accepted. "It wasn't a bad job, but after three and a half years I got bored with it because the patients were all somewhat similar and the bureaucracy was byzantine."

Jake Finesinger, who by now had left Harvard for the University of Maryland, offered Brody a job as a full professor with no administrative duties. Finesinger viewed psychiatric residencies as graduate education rather than as vocational training, a vision similar to Redlich's, and Brody accepted.

He was thirty-six when he arrived in Baltimore, in 1957. A year later, when Finesinger became gravely ill, Brody was temporarily appointed psychiatrist-in-chief of the University Hospital. He was only thirty-eight when he accepted the departmental chairmanship, despite his dislike for administration. "I was much too young for that position," he said recently. As chair, he was best at helping make a name for the department abroad and defending the department's turf within the medical school. He saw patients (including many doctors from Johns Hopkins), but his real interest was social psychiatry.

Brody adopted a relaxed style of chairmanship, traveling widely and often, especially in South America, leaving much of the administration to his friend and colleague, Russell Monroe, his first faculty recruit. In his book *The Lost Ones: Social Forces and Mental Illness in Rio de Janeiro* (1972), Brody made a case for the relationship between migration and mental illness, based on research he did from 1964 to 1968, as a visiting professor at the Federal University of Rio de Janeiro. As a visiting professor at the University of the West Indies in Jamaica and consultant to its National Family Planning Board (1972–75), he carried out the first national, psychodynamically oriented investigation of psychosocial factors determining reproductive behavior (*Sex, Contraception, and Motherhood in Jamaica*, 1981).

He brought psychiatry across international boundaries and was an important researcher and lecturer on culture conflict and the effects of minority status on mental health and community development. He allowed others to hatch and nourish programs—for example, giving Walter Weintraub complete license to develop the Combined Accelerated Program in Psychiatry (CAPP). Many programs flourished under his relaxed leadership, consistent with his own clinical values—respect for the complexity of the individual and appreciation of the individual's problems as arising in a social context that deserves to be understood in its own right.

"He was a strong department chair in the sense that he could intimidate the heads of other departments (which tended to look down on psychiatry) and defend the department's territory," says Weintraub. He was enormously bright, quoting scientific literature from memory, and if agreements were reached at official meetings, he would return to his office, summarize what was said, and send his

expertise, sophistication, and sensitivity as psychotherapists. "Gene was intimidating intellectually, questioning our work and demanding the best from us all," says Gary Nyman. "I remember him once quoting some obscure professional reference spontaneously in a conference. In my academically rebellious fashion, I hunted it down. Of course his photographic memory was accurate."

Brody saw the Psychiatric Institute as an academy—a miniversity—where bright people could discuss interesting issues. He was uncomfortable with the narrow view of psychiatry as a medical specialty; he wanted a department informed by psychoanalysis but also by neurology, biology, and the behavioral sciences—psychology, sociology, social psychology, and anthropology.

Believing the barriers between the mental health professions to be counterproductive, he hoped to help integrate them, maintaining strength within the institute in psychiatric social work, clinical psychology, and psychiatric nursing. He brought in a behavioral pediatrician, Stan Friedman, to run child psychiatry. MDs, PhDs, social workers, psychiatric nurses—all were respected. He encouraged an interchange among people in various subdisciplines—analysts, social scientists, biological scientists, and the people who worked with community groups—and was committed to ethnic and gender diversity.

summary out with a cover note, establishing a record.

Under his leadership, the department helped trainees develop clinical

Brody served as chair of the department from late 1959 to 1976. Many thought he would become dean of the medical school, and he was certainly a top contender, but in 1972 John Dennis, chair of radiology, was selected instead.* Brody was made associate dean for social and behavioral studies in 1973 and formed a Social and Behavioral Sciences Reference Group, bringing together people from all five professional schools on campus (law, medicine, pharmacy, dentistry, and social work and community planning) to network and hear presentations on various topics. From 1977 to 1986 he was professor emeritus.

His lasting concern with family planning in developing countries led to many consultancies, the last of which, before health issues forced his retirement from active travel, were in Yemen (2000) and Uzbekistan (2002). He also became a major advocate for human rights, especially for patients. He lectured at various South American universities, organized major conferences, and published books on minority group adolescents in the United States and on the mental health of migrants and refugees. His research career in social psychiatry yielded several books and more than two hundred academic papers.

He received many honors and distinguished fellowship appointments and was a consultant to the World Health Organization and the Pan American Health Organization. But he especially prized his leadership of the World Federation for Mental Health (WFMH), of which he was president (1981–83) and secretary general (1983–98). He gave his time and energy to WFMH because of its ecumenical nature, with citizens, patients, and professionals participating. He was also the very-long-term editor-in-chief of *The Journal of Nervous and Mental Disease*, despite being weakened by Parkinson's disease, working until a week or so before his death, March 13, 2010.

---

* The previous dean, John H Moxley III, had in his mid-thirties replaced an older, very traditional dean. Moxley—an impetuous, creative, and imaginative change agent— left after four years to become the first dean at the University of California at San Diego. Maryland's president, Albin Kuhn, a conservative agronomist, didn't want someone like that again so he considered three internal chairs for the dean's position: Theodore Woodward, the beloved chief of medicine; John Dennis, the chair of radiology; and Brody, who, says Frank Calia, was "an acquired taste: the classic scholar with a droll sense of humor, who would say the most outrageous things. A lot of people thought Brody would have made a hell of a dean." Dennis got the job.

(*continued from page 103*)
at least through the early 1970s, but nothing is simple and straightforward where psychoanalysis is involved.

Psychoanalysis was never directly part of either medicine or academia, and Freud and his followers wanted it that way. Academia can be limiting, and they had enough trouble with struggles for control in their own organization, says Jonas Rappeport (whose analyst was Sam Ingalls). "If they were connected with a university, they would never be able to do what they wanted to do." Psychoanalysts in training would be learning and talking about sexual drives, and for a long time university boards of trustees steered their institutions away from course content about sex. To avoid academic politics—including the university senate's being able to withhold approval of training—the institutes kept themselves separate from the universities. But many academic psychiatrists got training in psychoanalysis because it conferred status, and low-fee psychoanalysis was made available to many medical students and residents.

Not everyone who did talk therapy was a psychoanalyst. In treatment, a distinction is made between psychoanalysis (four or more days on a couch, in a structured setting and routine) and psychodynamic therapy ("insight therapy"), which is akin to, but is not actually, psychoanalysis—is shorter term and less ambitious in scope. Psychodynamic, or dynamic, therapy is psychotherapy with a psychoanalytic underpinning—with an emphasis on capturing and analyzing memories, understanding the unconscious meaning of symptoms to the patient, the patient's defensive structure, and factors involved in resistance to dealing with the illness itself, the description of the illness, or the medications prescribed for treatment. Dynamic psychiatry today would also involve understanding and dealing with the underlying problems, as opposed to running down a *Diagnostic and Statistical Manual* checklist of symptoms, assigning a rating, prescribing medication, but not really discussing or understanding the patient's attitude toward medication or seeing the doctor.

The classic model of analysis was based on depth psychology. It was focused on the unconscious, on infantile sexuality and the childhood origin of symptoms, on psychosexual stages of development and sexual dynamics, on analyzing the patient–analyst transference—all new concepts when Freud presented them. Harry Stack Sullivan, who was openly disdainful of Freud and classic analysis, greatly influenced his followers at Sheppard Pratt Hospital and Chestnut Lodge (a private mental hospital in Rockville, Maryland) with his analytic work with schizophrenics. In the classic Freudian view, analysis was not a proper treatment of choice for schizophrenics.

Frieda Fromm-Reichmann and Otto Will, who were also at Chestnut Lodge, were the Sullivanians most familiar to staff and residents at the Psych Institute. Indeed, Fromm-Reichman was one of the featured speakers at its opening. A gifted therapist and teacher, she had fled the Nazis in her native Germany and come to the United States in 1935. In the 1940s and 1950s she had helped create at Chestnut Lodge a psychoanalytically based therapeutic environment in which after long-term intensive therapy some patients with schizophrenia got better. Jake Finesinger probably disagreed with the Sullivanian influence on these outside supervisors from Chestnut Lodge, but never undermined them.

Psychoanalysts have a long tradition of disagreeing among themselves, and the members of the original Baltimore–Washington society were no exception. The issues on which they disagreed included ego psychology, revisions of Freudian theory, Harry Stack Sullivan's focus on the interpersonal aspects of psychodynamics, and the use of psychoanalytic theory to understand and treat psychoses. The more classic group of psychoanalysts,

Transference, in the past, had to do with the doctor–patient relationship; today it might also involve the patient and the health care system, in which patients often feel stymied.

In 1926 Frieda Reichmann had married the noted therapist and author Erich Fromm, fifteen years her junior and her former patient, from whom she later separated. "Analysts in Washington had long been considered anomalous because so many of them worked in hospitals and treated seriously disturbed patients," writes Gail Hornstein in an account of the work Frieda Fromm-Reichmann and her colleagues were doing at Chestnut Lodge. "Most analysts elsewhere worked only with outpatient neurotics." In the 1930s, however, the Washington–Baltimore psychiatric community had already "become a home for renegades, and experiments were taking place all over the region. Adolf Meyer was at Johns Hopkins teaching medical students to sit by the beds of psychotics until they could make sense of what their patients were trying to tell them. Harry Stack Sullivan was at Sheppard Pratt … running a special ward for schizophrenics and claiming recoveries in an astounding 85 percent. William Alanson White was in his twenty-eighth year as superintendent at St. Elizabeths, rounding out a career as psychiatry's most distinguished iconoclast by letting Edward Kempf try psychoanalysis with delusional patients." Gail A. Hornstein, *To Redeem One Person Is to Redeem the World: The Life of Frieda Fromm-Reichmann* (Free Press, 2000), pp. 97, 181.

believing the presence and power of unconscious forces to be at the core of psychoanalytic thought, viewed concern for the social and interpersonal aspects of psychodynamics as a defensive avoidance of unconscious issues.

Such disagreements led the original Baltimore–Washington psychoanalytic institute to officially split into two institutes in 1946. The new institute got formal approval by the national organization in 1952. Students and faculty who want training in psychoanalysis today can apply to either the Baltimore–Washington Institute for Psychoanalysis, historically if no longer the more classically Freudian of the two groups (originally at 827 North Charles Street, in Baltimore; now based in Laurel, Maryland), or to the Washington Psychoanalytic Institute. These are separate operations, neither with direct ties to any university. Fromm-Reichman taught at both institutes as well as at one in New York.

Psychoanalysis and various kinds of dynamic psychotherapy soon faced competition from other approaches to dealing with mental illness, particularly for the treatment of severe and persistent mental illness. As treatment for severe mental illness, dynamic psychotherapy would be set back dramatically by a malpractice lawsuit against Chestnut Lodge in 1982. And psychiatry's exclusive franchise on psychoanalysis would be eliminated in 1988 by the resolution of a longstanding lawsuit claiming that psychiatry's exclusive franchise was unfair. (Those two events are discussed briefly in the section on the 1980s).

Moreover, "there has been a revolution in psychoanalytic theory in the last twenty-five to thirty years, owing to baby research," says Léon Wurmser, who served on the faculty in the 1970s. Researchers are learning how complex the psychological development of the baby is, how early it begins, and how that affects everything that comes afterward.

The early conflict—even animosity—between the classic and Sullivanian schools of thought greatly diminished over time, says Warren Poland, with "appreciation of the fact that there can be no drive without an object to the drive and there can be no love object—a person, not a thing—without a drive.

Among those who talked to me about the local psychoanalytic institutes were Gene Brody, Herb Gross, Tom Milroy, Jay Phillips, Warren Poland, and Jonas Rappeport. "My first analyst, Otto Will, taught in the department," says Herb Gross, who was active in the department for decades. "When I was about to leave the army he suggested that the University of Maryland was better than GW or Hopkins. He left town to take a job in Massachusetts and I started up with Robert Cohen. Warren Poland taught me at the Washington Psychoanalytic Institute." Gross is president (2009–2111) of the Washington Center for Psychoanalysis.

"What Freud, Melanie Klein, and others hypothesized about early childhood has proven partly wrong, partly fantasy, and to some extent, but not terribly much, correct. Freud's theory of conflict and the treatment of conflict has stood the test of time; the theoretic superstructure, much less so."

Meanwhile, in 1964 there was still so much stigma associated with mental illness that when Joanne Greenberg published a semi-fictional account of her own psychotic breakdown and recovery at Chestnut Lodge, she published it as a novel—*I Never Promised You A Rose Garden*—under the pen name Hannah Green. The novel's sixteen-year-old heroine, Deborah, is taken to a private mental hospital, where she opens up to the fictional Dr. Clara Fried, a character based on Fromm-Reichman, who had been Greenberg's therapist. Fromm-Reichman apparently planned to write a joint account of the treatment with Greenberg, but died in 1957.

Also, Freud wrote about guilt, but ignored shame, says Wurmser, author of *The Mask of Shame* (1981). I feel guilty if I have harmed somebody; I feel ashamed if I have betrayed my own and others' expectations of me. One feels internal guilt out of an abuse of power. Shame is more external—about how we will be perceived, even by ourselves, in terms of weakness and failure.

Child psychiatry

Child psychiatry had a history in the medical school before it became an official division of the department of psychiatry. In response to problems of juvenile delinquency, mental retardation, and the need for child protection, juvenile courts and child guidance clinics developed in the community well before anything developed in academia. In 1921 the Commonwealth Fund began to support training and clinical services for a series of new clinics patterned after Boston's Judge Baker Guidance Center, and these became part of a national child guidance movement. By the end of the 1930s, more than five hundred community-based child guidance clinics were supported by local philanthropy—"rarely affiliated with a hospital, let alone a medical school."[6] They valued psychoanalytic thought and prescribed few if any drugs.

In 1930, Leo Kanner had started the first academic department of child psychiatry, at Johns Hopkins, under the leadership of Adolf Meyer. After passage of the National Mental Health Act of 1946, the U.S. Public Health Service in 1948 began to fund training in child psychiatry, and the child guidance clinic loosely affiliated with the University of Maryland became a training site for medical residents and various schools of social work. Whit Newell, a much-loved child psychiatrist (and president of the Baltimore Psychoanalytic Society, 1950–51) was director of the clinic near University Hospital. Training was provided by the clinic's multidisciplinary team: a psychiatrist, psychologist, and social worker. Then as now, there was a shortage of qualified child psychiatrists.

Once the Psychiatric Institute opened, an active child guidance clinic took residence on the terrace (basement) floor, where there were classrooms and play therapy rooms opening onto an outdoor play area. Inpatient care was in 4G, on the fourth floor, and there was a gym on the sixth floor. Residents from Maryland rotated through the busy clinic, managed at first by Clara Livsey, and residents from a fledgling child psychiatry program at Sheppard Pratt came over for supervision on selected cases. The clinic treated children sent from various social agencies around the city and held consultation conferences with their workers. After Newell's death in the mid-1950s, child psychiatry services were led, in turn, by Charlie Bagley (briefly, after serving as administrator), Marvin Jaffe, Joseph S. Bierman (acting director 1957–59). It is unclear who led in 1959–61.

The American Board of Psychiatry and Neurology (ABPN) ruled in 1957 that general psychiatrists must have six months of training in child

There was so much stigma associated with mental illness that Joanne Greenberg published a semi-fictional account of her own psychotic breakdown and recovery at Chestnut Lodge—I Never Promised You A Rose Garden—under a pen name.

For child psychiatry to become an official subspecialty of psychiatry, "the claim that child psychiatry was really behavioral pediatrics had to be refuted," write Flaherty and Brooks. This topic would be revisited in the 1970s.

For nearly thirty years, it remained "child psychiatry." It became "child and adolescent psychiatry" after a "push for more specialization within psychiatry," which "was hotly debated in the late 1980s and early 1990s," writes John E. Schowalter in his chapter on child and adolescent psychiatry in Menninger, *American Psychiatry etc.*, pp. 475–76. The American Academy of Child Psychiatry became The American Academy of Child and Adolescent Psychiatry in 1986, ABPN added "and Adolescent" in 1989, and the Accreditation Council for Graduate Medical Education (ACGME) did so in 1991.

psychiatry and that the child guidance clinics, which provided considerable training, must be administratively linked to approved general psychiatry training programs. The clinics were now to be called child psychiatry clinics, and Maryland's clinic became the Child Psychiatry Service. In 1959 the American Board of Medical Specialties issued its first certificate in child psychiatry, which for the next thirty years was the only psychiatric subspecialty the ABMS recognized—the next one being geriatric psychiatry in 1989.

In 1961, Brody recruited Frank Rafferty, a nationally respected child psychiatrist from Utah, an early maverick with a strong personality and strong opinions, to organize and develop the department's official new division. The division's first fellows—George Brown, William Battle, and Anthony Gillette—were joined in 1963 by Ulku Ulgur, one of four Turkish members in the department's early years.

The four Turkish members of the department (who knew each other but did not work together) were, in order of appearance, Saim Akin, Ülkü Ülgür, Basri Sila, and Alp Karahasan (originally Karahasanoğlu). His first two years in America, Ulgur kept the umlauts in his name; the third year, when he dropped them, he knew he was American.

Rafferty wanted to build a full child division, with training, research, and the extension of community-based services. "He was a visionary, ahead of his time," says Ulgur. He could see "child psychiatry as a profession with multiple tasks and roles, serving children, their parents, schools, and communities. When I arrived, child psychiatry was still in a very transitional phase and many of the psychoanalytically trained therapists were resentful of abandoning old styles and moving into this unknown new territory. Most of the staff was trained in psychodynamic psychiatry and treatment and more, because child psychiatry was different from adult psychiatry. Working with parents, schools, courts, and social services required additional skills, and trying to meet the needs of developmentally disabled children required skills in social and community work. Frank Rafferty was very good at all that." Everyone attended all major teaching activities of adult psychiatry, too.

Frank Rafferty established family therapy (a new concept) in child psychiatry and pushed for better community services for children.

Joseph "Joe" Noshpitz, an internationally known child psychiatrist, came to help organize the children's residential service, teach, and supervise. During lengthy case presentations and discussions, Noshpitz was able to dissect the information he was provided and return it, crystallized, to the residents. He was good at teaching the meaning, dynamics, and therapeutic value of child's play. A long-time advocate of treating children in residential centers, he "was interested in using the entire milieu of a treatment center as a way of helping a child to grow," said one of his colleagues, "not just squeezing or whipping a child into shape." Noshpitz, an analyst, paid attention to children's development, adaptation, and adjustment, not just the development of psychopathology, and his style and knowledge base made him a superb teacher, says Ulgur.

The colleague was Robert A. King, who coauthored a two-volume work on child psychopathology and development with him, quoted in Joseph Noshpitz's obituary in the *New York Times*. Noshpitz was a founding member of the American Academy of Child and Adolescent Psychiatry, serving as its president from 1973 to 1975, and was editor-in-chief of the *Basic Handbook of Child Psychiatry* (1987), among other publications. "Joe was incredibly good, and knew more card games and tricks than anyone can imagine," says Bernadine Faw. He would admit to anyone who complained about being in analysis too long that he was still in analysis after twenty-five years, though not with the same analyst.

In 1967 an Iranian psychiatrist named Taghi Modarressi joined the faculty. He became director of outpatient services; Naomi Grant, a well-known child psychiatrist from Britain, was director of the children's liaison service; and Ulgur headed children's residential services, replacing his supervisor, Mariano Veiga, another psychoanalytically oriented child psychiatrist. "It was the best learning experience in my life," says Ulgur.

Rafferty's office was on the terrace floor, Ulgur's on the fourth floor, and those of Grant and Modarressi on the first floor.

A multidisciplinary group ran an intramural school and residential service for fourteen severely disturbed children, whose average stay was two years. Their problems ranged from early infantile autism to schizophrenia and other severe disorders of childhood. The treatment team consisted of full-time teachers supported by the Baltimore school system (including Roland Queen, Carl Wilson, and Bill Hill), activity therapists (Kersley Vauls), social workers (including Stan Weinstein, Kay Donahoe, Cecelia McCue), psychologists, nurses (including Nancy Krauss and Kathy Cole), child care workers, and child psychiatrists. Rotating adult psychiatry residents and child psychiatry fellows were supervised closely as they learned various treatment modalities and provided intensive services to the children. At a certain point Ulgur shifted the therapeutic program from a seven- to a five-day week, so the children could spend their weekends at home. "Our greatest goal was to keep the families intact and to keep the children in their family settings. Although hospital stays were long, the children didn't live in isolation but in a carefully designed therapeutic milieu designed to meet their needs. We developed such a strong faculty that the school of nursing, school of social work, and clinical psychology assigned their own trainees to us. We had an ample number of PhD candidates." Under the new model of involving the family, the length of stay was shortened to one year.

In the summertime, they would take the kids to a camp, to go swimming. "There was something about getting in a pool with a bathing suit and no ties," says Stan Weinstein. "You just would relate, and kids loved water play. It's a great way for the children to regress. Back in play therapy days, we remodeled 4G once and put in a water play therapy room."

Eventually, says Ulgur, when health care became insurance-oriented, the long-term stays came to a halt. "The insurance companies said, 'If they can go home for the weekend, they probably don't need to be in the hospital, and five days is enough.' But at that time, just admitting a patient to the hospital was a lengthy process, requiring family interviews, a visit to the home environment, and then bringing the children in gradually. It wasn't zip in and zip out, but careful planning to determine the children's needs. We paid attention to the grouping. We didn't admit everyone who was in need; we made sure any child who was admitted would benefit from our existing therapeutic group. The discharge process also took time." After the child returned home and to the community, the child's therapist and the family therapist often continued their treatment for months. The division's preadmission and aftercare processes made the children's residential service a model for continuity of care.[7]

Rafferty was brilliant at recruiting. On the faculty roster were Murray Bowen, based in Georgetown, who came in to teach family systems therapy, drawing circles on the blackboard, Zelda Teplitz, a child analyst, and Lewis Holder, a prominent child psychiatrist. In 1967, Rafferty recruited the department's first director of child care, George Cohen, who had worked with Benjamin Spock and had a master's

"Our greatest goal was to keep the families intact and to keep the children in their family settings," says Ulku Ulgur.

degree in child care from the University of Pittsburgh (in itself unusual). Rafferty also recruited a number of child care workers, some with masters' degrees and PhDs, from the ranks of conscientious objectors doing health care service rather than serve in Vietnam.

Under Rafferty the division established a family therapy clinic (which was pretty radical at the time), worked on an NIMH-funded family therapy project, and helped train allied professionals in child psychiatry and child development. The institute had no adolescent inpatient unit, though adolescents were occasionally admitted to adult inpatient units and the division worked with the adolescent unit at Crownsville State Hospital. Rafferty sought partnerships in unlikely places. He was involved with VISTA and the Peace Corps, for example. "There was a high rate of psychiatric and psychological casualty among the Peace Corps workers," says Ulgur. "Frank became involved with that through Joseph English, chief psychiatrist for the Peace Corps." English explained that volunteers whose idealism and discontent led them to join the Peace Corps in the first place often had trouble reentering the country after living abroad for two years.

The Rouse Company was developing Columbia, Maryland, from farmland, and one day Rafferty told Ulgur, "Look, you could have a therapeutic preschool there. Go visit some schools and see what you could do." Rafferty envisioned a therapeutic school for emotionally disturbed children, providing early intervention for children who seemed to have problems. "Now every school district has a program of preschool intervention called Child Find. School-based mental health was one of Rafferty's visions that got realized later. He encouraged us to provide consultations in the schools, even though we didn't know the techniques yet. There were a few pioneers here and there, but we didn't have adequate role models, and the information wasn't well organized. We had to write our own books."

Before the concepts of specialized services had been fully developed, Rafferty encouraged faculty and trainees to get training and become leaders in community-based services for children, adolescents, and families. Ulgur consulted with various educational organizations and eventually became a consultant to the Howard County School System, then expanded to Baltimore City and Anne Arundel County. Those psychiatric consultations to schools, which became a model for school-based mental health services, were "a by-product of our early learnings in the department, whether as faculty or trainees."

Residents' experiences in the early 1960s

In 1961 Marcio V. Pinheiro, a Brazilian who had just finished his second year of residency in internal medicine at St. Agnes Hospital, was accepted as a first year psychiatric resident at the Psych Institute. Except for reading some of Freud's papers, he didn't know much about psychiatry.

His first assignment was Ward 3G. Residents were assigned up to ten hospitalized patients, each of whom they met with three times a week for fifty minutes. Pinheiro recalls the anxiety he felt at first, changing from internal medicine to psychiatry. Once a day he met with the ward administrator, Nathan Davis, who had switched from

"To this date the Institute of that time remains a model of a psychiatric hospital for me," says Marcio Pinheiro. "Psychiatry had an identity of its own, as a medical specialty that drew from many sources."

philosophy to psychoanalysis and was a student at the Baltimore–Washington Psychoanalytic Institute. He had daily community meetings with the patients and staff and became interested in milieu therapy—how the environment of a psychiatric ward could be organized to maximize a patient's recovery. Once a week he discussed his cases with his two supervisors, Kent Robinson and Bill Magruder. He participated in one seminar on psychotherapy with Otto Will Jr. and another on milieu therapy with Gene Brody.

The first year of residency was inpatient, under Walter Weintraub, director of inpatient services on four similar wards. During that year the wards became co-ed and autonomous—that is, the patients would enter and leave from the same ward instead of progressing from one to the others. Pinheiro especially remembers treating a very regressed schizophrenic psychiatric nurse, with whom he had many difficult meetings, at least three times a week. "When I approached her she would start to scream, asking me very loudly to leave. People would know when I was going to have a session of psychotherapy with her. In the course of psychotherapy she stopped eating and I decided to have lunch with her every day to show her that I was not concerned about the food. My supervisor suggested that maybe she thought the food was poisoned." She still refused to eat, so she was fed twice a day through a nasogastric tube, Pinheiro explaining to her that this was to prevent her dying. The residents were very involved with the patients, who were there for long stays, so as Pinheiro's first year residency ended and he moved on to outpatient care, he followed this patient at a distance, participating in the case conference presented by the next resident to care for her, Bernadine Faw.

For each case he began treating, Pinheiro had to present the patient's problems, writing a detailed complaint, history, and psychodynamic formulation based on psychoanalytic principles. The residents used fifty-minute sessions of talk therapy three times a week to treat patients with severe schizophrenia and manic–depressive psychosis (not yet called bipolar disorder). "Medication was seldom used," says Pinheiro. "Lithium was not used, and the antipsychotic medications, although already available, had not yet been well tested." The belief seemed to be that "a good therapist did not need to use medications." There were also group psychotherapy sessions, but they did not yet know the importance of working with families, "although we tried."

Their textbook, *Modern Clinical Psychiatry* by Noyes and Kolb, presented psychodynamic American psychiatry. They also read Freud's papers and *The Impact of Freudian Psychiatry* by Franz Alexander.

"One thing was always clear in our minds: what the patients needed. Within this framework, in an atmosphere of freedom, we tried and changed treatments as we learned which ones worked better. We started with inpatient and, in our second year of residency—when we went to outpatient treatment, under Gerald Klee—we could follow two inpatients whom we had been working with, so we could have an experience with long-term psychotherapy with the severely mentally ill. Patients who still needed inpatient care and were not being followed by residents were sometimes transferred to state hospitals for further inpatient care. The discharge of a patient to the community had to be very well planned, with good communication between the inpatient and outpatient psychiatrists. During my residency John F. Kennedy had his Action for Mental Health initiative and soon we had the help of community mental health clinics, to which we could refer our patients." Later, the Walter P. Carter Center would be built to meet community psychiatry needs.

Working with outpatients, Pinheiro became more anxious, perhaps "because I then was treating patients who were more similar to myself, and they would make me look more at myself as I listened to them. Not that this did not happen with the inpatients, but there, although I had much in common with them, I was able to separate myself better from their psychopathologies." He was already having once-a-week psychotherapy with Olive Smith, "a kind psychoanalyst from the Baltimore–Washington Psychoanalytic Institute." On her recommendation, he undertook psychoanalysis with Francis McLaughlin, seeing him four times a week for three years—a life-changing experience. "To this day, I put this experience with Dr. McLaughlin to good use."

> *"Medication was seldom used," says Pinheiro. The belief seemed to be that "a good therapist did not need to use medications."*

Often the residents needed psychotherapy to deal with what they experienced in their residency. "When I was a first year resident," says Bernadine Faw (Arnold), who was a resident from 1962 to 1964, "we were evaluating a woman who was going to be admitted. (The first person a patient saw was us, the least experienced people.) We were doing this intake, realizing she had postpartum depression and needed to be in the hospital, but nobody wanted to take her away from her baby, who was thin and pathetic. So Walt Weintraub got the idea of admitting the baby, too, and they were probably in the hospital two or three months. She became very good with the baby. Everyone loved him, he was getting lots of attention, and he was looking great.

"She got a lot better and was discharged, and the baby thrived. She was coming in once or twice a week. We were allowed to follow our inpatients as outpatients after they left, if they left—those were the days of long-term hospitalization. It was fascinating and we were planning to write the whole thing up—having a baby on the ward with other mentally ill people was very unusual—but it ended so tragically that nobody had the heart to write up anything. What made it so traumatic—I feel like crying still—is that after she was discharged she ended up killing herself. I was seeing her as an outpatient, and I think she wouldn't have killed herself if I had been more experienced. I had supervision but they can't pick up as much from what you're saying as if they'd seen her themselves, or they might have known not to send her home, to say, 'You've got to come back into the hospital.' But I didn't.

"Those were the days before much medication; I think she had Elavil and psychotherapy, but they weren't enough. We knew she was desperately depressed. We got her somewhat better, so she was able to go home and was doing pretty well for a while. One of the goals, besides getting her better, was to help her be a better mother and we sure reached that one. Her husband was off at work, she waited until he was about to come home, she had the baby sound asleep, clean, everything fine in the crib, and baby would not be alone very long, because daddy was coming right home. And she shot herself. She shot herself. It was the most traumatic thing that happened in my career. I was her doctor and I'll never forget her.

"Walter was as sad and upset as everybody. Nobody blamed me except myself. And at the time he probably helped me not blame myself quite so much, to understand that these things do happen and I couldn't have known for sure. I was absolutely shocked. It was my own narcissism, I guess—it didn't occur to me that she actually could do that, especially since she always assured me she wouldn't."

Faw says, "I can't say enough good things about Walt Weintraub. He was a good teacher, kind, gentle, warm, and caring—a good role model. He could tell you things you were doing wrong without your minding at all—and I was incredibly sensitive, so that was really something. He just knew how to handle people, and he didn't get rattled and excited and go wild because something was going wrong. He'd just listen, and it would end up getting fixed."

The residency program was run "super loosely," with little structure, as if you were expected to figure things out on your own, says Faw. In a sense, residents had both heavy responsibilities and, at the same time, not enough. In their second year of residency, a new resident joined the small group of residents doing outpatient residency. "It was clear to all of us that something was drastically wrong with him, and it kept getting worse. We kept trying to tell people something was wrong, that he needed help, that they needed to pay attention, but they pooh-poohed us. (We were mere residents; what

Many of the psychoanalysts who supervised "didn't tell us anything—expected us to figure it out for ourselves," says Bernadine Faw Arnold. "And we were very green."

could we know?) One day as we waited for a case conference to begin, he went up to the blackboard and in a booming voice said something like, 'I know it all now,' began writing and talking about God or Jesus, and became floridly psychotic, saying he was a prophet. Marcio Pinheiro took him by the arm and somehow got him to Sheppard Pratt Hospital, where he was admitted by Rolfe Finn, a fine psychiatrist. (Usually Hopkins staff came to Maryland for hospitalization and Maryland staff went to Hopkins, to minimize gossip.) Gerry Klee and Russ Monroe hustled everyone else out of the case conference meeting room. It was a traumatic event for all of us. It validated what we were thinking already: Why didn't they listen to us? It would have been so much better if he had been diagnosed and treated earlier."

As a summer fellow working in the adolescent clinic, Faw had had excellent supervision from Charlie Bagley and Jean Coyle (O'Connor). "They were friendly, personable, and helpful, and also tried to teach." She had a problem with psychoanalysts who supervised: "They didn't tell us anything—expected us to figure it out for ourselves. But when you don't know anything to start, it's a little hard to figure something out. We were very green and nobody was teaching us anything. In essence, some of the analysts treated us like analytic patients of theirs and some of the non-analysts seemed to be aping that style."

One evening a week Walter Weintraub and Gerry Klee provided training in psychotherapy for psychiatric residents in state hospitals, many of them foreign medical graduates. Language was a problem, so patients with good language skills were selected for the training sessions. Residents were taught to be warm and attentive while letting the patient do most of the talking. Interviews were audio-recorded, with the patients' permission, and the trainees played back their interview, with their supervisors suggesting ways they might improve their techniques. "Like even the most skilled therapists, the residents sometimes made meaningless remarks to which a patient might respond as if they represented profound wisdom," says Faw. "Such misunderstandings sometimes led to a therapeutic experience—a reminder that psychotherapy is not an exact science."

Otto Will continued as an important outside resource under Brody, coming to the institute once a month as a teacher and primary supervisor. Will was also the analyst for some members of the faculty, including Russ Monroe. Chestnut Lodge, where he was based, was at the peak of its experiment treating hospitalized schizophrenics with intensive psychoanalytic psychotherapy. Residents had one seminar on psychotherapy with Will (representing the more unorthodox Sullivanian school of interpersonal psychiatry) and another on the psychoanalytical theory of neuroses with Russell Anderson, a classic Freudian from the Baltimore–Washington Psychoanalytic Institute. Anderson also held a continuous case conference with neurotic outpatients, but after hospitalization for heart disease he was never quite the same.

"Like Walter Weintraub, Dr. Will was a good supervisor, very gentle," says Faw. "Every word he said was worth saying, which was true of Weintraub, too. Once a month, he came over from Chestnut Lodge for a continuing case conference, and nobody ever missed that one. He would sit at one end of the conference table, a dozen or so residents (and staff) would sit around the table—or at the back if the table was full—and one resident would present a case." During her year as inpatient resident, Faw remembers presenting a patient she had inherited from Marcio Pinheiro, a psychiatric nurse about twenty-five-years old whom Pinheiro had been seeing almost every day, patiently trying to help. The woman was now constantly mute—she could hear but wouldn't talk—and totally catatonic. She had a feeding tube in and was not taking medication. The emphasis at the time was still on psychotherapy and milieu therapy.

"Marcio, who was a year ahead of us, was laid back and could just be with her, trying to relate and be supportive," says Faw. "I really didn't know why anyone would expect you to be able to do anything. I was horrendously frustrated and upset. Chestnut Lodge, I think, was better at this type of treatment than Maryland. I started to present this case to Otto Will at the conference, asking in agony, 'What can we do? How long does this go on?' The state was paying for this, because she was training the residents. She had no family.

"Anyway, Otto Will actually agreed to medicating her so we put her on a small amount of the new neuroleptic drug, Stelazine, and she gradually came out of it and was able to talk before the year was up. I saw her then as an outpatient for a while. She didn't come often because she was living in Hagerstown, which was quite a distance, and we didn't have good roads then. But she kept coming, and afterward she wrote me a few times. She was doing well and had met a young man—she had never had a young man in her life before. Things seemed to be going very well. She had remained on Stelazine, being very impressed with how it had helped—and so was everyone else. That was a very good learning experience for us all. It was also a bit bizarre, but those were times of transition. I think people were shocked that Otto Will, of all people, agreed to try the medication, but he was a sensible guy. He knew people responded sometimes and that anything is worth trying instead of sending her to a state hospital (about which many of us held negative fantasies). I really admired Otto Will. He

Marcio Pinheiro was so impressed with her recovery that he asked for an interview with the patient. She told him that she remembered their meetings but was not, at the time, organized enough to respond to him verbally—was helpless to do so. To this date he wonders what impact his year of psychotherapy had on her. With such a patient today he would combine the use of neuroleptics with psychodynamic psychotherapy. One of the first things he learned in psychotherapy was to control the urge "to do something."

The Psychiatric Institute had a clear identity, separate from the school of medicine, physically next to the hospital but not quite merged with it.

was one of my heroes, not just because of that case, and because he was sensible, but because, unlike some of the analysts, you could understand what he wrote."

Although some revered him, Will apparently didn't take himself too seriously. Asked if he got anything out of his psychoanalysis with Harry Stack Sullivan, Will told John Haws, "Yes, my tennis game improved dramatically." Asked the same question by Pinheiro, he said, "In the end I played the violin a little better."

Walter Weintraub was in charge of inpatient psychiatry, Gerry Klee ran outpatient psychiatry, and Virginia Huffer ran the consultation liaison service. The specialty of liaison psychiatry, also known as consultative psychiatry or consultation–liaison psychiatry, developed when psychiatric care was introduced in general hospitals. If the primary care team on the medical and surgical units had questions about patients' mental health status, or felt their mental status was affecting their physical problems, they called Ginny Huffer. Huffer supervised all the third year medical students and residents who rotated through the service. Considered a brilliant psychoanalyst, she was also an outstanding supervisor and an interesting teacher, a "tough but fair lady, very task-oriented, who tolerated no nonsense."

"She would grill you on your cases, taking them apart," says Eliot S. Cohen (resident 1972–75), "and you would leave there thinking you were the worst resident in the world. But if you talked about a patient's dreams, especially his sexual dreams, she would loosen up and relax." She had grown up an only child in Boonsboro, Maryland, had never married but had many, many friends, and was an avid sailor with a place down on the Eastern Shore. In 1970, she spent time with the women on Mornington Island, Australia, later publishing the book, *The Sweetness of the Fig: Aboriginal Women in Transition* (1980).

Many residents valued the social atmosphere in the department. The Psychiatric Institute itself had a clear identity, separate from the school of medicine, physically next to the university hospital but not quite merged with it, says Pinheiro. The wards were quite comfortable, a garden surrounded the building, and there was a gymnasium on the upper floor. "To this date the Institute of that time remains a model of a psychiatric hospital for me," says Pinheiro. "Psychiatry had an identity of its own, not exactly the medical model but a medical specialty that drew from many sources—among them psychoanalysis, sociology, anthropology, and yes, the hard sciences too. A great emphasis was placed on dealing with people at all levels, patients and staff—perhaps the influence of Sullivanian interpersonal psychiatry. It was good to be part of that big family under Dr. Brody's leadership. There was a feeling that patients and staff were in the same boat. There were no white coats for doctors, nurses, or attendants."

There was also an atmosphere of intellectual freedom. "Although we were treating patients with severe mental disorders with very little medication, there were no prejudices in favor of this or that treatment or dogma, this or that author, or how we should look at psychiatry and psychiatric patients," says Pinheiro. "If I had gone for a residency in another geographical area, or even next door at Johns Hopkins, I would not have been exposed to the same comprehensive, humanistic, clinical approach." Hopkins was looking more at the brain than at the mind, taking a more biological approach to psychiatry. Elsewhere in the United States, "patients were receiving a lot of electroconvulsive therapy in short hospitalizations, with

Ron Taylor, who had experience with ECT because of its extensive use at Taylor Manor Hospital, says that Maryland's faculty was inexperienced with ECT (many had never seen it done), was reluctant to use it, was required to do it in an operating room (which made it more costly), and even had a hard time finding the ECT machine the department owned. The psychoanalytically oriented department put many obstacles in the path of using ECT, discouraging referrals for it.

no concern about the therapeutic milieu, psychotherapy, etc. Of course we did use ECT but only as treatment for a few selected patients. We felt free to try anything within the accepted psychiatric practices without having to follow an official ideology. Dr. Brody was a seeker of truth, open to any line of investigation."

Training was patient-oriented and hence problem-oriented. In addition to the classic case presentation and continuous case seminars, there were topic-oriented reading seminars (on psychoanalysis and schizophrenia, for example), journal clubs, and resident involvement in the teaching of freshman and sophomore medical students. Brody had graduated from the New York Psychoanalytic Institute, but like Finesinger he encouraged a healthy debate about psychoanalysis—often at his own home. Residents also lunched with John Reid, the staff philosopher, "whose mission was to be around to talk to residents." Every week, staff and residents met in the small auditorium for the Psych Institute's Friday conference—to which Brody invited interesting speakers on a wide range of topics. "He himself was present, frequently asking very intelligent questions," says Pinheiro.

After leaving the Institute Pinheiro worked for seven years at Sheppard Pratt, Springfield Hospital, community health centers, and in private practice before returning to Belo Horizonte, Brazil, to share what he had learned.

"Dr. Brody impressed me quite a bit, not only because he was very bright—close to a genius—but also because, a sensitive Brazilian, I sensed him to be a man free of prejudices against foreigners."

At the Friday conferences, experts sometimes spoke about their research. Bob Grenell, who in 1960 had organized the institute's neurobiology laboratories, was doing research on psychopharmacology. He and others sometimes spoke about new medications. Some staff members spoke about research with LSD and some about using LSD as part of therapy. One professor from Peru talked about love and psychotherapy. "The future of psychiatry rests with institutes and universities which, not bound solely by service needs and not adhering to any single doctrine of human behavior, can approach a problem wherever there is a lead," wrote Brody in 1961. After a Friday conference, the faculty and interested residents would lunch with the guest speaker. Often Gene and Marian Brody invited guests, staff, residents, and students to their Ruxton home for a long evening of cocktails, good food, and fellowship.

There were many discussions of William Caudill's influential book, *The Psychiatric Hospital as a Small Society*, about the importance to the patient's treatment of the social environment in the hospital. Caudill, an anthropologist, had entered Yale's Psychiatric Institute as a patient and stayed for a month or so, making interesting observations about the small society of the hospital and noting "collective disturbances" on the ward. At one point some patients ran away, others came back drunk, and the whole ward was disturbed as a small society; he traced the disturbance to underground conflicts between staff groups (doctors and nurses, for example) that had not come up for discussion. If the staff didn't make a consistent effort to acknowledge such conflicts, bring them into the open, and work them out, the patients would become disturbed and act them out. To make the ward milieu in Maryland's Psychiatric Institute therapeutic for the patients living there, the residents took these lessons seriously. They discussed similar issues from the book *The Mental Hospital*, written by a psychiatrist (Alfred Stanton) and a sociologist (Morris Schwartz) and from Elaine Cumming's *The Ego and Milieu*, a theoretical and practical guide to milieu therapy.

There were many discussions of William Caudill's influential book, The Psychiatric Hospital as a Small Society, *about the importance to the patient's treatment of the social environment in the hospital.*

"Of course the insurance companies and managed care in mental health later dismantled all of this," says Pinheiro. "Compared with the milieu in my residency days, the environment patients live in today is terrible, each one isolated in his room being 'treated' by white-coat docs called med checkers."

"It was slow-motion learning in those days," says Ulku Ulgur. "We were not in the fast lane. But it was truly a stimulating environment for learning and development, both in adult and child psychiatry, and I give Gene Brody, Russ Monroe, Walter Weintraub, and their staff credit for that. We all spoke on a first-name basis but were treated with utmost respect. Our medical students were very successful in the psychiatry portion of their national boards, and those who were trained in the department of psychiatry moved on and became leaders in their own states, so the department was highly regarded as a place of learning."

"We learned to seek the truth from any source," says Pinheiro. "Perhaps this was uncomfortable to residents just starting out in psychiatry." Encountering psychiatry, with all its uncertainties, new residents tend "to adhere to one author, to be a devotee to one school, one method of treatment, one line of therapy, one way to look at psychiatry. Not in the Psychiatric Institute. It was this open spirit that made the Institute an academy, open to all sources of knowledge. I felt lucky to be there."

Brody and Monroe were house officers together at Yale in 1944, after Monroe got his MD at Yale and Brody got his at Harvard. A trusted friend and sailing buddy (sailing on the Chesapeake Bay on Brody's sloop, *Sirena*), Monroe naturally assumed Brody's duties for extended periods the many times Brody was a visiting fellow elsewhere or traveling abroad.

Building a department

Brody's first hire, his medical director, was Russell Monroe, whom he had known at Yale and had brought up from Tulane. Monroe, doing research on the interface between neurology and psychiatry, injected a strong theme of neurology into the residency, hiring Barbara Hulfish half time in 1969 to direct the EEG part of Bob Grenell's neurobiology lab. Psychoanalysis was still the most highly regarded form of psychotherapy, but it was beginning to lose ground. There was intense interest in experimental approaches to understanding brain physiology and psychopharmacology. There was increasing evidence of the effectiveness of neuroleptic drugs in the treatment or alleviation of psychosis. Researchers were riding the first wave of the revolution in psychopharmacology, which was gaining strength but had not yet overpowered psychodynamic therapy.

Like departments of psychiatry elsewhere, the department expanded to include the systematic study of human behavior, the behavioral sciences. Brody began hiring psychologists, sociologists, anthropologists, experimental psychologists—even the animal psychologists got folded into the department of psychiatry. Basic research was considered an essential part of training. Researchers were trying to understand both the physical and chemical basis of psychosis and its reflection in language and symbolic processes. Areas under study ranged from verbal behavior during psychotherapy to the chemistry of isolated nerve cells.

Several new forms of brief and behavioral therapy were also gaining support. Ellen McDaniel ran a brief-therapy clinic for the medical students, as part of outpatient services. Psychiatry did not initially embrace—but would certainly be influenced by—the popular work of psychologists Carl Rogers (who championed a nondirective, client-centered, humanist approach to therapy, making use of encounter groups) and Albert Ellis (whose rational emotive therapy was a step toward cognitive behavioral therapy). The cognitive model had a popular following that would significantly, if not immediately, influence psychiatry. Behavioral techniques were leading to an increased emphasis on description

Like departments of psychiatry elsewhere, the department expanded to include the systematic study of human behavior, the behavioral sciences.

and symptoms and less emphasis on the theoretical issues emphasized in psychoanalysis.

From the mid-fifties to the mid-seventies, departments of psychiatry began hiring psychologists, sociologists, anthropologists, experimental psychologists, and psychopharmacologists, according to David Mallott. In 1980, when DSM-III came along and there was a push to medicalize psychiatry, "that's when you saw these folks going back into academia, into regular departments of sociology and anthropology. But during that twenty years, all the major departments had folks like that." The Psychiatric Institute prided itself on being open to new concepts and approaches in psychiatry as well as new approaches to teaching.

Not everyone was happy with the departure from a strictly medical approach to psychiatry. "To a medical student, the teaching of psychiatry left much to be desired," says Jonathan Tuerk (class of 1964). The Saturday morning "magic show with Eph Lisansky" taught the value of a good interview, but "here we were medical students learning anatomy, stuffing our head with facts and hard knowledge, and the psychiatry department wanted us to stop that and switch gears without any explanation. In one class the teacher got up in front of close to a hundred students and asked us why babies cried, which was to me outrageous. Nobody knew why babies cried. And in some interviewing classes, we were broken into small groups and we were supposed to interview a patient, and a chief resident or young staff

From the mid-fifties to the mid-seventies, departments of psychiatry began hiring psychologists, sociologists, anthropologists, experimental psychologists, and psychopharmacologists. In 1980, when DSM-III came along, you saw these folks going back into academia, into regular departments of sociology and anthropology.

member was supposed to be there to help us with this interview. The person who sat in on my group put his head down on the table and went to sleep while somebody was trying to interview a patient. It was the dark ages of psychiatry training. Dr. Brody and Russ Monroe were good, and when they gave a talk people listened because they had something to say. The other people seemed woolly and fuzzy."

Being a psychiatrist was the last thing Tuerk wanted to do. He loved internal medicine but didn't want a private practice; he wanted to be in a hospital treating critically ill patients. Today he could do that, but they didn't have hospitalists then. In his rotation on the psychiatry unit, Walter Weintraub and the chief resident made a big impression on him, and in his senior year (1964) "somebody came and talked about the *Diagnostic and Statistical Manual* and how you make a diagnosis, and that felt like some meat." He realized that his father, the much-loved Isadore Tuerk, had had a decent life, so in the end he became a psychiatrist despite his negative impressions in medical school.

Jonathan Tuerk finished a psychiatric residency at Yale in 1969, served in the Army until 1972, worked at Chestnut Lodge from 1972 until 1998, then went into private practice, retiring in 2006.

"It was an exciting time to be in training," says Walter Weintraub. "Attempts were being made to integrate the growing knowledge in these fields with older theories and

Isadore Tuerk (1908–89)

Isadore Tuerk helped decriminalize alcoholism, convincing the state that it was a disease. His Saturday morning group meeting for alcoholics regularly drew fifty to a hundred people.

When Isadore Tuerk was preparing to go to medical school, he got a job as a shop teacher at a junior high in Pimlico. Knowing nothing about shop, he let the kids do whatever they wanted while he read and studied. When he was in medical school, he made money playing ten people at checkers simultaneously, at Carlin's. "They each paid 10 cents to play him," says his son Jonathan, who also became a psychiatrist. "If they won, he gave them a five-cent cigar, so he couldn't lose. That was part of his cleverness." His standing as one of the most beloved psychiatrists in Maryland held steady despite his role in several major—even controversial—changes in Maryland psychiatry.

After graduating from the University of Maryland School of Medicine (1934), he worked with Hopis in the Indian Service in Arizona, returning to Maryland in 1939 to work at Eastern Shore and Spring Grove state hospitals. During World War II he served as division psychiatrist for General Patton, with whom he toured Buchenwald the day after it was liberated. He returned to Spring Grove in 1949 as clinical director and then superintendent, serving there until 1960. "The hospital at Spring Grove was horribly overcrowded, with thousands of patients and maybe five psychiatrists on staff," says his son. In 1949, Tuerk cooperated with the *Baltimore Sun* journalist reporting for the series "Maryland's Shame," helping them publicize the understaffing and thereby increase state funding. "The hospital experimented with lobotomy, with insulin shock (with Metrazol), with whatever they had to help these people. When the results weren't so good, he dropped some of the therapies," says his son.

From 1960 to 1968 he was commissioner of Maryland's Department of Mental Health and Hygiene. For many years psychiatric care in state hospitals had been racially segregated and all of the black patients went to Crownsville. In the early 1960s, when the Community Mental Health Act called for community care organized by catchment area, Tuerk oversaw desegregration of Maryland's state mental hospitals.

He also helped decriminalize alcoholism, convincing the state that it was a disease. Besides helping alcoholics in his private practice, he developed a Saturday morning group meeting for alcoholics at University Hospital that regularly drew fifty to a hundred people. "I went to his group and it was nowhere near the hotshot group therapy I had been taught," says his son. "It was sort of like Alcoholics Anonymous, but not exactly. They talked about lots of things, looking for my father's approval. When they were sober, he would smile benignly and nicely on them, and when they weren't, they wouldn't get that kind of gratification from him. That was a huge motivation for people to not drink. He treated alcoholics like human beings, people who were troubled and had an illness. My father was a very nice guy and his patients knew it and loved him for it."

Tuerk House, established on Greene Street in 1970 to help people with substance abuse problems, was one of three buildings named for him. The other two were at Spring Grove and Rosewood.

practices. It is true that there were opposing camps of theory and practice, with some hard liners on both sides claiming possession of the whole truth, but few of us believed that anyone had all the answers. As residents and later as teachers, most of us attempted to continue the tradition of synthesizing approaches from many directions. It worries me that psychiatry as it is taught and practiced today often has a much narrower base than before."[8]

Many of the medical students were drawn to psychiatry partly because of summer fellowships funded for a few years by the National Institute of Mental Health. NIMH gave the department grants to pay medical students to do several weeks of summer work that would introduce them to psychiatric concepts and, it was hoped, get them interested in psychiatry. Grants went to several freshmen, several sophomores, and several junior medical students. "We had lectures, we worked in the old outpatient clinic the first year, and later we saw inpatients," says George Gallahorn. "We each worked with a particular faculty member. Jane Cushing and I worked with

In 1962, the French were leaving Vietnam and the United States was about to get involved there. On about the third day in anatomy class, says Gallahorn, a freshman medical student in 1962, "a guy in a suit comes in and says, 'I'm from the Department of Defense. We have a plan for you which will guarantee that you can finish medical school and an internship. You may or may not be able to finish your residency before going in the service. If you don't want to sign up for this plan—the Berry Plan—you run the risk of being drafted out of medical school and going in as a private, whereas if you sign up for this plan, you will go in as a captain. So anybody who wants a form, they're right here on the desk.' Some people had already been in the military, but nobody wanted to risk being drafted out of medical school, so we all signed up for it. This was before Vietnam was seen as a threat." Gallahorn was lucky: he got deferred long enough to finish his residency and then put in two years in the Air Force. The draft and the Berry Plan influenced the paths of many medical students' careers.

Gene Brody, meeting with him weekly. Usually he would give us a reprint of one of his many papers to read and think about, but he also wanted us to do some research on prejudice. He got me involved in writing the first draft of a case report, about how prejudice essentially disappeared in a psychotic woman and then returned as she got better, with some ideas about what that might mean about prejudice. I took it in to him and the next week he said, 'Well, it's a bit primitive, but we can work on it.' We got it into shape, and it was published in the *American Journal of Psychotherapy* with Jane, Gene, and me as co-authors. The beauty of the summer fellowships, for which NIMH funding eventually ended, was that you could go in after the first year, second year, or third year and spend a summer learning about psychiatry, and some people who did them in the later years ultimately did become psychiatrists."

The early years of community psychiatry

Many of the alternatives to psychoanalysis became particularly relevant with the advent of community psychiatry. Many of the Psychiatric Institute's patients were from crime-ridden neighborhoods, and their mental problems seemed to be closely associated with common medical, social, and economic difficulties. "A depressed, diabetic woman, for example, might have a violent, unemployed alcoholic husband, a drug-addicted son who was in and out of jail, and an unmarried pregnant daughter infected with syphilis, all at the same time," says Gerry Klee, chief of outpatient care from 1959 to 1967. "That woman would typically have been referred to psychiatry by various medical and surgical clinics. A medical student or first year psychiatric resident's attempt to do psychoanalytically oriented psychotherapy was rarely, if ever, successful. It seemed obvious that a family approach, centered in the home and neighborhood, made more sense."

In 1959, the outpatient department had begun working with the Baltimore City Health Department. The headquarters of the Western Health District (WHD) was across Pine Street from the Psych Institute, and "its excellent public health nurses (PHNs) spent most of their time in homes

Gerry Klee with Anita Bahn (biometrics branch, NIMH) and Kurt Gorwitz (director of biostatistics for the Maryland Department of Health and Mental Hygiene)

helping families with the full gamut of health, social, and economic problems they faced," says Klee. Everyone, from kids in the street to the elderly, loved and respected the PHNs, who were easily recognized by their dark blue and white uniforms and the small black physicians' bags they carried. They already knew most of the Psych Institute patients, who visited WHD clinics for health education, medical attention, and help dealing with various agencies. The nurses also followed up on patients who were discharged from state mental hospitals. The Psych Institute's outpatient department developed a close working relationship with the WHD staff. "Our social workers collaborated with the PH nurses and spent time helping residents of public housing projects," says Klee. "Our staff contributed time to the well-baby clinics. Staff, students, and residents accompanied PHNs on many home visits. Several studies grew out of that collaboration. Except for a small amount of start-up funding from NIMH and the Maryland Department of Health and Mental Hygiene, this program ran for years without any additional funding. Our biostatistical research showed significant correlations between mental illness and biopsychosocial factors."[9]

The amount of outpatient activity increased in the early 1960s, when the new Open Clinic began taking walk-in patients. The walk-in clinic, initially supervised by Carl Schleifer, was open only weekdays to those with no appointment but an immediate need to see someone. At other times psychiatric emergencies went to the general hospital's Accident Room (later called the Emergency Room), where the psychiatric resident on call would see them—and where walk-in patients were seen before the clinic opened. Residents rotated in and out of the Open Clinic maybe once a week.

The clinic became a valuable training area, in which psychiatric residents and senior medical students learned to do intakes, often with severely ill people. A resident and one or two psychiatric nurses were on duty Monday through Friday, 9 to 5. Part of training was learning how to react to odd behavior—for example, the patient carrying a flatiron who explains, "Oh, I need that to hold me down."

Outpatient activity increased in the early 1960s, when the new Open Clinic began taking walk-in patients.

Because the Open Clinic was a training venue, patient interviews ran forty-five minutes to an hour. "In an emergency room, you ordinarily don't have that much time," says George Gallahorn, who in 1972 became director of the clinic, "and you don't have follow-up. You just have one-time exposure to a person and then they go on to the rest of the health care delivery system and you don't see them. Ordinarily it would be a quickie diagnosis, but this was a teaching session in which we opened up the interview to be much longer in order to see what was there. In that interview, you wanted to keep the patients from killing themselves, you wanted to get them on the right track in their treatment, you wanted to get as accurate a picture as you could of who they were."

There was a steady stream of patients, many of them psychotic, some suicidal and requiring hospitalization. For many reasons, financial and otherwise, the Psych Institute couldn't take most of them for inpatient care. Many were sent to state hospitals. "I'll never forget one man who was both suicidal and homicidal," says Klee. "He told us of his plan to board a commercial airline with a bomb, which he planned to explode in midair. He seemed dead serious and that overrode confidentiality, so I called the police and asked them for help." The police said they could do nothing because he hadn't broken any laws, and the staff had to let him leave.

"The most heart-breaking cases were the severely demented elderly patients brought in by their families, who could no longer care for them at home," says Klee. "In those days few nursing homes would or could take them even if they could pay. The P.I. was not equipped to handle such cases. We had no choice but to send them to state hospitals." Isadore Tuerk, as Commissioner of Mental Hygiene, was one of many who worked behind the scenes to promote more comprehensive and affordable care for the elderly.

In 1963 President Kennedy signed the Community Mental Health Act, reversing a century-long policy of federal noninvolvement in state services for the mentally ill. For 109 years, state-based approaches had emphasized long-term institutional care in large hospitals, with more custodial care than treatment. Now community psychiatry—being able to find mental health care near where you live, as opposed to getting treatment in a state hospital miles from home—had become federal policy. The NIMH was to oversee community mental health centers (CMHCs) for patients being discharged from state psychiatric hospitals. In theory, the federal government was committed to providing a variety of facilities for partial and short-term hospitalization, including clinics, halfway houses, and day hospitals.

Since 1854, when President Franklin Pierce vetoed the Indigent Insane Bill. In 1955, Congress passed the Mental Health Study Act, which led to establishment of the Joint Commission on Mental Illness and Mental Health. The ten-volume report *Action for Mental Health* (transmitted to Congress on December 31, 1960) assessed U.S. mental health conditions and resources, with an eye to arriving at "a national program that would approach adequacy in meeting the individual needs of the mentally ill people of America." The report caught the attention of President Kennedy, who established a cabinet-level interagency committee to study the recommendations and decide on an appropriate federal response. That commission's report became the basis of Public Law 88–164, the Mental Retardation and Community Mental Health Centers Construction Act of 1963, also known as the Community Mental Health Centers Construction Act, or CMHA for short.

After Kennedy's assassination in November that same year, President Lyndon B. Johnson signed into law amendments to the 1963 legislation, providing appropriations for staffing and authorizing grants to help pay the salaries of professional and technical personnel. "The federal CMHC program was based on a seed-money concept," writes Steve Sharfstein. "Local communities applied for federal funds that declined over several years (initially five years and then eight). Alternative funds, especially third-party payments, were expected to replace the declining federal grant. These programs were intended to serve catchment areas of between 75,000 and 200,000 individuals and to provide five essential services: inpatient services, outpatient services, day treatment, emergency services, and consultation and education services. The country was divided into three thousand catchment areas, and the hope in the 1960s was that the entire country would be covered by the mid-1970s. That did not come to pass."[10]

The process typically called deinstitutionalization should have been called dehospitalization, in Sharfstein's view. The idea was to replace institutionalization with community-based care, but some states simply used the law as an excuse for closing expensive state hospitals and didn't provide the community-based care. The community health centers were never adequately funded and never lived up to their promise of providing for the seriously mentally ill patients being discharged from hospitals. Many patients were released to communities that did not have the facilities, expertise, or will to deal with them. Many former patients became homeless or ended up in jails or prisons—without the mental health care they needed.

Another problem was that the centers assumed functions their promoters did not intend. "The treatment of choice at most centers was individual psychotherapy, an intervention especially adapted to a middle-class educated clientele who did not have severe disorders and which was congenial as well to the professional staff," wrote Gerald Grob and Howard Goldman.[11] "The result was that persons with severe and persistent mental disorders—the group with the greatest needs—were generally overlooked or else, forced to compete with other groups for resources, were often the losers." Goldman became a key figure in the department's later approach to community psychiatry.

In 1963 President Kennedy signed the Community Mental Health Act, reversing a century-long policy of federal noninvolvement in state services for the mentally ill.

Changes in the way health care costs were covered also presented a problem. As part of his Great Society agenda of domestic reform, in 1965 President Johnson signed bills creating Medicare, a system of health insurance for the elderly (under the Social Security program), and Medicaid, a similar system for the poor. Under Medicare and Medicaid legislation, poor patients in state hospitals were finally given partial benefits. This would have consequences: With the federal government covering part of the cost of general and mental health care, states would begin to feel less responsible for health care costs they had traditionally covered. At the same time, there would gradually and then suddenly be a shift from funding for a catchment area to fee-for-service funding.

Meanwhile, mental health care issues got mixed up with other issues. Under Isadore Tuerk, Commissioner of Mental Health from 1960 to 1968, the state's mental health facilities were desegregated. This major change was facilitated by the nationally mandated push for community mental health centers to serve all the patients in a defined catchment area. Crownsville, the hospital that had served all of the state's African Americans, in the early sixties began serving the catchment area for Anne Arundel County and some counties in southern Maryland—white, black, everybody.[12] Crownsville's adolescent patients were integrated in 1962 and the adult patients in 1963; the hospital's first African American superintendent, George Philips, was appointed in 1966.

That same year, Brody appointed Lindbergh S. Sata as director of the department's new Division of Community Psychiatry, the idea being to help develop a complex of grant-funded outpatient mental health clinics for patients previously treated in the state hospitals. Sata was to supervise planning for construction of the Walter P. Carter Center, one of the nation's first comprehensive community mental health centers. Serving patients in the university's catchment area, the Carter Center would be like a state hospital in the city, containing both inpatient wards and an outpatient clinic. Psychiatric staff would come from the Psych Institute. Sata's division also took charge of field testing treatment programs to be incorporated into the new center, which was expected to become operational by 1970. The Carter Center would be responsible for about a hundred thousand people (both "Negro" and "white" populations) in the western and southeastern health districts.

The Carter Center was to be the hub of the department's Inner City Mental Health Center program, drawing on grant funds. NIMH provided $217,000 to cover the salaries of 21 of 27 full-time workers (three-person teams with a psychiatrist, psychiatric social worker, and a psychiatric nurse on each), and the state contributed $72,000—with

Lindbergh S. "Lindy" Sata

Lindbergh Sata, born in 1927, was named for Charles Lindbergh, who'd successfully flown solo across the Atlantic that year. "Lindy was a quiet, pleasant, easy-going man, bright and articulate but not argumentative," says Bob Derbyshire. Sata was a second-generation Japanese American from California, whose family was sent to a Japanese-American internment camp during World War II. About his experiences as a Nisei, he later wrote, in "Musings of a Hyphenated American," "My parents, mindful of helping me gain an acceptable place in society, reminded me of the need to coexist with others unlike myself." In 1978 he left to become chair of the department of psychiatry at St. Louis University.

the proportion of federal support tapering off to zero in five years. Initially the service operated out of a storefront clinic on Eutaw Street, a couple of blocks east of University Hospital. The first of several Inner City Mental Health Centers, the Federal Hill Mental Health Center, opened in February 1967 at 1414 William Street, SW, the former Good Shepherd Methodist Church. Werner Kohlmeyer was medical director, with Basri Sila providing child and adolescent services on Fridays. The staff, which served a population of 95,000 in southwest Baltimore, worked with schools, local churches, welfare workers, the police, probation and parole officers, the Community Action Agency, and other community groups and agencies to identify and refer members of the community—including teenagers with a drinking problem—who might need mental health services. Many patients were referred by social workers, who routinely moved freely about the community.

The second center to open was the Redwood Hall Center for Mental Health, at 721 West Redwood Street, near the Psych Institute, with Clif Lamb as director. The federal Department of Health, Education, and Welfare gave nearly $800,000 toward building the third center, the Cherry Hill Center for Mental Health, at Fayette and Pearl. The Fayette Street outpatient clinic would be located in the Carter Center itself. The Morley Street Clinic also opened in West Baltimore, in an abandoned convent. The Federal Hill Mental Health Center became the Carruthers Center, which was in a former Roman Catholic Church leased from the Archdiocese of Baltimore at a very low rate.

All of the Inner City Mental Health Centers provided outpatient and emergency services, as well as counseling and education, and in July 1967 a seventeen-bed inpatient ward in the Psych Institute opened for all center patients, with Lutz von Muehlen as director. Only in extreme cases did patients stay longer than twenty-eight days, and the stays were tailored to the patients' practical needs. Some patients received partial hospitalization. Those who needed to work during the day could stay nighttime only, and parents who needed to care for their children at night could stay daytime only.

Even among those who participated in the community psychiatry programs, not everyone thought they made sense. "My goal was to become a psychiatrist in private practice and treat relatively affluent patients with an eclectic form of individual psychotherapy," says Clif Lamb, an African American therapist who was briefly director of the Redwood Hall Center. "I had little or no interest in taking on the depression, anxiety, and lifestyle issues inherent in communities of people suffering from society's ills." Lamb thought the government's interest in flooding underprivileged communities with mental health centers might also be a way of approaching the latent unrest that was in fact beginning to produce riots in some cities. He shook his head at recently hired social workers and "community workers" trying to organize block parties and rent parties and trying to teach barbers and bartenders to encourage people who needed psychiatric attention to go to community mental health centers. He believed that psychiatric treatment was appropriate only after such essentials as food, clothing, shelter, education, and employment were taken care of. Lamb had remained at the Psych Institute because he felt he could take from its eclectic offerings those that might be helpful. Insight-oriented psychotherapy was appealing but he'd been frustrated at getting so little guidance on how to treat patients with schizophrenia and doubted that the "double bind theory" or the "schizophrenogenic mother" accounted for the symptoms of florid schizophrenia. In fact, he was doubtful that psychiatry had a base in real science. "The nuts and bolts of therapy provided by Walt Weintraub and Jerome Frank's book *Persuasion and Healing*, recommended by Brody, provided the core of my understanding of what therapy was and how it worked."

"My goal was to become a psychiatrist in private practice and treat affluent patients with individual psychotherapy," says Clif Lamb. "I had little interest in taking on the depression, anxiety, and lifestyle issues of people suffering from society's ills."

Changing social forces of historic proportions brought a slowdown in progress on the Carter Center. In April 1968, after Martin Luther King Jr.'s assassination stunned the African American community, rioting broke out in many American cities and soon spread to Baltimore. The area west of what is now Martin Luther King Boulevard was in flames, and members of the community were outraged. Some of them sat on the advisory board of the Carter Center. They did not want the university to have anything to do with their community mental health center, says Gallahorn, "because they felt that university doctors experimented on patients."

There was some reason for such distrust. Beginning in 1932, the U.S. Public Health Service had carried out long-term studies of the incidence of syphilis, and the relative effectiveness of treatments for it, on a population of mostly poor African American sharecroppers in Macon County, Georgia. In 1932, the known remedies for syphilis were toxic and fairly ineffective and the idea was to learn whether syphilis patients were better off in the long run with those treatments or no treatment.

To "prevent the moral breaches that happened in Tuskegee from happening again," says the CDC on its website, www.cdc.gov/tuskegee, the federal government reexamined its policies. It was after the Tuskegee experiments that exacting federal standards were developed, for informed consent on research involving human subjects, and review of research by institutional review boards (IRBs). In 1974, Congress passed the National Research Act, which, among other things, required the establishment of IRBs to review all research involving human subjects funded by the Department of Health, Education, and Welfare (which became Health and Human Services). The regulations subsequently passed raised to regulatory status NIH's "Policies for the Protection of Human Subjects," first issued in 1966.

When Isadore Tuerk was Commissioner of Mental Health and Hygiene, he reported directly to the governor. Governor Marvin Mandel introduced a state Secretary of Health to whom the commissioner reported. This extra layer of bureaucracy diminished the power of the commissioner's office.

After World War II, penicillin became the standard treatment for syphilis, but rather than end the study and treat all the patients, or split off a control group and treat one cohort with penicillin, the Tuskegee scientists in charge of the study continued it for twenty-five years, withholding information about penicillin from the study participants. In 1966 an investigator in the Public Health Service in San Francisco called for an end to the study for ethical reasons, and an African American statistician in the PHS repeated that call in 1968, but the Centers for Disease Control, which by then controlled the study, kept it going. News of these protests appeared only in *The Drum*, a newsletter devoted to ending racial discrimination in the Department of Health, Education, and Welfare. Not until stories broke in the *Washington Star* and *The New York Times* in 1972 did the general public get wind of what the CDC now calls a moral breach. The study then ended immediately, but the black community's level of trust in public health and medical research—in doctors generally—never fully recovered. That distrust was particularly strong as the Carter Center began operating.

During a period of strong community activism, the advisory board for the Carter Center had an attorney from Legal Aid help file its objections to university control of the center. A public battle lasting more than a year went on before the new Secretary of Health and Mental Hygiene, Neil Solomon, who was not a psychiatrist, capitulated, agreeing that the state, not the university, would hire the psychiatrists.

"By that time, of course," says Gallahorn, "there were cost overruns." The original plans for the Carter Center called for eight floors, not seven, with a swimming pool and gymnasium on the eighth floor, and with offices all around the outside so that everybody would have an office with a window. As costs escalated, those features got lopped off and there were changes to the core of the building as well. When construction was finished there were four outpatient clinics in the university's catchment area, including the Fayette Street Clinic in the Carter Center itself, which also had inpatient units. The problem was, the state couldn't find enough qualified psychiatrists willing to work at the Carter Center, the other clinics, or the state hospitals. "In those days, most people who finished their psychiatric training went into private practice or worked at a private hospital," says Gallahorn. "They didn't go to work for the state."

Moreover, "at the time, there was a movement toward community ownership of services and a period of strong anti-psychiatry feeling," says Lois Flaherty. "The advisory board had basically thrown out the psychiatrists, believing

Architects from Texas had designed an expensive building [see page 146], adds Herb Gross, and when conflicts arose—especially when the state began worrying about patients jumping from open balconies—the state completely cut funding for the building. The Texas architects flew to Maryland and met with Gene Brody, who had to lobby to get the building built. The local community, which had seen small-scale models of the building, considered it a white elephant. The original design was open, the idea being to house many community-based activities. The state architects severely curtailed the open design, in effect walling the building off and making it harder to get into the Carter Center than it was to get into the University Hospital, says Gross.

"We want the community to flow through this building," said James Falick, associate partner of Caudill Rowlett Scott, the Texas-based architecture firm that designed the Carter Center. Five columns housed staircases and elevators in this model. As costs rose, many features got lopped off.

the community would be better served by people who came from the community and were in touch with it. The board was hiring 'indigenous paraprofessionals,' people who had grown up in the community and had gotten some on-the-job training and were functioning without a lot of supervision. Credentials were not considered important. There was the sense that psychiatrists didn't know more than these community workers."

Although the Carter Center was on the university campus, the university was not running the center. Things were not working at the Carter Center, but this was no longer the Psych Institute's problem. The university didn't want responsibility for something it had no control over, and the P.I. was busy with other developments.

Jonas Rappeport and forensic psychiatry

Jonas Rappeport, a founding father of the American Academy of Psychiatry and the Law (AAPL, pronounced "apple"), was, in turn, its first president, first medical director, and first executive director.[13] His is a story of passionate advocacy, solid work, smart choices, and the benefits of networking.

As a teenager in Windsor Hills, Rappeport began reading about psychiatry and the law while babysitting for the two children of Manfred Guttmacher, chief medical officer at the Court Clinic for Baltimore City's Supreme Bench and one of the earliest forensic psychiatrists.* In Guttmacher's library he found many books not on most adolescents' reading lists.†

Jonas Rappeport, shown here with his niece, Fern, began reading about psychiatry and the law as a teenager, babysitting for the children of Manfred Guttmacher, chief medical officer for Baltimore's Supreme Bench.

He finished medical school at Maryland in 1952, when Jake Finesinger's department was still new, and began his residency at the Psychiatric Institute. In his first year, he became interested in patients who assaulted the medical staff. Little happened to most of the residents, but one medical student, Sheppard Kellam, kept getting hit by patients.* Was it something Kellam did? Nobody knew, so Rappeport evaluated the incident reports. "It was crude research and I never published it,

---

* Forensic psychiatrists may help the legal system evaluate an individual's competency (e.g., to sign a contract, execute a will, stand trial, be eligible for execution), may testify about a defendant's mental status while committing an offense, and may help evaluate responsibility. They may be called as expert witnesses in criminal or civil trials (including divorce and custody work) and must be familiar with various standards for determining a person's mental status (M'Naghten rules, Durham rule, ALI test) and the problems with any so-called insanity defense. They may also be involved in the care and assessment of prisoners. Few forensic psychiatrists practice forensic psychiatry full-time.

† Among books Rappeport found in Guttmacher's library: Krafft-Ebbings's *Psychopathia Sexualis*. Rappeport also dated a girl who babysat for Eph Lisansky's children, and he was Cubmaster for the little brother of Riva Novey, with whose husband Rappeport would later work. Riva Novey herself was a social worker at the child guidance clinic associated with Maryland; she later became a psychiatrist. Manfred Guttmacher was twin brother of Alan Guttmacher of the Guttmacher Institute

---

* "The worst that ever happened to me," says Rappeport: "Once a patient threw a cigarette lighter at me in my private office. Once a patient grabbed me by the throat, but that was my fault; I had pushed him too far. Another time a patient said 'Don't come into this seclusion room or I'll throw this orange juice on you,' and he did. Shep Kellam, who married (and divorced) Jake Finesinger's daughter, later went into public health, working at the Blumberg School of Public Health at Hopkins.

but we talked about how many times people got hit, where and how and under what circumstances. There are so many factors to be considered; this is the problem with predicting dangerousness."

Later, when he got to the county courts, he did a follow-up study, with George Lassen and Frances Gruenwald, on what happened to the patients the court released throughout the state. "A doctor would say in court, 'This guy's too dangerous. He's in the hospital because he beat the holy Moses out of his neighbor; we've treated him and he's better but we still think he's dangerous.' One of the reasons the court ruled differently is that the court had a lot more experience with violent people than we ever had. Our 'violents' were psychotic. The court had violent people who were just angry. People who were psychotic were responding to delusions or hallucinations. They thought you were going to hurt them so they'd better hurt you first. None of them got into any serious trouble as I recall.

"I presented my study at the American Psychiatric Association meeting and it was published in the *American Journal of Psychiatry*. I discovered something then, which I tell my students: Pick out something nobody's done before or done well, do a good job, and your career is made."

Rappeport started his residency at Maryland in 1952 but finished it in 1956 at Sheppard Pratt, taking an extra year there, as assistant chief of service (chief resident). While at Sheppard Pratt, he was asked to testify at civil commitment hearings and worked with psychoanalyst Samuel Novey, evaluating juveniles for the Baltimore County Circuit Court and becoming the first court psychiatrist for Baltimore County.

Rappeport attended his first American Psychiatric Association meeting in May 1954. "Manfred invited me to come sit with the Psychiatry and the Law committee, the top dogs in forensic psychiatry: Colonel Albert Glass, Henry Davidson, Manfred Guttmacher, Karl Menninger, Herbert Modlin, John Ordway, John Torrens, and several others. They'd be talking and ask, 'What do you think, Rappeport?' They were so kind to this little squirt."

Rappeport served as psychiatric consultant at the Maryland Correctional Institution for Males and the Maryland Training School for Boys, and chief of the convalescent service at Spring Grove, as well as part-time director of psychotherapy. Spring Grove housed Maryland's only

"A doctor would say in court, 'This guy's too dangerous.' One of the reasons the court ruled differently is that the court had a lot more experience with violent people than we ever had."

Gene Brody and unidentified woman listening to Manfred Guttmacher, in 1965.

forensic psychiatry unit, in an old house on the hospital grounds. Forensic psychiatry was in its early stages, to say the least. A manhole in the basement floor led to a very small room, the punishment cell, where violent patients were housed. Isadore Tuerk, who was interested in forensic psychiatry, supervised Rappeport's evaluation and treatment of the forensic patients. In 1959, Rappeport set up a private practice.

In May 1967, after the death of Manfred Guttmacher, Rappeport became the chief medical officer for the Supreme Bench of Baltimore. His pay: $12,000 a year for five half-days a week. Like

Guttmacher before him, he provided most of the training in forensic psychiatry in the Baltimore area for some time. A medical student who got to shadow Rappeport as part of an elective got broad exposure to the court system, from divorce cases involving custody and access, to criminal cases, with Rappeport making clear how the justice system affected the psychological welfare of those caught in it. "He was passionate and very good about explaining different settings," says one former student.

For several years L. Whiting "Whitey" Farinholt, in the Maryland law school, and Manfred Guttmacher taught a

L. Whiting "Whitey" Farin-holt co-taught the Law and Psychiatry seminar, first with Manfred Guttmacher, then with Jonas Rappeport.

Law and Psychiatry seminar together. After Guttmacher's death, Rappeport co-taught the course with Farinholt and others in the law school. In 1966–67, Rappeport and the department of psychiatry launched a Psychiatry and the Law program, presenting a day-long seminar for state's attorneys, in collaboration with the law school. In 1967–68, the program presented the municipal judges of Baltimore City with a seminar on dangerousness, in cooperation with the Inner City Community Mental Health program. It also participated in a Conference on the Problem of Dangerous Behavior held in the law school, sponsored by the Maryland Department of Mental Hygiene.

Psychiatric residents had already been exposed to forensic psychiatry in the Baltimore county and city court systems. When the NIMH division of crime and delinquency decided to offer grants for people training in forensic psychiatry,

Rappeport applied for and, in 1968, the Psychiatric Institute got funding for a one-year full-time fellowship, which continues now under other auspices. Rappeport set up a six-week series of lectures in forensic psychiatry, which he gave to all of the residency programs in the Baltimore area. In 1972, again with a grant from NIMH's crime and delinquency division, Rappeport started a Special Offenders Clinic, which is still functioning. Residents today can still take an elective in forensic psychiatry as part of the forensic psychiatry fellowship program.

Although he had faculty appointments at both Hopkins and Maryland and was running Hopkins's forensic clinic, he felt the need for a national organization. In December 1967 he started getting in touch with directors of all fellowship programs in forensic psychiatry. After Rappeport and Robert Sadoff arranged for organizing meetings at the American Psychiatric Association meetings in 1968 and 1969, AAPL held its first official meeting in Baltimore on November 16, 1969. AAPL would have an informal relationship with the APA and—by unanimous decision—membership would be limited to APA members (that is, the organization would not be multidisciplinary).

At first it was a "mom and pop operation," with Rappeport's courthouse secretary helping him handle the correspondence. Rappeport, Sadoff, and Irwin Perr drafted the code of ethics and eventually helped organize the first certification exams, which all three passed. Rappeport became the first president of the board. The field was recognized as a subspecialty of psychiatry in 1992.

In the 1960s, the field was just starting to grow. "This was the heyday of hope for psychiatry," says Rappeport. It was the beginning of behavior modification, and "things were just jumping all over the place." People thought that psychiatrists might be able to cure criminals, change their behavior, predict dangerousness, and so on. A few court clinics had appeared, and there was talk about rehabilitating criminals, not just locking them up. "Unfortunately, the hopes were grandiose, and the public, particularly the legislature, is such that if you have a treatment program and you don't cure 100 percent of the people, or they get out and do something, then you're no damn good and we'll take all your money away."

During an active career, Rappeport consulted on most major forensic psychiatry cases in Baltimore City and on several national cases, too—including those of Arthur Bremer (attempted assassination of presidential candidate George Wallace), Sarah Jane Moore (attempted assassination of President Ford), John Hinckley, Jr. (attempted assassination of President Reagan), and John DuPont (murder of wrestler David Schultz). In the Hinckley trial, Rappeport and Will Carpenter, who'd been hired to direct the Maryland Psychiatric Research Center, testified on opposite sides (Rappeport for the prosecution, Carpenter for the defense).[*]

We take for granted now that what patients tell their psychiatrists is privileged, but in the 1960s, lawyers would often get subpoenas to browse through patients' psychiatric records. Psychiatrists began keeping two records for each psychiatric patient so that the general hospital record would not include sensitive information about the patient's history or assessment. Rappeport was an advocate for a Maryland statute guaranteeing privileged communications between a psychiatrist and his patient. The Maryland Psychological Association

Jonas Rappeport, a founding father of the American Academy of Psychiatry and the Law (AAPL), as well as its first president, medical director, and executive director.

---

[*] In 1972 Gene Brody testified for the defense at the trial of Arthur H. Bremer, who was convicted of shooting Governor Wallace in a Laurel shopping center. Rappeport testified for the prosecution, believing, as he said recently, that "Bremer was a sick boy but not so sick as to be considered not responsible. Dr. Brody believed that he was schizophrenic but not responsible. (Being schizophrenic alone does not make one not responsible.)"

lobbied against such legislation because their patients were not included, and the initial bill was vetoed in 1965. With Rappeport as president of the Maryland Psychiatric Society (1965–66), the psychiatrists and psychologists got together and a new bill was passed and signed, granting privilege to both professions.* With Nicholas Conti, Rappeport in the early 1980s developed Maryland's pre-trial screening program for all defendants

who raise questions about their competency to stand trial or about their criminal responsibility.[14]

Thirty-five people attended the first AAPL meeting in 1969; today the Academy has 2000 members, and 600 to 800 people attend the annual meeting. "Jonas invigorated it," says one of the many psychiatrists he mentored. By the time he retired, he had trained thirty-nine fellows and garnered many awards. AAPL created the Rappeport Fellowship in 1985 to offer outstanding residents with interests in forensic psychiatry a chance to attend AAPL's annual meeting.

---

* The Mental Health Association of Maryland and Delegate Jerome Robinson were important allies in finally gaining passage of this critical legislation, says Gerry Klee.

Years of protest

"Medical school was all about memorization," says Bob Derbyshire. "If you were a good memorizer, you passed through the system. As one faculty member in anatomy would tell the medical students, 'If the walls are green, you want to be green. Don't make waves. Just go through the system. Memorize what you have to memorize, get your competency, and move on. Then you can do what you want to do.'"

Four years of waiting for their medical lives to begin "didn't suit some of the younger people who were quite active," says Derbyshire. "I think the protests began with a group of freshmen in the class of 1968 (the students in the early 1960s were in some ways a lethargic group). The medical school wanted them to wear white coats and ties and they wouldn't. They went on the wards in jeans—dungarees, we used to call them—not the whole class, but the students who were actively against the war and fighting discrimination. They would flout every restriction the medical school put on them."

The quota for Jews was much higher, but a number of Jews also had some difficulty getting in, say Derbyshire and Rappeport. Sometimes they would enter the pharmacy or dental school and then go to the medical school. There was an easier entrée if you had a pharmacy diploma.

Many students were rebelling against discrimination, particularly that against African Americans but also that against gender. "When I first went there the quota system was three blacks and three women," says Derbyshire. "There was a lot of the good old boy system; they would deny that, of course, but being an Anglo-Saxon Christian was the game of the day. If you weren't that or some variation on that, there was a quiet but persistent denial that you were qualified for medical school." Some of the students were also very discriminatory. "To try to teach them something about what it was like to be black in America was very, very difficult. Some of them could pick it up easily and others had a difficult time, just like most white folks do."

The students did a lot to foster change. "They organized programs trying to educate the medical faculty about what it means to be black, and the medical faculty was very resistant. The students were saying that the treatment for black patients was different from that for white patients. The faculty wanted the patients to call the doctor 'Doctor,' but they wouldn't call the patients Mr. and Mrs.—they would call them Sam or Genevieve, or whatever. When the medical school began to admit more blacks, the medical faculty wouldn't just accept them on the basis of their record at another school—whether it was Morgan College or Harvard University. The black students would automatically have to take courses in anatomy, physiology, biochemistry, or whatever was necessary to prove that they could be there."

MCAT scores were the biggest factor in whether you got into medical school, so students well versed in physiology, biochemistry, or biology were more likely to get in. Second in importance was what your undergraduate professors said about you. Third in importance was what the interview committee at Maryland said.

"There was also age discrimination," says Derbyshire. "If you were thirty or older, they did not want to look at you. You had to be younger than thirty. Their philosophy was, We're spending four years and hundreds of thousands of dollars to educate these people so we want them to be around to do their work as a physician for x number of years. If you're thirty that means you're not graduating until you're thirty-four and they thought that was too late. Today I see things have changed tremendously. It's filled with women these days, which is wonderful—women make better physicians I think anyway—and there are many more African Americans and Asians than there ever were before."

In the second half of the 1960s, medical students at the University of Maryland were upset about a number of things—one of the first being the rumor that the department of medicine was doing research on cholera and on blackwater fever, using as subjects the prisoners at Patuxent Institution—research that would undoubtedly not be approved by IRBs that would be required after 1974. (Prisoners must now be addressed in a special way for informed consent.) Medical students protested about scuttlebutt that the microbiology department had contracts with the U.S. Army to develop potent strains of rickettsia, bacteria with potential for use in germ warfare. They protested about medical students being asked, in first year physiology, to dissect and do renal experiments on dogs from the pound, and one night some of the students set the dogs free. In particular they were concerned about how their medical education related to the real world.

Some medical students participated in protest marches about the Vietnam War held in Baltimore and Washington, D.C. "We organized a group called the Student Health Organization (SHO), a group of medical students who were committed to the notion that medical care was a right, not a privilege," says Jerald "Jerry" Kay (class of 1971). "For the anti-Vietnam war marches going on in Baltimore, we organized a group to serve as what was called 'medical presence,' meaning that the medical students marched along with the marchers, to ensure that if anything happened we would be there. The dean of the medical school was a retired bird colonel by the name of Stone, and he didn't like it that some of us skipped classes, put on white coats, and were out there in the streets."

William Spencer Stone, a career officer in the U.S. Army Medical Corps, was dean from 1955 to 1969. Stone was strong clinically and in research, but, says Derbyshire, was "socially conservative and ran a tight administrative ship. Many students and some faculty referred to those years as the Stone Age."

Many of the young students would meet in the medical school, trying to devise ways to get the medical school to make changes. "It almost reminded me of old communist cell meetings," says Derbyshire. "Jerry Kay was particularly active; he tended to be more socialistic than communistic.

Another guy was ready for revolution; even some of the students had a hard time with him."

Protests against the war were still going strong in 1969, when Nelson Goldberg (a ringleader in protest, in the class of 1973) started medical school. His class also had issues with the faculty and medical school. "The first two years of medical school were nothing but sitting in a classroom being talked to," says Goldberg. "We were twenty-two and felt it was time to actually learn how to do things; when Alexander of Macedonia was our age he had already conquered the world. Those of us who wanted to be surgeons looked to surgery as part athletic endeavor. We knew that most good athletes had begun their training in their late teens or earlier, and we weren't being shown how to do anything.

"The ethos of the medical school was that students should never call attention to themselves," says Jerald Kay, who, in an era of student protest, was particularly active in calling for change.

"This really hit home when the medical students at Maryland and Hopkins were asked to come serve as medics for the antiwar marches going on in Washington. As first and second year students we didn't know how to do anything, so we organized the first free medical school—for

Dean John Moxley III on the back of Nelson Goldberg's Triumph motorcycle, leaving for the 1973 graduation party. Moxley agreed to ride on the motorcycle if Goldberg, a ringleader in student protest, wore a tux.

Bob Derbyshire was part of that, as well as Dr. John Money, cofounder of a Sexual Disorders Clinic at Johns Hopkins. Known for his work on sexual and gender identity (he created the term "gender role" to replace "sexual role") and his belief in "sexual reassignment," Money was controversial for, among other things, saying that people who thought they were the wrong gender might be better off with a sex change operation than with counseling. Later, various faculty members helped teach the human sexuality course.

Hopkins and Maryland students. The American Red Cross came to Davidge Hall and taught us basic first aid, which most of us didn't know. We also had a combined class on sex education at Hopkins, another topic that wasn't taught in either medical school but was of great interest to young, sexually active students."

Those first-ever combined classes between Hopkins and Maryland were unofficial and student-driven. "We just wanted to get on with it," says Goldberg, who was class president his second year of medical school and student body president his third and fourth years. "We were egging each other on, because we didn't know how to do anything. Basically we were probably kids with close to adult ADD: We had high energy and we weren't being challenged enough. The bottom line was we wanted to do things to make a difference. Sitting in class and vomiting back nonclinical facts just didn't cut it anymore."

"Remember," says Kay—who for twenty years has been professor and chair of the psychiatry department at Wright State University in Dayton, Ohio—"the medical school was very conservative and a relative anachronism at that point. Things had changed very slowly, if at all, in American medical education since 1920, when the Flexner Report came out. Pedagogical techniques that were beginning to emerge in other fields were still unheard of in most medical schools, not just the University of Maryland. And Maryland also had the inferiority complex of growing up in the shadow of Hopkins. Medical school was still an aggressive, competitive environment. New medical students were told, 'Look to the right and look to the left; one of the three of you will not be here in four years.' The ethos of the medical school was that students should never call attention to themselves."

The psychiatry department played a key role in helping medical students channel their frustrations. Medical students saw the psychiatry faculty as notably more accepting of student behavior outside the norm than the average faculty member was. "The psychiatry department took the time to sit down and understand where we were coming from, what we wanted," says Goldberg. "They understood the conflicts that were going on between the medical school hierarchy and the newly empowered students. They tried to make the relationship between the students and faculty better. Several faculty members in the psychiatry department were our friends, counseling our students: Robert Derbyshire and Jerry Hunt, Ellen McDaniel, and Ephraim Lisansky." The psychiatry department was considered less academic than the rest of the medical school, more freethinking, and more receptive to the social consciousness that was so important to many students (and some of the teachers) in the 1960s.

More than 10 percent of the class of 1971 went into psychiatry, says Jerry Kay (probably one of the highest numbers in the country for that year). The seventeen Kay remembers are: James Bozzuto, Harold Cohen, Susan Cohen, Alan Dubin, Mike Edelstein, John J. (Jack) Haggerty, Jerald Kay, Richard Keown, Robert Lehman, Michael Maloney, Jeff Mitchell, Robert Neborsky, William Samuels, Robert Schreter, Marlene Schwartz, Stewart Shevitz, and Rena Victor (Kay).

Standards of physical appearance became a focus of much of the animosity between the medical faculty, which leaned toward strict dress standards, and the medical students, increasing numbers of whom leaned toward rebellion. Many teachers were disturbed by the students' clothing, hair style and length, and demeanor and tried to get them to behave and look more like the traditional concept of a physician. The students wanted to learn how to be doctors, felt they still were being treated like adolescents, and reacted accordingly.

"The night before I came to medical school I shaved the beard I'd had for many years," says Kay. "After three days, realizing they wouldn't throw me out for it, I grew it back. But articles were posted on the bulletin board and in the anatomy lab, saying that beards carried infectious agents." In 1970, as class president, Goldberg declared the first Freak Day, an annual day when students could dress however they wanted, and some came as hippies—a couple sipping wine in the back row.

When Goldberg came back to join the full-time faculty in 1981, eight years after graduating, George Balis and other old faculty members said they thought at the time the student rebels were a pain in the ass and troublemakers, but they realized in retrospect that those were the students who really cared. "Students in 1981 didn't care about social issues or the medical school; they just wanted to go through, get their degree, and be done with it.

"We weren't the dumb students by any stretch of the imagination," says Goldberg. "We got bad grades at first because for the first two years we decided just to ride the curve; we were taking courses we'd already gotten A's in, in college. We had our own newspaper and for the four or five issues we published it David Shiling wrote a column called *The Weather Report*" (see page 158).

What was taught also came under protest. There was, for example, a confrontation with the department of epidemiology, which was presenting "a new system whereby the doctors would be like computers or books and the P.A.'s and nurse-clinicians would actually give the care," says Goldberg. "Some of the students were offended at having to sit through lectures on epidemiology, which seemed very soft, non-practicing-medical stuff—and not real science. So we boycotted a lecture and I think an exam, too. Our main enemy, I think, was the chief of epidemiology."

Herb Gross, who first told me about the incident, said he met with Shiling afterward and helped convert him to more establishment ways. Goldberg went on to get his surgical training at Yale and became a clinical associate at NIH before joining the staff at Maryland. David Shiling got training in psychiatry at Harvard and in neurology at Georgetown and was at NIMH when Goldberg was at NIH. They started and jointly ran a government study on the use of marijuana as an antiemetic for children getting chemotherapy. Goldberg became a plastic surgeon who does mostly reconstructive surgery. He has made thirteen trips to third world countries to do reconstructive surgery on children with cleft palates and similar problems.

Generally, the students considered psychiatry their friend, but one year Herb Gross gave a final exam with such global questions that students felt like they were being asked to define the psychiatric history of man or the meaning of life. One student, Billy Landis, wrote in his exam book, 'This is meaningless,' and handed it in. David Shiling and Nelson Goldberg clipped the synopsis of the weather report from the front page of *The New York Times* and pasted it in the blue book. "We thought that was as meaningful as the questions they asked," says Goldberg. "We three were called in by the dean of students and told that if we didn't hand in a real exam we would not be allowed to pass on to the next year of medical school. We turned in our exams; they made us write what we considered nonsense and they passed us."

The idea that a physician's role was to educate patients was not common then, and the students wanted to understand and educate the patients about what was going on with them. Most of them came to understand about social class, minority status, and reference group: the group we aspire to be like or to not be like— how the black man was the negative reference group for lower-class whites, who could not get any lower, but could at least say, I'm not black. They understood how it was important for poor whites to keep blacks down so they could feel up, and how all of this affects people's ideas about medicine and medical care.

Greifinger later went into community pediatrics and was then head of health services for the state prison system in New York.

Jerry and Rena Victor Kay (they had married in the second year of medical school), Nelson Goldberg, the Student Health Organization, and other Hopkins and Maryland students recruited medical residents to volunteer at a free medical clinic for the disadvantaged and indigent. The clinic, on Greenmount Avenue in the Waverly section of Baltimore, was staffed by medical, nursing, pharmacy, and social work students, with some faculty volunteering their time as supervisors and consultants.

The Kays' group, which included Bob Greifinger, was convinced "that poor people received a different level of care at University Hospital than those who were hospitalized on the ninth floor, which was for private care. We undertook a study and looked at issues such as quality of food and some aspects of patient care. That developed into large town hall meetings, which the press got wind of, unfortunately. Despite the presence of *Baltimore Sun* reporters, in many respects we had never seen so many faculty and students together discussing what I like to think were critical medical issues. A significant number of people felt I had selected the wrong career and shouldn't be in medical school," says Kay, "nor should my wife and classmate.

"In all that happened, Bob Derbyshire was instrumental in protecting our hides—in advocating for the students. He was really an important figure for the medical students. He was always there to support us—our champion, our spokesperson, and probably the one most concerned with our welfare and well-being. Bob felt that protest reflected the tenor of the times, and medical schools should be no different—we were young people. He went to the promotion committee on my behalf and argued effectively that since I wasn't in academic trouble, there was no justification for sanctioning me or throwing me out. When someone asked how Rena was different from me, he allegedly responded, 'She doesn't have a beard.' He also supported me in my hearing for conscientious objector status.

"Whenever I wanted to drop out of medical school, which was 7.3 times each week," says Kay, "I would seek his counsel—not for psychotherapy, because he wasn't a clinician. We would talk about the virtues of staying in school,

Toward the end of his freshman year, Kay told Derbyshire he wanted to do the Near-Eastern Studies program at Hopkins and said he'd asked the medical school advancement committee if they would hold a place for him so he could come back afterward. This upset the advancement committee, which told Derbyshire they didn't hold places for people. He suggested they say, "Yes, go. We'll hold a place for you for a year, anyway." Why, they asked, would they do that? He explained, "Jerry's testing to see how rigid you guys are. If you say yes, he won't go." They granted his request, and Kay didn't go.

particularly in light of the Vietnam war draft. I gravitated toward psychiatry very early on in medical school, in part because of his influence."

Russ Monroe was also supportive. "We were looking for other kinds of intellectual stimulation, to counteract what we felt was the narrow anti-intellectualism in the medical school," says Kay "We mentioned this to Russ Monroe, and he began holding a monthly meeting on existential psychiatry, about which he knew a fair amount. He opened his house to seven or eight of us first and second year medical students, and he had us reading people like Ludwig Binswanger. That's the kind of guy he was—a real mensch. This stuff was totally out of the mainstream of American psychiatry. And Russ's own work, on the impulsive personality disorder, was in many ways ahead of its time."

Reluctant now to come across as an *enfant terrible*, Kay explains that what was going on in terms of social issues was exciting. "I chose not to do my residency at Maryland, but it was a meaningful time, and my wish to go into psychiatry and my commitment to psychiatric education may have been strongly influenced by my experiences there. Looking back, what I took away from my time at Maryland was the commitment of people like Derbyshire, Russ Monroe, Walter Weintraub, Herb Gross, and maybe George Balis—that they really gave a damn about the students."

"Not all of the experiences at Maryland were positive ones, as the medical school in general did not seem to know exactly what to make of us as individuals," says Victor Reus, a CAPP student who was there at the same time as Goldberg and remembered the incident with the epidemiology test, but not the reason for it. "My overwhelming impression, however, is that I received an excellent, well-rounded medical education and that I was allowed much more clinical responsibility across rotations than is certainly the case presently in the training of medical students. I am not sure that this was necessarily the best medical service

Bob Derbyshire led sensitivity training groups for medical and nursing students and some junior faculty.

provided to the patients involved, but it certainly did accelerate clinical learning."

Donaldson Brown weekends

All around the country people were starting up sensitivity training and encounter groups. Russ Monroe set up the first groups in the department. In the mid-sixties, he sent Lindbergh Sata to Bethel, Maine, for a sensitivity training program offered by the National Training Laboratory (NTL) early each summer, and Sata sent several residents, psychologists, sociologists, and anthropologists as medical and psychological consultants, who participated in the training at no cost (indeed, they received a small stipend from NTL).

At Maryland, Bob Derbyshire and later Jerry Hunt, together with anthropologists Jay Nolan and Laura Rhodes, and Dick Sarles (who came as a post-pediatric resident for training in child psychiatry), led small-group training. Douglas Weir supervised small-group teaching, using the department's television studio, which was set up in the basement near the experimental psychologists, in an area oncologists used temporarily, until space was provided for them in the hospital. From 1966 to 1976, Derbyshire helped provide sensitivity training groups for medical and nursing students and some junior psychiatry faculty. Jerry Kay remembers weekend-long marathon-type encounter groups for sensitivity training. "We'd come there Friday afternoon after school with a pillow and a blanket and do this kind of thing that everyone thought was hip," says Kay. "Bob was the faculty person who sponsored this stuff for us."

Soon after group leaders in the department had been trained by NTL, a tradition of fall and spring retreats was established, with residents from psychiatry and psychology meeting together at the Donaldson Brown Center. The fall retreat was the bonding retreat. Whether a spring retreat happened depended on whether the chief resident chose to make it happen. Occasionally retreats included spouses, also.

As you travel north on Interstate 95 toward New York, on the bridge across the Susquehanna River, look to the left. Sitting on the bluff atop a rock formation is the mansion. For more details, see: www.riverfrontcc.com/rfcchistory.htm and www.riverfrontcc.com

In 1935 Donaldson Brown, a prominent industrialist, had built an elaborate Georgian mansion on a two-hundred-foot bluff overlooking the Susquehanna River in Port Deposit, Maryland. In 1965, when he died, he bequeathed the mansion, together with twenty acres of scenic grounds, to the University of Maryland. Officially this site is called the Riverfront Conference Center, but the department's retreats were called Donaldson Brown weekends.

The bonding retreats were a way for the new residents to get to know the older residents and at the same time learn something about the group process. They offered a chance to see new ways of thinking and "enabled us to get in touch with ourselves," says the Reverend Denis Madden, now an auxiliary archbishop for Baltimore and vicar for the Neumann vicariates (ninety-six churches and sixty-five schools). "These weekends allowed a certain amount of trust to develop. For a while we didn't think of ourselves as 'Doctor,' or 'Father,' but just had a life experience as colleagues working together who more often than not became friends as well. There was also a great bonding between the residents in psychiatry and psychology. Henry Harbin, Howard Metzger, Brian Hepburn, and Paul McClelland—they were among the great people who attended these workshops. We enjoyed being with each other, and that ease was reflected in our work. Even outside these weekend experiences, I learned so much from senior faculty such as John Lion. Oftentimes, he would say something like, 'This guy just doesn't have a schizoid personality. He may meet all the criteria, but there is something else at work here.'"

Reactions to the T-groups varied. Some felt you got a sense of group process. Some found the process excruciating.

Sometimes the weekends were training weekends, and sometimes they were more experiential. T-groups, or training groups, based on the Tavistock theory of group process, were a little bit of both. The point of the T-group meetings, which were held on campus as well, was personal development rather than psychotherapy: self-insight (about such issues as tolerance, flexibility, independence, decisiveness), understanding what helps or hinders group functioning, understanding interpersonal relations in a group, and developing the skills to diagnose individual, group, and organizational behavior. The whole group—the "meeting group"—would break up into four or five small groups, organized in various ways: sometimes by year, sometimes with two representatives from each year, and so on.

Because they could be neutral about the group process, faculty members who were not well known to the residents were invited to sit in as consultants. They said very little, and what they did say might sound off the wall. Tom Krajewski recalls, "You might be talking about sports and they would make a comment like 'The guardian angels have come down from heaven.' We found out afterward they were making interpretations of group dynamics, so the comments weren't off the mark. In the end the consultants all got together with the strange clues they'd written down and would explain it all, so by the end of the weekend you got a good sense of how the group process worked and what kind of group it was, and you did learn a fair amount. At a wrap-up session on Sunday they would say, 'We wanted to give you clues without telling you exactly what the process was because if we told you what it was, you would stop the group process learning.' It was catch-22, in a way."

Reactions to the T-groups varied. Tom Krajewski was one of those who enjoyed and learned from them. "You could talk about anything," says Krajewski. "It was totally wide open and unstructured; the goal was to study group process. It might take the first day to define what the heck 'the goal' even means, when the goal's that vague, so it was kind of interesting. The small groups were supportive; you got to know everybody, and it was a lot more fun."

Others had a different experience. "The Tavistock Group that we ran was excruciating," says Elliot Cohen. "I don't think in this day and age they would do that. We would sit there in a T-group with whoever the trainer was. Everyone waited around. Nobody wanted to say anything. In my understanding the first person to say anything was killed off by the group. So a woman would speak up and we would all verbally attack her. Then the group leader would process and that was the end of that. I think group works as well if not better than regular therapy—I've used Yalom's books—but that was excruciating. We were too young, we didn't know what was going on, it was very passive teaching. And in that department, every time I brought up something they would psychoanalyze it."

Every year the theme was different. In the 1970s Jim MacKie organized highly memorable experiential weekends focused on spirituality and even the paranormal (with displays of Kirlian photography). The idea was to experience different ways of being, at times with the well-known Baltimore healer and psychic, Olga Worrall, a popular talk-show guest. Worrall had a real gift for healing, says Denis Madden, as well as a gift for seeing auras, or "the presence of people who have passed on." Explain it as electrical impulses or what you will, but one weekend Madden was seated next to Sid Cohen, who "was not especially receptive to these ideas," and was particularly skeptical when Worrall said that some spirits were there and that Carl Jung was among them. "Then she started going around the group saying things that she could not have known apart from the paranormal. She talked to me about Father Anthony, who had been a very big influence on me—he was probably one of the reasons I had joined the seminary. Father Anthony had been sent to Africa as a missionary and was killed in a terrible auto accident, and I happened to be the one back at the seminary to get the call informing us of this tragedy. I hadn't thought of him for years and I hadn't spoken to Worrall about Father Anthony. Yet she described him accurately and said he was very happy for the way things turned out and happy I was studying psychology. She did that for ten or twelve people and even one of the faculty. When she got to Ruth Newmann, she described how Ruth's grandmother used to put candies in her apron and say, 'Close your eyes, put your hand in, and pick whatever ones you want.' Olga was describing something that Ruth later said her grandmother would do whenever Ruth was having a hard time. Maybe Carl Jung wasn't there, but

"You remember the sixties?" says one senior faculty member. "Things got a litttle out of hand sometimes."

Worrall certainly made an impression on us with all these revelations."

After one of these powerful psychic weekends, "we asked Jim MacKie what to make of white magic," says Elliot Cohen. "He would present cases that could not be explained scientifically and we kept saying, what's the other side of this? One day he came in and sat us in a circle. He was a prim and prissy smoker and he sat down with a blackboard and pointer and said, 'We're going to learn about black magic.' While he's talking, the ceiling starts falling in behind us, and we all freak, and he just sits calmly smoking his cigarette. He says, 'Don't worry about it.' We refused to meet in that room again. About a year after we did this bizarre esoteric stuff he quit and became the Sufi master of an ashram in D.C."

"You remember the sixties?" says one senior faculty member who assiduously avoided the Donaldson Brown weekends, but would hear about them later. "Things got a little out of hand sometimes." In the 1960s and 1970s, on many weekends marijuana was the relaxant of choice. Once, in the 1970s, there were problems about a retreat on the theme of human sexuality, which involved a certain amount of nudity (in particular, a patrolling guard observed a couple "fornicating in the moonlight on the cliffs above the Susquehanna"). One year in the 1970s, three women refused to attend what many felt was essentially a male bonding weekend, and also refused to cover the ER, which junior faculty traditionally covered when the residents were at Donaldson Brown. Rebellion and power struggles took many forms in the 1960s and 1970s.

Then as things cooled down around the country, the Donaldson Brown weekends cooled down also, after being suspended for a while. "I think now it has a more respectable place in the program," says the senior faculty member. "The department tries to do away with the weekend but the residents have become very attached to it, as a symbol of something residents like, which therefore should not be taken from them." However, there is the perennial problem of who will cover clinical services over the weekend if the residents are all away.

Psychedelic research at Spring Grove

Research in pharmaceuticals, especially in the 1960s and 1970s, greatly increased hopes that medication could alleviate such symptoms as depression and anxiety and help control psychotic behavior. It also brought an upsurge of interest in how mind-altering drugs could affect states of consciousness. And for better or worse, one of the drugs for which researchers held high hopes was LSD, which became a part of U.S. and departmental history that many today would prefer to forget. Some still feel LSD holds great therapeutic potential.

D-lysergic acid diethylamide (LSD) was first synthesized in 1938 by the Swiss chemist Albert Hofmann at Sandoz Pharmaceuticals (now Novartis) in Basel, Switzerland.

Hofmann came to Maryland in 1970 to participate in a major symposium on serendipitous drug discoveries organized by Irving Taylor of Taylor Manor Hospital.

Hofmann at first put the drug aside, then looked at it again later, discovering its mind-altering properties in 1943. Dr. Humphrey Osmond, who later experimented with LSD for controlling alcoholism, coined the term *psychedelic* to convey "mind manifesting." In some it evoked a spiritual or mystical vision; in some, a kind of childlike joy; in some a bad trip. For a time it was "a drug in search of a use." By the late 1950s, said Robert Bernstein, former assistant surgeon general of the U.S. Army, "perhaps by coincidence, LSD was almost simultaneously recognized by the army as a military threat and by certain segments of our U.S. population as a means for self-fulfillment." [15]

Many at first believed that LSD could chemically induce a schizophrenic-like reaction that would open pathways for research.

Many at first believed that LSD could chemically induce a schizophrenic-like reaction that would open pathways for research. Also, "it was thought that perhaps the drug would open a way for the treatment of obsessive–compulsive personalities, people with a tremendous resistance to getting in touch with their feelings," says Marcio Pinheiro. "The hope was that LSD would open the doors to their inner world and overcome their obsessive defenses. Gene Brody invited two researchers to speak about their experiences using LSD to treat such patients. As I recall they would have the patient lie down after giving them LSD and would start asking the patient direct and very aggressive questions, trying to break through their defenses. . . . We know today that LSD did not go anywhere in psychiatry; all that initial hope went away."

During a twenty-five-year period beginning in about 1950, research on LSD generated many, many scientific papers and books and several international conferences, and the drug was prescribed to treat tens of thousands of patients. Medical students and psychiatric residents in the Psych Institute and other departments of psychiatry were often themselves encouraged to experiment with LSD in a controlled situation, so they could understand what a mind-altered state might feel like. The drug seemed to hold particular promise, in a therapeutic setting, for reducing recidivism in patients undergoing treatment for alcoholism. In 1963 a group of psychiatrists, psychologists, and social workers at Spring Grove State Hospital began exploring the effects of a brief course of LSD-assisted psychotherapy on "the drinking behavior, psychological condition, and social adjustment of alcoholics," with parallel tests on a control group of neurotic patients. The rationale of psychedelic therapy with alcoholic patients was the alienation-breaking potential of peak experiences induced by LSD. Depression and anxiety seemed to be particularly responsive to the treatment. LSD was found to be effective in the treatment of alcoholism in a double-blind study of three hundred patients at Spring Grove, funded by NIMH. The subjects who benefited the most were given a single high dose of LSD, together with psychotherapy. Most of the LSD studies emphasized that LSD alone was not effective; it had to be combined with psychotherapy and administered in the right setting, by people trained in the drug's safe and effective use.

In "The Use of Psychedelics in Treating the Terminally Ill," Bruce Sewick describes experiments in which researchers conducted tests to see if a "peak experience" with LSD reduced fear of death in terminally ill patients, bringing them relief from depression and a sense of isolation and alienation. Investigators included DiLeo, Goodman, Grof, Kurland, Pahnke, Rhead, Richards, Rush, Savage, Unger, Yensen. Only a few citations about LSD studies at Spring Grove are included in the bibliography; they can be found under the names Kurland, Pahnke, and Sewick.

Meanwhile, during the late 1950s the military and the CIA began conducting various tests on the use of LSD—initially for fear of its covert use against American military units. To familiarize officers with the drug, acid was provided as a supplement in the regular training program at various military bases, including the Aberdeen Proving Ground in Maryland—and some of the early research in the department was funded by the military. Elsewhere, the Army tested LSD's usefulness for brainwashing and for inducing prisoners to talk more freely, and later the armed forces stockpiled it in large amounts "for possible use in disabling an enemy force."[16] By the mid-1960s nearly 1,500 military personnel had served as research subjects in LSD experiments conducted by the U.S. Chemical Corps. Some GI veterans claimed they had been coerced into taking the drug, but there were also reports of LSD being taken from army laboratories and used for recreational purposes. "Some of these men had taken their first 'trip' (the word originally coined by army scientists to describe an LSD session) when acid was given to unsuspecting GIs at mess parties."[17] Military interest in LSD waned when psychoactive chemicals capable of producing even more bizarre effects were developed. LSD was more effective ingested than inhaled, so the army never found a way to deliver it effectively as a weapon.

Charlie Savage was doing research on hallucinogens before they became a social drug, when researchers first hoped they would lead to a breakthrough in understanding psychosis

The seeds of trouble were sown fairly early in the LSD studies. At Harvard, Timothy Leary and Richard Alpert (who later changed his name to Baba Ram Dass) began experimenting with botanical pharmaceuticals with psychoactive properties, especially psilocybin (contained in certain mushrooms) and LSD. Pre-med students knew that if they took a well-known gut course called economic botany, they could take things like LSD and peyote and record their responses. Leary and Alpert were kicked out of Harvard in 1963, and Leary later spent some time in prison, but Leary became a passionate

Savage, Gene Brody, and Russ Monroe had all been psychiatric residents together at Yale. After he left the MPRC, Savage went to work for Veterans Affairs, establishing one of the first long-acting methadone clinics. In describing him, several people used the word *brilliant*.

proselytizer about psychedelic drugs' mind-expanding qualities. Leary, given to self-promotion, turned LSD into a commodity, a recreational drug. The novelist Ken Kesey and his Merry Pranksters expanded on the freak aspects of drug use and further popularized LSD as a street drug.

Charles Savage was a principal investigator in studies at the original Maryland Psychiatric Research Center at Spring Grove, when it was controlled by the state of Maryland. "Timothy Leary could only walk in his shadow," says Gary Nyman. Savage, who was fluent in Latin and Greek, could also discourse for hours about scuba diving. "Charlie was carefully, with U.S. government approval, experimenting with hallucinogens at MPRC well before it became culturally popular," says Nyman.

After Savage's defense of the LSD studies, the research continued another ten years—in particular the studies of LSD and alcoholism.

"In recent months, both the lay and medical press have been filled with warnings about the dangers and harmful effects of the hallucinogenic agents such as LSD-25, mescaline, and psilocybin," wrote Savage and Myron J. Stolaroff in a journal article in 1965. "These warnings have risen in response to flagrant misuse of the substances by illicit operators using black-market materials for parties and 'kicks,' and by irresponsible investigators who, enthralled with the remarkable possibilities of these chemicals, have sponsored and encouraged their widespread use under improperly controlled conditions without medical supervision. In the furor, sight has been lost of the great value of these agents." Unfortunately, the dramatic appeal of the psychedelic experience had attracted "the 'beatnik' crowd seeking new experiences or escape

Based on his experience taking mescaline, Aldous Huxley wrote in *The Doors of Perception* (1954) that the brain and nervous system normally serve as a screening mechanism, transmitting only the kind of information needed for survival. Using a mind-altering drug to temporarily suspend the screening mechanism and open the "doors of perception," Huxley felt, could lead to a transformative experience. After trying LSD in 1955 he became deeply interested in the power of psychedelic drugs to bring about mystical and religious experiences. Believing that "the last rites should make one more conscious rather than less conscious, more human rather than less human," in 1963, when he himself was dying, he asked his wife, Laura, to give him 100 micrograms of LSD—as he had given the drug to his first wife, when she was dying. Huxley believed in the power of the drug to lead one to self-transcendence, grace, "a deeper understanding of the nature of things."

from the established and the humdrum, the unsavory elements sensing an opportunity to expand narcotic traffic, and persons genuinely seeking greater knowledge."[18] After Savage's defense of the LSD studies, the research continued another ten years—in particular the studies of LSD and alcoholism.

In 1965 researchers at Spring Grove turned their attention to the needs of terminally ill cancer patients. "K," a professional member of Spring Grove's research team, had undergone a radical mastectomy for breast cancer, which had metastasized to the liver. Psychologist Sidney Wolf suggested that LSD therapy might relieve her anxiety, depression, and despair, and she agreed to try it, with Wolf as "sitter." After extensive preparation, 200 micrograms were administered in a therapeutic setting that focused on issues of personal identity and current personal relationships. The experiment was a success, giving "K" greater peace of mind. Psychologist Sanford Unger and others joined the team, which expanded the research on using LSD to alleviate the physical and emotional suffering of terminally ill patients, using patients referred by surgeons at Baltimore's Sinai Hospital. Stanislav Grof joined the research team, and Walter Pahnke (a graduate of Harvard Medical School, with degrees in divinity and comparative religion) became principal investigator on the cancer study. The researchers found that in two thirds of the subjects LSD was effective in lowering anxiety, depression, and the fear of death as well as in lowering the amount of pain medication required. It didn't help all of the patients, but it appeared to harm none of them. "The most memorable use of LSD," says Gene Brody, "was with one colleague's daughter, who was dying of cancer and was terribly concerned about leaving her children. Charlie Savage gave her LSD, which reduced her anxiety to more tolerable levels and gave her an 'oceanic' feeling, being one with the universe and feeling less concern about 'leaving' her children."

Stanislav Grof and Joan Halifax, *The Human Encounter with Death*, Chapter 2. Grof's use of LSD with dying patients was also written about in a special section of Time magazine (April 2, 1973) on "The Rediscovery of Nature," available online, which also mentioned research on alpha waves and biofeedback training as a way of learning to control certain aspects of one's own physical and mental state. As a medical student, Nelson Goldberg (class of 1973) worked one summer at Spring Grove, putting electrodes on the heads of patients participating in research on the use of alpha-wave feedback machines. The doctor in charge of alpha-wave feedback was a professional musician turned psychologist.

"I had spent the summer of 1966 working for Al Kurland doing research in a program that was evaluating the use of thin-layer chromatography on addicts who as part of their parole agreement were being monitored via urine testing and were required to attend group therapy," says Ronald Taylor (resident 1973–76). The LSD research at Spring Grove had become associated with Cottage 13, one of the cottages where some of the hospital doctors used to live. Cottage 13 was used in a number of studies, especially in the use of LSD with alcoholic patients.

Al Kurland was in charge of biological research at the Maryland Psychiatric Research Center, in its early years.

After the Spring Grove Research Building was built, while Al Kurland was still in charge of the research, Cottage 13 was no longer used, and all LSD research was done in the research center. After his first year of residency, Taylor participated in one segment of LSD research there, as part of training for mental health professionals. "They had a living room set up there so you were lying on the sofa, your eyes blindfolded, headphones on, listening to classical music. All the 'visual' stimuli were in your head, so you became intensely aware of everything that was happening and you had a chance to look at your thoughts with few external stimuli. They would also take off the blindfold and take you outside, let you look at the trees. You were really hallucinating, but in a well-controlled environment, with professionals immediately available. For me it was a wonderful experience. I was given a pharmacologically pure dose, which is not what you would normally get from the street. It was a whole-day event, very closely monitored, so the residents could have the experience in a controlled environment. I would definitely do it again under the same circumstances." Experiments suggested that a pleasant environment had a positive effect on the LSD experience.

One theme that "characterized the times for many of us in the class," says Victor Reus, "was an interest in states of consciousness and the role of mind-altering substances in therapy and in personal growth. A number of us had, during our college days, experimented with such things, and we were overjoyed to discover that the department of anesthesiology was eager to recruit medical students to evaluate a new anesthetic, ketamine, which had recently come into usage. It had the benefits of not depressing respiratory function or inhibiting the gag reflex, but had the unfortunate side effects, from their perspective, of causing disorientation and hallucinations, particularly during the recovery period. Young children and older individuals seemed to do reasonably well with it, but many others found it an aversive experience. Since it was a racemic compound, the department wanted to see if separating the 'd' and 'l' isomers might also separate the therapeutic anesthetic effect from its behavioral side effects.

Residents could experience quick immersion in the Lilly tank, the sensory deprivation tank used to elicit out-of-body experiences.

"Approximately a dozen of us in the class of 1973 signed up for a series of IV infusions that were conducted in the recovery room. It was truly an amazing alteration of consciousness and certainly the most potent hallucinogenic experience that I ever had, quite exciting, and made even more so by the fact that we were paid to participate. We did not realize at that time that ketamine would go on to receive a widespread fame through the writings of John Lilly, MD, the dolphin guru, or that it was closely linked in molecular structure to PCP, which would have its own effects on American life. Interestingly, we now seem to have come full circle, with ketamine being promulgated as a possible therapeutic intervention for treatment-resistant depression.

"In any event, as a result of these experiences, John Neill and I went on to become interested in the activities of several faculty at the Maryland State Psychiatric Research Center at Spring Grove. We got Dr. Walter Weintraub and Dr. George Balis to have us assigned out there, knowing that several individuals at that site (Dr. Stan Grof, Dr. Charles Savage, and Dr. Walter Pahnke) had been giving LSD to schizophrenic patients and to terminally ill cancer patients in an effort to develop it as a therapeutic agent. I do not recall that we actually were able to get involved in any particular protocols ourselves there, but we were able to meet all these individuals and hear first-hand what their experiences in doing this research were.

"I also recall being able to take a quick immersion in the sensory deprivation tank that was used to create nondrug out-of-body experiences." Many others also recall the Lilly tank.

At the time, the Maryland Psychiatric Research Center at Spring Grove was run by the state health department, not by the department of psychiatry. It had become a center for psychedelic research worldwide, and the researchers had FDA approval for what they were doing: testing different compounds to see what impact they had on people's brains and doing a variety of clinical studies as well.

Among many Maryland researchers who worked on the LSD studies, the best known were Charles Savage (whose name appears on twenty-five papers, from 1952 to 1973, not all of them at Maryland) and Al Kurland (whose name appears on many papers from 1967 to 1977). An early round of investigators included Gerald Klee, Joseph Bertino, Enoch Callaway III, R.R. Griffiths, Arthur B. Silverstein, and Walter Weintraub. One paper, "Clinical Studies with LSD-25 and Two Substances Related to Serotonin," was published in *The British Journal of Psychiatry* in 1960. Bibliographies of later research with LSD, particularly at Spring Grove, include the names of these investigators: Francesco B. DiLeo, Judith Floam, Louis Goodman, R.R. Griffiths, Stanislav Grof, Nancy Jewell, Al Kurland, Ann Lansinger, Karen Leihy, Russ Monroe, Walter N. Pahnke, John C. Rhead, Ilse Richards, William A Richards, Lockwood Rush, Charles Savage, John W. Schaffer, Arthur B Silverstein, Sanford Unger, T. Glyne Williams, and Richard Yensen.

Legitimate research was being conducted, and many papers were published.

In the end, however, with all of the hysteria and backlash against drugs in the 1970s, the FDA ended its approval, apparently deciding there were better ways for researchers to spend their money. The increasing amount of drug abuse in the 1960s and 1970s unquestionably affected attitudes toward research on LSD. Timothy Leary, Ken Kesey, and other promoters of the psychedelic experience must shoulder much of the blame for killing legitimate scientific research. But the media also ran stories about the CIA testing LSD on unwitting subjects, at least one of whom (Frank Olson) apparently committed suicide because he didn't know what was happening to his mind.[19]

Sandoz stopped producing pure LSD in 1965, after the government became concerned about the proliferation of LSD as a street drug. In 1966 possession of LSD for recreational purposes was prohibited by law, and the conditions under which research could be conducted were so strict that it was difficult to get funding or permission to do the studies.[20] The research at Spring Grove came to an end in the mid-1970s.

Denis Madden tells a story that provides a fitting end to the LSD period of the department's history. The state, as part of a negotiation to get the department to provide training for state psychiatrists, had turned control of the Maryland Psychiatric Research Center over to the department of psychiatry. Russ Monroe had just hired a prominent researcher named Will Carpenter Jr. to transform the MPRC into a world-class center for studies of schizophrenia and other forms of serious, persistent mental illness. Madden, in his Baltimore office, had gone through standard procedures for requisitioning a filing cabinet for his office. The used filing cabinet that arrived (presumably cast off by the MPRC) shocked him; he looked inside, quickly locked it, and reported to the department's new chair, "Russ, you won't believe this, but my filing cabinet is filled with drugs." Monroe, who had participated in the LSD studies, recognized them. "He took them and I don't know what he did with them—he probably burned them," says Madden.

Clearly, the era of psychedelic research was over.

5

From CAPP to the Carter Center

1970–1985

If the decade of the 1960s was a time of social activism characterized by faith in the possibility of social progress through social
programs, the decade of the 1970s was a time of disillusionment.[1]
Psychiatrists were leaving community mental health centers, not
joining them. But something different happened at the University
of Maryland. A wry, benevolent psychoanalyst named Walter
Weintraub (with the help of George Balis) launched an advanced
track in psychiatry that became a model for how to attract more
medical students to the field. Then Weintraub helped some idealistic medical students from the sixties negotiate a model of state–university collaboration called the Maryland Plan, which transformed
Maryland's state hospital system and changed attitudes about psychiatry in the public sector. A wise and charismatic Peruvian by
the name of Jose Arana reestablished leadership at the Walter P.
Carter Center, where leadership was sorely needed, serving also as
a role model for compassionate, intelligent clinical care for destitute,
often homeless, psychotic patients. After the era of disillusionment,
a more realistic concept developed, of providing the best possible
services to a defined service area—in particular, care of patients
with serious, persistent mental illness.

Sustained inflation in the 1970s had an effect on the economics of health care and medical schools. Budgets tightened and priorities changed, but members of the department still had time to spend
with patients. Managed care had not yet come along, so a patient
with no health insurance could still be admitted as a "teaching case."
That would change in the late 1980s.

As a CAPP student from that time puts it, the "biological dimensions of psychiatry were of secondary status in the early seventies but rising, and psychoanalytic thinking was falling in status."
Change was in the air. Some experiments would work, some would
not. Child psychiatry at Maryland would, for a while, be led by a
pioneer in behavioral pediatrics. And the flood of new approaches
and techniques for addressing mental health
problems that had begun in the 1960s would
continue. At the University of Maryland, it
was an exciting time to be on the psychiatry
faculty or in training.

Chairmen of the department

Jacob E. Finesinger	1949–59
Eugene B. Brody	1959–76
Russell R. Monroe	1976–85
John A. Talbott	1985–99
Anthony Lehman	1999–

n 1969, the university's board of regents voted to expand the medical school's incoming class size from 100 to 200, in response to the need for more physicians in Maryland. Enrollment, which increased steadily, peaked in 1980 at 185 students. "It was awful," says Frank Calia. "We had too many students and not enough patients, faculty, residents, or space." By the 1990s, "it was rolled back to 150."[2]

Typically, the first year of residency was inpatient care, the second was outpatient care and hospital consultations, and the third was a mixture of various services. Ron Taylor (chief resident, 1975–76) recalls there being twelve residents each of those three years, not counting the ones who spent their time mainly at Spring Grove Hospital (for whom the department assumed responsibility), and three chief residents (outpatient, inpatient, and child). In their fourth year many residents did child psychiatry fellowships. The chief residents were members of the psychiatry faculty, as instructors. "Some of us also gave lectures to the medical students and led group meetings of medical students," says Taylor. One quickly went from learning to teaching. The general idea in residency training anywhere is "see one, do one, teach one."

One quickly went from learning to teaching, says Ron Taylor. The idea in residency training was "see one, do one, teach one."

Two first year residents were assigned to each inpatient ward. Each had a "patient" room on the floor; they also used their room as an office for seeing patients and families, and as a sleeping room when they were on call. One first year resident was on call each night, with a second year resident as backup, in turn backed up by their chief resident. The offices of the second and third year residents were on the first and ground floors.

The Psych Institute "was like a large family—very close," says Taylor. "We loved being there and we had fond feelings for the faculty, who were almost like older siblings. I absolutely loved the place and faculty (with a few exceptions). Each year, the residents

Poe's grave is in the courtyard of the Westminster Hall and Burying Ground, which now belongs to the law school.

met at Poe's grave, at a church at the southeast corner of Greene and Fayette streets, and took pictures. Sometimes the residents did skits making fun of the faculty and each other."

CAPP, The Accelerated Psychiatric Track

Many of the medical students who came to orientation in 1970 listened with interest as Walter Weintraub, the new training director, made a pitch to the whole class about the department's new Combined Accelerated Program in Psychiatry (CAPP). In exchange for intensive extracurricular work studying psychiatry beginning in the freshman and sophomore years, medical students could shorten the period needed to complete psychiatric training, yet did not need to commit to psychiatry. CAPP students would begin clinical training in their freshman year and supervised psychotherapy in their sophomore year, and they could choose to be treated in psychoanalysis at a low (sliding scale) price. Psychoanalysis was still highly valued, both personally and professionally, so that opportunity alone drew some medical students to the program.

"We took twelve people from the freshman class," says Weintraub, "trying to get the best of the recruits, people who would not ordinarily have the opportunity to do such things—and started teaching them psychiatry from the very beginning. They got extra courses (on theory of psychiatry,

"If I had to do one thing again that's what I would do: CAPP," says Walter Weintraub.

for example), they learned how to interview patients, and they had an opportunity to treat patients in psychotherapy, under supervision. We did a lot of what is done in residency training but we did it earlier, so they could have an experience medical students generally don't have. By the time they graduated they would know a fair amount of psychiatry." The CAPP students did all the work required of medical students plus the extra work for CAPP.

How did they find candidates? Gary G. Bawtinhimer (CAPP class of 1979) recalls his first few days as a first year medical student, in 1975: "Like so many in the classroom, I was scared to death about the educational endeavor

Spice, a long time companion to Gary Bawtinhimer (CAPP 1979), attended classes and helped the young resident build connections with severely ill patients at Springfield Hospital.

upon which we had embarked. During several of those first-week lectures, there was a man standing along the side of the lecture room, near one of the exits, casually taking in the class as he compulsively ate sunflower seeds. It seemed somewhat odd for him to be standing there. I thought he must have been one of the faculty, though he didn't dress like one (no white coat) and seemed especially calm, if not nonchalant. At the end of the class he would disappear, without saying anything to anybody. About two weeks into the start of the new school year, Dr. Walter Weintraub approached me after a class. He introduced himself, said the department of psychiatry was having a dinner meeting, and asked if I would like to attend." Having no idea why the invitation was extended, but looking for a break from the tedium of lectures, Bawtinhimer went to the dinner and noted the difference between the psychiatry faculty and residents and the other faculty he had encountered.

In exchange for intensive extracurricular work, medical students could shorten the period needed to complete psychiatric training, yet did not need to commit to psychiatry.

During those first-week lectures, there was a man standing along the side of the lecture room, casually taking in the class as he compulsively ate sunflower seeds. At the end of the class he would disappear, without saying anything to anybody. It was Dr. Weintraub, recruiting for CAPP.

"Dr. Weintraub had been attending those early lectures to scope out the freshman class, discerning who within the new flock had that something about them which indicated that they might just be interested in psychiatry and might have what it takes to become a psychiatrist. That was my first introduction to Walter Weintraub and to his principle that intuition is a good psychiatrist's most important asset.

"Through the CAPP program, with its many hours of teaching and supervision of patient care, by the time I graduated from medical school I had already had four years of specialty training in the field and had built a myriad of clinical skills, which I rely upon until this day. I calculate that in my thirty years as a psychiatrist, I have had well over 75,000 patient contacts. Each one was heavily influenced by my training in the CAPP program from 1975 to 1979—in particular, the tutelage of Walter Weintraub."

However they were recruited, year after year the CAPP students excelled. Members of that first official CAPP class (1970–74) included Barbara Cochran, who became an internist specializing in psychosomatic disorders; Jay Phillips, who became a training analyst and still teaches at Maryland; Bruce Rounsaville, who became head of Yale's Clinical Research Center on Behavioral Treatments for Drug Abuse; and Stephen Xenakis, who became a brigadier general with the U.S. Army Medical Corps.

"We were the first of the accelerated psychiatric track people," says Steve Fleishman, a member of that first group. These bright students were all motivated, he said, "because they wanted this venture to succeed. They wanted to document to the scientific community that if you start training people early in their psychiatric career they are ahead of the curve. .... It was exciting because it had never been done before; it was not going on anywhere else in the country. It was a new experience for everybody. We started learning about psychiatry in our freshman year of medical school and we also started seeing patients, which in those years was unheard of. We were working hard to learn gross anatomy, but we were doing psychiatry too." Fleishman, a self-described country psychiatrist, says, "They didn't know what a child psychiatrist was. So I pioneered child psychiatry for southeastern North Carolina."

"I had majored in psychology at Yale and planned to become a psychiatrist right from the beginning," says Bruce Rounsaville (CAPP 1970–74). "When I found out that I could start doing psychiatric work and advanced readings right from the start of medical school, I thought I had died and had gone to heaven—it was nearly that exciting. In that first class, we were offered an incredible array of benefits at no extra charge: an interviewing seminar with Walter Weintraub, a continuous case seminar with Herb Gross, an opportunity

"When I found out that I could start doing psychiatric work and advanced readings right from the start of medical school, I thought I had died and had gone to heaven," says Bruce Rounsaville (CAPP 1974). A professor of psychiatry at Yale, he is also director of the VA's New England MIRECC.

to become engaged in our own treatment free of charge (or at a reduced rate), and the opportunity to pick up one or two psychotherapy cases and get an hour per week of supervision. We read Freud, Piaget, and other major psychological and psychiatric thinkers and, spending around four hours a week with other CAPP students, we bonded together as a group in a way I had not experienced in any other part of my education.

If you start training people early in their psychiatric career they are ahead of the curve.

"At the time, I did not appreciate the fact that the CAPP faculty were all donating time to the program that was above and beyond their ordinary educational and clinical duties. That degree of generosity and devotion of resources to medical student education was unique then and now. This program made medical school an exciting time while I was slogging through a great deal of education and training that did not seem all that relevant to what I was ultimately going to do. Of course, psychiatry has become more medicalized, and I am glad to have gotten the medical training—even learning all that anatomy.

"From the University of Maryland, I went on to the Yale psychiatry program for residency training and have stayed on the faculty ever since. I don't think I could have possibly been accepted in the Yale program without the CAPP program, as my grades in anything other than psychiatry were mediocre. I have been able to have a degree of success in academic psychiatry that I would never have anticipated, and the CAPP program made this possible." Rounsaville, a professor of psychiatry in Yale's medical school, is also director of the VA's New England Mental Illness Research Education and Clinical Center (MIRECC).

What was CAPP's purpose? "The CAPP program was one way of resisting the anti-psychiatry bias of the medical school," explains Weintraub. "We were able to counter that by the training we gave the CAPP students. CAPP students were more apt to go into psychiatry as residents than they would otherwise. We think it had to do with people not being turned off by psychiatry, as they would ordinarily have been in the medical

"CAPP program" is redundant, but everyone says it, including CAPP's founder.

school. At that time, and from time to time, there was a shortage of psychiatrists, and we were able to demonstrate that going through this program made it more likely that someone would go into psychiatry."

The program was also seen as a way of compensating for "the sketchiness of the behavioral science foundation" then accepted as standard for students graduating from medical schools, and of providing "as good a background in the behavioral sciences and psychiatry as they receive in the other medical disciplines." The idea was to "introduce a pedagogic approach different from the existing fragmentation of the educational process" and to experiment with "an innovative model of integrated medical–psychiatric education."[3]

In "Tracking: An Answer to Psychiatry's Recruitment Problem?" Weintraub, Balis, and Donner (1982) show that University of Maryland freshmen who preferred psychiatry were more than four times as likely to enter psychiatric residency training if they participated in CAPP than if they pursued the regular undergraduate psychiatry program. "The authors believe that an enthusiastic psychiatric faculty intimately involved with students over an extended period of time was the crucial factor neutralizing antipsychiatric socialization experiences in medical school." Moreover, "the University of Maryland maintained the percentage of its graduates who chose psychiatry during the mid-1970s when the national percentage was declining by an estimated 25%."

While all first year medical students were studying anatomy, for example, CAPP students also took a life-drawing class for a few weeks. Those years were a time of creative ferment, says Robin Hatcher. Weintraub, with his training agenda, ran into a Goucher art professor, who happened to have heard Betty Edwards lecture (before publication of her book, *Drawing on the Right Side of the Brain*). She "was coming from a different starting place than Weintraub but with a remarkably similar hope: providing opportunities for trainees in very different fields to document their experiences with a nuance and a confidence that previously were beyond their reach." First they viewed many images of the nude body throughout art history and heard some theory. Then they were given drawing tasks, with professional nude models as subjects, designed to exercise the right side of the brain, "which at that point in our lives was being thoroughly neglected," says Hatcher. They drew

Looking around the room for a student example during his lecture on OCD, William Holden spied Robin Hatcher's meticulously outlined and underlined notes and picked her twice, in both her first and fourth years as a CAPP student. Robin also learned to draw on the right side of the brain.

without looking at the paper; they drew on newsprint; they drew big and rapidly, from their shoulders instead of their wrists. You're not sitting down to do something perfect, the art teacher told them; this is about giving your brain time to play or flex itself. One classmate left the class fuming. "Maybe he thought it was sacrilegious or a waste of time; maybe he couldn't let himself draw. But it gave me access to something inside me—a process of perception and expression—of which I had been unaware. It really was a road to the unconscious," says Hatcher.

"Not only did the CAPP program change the department's standing in the medical school, but the effect was felt all the way to Annapolis," says Weintraub. "The legislators looked at the budget very carefully each year and were astounded to find that there was so much teaching going on. The rap universities have in Annapolis is that doctors are allowed to do clinical work but they don't want to teach. This program was getting more teaching done than any other kind of program, and the legislators were impressed."

"The stated goal for CAPP was to train everyday physicians to embrace psychiatry, understand it, and understand psychiatric patients," says Walter's son, Eric Weintraub, who became CAPP's director in 1993. "The idea was to train physicians to be friends to these patients and to give them good care, because there is a lot of prejudice against psychiatric patients. The department never expected the CAPP students to go into psychiatry, and only an estimated third or so do. Recruitment into psychiatry was not so much a goal as an unstated benefit of the program."

"I think CAPP was the second program of its kind," says Walter Weintraub. To his knowledge, the only similar program that existed in this country when CAPP started was a program in Cleveland, about ten years older than CAPP, in which freshmen were assigned to a pregnant woman, whom they followed as she gave birth—and then they followed the child. Family medicine was the only other discipline in the medical school that tracked students in a program like CAPP, offering training even to students who weren't planning to choose that discipline, and family medicine's program came much later, says Michael Plaut, a faculty psychologist who

James Gamble (CAPP 1975) in 1975 (left) and 2010 (above), influenced by his CAPP training, teaches what he calls orthopaedic psychotherapy to his orthopaedic surgery students at Stanford.

became assistant dean for student affairs. "The idea was that they would be better at working with patients no matter what discipline they chose." Pathology offered a similar program.

"If CAPP had two candidates and one was better suited for the program but not interested in psychiatry," says Eric Weintraub, "and the other candidate was being considered solely because they were interested in psychiatry, CAPP would take the better-suited candidate, even if their intention was to become a surgeon."

Indeed, CAPP graduate James Gamble (CAPP class of 1975) is now a prominent surgeon at Packard Children's Hospital and professor of orthopaedic surgery at Stanford University medical school, specializing in pediatric orthopaedics and adolescent sports medicine. As a postdoctoral fellow in the biochemistry department at Johns Hopkins, with a PhD in biochemistry, Gamble came to Maryland to get a medical degree. "The CAPP program was one of the best learning experiences in my medical school career," says Gamble. "Walter Weintraub, Jim Lynch, and the other CAPP instructors had a profound influence on my education and subsequent career. And I am pleased to report that the CAPP experience has influenced orthopaedic education at Stanford.

"In my practice of pediatric orthopaedics, I see many children with developmental conditions that cause parental concern but that will resolve with time," says Gamble. "Parents are concerned and seek treatment, and often multiple opinions, for the management of these conditions, not wanting their children to grow up with a deformity." To address this problem, Gamble teaches what he calls orthopaedic psychotherapy. Rather than gloss over the condition and tell the parents not to worry, Gamble suggests four simple steps:

- First, listen to the parents' concerns.
- Second, acknowledge their concerns, as in 'Yes, I see what you mean.'
- Next, educate the parents. This involves a conversation, not a lecture. Ask for and answer all questions.
- Finally, offer follow-up. Gamble recommends eight to twelve months for follow-up.

These simple steps of listening to the parents, acknowledging concern, educating, and following up are not self-evident to surgical residents, who commonly need training in interpersonal skills. So CAPP training from thirty-five years ago is influencing today's Stanford orthopaedic residents and other faculty Gamble has trained.

CAPP's first year program. "The most useful thing the first year was the seminar on interviewing a patient," says Walter Weintraub. "All CAPP students had an opportunity to interview a patient and be observed by their cohorts."

Margo Leahy (class of 1973, and a participant in a pilot year of CAPP in 1969–70) remembers "reading a great deal of Freud and receiving case supervision from very good faculty who were also analysts." A psychiatric analyst who practices in San Francisco, Leahy remembers the pilot program as being "well grounded theoretically. This was long before there was a post-Freudian body of work like there is now, so the

Margo Leahy went on to do her residency and child psychiatry fellowship at Stanford and was later hired out of the fellowship as one of the youngest faculty members to develop a new outpatient child psychiatry clinic in conjunction with the children's hospital program. Then, instead of pursuing an academic career, she did psychoanalytic training in London and San Francisco. She is now establishing a child analytic training program at the C.G. Jung Institute.

material was very traditional, Brennerian in nature. I had an extraordinary education in psychiatry that I could only fully appreciate after my later training."

In addition to acquiring a body of knowledge in psychiatry and the opportunity for two or three years of supervised psychotherapy, the CAPP students had greater access to jobs, fellowships, faculty, and frequent dinner parties in the homes of psychiatry faculty. "I had those students to my house probably once every two months for dinner," says James Lynch, a popular psychology instructor in CAPP's early years. "It was an era that permitted that kind of luxury. They were twelve kids, wonderful, wonderful people, and I'm still in touch with many of them."

Above all, the CAPP students had peer support from CAPP participants in all four classes, offsetting the bias against psychiatry projected by other students and nonpsychiatric faculty and house staff.

Summer practicum. "CAPP also gave us an opportunity to experiment with psychiatry teaching," says Weintraub. "For example, medical students are off in the summertime, so we sent CAPP students all over the world—to England, Italy, Switzerland, and Turkey—to do things we couldn't do in the regular program. The summer elective for CAPP students the summer between their first and second year—the only summer medical students have off—still involves a practicum."

"That is the only summer the students have anymore that they can do whatever they want," says Michael Plaut, "so those in the CAPP program will spend eight weeks in a psychiatric hospital anywhere in the world, and the department helps them find a place." CAPP students were supposed to work in psychiatry in the summertime. Not all of them could afford to just spend the summer volunteering, so the department would get the students who needed it money to allow them to do the summer work. Part of an NIMH grant the department got helped pay the students for their summer work, and they got credit for it at the university.

Even before CAPP, medical students interested in psychiatry issues could take a summer fellowship, says Alice Heisler (class of 1963). Heisler saw a hospitalized patient every day for a while, tapering off to three times a week—in the days when hospital stays were much longer. "We had excellent, excellent supervision," says Heisler.

Second year CAPP program. In the second year, says Walter Weintraub, "we'd try to get them to actually treat a patient under supervision. Again, supervisors never turned me down because these were students who wanted to learn and were volunteering and doing extra time." This began in the pilot year, before CAPP was formally organized.

In the pilot year, says Victor I. Reus (class of 1973), medical students who were interested in psychiatry were allowed to take on additional experiences in the field. "Without any

John Neill, left, and Victor Reus (CAPP class of 1973) were assigned to John Lion, an expert on violence, and helped him assess recurrently violent individuals as part of research and clinical activities. Reus ran a group at a Maryland penitentiary.

particular formal training, but with considerable enthusiasm and interest, I was allowed to become a psychotherapist for several outpatients at Sheppard Pratt." Reus got intensive supervision from several faculty at that site (including Art Hildreth), using taped recordings of his sessions. "These were not easy cases. My first patient was a rather disturbed and rageful young seminarian, trying to come to terms with his chosen profession as well as his homosexuality and his earlier experiences of clergy abuse. I did not realize it at the time, but many decades later I would actually serve as an expert witness in litigation on these cases of clergy abuse."

In the first or second year of medical school, with no prior experience in group therapy, Reus was assigned to conduct a group therapy program for inhabitants of the Maryland State Penitentiary. "I remember asking a number of individuals how I should structure this activity, which consisted of ninety-minute group meetings on Wednesday nights for a period of four to six months. Getting into the facility took some time and required traversing numerous locked passages. My recollection is that this turned out reasonably well, with many of the participants feeling that the experience had been useful to them, for reasons I am not quite sure of. Several of the individuals had life sentences, and the group therapy experience at least provided some social stimulation for them." John Neill (another CAPP participant) and Reus were assigned to John Lion, an expert on violence, and helped him assess recurrently violent individuals as part of his research and clinical activities. "This was my first experience with the concept of episodic dyscontrol syndrome and the thought that there may be a neurological underpinning to such things as explosive personality and impulse control disorders. I began to appreciate the clinical benefits of anticonvulsants in the treatment of behavior decades before they entered mainstream usage in our field. John was a remarkably gracious and effective teacher for us in this area, as was Dr. Russ Monroe."

"It was an exciting time," says Reus. "The early experiences that I had, and the sense of responsibility and trust that was given to me, were instrumental in solidifying my commitment to academic psychiatry and the feeling that it was a choice that I would be comfortable with over a lifetime."

Victor Reus, a director of the American Board of Psychiatry and Neurology, is current chair of the Residency Review Committee for Psychiatry of the Accreditation Council for Graduate Medical Education (ACGME). In 2009 he received the APA/NIMH Vestermark Award for Psychiatric Education.

Did the patients benefit? "Oh absolutely," says Steve Fleishman, "because we were very closely supervised, and the patients knew they were being charged a very low cost or nothing and this was all part of a teaching experiment. All told, they got good psychotherapy or psychiatric treatment, whichever you want to call it."

We went to school all year round, so we got to graduate six months early," says Fleishman. "In those years to have a psychiatric residency you did not need to have an internship, but because we graduated early we all had a six-month internship. Some chose to do internal medicine. I chose to do pediatrics at South Baltimore General

"The regulations for psychiatric training changed a year or two afterward," says Fleishman, "where you had to have a year's internship and then three more years if you wanted to be an adult psychiatrist and four more years if you wanted to be a child psychiatrist (for a total of five years).

Hospital, a community hospital affiliated with the University of Maryland Hospital System."

The importance of volunteer faculty. "What astonished people across the country is that this program didn't cost anything," says Walter Weintraub. "In fact, people kept telling me to stop advertising the program as not costing anything, because it made things harder for them. I shouldn't say it didn't cost anything," says Weintraub, "because with both the CAPP program and the Maryland Plan, volunteers were doing most of the work, and their efforts were certainly worth something. Sometimes they would do the work for my sake—because I had done things for them and I was asking for an hour a week from each of them. But it was more the idea that for the first time in their careers they were working with students who enjoyed doing psychiatry, which is a big deal."

"The only outside financial support CAPP got was in the early days, says Weintraub, when, for about five years, NIMH supported a summer fellowship, to give CAPP a start. And when medical students are assigned to a state hospital, sometimes the site where they are assigned puts up some money, to help them survive. "The economics of being a medical student are awful."

The CAPP students, learning that faculty time was volunteered, were appreciative. The entire program was "extremely generous," says Jay Phillips. "We were at faculty members' houses once a month in the evening for social activities, where people would present their cases. They really put a lot of themselves into that program, and it really made a tremendous difference in my life. Walter Weintraub and George Balis were instrumental in my developing the way I did as a professional. I owe them a lot. I was glad to do the CAPP seminar for years just on the basis of repaying the debt I felt I owed to those two."

Among many volunteers who provided instruction and supervision were Jose Arana, George Balis, Bob Derbyshire, Herb Gross, Bill Holden, Virginia Huffer, Jerry Hunt, Dan Johnston, James Lynch, and Walter Weintraub. Many psychologists and social workers participated as well.

What made someone a good teacher? "First, the teacher has to listen to the trainee present clinical material and decide at what level the trainee needs help," says Phillips, who later joined the faculty. "Some trainees need help at the most basic level of sitting in the room with the patient and tolerating the task of listening to a patient's story. Others need help with the listening—deciding what's more important, what's less important, and how to make those distinctions from the raw material the patient provides. Then the task gets more refined: Listening to content vs. process, conflict and compromise, indications of transference, which may happen at different levels of awareness to the patient (what's closer to the surface, what's further away). The things we deal with are the most complex readings of human mental functioning. It takes a fair amount of experience to appreciate that and a fair amount of empathy to be able to help somebody learn it."

In 1971, after much debate, the department changed its name from the Psychiatric Institute to the Institute of Psychiatry and Human Behavior (IPHB). When the department left the IPHB building, it reverted to the simpler name, Department of Psychiatry.

The Psych Institute broadens its identity

In 1971, after much debate, the department changed its name from the Psychiatric Institute to the Institute of Psychiatry and Human Behavior (IPHB), reflecting an effort to be interdisciplinary and to address issues of mental health and mental illness as aspects of behavior in all its sociocultural and neurobiological dimensions. The new name suggested both a clinical identity and a research and scientific identity—moving along a track encouraged by the NIMH. Departments elsewhere were also changing their names to the equivalent of "department of psychiatry and behavioral science."[4]

The shift away from a strictly medical model was part of a national trend. In 1970 the American Board of Psychiatry and Neurology (ABPN), in a controversial decision to which the APA and many departments of psychiatry objected, announced that it would no longer require the internship year, involving six months of general

"The Association of University Professors of Neurology website reports: "Just one year before the AUPN was founded, the AMA Council on Medical Education released the Millis Report, which recommended abolition of the internship and combination of the internship and residency years into a unified whole. In July 1970, the American Board of Psychiatry and Neurology sent a notice to program directors that the ABPN would no longer require the completion of an internship as a requirement for eligibility for certification. 'High-handed' was one of the kinder descriptions of this directive among AUPN members and it was unofficially agreed that neurology programs would continue to require a preliminary year in general medicine."

medical experience as part of a four-year psychiatry residency.[5] The result, says John Talbott, was that "this bunch of people who came up then didn't know how to palpate, didn't know how to diagnose, didn't know how to do anything. It's sad. Also, there was a whole movement to have a profession of psychotherapy, so that you identified yourself as a psychotherapist," whether you were a psychiatrist or something else.

"What is really happening to American psychiatry today?" asked John Imboden, president of the Maryland Psychiatric Society, in the first issue of *The Maryland Psychiatrist*, in 1974. "Is it undergoing an identity crisis? Can psychotherapy be done by just anybody?"

Psychoanalysis earlier in the century had created such excitement that psychiatrists had begun leaving state hospitals (once their principal place of employment) and organizing their work around an outpatient psychoanalytic practice, seeing patients four or five times a week in a private office. And for twenty years the department had been heavily influenced by psychoanalytically oriented psychotherapy. By the 1970s, however, belief in the supremacy of psychoanalysis was diminishing, new treatments appeared increasingly to be effective, and the department had begun relaxing about who could do therapy.

In the 1950s and 1960s, those who were not on the psychiatry track—faculty such as Bob Derbyshire and Jerry Hunt, who were PhDs, not MDs, and who were brought in to teach and do research in the behavioral sciences—had not previously been allowed to practice psychotherapy in the IPHB. "In a medical setting, a person with a PhD was a second-class citizen, because they didn't have the patient contact that gave them credibility," says Hunt. By 1973, when Michael Plaut, another PhD, was hired by both behavioral pediatrics and child and adolescent psychiatry, PhDs were becoming more involved in therapy, partly because facilitators were needed for the small groups then in common use and partly because the child psychiatry division began bringing in experts to provide training in family therapy, a field not dominated by psychiatrists. (Psychiatrists spoke of their "patients"; other therapists spoke of their "clients.")

"I found that this department corrupts you in different ways, and I'm saying that in a positive sense," says Plaut, who had come to do animal research in psychosomatic medicine. "Joan Scratton, an Australian who was our director of social work at the time, warned me soon after I came that this department has a way of making clinicians out of everybody.[6] The department was structured very differently back then, and I soon found myself getting involved in the teaching of medical students and working with student programs." In 1975 he began helping on the new sexuality course, which needed group leaders.

Those who saw patients about sexual problems saw mostly the "worried well"—people who could afford private health insurance. The people residents saw on the wards every day could not typically afford to see a therapist if they had a sexual problem—patients on Medicare, perhaps, but rarely patients on medical assistance.

By the mid-1970s, social workers were pursuing the right to provide psychotherapy without a physician's supervision and, despite active lobbying by the Psychiatric Society, brought about a change in the laws that allowed them to do so.[7] Psychiatry then became so preoccupied with pharmacological solutions that clinical psychologists and social workers increasingly stepped in to fill a gap and began doing much of the talk therapy nationally.

Student Mental Health Service

The Psych Institute did its best to handle the increasing load of problems—such as stress, anxiety, and depression—presented by medical students and students in all the professional schools (law, dentistry, nursing, pharmacy, and medicine). "When I first got to Maryland, medical and nursing students were being seen all over the department," says Gross. "These patients were smart, verbal, and interesting. I'd see them and then dole them out to the residents, for whom they were important and interesting teaching cases." In 1969, the department got funding for student mental health, and in 1970 Gene Brody and the director of the student health service hired part-time faculty member Thurman Mott as the first full-time director of the student mental health service. A former chief resident, Thomas Cimonetti, worked with Mott to establish (in 1971) the mental health services at the University of Maryland-Baltimore County. As student health psychiatrist, Mott did evaluations and provided brief

In 1960, while he was serving as director of psychiatric education at Springfield Hospital and director of education for the state's Department of Mental Hygiene, Mott began spending one day a week in the department working with adolescent outpatients. Gene Brody, knowing of his interest in adolescents, asked him to join the faculty, working half-time in the student mental health service and half-time teaching medical students and residents. For many years the student health service was a separate entity, its director responsible directly to the dean. Later it was under the department of medicine, and in the late 1980s responsibility for it moved to the family practice department. Mott's functions remained unchanged, and student mental health remained the responsibility of the department of psychiatry. Note that this "student mental health service" is different from the one that developed later in child psychiatry, providing onsite professional help in the Baltimore city school system.

therapy for students from all the professional schools, for everything from adjustment reactions, exam anxiety, and relationship problems (especially if they interfered with the students' work) to depression and occasionally psychosis. Student Health initially paid for twelve sessions of therapy, raising that after a few years to twenty sessions. When students required longer-term therapy, Mott referred them to psychiatric residents. In the late eighties, Student Mental Health expanded, adding a second psychiatrist, Katherine Ackerman, and a psychologist, Morris Roseman.

Alcohol and drug abuse programs

Programs dealing with alcohol and drug abuse took a while to find their permanent home in both Maryland's medical school and the federal government. Alcohol abuse and alcoholism were acknowledged to be a major public health problem in the mid-1960s, when the National Center for Prevention and Control of Alcoholism was established as part of NIMH, but opinions vacillated on whether it was a mental health problem. NIMH inaugurated the Center for Studies of Narcotic and Drug Abuse to do research on drug abuse. In 1970, the National Institute on Alcoholism and Alcohol Abuse (NIAAA) was created as an independent federal agency. In 1974 NIAAA became part of the Alcohol, Drug Abuse, and Mental Health Administration (ADAMHA), established in 1973 to bring together existing and new groups. ADAMHA was abolished in 1992, when the three participating groups resumed their independent identities: the National Institute on Drug Abuse (NIDA), the National Institute on Alcoholism and Alcohol Abuse (NIAAA), and NIMH. This national game of musical chairs doubtless had an effect on what went on at Maryland.

In 1969, Russ Monroe and George Balis started a division of alcoholism and drug abuse as a general University Hospital program—its precursor being Isadore Tuerk's

Léon Wurmser

Saturday morning group for alcoholics. In 1971, the alcoholism and drug abuse program, under Willem Bosma, was moved from the department of psychiatry to the office of the dean of the medical school, where it would stay until the mid-1980s. Wendy Maters was part of the clinical leadership, especially at the quarter-way houses. James O'Donnell and, after 1973, Frances Fitch, were primary workers in the program on alcoholism counseling.[8]

In 1971, Léon Wurmser came to Maryland as scientific director of the division and to head the drug addiction part of the program—especially the methadone clinic. A Swiss-born psychoanalyst, Wurmser had come to the States in 1962 to get more solid psychological training than was available in Europe after Hitler's regime. He had had to start his psychiatric residency and psychoanalytical training all over again in Maryland, and to support his family he had moonlighted, working with drug addicts. In 1969 Johns Hopkins had hired him to build up their drug abuse program in two basement rooms "uninhabited, except by rats." Hopkins's emphasis was on drug education, which Wurmser viewed as inadequate for the heroin problem the state was facing.

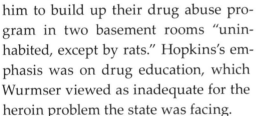

Wurmser's primary interest was psychoanalysis, which Gene Brody allowed him to practice as an associate professor; Russ Monroe, with whom he was not in favor, did not allow it and banished him to a space in the basement.

In 1977, when Bosma left, Wurmser was put in charge of the whole alcoholism and drug abuse program. In 1978 he published *The Hidden Dimension: Psychodynamics in Compulsive Drug Use*. He was already working on *The Mask of Shame* (shame not having figured in Freud's theory). Wurmser saw drug addiction as a symptom of a deeper psychological disorder that was treatable but hard to treat; it had to be seen in the framework of serious neurosis. "In virtually all the patients with drug addiction, I found severe child abuse—mostly horrible violence or horrible humiliation—disturbed human dynamics, sometimes behind a shining façade." In another time these patients would have turned to violence, but with the easy availability of drugs, they found their way to drug addiction instead, says Wurmser.

This was not the only division in search of a firmer identity.

The perennial shortage of child psychiatrists

In 1972, there were about 800 child and adolescent psychiatrists in the country; now there are about 7,500. Then as now, the supply fell far short of demand, and the shortage remains particularly severe in rural and poor urban areas.[9] Why is there a shortage of child psychiatrists? Recruitment into child psychiatry is tough because the field is competing with both pediatrics and other fields of psychiatry. A potential recruit has to want to work with children, so right away has to decide, *Do I want to be a pediatrician or a child psychiatrist?* The pay differential is not that great: a child psychiatrist makes more than a pediatrician, but not much more than a general psychiatrist, although the training time is longer. Pediatric training takes three years; child psychiatry training, five years—one year more than general psychiatry. Generally residents do two years of general psychiatry before they do child—three, if you include the internship year (now called post-graduate year one or PGY-1). Because in some ways child psychiatry is so different from general psychiatry, at that point students are thinking, *Do I want to do all this training and then basically start over again?*

The field has struggled to find ways to address its personnel shortage. Attracting more people from pediatrics into child psychiatry is one approach. Organizations are looking at ways to give earlier exposure to child psych in residency training—for example, letting a rotation in child neurology count as a core neurology requirement.[*] They've also been trying creative new tracks of training. In the 1980s, the American Board of Psychiatry and the American Board of Pediatrics began a pilot effort at a triple board program, allowing residents who trained in approved combined programs for five years to be eligible to take board exams for certification in pediatrics, psychiatry, and child psychiatry.

There has only been one track into child psychiatry, and that is through adult psychiatry, says David Pruitt, current chief of child and adolescent psychiatry, "and as they get into adult psychiatry residents often aren't sure they want to train two more years. It would be better, in my opinion, to have different avenues into the field of child and adolescent psychiatry—if we were able to bring trainees out of pediatrics."

> *Recruitment into child psychiatry is tough because the field is competing with both pediatrics and other fields of psychiatry.*

[*] This means that more time could be spent during the child psychiatry training period on other things, such as infant psychiatry or a research experience. The issue of double dipping has been a contentious one, as general psychiatry residency directors don't want their residents taken away from rotations on adult services, where they are needed. For example, allowing a pediatric consultation–liaison experience to count for general psychiatry would take the residents away from the adult CL service.

Power struggles in the child psychiatry division

Dick Sarles trained in child psychiatry in the late 1960s, when many child psychiatrists came out of pediatrics, as he did. After graduating from the University of Maryland's medical school in 1961, Sarles trained in pediatrics under the Berry plan. He became interested in child psychiatry during the three years he served as an Air Force pediatrician in Germany, taking care of military dependents. Returning to the States for training in psychiatry, in 1968 he chose Maryland over Hopkins, because the Psych Institute wanted to expand its pediatric liaison work. The department constructed a flexible training program for him that suited his background and the department's needs. Psychiatry paid half his salary and pediatrics paid a quarter, "which was a huge commitment on their part," said Sarles, who also kept seeing private patients. This setup, with a foot in both departments, was ideal for teaching and for developing the pediatric consultation–liaison (CL) service.

Sarles started in outpatient adult psychiatry but took child psychiatry seminars his first year, then did child psychiatry his second year. He did inpatient adult psychiatry his third year, which is normally done the first year, and kept attending child seminars and carrying child patients.

Training programs in child psychiatry at the time were influenced most by psychoanalysis, by the child

Dick Sarles (shown here in 1972, with hand at chin) trained in both pediatrics and child psychiatry.

guidance movement, and to some extent by the family therapy movement. "In my early training, the child psychiatrist would see the child, the social worker would see the parents, and the child psychiatrist and the social worker might or might not talk once a week," says Sarles. "Their roles were separate. Psychopharmacology was primitive. There were the stimulants (mainly Ritalin and Dexedrine), imipramine for bed-wetting, and some other antidepressants, but the use of medication in the early seventies was still minimal.

The length of stay was similar at Menninger (in Topeka), Sheppard Pratt, the University of Pennsylvania, the Institute of Living (in Hartford), and the Brown Schools (in the South), says Sarles. Did the kids profit from the longer stays? "The question is, how long is an adequate length of stay? Managed care took things from the sublime of a nine-month stay to a three-day stay. Was nine months too long? Kids certainly got better and did very well. Would nine weeks have been better? Nine days? The wave of change, driven by economics, went from long-term to very short-term and then bounced back somewhat, so that on most children's inpatient units now probably the length of stay is a week. You don't see too many three-day stays anymore, although some insurance companies force you to get a kid out in three days. Then the question is: What good is a three-day stay?"

"The prevailing treatment was long-term, intensive, psychoanalytically or psychodynamically oriented care. The average length of stay on 4G, the inpatient unit for a latency-age child (six to twelve years old, and occasionally five), was about a year and a half. These kids were seen three times a week in individual therapy, once a week in family therapy, and then all the rest of the therapies—and they went to school here. On outpatient you'd see them once or twice a week.

The mode of treatment then was different from what we see today."

Children were admitted to the hospital for long stays. Every summer young patients were discharged and new patients were admitted to fill the unit, and it was important to discharge them properly, says Stan Weinstein, a social worker with a PhD in human development, who interned as a student social worker on 2G (an adolescent and adult inpatient unit). In 1968, when he graduated, Ulku Ulgur recruited him to 4G (children's residential services) as intake supervisor ("director of admissions") and to do family therapy. "Obviously, providing good service to patients was primary, but one factor in deciding who to admit was, Would this be a good training case to learn from. Money wasn't a big issue, and training was a priority. In those days the hospital always lost a lot of money and assumed the state would be able to manage, and the state usually did. Also, the department had more money then. NIMH was funding training programs, and the federal government was more generous then. So when we evaluated a child for admission, the question seldom arose as to insurance or ability to pay. It was much more, Did the patient need that level of care, and was it a good training case."

Weinstein supervised psychiatric residents, child psych fellows, psychology and social work interns, and nurses completing their master's degree. To complete work for his PhD, he studied attitudes toward death and dying in senior medical students at five medical schools. Under federal legislation creating counseling and information projects around the country he led a grant to study families who lost babies to sudden infant death syndrome (SIDS) and to provide educational services to help professionals understand how to help families prevent the loss of this child from causing further psychiatric and other problems.

The department had established a special school for children with special problems, inside the Psych Institute but supported by the school district, with two full-time teachers serving fourteen children. At the time, the department had its own psychiatric social work program (headed by Len Press and then Don Blumberg), its own child psych nursing program and supervisor, and its own activity therapy and psychology staffs (that would change later). Under the supervision of Weinstein and others, they all provided services to the young patients, as did rotating residents and child psychiatry fellows. When the kids began to improve, their improvements showed up first in the school setting—perhaps because the school provided structure, tasks, and controls.

When the attending or resident in another department called child psychiatry to say, "I think we need a CL consult on this child," it might be a patient who stopped eating for no discernible reason, and they weren't sure what was going on or how to coax him to eat. Or there might be a difficult parent or a child in renal failure who was not only sick but also worried and depressed. The outside resident would present the case, then Sarles would ask pertinent questions and bring clarity to the situation. The residents needed to get a family history because they needed to know the premorbid status and behavior to determine if the problem had been a problem before the child was ill or if it was caused by the disease or the hospital. Most of the child and adolescent psychiatric consults were in pediatrics, but they'd occasionally get called for a teenager in ob–gyn or shock–trauma (up through the age of eighteen or nineteen). Eventually the psychology interns and behavioral pediatrics residents joined Sarles on his rounds, too.

The experiment with behavioral pediatrics

"Dr. Brody, who was a psychoanalyst, said he was disappointed that child psychoanalysis didn't really deliver mental health services to kids, as it had promised," says Sarles, "so he hired Stan Friedman, a behavioral pediatrician with no training in child psychiatry, as chief of the division of child psychiatry. Dr. Friedman had been doing psychosomatic research up at Rochester and was interested in community mental health. Dr. Brody took a big risk hiring a behavioral pediatrician, which was somewhat anathema within the psychiatric community and didn't go over too well in the department, which was highly psychoanalytic at the time." Brody wanted to shake things up, and he did.

"I don't know whether I made a mistake in hiring Friedman or not," says Brody. "He did what I hired him to do: He built a division and he got basic objective research going in a lot of different areas, including animal research and sudden infant death syndrome. The trouble with the psychoanalytic stuff is that so much of it is inferential—is intuitive guesses about what's happening."

Like Sarles, who had set a precedent, Friedman had a dual appointment in pediatrics and psychiatry. He was responsible and responsive to two chairmen, Gene Brody in psychiatry and Marvin Cornblath in pediatrics, and he made a deliberate effort not to play one against the other.

During his tenure, the fellows in pediatrics and psychiatry did many things jointly, including an interesting weekly meeting of all the trainees in pediatrics and child psychiatry—twenty or twenty-five people.

Pediatrics as far back as the early 1900s had emphasized family dynamics and how families responded to a child's illness. Early studies emphasized the importance, with abdominal pain, of looking at family function, says Friedman. A British researcher who had looked at a hundred cases of children with abdominal pain found no physical or organic cause for the pain in most of them. In about 90 percent of the cases the problem was family dysfunction or what would later be called psychosomatic causes.

Gene Brody hired Stan Friedman, a pioneer in behavioral pediatrics, to direct child psychiatry and shake things up. That he did.

Behavioral pediatrics, a new field in the 1970s, emphasized treating the whole child (as part of a family) and learning more about the behavioral aspects of diseases, especially the effect of chronic diseases on children and their families. Behavioral pediatricians specialized in treating common behavioral problems and non-severe emotional and mental health problems, such as ADHD, family problems, development issues, and various learning disorders. Behavioral pediatricians are fully trained as, and are eligible to be board certified as, pediatricians. In the early days, there were no formal boards in the subspecialty of behavioral pediatrics; now there are, and they must conform to the American Board of Pediatrics rules for certification, which require three years of fellowship training in behavioral pediatrics. The line between behavioral pediatrics and child psychiatry is blurred, but behavioral pediatricians do not generally see kids with schizophrenia or psychotic problems. Both behavioral pediatricians and family social workers might do short-term counseling with parents on behavior management (when, for example, the parents don't know how to handle a child who is throwing tantrums) or might do evaluations and counseling in the schools for children with performance or behavior problems. Behavioral pediatricians also do evaluations for children

"Behavioral pediatrics in Maryland was different from elsewhere," says Lois Flaherty. There were no ACGME or American Board of Medical Specialties (ABMS) requirements, so programs differed around the country. "When I moved to Pennsylvania, I interacted with behavioral pediatricians who primarily worked with developmental disabilities or with neurological conditions. The idea at Maryland was that the behavioral pediatricians would focus on the mainstream pediatric patients who also had the more common psychiatric disorders, such as ADHD, and, as Stan pointed out, the whole child and family."

with problems such as autism and cerebral palsy, when the parents sense something is wrong but don't know quite what it is or how to find the proper services to help the child.

Stan Friedman was considered a pioneer in the field. He had started the first behavioral pediatrics fellowship program when he was at Rochester, just before he came to Maryland. Besides starting another behavioral pediatrics fellowship at the University of Maryland, Friedman persuaded the W.T. Grant Foundation to fund a training program to teach behavior and development to pediatric residents. That led to the funding of eleven other programs in the country. Marianne Felice, one of the first fellows in the behavioral pediatrics program, designed and implemented the training program, which David Bromberg and Alice Heisler inherited and continued when she moved on. Mary Jo Albright taught family dynamics, Nancy Kohn Rabin taught child development and psychology, social worker Judy Haran talked about psychiatry, Thomas Kenny taught pediatric psychology, and later C.T. Gordon, who had been a CAPP student, talked about psychopharmacology. "I learned so much," says Alice Heisler, a behavioral pediatrics fellow (1976–79). "Psychologists would talk about their tests, so we learned about evaluating children and about differential diagnoses (is it this or this or this—which things do you rule in and which do you rule out?). The psychiatrist might say, 'I think you're describing signs of anxiety. Children may act out because they're anxious; anxiety in a child doesn't always show up like anxiety in an adult.'"

Felice and Gregory Prazar were the first two behavioral pediatrics fellows (1974–76). Felice joined the faculty and stayed another three years. There were also fellows in adolescent medicine and in school health (under Murray Kappelman, who felt pediatricians trained in behavioral medicine were better suited than child psychiatrists to deal with pediatric issues).

"I had been a critic of child psychiatry and I thought, rather than just criticize, let's see if I can do anything better," says Friedman, who felt there should be more social responsibility and sound research. "Gene Brody wanted to bring some research into the Psychiatric Institute. That's why I went there. I think he hoped not only that child psychiatry would do some research but that it would spread to the general psychiatry people. Mike Plaut, a grad student in psychology, came with me, and we started out in both psychiatry and pediatrics."

"Stan was smart—maybe brilliant—and dynamic, and he could conceptualize and negotiate new programs out in the community," says Heisler, who participated in one of those programs—providing parenting classes to women living in transitional housing.

"Most of the people who do behavioral pediatrics now are people who are interested in developmental disabilities," says Lois Flaherty, who would later chair the division, "but at Maryland Stan basically viewed them as equivalent to child psychiatrists; in fact, he thought they were better than child psychiatrists because they had pediatrics. Child psychiatrists tend to feel that behavioral pediatricians aren't as well trained and can get in over their heads, but the ones who came through the program at Maryland were well trained and I think that's partly because they got a lot of supervision from the psychiatry faculty. That wasn't always the case elsewhere."

In 1970 Congress passed the National Developmental Disabilities Act, which brought "retarded, crippled, and neurologically handicapped" children into one program.

"In the seminars and the day-to-day work we emphasized working together, and we really had a lot of cooperation," says Flaherty. "Inevitably there was some competition for resources—who got what offices and what toys went into the playroom—but even after Stan left, child psychiatry continued to have a lot of interaction with behavioral pediatrics. When he was still there, there was probably more integration of seminars. During supervision, the behavioral pediatricians became more separate, but there was still a fair amount of working together."

Child psychiatry had its roots in community psychiatry—its legacy as a "soft" specialty comes partly from its start in the child guidance clinics, not in an academic environment—but it had gotten away from community involvement, says Flaherty. And most of the early child psychiatrists started out as pediatricians. When the American Academy of Child Psychiatry began, in 1959, about half the members were trained in pediatrics. "Stan strengthened the connection between pediatrics and child psychiatry," says Flaherty, "but he had an ambivalent relationship with psychiatry. He and others argued that child psychiatrists were too small in number and too insular to be a viable specialty."

Friedman wanted to show that child psychiatry as a field could be relevant to the community—in both training and services. He initially had trouble finding the child psych fellows, who spent most of their time moonlighting, so he put a strict limit on this activity, saying full-time psych fellows could moonlight only if it made educational sense (offering an experience they couldn't have otherwise). He also insisted that fellows in the training program be observed directly and not just supervised based on what they reported happening. "No one had ever seen them interview anyone or play with anyone in play therapy. They would tell the supervisor what they were doing and the supervisor would make suggestions, and that's okay as far as it goes, but it's selective. You tell the supervisor what you want to tell them, either consciously or unconsciously, which might or might not equal what's going on in the actual interaction." Friedman made it a practice to have direct (sometimes videotaped) observation at weekly meetings, but actually watching fellows in practice was difficult to achieve. Fellows resisted it because it was time-consuming and it was not standard practice.

The various fellows learned a lot together but also had to learn more about their subspecialties. "The people in school health had to learn about the structure and function of schools and school systems, what kind of permission you needed to examine kids in the school, and all that jazz," says Felice. "The people in adolescent medicine had to learn about gynecology and all the medical issues of teenagers. The people in behavioral pediatrics had to learn about the psychosocial effects of certain diseases of children. And child psych fellows had to learn what psych medications to use for children. There was overlap, but we all had slightly different concepts and skills to learn."

Child psychiatry ran a behavior clinic, which was especially helpful for inner-city families whose children had ADHD and no regular pediatrician to evaluate or coach them. Pediatrics ran a central evaluation clinic, to evaluate children with developmental disabilities or diseases such as cerebral palsy. It could take a while to figure out if a child's problem was a hearing, speech,

The evaluation clinic was headed by Ray Clemmens, who led and supervised a staff comprising a pediatrician, a psychologist, an educational specialist, and, when needed, a consulting psychiatrist.

learning, or mental health problem. Psychiatrist Ted Kaiser and later Alp Karahasan provided invaluable consultation at the weekly case conference, helping to teach about systems, resources, and principles.

In her second year, Marianne Felice was asked to run the adolescent medicine clinic. There were special clinics for victims of adolescent rape, for pregnant teenagers, and for kids who had attempted suicide. In the suicide attempt follow-up clinic, Dick Sarles supervised rotating medical students, pediatric residents, and fellows in adolescent medicine, child psychiatry, and behavioral pediatrics.

"Having that kind of overlap in training all in the same clinic was a rich experience for everybody—particularly the patients," says Felice. "It was considered one of the best training programs in behavioral pediatrics at that time, and the close relationship between pediatrics and child psychiatry succeeded partly because our immediate supervisor, Dick Sarles, did an outstanding job teaching all of us. It was exciting because we were blazing new trails. At first, few institutions had behavioral pediatric fellowships, and there was no single way to structure the fellowships. At Maryland, with Stan a member of the psychiatry faculty, we went to both psychiatry and pediatrics faculty meetings. He said we had to be able to bridge both worlds, and it never occurred to me how unusual that was. I loved it." At a retreat about the future of behavioral pediatrics convened for child psychiatrists and behavioral pediatricians on Maryland's Eastern Shore, Felice stood up and said, "The fields of pediatrics and child psychiatry have always been close. We bicker a lot, but in reality we both care about children. We may not have to get married, but we at least need to get along for the sake of the children. We will harm children if we do not work together." Years later, she adds, "I would never have had the nerve to say that publicly if I had not felt so comfortable and so embraced by the department of psychiatry."

"Taghi Modarressi was one of our supervisors," says Heisler. "He taught the fellows the emotional issues and dynamics of mothers and infants, and I don't know where I would have ever learned that otherwise. You can read a book, but he brought it to life. We brought in cases to present,

Taghi Modarressi and his wife, Anne Tyler, the novelist. "Taghi was ahead of his time in trying to take a structured look at infant behavior. He recorded infants and children crying and left the door open to see who would come in and check on the crying. He had a sense that babies cried because of certain behaviors."

and he talked about what the dynamics might be, also tying different theories together. In individual supervision, you would bring in the case you were working on, and he would guide you: Did you think of this, or ask about that? If he said it might be something between the brother and sister, we'd guide the patient to tell us a little more about that. Taghi was an excellent, very supportive supervisor and teacher."

Modarressi had joined the department in 1965, while Frank Rafferty was director. Ulku Ulgur ran residential services, Modarressi ran the child inpatient unit for a while, and Naomi Grant ran the children's liaison service. Rafferty left to direct the Institute for Juvenile Research in Chicago in 1971, and for two years (1971–73) Modarressi served as acting director of the division while a national search was conducted for the permanent director. "As an acting director, he was extremely good," says Ulku Ulgur. "He was gifted. He stimulated the faculty to do more teaching, to publish more, and to be more active. But he did not like administration; he preferred to teach and do research."

Rafferty went on to become medical director of the Brown Schools in Houston, Texas.

"When I first got there," says Friedman, "I met with each of the staff and asked if there was something I could do that would be meaningful to them professionally, and Taghi said, 'Yeah, give me your job.'" Modarressi, as acting division director, had been passed over for the permanent position, about which he was at best ambivalent, but he had been made training director, a position psychiatric trainees often relate to more than the division director.

Modarressi taught everyone the importance of bonding and nurturing to children's mental health. "Nobody talked that language then, and he was a role model for looking for bonding and nurturing in the families we were seeing," says Heisler. He would show films demonstrating variations on bonding problems: one mother would be overstimulating the infant; another fed her child but depression kept her from being nurturing; in one home, chaos and screaming kept one mother unavailable for nurturing; in one, a baby's illness made it too ill to hold and nurture and the parents didn't know what to do.

While Modarressi was in charge of the residential children's unit (4G), Stuart Tiegel was hired as faculty to recruit for admissions, supervise family therapy, and oversee the psychology interns and child psychiatry fellows in family therapy training. "Taghi was a champion of children's treatment," says Tiegel. "We also had George Cohen, a childcare worker with a master's in childcare on the staff." (In those days the Child Welfare League of America was involved in oversight of residential treatment all over the country.) "We ran an interesting, intimate, twelve-bed unit. The children would come in on Monday and leave Friday at noon. We had to know where everyone lived, because during a major snowstorm we had to get the volunteer fire department to deliver the children's medicine to them."

The unit accepted both boys and girls, some with the beginnings of childhood schizophrenia, and no adolescents. "We had time to work with kids then," says Tiegel. "There was

Modarressi taught everyone the importance of bonding and nurturing to children's mental health. "Nobody talked that language then, and he was a role model."

a child life staff, a nursing staff, and a school. The milieu was largely the responsibility of the childcare workers and the nursing staff, and therapy was the domain of the child psych fellows, child psychiatrists in training, some of the psychology interns, and me." Tiegel had a one-way mirror built into his office, with an observation area on the other side. Observers watched all admissions through the one-way mirror, and Tiegel also used it to supervise family therapy training.

Taghi Modarressi, Stanley Greenspan, Reg Lourie, E. James Anthony, Erik and Joan Erikson, at 1982 symposium, The Infant and the Young Child.

Everyone mingled: the psychology interns, the child psychiatry fellows, and interns from the University of Maryland's and Smith College's graduate schools of social work. (Smith used to do field placements at Maryland.) "Taghi had a phenomenal seminar on human development that interns and fellows were required to attend," says Tiegel. "He grew very animated talking about the inner life of the child. In those days parents had to be treated separately because they would mess up the treatment the child psychiatrist provided. We used terms like 'schizophrenogenic mothers' and blamed mothers a lot, which led to interesting discussions. We did a lot of well-intentioned arguing. I believed that kids needed to be treated with their families; Taghi would never allow a resident who was treating a child to also treat the family. We had a blow-up about a badly encopretic kid; the resident was treating the kid, someone else was seeing the family, the resident's wife died, and Taghi asked me to take over the case. I said I would do it only if I could do it my way, seeing the family with the kid, and we kind of broke that barrier then.

"Not long after that," says Tiegel, "the unit as we knew it ceased to exist. The insurance companies were telling the hospital administrators that if the kids could go home on Friday, they didn't need to be in the hospital. This was in the early eighties, when the concept of medical necessity started driving care. Taghi, George Cohen, Marie Constantini, the head nurse, and I turned over control of 4G, the four-and-a-half-day unit became a seven-day acute care unit, and we all found other things to do. George continued on the inpatient unit, Taghi started the Center for Infant Study, and I secured a grant to do marital and family therapy training as a combined program between the department of psychiatry and the state Department of Health and Hygiene."

"Taghi had worked in the Carter Center for a while, seeing that as an opportunity to develop a program independent of Stan Friedman," says Flaherty. Friedman and Modarressi's views and personality were so different that Modarressi, with Russ Monroe's permission, developed a new program independent of the division: a center to study infants, in a separate building on Lombard Street. Modarressi began holding conferences and symposiums, bringing in such pioneers in child psychiatry as E. James Anthony and Stanley Greenspan. Erik Erikson came for the conference "at the end of our run as the children's residential service, when Taghi was raising money for the center for child and infant studies," says Tiegel. The Center for Infant Study was launched in 1982 (initially as the Center for Child Study) with a symposium on The Infant and the Young Child: Developmental and Psychopathological Issues. In 1985, the center (with co-chair E.J. Anthony) hosted an evening symposium, Resilient Children, and in 1988 the center held a second symposium, The Roots of Creativity in Infancy: The Beginnings of Imaginative Life.[10]

In 1977, when he was at Hopkins's Phipps Clinic, Tiegel had begun intensive one-day-a-week training in family and marital therapy in D.C., with Jay Haley. He did his second year of training when he came to Maryland. "It was a long, grueling day, but Taghi approved it because he felt the staff would reap the rewards." He then spent two years at the Finan Center in Cumberland, learning to train the trainers. "There aren't any training institutes anymore." Under this training grant, Tiegel, who reported to Henry Harbin, led ten other trainers. For about thirty-six weeks a year, they provided six hours of live supervision in clinics and hospitals one day a week, with the express purpose of reducing acuity in the outpatient programs or reducing admissions in inpatient. They spent time with psychologists, psychiatrists, or social workers at Springfield, Spring Grove, and Crownsville hospitals, and held two conferences a year for all the trainees—usually in the auditorium of the school of social work.

Russ Monroe, with Modarressi in the background.

Friedman was not sympathetic to what the center was doing. He viewed Modarressi as being more interested in learning from patients than helping them. "Taghi did know the value of research, and in some respects he was ahead of his time in trying to take a structured look at infant behavior," says Carol Norris-Shortle, the current infant mental health consultant for the therapeutic nursery. "George Cohen told us that Taghi had recorded infants and children crying and left the door open to see who of the staff would come in and check on the crying. He had a sense that babies cried because of certain behaviors. Taghi was not hands-on with the children, but he saw the importance of the parents bonding with the children. Instead of his picking up the baby and calming and soothing it, Taghi wanted the mother to pick the baby up and calm and sooth it. Maybe Dr. Friedman perceived that as not working with the child. My understanding of how crucial attachment is to a relationship really emanates from Taghi, who introduced me to Selma Freiberg, who originated the work we're going back to study now."

In 1972 Modarressi had asked research associate Duncan McCulloch to investigate prelingual vocal communication in child development. McCulloch later became research coordinator for the Center for Infant Study.

When the Center for Infant Study opened, residents and fellows often asked if their patients (mother and infant) could be seen there. Modarressi got grants from the city and state to take care of at-risk children. He also had the strong support of his wife, Anne Tyler, the well-known Baltimore novelist. (He eventually wrote four novels himself.) The fee-for-service approach by then required by the university was a challenge, as services to small children and families takes more time—the "patient" including not just the child but one or both parents and sometimes siblings. From the start, the center relied on grants, extensions, private funds, and the determination and financial acumen of the center's modest and competent administrator, Alma Troccoli, who, all agree, was "the main reason the center survived the financial landmines of its first fifteen years." In 1984–85, the center got a three-year training grant, and in July 1986, in the third year of the training grant, the center opened a clinic for infant mental health in Howard Hall, on Redwood Street. Three years later, it began providing services to Head Start at Pimlico Elementary School, which led to a Head Start

"For twenty-five years Alma spent long hours tracking the finances of the center and securing grants and philanthropic support to ensure that the center continue its mission," writes Carole Norris-Shortle. "Through the toughest days, when it seemed the center would not be able to financially make it another year, Alma soldiered on to find resources to continue. Generations of staff, trainees, and very young children and their families owe a great debt of gratitude to Alma."

Therapeutic Nursery Program, launched at the Cold Spring Head Start Center.

"I think Taghi felt he needed as much independence as possible to protect himself," says Lois Flaherty, "initially because he disliked Stan Friedman but he also wanted not to have to report to me when I became division director. When I came there, Taghi was the most academically oriented person in child psychiatry. He had published, he was doing some research on early development, and he was involved with the Academy of Child Psychiatry. Then he drifted off on his own and became less involved with the academy. Although he viewed his center as an academic research center, its basic focus was providing services for infants and young children."

For a long time the research base was almost nonexistent, says Flaherty. Early issues of the *Journal of the American Academy of Child and Adolescent Psychiatry* contained mostly case reports, descriptions, and programs—not much on research. The knowledge base has improved, research is now exploding (in neurobiology and brain function, for example, and services research), there are some research fellowships, and the field seems to be more respected. Public and private grant support has increased, and there are now many endowed chairs in child psychiatry in the country, where for a long time there were none.

According to the American Academy of Child and Adolescent Psychiatry, as of December 2009 there were eighty endowed positions in child and adolescent psychiatry in the United States.

Work with schools continued and expanded within behavioral pediatrics. Murray Kappelman, who had a joint appointment in behavioral pediatrics and child psychiatry, began going into the schools to do consulting. Friedman supported and extended that consulting role. "Someone somewhere in the system would request an evaluation of a child or family and the trainees would take these in order," says Friedman. "It might be a trainee in pediatrics or someone from psychiatry. The supervision was a little different, depending on their field, but there was a common pool of resources for consultation requests, and I thought that worked very well. There is some data to show that people who train together do a lot more cross-fertilization after they train; it sort of sets up the model."

Friedman brought in people like psychiatrist Al Powell to teach the fellows how to speak the language of the school system, which was different from the language of the medical system. The school system had its own culture and perspective on the kinds of problems kids had and what needed to be done. The schools didn't necessarily look at children as having a DSM[12] diagnosis, but rather as fighting, being defiant, not paying attention, and so on. To work in a school you had to understand that what's important to the teacher may be different from what the resident or the fellow sees. If a teacher sent a child to the school nurse because the child was falling asleep all the time, for example, testing might show that the child did not belong in a special education class but was bored—or was perhaps depressed. A school might refer a child thinking she had attention deficit disorder, when the child was actually preoccupied because her father had just been incarcerated, or maybe she was taking care of younger kids at home because her mother was ill.

A social worker or psychologist in the school, with a psychiatrist available for consultation, could either refer the child for treatment somewhere else or, more often, do the treatment there, even if medication was needed. "Part of setting up these programs was trying to make sure a full range of services was available, some in the school and others outside," says Friedman. "Every year a couple of kids would end up being hospitalized—not many, considering how many kids we saw—but we had that ability to hospitalize them.

"We had about a million dollars in grants and contracts, which in today's world would be a lot more money. A million dollars went a lot further then." Much of that came from the Baltimore city and county school districts, but especially from the city. Trainees spent time in the schools seeing kids with problems, especially learning problems. For the most part it was a diagnostic service, and they would refer kids back to the classroom, perhaps with recommendations.

Friedman saw few patients but brought in money by consulting with various community groups, which was part of training. If a fellow went to a school district to see kids with learning disorders, the division of child psychiatry got paid;

those service contracts helped pay the fellows' salaries. On Friedman's watch, child psychology and the children's in-patient unit, which had both been losing money, began to make some. "We went from losing half a million dollars a year to making half a million dollars a year, while the other units were losing money," says Friedman. It was mostly a matter of collecting money that was due. "Psychology was losing money because it was not billing. They had no records; no one knew who was seeing whom. They were moonlighting all over the place. But in child psychiatry the psychology group was making money. It was just a matter of paying attention. Then the department decided to have a single psychology group, which included the psychologists in child psychiatry." Each time the division became solvent, the department would fold division income into general psychiatry income, which was discouraging to Friedman.

A school might refer a child thinking she had attention deficit disorder, when the child was actually preoccupied because her father had just been incarcerated, or maybe she was taking care of younger kids at home because her mother was ill.

"One source of tension, I think, for the child psychiatry faculty, was the fact that the two programs were different in terms of their competitive attractions for trainees," says Lois Flaherty. "The child psychiatry program, like similar programs elsewhere, had to struggle to fill its positions from a relatively small group of applicants—and the fact that Stan was not a child psychiatrist didn't help with recruitment. Behavioral pediatrics, on the other hand, attracted excellent candidates from all over the country. The two groups were not on the same level academically. Stan was generally seen as favoring the behavioral pediatrics trainees—understandably, considering their caliber. It was really like a sibling situation in which one sibling is favored over the other."

After 1983, Stan Friedman no longer ran the child and adolescent psychiatry division, though he remained head of behavioral pediatrics. Lois Flaherty became acting director of child psychiatry. Friedman left the university in 1985.

Variations on a spiritual motif

It was an ecumenical department in more than one sense of the word. Not only did the department encourage a variety of approaches to mental health care, but in the 1970s in particular it was associated with interesting practitioners from different spiritual traditions. For example, Sister Carla, an ex-nun from Pennsylvania better known as Marianne Felice, was heavily involved in training activities jointly conducted by behavioral pediatrics and child psychiatry.

As Sister Carla she got advanced education because of the Sisters of Mercy. As Marianne Felice, she chairs the department of pediatrics at the University of Massachusetts medical school.

"In my Italian family, the boys were encouraged to become somebody and the girls were not," says Felice. "My father had money put away for my brother to go to college, but not for me. I was of the generation where girls could become a teacher, a nurse, or a secretary, and I wanted to be a nuclear physicist, an astronaut, an anesthetist (I liked the sound of it), or a ballerina. I knew I wasn't going to stay around home and be just anything." Her mother had died when she was ten, and she identified strongly with the nuns who educated her. "They were the ones who told me I was smart and could be whatever I wanted to be—not my own family. So after I graduated from high school, I entered the Pittsburgh convent of the Sisters of Mercy." In the early sixties, Pope John XXIII opened the doors of the church to let in fresh air and modern ideas, such as nuns wearing modern habits. Many priests began leaving the priesthood and nuns the convents. Felice, now Sister Carla, joined protest marches in her habit. At Mount Mercy (now Carlow University), she was being groomed to become a chemistry professor, but while applying for graduate school she learned that her transcript had been signed out by her mother superior—who sent for her and asked if she would like to become a medical doctor.

Mother Thomas Aquinas was having trouble finding good counselors for the nuns troubled about leaving the convent. Most counselors at that time—whether psychiatrists, psychologists, or social workers—were men, who didn't understand why an attractive young woman in her twenties would be conflicted, given a choice "between staying in the convent with vows of poverty, chastity, and obedience or leaving, maybe getting married, maybe having children, but at least having her freedom." Their counseling was doing the nuns no good. The mother superior's brother (a psychiatrist on the faculty of the University of Pittsburgh medical school) suggested she find a nun who was a psychiatrist. "What we do in academic medicine when we don't have a specialist is we grow our own," he said. "Find somebody you think would make it in medical school and groom her to become a psychiatrist for the nuns."

Felice was eventually accepted into the second class at the new Pennsylvania State University College of Medicine at Hershey. Halfway through medical school she decided to leave the convent and, with Mother Thomas Aquinas's blessing, allowed her temporary vows to expire. Nine nuns showed up at her medical school graduation to congratulate her.

"I feel as if my entire career has been built around doing exactly what God intended me to do," says Felice. "If my mother hadn't died, I suspect I would never have become so close to the nuns, or entered the convent, and that's where I got the courage to think, *I can be anything I want to be.* And then the nuns sent me to medical school." She came to Maryland as one of the first fellows in behavioral pediatrics, under Stan Friedman, and became a pediatrician rather than a psychiatrist. She is now chair of the department of pediatrics at the University of Massachusetts medical school and physician-in-chief at the UMass Memorial Children's Medical Center. She repaid the convent for the money it spent on her education.

Then there was Denis J. Madden, who has risen rather high in the Catholic Church. After earning an undergraduate degree at St. Benedict's College in Atchison, Kansas, Madden was ordained a Catholic priest in 1967 and sent by

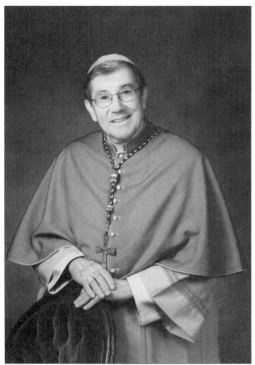

Denis J. Madden, a Catholic priest and clinical psychologist, worked with John Lion and violent patients in the interest of nonviolence—and later at Tantur, trying to advance peace in the Middle East. Today he is auxiliary bishop for the church's Baltimore archdiocese and vicar for the St. John Neumann vicariates.

the Benedictine order to earn a master's degree in psychology from Columbia University and a PhD in clinical psychology from Notre Dame. The idea was that he would serve as psychologist for a Benedictine seminary. The closing of the seminary and his encounter with a violent peace march in Manhattan led him down another path.

Madden was a graduate student at Columbia during a time of many antiwar demonstrations, and one march in particular down Fifth Avenue stuck in his memory. The police had cordoned off the avenue, half for marchers and half for traffic. "One cab driver let loose with his view of the marchers and their mothers, and a group of marchers responded by taking the driver out of his cab and punching him," says Madden. "They had him on the ground, beating him." In one place, some marchers were beating the unfortunate cab driver and others were holding aloft signs saying "Peace Now!" and "Make love, not war." As Madden walked back to campus, he thought, *There's something wrong here.* While finishing his doctorate at Notre Dame, Madden decided to learn more about the psychology of violence.

This led him to John Lion, an expert on how to recognize and prevent violence in patients, who was working with violent patients at Maryland's Institute for Psychiatry and Human Behavior. In 1972, the IPHB had established a research unit built around a specialty clinic, the Clinical Research Program for Violent Behavior. Led by Lion, this program grew to national prominence. In 1973, after an internship at DePaul Hospital in New Orleans, Madden

Among Lion's many publications over the years: *Evaluation and Management of the Violent Patient: Guidelines in the Hospital and Institution* (1972); *Rage, Hate, Assault and Other Forms of Violence,* by Denis J. Madden and John R. Lion (1976); *Assaults Within Psychiatric Facilities* (Lion and W.H. Reid, 1985); and Clinician Safety: Report of the American Psychiatric Association Task Force on Clinican Safety (Task Force Report No. 33, by William R. Dubin and John R. Lion, 1993).

came to Maryland as an intern in the department's psychology division. He felt that postdoctoral work with Lion and violent patients would help in the understanding of violent behavior and might in a real sense be working for nonviolence.

Madden also worked part-time as a marriage and family counselor for Associated Catholic Charities, celebrated Mass at St. Martin's in West Baltimore, and provided long- and short-term counseling to priests and religious sisters in the archdiocese.

John Lion was a "wonderful teacher and a wonderful man, very human—an excellent therapist, but with a great ability to conceptualize," says Madden. Lion was also interested in, and wrote a book about, the art of psychiatric medication—not just looking things up in the *Physicians' Desk Reference*. He said, for example, that there were certain times when you might be almost approaching a toxic level but you had to go there, with all the safeguards, if you were going to help the patient.

Lion's violence clinic was mainly an outpatient clinic, for patients referred by the courts. "Many of them were not there voluntarily," says Madden. "They were given the option of therapy or jail. John would say, 'Because of their histories, nobody wanted to treat these people.' Recognizing the importance of small victories, John felt that if they had been fighting four and five times a week and we got them to fight only two or three times a week, we were going in the right direction. It was amazing: You could really help people make changes in their lives." The basic idea—which was new for this group—was to help them gain some insight into what triggered their violence and to get them to immediately separate themselves from the situation—by counting slowly to ten, for example, or by removing themselves from the scene physically—so they didn't have to react the way they usually would in similar situations. In therapy, they would talk about their challenge, and the majority of them seemed to make some progress. Some, however, would say, 'I should have gone to jail; it would have been better than sitting here talking to you.' "

"I learned so much from John," says Madden. "If I felt uneasy about a patient or didn't know what the problem was, John would say, 'He seems to meet all the criteria for a diagnosis

John Lion

but it's not that. There's something else there.' You learned intuition from working with these people. John used to say that, naturally, you used good practice and good clinical judgment, but what was critical was to be consistent and to genuinely care about your patients."

Madden had joined the department six years after becoming a Catholic priest. His two fellow interns in psychology in 1973 were Henri "Hank" Montandon and Carol Weyland (Conner). Around the same time, Madden and Henry Harbin did some research on kids who had physically assaulted and sometimes even killed their parents. "One of the things we learned," says Madden, "was that in most if not all of these families they felt it was important that you not violate family secrecy: 'What went on in the home, went on in the home, and should stay in the home, whether people were abusing each other, using drugs, or doing anything else.' You had these tragedies occurring because tensions would build up to such a level that the adolescent in some instances might actually kill the parent.

"If they had been fighting five times a week and we got them to fight only three times a week, we were going in the right direction." The idea was to help them learn what triggered their violence and get them to separate themselves from the situation.

"With such patients, we felt the therapy had to include the family. Often the parents didn't want to come in, so we'd say, 'If we are going to treat your son or daughter, you have to be there.' That was the only way you could get them to come in." Often it was the son or daughter who would reveal the family dynamics. "In one session a father was playing the role of stern father, admonishing his son, 'You know what'll happen if you don't get in here by midnight,' and the son said 'I know. Nothing. *Nothing.* We're playing a game for the doctor.' That threw the father for a loss, and then the mother said, 'Well, maybe we don't do all of the things we say.' It's a long road. You have to help them to see that unless these things get talked about, you make yourself vulnerable and you're at risk of losing control."

Madden loved working with, and learned a lot from, Ruth Newman, "an excellent and compassionate psychologist and supervisor," who supervised group psychotherapy.

"We had a group for the violent patients in our clinic and Jonas Rappeport had another clinic for the Psychiatry and the Law program. Our patients were ordered into therapy. Jonas worked directly with the court system. He used to have once-a-week groups, and his was a slightly different model. I think in addition to his therapist, he actually had either probation officers or people who worked with the probation officers intimately involved in the therapy." In addition to those programs, in 1972 Russ Monroe initiated research on impulsive behavior for repeat offenders, as part of his work on episodic behavioral disorders.

After the Maryland Plan was launched (see page 273), Madden and Brian Hepburn got a grant from the state to train personnel in the state hospitals on how to deal with violent psychiatric patients. "Brian and I would talk about the therapy part of the program—the interview, diagnosing, and treatment—and we had two nurses, a man and a woman, who taught how to physically restrain patients. That gave the staff more confidence, and as a result both they and the patients were less likely to get hurt."

"Being at Maryland was one of the most positive experiences of my life—an outstanding time. There was a great atmosphere, a spirit of collegiality. You were teaching, working with patients, and doing research; it was the perfect combination. I liked them all, but especially the teaching and the therapy, working with the patients. I loved it there. A lot of what I learned—about loving people, being patient, and not taking myself or things too seriously—came out of our fraternity at the Psychiatric Institute. Leading psychiatrists were there and we laughed and enjoyed each other."

In 1988, on the suggestion of Father Ted Hesburgh, past president of Notre Dame University, Madden left for a "brief" sabbatical at Tantur, an institute for ecumenical studies in Jerusalem where clergy and laymen go on sabbatical to take refresher courses in theology or work on a scholarly project. "It was also a place where people could come together for dialogue, especially about peace in the Middle East. However, I soon noticed that it was the same folks coming for the dialogue, and not much seemed to be changing on the ground," says Madden. He and some friends decided to found the Accord Foundation, a humanitarian organization that got Palestinians and Israelis to work together on things they could all agree were important, such as the welfare of children, health, education—the idea being that in working together they would come to know each other and demonstrate that indeed they might not be that far apart.

"We took what I thought was a novel approach. We had Israeli doctors coming down to the Gaza and Palestinian doctors doing training at Hadassah. We had Jewish librarians from Jerusalem going down to Gaza to help set up a library for the sixty or seventy thousand people living in the Jabalya refugee camp." Madden stayed in the Middle East for nine years, serving as director of the Pontifical Mission for Palestine in Jerusalem, and then moved to New York as associate secretary general of the Catholic Near East Welfare Association.

In 2005 Madden was the first American bishop appointed by Pope Benedict XVI, as auxiliary bishop for the Catholic Church's Baltimore archdiocese. As vicar for the Neumann vicariates, he oversees ninety-five churches and about sixty-five schools, covering all of Baltimore city and Baltimore and Harford counties. He is still a licensed clinical psychologist in the State of Maryland and the District of Columbia. He has participated in the marriages of, and performed memorial services for, several of his classmates.

Madden and his fellow interns when he came to Maryland—Henri Montandon and Carol Weyland—were supervised by James S.B. MacKie (pronounced Mahk-EYE), head of the psychology division. "Jim MacKie was a bright man, deeply involved in mysticism and eastern religions, and one of the most skilled therapists I've ever seen," says Madden. "He was also one of the holiest and most generous persons I've ever met. He would go up on the wards and talk

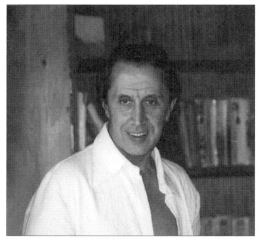

James MacKie, head of the psychology division, supervised Denis Madden, Henri Montandon, and Carol Weyland as interns. Deeply involved in mysticism and eastern religions, MacKie and Weyland both went West and became leaders in Sufism Reoriented.

with patients who were somewhat combative or belligerent, and he had this great gift of calming them down."

"Jim MacKie was a brilliant psychologist," says Henry Harbin. "He knew the literature—everything. You could throw out a topic and get an hour's lecture." At one point MacKie began coming to grand rounds dressed all in white, including white ballet slippers. "We thought he was just a flaky mental health person," says Harbin, "but he was becoming a full-time Sufi." He moved to California and became involved with Sufism Reoriented, an American version of Sufism, serving from 1981 until 2001 as its *murshid* (guide or spiritual teacher). On his death, Carol Weyland Conner became murshida for Sufism Reoriented. It was clearly an ecumenical department.

Sufism is an ancient mystical tradition that emerged from Muslim beliefs. Sufism Reoriented describes itself as "a universal spiritual school that recognizes a central core of divine love at the heart of all spiritual systems." See www.belovedarchives.org/glow _international/art008_01.html.

An explosion of therapies

There was an explosion of therapies from the sixties through the eighties: family therapy, group therapies, biofeedback, hypnosis, Rolfing, medications (reluctantly, at first, because of the department's psychoanalytically oriented tradition)—even "being" together. Carl R. Rogers, the author of *Encounter Groups* (1970), argued that by valuing certain (*main text continues on page 227*)

Russell R. Monroe, MD

Officially Russ Monroe chaired the department from 1976 to 1985, but starting in 1975 and for several earlier years, he functioned as acting director during Gene Brody's frequent sojourns abroad.

The achievement Monroe prized most was getting the Maryland legislature (in 1977) to shift control of the Maryland Psychiatric Research Center (MPRC) from the state's Mental Hygiene Administration to the department of psychiatry, and then recruiting Will Carpenter to develop and run a totally transformed MPRC. Monroe had participated in LSD experiments at Spring Grove, but when that path of research became problematic, he took the lead in getting Will Carpenter to set up a research center with a totally different focus. He fully supported the MPRC's shift in emphasis to the study of schizophrenia and other psychotic disorders and fought to get the funding that made possible its many important contributions.

As part of the same state–university negotiations, Monroe signed a contract with MHA establishing a unique collaborative state–university arrangement (the multi-award-winning Maryland Plan), under which the department would provide residency training in three state mental hospitals (Spring Grove, Springfield, and Crownsville) and would provide residency training in, and psychiatric services for, the Walter P. Carter Center, a community mental health center downtown.

After growing up in Des Moines, Monroe graduated from Yale (1941), got his medical degree there (1944), interned

Russ Monroe, who studied temporal seizures and episodic dyscontrol phenomena that led to episodic psychosis, helped sign the deal that launched the Maryland Plan and brought Will Carpenter and a strong scientific and clinical research program to the MPRC.

at Yale–New Haven Medical Center, had psychiatric and psychoanalytic training at Columbia University, served two years (1945–47) as a captain in the U.S. Army Medical Corps, and finished a psychiatric residency at Rockland State Hospital in New York. As an associate professor of psychiatry at Tulane University (1950–60), he helped establish a branch of the American Psychiatric Association.

Monroe had come to Maryland as a full professor and training director in charge of the psychiatric residency program. "He was a real gentleman," says

Gary Nyman, "an intellectual, caring, compassionate researcher–clinician. As a supervisor, he encouraged me with certain patients to try not to say anything for the first twenty minutes of a session and just see what happened. He was an intellectual who was interested in trying to help people. He didn't ask for anything for himself." As chair, he gave free rein to his own strong leaders in training: Walter Weintraub for residency training, George Balis for medical school training in psychiatry, and both of them for CAPP.

At Tulane, he had been part of a research team that implanted semi-permanent electrodes deep in the brains of volunteers, to explore whether electrical storms in the primitive part of the brain might lead to impulsive, aggressive, or violent behavior in some. The probes detected those storms and researchers could link them to impulsive behavior. "Such impulsive behavior is usually driven by primitive feelings," Monroe later told a science reporter. "The primitive emotions are fear or rage. Often those people are aggressive and homicidal, but many times they are suicidal. I'd say most often they are, in fact."[*]

Such impulsive violence could result from storm activity in the brain or from a lifestyle in which people never learned to think of consequences. Monroe's research tried to distinguish between the two. In the brain storm group, he said, "the capacity for planning is impaired. One factor is probably confusion, or a lower level of awareness during the impulsive behavior." Throughout his career, Monroe remained interested in brain chemistry, electronics, and functioning—particularly in temporal seizures and other episodic dyscontrol phenomena that led to episodic psychosis. He did EEG studies of patients with violent histories, administering alpha chloralose to a level that almost triggered seizure-like activity, to see if there was a relationship between their brain activity and some of their aberrant behavior. He wrote many papers on violence, epilepsy-like phenomena, and treatment for mental disease, as well as on medical hypnosis and family therapy. His published books were *Episodic Behavioral Disorders: A Psychodynamic and Neurophysiologic Analysis*; *Brain Dysfunction in Aggressive Criminals*; and *Creative Brainstorms: The Relationship Between Madness and Genius* (in which he examined the episodic madness of such artists and writers as Vincent Van Gogh, Emily Dickinson, and Virginia Woolf).[*]

He also did some hypnotherapy. "We had a patient, a teenager who was very, very badly burned," says Jonathan Tuerk, "and we couldn't give her enough

---

[*] Jon Franklin, "Electric Storms Deep in Brain Studied by Researcher," *Baltimore Sun*, 1972. "The storms are too deep in the brain to show up on the electroencephalogram, which records electrical activity in the outer cortex," wrote Franklin.

[*] At grand rounds he made the case that Van Gogh's psychosis might have been a form of episodic dyscontrol. He theorized that Van Gogh's seizures may have resulted from the substance thujone, in the liqueur absinthe, which was favored by artists and intellectuals.

pain medicine to help her. We asked him to come in and help us with her, and although he didn't put her entirely into a trance, he did teach her techniques so that she could relax and decrease the amount of pain that she was experiencing, which was extremely helpful for that patient."

He was an inspirational leader with a different style—a twitch in his eyebrow adding to a mild air of quirkiness. At his home, he hosted discussions on arts and psychiatry for medical students. "To be invited to a faculty member's home for pizza and art discussions just fueled the psychiatric heat," says James C. Bozzuto. The department under Russ was an eclectic group, with interesting people focused on teaching. "Teaching was Russ's big thing—that and research," says Dennis Kutzer. "Russ really wanted people to learn."

Monroe and Brody were good friends who shared a love of sailing, but Monroe was a quieter, more private and reticent man. A biological psychiatrist, Monroe was smart and studious—and, like Brody, saw the Institute as a miniversity. He had as little interest as Brody in administration, and he hated politics and interpersonal crises, of which there were a fair number.* When he became chair,

he hired business manager Steve Valerio to help run the department.*

Monroe, a kind, well-liked gentleman, hated confrontation; in 1984–85, major changes taking place on campus were unfavorable to the department. University Hospital became a private not-for-profit hospital complex, the budget for psychiatry shrank, and a new shock–trauma group, clearly, was going to take over the space where the Psychiatric Institute had kept its independence. Outraged that the university wasn't going to replace the old building, Monroe resigned.

John Talbott, who was recruited as the new chair and spent his first weeks living in Monroe's home, remembers Monroe saying, "I think I've left things in pretty good shape. I'm going to get out of your way and work in my lab. I won't bother you. I'll never give you advice and I'll never ask you a question. I'll stay completely away." (And he absolutely did, says Talbott.) "There are just three people who are problems. I should have fired them but I couldn't do it." Talbott gave the three a year to get funding, and they left the department.

After stepping down as chairman, Monroe, who was married, with three children, stayed in Maryland a few years, seeing private patients, until his wife died. Then he moved to San Francisco, where his son, Russell R. Monroe Jr., also a psychiatrist, lives. He died there on April 4, 2003, of complications from pneumonia, at eighty-two.

---

* "But he stood by me in a very difficult confrontation with Stan Friedman, who was a lightning rod as head of child psychiatry," says Stuart Tiegel. Tiegel had gotten a state grant to do child and family therapy training, and there were some issues with the funding. "Friedman essentially wanted to get rid of me and Russ wouldn't let him do it," says Tiegel. "He was very supportive through it all, saying, 'You're not going to be on the street.'"

---

* Valerio later left to work for Nobel laureate David Baltimore at Harvard and in New York and had a successful career himself.

Photo from 1972–73 department of psychiatry *Bulletin*.

(*continued from page 223*)
core conditions—especially genuineness (congruence), acceptance, and empathy—group members could humanisti-
cally open up and authentically encounter each other and
themselves. "They could begin to trust in their feelings and
accept themselves for what they are."[12]

"It was not just the medical students and residents
learning about new models," says Stan Weinstein. "It was
students in social work, psychology, and nursing. There
was this excitement. Grand rounds was always packed, often with outside speakers coming in to talk about the new
therapies, new approaches—and sociologists talking about
cultural influences."

Theorists and practitioners of family therapy began shifting the focus of therapy from the solo patient to the patient in social context, especially the family. The newly renamed Institute for Psychiatry and Human Behavior (IPHB) hosted many training workshops for residents and faculty members, featuring such pioneers and master trainers in family therapy as Jay Haley and Cloé Madanes (who started the Family Therapy Institute in Chevy Chase, Maryland, in 1974), Salvador Minuchin, and Virginia Satir.

Virginia Satir, one of the best known family therapists, came for a weekend training workshop. A tall, imposing woman with a dynamic personal style, a gift for role-playing exercises, and a good sense of humor, she had such powerful interactions with faculty members that many who hadn't believed in family therapy began to change their minds. "She led seminars with faculty, social workers, psychologists, everybody—and she held everyone spellbound," says sociologist Bob Derbyshire. "Some of the residents decided they wanted to do some family therapy, and some of the social workers, who were already trained as family therapists, became much more prominent in the process. Up till then, in Freudian and some other forms of psychiatry, your psychiatry patient was *your* patient, and you could not be concerned about anyone else, which of course is kind of crazy. If a psychiatrist got a call from the patient's mother or wife, he would say, 'I can't talk to you, but here's a social worker who can.' The social worker would talk with family members, but the family never met the psychiatrist—and of course some families felt that with a social worker they were getting second-rate treatment, but that's the way it was done." As systems theory, family therapy, group therapy, and other new approaches took hold, that old model of the psychiatrist as kingpin at the top of a psychoanalytically oriented hierarchy began to loosen. At Maryland, treatment approaches were starting to become more integrated by the early 1970s.

Master teacher Jay Haley, author of *Uncommon Therapy* (1973), believed in brief therapies to solve immediate, concrete problems rather than in probing the past for root causes. He felt it was the therapist's job "to change the patient, not to help him understand himself." He broke therapy down to a

Master trainer Virginia Satir, leading exercises in role playing, held seminar participants spellbound. Social workers were already being trained as family therapists; now psychiatric residents became interested in the field.

practice of simple ideas, skills, and techniques, which was "quite different from the nondirective ideology the field had when I first got into it."

Those who trained with Jay Haley and his then wife Cloé Madanes were observed through a one-way mirror, which the patients knew was happening. "While you were in the therapy room with the patient, Jay or Cloé would phone in with a directive, such as, 'He's talked about that three times, move off that, or try this,' whatever it was," says Denis Madden. "Sometimes I'd use the same process when I was working with students. One time I was observing a senior medical student who was a little stuck, and I didn't phone in right away because I thought he could work his way out of it. The medical student kept looking down at the phone and finally the patient said, 'I don't think he's gonna call.'" Madden called then and said he was doing fine. "This calling-in business was their novel approach to family therapy. It made you self-conscious at first, but then you got used to it, because you wanted to learn."

"Haley did all kinds of things that were counterintuitive," says Madden. If someone had a problem setting fires, for example, he might set a trash can on fire—"somehow he knew how to do it at the right time. He got you thinking about ways to help this person most—he gave you freedom to step outside the traditional mold." Haley himself, for example, had no degree in psychology. He had a bachelor's degree in theater arts from UCLA, a bachelor's degree in library science from UC Berkeley, and a master's degree in communications from Stanford University.

"Jay taught us about how the family system supports itself—how, for example, a 'sick member' may enable the family to stay together," says Madden. "You could actually see that and graph it: When an adolescent got sick (was down) and had to be hospitalized, the family was very stable. As he got strong, independent, and didn't need that family, the family would fall apart, become disruptive, or whatever that family did (bringing it down), so essentially he'd almost be forced to play that sick role again. You would try to break that cycle so the son or daughter could be healthy and the family could be healthy—it didn't always have to be one up and one down. Jay didn't believe in going on forever with these things. You would go along and get those moments when things shook loose and a moment of insight would happen. Then you might say, We're not going to do that again for a while."

Disillusioned with long-term approaches focused on retracing memories of the past to gain insight into unconscious drives and emotions, Aaron Beck, a psychiatrist at the University of Pennsylvania, developed an approach that focused on cognitions (current thoughts or feelings), to define underlying *schema*—assumptions and ways of processing information—that guide our behavior. Cognitive therapy addressed negative schema and cognitive biases and was first developed for use with depression, but was also useful with phobias, eating disorders, obsessive–compulsive disorder, and personality disorders. Behavioral modification and cognitive therapy techniques were eventually combined in cognitive behavioral therapy, which would become an important tool in working with patients with severe and persistent mental illness.

"Jay taught us about how the family system supports itself—how, for example, a 'sick member' may enable the family to stay together."

Thurman Mott used hypnosis in some of the short-term therapy he did with the professional students who came to Student Health. He'd become interested in hypnosis in the late sixties. He knew it could be useful in psychiatry and to some extent in family practice medicine and anesthesiology, but not many people in the department were using it—Russ Monroe being one of the few (and he was apparently good at it). Few psychiatry departments offered formal courses in its uses in psychiatry. After taking some courses on the subject, Mott began giving a course—first as an elective, then as a regular course for second year residents of twelve to fifteen two-hour sessions, with an elective advanced seminar for those interested in knowing more—for psychiatric residents, including Elliot Cohen, who took the advanced course in hypnosis on Friday afternoons, when students were tired and particularly susceptible.

Mott lectured on hypnosis to second year students in medicine and dentistry and taught psychiatric residents the basics of hypnotic induction and the uses of hypnosis in psychiatry. Hypnosis could facilitate psychotherapy, especially for retrieving memories and for treating phobias—including a severe phobia of dentistry. "People can actually have major surgery done with hypnosis as the only anesthetic, but that requires someone who is quite hypnotizable, and not everybody is," says Mott. Hypnosis was particularly useful for helping people stop smoking. (It was less helpful fighting obesity; it's a lot easier to stop smoking than to stop eating.)

Russell Monroe, with his interest in temporal lobe epilepsy, injected a strong theme of neurology into the residency. Barbara Hulfish, who joined the department in 1958 and served on the faculty for more than two decades, held joint appointments in neurology and psychiatry. She taught many residents how to do cognitive testing as part of routine psychiatric evaluations, so they could pick up even the most subtle brain dysfunction, says Andrew Rudo (resident 1976–79). She was doing interview research on how many of the medical school faculty had ADHD, which at that time was called minimal brain dysfunction. Her theory was that most doctors have it: that's why they're so obsessive.

Laurette Bender, the child psychologist known for developing the Bender Gestalt Visual Motor Test in 1923, had retired to Saverna Park to live near her son. She came to the department once a month or so to talk about her test, which was widely used, says Stan Friedman.

Behavioral modification and cognitive therapy techniques were eventually combined in cognitive behavioral therapy, which would become an important tool in working with patients with severe and persistent mental illness.

To test for dyspraxia and apraxia (the partial or complete loss of ability to perform certain purposeful movements and gestures) she would take a stapler apart (the kind with the staple remover snapped on) and ask the patient to put it back together. Observing the patients with her stapler kit, she could pick up certain cues. "She taught a lot of soft signs that they're just now figuring out how to measure," says Henry Harbin. "She was ahead of her time. Back then we didn't have imaging. What is now standard for neuropsychological testing, she taught us to do as residents."

"I still carry around the tools she taught us to use to conduct this testing for subtle cognitive dysfunction," says Andy Rudo. "I remember how sensitized we were to this borderline area between psychiatry and neurology, so much so that when we were on call to the ER, it was not uncommon to evaluate a 'psychiatric' patient and suspect strongly neurological problem, only to summon the on-call neurology resident, who after a cursory exam would declare, 'no neurological disease.' We often then would need them to admit to our service just to treat the probable neurological problem, such as temporal lobe seizures."

Many departments of psychiatry are highly competitive, says Madden. Maryland felt very human. "The other thing I felt, which I don't notice so much in other programs, especially today, was a great bonding between the residents in psychiatry and psychology. We were all very close. That gave you a great sense of security in the hospital and trust in the people you worked with."

Social psychiatry, fostered initially by the community mental health movement, led to a re-engagement with state hospitals and a sea change in the integration of state hospital and community psychiatry. After the state brought in Gail Fidler, a psychiatric occupational therapist, to redesign rehabilitation services at Springfield State Hospital, hospital services were then paired with some of the new psychosocial rehab programs developing in the communities.

"It was a wonderful time to be teaching psychiatry or to be a psychiatrist in training," says Jon Book, one of the pioneers in the Maryland Plan (see chapter 6). "At University Hospital and elsewhere, the patients were already cycling through too fast, so residents didn't have a chance to get to know them." Doing a six-month rotation in a state hospital was an advantage for residents training in the late 1970s and later, said Walt Weintraub, because they could take the time to talk to the patients, understand them, and see if talking might help guide their treatment. Says Book, "It wasn't that Walt was against medication, but you didn't have to medicate patients immediately and then ask questions later."

"It was a time of so many transitions that in training you might get very different advice, depending on your supervisor. If your supervisor was an analyst, when you talked about evaluating a new outpatient, you might be advised, 'Don't medicate the person too fast; their anxiety is what got

"We'd been using meds at that point for thirty years, but now we weren't apologizing for it anymore," says Frank Calia, vice dean of clinical affairs and former chair of the department of medicine. DSM-III put psychiatry back squarely in the culture of medical school.

them to come to you. If you medicate them too quickly, their symptoms may improve, you will relieve the suffering but only superficially, and they won't come back for treatment. You won't help with the fundamental underlying problems so the problems will persist, and the patient will be admitted again later.' A more psychopharmacologically oriented supervisor would say, 'This patient has this problem, this medication will work, let's start them on it and help them. What are you waiting for?' A supervisor geared to family therapy might say, 'Something is going on in the patient's family system. We'll be missing the problem if we don't treat them more broadly.'

"For a while, in the 1980s, we went through an awkward stage of having bailiwicks," says Book. "If you had a right-toe problem you had to go to a right-toe doctor; you couldn't take your problem to a left-toe doctor. In the eighties, analysts did analysis and psychopharmacologists did psychopharmacology. Analysts didn't medicate and often felt they shouldn't medicate. If the patient needed medication somebody else should give it to them. And the psychiatrist comfortable with psychopharmacology didn't necessarily want to spend time talking with patients. We've largely come out of that period of bailiwicks, but not quite. We still suffer from the psychopharmacologists who do the fifteen-minute med checks. Managed care may have facilitated that, but it was happening anyway."

Some things were lost, but there were also big gains. There were exciting new tools for evaluation and diagnosis, for example. In 1980, the American Psychiatric Association published the third, totally new *Diagnostic and Statistical Manual of Mental Disorders*. DSM-III, as it is known, provided a new, more descriptive diagnostic nomenclature that would be helpful for training, research, and treatment. "DSM-III was the endpoint of a process that started in the late sixties to reclaim psychiatry as a purely medical specialty," says David Mallott. "Clearly there'd been people all along the way who had chafed under the purely psychologic, psychoanalytic view of psychiatry—after all, Thorazine was introduced in 1954 and the antidepressants a few years later—but the pressure for change built up through the 1970s. The APA's publication of DSM-III made a statement: we're a medical specialty, we have identified specific diagnostic categories of mental disease, our diagnostic system describes illness in terms of symptoms, relief of which is the aim of treatment. And reducing symptoms is an acceptable measure of success. Mental illness was the result of organic problems in the brain or chemical imbalance, not psychosocial experiences. We're not a psychologically based organization anymore."

After considerable argument about whether to eliminate the word *neurosis* (as vague and unscientific), the DSM compilers arrived at a compromise, inserting the word parenthetically after disorder in some cases

"There's been some criticism about its usefulness for research," says Jon Book, "but for someone who is primarily a clinician or administrator, DSM-III worked out well. You could look and find a treatment in the research—say, for hallucinations in schizophrenia—that matched what you needed to treat."

"We'd been using meds at that point for thirty years, but now we weren't apologizing for it anymore," says Frank Calia, vice dean of clinical affairs and former chair of the department of medicine. "DSM-III put psychiatry back squarely in the culture of medical school and the academic medical community. But as a result, a lot of interesting, smart, fascinating folks began leaving, retiring, not to be replaced. By the time 1990 rolled around, the idea that psychiatry departments were full of psychologists, sociologists, anthropologists, and philosophers was gone, for good and for bad—the bad part being that we lost a wonderful group of teachers."

Meanwhile, the variety of effective medications had expanded to include psychotropic medications, antidepressants, and anticonvulsant medications (helpful as mood stabilizers). In 1982, Dr. Rafael Osheroff filed suit against Chestnut Lodge, where he had admitted himself as a patient in 1979, because the physicians had not given him antide-pressants at the facility when he was suffering from severe depression. Osheroff claimed negligence on the Lodge's part, for treating him with psychotherapy alone. Pharmacologist Gerald Klerman testified, arguing "that there was no scien-tific evidence for the value of psychodynamically oriented intensive individual psychotherapy in a severely depressed person." [13] After the Osheroff case, empirical studies became important for all psychiatric therapies.

In this period, the first of a series of powerful new im-aging technologies was becoming available. During his early days at Springfield Hospital, for example, Jon Book's office was at the end of a long hall, and a patient new to the unit walked down that hall with what nurses described later as an ataxic gait. "He walked into my office and around my desk and peed in my trash can, which was a little weird," says Book. "He seemed somewhat demented, was indeed ataxic, and was incontinent but not in the classic way: He peed in inappropriate places. At the time, nobody at Springfield was getting CT scans—not just because Springfield had no scan-ner but because it wasn't part of the practice. But we had just come from a training program where there was a CT scan-ner, and this patient was one of the first we sent to the uni-versity for a scan. The images of his brain made it clear that he had normal-pressure hydrocephalus, for which there is a cure. He went into neurosurgery and got a shunt to drain the extra fluid from the brain. You had to have a high suspi-cion of why he might be demented, but it was easy enough to get a CT scan, a neurological workup, and a diagnosis. Imaging made it possible to detect structural and anatomic neurological problems few would have picked up before.

"It was an exciting time because there was no single way to see things and put them together. The state hospital was seen as a setting where you could integrate all these new approaches—where, if the patient had a family, you might do family therapy, and if the patient was willing to talk you could do, maybe not analysis but more exploratory psycho-dynamically oriented psychotherapy. You could decide what medications were appropriate and take some time to watch them work—as many medications take more than a few days or a few weeks to work optimally. You could see if group therapy or psychiatric rehabilitation engaged a patient and who they might be useful for." Adding to the excitement later would be the blossoming of genetics, which would inform everyone's understanding of illness, of possible treatments, and of reactions to treatments.

"Struck by the widespread apparent efficacy of what were claimed to be disparate methods, thinkers such as Strupp, Frank, and Garfield in the late 1970s and early 1980s focused on the question of whether the various therapies were as different as they were claimed to be, or whether instead their power rested in elements common to all . . . a healer–patient relationship, acceptance and support, the opportunity to express emotions, rituals of treatment to be observed, and a system of explanation."[14]

Human dimensions in medical education

In response to student demands in the 1960s, in the 1970s there was much inter-school coursework. In January and June, students could participate in "minimesters," short courses that brought together students from the five professional schools. "The sexuality course was part of a wave that was sweeping the country," says Michael Plaut, who in 1978 became assistant dean for student affairs. "We had one required course for medical students and an elective course for all students on campus. People realized that sexuality is such a difficult, sensitive topic that you can't just teach it didactically; students need a chance to explore their feelings and attitudes in a protected environment. We had lectures and presentations and guests such as gay physicians or health professionals who worked with handicapped people around sexual issues. We showed audiovisual materials—many of them sexually explicit—so students could discuss the impact those had on them."

Similarly, the psychiatry department became active in the Human Dimensions in Medical Education retreats for new medical students, which needed leaders for the small-group discussions commonly used by them. The HDME retreats, conceived in 1976, were run out of the dean's office for twenty-five years. Murray Kappelman ran the program for a few years, and then

The Intimate Human Behavior course was part of an interprofessional elective system, "which lasted until the deans retreated into their previously isolated states," says Plaut, who later served on the licensing board for psychology in Maryland. "I was shocked by the number of sex-related cases we saw on the board. Nobody talked about the whole idea of therapists becoming sexually involved with clients and patients, and I realized not only that so much of that was going on but that we weren't doing anything to prepare our students for the risks that lead people into those situations. So we introduced that topic into the sexuality course." Plaut returned to Cornell on a fellowship (1987–88) to develop his clinical skills, became a sex therapist, was editor of a sexuality journal, and president of a sexuality society. He later began consulting, teaching, and doing rehabilitation work, for all the licensing boards in Maryland, with professionals found in violation of sexual boundaries.

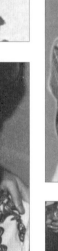

Clockwise, from top left, at retreats in the mid-1970s: Mort Rapoport; Barbara White and Jon Book, medical students; Rosalie Rapoport; Mary Jo Albright; Mike Plaut and Fran Fitch.

Left to right, Marianne Felice, [?], Jay Nolan (anthropologist, department of psychiatry), Tom Hobbins (department of medicine)

Michael Plaut took over. After a series of planning retreats (at Belmont and Donaldson Brown), the retreats opened to students in 1977. After that, every August a three- or four-day retreat was held at a resort at Wisp or Deep Creek Lake in western Maryland. These were attended by faculty, incoming medical students, some upper-class medical students, and often partners of both the faculty and students.

The HDME concept was originally developed at the Carl Rogers Center for the Study of the Person in La Jolla, California, says Jerry Hunt. A secretary in Rogers' office was married to an alcoholic physician who committed suicide. She attributed his suicide to his detachment from his own and his patients' humanity, and she felt that more attention early on to issues such as substance abuse and the professional violation of sexual boundaries would help prevent greater problems later.

Rogers and his colleagues tried humanizing medicine in some of California's medical schools, using small-group techniques, says Hunt, who went out to California, got training, and, with his wife, Lorraine, became actively involved in the HDME program. NIMH training funds were beginning to dry up but, after a little lobbying, the National Institute of

Child Health and Human Development (NICHD) provided start-up grants for teaching behavioral science and for the first year or two of HDME programs. John Dennis, dean of the medical school (and a radiologist), was willing to help fund a program of retreats for people in medical education. The office of medical education drew most of its group leaders from the ranks of psychiatry, pediatrics, internal medicine, and family medicine, "the traditional nurturers on the faculty," says Plaut, "but we also had faculty from surgery, pathology, biochemistry, and anatomy."

Consultants were brought in from the Center for the Study of the Person to lead training retreats at Donaldson Brown for major faculty, including some administrative leaders. "We were doing essentially Rogerian encounter groups, asking, 'Okay, you're Dr. So-and-So, you wear a white coat, but who are you, really?'" says Hunt. "When you're with neurosurgeons and that question is on the table, it's an amazing experience. A patient comes to a neurosurgeon wanting someone with skilled hands, who knows chapter and verse about neuroanatomy, neurochemistry, and neurophysiology, but when the surgeon comes back into your room after the surgery is over, that's the point at which you want a human being."

Later, when the retreats were opened to medical students, Hunt interviewed senior staff. For example, he asked Carl Soderstrom, from shock–trauma, "How do you tell someone that their loved one is dead? What issues do you face when you do it, what issues does the family face, what does shock–trauma provide?" He asked an internist, "You have a patient who smokes, drinks, and has diabetes. How do you address those issues?" After putting questions about the human aspects of medicine on the table, facilitators would open the discussion to students in small groups.

Students learned about small groups by being in one. Mike Plaut also provided handouts on small-group dynamics and well-organized facilitator training for the small-group leaders. Students unfamiliar with small groups often wanted to know "What are we going to cover?" and were sometimes bothered when told it was their group and the group could go where it wanted to go. Facilitators learned to offer their own experience to model how to share, gently encouraging the one or two who said nothing, supporting those who were reluctant to share or who shared something they regretted because it led to feelings or memories, encouraging those who talked too much to give others a chance, supporting what people said by restating or summarizing it. "It was gratifying to be a part of a group's experience from first introductions to increasing levels of participation and sharing," says Alice Heisler, one of several group facilitators who also participated in a vertical advisory system for the medical students. The HDME retreat gave student advisors an early chance to meet the freshman advisees who, back on campus, would join their group, which also included sophomores, juniors, and seniors. There was also a weekend seminar on human sexuality for the medical students, physical therapists, and their significant others, where people would speak about sexual issues, including homosexuality.

Taking charge of the Carter Center

Few community mental health programs were run by physicians. Psychiatrist Carl Segal, a leader in Maryland psychiatry and community mental health, was almost a lone soldier running Howard County's community mental health program, in Springfield Hospital's catchment area. With Segal supervising, several fourth year residents got a chance to train both at Springfield and in the community. One of those fourth year residents (and a former CAPP student) was Maxie Collier, a charismatic African American clinician and leader who, in a life dedicated to public service, eventually joined the Springfield staff, served for a while as the commissioner of mental health and addictions for Baltimore City, then left to be director of a Baltimore City community mental health clinic called the Liberty Medical Center (now closed). "People loved to work with Maxie," says Jon Book.

Work on the Walter P. Carter Center had begun in 1966 as a collaboration between the psychiatry department and MHA under the Federal Community Mental Health Act. The relationship between the two had faltered and nearly ended when community activism took an anti-psychiatry turn and federal funding was phased out. The community group in charge of the Carter Center—a state hospital in the city—had thrown out the university psychiatrists in the 1960s, but in the mid-1970s the Carter Center became part of negotiations for the Maryland Plan, because the state needed a reliable source of mental health professionals to run the place.

Early on the aim of the Maryland Plan was to train psychiatrists to work both in state hospitals and in community health centers. The problems were different in the community mental health centers (CMHCs), which had been sold to the public as curing many ills under a vague, broad definition of mental illness. By the 1970s, they were increasingly oriented to social and community services and less to caring for patients with severe mental illness. This demedicalization made it difficult to recruit psychiatrists to work in the centers. And without psychiatrists, the centers could not and did not adequately serve the severely and persistently mentally ill, the patients most in need of help.

In 1976, Gary Nyman, who had completed his psychiatric residency and had spent a couple of years directing a small Hopkins-based community mental health program, became director of the state's Mental Hygiene Administration, which had authority over the Carter Center. Nyman decided that the only way to get the Carter Center staffed with psychiatrists was to reestablish the agreement under which the University of Maryland's department of psychiatry would provide both psychiatrists and psychiatric residents. Russ Monroe, the department chair, asked George Gallahorn to work with Nyman on developing a special services contract, one that specified that the university would provide psychiatrists and psychiatric residents for the Carter Center—and the state would hire the nurses, nursing assistants, social workers, and administrative staff.

The community advisory board still objected to having the university providing psychiatric staff, so Gallahorn and Nyman began meeting with the board at least once a month. Without planning to, they developed a bad cop–good cop routine, with Gallahorn (representing the university) playing the good cop. "Gary would be the one having a fit and getting angry, and I'd be trying to calm him down. Eventually we convinced them that the state wasn't able to attract psychiatrists willing to work for the state and, without psychiatrists, families in the neighborhood they represented would not be able to get care close to home and would have to travel to Spring Grove, Springfield, or Crownsville." Reluctantly, the advisory board was persuaded to approve a formal contract. A new contract signed in 1976 rejuvenated the center, and the Maryland Plan provided funding for training and staffing.

In 1976, Gallahorn started functioning as medical director at the Carter Center, later becoming clinical director. The department appointed Jose Arana as director of inpatient services (and of 7C, the center's first inpatient ward) and Bob Cummings as director of emergency services. Fereidoon Taghizadeh was director of the adolescent inpatient unit, which began admitting patients in 1979. For a while Gallahorn was shuttling back and forth between the Open Clinic and the Carter Center, which were only a block and a half apart.

Gallahorn was also doing psychoanalytic training, sometimes in Washington, sometimes in Baltimore. He enjoyed the administrative work at the Carter Center, but it was demanding, and he often had to cancel patients for things like emergency budget meetings in Annapolis. Like many others involved in public psychiatry, he had to decide: Do I want to be an administrator or do I want to do clinical work? Choosing the latter, he resigned from the Carter Center, but "it was not an easy decision."

Meanwhile, Gallahorn was busy running the Open Clinic, the ambulatory clinic in the Psych Institute. "Even when I took over, Open Clinic and Phipps were the only two places in the city where people could walk in and get

Left to right: Russ Monroe, George Gallahorn, and Gene Brody, after medical school graduation in June 1966, at which George Gallahorn was awarded the department's first Jacob Finesinger Award for Excellence in Psychiatry.

a psychiatric evaluation. None of the community mental health centers were up and running at that point, so we had over 2,000 visits in 1972, the first year I was there. Psychiatric residents worked there four days a week; family practice residents learning psychiatry, one day a week, doing evaluations. Medical students also did rotations there.

Gallahorn's staff included three psychiatric nurses, two social workers, and Ann Bailey, the secretary–receptionist (the term used then, although "she kept the place running"). Staff included nurses (Gail Pomerantz, Margie Shultz, Judy Bankhead, and Lorraine Pride) and social workers (Norma Jones, Katie Genut).

"Some patients were psychotic and a few dangerous. Others were patients who in those days were called neurotic"—with depression, for example. But with the state's passage in 1974 of Regulation D, "any patient who was certified, committed to a hospital, had to have an evaluation by a hearing officer. At first the hearing officers would naively release all sorts of patients who supposedly weren't an acute danger to themselves or others, not understanding the subtleties of these patients' illnesses and how they might be considered a danger to themselves or others. So suddenly many people were being released from hospitals who very quickly would go off their medications, become psychotic, and end up being readmitted. They got readmitted through the Open Clinic or Hopkins or eventually some other community mental health centers. But the number of psychotic and out-of-control patients increased markedly, starting in about 1974."

"It was a wild place," says Denis Madden. "People just walked in there, some of them hallucinating. Our offices were on the same floor, and every once in a while there'd be a little bit of a disruption and they'd have to get some security people or therapists down there to calm the thing down."

Herb Gross requested an alarm system, but was given a panic button that set off a tiny ringing noise in the waiting room, where you didn't actually need to be told there was a problem. Eventually they installed a system that communicated with the head office and security.

In those days, three elderly men in uniform provided security, says Gallahorn, who had to beef up safety measures because the neighborhood was changing and more difficult patients were coming in.

With the opening of community mental health centers, the number of people coming to the Open Clinic diminished significantly. With a decline in the patient population, the clinic wasn't paying for itself. "At the time, the charge was forty dollars a visit," says Herb Gross, who was in charge of outpatient services. "The Carter Center had the same kind of setup, also run by our residents, and there was no charge there. So we were running ourselves out of business." Moreover, as an indirect effect of Regulation D, there were proportionately more disturbed patients who needed to be managed in a setting more appropriate than the rather open setting of the Open Clinic—which had no separate quiet room in which someone could be held. The Open Clinic closed on April 1, 1977.

The department had done some research in cross-cultural psychiatry, which showed that the residents working in the Open Clinic tended to diagnose patients from diverse cultures with more severe illnesses than warranted because they didn't understand them or were afraid of them. (They might, for example, diagnose schizophrenia in a person who was simply experiencing hysteria.)[15] After the walk-in clinic services moved to the Carter Center, Gross co-interviewed there with a retired colonel from human resources, an African American whom he knew from the medical school's ambulatory services committee. Much of the staff didn't understand African American men, who were underrepresented in the clinic population and were often very uncommunicative. "To help the residents understand, we would interview people, all of us, in a small room. If the patient was truly psychotic, the colonel didn't understand him as well. If the patient was more neurotic, the colonel understood him better." In the Open Clinic, which had no catchment area and drew residents from around the city, the patients had been about half black and half white. In the Carter Center they were more often black, because they were referred there from clinics and community mental health centers in the Carter Center's catchment area.

Some of the psychiatrists the Carter Center was trying to hire had to be persuaded that community psychiatry was workable. One initially reluctant recruit was Lois Flaherty, who had been a child and adolescent psychiatrist in the outpatient clinic at Sinai Hospital. "The notion of community psychiatry was radical and didn't make any sense at all from what I read about it," she recalls. "In those days, the idea of community psychiatry still seemed nebulous: as if, by intervening in the community you were somehow going to eliminate poverty and all the social ills that went with it." She hated the vague, grandiose ideas, the belief that disorders didn't exist, that mental illness was all social. "In fact, disorders do exist, and they exist more in disadvantaged communities." She couldn't see how community mental health centers could work if they were not going to actually treat patients for psychiatric disorders.

Taghi Modarressi persuaded Flaherty to take a job at the Carter Center. "At that time the Carter Center was in the process of being resurrected from its ashes, after having gone through a very difficult time." She was skeptical, but Gallahorn, a Yale graduate trained in psychoanalysis, was different from any community psychiatrist she had met. "Our mission is to remedicalize the Carter Center and community mental health," he told her. "We're going to really need people who want to do more traditional psychiatry."

She joined the child and adolescent psychiatry division as part-time faculty in 1978, based in the Carter Center. "It was a wonderful job," says Flaherty. "I loved it, and what they were doing—working with individual patients and families, but in a community context—made sense."

Under community control, social workers provided much of the therapy for their "clients." With the department of psychiatry in charge, they were again called "patients," says Herb Gross.

Part of Flaherty's job, as director of children's services at the center, was to help bring back psychiatric leadership. She helped open an adolescent inpatient unit and expand services to children and to schools. She promoted training and the connection with the department's child psychiatry division, becoming its training director in 1981, while still working at the Carter Center. "In a sense it was kind of a parallel universe to the department in that it had its own inpatient unit, outpatient services, a day treatment program, and an emergency room, which had a whole continuum of services," says Flaherty. "It had its own staff and faculty (all University of Maryland department of psychiatry faculty). To begin with, the Carter Center and the department were more separate; they had a sort of tiered system, but the Carter Center gradually became more involved in the academic mission of the department. There had always been residency training there, but then there was research as well, and I think over time things got more closely integrated. When I was both training director and head of children's services, I think I was the first person who had feet in both aspects of it, and I tried to integrate them, but I think later they became much more integrated."

In 1980, when Gallahorn left the Carter Center, Jose Arana became clinical director, serving until his death in 1991. Among others, Arana hired Jay Phillips, who had been working in Student Mental Health. "Our population was an inner-city general psychiatric population," says Phillips. "There is no typical patient at the Carter Center, but many of them were chronically severely mentally ill; many had acute psychiatric disorders of less severity. Generally their disorders were compounded by poverty, social disorganization, lack of educational opportunity, and the usual woes of the bottom fifth of American society. I think we did a lot of good. The Carter Center survives because it continues to do good. It certainly serves a need that's not going to be wished away."

Jay Phillips was director of outpatient services at the Carter Center from 1980 to 1985, before moving to private practice full time. He returned to work at the Carter Center as a part-time clinician from 1994 to 2001, when Eileen Hastings was clinical director. "I had nothing but the highest regard for the services provided at the Carter Center. The pressure to provide services to the most severely ill had increased under financial constraints, which were even more apparent when I returned and got worse right up to the time I left. The state demanded more paperwork, to demonstrate the efficacy of the staff's work, which only added to the pressure on staff. Doing public sector mental health work got to be very hard, and the people who do it deserve all the respect and support that can be thrown their way."

Researching the effects of touch

Psychologist James Lynch became well known nationally for his research on the implications of human loneliness and social isolation, writing books that rose to a level of popularity few academics' books achieve. Lynch joined the faculty in 1969 as director of the department's behavioral laboratories. As a postdoc student at Johns Hopkins medical school, he had worked with W. Horsley Gantt, Ivan Pavlov's last American student, trying to create hypertension in animals, with an eye to developing drugs to control human blood pressure. He'd observed that petting a dog lowered the dog's blood pressure significantly and that the heart rate also dropped.

W. Horsley Gantt

(*main text continues on page 250*)

Jose Arana

Jose Domingo Arana was born in Lima, Peru, in 1939, the younger of two children. Trained in Peru and Berlin, he completed a psychiatric residency at Maryland in 1972, coming to the Institute for Psychiatry and Human Behavior, as it was then known, because Gene Brody had written about immigration. After serving as ward administrator in the IPHB, he went to the Carter Center as director of inpatient services, became clinical director in 1980, and served there until 1991.

"On my first day as an intern, at our first meeting," says Samuel Goldberg (class of 1978), "Arana said, 'We have three basic principles here, in decreasing order: patient care, teaching, and research.'" Goldberg finished his residency in 1982, interned at the Carter Center, then worked at the Cherry Hill outpatient clinic until the early 1990s. Jose Arana "was the best psychiatrist I ever met, my ego ideal of a psychiatrist, an extremely warm, wise, and supportive person who knew about psychodynamics, pharmacotherapy, and diagnosis. He knew how to make judgments and decisions and take actions for the organization as a whole that always seemed to be the right ones. Many of the patients were psychotic—extremely disturbed, needing hospitalization—but he encouraged us to talk to the patients, to listen to their stories, to do psychotherapy with all of the inpatients. (Nowadays that's not possible.) He had never had psychoanalytic training but saw the psychoanalytic perspective as the most humane, thorough, and appreciative of patients' human story and experience—even poor, drug-addicted, psychotic, homeless people. He was able to empathize with them as human beings."

Arana was pragmatic about broad things like poverty and how the system worked, but above all he was humane. "We had truly destitute, homeless patients here, living in the worst kind of poverty and on top of that afflicted with mental illness," says Goldberg. "Sometimes they were obnoxious—spitting, cursing, threatening, smelly, alcoholic. He was always able to keep a clear, physician-like caring perspective on them, where they came from, their needs and their suffering. Patients benefit when the clinical staff has that model of a caring, compassionate clinical concern."

"Jose was well informed about the biological dimensions of psychiatry, which were of secondary status in the early seventies but rising. Psychoanalytic thinking was falling in status," says Jay Phillips, who was a CAPP student when Arana was a resident, and became a resident when Arana was ward administrator. "Jose was good at both, which made training that much richer an experience." Arana was a warm, thoughtful, intelligent man, completely devoted to the welfare of severely ill, impoverished people. "He cared about them deeply and wanted to provide the highest quality clinical care to that population but also to study how to improve that care," says Phillips. "He was always thinking carefully and deeply but not ponderously about any situation. He was creative and delightful."

He hired Phillips because of his clinical strengths, making it clear that, while he had an agenda of research and improving services through new knowledge, his primary value was clinical excellence. "I could never meet with him enough," says Phillips, "because he was busy doing so many different things, but meeting with him was the highlight of my week. He knew the psychiatric literature in three languages and he was astute about organizational problems and how they related to the actual care of actual patients."

A good-looking man with a sense of humor, Arana was able to listen to problems, understand, and come up with creative solutions. He was kind, humble, and humane, yet a good leader, say his colleagues—a great teacher, a prolific writer, a popular lecturer and consultant, a fabulous clinician, a superb administrator, "the most wonderful boss I ever had."[*] He collaborated with other faculty in establishing at the Carter Center a continuous care program that would provide intensive mobile services to homeless Baltimore people with serious mental illness, a program to treat patients with the dual diagnosis of mental illness and substance abuse, and a formal research program focused on some of the most pressing problems he saw among the patients at the time.[†] He was president of the Maryland Psychiatric Society (1985–86), president-elect of the American Society of Hispanic Psychiatrists, and (at the time of his death) a consultant in mental health services to the Pan American Health Organization.

Arana had had surgery for a pituitary tumor. On a visit home to Peru, he died quietly in his sleep, February 3, 1991. His unexpected death in his forties was a devastating loss to the staff of the Carter Center.

---

[*] Arana wrote several chapters in *Psychiatric Foundations of Medicine* (1978), edited *Health and Behavior: Research Agenda for Hispanics* (1987, with M. Gavirta), and contributed to several psychiatric journals. Others who worked at the Carter Center when Arana was there, said Lois Flaherty at his memorial service, included Wardell Barksdale, Rolfe Finn, Earlmae Green, Brian Hastings, Eileen Herron, Mary Hodgson, Gwen Johnson, Pat Kendall, Helen Lann, Tony Lehman, Leon Levin, and Vondalear Smith.

[†] Arana and John Talbott hired Tony Lehman, the current chair, as director of that research at the Carter Center.

(*continued from page 247*)

But Christiaan Barnard, who saw the heart as a pump, had just done the first heart transplant, and few cared how a dog reacted to petting.

After losing a bet with the owner of a horse farm he met at a cocktail party attended with Jim MacKie, a horse lover, Lynch did research showing that a horse's heart rate dropped even more than a dog's in response to petting—from forty beats per minute to as low as fifteen to twenty beats per minute on the first horse measured. He began to wonder, Could human hearts be affected in similar ways?

Russ Monroe suggested Lynch seek support from the dean of the medical school. Dean Moxley agreed to support his research but suggested Lynch look at its clinical implications by doing something with heart patients in the coronary care unit. Soon after their discussion, Mary Etta Mills and Sue Thomas, clinical specialists with an interest in coronary care, knocked on Lynch's door asking for help with research design, and a collaboration was born.

After earning her doctorate at Johns Hopkins, Mills became the vice president for nursing at the UMMC, later joined the nursing faculty, and became associate dean for academic affairs. Thomas earned her doctorate from Maryland, joined the nursing faculty, and became assistant dean for doctoral studies.

They began to monitor patients around the clock, consuming miles of paper (in the days before digital data recording). What happened when a wife sat by the patient's bedside, for example, or when a nurse took a patient's pulse? One day Lynch observed a man in a shock–trauma unit on whom "they were pulling the plugs. He was being terminated; he was in fibrillation. A nurse took the patient's hand and said, 'Don't worry. I'll stay with you.' He went back into normal conduction. It was the most dramatic thing I ever saw in my life, and it made me ask, 'If transient human interactions, just a little touch, does this, what does the chronic absence of human contact—loneliness—do to us? How in the world do you go

James Lynch, a favorite with CAPP students, became popular on the lecture circuit and appeared on *60 Minutes* after publication of his book, *The Broken Heart: The Medical Consequences of Loneliness.*

from being lonely to becoming hypertensive or having coronary heart disease or cancer?' I was still thinking in terms of mechanisms and variance equations: one part cholesterol, two parts hypertension, three parts loneliness, and voilà! You get coronary heart disease!"

In 1970, the first statistics were coming out of the 1960 health census, the first ever to record marital status, which until then wasn't considered an important health variable. Lynch observed that the single, widowed, or divorced had death rates two to ten times higher than married people, which was true for all ages, all races, and both sexes, across the country—but the effects were especially pronounced with heart disease. Based on what he'd learned, he wrote his first book, *The Broken Heart: The Medical Consequences of Loneliness* (1976).

His manuscript, geared to scientists, was rejected by twenty-five publishing houses before it was accepted. With many rejections came letters critiquing the book. Lynch rewrote the book and sent it out again. Basic Books published it, and the *New York Times* ran both a withering review and a glowing review. Lynch became popular on television and the lecture circuit. Stories about him made the cover of *U.S. News and World Report* and appeared in *Time*, *Newsweek*, *People*, and other media. His book "hit a nerve in the culture. I never will know how all of that publicity affected the powers at Maryland. I had the feeling they were uncomfortable with it somehow, because nobody really believed that loneliness was such a killer back then. I'd written that book defensively, preparing for a medical attack that never came." A year later *JAMA* published two editorials urging every doctor in the country to read the book, which was eventually published in twelve countries and eleven languages.

After automated blood pressure machines came out, Lynch's researchers could talk to patients while studying their cardiovascular systems. "We noticed that talking had profound effects on blood pressure. One of my students, Ken Malinow, did a study showing that the more rapid your speech, the higher your pressure goes. At first it looked like a paradox, that loneliness kills, but Malinow, an internist, psychiatrist, and passionate defender of the state of Israel, told Lynch he wanted to publish the paper in Hebrew in the *Israeli Medical Journal*. "We were free as birds back then," says Lynch.

that when you talk your blood pressure goes way up. We saw that many people talk without putting commas in their sentences—they didn't breathe, so they weren't getting enough oxygen. Blood pressure went up more when people talked than when they did violent exercise. And it was the very people who had the largest pressure rises when they spoke who tended to withdraw from human contact—because of this unfelt stress. In many men whose wives thought they didn't care, these tremendous surges were going on underneath. We began to change the way they were breathing. We began to understand heart disease as in part reflecting human communication disorders."

In the early eighties, Lynch got a call from the producers of *60 Minutes*, asking him to do an interview for the show. He agreed, if they would put his ten-year-old daughter on. "What's she got to do with loneliness?" they asked. He wanted to show them how children react when they pet a dog. Three days later a CBS crew showed up and Harry Reasoner did a story on how pets affect health. Viewers saw Lynch's ten-year-old daughter's blood pressure rise as she read poetry and fall by half after she put Rags, her dog, on her lap. The messages: when you speak, your blood pressure rises; when you listen or attend to others, it falls; and pets lower blood pressure. CBS rebroadcast the segment several times, and retirement homes began bringing pets in as therapy for elderly residents. Lynch saw heart disease as a communication disorder. "But how do drug companies make money out of that?" His second book, *The Language of the Heart: The Human Body in Dialogue*, came out in 1985.

In *A Cry Unheard: New Insights into the Medical Consequences of Loneliness* (2000), Lynch argues that "school failure is the leading cause of heart disease, not economic disparity later in life. When you can't communicate, when every time you open your mouth you feel stupid, your pressure goes into overdrive, and the only thing that knocks it down is narcotics, alcohol, or to disconnect from society. If you drop out of school, you lose your capacity to talk without stress, and you die prematurely. Maryland and Hopkins are surrounded by a population in which the black male's average lifespan is fifty-nine years. We have the finest research institutions in the United States looking for the sources of disease, when it's all around them."

Lynch next did a study of the effects on blood pressure of status and self-esteem. Medical students were asked first to read quietly to themselves and then to read to another person. For half of the med students, the "other person" was dressed in dungarees and a sweatshirt and said he was a grad student working in one of the labs; for the other half, the other person wore a suit and white coat and said he was the chief medical resident. Basal pressures went up 15 to 20 percent when they read aloud—with the increase doubling when they were "talking up" (to someone of higher status).

"Gene Brody and Russ Monroe," according to Lynch, "never once wavered in their complete support of my research—not once. I could never have done all of this research without them and without being at Maryland. And of course with the medical students—especially the CAPP students—there was always this dynamic energy. I had those wonderful students to my house probably once every two months for dinner. It was an era that permitted that kind of luxury."

"Jim Lynch had a profound influence on my education and subsequent career," says James Gamble (CAPP class of 1975). "Discussions with him were always an infusion of fresh intellectual air—he had a wonderful way of thinking. He was a humanitarian and a scientist, to be sure, but he was also absolutely intolerant of diffuse language and sloppy thinking. He taught me the value of honest, critical thinking in an environment (medical school) that often demanded blind acceptance and memorization of fact and theory."

Changes in medical economics

For insights into how changing medical economics affected the department I thank, but do not blame, for their observations and explanations, Frank Calia, Lois Flaherty, Howard Goldman, Herb Gross, Mike Plaut, Tony Lehman, James Lynch, and John Talbott.

Early in the 1970s, residents got one half-hour session with faculty member Nate Schaper on psychiatric business practices, says Elliot Cohen. "Our entire training on how to run a business office was to put the cost of treatment down on a five-by-eight card. It was cash pay—at that time thirty dollars an hour—and that was the extent of our bookkeeping. Later, of course, the rate was higher and things were far more complex. I have fond memories of Nate trying to make it that simple." Even then, change was in the air.

From the beginning, there was a marriage between the community's need for care and the medical school's need for teaching cases. Under the state charter for the medical school, the patients in the surrounding community were to be the teaching cases for the medical students. That relationship persisted, says Herb Gross, until the Maryland legislature learned that the state of Michigan had decided its state hospital would pay for itself (instead of relying on

"Our entire training on how to run a business office was to put the cost of treatment down on a five-by-eight card. It was cash pay—at that time thirty dollars an hour—and that was the extent of our bookkeeping."

state funding), and decided, "Me, too." The state of Maryland hired a consultant, Ray Dearborn, to chair a commission to review the way medical services were paid for at University Hospital. Dearborn reported, for example, that outpatient services, at least, was good at issuing bills but not at collecting money. At the end of the year the university added up the bills and sent them to the state legislature, which added up the totals and gave the university an appropriation, to defray the teaching cost of a university hospital caring for poor patients. This approach didn't require the hospital to develop fiscal systems.

In the mid- to late 1970s—during a period of general inflation, and before managed care came in—there was an intentional change in the culture. "The dean and the hospital director wanted each department to form a corporation, so they could control what the department's doctors were earning and take a piece of it," says Gross. The first department to do so was ob–gyn.

Bringing financial discipline to the hospital meant changing the way the physicians were reimbursed, and getting the hospital billing system up to speed took a long time. Outpatient services, for example, which had about 150,000 patient visits a year, got credit for only 75,000. For some of the low-fee patients, the residents could bill on a sliding scale, but they had to learn how to bill, how to collect the money, and how to get it to the hospital. Later, there was a uniform charge of eighteen dollars for each outpatient visit, based on square footage. "Over the course of years the deans took a bigger and bigger percentage, we could no longer fund our research, and the younger faculty had a hard time getting permission to fund their psychoanalytic training," says Gross.

Budget problems also brought a change in the ratio of faculty to students. Earlier there had been 200 faculty

Herb Gross, then and now. "Over the years the deans took a bigger and bigger percentage, we could no longer fund our research, and the younger faculty had a hard time getting permission to fund their psychoanalytic training."

members for ten to twelve psychiatric residents a year. The department was now spread out across the city, so more residents were needed; they helped support the department by seeing patients.

In 1974, the department of psychiatry established a faculty practice plan, a new national economic model facilitated by the enactment in 1965 of legislation authorizing Medicare and Medicaid, which "converted the poor and elderly from subsidized to paying patients, with reimbursement from the federal or state government." New patient care revenues generated through the faculty's clinical activities helped offset departmental expenses and "the dwindling of direct federal support for medical education."[16] Psychiatry Associates, the medical service plan for the department, emerged under university guidelines.

In 1975, the department was down to seven psychiatric residents, says Tom Krajewski. (This would change with introduction of the Maryland Plan.) There was also some controversy that year about whether the residents chose, or the faculty appointed, the chief resident (or both).

Most medical schools and hospitals now have something like Psychiatry Associates, an arrangement similar to a private group practice. As an associate, when you reach a

In 1974, the department of psychiatry established a faculty practice plan, a new national economic model facilitated by the enactment in 1965 of legislation authorizing Medicare and Medicaid.

certain level of income, any additional revenue you bring in goes into a general pool, which is divided equally among the seventy or so associates. This kind of arrangement held less attraction for several members of the faculty. John Lion, for example, who was in big demand for speaking and consultations, eventually decided to go into private practice.

At first, only the physicians were required to be part of the hospital's new medical service plan. "Psychologists and social workers were not, so many of the psychologists would disappear part of the day to see private patients, with no control on their income," says Plaut. "That stopped once we all had to be a part of the medical service plan. Making all faculty accountable was comforting to the medical faculty, because it put everyone on the same playing field. Yes, those who wanted to make more money left, but there had to be some accountability, whether with faculty time, research funding, or clinical service."

The structure was the same throughout the department: faculty members got a base amount that provided part of their salary, and they were expected to generate the rest through some combination of private practice, grants, and consultation. The relative amount of the base salary tended to go down over the years, which was how the department coped with decreasing funds. In 1977, when Lois Flaherty started, she says, "I think the base salaries were about 70 percent of income, and then progressively diminished, to 60 percent and then 50 percent. A cap was set on your salary. If your cap was $100,000 and the base was $60,000, and if on promotion your cap increased to $120,000, your base might stay the same (though as a percentage it declined), so the amount you had to generate on your own would go up.

"This was not an uncommon arrangement in academic departments. The problem is, it is destructive to research.

You're so busy figuring out ways to generate money that you can't give researchers any protected time—and of course you can't generate funding for research unless you already have some research."

To keep the clinical faculty in a medical school honest, the faculty must all have an approved salary, says Plaut. "How we earn that depends on our situation."[17] Some of it may come from hard money—state funds that go to faculty for teaching purposes. The hospital may fund faculty salaries because residents are taught, or faculty may be expected to bring in a certain percentage of our approved salary through our own devices, whether it's clinical work, contracts, or consulting. "We have to be accountable for everything we do. We have to report every year on consulting we do, whether it's paid or not, so that all of our time is accounted for. They don't make us accountable for every minute of the day, but there's a significant difference in the way things are done now."

Before the introduction of "accountability," faculty and staff had more flexibility. Ulku Ulgur could ask Russ Monroe to go to the hospital directors to provide funding to keep a certain child in the hospital. "We had flexibilities then that we didn't have later," says Ulgur. "When we sent kids to summer camps, I would go to dietary and ask them to prepare package lunches they could take on the bus (instead of serving them in the inpatient unit) and I could divert certain funds to good causes. Those kinds of flexibility were lost later. Now, 'if you're going to give kids hamburgers, you're going to give them hamburgers. You can't change the menu.'"

Schools like Harvard have the resources to provide grants to young faculty. The University of Maryland was at a disadvantage in that, because it was a state school, people assumed the hospital was supported by the state, which at one point was true. "During my tenure, that ended," says Flaherty, "so the hospital went through a turbulent time. When Taghi was in charge of 4G, before he went to the Center for Infant Study, kids could come and stay there for a year because their stay was being paid for. Suddenly these units were supposed to be self-supporting, and they never could make money. Psychiatry and pediatrics departments don't tend to generate enough money to pay their own way. They tend to serve people in the surrounding communities, which are not usually wealthy communities. It is the departments that offer expensive (often surgical) procedures that tend to make money."

During Brody's tenure as chair, fairly generous and steady funding for both training and research was available from NIH, NIMH, NICHD, and the state of Maryland. Russ Monroe took over the chairmanship at about the time funding dried up, and the economic base was changing in other ways, too. For one thing, with dehospitalization, by 1975 the population of U.S. mental hospitals had dropped by 80 percent. Maryland was still providing patient care at several state hospitals, including the Carter Center, but the promised federal support for community mental health centers around the country had not been sustained, and the mental health centers were not taking care of the persistently and severely mentally ill patients.

Also, medical schools across the country had expanded in 1969, says Lois Flaherty, partly in response to federal funding provided to support acceptance of U.S. citizens who had completed two years of education at foreign medical schools. Several new schools were created to increase physician numbers in the United States.

Monroe, who had little interest in finances, hired Steve Valerio, a tough and accomplished administrator with a finance degree, who some considered the de facto chair of the department. But one of Monroe's chief personal accomplishments, as part of negotiations for a collaborative arrangement called the Maryland Plan, was to get the state legislature to transfer control of the Maryland Psychiatric Research Center from the Mental Hygiene Administration (MHA) to the department of psychiatry. That transfer, in 1977, reflected a major change in how research in the department could be done and what it would focus on.

As of 1990 MPRC would be indexed at 1 percent of the state mental health budget. "That didn't last or even really take effect with the budget office," according to Will Carpenter.

Russia's launching of Sputnik in 1957 had led to a space race in the 1960s, one unintended consequence of which was to shift the emphasis in U.S. universities away from the liberal arts toward the sciences, says Jim Lynch. When universities discovered the phenomenon of overhead rates (the university getting $100,000 in overhead for each research grant of $100,000), they also tended to replace the monastic tradition of knowledge for knowledge's sake with the tradition of knowledge as a business. The net effect was to diminish the importance of the humanities in universities, with medicine becoming a big business driven by grants from the federal government.[18] "When I left Hopkins in 1968," says Lynch, "one professor hit the table one day, angrily, and said, 'The sooner you guys learn that research is big business, the better off you'll be.'"

Those like Lynch who were uncomfortable with dependence on grants found doing research more difficult in the new environment. At Hopkins, Lynch says, "I had shared in a multimillion-dollar grant from the Heart Institute, which wasn't renewed, so everybody suddenly lost their jobs. I vowed I would never structure my life to be dependent on the whims of a few people deciding whether your work is worthwhile. When I came to Maryland, my primary job was research. I structured it around clinics and generated enough money to pay for the research and personnel to carry it out. The problem was, the university didn't get any overhead, so when times changed, they changed. I refused to apply for a grant." A few months after John Talbott came in as new chair of the department, Lynch left the university, saddened by "the industrialization of academia," and, with Alp Karahasan, set up a private clinic in Columbia and Towson. He had no interest in stepping onto the grant treadmill and now treats a number of academic physicians "for the stress of constantly needing to win NIH RO1 grants. Universities are under terrible constant pressures to get money, separate from clinical work, mostly from block grants and that kind of thing."

Will Carpenter, recruited in 1977 to run the MPRC, had both the solid scientific reputation and the leadership skills to succeed in the world of grants, but surviving in the world of soft money and grant cycles would be a constant headache.

> *"We had flexibilities then that we didn't have later," says Ulgur. "Now, 'if you're going to give kids hamburgers, you're going to give them hamburgers. You can't change the menu.'"*

"Almost every year," says John Talbott, who became chair in 1985, "it was the Perils of Pauline. The budget would go to bed, and at midnight some budget guy in Annapolis would see this line item in the budget ('Research in the Department of Mental Health') that didn't look like it belonged and would draw a red line through it. Then Will and I would go into high gear, call legislators, even threaten to transfer MPRC back to the state. Many states fund little or no research through their departments of mental health; all their research money comes from NIH, NARSAD, whatever. The big, relatively rich states—California, Illinois, Maryland, Massachusetts, New York, Texas—traditionally support research adequately, so we're not unique by any means. All the algorithms for schizophrenia treatment were developed at Texas with state monies. Places like Langley Porter, Illinois Psychiatric Institute, Texas Mental Health Institute—we're not alone. The research can't be airy fairy; it has to back the mission of the state, which is why schizophrenia research is so very appealing and fundable. But there are legislatures that say hospitals should be treating people, not doing research. The education process is endless." During the periods when research grants are not in effect, there is a scramble for bridging grants, to support and retain research faculty.

> *One of Monroe's accomplishments, as part of negotiations for the Maryland Plan, was to get the legislature to transfer control of the MPRC to the department of psychiatry.*

After the state hospital system stopped "warehousing patients" (keeping them for a long time, with little treatment) and began expecting to treat them as outpatients in the community who might be able to lead a more normal lifestyle, the emphasis in the department and in training changed. This happened nationally, not just in Maryland. Dehospitalization hugely affected medical economics. Mental illness tends to run in families, poverty gets passed from one generation to the next, there are many disturbed people in the community, and people who are seriously mentally ill clearly can't be gainfully employed, so they tend to be both poor and either uninsured or underinsured. "That is why since the late 1970s the department has always had one kind of partnership or another with the state," says Frank Calia.

There is always a struggle about who's paying for mental health care: the federal government, state government, or local government, says Howard Goldman. "With community psychiatry, there was a shift in emphasis, which worked or didn't work, depending on where you were. It seemed to work better in Maryland than it did in a lot of places. The Maryland Plan enabled us to train a lot of our residents in the state hospitals and, partly because of that, a lot of our residents became leaders in the state mental health system—which from the late 1970s into the 1980s was a rich environment."

A return from federal to state funding for mental health care, and major changes in funding and reimbursement for all health care, now greatly influenced university strategy. In 1981, arguing that the hospital would never get the technology it needed unless it privatized, the new chancellor, Albert Farmer, persuaded the legislature to bring about privatization. The hospital had originally been a private medical college. The fifth oldest medical school in the country was launched in 1807 in Baltimore, by a group of physicians trained in Scotland, England, and France. It was a proprietary medical school, created with the idea of making money. In 1823 the doctors at the medical college raised some money and built a dispensary in which to teach more medical students and young MDs who wanted more training.[19] Because the young MDs lived in the dispensary, they were called residents, says Calia. In 1920, the medical school had financial problems and, with promises of financial backing from the state, became a public institution. When times were good, it thrived; when they were not, it didn't; and it was now operating with a substantially shrinking subsidy. "When I got here in 1969 it was a state medical school and a state hospital, and the hospital was a dump," says Calia. "It *looked* like a state hospital."[20]

In 1984, University Hospital, after sixty-four years as a state hospital (1920–84), was reprivatized and revitalized. It became a private not-for-profit 501(c)(3) hospital complex, the University of Maryland Medical System (UMMS), with Morton I. Rapoport as CEO. Under the new plan, all hospital physicians were recognized as medical school faculty. Nonfaculty employees could continue as state employees or become members of the new corporation. New personnel automatically became corporate employees.[21]

One of the nation's oldest teaching hospitals, this 731-bed facility is home to the University of Maryland Marlene and Stewart Greenebaum Cancer Center, the R Adams Cowley Shock Trauma Center, the University of Maryland Hospital for Children, and the University of Maryland division of transplantation.[30]

The medical school remains a state medical school. "However, the school gets less than five percent of its operating budget from the state," says Calia, "and even though the hospital is no longer a state hospital, it gets money from the state for certain building programs. Our shock–trauma unit, which is private, is world class; the police and fire department depend on it for all motor vehicle accidents. So the state wouldn't think of not supporting it. Similarly, because mental health is a big problem, Tony Lehman can say to the state: 'These people can't pay. What are you going to do? Abandon them? You've got to pay for it.'"

In 1987, the university's faculty practice plan was privatized as a 501(c)(3) corporation. "At this juncture, the hospital and practice plan have limited experience with capitation," wrote Meyer and McLaughlin.[22] University Hospital was separate from the Carter Center, which was state-run until 1993, when the state decided to privatize its outpatient services.

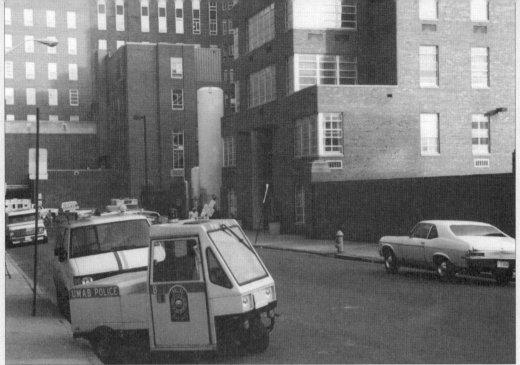

The Psychiatric Institute shortly before it was torn down. The courtyard wall is on the right.

Shock–Trauma

Psych Institute overcome
by shock–trauma

Once University Hospital became a private hospital, "it grew like Topsy," says Herb Gross. "It got into the modern era and built a lot of buildings." One of those buildings in particular would alter the fate of the Psychiatric Institute, as would the ascending star of a surgeon from Utah by the name of R Adams Cowley. A charismatic cardiac specialist, Cowley had graduated from the University of Utah, earned a medical degree from Maryland, and done his residency at University Hospital. After doing thoracic surgery elsewhere he returned to Maryland as director of the medical school's cardiopulmonary lab. In 1956, when he was head of thoracic and cardiovascular surgery, shock was a problem with many patients, so the department built a shock laboratory in the Bressler building to study shock's effects on dogs, cats, and rats. Concluding that species differ in their responses to shock or stress and that the problem couldn't be studied by surgeons alone, Cowley established a multidisciplinary team to systematically observe and measure what happens during shock. It wasn't easy to make meaningful measurements in patients under treatment for shock, because the patient wasn't stable: "His temperature was moving up (and we were treating him to get it down) or it was moving down (and we were treating him to get it up)." In those early days, the cardiology team had to make its own valves, grafts, or artificial blood vessels (from nylon fabric purchased at the nearby May Company) and most of the patients they were studying in treatment were "derelicts—who were almost dead at the outset."[23]

Getting funding was not easy, either. NIH, which wanted numerical data, was reluctant to fund shock studies because getting measurements was so difficult. "The Army in 1958 was both enthusiastic and afraid of our shock research proposal," said Cowley in 1978. Cowley's teams were putting cannulas in the radial artery and venous system to measure heart pressures, which the Army felt was impossible and dangerous, and Army people would show up unannounced to see what they were doing. Cowley's studies sounded too experimental at a time when Nazi experiments on Jews at Dachau and elsewhere were a fresh and distasteful memory. They were awarded a contract for $100,000 to study shock in people, the first such award in the country—which allowed them to develop the first clinical shock–trauma unit as part of surgery. In 1960 they began training people and getting equipment. Early in 1961 they were working from a two-room hospital laboratory on the fourth floor of the Psych Institute, a room that had been extremely well-equipped for heart surgery. To monitor and study the act of death in humans, the shock–trauma unit would

R Adams Cowley, standing, with Nate Schnaper, who spent a fair amount of time moderating tense encounters in the ER. "He could be difficult," says Schnaper of Cowley, "but he could also be gentle and sensitive."

take one dying patient at a time from the general hospital and monitor the patient with sophisticated equipment (used nowhere else then, and now in common use). Research was the purpose of monitoring these dying patients, who were in shock and "could not have been saved in the general hospital"—but about half of them lived. They were so ill that most of them died within weeks or months, but Cowley had his numbers.[24]

Gradually, their research confirmed the golden hour hypothesis that Cowley had begun to form while serving with the U.S. Army in France—that many severe injuries could be stabilized if the patient could be transported to a well-equipped site with a surgical team skilled in dealing with traumatic injuries. "There is a golden hour between life and death," explained Cowley in an interview. "If you are critically injured you have less than sixty minutes to survive. You might not die right then; it may be three days or two weeks later—but something has happened in your body that is irreparable."

From two beds the unit went to four, and in 1963 Cowley got an NIH grant to develop the first shock–trauma center, to study shock in detail. In the early to mid-sixties the Center for the Study of Trauma, as it was known, needed a way to get more patients in. Patients were beginning to trickle in, referred by other physicians, but as they came in dying, the unit became known as the death lab. Most doctors were reluctant to lose their patients to this special team, and on top of turf concerns, 70 percent of deaths from traffic accidents were rural (and hence some distance away).

To take better advantage of that tiny critical window of opportunity when a life could be saved, Cowley persuaded the state of Maryland to purchase helicopters (with a Department of Transportation grant) that he would share with the Maryland Police. Cowley's group cut the mortality rate for direct admissions to the

Unfortunately, the natural site for the new Shock Trauma Center appeared to be right where the Psych Institute—now the IPHB—stood. The psych building at that time was old and run down, but still led onto a beautiful and serene courtyard, an enclosed green space for the patients. Helicopters landing in that courtyard were the first signals of trouble for the IPHB. Shown here, beyond the courtyard, the old Pharmacy Society building, also later torn down.

trauma center radically. A savvy lobbyist with a good cause, he negotiated directly with the legislators for a new Shock Trauma Center building and eventually for a statewide emergency medical services system. The survival of a close friend of Governor Marvin Mandel, a state official who was brought to the center nearly dead in 1970, made Mandel a strong supporter of the Center.

Unfortunately, the natural site for the new Shock Trauma Center appeared to be right where the Psych Institute—now the IPHB—stood. The psych building at that time was old and run down, but still led onto a beautiful and serene courtyard, an enclosed green space for the patients. Helicopters landing in that courtyard were the first signals of trouble for the IPHB. "The helicopter would land in our yard, and the stretcher would come rolling through our hallway into our elevator. It was like being in a war zone. It was prophetic to have those damned helicopters land and to run their patients through our halls, traumatizing our patients," recalls Herb Gross, who was still chief of the adult outpatient service. "The gym our kids in the children's unit used to play in became a storage unit for shock–trauma. Now my old office is the entry to a hyperbaric chamber and the old 645 West Redwood is attached to the big blue shock–trauma building."

They didn't knock the Psych Institute down. They built in and around the courtyard and up and over the Psych Institute. The courtyard ran from Redwood Street on the Penn Street side to where the ambulance entrance to the current Shock Trauma Center is. Destroying the courtyard to accommodate the new trauma center seemed to epitomize the disrespect the administration had for psychiatry at the time.[*]

It didn't help that on Thursday evening, July 10, 1975, a cloudburst and a backup in the city's drainage system caused the worst flooding in University Hospital since Hurricane Agnes.[†] "It was a heavy downpour," recalls psychoanalyst Léon Wurmser, who, five minutes before the flood, ran to get Connie Sakles and sprinted to the parking building. "That was my saving sprint," says Wurmser. It rained so hard that the sewage system couldn't handle it, manhole covers popped open, water filled up the window wells on the basement level, and water totally filled three offices at the north end of the floor: Wurmser's, Jay Nolan's, and Jerry Hunt's. The water got so high it split the doors on those offices and then a wave came through. The flood swept through Wurmser's office with such force that his steel desk was carried down the

* "In all fairness," says Michael Plaut, "long before the shock–trauma building went up, the landing site was moved to the roof of the university parking garage that used to be across the street. Ambulances would run up the seven levels on the down ramps as they could not negotiate the angles on the up ramps. Red lights would flash, bells would go off, and all cars had to stop. The ambulance would meet the chopper on the roof, take the patient down to the street level and then to the hospital entrance—a good part of that all-important golden hour."

† Terry Capp. "Recent cloudburst causes extensive flooding in Psych Institute," UMAB Happenings, 4:42, The University of Maryland at Baltimore, July 22, 1975. Mike Plaut and Léon Wurmser provided details about the flood's effects.

It didn't help that a backup in the city's drainage system caused the worst flooding in University Hospital since Hurricane Agnes. The flood swept through Léon Wurmser's office with such force that his steel desk was carried down the hall toward the other end of the building.

hall toward the other end of the building. "If I had been in that room, I would have drowned, because the flood quickly reached the ceiling." Documents and patient records were scattered in the courtyard. "That was symbolic for everything that went on."

On the less affected end of the floor, across from Stan Friedman's office, Mike Plaut was on the phone with his wife, talking about going home until things quieted down, when the doors at the end of the hall burst and a wall of water, bearing furniture, came toward him. As the water rose, he stacked file cabinet drawers on his desk and sofa, leaving when the water climbed as high as the electric outlets.

The fire department had the water pumped out within an hour, and the flood damage was clearly visible. Gerry Hunt's office was a shambles, Wurmser's office was no longer separated from the adjacent office by a wall, and mud covered Jay Nolan's office, destroying more than a thousand of his books. The terrace level of the IPHB was covered with seven to eight feet of water, covering the kitchen, laundry room, medical records, and other basement-level offices. Ten elevators were out of commission. Many of the staff were moved out of the building to healthier accommodations. Stan Friedman swore he would not stay on that floor anymore and he and some other (but not all) members of child and adolescent psychiatry got space in the Medical School Teaching Facility (MSTF), a building on Martin Luther King Boulevard. They held that space for many years.

"It took us a week to clean up," says Plaut. To deal with the mud and dry out the books and papers, they used material the Library of Congress had developed after the flood in Florence, Italy, a few years earlier. "Russ Monroe, Norm McCleod (our administrator then and a great guy), and the hospital administration were very helpful. So was the fire department."

Before one end of the IPHB was torn down, there were turf wars to be fought on many fronts, questions to be answered, a decision to be made. Would the shock–trauma center be built at Maryland General or at University Hospital? Would the shock–trauma doctors be academic enough? Would they write papers? Cowley might have preferred Maryland

General, but it was felt that University Hospital added more value to the center. To get the trauma center, University Hospital had to make some concessions. The surgeons in the trauma center had to get their credentials and promotions approved by the chairman of surgery, who was in the medical school and University Hospital.[25]

It fell to Tom Krajewski to sign off on tearing down the IPHB. Krajewski, who had helped launch the Maryland Plan, was from mid-1984 to mid-1986 assistant state secretary for health and chief physician for the state of Maryland. Krajewski, to whom as state physician shock–trauma would report, recalls the irony of the situation. In 1952, when it opened, the Psych Institute had also been the state's bright new hope. It too had started as an entity independent of the university, set up through separate state funding. It too had ruffled a few university and medical school feathers. Now it was being replaced, physically, with the state's new darling. Mort Rapoport, hospital CEO, said, "Tom, you need to understand, these people are very resentful of shock–trauma. They get all the special awards and all the grants, and they can go outside of the system."

"Now shock–trauma was under me, in that the state funded it when I was chief physician, and they were going to build a building," says Krajewski. "We looked at different sites and I hated to say it, but the best site was where the IPHB was. Being primarily outpatient, IPHB didn't need to be adjacent to the hospital, and as it was an old building it was going to have to be replaced anyway. Trauma had to be inpatient. We couldn't put the trauma center two or three blocks away and have people carted over—and we couldn't have specialists driving two or three blocks to do a consult. But boy did I feel guilty. It was going to happen. I tried to make it happen in the least problematic way, so that it was a win for everybody."

Krajewski got commitments to have other buildings built. The department of psychiatry would now move into a sturdy building at 701 Pratt Street that was being renovated for the purpose. The department's old guard had prided itself on IPHB being independent of the hospital, but to some extent psychiatry was viewed as not part of medicine at a time when there was some pressure to medicalize it. Krajewski's pitch was, "Let's have these buildings built for outpatient, but let's incorporate the inpatient into the regular hospital, like we want to incorporate psychiatry into mainstream medicine—to get away from the old stigma that psychiatry isn't really part of medicine."

And the reality was that the IPHB wasn't independent anymore. It was now Dr. Cowley who could go around the medical school and go right to the legislature. In 1973, when Krajewski was a psych resident, the university had allowed enough training money for psychiatry patients to stay in the hospital for six months, so the resident who treated that patient every day could learn. "But in this day and age, would you want to be in the psych hospital for six months for me to learn from you? The university had started cutting back on that training money. So they were really in control at that point," says Krajewski. "I think the loss of the building was symbolic of what they had already lost." And of course psychiatric inpatient stays were down all around the country, not just in Maryland.

Finally the old Psych Institute had to go. "They tore it down," says Walter Weintraub. "They murdered it. They spread us out all over the place." Inpatient went to the other side of the university hospital where medicine and surgery were, and outpatient went to 701 Pratt. The era of nearly everyone working together in one special building was over.

Herb Gross did the first psychiatric consult with the new shock–trauma center. He was called in after a young man had drunk himself into oblivion and become involved in a car accident. He was asked to help the staff deal with the stresses "of taking care of a guy who normally would have been dead but who now, because of the shock–trauma center, was being kept alive—in a coma—despite an outcome that was anything but certain."

Previously, the medical school had been a protected enclave, financed by federal funds, by the hospital, and by generous teaching funds from the state legislature, supplemented by the University of Maryland. "We could keep people on the wards for longer stays and we could admit patients who were useful for training," says Herb Gross. "But with this transition, the hospital required us to meet a more medical model: our length of stay got shorter, our census went down, and, most important, they costed us out as if we were a surgical medical service."

The battle over square feet had begun as soon as the Psych Institute was built. Now Bill Jews,* as associate hospital director, complained to Herb Gross that the psychiatry department had more

They didn't knock the Psych Institute down. They built in and around the courtyard and up and over the Psych Institute. Destroying the courtyard to accommodate the new trauma center seemed to epitomize the disrespect the administration had for psychiatry at the time.

square feet per patient than anyone else. Gross explained that psychiatry patients don't usually spend most of their time in bed and needed space to move around

* In 1993 William L. Jews became CEO of Blue Cross and Blue Shield of Maryland.

in. Moreover, he said, "the actual cost per square foot for a psychiatry room should be lower, because it's really the cost of running a motel, plus some doctors. You don't have to sterilize it; you just have to vacuum it. But you're charging us the same for a square foot that you charge the department of surgery for its operating room." However, Maryland's Health Services Cost Review Commission mandated one price for the hospital. "Before that, I think they charged us by the square feet appropriate to us. There always was a problem costing us out, but it became even a bigger problem when a uniform charge was applied throughout the whole hospital."

In May 1982, Russ Monroe wrote a letter to T. Albert Farmer, the chancellor of the university, about the demise of the department because of changes in the way the hospital regarded and funded the institute. With the physical demise of the institute itself, he tendered his resignation as chairman of the department.

By then, managed care was about to effect an even greater change in medical economics and mental health care.

Last days of the Psychiatric Institute (IPHB).

6

The Maryland Plan
When Idealism and Pragmatism
Struck a Deal

University-trained psychiatrists often avoid public sector employment because they see it as inferior, and many states struggle to recruit adequate psychiatric manpower. In the mid-1970s, a group of bright, idealistic young University of Maryland–trained psychiatrists with a strong interest in the public sector informally developed a groundbreaking project called the Maryland Plan, an effort to recruit more university-trained psychiatrists into public service—which typically meant going to work in a state hospital. The recruitment team for the Maryland Plan adopted a sixties-style inspirational strategy to temporarily destigmatize state psychiatry, elevating poorly paid and sometimes unpleasant work to a noble cause. The emphasis in this university–state collaboration was to train (and thereby perhaps recruit) psychiatrists to work in the public sector, especially to provide care for the patients with the most severe and chronic mental illness. Four times as many graduates from Maryland's psychiatric residency program entered state psychiatry in the fifteen years after 1978, when the plan was implemented, than in the eight years before. A new generation of leaders changed and expanded the scope of the plan. What enabled this training partnership to work makes for a compelling story, with an interesting cast of characters and many valuable lessons learned.

When John Talbott was running for president of the American Psychiatric Association in 1983, he assembled a national group of psychiatrists with a special interest in chronic and severe mental illness to plan what he would do if elected. One of the ten items included on his agenda as APA president was to encourage states and universities to collaborate on providing training, research, and clinical service. "It became clear that two groups were out ahead of everybody else in the country: a group in Oregon that was involved in providing training for community mental health centers and a group in Maryland that was focused on supplying manpower to the state hospitals," says Talbott, who soon after being elected APA president came to Maryland to chair the psychiatry department.

That "group in Maryland" included a core group of young psychiatrists who grew up in the sixties and graduated from the University of Maryland psychiatry department's residency program, inspired, mentored, and led by the greatest recruiter in department history: training director Walter Weintraub. How this group changed the nature of public psychiatry in Maryland is a story central to the history of the department and a fascinating study in how getting something difficult accomplished depends a lot on who you know, how well you trust each other, and how much you want to make a difference.

The two-track system of residency training

The year was 1976. "In those days, and to some extent even today, there was a two-track system of residency training," says Walter Weintraub. "Residents who had graduated from American medical schools and were being trained as residents in university centers were getting the elite training. Another kind of training was going on in the state hospitals, where most of the foreign medical graduates did their residency." It seemed to Weintraub that there was something wasteful, unrealistic, and inherently undemocratic about a system in which the sickest patients were in the state hospitals, where the least-trained (mostly foreign) doctors were, and the university-trained people were getting the patients with the least severe mental health problems. Weintraub had a notion that if there was enough money lying around to support a two-tier system of residency training, there was enough to support a more sensible single-track system where all residents would have similar kinds of training experiences and where everybody would have an opportunity to treat the very sick patients.

Walter Weintraub, interviewed in August 2007 and December 2008. All quotations from Walter Weintraub are from these two interviews and follow-up questions, unless otherwise noted. Others interviewed for and quoted in this chapter include Jonathan Book, Henry Harbin, Brian Hepburn, Dave Helsel, Dennis Kutzer, Tony Lehman, Gary Nyman, Tom Krajewski, John Talbott, and Stanley Weinstein. Historical information also came from journal and newspaper articles, including articles written by Weintraub and others for the *American Journal of Psychiatry* and *Hospital and Community Psychiatry*, full citations for which can be found in the bibliography at the end of the book.

"So when I became training director," says Weintraub, "I decided to see what I could do. I was certain it would work. One reason I thought so is that the people who had to carry it out were people I had trained. I had trained people for twenty years, many of these people were working all over the place in Maryland, and I thought that they would trust me and be willing to go along and try this experiment."

The Maryland Plan was Walter Weintraub's brainchild

This may have seemed an experiment unlikely to succeed, because, as Weintraub observes, "the university programs tended to be snobbish and to see themselves as elite programs. They were mostly psychoanalytic in scope and therefore more interested in treating neurotic patients who were not that sick than in treating the schizophrenics and manic–depressives. You can't blame the elite program. They would claim that at least we know how to treat these people; the others we don't know how. But as new medications came along and these sick patients became more treatable, it was a little easier to begin a program like the Maryland Plan."

Twenty-five years after the "Maryland's Shame" series had run in the *Baltimore Sun*, the state's mental health facilities were still overcrowded and poorly staffed, and the state, with vacancies to fill in half of the state and hospital positions, still had problems recruiting and retaining psychiatrists. Psychiatrists in state facilities had huge responsibilities without authority and limited resources and support systems to care for often difficult patients. Their low-prestige "work was made more difficult by such factors as administrative restrictions, public scrutiny, political manipulation, and the impact of judicial decisions."[1] Salaries for psychiatrists were among the lowest in the nation, and the state mental health system was "a dispirited, stigmatized organization" which had trouble recruiting good doctors. About 70 percent of the state psychiatrists and all of the psychiatric residents in state facilities were foreign-born graduates of foreign medical schools, and they were state-trained, not university-trained, in psychiatry.[2] Many of them were not fluent in English and had problems blending in with American culture, which affected their ability to treat patients.

"It wasn't totally a wasteland," said Sherrill Cheeks, a psychiatrist at Springfield State Hospital and one of the few university-trained psychiatrists in the state system before

1976. "There were islands of individuals who could match anyone. . . . Many were bright," he said of the foreign-born doctors who once made up the bulk of the staff. "But they didn't speak English and didn't have connections. There was a feeling of first- and second-class psychiatrists. The university psychiatrists were the crème de la crème. The state hospital psychiatrists were not so hot."[3]

Psychiatrists trained and working in state hospitals for the most part practiced "custodial institutional care," particularly for the severely mentally ill, by contrast with young, mostly American, university-trained psychiatrists who were "practicing therapeutic institutional care," wrote Pearl Katz, a University of Maryland anthropologist who studied the recruitment program's effects on patient care.[4] University-trained American doctors benefited from solid academic training but got little direct experience with the more difficult types of psychiatric patients found in the state hospitals, said Alp Karahasan, who would eventually become state director of mental health. The foreign-born doctors in the state hospitals got experience with those patients but not much academic training in how to deal with them, much less treat them, effectively.[5] "Many patients spent years in hospitals yet received little treatment or were dumped, ill-prepared, back into the community," reported the *Washington Post*.[6] There were too few doctors (roughly twenty-five) for far too many psychiatric patients—roughly 1,600 at Springfield, where Cheeks had worked for twenty years.

The main problem was recruiting more university-trained psychiatrists to work in state mental health facilities. A secondary problem was training (and thereby, it was hoped, recruiting) young psychiatrists from the elite schools to work in the state mental health facilities and to provide good training for the doctors already working in the hospitals.

Previous recruitment efforts, offering the carrot of additional income, had failed to retain new recruits. Between 1965 and 1975 the state and university had offered a five-year career training program in which, in return for a substantially higher stipend during residency training, residents agreed to spend eighteen months of their training in state units and to work for two years in state facilities after graduation. All but one of the nineteen residents who participated completed the program but most stayed only long enough to fulfill their two-year service obligation.[7]

"The jobs were lousy," said Weintraub. "A person gets into one of these jobs and finds himself away from people he respects. His superiors demand loyalty more than professionalism. They become more politicians than psychiatrists. They were dead-end jobs." Recruiting attempts failed in the past, he said, "because the state never changed the job descriptions. You get into a long seniority line, and you have all the disadvantages of a bureaucratic job. If you can go into private practice or a university hospital job, then why would anyone in their right mind take a job like that?"

Much of the psychiatric training in the universities focused on the private sector, says Tony Lehman, the department's current chair, so much of the residency training went on in large private hospitals and psychiatric institutions such as Chestnut Lodge, Sheppard Pratt, and the Institute for Living. "Even the University of Rochester, where I came from," says Lehman, "was a private university. I actually went to Rochester because the chairman of the department wanted me to set up a training program for residents in the state hospital, which I did. Some people thought it was great, and some people thought it was a betrayal, a dumbing down. Working with people with severe mental illness was not very attractive for most psychiatrists, because they

Gary Nyman and Jon Book in 1994

don't have any money, and you can't just sit with them in your office for an hour and do talk therapy. So what was notable about Maryland even back in the sixties was that people like Walter wanted to do something for those patients in the public sector with severe mental illness. That's a major theme in the department's identity."

But recruiting well-trained psychiatrists to work in the state hospitals wasn't easy.

And that's where Gary Nyman, one of Walter Weintraub's bright young protégés at the University of Maryland comes into the story.

An enterprising young psychiatrist takes an unlikely job

Weintraub had recruited Gary Nyman (a fourth year medical student at the University of Virginia) to start as a resident in psychiatry at Maryland in 1969. "As part of my interview, Walter took me for lunch to the Lexington Market, where we had Polish hot dogs and an Orange Julius. He was straight talking, honest, and real. A week later I received his three-page, single-spaced, personal letter accepting me into the training program and telling me why training in his program was right for me. I accepted. Now, forty years later, the rightness of it is even clearer. Walter had, and still has, a charm and sincerity that brings out enthusiasm for the profession and the best in everyone."

After Nyman finished his residency, which was interrupted by military service, he spent some time directing Johns Hopkins's Community Mental Health program. In 1976 a vacancy came up in Maryland's Mental Hygiene Administration. MHA was looking for a director at the same time that it was going to cut the mental health budget by a fifth. Encouraged by Weintraub and Russ Monroe, Nyman applied for a job that for obvious reasons nobody else seemed to want. "I was hired at $38,000," says Nyman, "but who worked for money in that era, anyway? This was an exciting chance to see what could be done."

Nyman has been described as astute, idealistic, visionary, brash, and abrasive. Most agree that without him and Walter Weintraub the Maryland Plan wouldn't have happened.

Lingering memories of the *Sun*'s 1949 exposé of the state mental hospitals may have been a factor in the remarkable collaboration that now developed. The American Medical Association was gradually withdrawing accreditation across the country for autonomous state hospital training programs, and an AMA committee had recommended disaccreditation of the state-run psychiatric residency training being done at Maryland's two largest state hospitals, Springfield and Spring Grove—as if prospects for recruiting young psychiatrists for the state hospitals weren't already grim enough.

In 1976 a task force from the American Psychiatric Association (APA), studying Maryland's system at MHA's request, found that "inadequately trained foreign medical school graduates carry considerable clinical responsibility in both state and local mental health programs." The APA task force recommended that psychiatric training programs in the state's hospitals be integrated into the residency programs run by Maryland's medical schools.[8]

A deal is made to launch the Maryland Plan

New in his post as director of MHA, and sensing the potential for disaster in the state hospital system if things stayed the same, Nyman supported the APA task force recommendation. He and the team he began building at MHA believed that academic psychiatry could do much better than the state did with public sector psychiatric research and education. During 1976 and 1977, he helped negotiate a deal. He asked the University of Maryland to integrate the training programs of the Springfield and Spring Grove state hospitals with that of the university and also to recruit psychiatrists for the inner-city Walter P. Carter Community Mental Health Center. He, representing the state, and Monroe and Weintraub, representing the university, set about negotiating what would become known as the Maryland Plan. Essentially the department of psychiatry was saying, We want to do this joint training. The state was saying, We have only so much money and we want this to happen. Russ Monroe was primarily interested in strengthening research but would say yes to the training if he could get what he really wanted: the state's publicly funded psychiatric research program, the Maryland Psychiatric Research Center, in Catonsville. With MPRC officially part of the department, research would blossom, especially if Monroe could hire noted schizophrenia expert Will Carpenter to run it, as he hoped to do. "Walt's passion was psychiatric education and so was mine," says Nyman. "Russ was willing to take a chance with education in part because he knew he had our (MHA leadership) support for Will and MPRC research."

> "The state public health system and the university system warily agreed and then danced together elegantly."

The Maryland Plan required concessions from both sides. The plan the state negotiated with the department was this:

- The Maryland Psychiatric Research Center would be transferred from the state's Mental Hygiene Administration to the department of psychiatry.
- The university would integrate state psychiatry residency programs with its own and would recruit psych staff and residents for the new inner-city mental health center (the Carter Center) being built near University Hospital. The state hospitals would no longer hold autonomous residency training.
- The state would provide stimulating working conditions for its psychiatrists—providing generously for continuing education and participation in university teaching programs. It promised rapid promotions to positions of authority according to ability rather than seniority.
- All state psychiatrists working in university-affiliated hospitals and clinics would be available one half-day a week for volunteer teaching at the university hospital during state working hours. State psychiatrists working on university training units had to be approved by the universities.
- University residents would have six- to twelve-month rotations in a state hospital or community mental health center—with the university monitoring all aspects of their training. In their final resident year they could choose an elective assignment in specialties such as forensic, adolescent, community, or administrative psychiatry—with training as assistant ward administrators for the last.
- Faculty and trainees would thereby have access to a new psychiatric population. If state mental health systems began to attract more competent psychiatrists, those psychiatrists could become part-time faculty at no cost to the university. With an integrated network of hospitals and clinics, there would be greater opportunity for providing continuity of care for patients.

University researchers would have larger cohorts of patients for clinical research. Moreover, the cooperation of state agencies and clinical facilities was needed for programs involving the care of children, adolescents, criminals, and handicapped people.

- Residents' case loads would be limited to five carefully selected inpatients. Full-time staff would be responsible for treating patients not assigned to residents. Training wards would be administered by full-time psychiatrists holding university appointments. Most consultants to the training units would be full-time university faculty.
- The university's department of psychiatry would make decisions about education, and the MHA would make decisions about service programs.[9]

Monroe, Weintraub, and Nyman were excited about this significant redirection of two programs. MHA agreed to the deal, and Nyman planned for the transition of the MPRC and the state's psychiatric education programs to the Institute for Psychiatry and Behavioral Science (IPHB)—the official new name of Maryland's department of psychiatry. Higher-ups in both the Department of Health & Mental Hygiene and the University of Maryland approved.

"They may not have believed that such interstate agency cooperation would work because the average national MHA director's tenure was eighteen months, I was new and inexperienced, and nothing was possible in that short a time span," says Nyman. In short, the state was willing to take a chance because they didn't think Nyman would last eighteen months.

"Previous attempts to merge university and state cultures were short-lived, highly resisted, and ultimately unsuccessful," wrote Pearl Katz, a University of Maryland anthropologist who studied the bureaucratic links that formed between the two cultures, Maryland's state and university mental health systems.

"The new director committed the prestige of his office to the implementation of the APA recommendations," wrote Weintraub and others in the *American Journal of Psychiatry*.

More frankly, Weintraub told *Washington Post* reporter Christine Russell, "It was considered a hopeless situation. Having no previous experience in state government, [Gary Nyman] didn't realize he couldn't do anything."[10]

Weintraub and colleagues wrote that they had decided on "a strategy of inspirational recruitment" to "buy time to improve state psychiatrists' working conditions. To fire the imaginations of university graduates, the public sector was to be romanticized as the place to be, the place where the action is." The plan leaders "sounded a high moral note by announcing their intention to recruit the most capable graduates of Maryland's residency training programs," on the grounds that "access to university-trained psychiatrists was the right of the poor and the chronic mentally ill." Calling the program the Maryland Plan sounded a patriotic note.[11]

"Attempts to merge university and state cultures were short-lived, highly resisted, and ultimately unsuccessful."

"Walt would sometimes quote St. Paul's Epistle to the Corinthians," says Nyman, "about recruitment as having four components: belief in the cause, belief that something better will evolve in the future, flexibility: be everything to everyone, and fellowship."

Everyone wondered, Would it work?

Nyman recruited other key personnel from the school's faculty to help run the MHA. Henry Harbin, who created the position of state training director, would later have Nyman's job, and so would Nyman's deputy director, Alp Karahasan, a thirty-one-year-old MD–PhD who had both "impeccable credentials in research and child and adolescent psychiatry" and a winning personality. "It was impossible to be angry with Alp," says Nyman. "He was uniformly loved, respected, and admired."

"It was a challenge," said Karahasan. "The chronically ill patients were getting no care. The role of the physician had deteriorated into a minimal duty person who just signed prescriptions. It was horrendous." But, he told a reporter, it was also an opportunity for an "aggressive, arrogant but competent bunch of people" to test the system. "We had our roots in the 1960s student movement. . . . We smelled blood a little bit. There was going to be an old school–new school fight as people-oriented physicians took over."[12]

"Frankly, I didn't really know what an MHA director was 'supposed' to do," says Nyman. "For example, at the time I didn't even know that unused funds from the hospitals couldn't readily be shifted to community programs to 'follow the patients being discharged.' I had just come from being director of a small, academic community mental health center, with a $250,000 budget and ten employees. Almost overnight, I was the thirty-four-year-old Maryland MHA Director with a budget of $110 million (in 1976 dollars), supervising over 6,500 employees in eleven hospitals and fifty-plus community programs. Fortunately, I trusted my mentors, Walt and Russ. And their advice and behavior consistently validated that trust, for the benefit of the program and patient care. I gradually learned the job, even going through the Executive MBA Weekend Program at the University of Pennsylvania's Wharton School in 1978–80."

Changing the culture

To improve the state hospital system, where patients were generally receiving inferior treatment, these "inexperienced bureaucrats" with an "antiestablishment bent" had to "replace some of the foreign medical graduates and more poorly trained American physicians on the state hospital staffs with 'the best and the brightest' psychiatric graduates," Alp Karahasan told *Psychiatry News* in 1984. "Attracting them, however, meant changing the way the system traditionally operated."[13]

Well into the 1970s, said Nyman, recruitment of state hospital psychiatrists and nurses was difficult both in Maryland and nationally. "Half of the professional positions (thirteen of twenty-six) in Maryland's MHA central office were vacant when I was appointed. Close to that number of psychiatrist vacancies existed at Maryland's big three state hospitals. Nursing vacancies were

"Our idea was to change the culture—to change the value system."

also a significant problem. Criticism of the quality of psychiatric care in these hospitals was uniform—a national trend. And the MPRC had the same problems. Hospital units were understaffed and psychiatric professionals understandably did not have a community treatment orientation to patient care." Continuity of care for patients released into the community was a luxury doctors with too many patients and too little time could not provide.

Other problems with staff emerged, said Nyman. "I remember going to one facility on a Friday at 10 a.m. and finding that thirteen of the fourteen psychiatrists had already signed out at 4 p.m. A grand jury investigation was already brewing.

"Our idea was to change the culture—to change the value system. Many of the psychiatrists working in the state hospitals previously had higher priority for other work activities elsewhere. They did not value spending time to try to change the hospital's work approach and culture. We brought to the state system a group of psychiatrists expecting to make things better." Starting in a few state hospital units, Nyman and his team began systematically trying to transplant the psychiatry department's idealistic value system into Maryland's psychiatric hospital and community programs in the late seventies and early to mid-eighties.

"One Saturday morning in the spring of 1977," says Nyman, "after I'd been at MHA for close to a year, I was with my son at the Mt. Washington post office and ran into Walt. I remember him asking, 'So when can we begin sending Maryland psychiatric residents out to Springfield?'" Springfield State Hospital was a rural hospital near Sykesville, in Carroll County, about forty-five minutes west and slightly north of Baltimore. With more than 1,700 patients, it was Maryland's biggest state psychiatric hospital.

"'How about Monday?' said Nyman.

It took longer than that.

Krajewski and Book take on a challenge
The first class targeted for recruitment was psychiatrists finishing their residency in 1978. The two men Weintraub chose to begin the program had begun their psychiatric residency

Psychiatry residents, 1977. Standing (l to r): John Carroll, Bruce Regan (inpatient chief resident), Ruth Silvano (secretary coordinator of outpatient clinics), Daniel Freedenburg (faculty, director of psychopharmacology clinic), Stephen Starr. Seated (l to r) Michael Fox, Rochelle Herman, Samuel Adler, Jon Book, Tom Krajewski, Barbara Hulfish (faculty, neurologist), Jay Phillips (outpatient chief resident), Mary Furth.

in 1975, as two of seven first year residents. In their final year of residency, Tom Krajewski, a former high school teacher, and Jonathan Book, who went straight from college and medical school to psychiatric residency, were selected by the other residents and their professors as chief residents—"the best of the best," said Weintraub, "the ones who get all the offers."

Krajewski was thirty; Book, twenty-nine.

"I'm sure Gary Nyman introduced the idea to me," says Book. "He came to talk to me about this project that was going to start up and asked if I would be interested in doing it. I gave it some thought. Tom Krajewski and Henry Harbin—who was a couple years ahead of us and was already an attending psychiatrist on 3F—we got together and each of us said, 'I'll do it if you'll do it.' " Harbin started first, as training director for the state, and then, after going to Springfield a couple of times to meet the people and talk about the plan, on June 28 Book and Krajewski started work at Springfield Hospital.

"Nature abhors a vacuum," says Book, "and we got sucked into the administrative part of this. From the time we were chief residents together, Tom and I were interested in administration—in systems of care and the organization of care, and not only in the assessment and treatment of individual patients—so we quickly took to the opportunities at Springfield, which Gary Nyman chose partly because he thought the leadership there was more committed to the success of the training program—especially Sherrill Cheeks, the division director in charge of the tri-county and Montgomery County units where the training unit would be launched. Gary said, 'There are several people you need there,' and he was right about that." Nyman also knew that the superintendent and clinical director were going to retire, which would give him a chance to promote either Book and Krajewski or people internal to Springfield who would support the training program.

Krajewski and Book were to be the first University of Maryland team working as unit psychiatrists on the staff of the tri-county unit at Springfield, where some of the most seriously mentally ill patients were admitted from Carroll, Howard, and Frederick counties. In July 1978, their residency completed, the two chief residents began setting up the university's first new training unit.

Jon Book got a sick feeling in his stomach, a combination of butterflies and fear.

"Their mission was as straightforward as it was impossible-sounding," reported Patrick Maguire in a long *Baltimore Sun* story. "Take over a ward—about 45 patients—at Springfield, establish new levels of care, and then create a training program that would bring droves of other young psychiatrists into the system. And to comfort them on this quest? The knowledge that ambitious plans like this had been tried before and had always failed. . . ."[14]

The day they started as attending psychiatrists, Book drove out Liberty Road toward Springfield and rounded the bend at Route 32. He got a sick feeling in his stomach, a combination of butterflies and fear. What was he getting himself into? In all their years of training, whenever patients were

Partial view of the Springfield Hospital Center in the sixties

treatment-resistant, they were sent to the state hospital. "We knew these patients would go into the state hospital, but we didn't know what happened to them. They were too difficult to treat, so we didn't have any direct experience evaluating and treating them. And now I was going to the state hospital where we sent all these treatment-resistant folks. I had a horrible feeling that I was making a mistake. I wondered if the treatments I had learned about would work." Krajewski was also having second thoughts.

Starting with a radical change

There was a hierarchy of care among Springfield's patients, depending on the projected length of the patient's stay. Some of the older buildings on the edge of campus held the long-term, chronically ill patients who had little expectation of leaving the hospital and for whom "moral treatment" had been the original objective when the buildings were new. Patients who were likely to respond to treatment and to be able to return to the community after a moderate- to long-term course of treatment were assigned to convalescent cottages—so called not because they looked like cottages (they looked more like two-story school buildings) but because patients were expected to stay there for months, not years.

The convalescent cottages were open cottages. New patients were taken to admission units, which were locked.

The training unit would not work with the hospital's entire patient population. It would start with a carefully selected group. Cheeks had already decided that if the first training unit was going to be an admission unit for acutely ill patients, it would be better to start in a locked building where the patient rooms and the day area were all on the first floor, making it easier to observe and supervise the patients. As they expanded the number of training units, they would add convalescent cottages.

The tri-county unit, where they launched the training unit, consisted of two contiguous admission units plus two convalescent cottages that held forty patients each.

They started with the two contiguous admissions units, limiting the number of patients in them to forty-two. Then, says Book, "We did a couple things that were innovations here, not because we were trying to be innovative but because we wanted to make this work." The units at Springfield were segregated by gender, and "what we did was open the doors, allowing men and women in two contiguous units to share the whole space of the two units, which offered some advantages and some disadvantages." Letting men and women share space in the training unit demonstrated concretely that "this is not just a training unit. Something different is happening here." Women still slept in the women's section and men in the men's section, but in the daytime they shared the same space.

"The reaction from most of the staff on the units was supportive," says Book. "There was some concern about whether everybody would have to let men and women share space, which they did eventually. The admission units made the change fairly quickly in state hospital time. The long-term units took years. They were introducing several changes at once, with some resistance from outside the units. Krajewski and Book did what they could within the limits of the state hospital culture, but, says Krajewski,

"This is not just a training unit. Something different is happening here."

"Our psychiatric training unit worked because it was isolated from the other units, because it was different. And in fact we preferred to stay isolated—to stay away from all the conflict. That posed some problems. If we needed to transfer a patient into another unit, it wasn't always easy—we really had to make our case. At the time we thought it was because we were the golden boys, but I found out over the years that we were just being exposed to the same kind of routine day-to-day conflict that goes on in all state facilities, where everybody feels that they're getting the worst of the worst and when you're trying to transfer somebody they feel like you're trying to get away with something. Any time you need to transfer somebody for whatever reason, it may make sense for the patient, but there's a lot of paranoia in the state hospital: 'If that patient's so good, why don't you keep them? Why would you want to dump a difficult patient? You're trying to give me the worst patients and you keep the easy ones.' When I retired, the same kind of dynamics were still going on in the state facilities. I'm not sure it'll ever change. I think it's human nature."

During that first year they recruited to expand first into the open tri-county cottages and then into Montgomery County admissions and open cottage units. The training itself remained on the tri-county admission units. They were trying to recruit mostly graduating residents from the University of Maryland, but graduates from other residency programs also came. "We weren't recruiting from internal to Springfield, and probably that became a problem, because folks were feeling displaced. As we recruited somebody to a unit, we were asking somebody else to move, which was hard both for the staff and for us."

Within two years of their starting the training unit, Tom Krajewski became clinical director. Three years after their starting day Krajewski became hospital superintendent and Jon Book became clinical director, the job he loved most of all. "Taking responsibility for the whole ball of wax" made things workable, says Book, though

Alp Karahasan, being interviewed by a writer.

perhaps it didn't seem so from some other people's point of view.

Encountering us versus them tension and resistance

Nyman had arranged a meeting with the entire medical staff, at which he was accused of being anti–foreign medical graduates. Part of the heated exchange was conducted in Turkish, as Nyman's deputy, Alp Karahasan (originally Karahasanoğlu), was one of those foreign medical graduates. "A lot of anger was generated as we insisted on a change in 'the system,'" says Nyman.

"Remember, we were fresh out of training and the medical staff was mostly foreign medical graduates; most were well older than we were," says Krajewski.

Several dynamics played out among the medical staff. There was the dynamic of university versus public sector staff. There was the town–gown culture clash: the ivory tower psychiatrists versus the practical how-do-you-provide-services-to-people public psychiatrists. And there was tension between the American medical school graduates and the foreign medical school graduates, says Book, "which had a lot of feeling to it. The foreign medical graduates felt discriminated against and said so openly. These issues overlapped, and it was hard for people to get a helpful perspective. Dr. Weintraub came out on more than one occasion and said to the physicians here, 'This is not an American versus foreign medical graduate issue. I'm a foreign medical graduate, as are other doctors doing their residency at the University of Maryland.' In part it was a culture clash, in which they were asking, 'Were people from other cultures and other backgrounds, including other training experiences, valued any longer, or only those who had followed a particular path?'"

Dr. Deusdedit Jolbitado, who was the director of education at Springfield in 1978, when Krajewski and Book came, had been not only director of the autonomous psychiatric residency training program but also director of the continuing medical education program at Springfield. But the residency training program had already lost its accreditation. "It didn't lose it because we came," says Book. "It lost it because the hospital was not meeting the training requirements of the Committee on Graduate Medical Education, the national accrediting body. At one point I took over as director of education, which meant that Dr. Jolbitado—a full-time state employee who was well respected by Springfield's medical staff—was in essence being deposed, both as director of residency training and as director of continuing medical education. He moved on to other roles at the hospital, but he certainly felt underappreciated."

"They were viewed with suspicion," wrote *Post* reporter Christine Russell. Doctors from the old guard formed a Responsible Concerns Committee to keep an eye on the new psychiatrists. "They saw them as ivory tower people who didn't know how to manage very sick people," said Sherrill Cheeks.[15] Most of the staff viewed the arrival of the two young psychiatrists with fear, skepticism, and resentment, rightly fearing they could lose their jobs. Rumors spread that the state was pumping money into the project. "It wasn't true, but it didn't stop their colleagues, who'd greeted them with icy disdain, from referring to them sarcastically as 'The Golden Boys,'" wrote Maguire, in the *Sun*.

"We started to go to the meetings there," says Krajewski, "and we tried to work with them, but there was a great deal of resistance. They felt like, 'Who are these people who are specially recruited to come in and start a training unit?' I think they were upset that the university didn't put together a training unit using them, but none of them were on the faculty of the university. This was the plan the university put together."

Although the state had a poor training system, some really talented people worked there under almost impossible circumstances, with inadequate financial support, and this new administration was more focused on changing the way patients were treated than on appreciating the contributions of these talented members of the old guard, says Stan Weinstein, a social worker with a PhD in human development who accepted a position as state director of mental health manpower.[16] For their part, the old guard perceived the new psychiatrists as too young, as not having paid their dues.[17]

When Krajewski and Book arrived at Springfield, all of the psychiatric residents and three quarters of the staff psychiatrists were foreign medical graduates, and less than a third of the staff psychiatrists were board certified.[18] After a few years, nearly half of the hospital's forty psychiatrists had been replaced by university-trained psychiatrists. The proportion of board-certified psychiatrists greatly increased over time. There was a lag because they had to be out of residency before they took their boards, but all of the university physicians were certified at the earliest possible date. New graduates were given assistance—supervision and practice—as they prepared to take the boards.

The idea was not to get rid of the old guard, says Book. "This whole project wouldn't have worked if there had not already been remarkably conscientious and capable people at Springfield interested in change. They were already here, they joined in, they saw the Maryland Plan as a validation and a shot in the arm—a validation that public service is a good thing to do, and here come more troops to help, with maybe a little different emphasis or a little different experience and expertise. I didn't feel like we fell into a pool of unmotivated, inexperienced, or inexpert staff. My view now after years of working in the state system is the same as after I'd been here maybe only a year: At one end of the spectrum, public service attracts people who are remarkably bright, dedicated, conscientious, and hard working. At the other end are some who are like deadwood, just waiting for their retirement to come through. And I think there are more of the diligent and conscientious staff than the other, but the nonperforming staff does exist and tends to be able to hide at a place like Springfield, in a way that probably wouldn't be tolerated in a private facility."

Certainly there wasn't a long line of people waiting to assume command. "It's not as if we were competing with a group that coveted positions being filled by Maryland Plan people," says Jon Book. "In my experience, only a small group of people are able and willing to take on administrative

"Only a small group of people are able and willing to take on administrative responsibilities."

responsibilities and are encouraged to do so. Tom and I became interested in administration and systems change as residents and got encouragement from Gary Nyman, Henry Harbin, and Walter Weintraub. It's still a struggle to get psychiatrists to take an interest in the system, and not just in individual patients."

To develop strength in administration, Krajewski and Book also created their own course on administrative psychiatry. "The American Psychiatric Association has a certification program in administrative psychiatry, and we got those materials, identified what one has to show proficiency in to become board certified, and set up our own course. We found experts to cover each of the main content areas and offered the course to anyone who was interested. We probably had eight or ten psychiatrists participate, and after eight to twelve weeks (I can't remember how long) we had the whole group take the exam. Not everyone passed on the first go-round, but they did on the next. It was our way to encourage, stimulate, and support people feeling comfortable in administrative psychiatry. After the first year it expanded and we got more institutions involved, so it wasn't a Springfield-centered project. We did it a couple more times before we ran out of candidates interested in taking it."

Presenting treatment-resistant patients as training cases

Despite considerable resistance from the old guard, Krajewski and Book made progress. "The Maryland Plan worked in terms of what it was supposed to do," says Krajewski. "The goal was to bring residents and medical students in to train. Once you brought them in and trained them in the state hospital environment, they wouldn't be scared to work there. People were scared to work there for a number of reasons. First, the patients are the worst of the worst, there's no question. If you are on the psych unit of St. Joseph's Hospital, let's say, and if the patient becomes exceedingly violent, they'll say, 'Let's send them to the state hospital.'

"Secondly, the residents didn't want to go out there, because they would have been loners: an English-speaking, American-trained psychiatrist basically in a foreign nation. There were two or three American-trained psychiatrists on a staff of maybe thirty, but that was unusual. And there was the perception that those English-speaking, American-trained people were less than adequate and couldn't make it elsewhere. I learned that that was not necessarily true—that some of those people were there for a reason: they wanted to work with the more difficult patients; they found it more challenging."

The idea, says Krajewski, "was to bring people in, familiarize them with the environment, and then try to help them integrate into it after they graduated. Not only was there the education but there was a support system too. And Dr. Nyman could not have picked a better unit to start out on. They were very friendly, it was a good cross-section of socioeconomic groups and a good cross-section of diagnoses, so you saw everything. The patients and the clinical material were far superior to what we had seen as university residents—very disturbed, very sick patients. For example, out there I had a patient who was post-lobotomy. At a university you would not see the chronic, very difficult, and dangerous patients—the classic severe cases you read about in textbooks; they were sent to the state hospital. The really sick patients at Springfield were great teaching cases."

Psychiatric residents, 1978. Back row (l to r): Stephen King, Andrew Rudo, John Carroll, Robert Konkol, Thomas Krajewski (out-patient chief resident), [?], Maxie Collier, [?]. Middle row: Mary Furth, [?], Robert Schwartz, Eva McCullars, Dennis Kutzer, Paul McClelland, Diane Yauk, [?], [?], Barry Rucnick, Meena Vimalananda, Nasreen Hafiz. Front row: David Student, Kenneth Malinow, Beverli Goldberg, Jonathan Book (inpatient chief resident), Raymond Wertheim, Alan Gold, Gary Seligman

Krajewski and Book began their training program. First, they enrolled the hospital residents who had not completed their training in the university's residency program, so they could complete their residency in an accredited program. By July of 1979, seven more university psychiatrists had joined the staff, and residents from the university began going there in six-month rotations. Eventually the students themselves began requesting a stint at Springfield over the once-sought-after slots at University Hospital. "A lot of good residents came through the program, and many of the residents who trained there stayed on and worked there." One of the first residents was Brian Hepburn, who now heads the state's Mental Hygiene Administration.

> *"Well, Jon, we've taken over the administration building," said Regan. "Now what do we do?"*

Previous efforts to lure residents into working for the state had been based on financial incentives. Weintraub was having none of that. As *Psychiatric News* would report, "To lure these psychiatrists into the state system, the residency training staff at the medical school, headed by Walter Weintraub, promised the graduates a lot of hard work, unimpressive salaries, excellent clinical supervision, and administrative protection when some of their innovations were blocked by the remaining 'old guard' staff, Karahasan said. The new staff were allowed after-hours private practice. In addition, the state administration became more specific about appropriate care standards for public facilities as a way of improving care and making work in these facilities more attractive." [19]

Now, what do we do?

In 1980, when Krajewski, two years out of training, was made clinical director of the hospital, he was directing physicians who were on average twenty years older than he. The next year, Krajewski was made superintendent and Book became clinical director. Their predecessors had retired at more than twice their age. The two men took on a second training unit, then a third, until they had five: two acute units, one geriatric unit, one adolescent unit, and one chronic care unit.

Henry Harbin and Gary Nyman persuaded Dennis Kutzer, chief psychiatric resident at the university, and Gary Seligman to join the training team at Springfield in 1979. After a year they made Kutzer director of the tri-county unit.

Book recalls a visit from Bruce Regan, a former Harvard peace demonstrator who by then headed the state's psychiatric education and recruiting program. Regan walked into Book's office, sat down, and said, "Well, Jon, we've taken over the administration building. Now what do we do?"[20]

Book and Krajewski began making administrative changes, relieving overcrowding in admissions wards and establishing new wards with a different focus of care for longer-term patients. They also worked at getting the message out to judges and police agencies and other hospitals that only the truly psychiatrically ill should be taken to Springfield.

"One of the things that became clear to us," says Book, "was that folks were being sent to us for all kinds of reasons, some of which didn't make sense. We were not the best place for every person to get what they needed. There were only three places open twenty-four hours a day, seven days a week: hospital emergency rooms, the jail, and us. If there was any social, criminal, or medical problem, those were your choices. That's still true. If you think of it that way, then there is different decision-making about who goes where, when. There's concern in the country still about people inappropriately using emergency rooms and people going to jail when they ought to be going somewhere else. It is much harder to get into a state hospital now, but the doors were very open when we first came here. I had just come from a setting where I had a waiting list, and in order to get into my training unit, you had to convince me that this was a good training case, so this was a bit of a culture shock for me. Anybody could send anybody here."

Krajewski and Book had to find a way to deal with all the judges, emergency rooms, families, and other state agencies making decisions about patients that Springfield should take—including patients from outside the hospital's catchment area, sent there so they could get the special treatment of a training unit. "We had to say, 'No, no, no, no, no. We can't serve all comers.' We didn't have enough resources."

How did they decide which patients belonged there? "We tried our best to decide based on clinical need: who needed a psychiatric hospital service," says Book. "For example, it was common at that time for homeless 'troublemakers' to be told in an emergency room, 'Why don't you go out to the state hospital, ask to be admitted voluntarily, and as a volunteer patient you can leave if you want. Or, if they don't agree, we'll certify you for involuntary admission.' Lots of people who came to our door had been given that pitch. They didn't have a place to live, and the community mental health movement had been oversold in terms of being able to solve all social problems for people who might have a mental illness. If you were homeless and you had a mental illness, 'Gee, that's your ticket; I can put a diagnosis on a piece of paper and you can have somewhere to sleep tonight.'

"So we had to have this discussion with lots of people, not just judges. Folks would drive family members out and just dump them on our doorstep. That wasn't because of the training unit; that was how it was in state hospital psychiatry. It was a different discussion if a judge sent a person out than if a social or medical organization sent a person out. It had a whole different sense about it when the judge would say, 'I'm going to order this person to Springfield. Did you want to be in contempt of court?' The issues could get pretty heated."

"There is a certain philosophy," Krajewski told a reporter at the time, "that state hospitals should be a dumping ground. Out of that comes a martyrdom complex: 'What else do you expect? They send us twenty patients whether we can handle them or not.' We were the first to challenge that."

"They began refusing to accept former patients who had gotten drunk or lost their paychecks—routine admissions that had swamped the hospital in years past and led to patient reliance on the system," Maguire reported. Police agencies were angry at first, as were judges and other social and health care providers and agencies that began getting calls from the two doctors explaining why a referral was inappropriate. They offended some traditions, but they cut back on inappropriate admissions.[21]

The number of patients confined at Springfield was reduced by 30 percent, with hospital psychiatrists coordinating follow-up care with neighborhood community health centers.[22] Krajewski and Book institutionalized a system that Cheeks had initiated, providing more continuity of care, assigning a single staff member to follow each patient. "In the old days," Cheeks told the *Post*, "people who made all the noise got all the attention. That does not happen anymore. The [new] system provides for no patient being overlooked."[23] Over five years they had fewer violent assaults, fewer locked wards, and fewer patients needing seclusion after violent episodes.

Residents working in the state's psychiatric hospitals were assigned only five patients. "In the old days," said Regan, "a resident could be given responsibility for as many as sixty patients at one time. It used to be all service and no learning."[24] Still, many of the residents supplemented their clinical work with research and teaching assignments at the university.

Many patients were reevaluated and their diagnoses, medications, and treatment changed. Rather than assume that a long-term patient diagnosed years before as incurable was indeed incurable, they did a complete review of the patient histories in their units. New diagnoses were sometimes applied to old patients and those who had been in and out of hospitals. Many patients diagnosed with schizophrenia and hospitalized for decades, for example, were found to have been consistently misdiagnosed. In some cases, the drugs routinely prescribed for schizophrenia were actually masking symptoms of what was called at the time manic–depressive syndrome, more commonly called bipolar disorder now—a mental illness that was by then found often to respond to lithium, which meant some of those patients could leave the hospital.

"Many patients had been misdiagnosed. Many were overmedicated."

Many patients were simply overmedicated. Book reviewed the record of one patient who had been on a locked ward, depressed and confused, banging her head on the floor. She had been in the hospital a long time, diagnosed with schizophrenia. His review of her record suggested that her erratic behavior became more frequent as her drug doses escalated. As she began to feel bad or anxious, she would be given more medication and would get worse. Low doses seemed to help her but higher doses caused confusion. Book stopped all her drugs. "Suddenly she looked like a nice old lady who could talk coherently," Book said. "After a couple of months of being quite stable she said, 'I really don't need to be here,' and left. She'd been in the hospital for twenty years.

"It's not that we brought some brilliance out here that didn't exist before. There were smart and well-intentioned people here who were terribly overworked in an impoverished, under-resourced system. One of the advantages of having students come here was that they could take the time to go back through a lot of records and paperwork and sort things out, taking the long-term view. One of the advantages of bringing academics here was questioning, 'Well, if it hasn't been going well, what's wrong? Maybe we're not thinking about it right.' It wasn't that a lot of new resources were infused into the system—but some new resources were infused. And certainly new people who were ready to take a fresh start came in and got to pay new and different and additional attention, so of course some things were discovered."

"I remember one gentleman who had spent pretty much all of his days on his hands and knees," says Krajewski. "He was diagnosed with schizophrenia, with a secondary diagnosis of pica, which meant that if a cigarette butt was dropped, he would go on all fours, grab it, and eat it. He would eat anything that fell on the floor. I said to Erica Dibietz, a respected social worker at Springfield, 'I don't know if this guy's the ideal candidate to put in the community. What's he going to do, go on the streets and eat out of the gutter?' Well, the social workers started to work with him. They took him for bus trips, and we adjusted his medications, because when somebody goes into the community they get very anxious. This gentleman literally went from crawling around on the floor all day long to doing a volunteer job in Frederick. He was able to take the bus on his own, he lived in a supervised facility, and he was off all fours. It was almost as if, 'We don't expect you to do that anymore.' That patient was treated with a combination of medication and talk therapy. That's where I think psychiatry's real future is. You really need both. Many times medication alone is just not the answer."

Springfield added treatments: family therapy, group therapy, art, dance, psychodrama, vocational rehabilitation, and instruction in basic living skills. Patients had more access to doctors, who took a fresh look at their case records. More effort was put into preparing patients to return to the community and to provide greater continuity of care when they left. Psychiatrists who passed up higher-paying positions to work in the state hospitals liked having a chance to put into practice the theories they'd just learned, with a varied and difficult patient population. "We give our staff the ball and let them try out their own game plan," said Krajewski. "We give a lot of flexibility in choosing therapies, and we try to give a lot of support."

"It was a creative kind of time," says Kutzer. The residents sometimes learned what worked through trial and error. The first year Kutzer was there, resident Bob Atkins had a patient in postpartum psychosis who was "manic as all get-out." They tried lithium, haldol—nothing was working. A year earlier, Robert Post of NIMH had come and given an unpublished paper on Tegretol to the residents, so Kutzer read up on the drug, got permission from the family, and tried it on this woman. In three days she was better. Kutzer was supervising Atkins for the medication, an analyst was supervising him for psychotherapy, and someone else was his family therapy supervisor. The family therapy supervisor said she got better because Kutzer shifted family dynamics. The analytic supervisor said it was a transference cure. Kutzer said, "All right, let's see."

The traditional hopelessness associated with state hospitals was replaced with "a surprising degree of hope."

Jon Book, speaking at a lunch for Springfield volunteers in 1985. David Chasen, clinical director at Springfield is seated to the left of Book. "They were too young to know that what they wanted to do was impossible."

They took her off the medication and in forty-eight hours she was sick again. Now they knew what would work.

The traditional hopelessness associated with state hospitals was replaced with "a surprising degree of hope."

Commissioners of mental health in other states began holding Maryland up as a model for getting psychiatrists trained in American universities into the public system. "Previously, service in the state system was not highly regarded; people thought that the best psychiatrists went into private practice. But in Maryland today the state system is one of the prestigious places to go. It's a remarkable reversal," said Dr. Harold McPheeters, director of the Commission on Mental Health and Human Services of the Southern Regional Education Board, Atlanta.[25] McPheeters told the Post about the "brash optimism" he'd encountered on a visit to Maryland. "Obviously that kind of enthusiasm makes it work. Most states have been having a real problem in losing psychiatrists from the state system. Maryland is gaining young, American university–trained psychiatrists. It's a very impressive countertrend to what's going on nationally."[26]

"They were exceptional people and first-class shrinks," said Gary Nyman. "They were willing to gamble, to take a chance."

"They were too young to know that what they wanted to do was impossible," said Walter Weintraub.

Other changes in staffing and services

With Krajewski and Book rapidly promoted to administrative positions overseeing the work of all the departments, they were able to attract trainees in all the disciplines to the training units. Within Springfield, staff were given a choice about working on the tri-county or Montgomery County training units. Staff could either volunteer or be asked to be moved out. Some found the training atmosphere challenging, interesting, and desirable. It wasn't just in psychiatry that there was excitement, enthusiasm for change and innovation, and some academic support for looking for better ways to do things—allowing for experimentation and creativity, pushing back against those who will push against any change, says Book. They had little trouble attracting new staff in nursing, social work, psychology, social work, and occupational therapy.

Nursing all over the country was becoming more professionalized—more based in the academy, says Book. Nurses came from various streams of training—in particular, the registered nurses, who went to a university and got a bachelor of science degree in nursing, and the so-called diploma nurses, whose training was more in-house, hospital-centered, and clinically based. The head of Springfield's department of nursing was about to retire, and Kay Sienkilewski, the new director of nursing, was a master's-level clinical nurse specialist. She then recruited other clinical nurse specialists into the nursing leadership. Both the master's level in nursing and the clinical nurse specialists in psychiatry were fairly new then, so nursing had its own excitement and links to academia. By 1983, it was hard to find a staff opening at the hospital, and the qualifications for nurses improved. From 7 percent registered nurses in 1979 the number rose to 21 percent in 1983, there were no openings for nurses, and the last twelve nurses hired had master's degrees.[27]

Springfield's department of social work already saw itself as an innovator in psychiatric social work. Henrietta DeWitt, an untrained social worker assigned to Springfield in the 1930s who later trained at the University of Pennsylvania, had helped establish psychiatric social work as a major discipline in Maryland's mental hospitals. In the late 1940s and early 1950s, after the "Maryland's Shame" article brought more funding to the hospital, DeWitt helped establish one of the first foster home care programs in the country—placing youths who could not live at home in homes with foster parents who had been trained to provide a structured environment that would help them learn social and emotional skills.[28]

It was great good luck, says Book, that as the Maryland Plan started and gained strength, the state also brought Gail Fidler in from New Jersey as a specialist in psychiatric occupational therapy to consult with the Mental Hygiene Administration about modernizing and professionalizing rehabilitation services for the whole state. Guided by Alp Karahasan, Fidler selected Springfield as the place to start such a training unit. Previously, says Book, state hospitals had used activity therapy—chiefly arts and crafts (basket weaving, beadwork, and the like)—to teach patients how to make productive use of leisure time. Patients with severe and persistent mental illness have generally spent a lifetime not using their leisure time well, so activity therapy was important for them.

But psychiatric occupational therapy, as Fidler helped develop it at Springfield, paid more attention to developing meaningful skills—not just leisure skills, but how to make your bed, take a bath, go to the grocery store, plan a menu, shop for food—all the practical skills you need to live in the community. After all, the federal government was funding community mental health programs and depopulating the state hospitals but the people leaving those hospitals either never had learned or had to relearn skills needed for living well in the community. Someone who had spent the better part of a lifetime in a state hospital needed to be taught how to find a bus stop, get on the bus, and put money in the fare box—not to mention the vocational skills needed to make money. Fidler developed a solid training unit in rehabilitation services and was also good at developing academic relations, so after thirty years Springfield is still getting trainees from all over the country in psychiatric occupational therapy.

What changed at Springfield and elsewhere

"What changed," says Krajewski, "was that the people here in the psychiatry department had a place to go practice on a different kind of patient." This is odd to talk about now, but "going back thirty years, you could spend a year on the units at University Hospital and never see a patient with the neuropsychiatric problems of tertiary syphilis or a patient with Huntington's chorea," says Book. You would see these and more at the state mental hospitals, which was where tertiary care in psychiatry was done in 1978.

"And the American-trained psychiatrists provided much better care," says Krajewski. "You may find debate with the foreign medical graduates, but the fact is, we were bringing in young, energetic people. The folks who were there—I'm not saying they were not intelligent or well trained, but they were burned out. The young psychiatry residents were more energetic. You got more sense of hope. After you work with those patients for such a long time I can understand where you lose that sense of hope, and you could see it in their faces: 'Well, what do you expect?' When you're dealing with psychiatric patients, that's not the kind of attitude you want to contribute. They may deny that they were that way, but that's what they appeared to me. Not all of them, but with a handful of them, they would throw their hands up: 'I guess the [difficult patients will] be here forever.'

"But they weren't there forever. Springfield's patient population peaked in the mid-1950s at about 3,600. When I took over the hospital we had almost 1,600 patients. When I left the hospital [four years later], we were down to about 1,300. When Jon Book took over after me, that census came down more. The census at Springfield today is in the 200s, Spring Grove's census is in the 400s. They may say this is due to other factors, but I think the Maryland Plan played a substantial role, because we put people in who energized the process of getting patients back into the community. And these patients were not just discharged to the street.

"In 1978, tertiary care in every discipline but psychiatry was provided in university hospitals," says Jon Book. "In 1978, if you wanted involuntary admission of a psychiatric patient too difficult for University Hospital or Hopkins to handle, you took them to a state hospital. That made state hospitals the perfect place for inpatient residency training. Today University Hospital and Hopkins are taking on more of the sicker patients."

They had supervised housing, they had all the supports they needed to succeed. Whenever there was a failure, and there were some—patients who would go psychotic in the community and have to come back—I could see the faces of some of those people saying, 'See what we told you?' But many people stayed out there and did really well."

At first, patients resisted leaving the hospital and going out into the community. The staff began "sending groups out to visit shopping centers, eat at McDonald's, ride the Metro, and visit outpatient facilities." They were taken to a "psychosocial rehabilitation center," to learn how to behave like "normal" people. A Frederick group called the Way Station, founded by Grady O'Rear, had set up one of the first community rehabilitation programs in the nation for people with chronic mental illness. Springfield lent them an occupational therapist, who would take the patients out to the Way Station a few days a week to prepare them for moving into the community.

"Whenever we sent somebody out, they had supervised housing, they had a day program to go to, we had their day structured so that they would have the community support they would need to succeed," says Krajewski. "There were not anywhere near the number of homeless you would see in other states and cities where they discharged people without a discharge plan. We had a discharge plan. They always would have somebody: They would have a place to stay and they would have structured and supportive services wrapping around them. We did it that way because we knew that that was the only way they were going to succeed. It doesn't help us to send somebody into the community only to have them readmitted and be back on our service." Funding problems and legal issues interfere with the best of state intentions, says Krajewski. Good local advocacy groups are helpful in that regard. NAMI and the Mental Health Association of Maryland were instrumental in providing community and political support in this endeavor.

Part of Weintraub's deal with Nyman was that the state jobs would be changed to allow creativity and flexibility. The result, said Weintraub, was that from "Cumberland to Chestertown every inpatient mental health facility has been captured by one of these young people."[29]

The state of Maryland was willing to invest close to a million dollars in training under the Maryland Plan, says Weintraub, because "they lived in fear of not having personnel to treat their patients in the state hospitals. The university, in a way, has promised the state that we won't let them down if they have a recruitment problem—that we'll help with their recruitment problem—and that's been enough to satisfy them, at least up until now. Before, the elite psychiatrists (at Maryland, Hopkins, and Sheppard Pratt, for example) never went out to the state hospitals—didn't know what a state hospital looked like. State hospitals were considered as offering second-rate treatment—old-fashioned psychiatry. But most students want to see very sick patients and want to see what a state hospital looks like, with its huge terrain and big buildings. So we began to send our elite recruits into places they had never been before."

At the state hospitals, residents began to be supervised by university-trained people working for the university; they would meet them at the state hospital to go over their patients with them. The state had always paid for supervision of the foreign medical graduates; it now paid for university-directed supervision, all residents got experience with the very sick patients,

Now every first year resident goes to the Carter Center for part of their first year of training, and several go out to Spring Grove. Some who have fellowships can go to the more distant state hospitals, but at least every resident has seen some very sick patients.

and the department's residents got higher salaries because they were treating patients in the state hospitals.

"We had room for everybody who finished training and wanted in," says Gary Nyman. "The state Mental Hygiene Administration system was huge . . . with scores of vacancies. If someone wanted to emphasize behavior therapy, there was a need. If someone else wanted to combine medication with psychodynamic treatment, there was also a need. With more newly trained, multidisciplinary young psychiatrists, we noted that recruitment of psychiatric nurses became easier. Other professional disciplines, at first wary, collaborated with increasing enthusiasm. The pay increases didn't come until later, when administrators approved salary increases, first for nurses and then for physicians and other professional disciplines, as now seemed justified (to the administrators)."

"We had some marvelous people," says Nyman, including Alp Karahasan, as deputy director, and Henry Harbin, who created the job of state training director. Nyman served as MHA director for five years (1976–81), Karahasan assumed the position next (1981–85), and then Henry Harbin (1985–88) served. Tom Krajewski and Jon Book were joined by others like Maxie Collier and Sunday June Pickens. George Gallahorn and Jose Arana continued as full-time psychiatric faculty but took over professional leadership of the state's Walter P. Carter community mental health center, next to University Hospital. "Many, many more psychiatrists joined the Maryland Plan and helped improve public sector psychiatric care," says Nyman. "No one psychiatrist was assigned to begin at a unit alone. Eventually, a critical mass formed, and the culture began to change as a whole."

Maxie Collier

"At administrative levels, like anything else, it's who do you know and who do you trust," says Stan Weinstein, "and do you have to have formal relationships or can you get a lot done with meaningful informal relationships?" The success of the Maryland Plan came about largely through informal relationships and despite the American versus foreign conflict, which went on for years.

In 1981, after he was "asked to leave" as director of MHA, Gary Nyman personally convened and paid for a group lunch in a private dining room in Danny's Restaurant (close to Mental Hygiene's central office), to discuss how concerned psychiatrists could become knowledgeable enough about the system to influence legislation that would affect how the public sector was run. "Do you know who your state legislator is?" he asked, urging the lunch group to call their representatives or go to their offices and meet them. For several years, Nyman's campaign of monthly meetings gave a dozen psychiatrists a chance to learn from each other who the state legislators were, what their positions were, who was interested in mental health, and how to influence them. This wasn't about lobbying for a particular bill; the Maryland Psychiatric Society or MHA itself got involved in specific legislation. It was more about how to educate legislators about the issues in public psychiatry and how to educate psychiatrists so they could participate in policy change. "Gary was an out-of-the-box thinker," says Jon Book. "I suspect there's not another example like that in the country, and it was an important idea in public psychiatry. Gary hosted this lunch through Alp Karahasan's and Henry Harbin's tenures as director of Mental Hygiene—and possibly a bit into Stu Silver's tenure."

The Maryland Plan expands

In 1982, George Balis persuaded Dennis Kutzer to go from Springfield to Spring Grove as clinical director, to help start a training unit there.

Soon after Kutzer started, two Justice Department officials arrived to investigate violations of patient rights— under the previous superintendent and assistant superintendent. Kutzer's team had to redo all the pharmacy forms and change seclusion policy, with the Justice investigators arriving at 2 a.m. for site visits. They also had an asbestos crisis and other management problems. Alp Karahasan, who was director of MHA at that point, helped push through changes, Kutzer became superintendent, and things started improving. Interstate 95 had been built in the late seventies, so you could get to Spring Grove in twelve minutes from the university, and many residents chose to go there rather than Springfield. As Spring Grove's program expanded, Springfield's coalesced into fewer training units.

Dennis Kutzer helped start a training unit at Spring Grove.

Meanwhile, the training program expanded into another state hospital. One Thursday a year or so after Kutzer helped set up a training unit at Spring Grove, Dave Helsel was eating his corned beef sandwich with the other psychiatric residents gathered in the Surfboard Room (so-called perhaps for its oddly shaped conference table) when a senior resident ran into the room, saying excitedly, "Can I have everyone's attention?! I've just received word that we've established a beachhead at Crownsville!" Russ Monroe, the department chair, followed, repeating the announcement. Some of the residents clapped. Many, like Helsel, stared or looked puzzled, having no idea what Crownsville was or why they would be establishing a beachhead there—or anywhere.

Crownsville Hospital Center, near Annapolis, had opened in 1910 as the Hospital for the Negro Insane of Maryland after the Maryland State Lunacy Commission reported in 1908 feeling "shame and humiliation" about the horrible cruelties being practiced on the "negro insane." Howard Norton, in his *Maryland's Shame* series in 1949, said Crownsville had become "the dumping ground for feeble-minded Negro children and epileptics. ... Sex offenders, ex-prostitutes, epileptics and idiots are thrown together with young children who are only feeble-minded or mentally retarded." Crownsville had been integrated in the early 1960s.

Crownsville had not previously served as a training site for Maryland residents, and now Eva McCullars and Phyllis Greenwald were heading up new training units there. Crownsville's administration had just signed an agreement to affiliate with the department's training program, so some of the residents could now expect to be able to rotate there. "Even after the explanation, I still had no idea why that was particularly exciting news," says Helsel, one of many residents who would personally be affected by what he calls the "expansive nature of the department back in the early 1980s, a period that might be called the heyday of the Maryland Plan."

When Crownsville closed (June 30, 2004), its clinical staff and 200 patients were transferred to Spring Grove and Springfield.

"Under the Maryland Plan," says Helsel, "our incomes as residents were supplemented by a certain dollar amount if we agreed, in advance, that we would work in the public sector for a period of two years (I think) immediately after residency. Furthermore, much of our time as residents in the 1980s was spent working at state hospitals." Many residents had jobs moonlighting nights and weekends as on-duty physicians in the state hospitals, and in their last year of training some were encouraged to work in state hospitals as junior attendings. Helsel worked a full year and a half of his four resident years as a resident at a state hospital.

"Back then, residents in psychiatry at the IPHB were being actively encouraged to think of ourselves as soldiers in the battle against the outdated and uninformed practices that were assumed to exist in public sector psychiatry in Maryland," says Helsel. "We were all given the impression that, armed with the credential of a university training certificate, we, the future graduates of the IPHB, would be the instruments through which public sector psychiatry in Maryland would be dramatically reshaped and reformed."

"We felt as if we were bringing the Promethean light of modern psychiatric science to these backwaters," said another psychiatrist who served as a resident in the late seventies and early eighties.

"I'm afraid," says Dave Helsel, "that the Maryland Plan quite possibly included

Dave Helsel, superintendent of Spring Grove Hospital

some unspoken xenophobic elements, since [most] of the long-term psychiatrists at the state hospitals had been born and educated abroad." Still, "the basic goal of the Maryland Plan was to encourage newly trained psychiatrists to enter public service—and in that sense the plan accomplished what it set out to do. I'm an example of the Maryland Plan: I have spent the twenty-three years since I completed my residency working at the Spring Grove Hospital Center." In 2003, Dave Helsel became superintendent of Spring Grove.

Overnight, a role model for recruitment

Most states had been losing psychiatrists during this period. Maryland was gaining them. Several articles in the 1980s spoke of a revolution in Maryland's mental health system whereby, starting in 1976, more than 200 young university-trained psychiatrists chose to work in the state mental health system, and more than half remained in the system more than five years—several becoming ward chiefs, superintendents, clinical directors at various hospitals; some working at community mental health centers; and several holding high administrative positions in the state's Mental Hygiene Administration.

"In the first seven years of the Maryland Plan, young, recently graduated, university-trained psychiatrists were appointed to most of the key central office positions in the Maryland Mental Hygiene Administrations: director and deputy director of the MHA, two of the three regional directors of mental health, and the state's director of psychiatric education and training. From the same cohort of young, university-trained psychiatrists also came clinical director or superintendent, or both, at each of twelve inpatient psychiatric facilities, most of them recent graduates with excellent records but little administrative experience. Successful recruitment continued after Dr. Nyman resigned, four years after launching the Maryland Plan. The program also branched out, trying to improve nursing, psychology, social work, and other aspects of patient care. The university's pool of part-time teachers grew, as the department added about 200 hours a week of teaching time *volunteered* by state psychiatrists."[30]

At a time when fewer students were choosing psychiatry around the nation, total enrollment in Maryland's psychiatry residency program doubled, from twenty-five to fifty. Employment in state psychiatric hospitals "became a prestigious and sought-after assignment for chief residents and other top-notch graduates from Maryland medical schools."[31] Improvements in the caliber of staff affected not only psychiatrists but also social workers, psychologists, and nurses. The number of recruits into public service greatly increased partly because residents working in clinical and administrative settings in state hospitals were strongly influenced by working with competent, contented psychiatrists, especially young, confident, university-trained psychiatrists whom the residents already knew as part-time faculty at the university. "We are getting the best and the brightest new psychiatrists coming out of the Maryland schools," said Henry Harbin in 1983. "We have twenty-seven psychiatrists on our staff who were chief residents; this is a huge percentage."

Editorial, *Baltimore Sun*, 1982

State hospital psychiatry in the United States often is seen as a depressing, discouraging line of work. Too often it has attracted unimaginative practitioners whose vision is even narrower because they got their training in hospitals like the ones for which they work.

Now, in Maryland, this is changing.

Over the past few years, experts agree, the quality of care in Maryland's state hospitals has improved immensely. The key has been getting highly skilled, university-trained psychiatrists into the system. With 87 of the Maryland hospital system's 130 psychiatrists now in this category, these 'first-class shrinks" (in the words of a state health official) are attracting their own kind, and Maryland's high-quality system has enough critical mass to sustain itself. Maryland state hospitals are becoming models for the nation.

This revolution was partly a product of a fortuitous convergence of factors. Young psychiatric residents in university hospitals in recent years often have been idealistic "Sixties kids." At the same time, new therapies have been developed—more sophisticated psychiatric drugs and more precise ways to prescribe these substances; emphasis on treating entire families instead of seeing patients in isolation as though their illnesses had come out of a social vacuum; community treatment to help patients rejoin society sooner.

In Maryland, imaginative officials in the state health department and the University of Maryland medical school seized the opportunity. They designed a new system under which the university would train the idealistic young psychiatrists to work in the state hospitals, and the state health department would support them in creating a revolution when they got there. In 1978, the university began sending psychiatrists to the hospitals although the pay is far less than they would get elsewhere. This has not deterred the physicians a bit. Johns Hopkins University and Sheppard-Pratt Hospital now also are training residents for the program, and Georgetown University has become involved.

Much must still be done. Some state hospitals have improved more than others. The community treatment programs are far smaller than they need to be. Some discharged patients still wander the streets homeless. But perhaps for the first time in this state, most of the people operating and staffing these state facilities glow with optimism. Providing good treatment for the very sickest is coming into the mainstream of psychiatry. That accomplishment deserves the highest praise.

This editorial ran in the *Baltimore Sun*, Sunday, December 26, 1982. Copyright © 1982 *Baltimore Sun*, reprinted by permission;.

Overall, the *Sun* reported in 1982, the Maryland Plan produced "a vastly improved hospital system, an upgrading in the quality of diagnoses of patients there, and the enlisting of young doctors motivated by the prospects of a challenge and not prestige." Mental health professionals from around the country came to Maryland to see what they could learn to improve their own state systems.[32]

The Maryland Plan got a lot of press attention in the 1980s. The highlight of the good publicity for Tom Krajewski was his appearance on *Nightline,* Ted Koppel's late-night news program on ABC, April 1, 1984, when it featured the Maryland Plan. In contrast, "we had CBS Evening News come out and look at what we were doing at Spring Grove," says Dennis Kutzer, "but they were more interested in bashing Ronald Reagan than in talking about what Maryland was doing."

"Reagan had told the Social Security Administration that under no circumstances were they to approve disability payments for mental illness , especially on the first round," says Kutzer. "Patients should automatically have to appeal, and we're talking about people who are not really organized, so they never got disability."

In 1985 the American Psychiatric Association gave the state and the University of Maryland one of its annual awards for outstanding mental health programs. The citation, said Dr. Carolyn Robinowitz, APA's deputy medical director, was for "a program that involves training psychiatric residents, American medical school graduates, at little extra cost."[33]

The secrets of success

What's interesting about why the Maryland Plan worked, when similar efforts elsewhere failed, is what the program's leaders felt was *not* important. Speaking at a conference in 1984 on collaborations between state mental health programs and university psychiatry departments, Weintraub said he was surprised to hear people from other states say that "a similar program would never work anywhere else." The Maryland program was practical, he said, because it was carried out with no major changes in the state mental health operation or in the way the university's psychiatry department was run. Weintraub told *Psychiatry News* that several popular myths were shattered by the success of this program, including the following:

- Low salaries will make it impossible to attract top-notch staff.
- University-trained psychiatrists will not work with chronic patients.
- Psychiatrists won't work in rural areas (the first hospital staffed largely by this new crop of psychiatrists is rural).
- Psychiatrists on university staffs will not go into state hospitals to supervise residents.
- Serious progress cannot come about as long as elected officials can pressure departments of mental health (they still do, he said).
- Integrating training and making state hospital opportunities more attractive are expensive propositions.[34]

The Maryland Plan proved these myths wrong.

The Maryland Plan was Walt Weintraub's brainchild. He was sensitive to the needs of state hospitals in a public mental health system and had a vision for change. As important as his vision, perhaps, was his flexibility. You don't see that kind of flexibility in most medical schools, says Henry Harbin. "When I was the director of the state mental health authority, I tried to forge relationships with several universities for a more limited residency program called psych education, and it was difficult to deal with traditional academic

Tom Krajewski appeared on Ted Koppel's late-night news program, *Nightline.* Dick Springer, assistant superintendent at Springfield, is on the right.

departments except Maryland. We would say, 'We're going to give you three residency slots for the state and we would like you to hire the residents. We want you to rotate people through our program so they get a little exposure to this population and this system.' And some of them would say, 'I'm sorry, we have all our lectures on those three days. We can't free anybody up to come over there that day.' I would ask, 'What do you mean? Can't you move them for two days? Don't you have a little flexibility?'

Roger Peele, Henry Harbin, Governor Harry Hughes, Walter Weintraub, and Chet Schmidt, with one of many awards. "As important as Walt's vision was his flexibility."

"'Nope, we can't do that.'"

Changing schedules was not an issue for Walt, who also felt no town–gown split. He was integrating the VA, the state, and the university and had the leadership to say, "Our mission is to do this right and get good training but be flexible." Any of these departments could have done that, but it isn't the academic way, says Harbin. "Walt had the vision to see that it was a good role for any university, to train residents to work with the patients in the state facilities, because otherwise the residents might not have been exposed to some of the really sickest patients. He also had the vision to see that a state university could be of help to the public health system in Maryland and to say, 'Hey, we'll do this as a partnership.' Other states and universities have done pieces of this, but never to this extent or with this enduring nature." Harbin had recruited Brian Hepburn into the system when Harbin was director of state mental health, and three directors later Hepburn became MHA director. Weintraub taught his protégés how to recruit for the long term.

Another key factor in the program's success was that many of the state agents of change had been trained at the same place. Three psychiatrists in a row who were trained at the University of Maryland became directors of the Mental Hygiene Administration: Gary Nyman (from May 1976 to November 1981), Alp Karahasan (1981–85), and Henry T. Harbin (1985–88). "You could well have said, 'God, they shouldn't have had the responsibility,'" says Stan Weinstein. "They were

Nyman was able to "last" for close to five years by quietly transitioning through three changes in the governorship. The Maryland Plan was launched under Gov. Marvin Mandel (1969–79), gained strength under Acting Gov. Blair Lee III (1977–79), and experienced its greatest growth under Gov. Harry R. Hughes (1979–87) young, inexperienced psychiatrists with no administrative experience to speak of. 'What were you doing, making them directors of a statewide agency responsible for thousands of patients?' But it happened," says Weinstein. "And they turned the system—they really did. Part of it was paying attention to the kind of people providing the services. There was a spirit of 'We're going to make it work, we're going to turn this system around; poor people deserve this.' Part of it was the excitement that it all coincided with the civil rights movement. They still had this sixties commitment to public service."

"It was the mutual personal trust among us (me, Walt, and Russ) that made it work," says Nyman. "Walt Weintraub seamlessly incorporated the state psychiatric residency training program into the department's. Two systems that historically were administratively separate from each other—the state public health system and the university system—warily agreed and then danced together elegantly."

The young leaders of the Maryland Plan had faith in their mission. What made them believe they had more to offer than their predecessors? "Part of their confidence was a result of youth and inexperience," wrote Weintraub and colleagues in 1994. "All were under forty; none had previous state experience. Bright and aggressive, they believed they could create a public sector constituency and obtain new resources for their program."

Many changes occurred because Weintraub and his protégés had established a strong level of trust. But other factors at work created the right climate for change, says Stan Weinstein. The state was under pressure because it couldn't get psychiatrists to work in the system, says Weinstein, and the university was under pressure because it needed money. During Gene Brody's tenure as department chair, there had been a generous amount of federal support. By the time Russ Monroe took over, that funding had dried up. "My memory is that the year Russ became chairman he had to cut his budget by something like half a million. There

"They were young, inexperienced psychiatrists with no administrative experience, and they turned the system— they really did," says Stan Weinstein.

was a sudden and dramatic shift in the fiscal future of the department."

The state had been running its own poor-quality residency training program, which it now stopped doing. There were vacant state positions at all levels, so the Plan leaders could match recruits' needs with vacancies in the system. "We were able to demonstrate," says Weintraub, "that, although the state had had problems recruiting psychiatrists before the Maryland Plan, afterward they had no recruitment problems—we have been able to fill the ranks, and that's very important to the state. The state is very sensitive to bad things happening in state hospitals and having sympathetic people run the state hospitals makes a difference." The attitude of elected officials in Maryland was generally one of "passive support" with limited resources, said Nyman in 1983. "As long as we did it ourselves, they didn't kill it." [35]

The university now got the money the state had saved, which allowed it to expand and move much more into the public mental health system. [36] In terms of cost-effectiveness, the Maryland Plan was a huge success for both state and university. "The Maryland Plan has cost the state nothing," wrote Weintraub and colleagues (1984). "Resources for resident stipends and teaching have been taken from already existing, poorly utilized items budgeted for the same purposes. Bonuses, formerly a part of state recruitment efforts, are not part of the Maryland Plan, so that money is actually being saved. . . . State hospital assignments have proved to be so popular that the university's ability to recruit good trainees has not been negatively affected." [37]

In fact, more and more young psychiatrists rotated as residents to state hospital units, says Nyman. After their university training, they were excited about working on units of their own. Indeed, Nyman, Karahasan, and Harbin remained active part-time teachers of residents even after they rose to state leadership, and as state leaders, they encouraged all state hospital psychiatrists to teach Maryland students and residents half a day a week. "It was the best recruitment tool we had," says Nyman, "as over a hundred new psychiatric staff joined the system."

Certainly higher salary was not the magnet that drew new psychiatrists to the system. Maryland's salaries for psychiatrists still ranked in the lowest third nationally, rising from $35,000 a year to $43,000 a year in the early 1980s.[38] The Maryland Plan was most successful in the years before starting salaries increased, and "doubling stipends did not prevent many recruits from leaving state service."[39] A post-war Veterans Administration recruiting effort based on financial incentives had failed, and from that Weintraub had learned that such surface measures were inadequate. The Maryland Plan team concluded that no recruitment program could succeed without dealing with the morale-eroding problems that caused the recruitment problem in the first place.[40]

Familiarity with and trust in an institution's administration seemed to be the most important factors determining a candidate's choice of program. "Recruitment efforts are hurt rather than helped by strategies that stigmatize the state system," wrote Weintraub and colleagues. "Payback schemes and bonuses suggest to applicants that state service is inferior to other choices. Rotating university residents through inadequate state training facilities will only strengthen their resolve not to seek state employment."[41] There were no major changes in curriculum for the residency training program. On-the-job training in administration supplemented the clinical training residents received. "We believe that ambitious programs in administrative and community psychiatry are irrelevant to recruitment and retention," Weintraub and colleagues wrote in 1984. "We have found that the most effective and economical way of recruiting leaders for state psychiatric programs is to attract natural leaders."[42] In the first seven years of the Maryland Plan, seventy-

"As long as we did it ourselves, they didn't kill it."

three new physicians with university training came to work in state inpatient hospitals—"including about twenty chief residents who could have their choice of jobs elsewhere."[43] By 1984 Maryland was boasting twenty-seven former chief residents among the 116 psychiatrists the state had recruited.

As word of the program's success spread, mental health specialists from around the country came to see why Maryland's program was succeeding. According to participants, several conditions in Maryland made this successful collaboration possible:

- A crisis in the state hospital system and the state's fear that an exposé like the one the *Sun* ran in 1949 could happen again
- A strong level of trust between the state and university leaders in mental health and shared values about training
- Longevity and flexibility in leadership: only three leaders at the head of the state's Mental Hygiene Administration from 1976 to 1988—leaders all committed to basic change—working smoothly with a training director in the university psychiatry department who was there for the duration and who was flexible enough to accommodate irregular scheduling needs
- MHA's willingness to support young psychiatrists in new positions and to offer the university attractive incentives
- Timing—among other things, launching the transition to university-based residency training in the state hospitals when there was a high vacancy rate at all levels in the state hospital system
- First-rate psychiatric education and a large and stable residency program at the University of Maryland
- The beginnings of first-rate psychiatric research at the newly constructed Maryland Psychiatric Research Center (MPRC) under Will Carpenter
- A "we can do it" crusading spirit left over from the 1960s, fueled partly by the confidence of "youth and inexperience"
- A bit of luck

What about retention of psychiatrists in the state hospitals?
The professors who mentored the new state leaders only partly shared their young colleagues' faith in the inspirational approach to recruitment. "They were confident that

combined state–university residency training would succeed, but they were doubtful about the long-term prospects of a statewide recruitment program," wrote Weintraub and colleagues in analyzing the impact of the Maryland Plan for *Hospital and Community Psychiatry*. They asked: "What motivated University of Maryland graduates to enter a highly stigmatized organization? How long did they remain in the public sector? What prompted those who left to make other career choices? Where did they go?"

Here's some of what they learned, as reported in 1994:

Significantly more graduates entered state psychiatry in the fifteen years after 1978, when the plan was implemented (78 of 164 graduates, or 48 percent) than in the eight years before (7 of 57 graduates, or 12 percent). Of these 164 graduates, 135 (82 percent) were American medical graduates.

Of the Maryland Plan recruits,

- 42 of 74 women (57 percent) entered state psychiatry, compared with 36 of 90 men (40 percent)
- 8 of the 78 recruits (10 percent) chose rural recruitment, more than an hour's drive time from Baltimore or Washington (compared with none before)
- 11 of 31 chief residents nationally entered state psychiatry (compared with only 1 of 14 before)

As for retention, of the 78 graduates who chose state psychiatry,

- 35 (45 percent) were still state employees in 1992
- More women (25) stayed than men (10)
- 16 of the 30 psychiatrists who started in outpatient clinics (53 percent) stayed through 1992, compared with 13 of the 48 who started in state hospitals (27 percent)
- Only three of the eight rural recruits stayed with the state ("Four of the five who left state service remained in their distant locations but entered private practice")

What had brought them to the state sector in the first place? In 1992, based on a survey of twenty-five recruits and on interviews, Weintraub and his colleagues categorized the recruits as follows (the average recruit identifying with more than one category):

Crusade leaders. Some of this group were "true believers in state psychiatry, . . . convinced that the incentives for treating the poor and neglected existed only in the public sector. Others were not converts to public psychiatry but were intoxicated by the exercise of power. They wanted to 'shake up the system' and make it more responsive to patient needs."

Seekers of temporary jobs. Many graduates of residency training seek temporary salaried positions while building a private practice. Destigmatizing public psychiatry made state service more of an option for this group.

Middle-level managers. Recruits drawn to administration of inpatient and outpatient units (but not to central-office and top hospital positions) "proved to be among the most stable of recruits."

Sixties-style idealists. Recruits in this group got a chance "to renew the struggle with authority" that characterized the student revolt and counterculture of the 1960s.

Peace Corps types. Some recruits had no interest in a career in public psychiatry but wanted an "experience," a chance to "participate for a while in an intoxicating social movement" (like joining civil rights demonstrations in the South or enrolling in the Peace Corps).

University affiliates. Some recruits were attracted to academic opportunities that didn't require a full commitment to university discipline—"these graduates enjoyed teaching medical students, supervising residents, and spending some of their time on the university campus."

"Reasons for leaving state psychiatry are closely tied to motives for entering the public sector," Weintraub and colleagues concluded. "Crusade leaders left when their attempts to rehabilitate state psychiatry under medical leadership were thwarted by their Health Department superiors. Many 1960s-style idealists left with the crusade leaders to whom they were closely tied. Numerous temporary job-seekers and Peace Corps types resigned after a few years, just as they had planned to do. Mid-level managers and university affiliates were the most likely to stay on because they were able to realize their aspirations in the public sector. Some recruits remained because of collegial relationships and because, after ten years, future retirement benefits made continued state employment a practical option."

Dennis Kutzer, for example, left the system because of his disillusionment with the political dishonesty of the budget process.

Fifteen years after the Maryland Plan was launched, "University of Maryland graduates were still entering the public sector in respectable numbers—about 40 percent of the class—even though the original leaders were no longer directing the program." However, working conditions didn't improve enough to satisfy many recruits, and a majority of the people surveyed—more than two-thirds of the men— left state service. That more women were retained may be related to the MHA policy of "allowing mothers to expand and contract their working hours to accommodate changing family responsibilities."

Among other problems in recruitment: rapid promotion of university-trained psychiatrists up and out of the state hospitals left new recruits inadequately supervised; residents were given permission to teach at the university but their clinical responsibilities weren't reduced, so they had to work late on unfinished chores; and academic psychiatrists competing for residents to supervise were favored, which the psychiatrists without trainees resented, creating a class system and lingering resentment.

The fact is, change was not complete. "A university culture crept more and more into the state culture," wrote Pearl Katz, but ". . . many aspects of the state hospitals have not changed drastically. The conflicts lie dormant and are expressed largely by long-term state psychiatrists who continue to perform the minimum legally mandated actions. The state system of seniority still protects long-term employees from losing their jobs."[44]

One indicator that the Maryland Plan succeeded, however, was that the state was able to recruit an adequate number of well-trained psychiatrists into hospitals, clinics, and administration in the public mental health system. Another indicator was that working in the state hospital was now recognized as a positive career move. Psychiatrists who worked for a time in a state hospital moved on to other valued positions in academia, administration, and private practice. "When Tom, Henry, and I were considering working with the state hospital system," says Book, "we consulted with a number of respected senior psychiatrists. They typically questioned why we would want to do that, with a clear implication that it might be an undesirable choice in terms of career planning. One psychiatrist said that going to work at a state hospital was 'professional suicide,' meaning that it would be seen as a disadvantage in moving back into mainstream academia or into private clinical settings. Clearly it is not professional suicide to come to work in the public mental health system today. It seems odd that that was ever a serious consideration before, but it was."

Director, Maryland's Mental Hygiene Administration

Gary Nyman	1976–81
Alp Karahasan	1981–85
Henry T. Harbin	1985–88
Stuart B. Silver	1988–97
Oscar Morgan	1997–2002
Brian Hepburn	2002–

7

The MPRC Becomes a Center for Schizophrenia Research

The history of the department of psychiatry at the University of Maryland School of Medicine is the story of two cultures. The first culture flourished under Jake Finesinger, Gene Brody, and Russ Monroe, the first three chairmen of the department. But it was Russ Monroe, who arrived in Maryland with the psychoanalytical credentials important to that first culture, who used a few departmental bargaining chips to lure an up-and-coming physician–scientist named Will Carpenter to Maryland to develop a strong center for basic and clinical research. In 1977, under Carpenter's leadership and with the full support of the department and the state of Maryland, the Maryland Psychiatric Research Center (MPRC) began conducting focused research in biological psychiatry, especially on schizophrenia and related severe and persistent mental disorders. The MPRC's transformation into a leading research center focused on the most debilitating form of mental illness attracted John Talbott and Tony Lehman, the two chairmen who, in turn, have led the department since 1985. The culture that developed was the byproduct of a clear and shared focus, effective collaboration, serious intent, and an entrepreneurial approach to research management.

Credit for the transformation that ensued goes also to Maryland's state leaders in mental health, who for decades have supported an extraordinary state–university partnership. There's a reason for the state to be involved in such research, says Brian Hepburn, current director of Maryland's Mental Hygiene Administration. "Historically it's the state and public agencies that have ended up taking care of the most severely ill populations."

The story of the MPRC is the story of an awakening—the blossoming of a research center. "Will Carpenter became director of a floundering research program on a state hospital campus with no direct responsibility for patient care, no brain collection, and no competitively funded investigators," says Tony Lehman, current chair of the department of psychiatry. "The MPRC now has forty-two research beds, three research clinics, a human brain collection of extraordinary quality, several neuroscience laboratories, and core resources in genetics, clinical biology, neuropsychology, psychophysiology, and biostatistics. (In addition, with newly funded resources it will soon have a neuroimaging center dedicated to brain research.) The faculty members Will recruited compete successfully for funding for peer-reviewed studies. The exceptional intimacy that exists between basic and clinical scientists has made MPRC a world-class center for translational research. Will and his staff established a model collaboration with industry, under the largest grant in the University of Maryland's history, creating new opportunities for public science. And Will has been the principal investigator for five NIMH centers."

With its close relationship to the state, the department was always associated with public psychiatry, but Carpenter's decision to take a chance on the MPRC was an important first step toward the department's developing a sharper focus on the training, research,

"Will Carpenter became director of a floundering research program on a state hospital campus with no direct responsibility for patient care, no brain collection, and no competitively funded investigators."

Will Carpenter (shown here in 1981) wanted to play pro football more than he wanted to go to medical school, but "playing for money on Sunday instead of doing what you're supposed to do just seemed wrong. I couldn't do it."

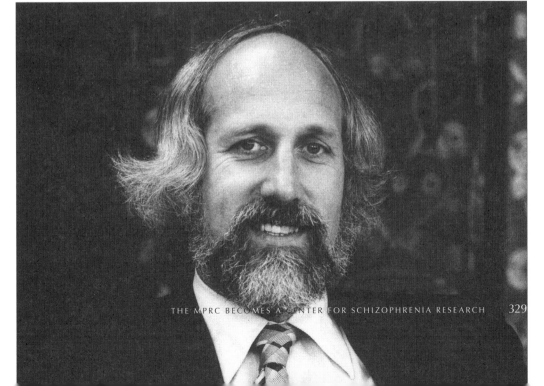

and clinical care needed to help patients with chronic and severe mental illness—in particular, schizophrenia.

A change in paradigm

This part of the department's story, then, starts with William T. Carpenter Jr., who arrived in Maryland in early 1977. At six foot six, the biblically striking former athlete was hard to miss. A native of western North Carolina, he had attended Wofford College in South Carolina on a football scholarship—choosing Wofford because it had both a good football team and a good premed program. After playing football (tight end) and basketball in college, he then faced a decision. The Baltimore Colts, eager to recruit him, offered to put him through medical school in Tennessee. He wanted to play pro football more than he wanted to go to medical school, but his upbringing had been fairly religious, and in the end, "playing for money on Sunday instead of doing what you're supposed to do just seemed wrong. I couldn't do it." (His sport now is tennis.)

He graduated from Wake Forest University School of Medicine,[1] intent on going into psychiatry. "I guess that was my mother's influence, although she was far too subtle to let me catch her at it," says Carpenter. Before college, "Mother had me tested by a psychologist, who told me I was interested in science and music. I had no talent in music but he said I would go into medicine, would specialize in psychiatry, was naturally lazy, and would have to work hard. He was right, of course. There probably wasn't a psychiatrist within fifty miles of where I was growing up, but when the psychologist told me that's what I was going to do, it seemed to fit like a glove. He was absolutely specific, so I now suspect my mother told him what to tell me."

After a medical internship at the North Carolina Baptist Hospital, Carpenter did his residency at Strong Memorial Hospital, at the University of Rochester School of Medicine. John Romano was chair of psychiatry, George Engel was there, and Rochester had a very strong training program with an emphasis on the biopsychosocial medical model. "I loved it there, wanted to be an academician, and knew you needed to find some way to do research and publish. Most importantly, I learned to think critically and avoid ideology."

From Rochester, in 1966 Carpenter went to the NIH—for two years that stretched into nine. Working in the depression unit of the National Institute of Mental Health, with William Bunney, he shared an office with Dennis Murphy, Fred Goodwin, David Janowski, Dave Anderson, and John Davis, testing whether abnormalities in the hypothalamic–pituitary–adrenal axis contributed to the cause of depression in patients with manic–depressive illness ("still the best name for it, although now it's called bipolar"). This was his first experience getting negative results where other people got positive results, but they were working in a stress-sensitive system. "People are distressed when they're depressed and less distressed when they're over it, so whether you're looking at disease or a stress phenomenon was problematic."

At the invitation of NIMH branch chief Lyman Wynne, Carpenter joined John Strauss on a nine-nation pilot study of schizophrenia sponsored by NIMH and the World Health Organization—to determine whether schizophrenia appeared in similar ways in quite divergent cultures. At the time, the main instrument used was the Present State Examination, a lengthy inventory of signs and symptoms. A study had shown research diagnoses of schizophrenia in London overlapping almost entirely with clinical diagnosis. But the results were different when the same study was done in the New York City area, partly because diagnoses in the United States were overly broad and intuitive: "Someone was schizophrenic if you felt the hair on the back of your neck rising." There wasn't much interest in diagnosis in America until there was a pharmacology that seemed to relate to diagnosis, says Carpenter. There was much more interest in getting at what underlay schizophrenia than at symptom manifestations on the surface. Differential diagnosis wasn't as important as understanding

"There probably wasn't a psychiatrist within fifty miles of where I was growing up, but when the psychologist told me that's what I was going to do, it seemed to fit like a glove."

the individual—except at Washington University in St. Louis, which had worked out operationalized criteria and was taking a real interest in diagnosis.

Carpenter worked seven years on the international schizophrenia study. The last four years he was also in charge of an inpatient unit at the NIH Clinical Center, which was recruiting and performing a number of studies with fairly young patients, who were floridly psychotic with schizophrenia but with the potential to get better. In one important study, Carpenter, his colleague John Strauss, and their research team examined patterns of outcomes for patients with schizophrenia. They studied three dimensions of outcome—symptoms, social functioning (or social relationships), and occupational and educational functioning.

Based on that research, Carpenter and Strauss challenged the single-disease model for schizophrenia. In papers published in 1974 and later, they proposed a new paradigm for schizophrenia—studying it as a syndrome with three separate and specific domains (or "axes") of pathology, involving relatively independent processes, each with its own trajectory: (1) positive symptoms of psychosis, such as specific hallucinations and delusions; (2) negative or deficit symptoms, such as flat affect; and (3) level of social and work functioning. "We knew this was critical in treatment," says Carpenter, "because we had seen no evidence that the treatments developed for psychosis so far had influenced these other domains of pathology. Psychiatrists had addressed the problem of schizophrenia by prescribing antipsychotic drugs, but medications effective for the positive clinical symptoms of psychosis, the hallucinations and delusions, didn't affect the underlying negative symptoms and cognitive impairment. And functional outcomes appeared to be principally related to negative symptoms and cognitive impairment."

Carpenter and Strauss challenged the single-disease model for schizophrenia. "We had seen no evidence that the treatments developed for psychosis so far had influenced these other domains of pathology."

European scientists in the twentieth century tried to reduce the extreme variation in diagnosis among patients with schizophrenia—in terms of symptoms, neuropathological findings, and other factors—by distinguishing between *true* or *nuclear* schizophrenia and other psychotic disorders. In Europe, says Carpenter, there was a strong sense that you captured the illness's progression, manifestations, recurrent episodes, gradual deterioration, and end-state defect if you knew how to identify and differentiate between nuclear or true schizophrenia and pseudo schizophrenia. You made that diagnosis using Kurt Schneider's influential system of first-ranked symptoms or the similar approach used by Gabriel Langfeldt. Nuclear schizophrenia was defined in terms of symptoms of reality distortion—especially hallucinations and delusions—and these mid-century distinctions would be reflected in DSM-III, the third edition of the *Diagnostic and Statistic Manual of Mental Disorders*, released in 1980.

"Everyone in the international pilot study of schizophrenia except John Strauss and me seemed to know that Schneider's first-rank symptoms defined a disease entity," says Carpenter. "We were young and probably didn't know that much but we thought that if we were doing this study we ought to measure developmental history and different prognostic factors from before the illness. The other countries didn't agree.

"In the United States, there had been more emphasis on the difference between good-prognosis and poor-prognosis schizophrenia and associating those concepts with developmental history, some of which fit with our

The Schneider and Langfeldt systems were a radical change from Kraepelin's earlier concept (1896) of "avolition combined with dissociative pathology," says Carpenter. Emil Kraepelin in the late nineteenth century had identified the two main "functional psychoses" as a single-disease entity with two constructs: dementia praecox (what we call schizophrenia, which tended to have an earlier onset and ran a deteriorating course) and manic–depressive psychosis (which had a better prognosis and a more episodic course). Dementia praecox had different phases and might manifest itself differently over time, but Kraepelin saw it as a single disease, whose main features were dissociation within thought, between thought and action, and between thought and emotion. He spoke also of the weakening of the wellsprings of volition, which leads to emotional dullness, a lack of drive, willfulness, and engagement. He associated a diagnosis of dementia praecox with a poor outcome.

Eugen Bleuler saw dementia praecox not as a disorder with underlying dementia but as a disorder with variable features, with dissociative pathology present in all cases. He renamed the syndrome schizophrenia, based on the dissociation within thought and between thought and emotion and between thought and behavior. With dissociative pathology as the core condition essential to all cases, hallucinations and delusions were viewed as secondary phenomena.

Adolf Meyer, at Johns Hopkins, saw schizophrenia emerging when a patient with a biological predisposition experienced the kind of environment and life events that would produce illness. Life events alone, he believed, would not produce schizophrenia, but given that predisposition the illness could develop in reaction to life events.

work. We quickly pulled items from existing prognostic scales,[2] and were the only one of nine countries to measure prognostic factors. When it came to measuring the two- and five-year outcomes, we thought we ought to have a diversified measurement of outcome—that it was not enough just to know how psychotic the person has been and how long they've been in the hospital during the last two years. We also wanted to know something about their social and occupational function. Investigators from other countries did not believe this was necessary."

Carpenter and Strauss looked at patterns of outcomes for people with schizophrenia, in particular along these three dimensions of outcome: symptoms, social relationships and functioning, and occupational and educational functioning. They found that those domains tended to be independent of each other—that, for example, a patient might experience a reduction in symptoms yet no improvement in their social or work functioning. Or their work functioning might improve but they might show no improvement in their symptoms. At the time, this "deconstructing of schizophrenia," as a syndrome that can be subdivided, was a new concept.

A similar process is probably true for many brain diseases—indeed, many diseases, period, says Robbie Schwarcz. This creates problems for innovative treatments. What incentive does a drug company have to spend $800 million on the development of a new drug that will work for only a very select patient population?

The discovery of separate dimensions of outcome suggested that there were also probably separate dimensions of pathophysiology and etiology.

DSM-III, then in development, was being influenced both by the work being done at Washington University and by the Europeans—especially the Schneiderian first-rank symptoms, which were thought to indicate the presence of schizophrenia: for example, hearing your own thoughts spoken aloud, hearing two or more voices maintaining a commentary about you in the third person, hearing a voice comment on your actions as they're taking place, experiencing your actions as being caused by external influences. But Strauss and Carpenter's studies were showing this paradigm to be inadequate. "In the first place, these symptoms occurred in other psychotic illnesses (including manic and depressive conditions) and were not unique to schizophrenia," says Carpenter. "They were more prevalent in schizophrenia but it wasn't clear how much of that was because that's how doctors were taught to diagnose.

"More important, dividing our broadly diagnosed schizophrenics into true and pseudo schizophrenia using the Schneiderian or Langfeldt criteria made absolutely no difference in predicting outcome, nor was it associated with the developmental picture. Instead, we found that the pattern of psychosis predicted the future pattern of psychosis, the pattern of social relationships during development predicted future social relationships, the pattern of educational and occupational role functioning predicted future success or failure. It didn't matter whether the patient had true schizophrenia or pseudo schizophrenia."

The medications in common use were relatively effective for the clinical symptoms of psychosis, the hallucinations and delusions, but had no effect at all on the patients' underlying cognitive impairment or their capacity to function well in the world. Those functions seem to be affected by some other underlying pathophysiology.

There were many exchanges of letters and criticism after the 1974 paper by Strauss and Carpenter came out. They were proposing a paradigm change, which took the field a while to accept. "We didn't have the slightest influence on DSM-III, except that they did add axes four and five, which were supposed to somehow capture the functional outcomes. In our own studies, we found the most discriminating symptoms to be flat affect, poor rapport, and poor insight, not the Schneiderian symptoms." Bob Spitzer, who was in charge of DSM-III, told Carpenter, "Those can't be judged reliably." Carpenter argued that if they hadn't

"We thought it was not enough just to know how psychotic the person has been and how long they've been in the hospital during the last two years. We also wanted to know something about their social and occupational function. Investigators from other countries did not believe this was necessary."

been reliable, they wouldn't have come out in the analysis. "It was more a question of attitude about what's in and what's out. I think everybody now considers the outcome of schizophrenia to be heterogeneous—that you have to look at different functional areas, which are not predicted very robustly by psychosis. Even with the negative symptoms added back as criteria in DSM-IV (published in 1994) you could still be diagnosed with schizophrenia if you had just Schneiderian first-rank symptoms."

Launching state research on schizophrenia

Carpenter left NIH in 1975 and, after eighteen months working with Ed Sachar on neuroendocrine approaches to understanding the brain (at Jacobi Hospital and Columbia, during a New York fiscal crisis), he applied for an opening at Spring Grove Hospital in Maryland. Carpenter knew that taking such a position was risky. He would be a member of the faculty of the University of Maryland School of Medicine and director of the MPRC. "Knowledgeable people advised me against it," he says, "and for good reason: Science just doesn't work in state systems and on state hospital grounds." Colleagues warned him that the state could just come in and shut a group down, so he knew it would be difficult to recruit good people to a state hospital. Some research units in state hospitals had been good for the state, the system, and increasing awareness, but not so good at advancing knowledge. Spring Grove had been one of several centers at which controlled studies with chlorpromazine (Thorazine) were done in the 1950s, so the hospital had used the new antipsychotic drug well before it was in widespread use. But Carpenter was not interested in being at a site where pharmaceutical companies tested drugs. He wanted to assume intellectual leadership in contributing

Carpenter was not interested in being at a site where pharmaceutical companies tested drugs. He wanted to assume intellectual leadership in contributing new knowledge or developing new compounds and therapeutic approaches.

new knowledge or developing new compounds and therapeutic approaches.

Carpenter kept thinking about what John Romano used to say at Rochester: "The best people end up in Park Avenue practices, when our patients are in these large state hospitals and communities. We should be devoted to the care and study of persons with schizophrenia, which is our lead disease." The message had registered deeply, and, says Carpenter. "When I finally landed here on the grounds of a state hospital with a focus on schizophrenia, I could finally relax and feel like I was doing the right thing."

For his part, Russ Monroe said, some years later, "I knew of Will Carpenter's work, and I knew that he was ripe to move, so I was right there, ready to grab him."

Carpenter arrived at the Maryland Psychiatric Research Center, on the grounds of the Spring Grove Hospital Center, early in 1977, ready to lead the MPRC to greatness. He had a building and a few scientists whose contracts he did not plan to renew. He had an initial budget of under a million dollars, which was literally a line item in the state budget, subject to elimination. "I was about forty-one," says Carpenter, "I

Monroe is grinning as he says this, on a video made for the MPRC's 25th anniversary. "Russ's passion was psychiatric research," says Gary Nyman, director of the state's Mental Hygiene Administration during Carpenter's early years at the MPRC. "He wanted the MPRC to blossom, and it did, with his support and under Will's direction. Will Carpenter, newly appointed, commanded our respect and trust. He changed the MPRC's direction, hired first-rate clinical researchers—and the rest has become history. He has done a wonderful job for Maryland, significantly advancing our knowledge about schizophrenia."

Ann Summerfelt's event-related potentials (ERP) lab, with state-of-the art technology in 1978.

hadn't done anything like this except run a unit at the NIH Clinical Center, and I wasn't prepared for it. But certain basic principles were self-evident. There would be a focus on schizophrenia and on growing strength in both basic neuroscience and clinical science. I wanted to develop faculty who were independent researchers but would naturally engage and collaborate with each other. My experiences at NIH had convinced me that you want people who have to succeed on their own, not work under someone else's direction, having their work prescribed in an authoritarian way."

"We started with humble beginnings," says Carpenter. The Friends of Psychiatric Research, a group previously set up as the grant-receiving organization for the center, owned all of the neuroscience laboratory equipment. "Without the gift of this equipment, we would have had to recruit neuroscientists without even the basic furnishings for laboratory work." And before Carpenter could begin hiring new staff, he had to settle litigation with several scientists from the old MPRC, who chose to stay but weren't considered appropriate to the new research program. Carpenter had to get through both litigation and a state subcommittee hearing about staff issues before he could get to work. The judge presiding over the litigation ruled that although the center did not have to give due process to the employees being let go, it had done so. As a line item in the state budget at the time, the MPRC did not have to preserve the slots for those scientists' positions. (On the other hand, its entire payroll could be wiped out by the stroke of a pen.)

The state did not have the flexibility to deal with grant money. When grant money runs out, the jobs run out, and the state was all about protected jobs.

Carpenter's next big task was to recruit cutting-edge scientists to the grounds of a state hospital that had not been doing either schizophrenia research or competitive science (winning grants)—that is, to a center that basically consisted of himself and a building. "It was probably nothing but immaturity and arrogance that led me to think we even had a shot at success."

He used his starting budget to convert the first floor of the MPRC (which was built in 1968) into an outpatient program. As the old scientific staff departed, Carpenter recruited Joe Stephens from Hopkins to head the outpatient clinic.

Doug Heinrichs got in touch from Cincinnati and asked if he could finish his residency in Maryland. He came as MPRC's first postdoctoral fellow, stayed on for nine years, became an RO1-funded faculty member, and was helpful getting grant funding to develop and run the outpatient unit. Heinrichs eventually succeeded Stephens as director of the outpatient clinic.

To build and run his neuroscience program, Carpenter hired Jon Stolk, a funded investigator from Dartmouth. "Jon ran a number of genetic studies on catecholamines in the brain, which involved cross-breeding and carefully examining many generations of animals. It was demanding science. With Jon, we were able to recruit people like Robert ['Robbie'] Schwarcz, who in 1979 joined us from the Karolinska Institute in Stockholm as the first assistant professor and who now heads the neuroscience program. If Robbie hadn't come here, his natural starting point would have been a degenerative disease such as Huntington's chorea (now Huntington's disease) but because he's here he's also interested in schizophrenia."

"From early on, we decided that the neuroscience program should be organized as independent laboratories, to deal with various domains of basic science that could be informative for understanding schizophrenia," says Schwarcz. "The only thing we knew for sure was that it was a brain disease. In the nineteenth century and before, that wasn't so clear; it was the liver, it was bile, it was gout."

Indeed, the MPRC's first NIMH grant under Carpenter (working with nephrologist John Sadler) was a controlled study of whether hemodialysis would cure schizophrenia. Blue Cross of West Virginia had approved dialysis for treating schizophrenia patients, and in Maryland there were advocates for setting up a dialysis unit for schizophrenia patients at an Eastern Shore hospital. Carpenter persuaded people responsible for the state budget to await the results of MPRC's controlled study, the conclusions from which were unequivocally negative. The paper reporting the study results was

Al Kurland, who had successfully advocated for building a centralized state research facility in the first place, and who had been superintendent of the Spring Grove research unit, was retained on staff for two years so he could be eligible for retirement. Kurland helped recruit and evaluate patients for Carpenter's first NIMH-sponsored study. "He was good with patients, good at getting things done, and good managing a protocol," says Carpenter.

accepted as a negative study by the *New England Journal of Medicine*. Most of the press ignored the press conference held the day the journal article appeared, flocking instead to the Chesapeake Bay, where a Russian trawler had hit a whale. "But I think I got some good credit with the budget people by encouraging them to delay their decision about the dialysis center until our study either supported or discouraged devoting resources to it," says Carpenter.

"The only thing we knew for sure was that schizophrenia was a brain disease," says Robbie Schwarcz. "In the nineteenth century and before, that wasn't so clear; it was the liver, it was bile, it was gout."

The state gave Carpenter additional money so the MPRC could run its own inpatient research unit at Spring Grove, and he recruited Carol Tamminga, a young scientist from NIH, to develop it. Scientists in the inpatient program study causes and treatments for mental illness severe enough to require hospitalization and examine the effectiveness of new medications. Many of the patients have not responded to traditional treatments and are willing to participate in research to find out why. What people with schizophrenia got at the MPRC, says Tamminga, was a chance to interact with scientists and physicians who knew the very latest not only about new drug treatments but also about combinations of drug treatments, and combinations of drug treatments with psychosocial treatments. "These are physicians who think deeply about what can be helpful to people with schizophrenia," she says.

"The MPRC was a very special place," says Tamminga. "I spent a marvelous twenty-five years there. We were associated with the university's department of psychiatry but were located on the grounds of a state hospital and had people from the state's Mental Hygiene Administration on our governance board. That was important, because it meant that patients with schizophrenia in the state of Maryland were within our network. My research was in one of Spring Grove's wards, and I did a lot of productive work there. Will Carpenter had a passionate interest in gaining new understanding of schizophrenia and finding new treatments for people with the illness."

The University of Maryland medical school was very much oriented to clinical care, so there were years when research, even clinical research, was not highly valued there, says Tamminga. This disadvantage was offset by the MPRC's location in Catonsville, Maryland, just off Interstate 695, the Beltway circling Baltimore. The MPRC is situated half an hour southwest of Hopkins and an hour northeast of NIMH, the National Institute on Drug Abuse (NIDA), and the other institutes on NIH's Bethesda, Maryland, campus. The area between Baltimore and Washington is rich in government, university, and private research. "One value of the MPRC was that we could be nimble in collaborations," says Tamminga. "I did all of my human brain imaging at Johns Hopkins. Many of us did our molecular work in collaboration with scientists at NIH." The Spring Grove campus is also ten minutes southwest of the downtown Baltimore campus, close enough to get there easily when necessary, but far enough from the downtown campus that distractions like committee meetings don't intrude too heavily.

The MPRC was established as a joint program with the state's Department of Health and Mental Hygiene. Russ Monroe had argued for transferring the center with that status. "He felt there was no way to get funded research in the department downtown," says Will Carpenter. "You couldn't create the resources through the medical system. The joint program status is vitally important to us. We have the use of two inpatient units that cost a lot of money, which we don't have to provide. We provide the research staff and faculty. Having all our researchers together on this campus is important for the integration of studies and the collaboration important to translational science."

A center for translational research

A major feature of the MPRC from the start was the combination of clinical researchers and basic scientists working together in close proximity, a pattern rare outside the NIH Clinical Center (where intramural clinical researchers also collaborate in space shared with bench scientists). Clinical

Carol Tamminga established a name for herself with her glutamate hypothesis of schizophrenia.

research was conducted with both inpatient and outpatient subjects. Crosstalk between specialties was particularly important at the MPRC because of the complex nature of schizophrenia, both as to causes and manifestations of the disease. "We did translational research from the beginning, before the term was coined," says Schwarcz. "And when the term was coined, we said, 'Wait a minute. That's us!'"

Everyone at the MPRC is expected to work independently, yet in a collaborative spirit. Some people are doing mainly inpatient work, some outpatient (with humans), and some basic science (with human tissue or animal models), but the ethic of collaboration and cooperation in research is important to everyone. "'Research commune' would not be quite the right way to say it, but we all really worked together," says Tamminga. "There was a high expectation for collaboration, for helping each other out, for sharing resources—far more than at other places."

Tamminga, for example, established a name for herself with her glutamate hypothesis of schizophrenia. Glutamate is an excitatory amino acid that influences most of the brain's neurons. Her hypothesis was that there is too little of it in the brain of a person with schizophrenia.[3] This idea evolved from discussions with Schwarcz, whose laboratory was—and to some extent still is—concerned with the molecular and cellular mechanisms that underlie nerve cell death in the central nervous system, and who had been investigating the role of excitatory amino acids in animal models for the neurodegenerative disorder Huntington's disease.

"To simplify a bit, in Huntington's disease, glutamate is a bad guy (and there's too much of it)," says Schwarcz, "and in schizophrenia, it's a good guy (but there's too little of it). The bigger point is that this is how we learn from each other. That's why I love it here: I learn from my clinical colleagues and they're very open to learning from me, which is not so true in Europe, where I was brought up and where academics are more hierarchical, especially in clinical departments."

"I believe Robbie was the first person to introduce the concept of neuroprotection and maybe the first patent in that area, years ago," says Carpenter. Since the 1970s, Schwarcz has been exploring how *excitotoxic* processes, triggered by an overstimulation of excitatory amino acid receptors, might be causally involved in the pathophysiology of several neurological and psychiatric diseases—especially Huntington's disease, temporal lobe epilepsy, and schizophrenia. "Robbie has been a leader in studying excitotoxicity and neurodegeneration," says Carpenter, "a mechanism by which a brain cell basically gets excited to death."

Tamminga, a clinical researcher, conducted many novel medication studies. Her studies of partial dopamine agonists were the foundation for new drugs such as aripiprazole. She also investigated GABA agonists and their role in treating motor disorders. Like others on the staff, she often collaborated with Johns Hopkins, which has excellent brain imaging, PET, and MRI resources. "They were happy to do experiments with us," says Tamminga. "My team was taking care of the clinical part, but we also had a hand in collecting postmortem brain tissue, which was useful for molecular studies of the illness."

Robert Schwarcz (shown here in 1983) has been a leader in studying excitotoxicity and neurodegeneration, a mechanism by which a brain cell basically gets excited to death.

Discussing the future of schizophrenia research over coffee in the mid-1980s, Tamminga and Schwarcz decided that researchers at the center needed to be able to study the human brain in the laboratory. They set about establishing an unusual and important resource: the Maryland Brain Collection. With the consent of family members, brains are collected postmortem from individuals with schizophrenia or related disorders, with the goal of using the tissue for studying the biological and genetic bases of mental illnesses. Brain tissue from individuals with no history of mental illness is also collected and serves as a control. The Maryland Brain Collection is a collaboration with Maryland's chief medical examiner and is critically dependent on the generosity of organ donors and their families.[4] The tissue is dissected and assigned a code, usually within twenty-four

Bob Buchanan, Robert Schwarcz, Paul Shepard, Rosie Roberts, Carol Tamminga, and Will Carpenter (1995) at Neuroscience Day, an annual day of research presentations at Overhills Mansion in Catonsville, Maryland.

The Maryland Brain Collection, dreamed up over coffee by Tamminga and Schwarcz, is a resource for researchers worldwide. Brains are collected postmortem from individuals with schizophrenia or related disorders, to provide tissue in conjunction with clinical information for hypothesis-driven research.

hours of death, and is then either frozen or chemically preserved for further study.

The main goal of the collection, which is maintained and funded through collaborative studies, is to provide high-quality tissue, together with comprehensive clinical information for hypothesis-driven research. It is invaluable for researchers, in Maryland and elsewhere, but is expensive to maintain, requiring an infrastructure for consent procedures, social workers to interview the family and gather clinical data, and a huge facility for tissue storage at minus eighty Celsius. Rosalinda "Rosie" Roberts, who joined the staff in 1990, was director of the brain collection for seventeen years.

Tamminga, who provided much of the energy for setting up the brain collection, used brain imaging to identify functionally abnormal areas in the brain of individuals with schizophrenia. She would then examine those same brain structures in postmortem tissue from the brain collection to try to unravel the molecular mechanisms underlying those functional abnormalities. Her focus was on the hippocampus, a brain structure critically involved in learning and memory. Researchers at the MPRC and their external collaborators now use this tissue to examine a wide variety of disease-related chemical and genetic defects. They also study the minuscule ultrastructure of brain cells, visible only through the MPRC's high-power electron microscope, to determine anomalies in brain tissue obtained from people with schizophrenia and other mental illnesses.

Gunvant "GK" or "Guni" Thaker joined the MPRC in 1982, completed his fellowship, and then launched a statewide motor disorders clinic. He is now chief of the Schizophrenia-Related Disorders Program (in the Tawes Building, on the far end of the Spring Grove campus), which comprises a first-episode clinic (for young patients experiencing psychotic symptoms for the first time) and a side effects clinic. Thaker and David Ross have tested innovative treatments for tardive dyskinesia (a common side effect of antipsychotic drugs). They also demonstrated that schizophrenia patients have abnormal eye movements and that these abnormalities are particularly pronounced in deficit syndrome patients.

Thaker is lead investigator for B-SNIP, a five-center study (with four other universities) relating genotypes to phenotypes, trying to understand how the risk for schizophrenia, schizoaffective disorder, and bipolar disorder can be transmitted in families, and to identify traits such as variation in cognitive abilities, brain structure, and brain function (intermediate phenotypes) that might be associated with risk for these illnesses.

B-SNIP, the Bipolar Schizophrenia Network on Intermediate Phenotypes. Intermediate phenotypes are biological traits related to genetic factors that increase risk for an illness but do not necessarily result in symptoms of the illness. Because they occur both in patients who have the illness and some of their relatives who do not, they represent an intermediate step in a pathway leading from risk genes to the clinical signs and symptoms of the disease. Carol Tamminga, who worked at MPRC for twenty-five years, is a lead investigator at the University of Texas Southwestern site, in Dallas. Thaker is PI for the whole five-center study.

Alan Breier, recruited from NIMH, directed the outpatient research program for six years before returning to the NIMH intramural research program. He later became medical director for Eli Lilly and Company. Bob Buchanan, who was doing service payback time on the Eastern Shore, got permission to spend

Guni Thaker is trying to understand how the risk for schizophrenia, schizoaffective disorder, and bipolar disorder can be transmitted in families, and to identify traits that might be associated with risk for these illnesses.

a day a week at the MPRC, then stayed on as a research fellow. He has been at the MPRC since 1985, directs the outpatient research program, has been a central figure in MPRC's success with NIH center grants, and is a national leader in clinical trials. He has a particular interest in finding new medications to alleviate the persistent negative symptoms and cognitive impairment associated with schizophrenia—the primary determinants of poor social and occupational functioning, which are not treatable with the currently available antipsychotic drugs.

"We take care of more than one hundred outpatients," says Bob Buchanan. "At any given time, a majority of them are in research protocols." Through clinical interactions, researchers learn what patients' needs and most pressing issues are, and what they struggle with in their daily lives, which informs the research. Elaine Weiner is medical director for the MPRC's licensed outpatient community mental health clinic. Contributing to patient care are a pharmacist, nursing staff, and social workers—and transportation is provided for patients who live in the community. Outpatient care and some outpatient investigators are based on the first floor of the MPRC's main building. Biostatistics, neuropsychology, and administration are upstairs.

"The importance to me of being in Catonsville," says Tamminga, "was that we could fully exploit the hospital setting and the resources of the state hospital. It was important for me early on that I had an inpatient ward available, so I could treat subjects in an inpatient setting. I had the opportunity to take patients off their usual medications. When you are testing new drugs, it's valuable to be able to start from a drug-free baseline, because there's such a huge medication confound. That was an important aspect of the work at the MPRC. As time went on, the resources of the state hospital dwindled and care for the mentally ill changed, shifting almost entirely to an outpatient setting, some of the advantages faded and I began to see the MPRC's separateness from the medical school as more of a problem than a benefit. All of my studies at that time were focused on inpatient work, so it was a disadvantage to my work when there was a shift toward community psychiatry and a lot of the patients left, or moved off campus (though I think it was probably an advantage to the patients)."

Ideally, for many schizophrenia studies, researchers should study subjects who are not on antipsychotic drugs, which can confound the research. "If you are asking whether there is reduced blood flow in a certain part of the brain during a psychological task, and whether this is more true for people with schizophrenia than for controls, you also have to ask whether the difference was caused by the medication or by the disease," says Carpenter. "In studies we're doing now, we're interested in whether the reward system that's so important in learning and in life gratification is heavily dependent on the dopamine system. There is a lot of reason to think it's abnormal in schizophrenia, so we're doing imaging studies that would get at that. But if they're taking anti-dopamine drugs while we're imaging, if there is a true signal we may miss it—because the signal may be caused by the drug instead of the disease."

Bob Buchanan is looking for new medications to alleviate the persistent negative symptoms and cognitive impairment associated with schizophrenia.

Off-medication treatment was not easy to carry out when state support of a dedicated inpatient unit, which is very expensive, started to fade. Also, "we're in an era where everybody thinks it's difficult to justify off-medication research," says Will Carpenter. "I personally believe there is overwhelming evidence that you can do it safely and meet high ethical standards. But I lose this argument. Everybody in the field is convinced it's not worth the effort, because it's wrong to withhold treatment known to be effective."

Carpenter argues that in nature a huge proportion of schizophrenia patients stop taking medications anyway, so it's not an unusual experience for them—what would be unusual is stopping medication under supervision. The disease process doesn't make the disease worse in the long run, he says. Psychosis per se doesn't generally create a long-term problem, unless having a breakdown prevents you from graduating or keeping a job. Moreover, the exacerbations are likely to occur over the next two years. "Almost none of them occur over the next two weeks, so it's unlikely to be a window of high danger. And you can monitor people very closely, so if they start to have a minor problem, you can intervene with drugs, which is almost always effective."

Not only is it an uphill struggle to do off-medication clinical research but the burden of doing business has grown so much, says Carpenter, that "we now have to hire extra staff just to keep everybody in compliance, without any evidence that it's made things safer or better. It costs much more to do projects, and there are many missed opportunities in research. Even for low-risk protocols, gaining approval and maintaining records is a significant burden. Meeting high ethical standards is always critical, but it is unclear that the extraordinary burden of compliance details increases safety or research ethics. Just to get approval of an informed consent procedure can take us six months. Until recently, if we planned an imaging study with NIDA, the research protocol had to be reviewed by a state IRB, a university IRB, and a NIDA IRB—three separate committees, all with different views, and none deferring to the others. We recently succeeded in getting the state of Maryland IRB and the university IRB harmonized."[5]

"We're in an era where everybody thinks it's difficult to justify off-medication research," says Carpenter. "A huge proportion of schizophrenia patients stop taking medications anyway—what would be unusual is stopping medication under supervision."

With funding from NIMH, in 2010 the MPRC set up a dedicated brain research imaging center with MRI capabilities (including a 3 tesla magnet) next to the Tawes Building. Up to now, researchers often worked with cameras, scanners, and collaborators at NIDA or at Hopkins, as the university had not developed research-dedicated brain imaging. "We were successful using the equipment at Johns Hopkins, but it's not the same as having a commitment for such equipment from your own university or enterprise," says Carpenter.

The Tawes Building houses the inpatient-based Treatment Research Program, the Functional Neuroimaging Laboratory, the Schizophrenia Related Disorders Program, and the First Psychotic Episode Program. Some aspects of the analysis of imaging and electrophysiological data are handled in one of the small houses originally set up as residences for caregivers.

Addressing deficit symptoms of schizophrenia

Carpenter and his MPRC colleagues introduced the concept of deficit schizophrenia. Research at the MPRC led them to distinguish between the primary, enduring negative symptoms of schizophrenia (*deficit symptoms*, such as restricted affect and diminished social drive) and the more transient, secondary, negative nondeficit symptoms, which can occur for a variety of reasons but are not caused by the schizophrenia itself. "This is the first time researchers have met the hundred-year challenge to define a disease entity within the schizophrenia syndrome," says Lehman.

The deficit schizophrenia subgroup, with primary negative symptoms, comprises about 25 percent of cases. The deficit symptoms are more likely to provide a basis for meaningful subtyping of the schizophrenia syndrome, and the nondeficit symptoms are more likely to respond to currently available treatments. Those same medications are not effective for addressing the problems of impaired cognition and other negative symptoms highly associated with poor functional outcomes. Certain schizophrenia pathologies (such as impaired cognition and negative symptoms) are observed before psychosis, so developing drugs effective in those domains may increase the possibility of early intervention and secondary

The deficit subgroup was validated with functional and structural imaging, postmortem pathology, pharmacological response profiles, and tests for neuropsychological impairment. Positive (psychotic) symptoms include delusions or delusional ideation, hallucinations, disturbance of association, agitation, suspiciousness, and feelings of being influenced by aliens. Negative symptoms include restricted range and intensity of emotional expression, limited ability to think and speak, social withdrawal, and reduced initiation of goal-directed behavior (often called flat affect, alogia, diminished drive, anhedonia, and avolition). Schizophrenia is also associated with cognitive impairment, disorganized speech and behavior, and poor attention.

prevention—and may be helpful for other classes of disease.[6] Addressing impaired cognition and negative symptoms could improve patients' quality of life and prepare the field to address possibilities for recovery, cure, and prevention.

Brian Kirkpatrick, in the outpatient research program, developed a structured interview that operationalizes criteria for defining the deficit syndrome, enabling researchers to distinguish patients who suffer from primary negative symptoms (restricted affective expression, diminished emotional range, poverty of speech, curbing of interests, diminished sense of purpose, and diminished social drive) from those who suffer from secondary negative symptoms (the result of untreated psychosis, side effects from antipsychotic medication, or the byproduct of living an isolated existence). Compared with nondeficit schizophrenia patients, deficit patients are less likely to have histories of depression and suicide, delusions with social content, or substance abuse, and are less likely to have insight into their impairments. Deficit patients are more likely to have histories of asocial development.

Although conventional antipsychotics (such as fluphenazine, haloperidol, and perphenazine) and second-generation antipsychotics—the newer antipsychotic medications that became available, beginning with clozapine (medications such as risperidone, olanzapine, quetiapine, ziprasidone, and aripiprazole)—are equally effective in the treatment of positive symptoms in treatment-responsive people, there are few options for those who fail to respond, says Buchanan. Only clozapine has been shown to be effective in people with treatment-resistant positive symptoms. For the 40 to 60 percent of those treatment-resistant patients who don't adequately respond to clozapine, the most common practice is to add a second antipsychotic, a practice for which there is little evidence of effectiveness. Buchanan led a large study to evaluate the efficacy and safety of adding risperidone to clozapine in patients who did not have an adequate response to clozapine alone.[7]

Second-generation antipsychotics have brought an increased incidence of weight gain, metabolic abnormalities, and concern about cardiac complications, and schizophrenia patients tend not to receive the best medical care. MPRC researchers are trying to devise more effective strategies to ensure adequate medical monitoring, as well as better interventions to treat co-occurring medical and medication-related conditions. "Should we encourage people with schizophrenia who have gained weight, or have developed hyperlipidemias or glucose dysregulation, to switch to a different antipsychotic, or treat the secondary medical condition?" asks Buchanan. "We are currently conducting a study on the efficacy of adjunctive rimonabant, a cannabinoid (CB1) antagonist, for weight gain and metabolic abnormalities."[8]

Jim Gold has discovered that representation in memory is intact in schizophrenia patients; the deficit is in memory storage.

Jim Gold, who was recruited from NIMH in 1995 to head neuropsychology, studies the functional relevance of neurocognitive impairment in schizophrenia. He has shown the profound effect of impaired mental processing speed on vocational functioning. In cognitive studies, he examines different aspects of memory function in schizophrenia, especially the nature of working memory impairment and the extent to which such impairment mediates the generalized deficit observed in schizophrenia. He has discovered that representation in memory is intact in schizophrenia patients; the deficit is in memory storage.[9] His work has led to new understanding of the reward system and its role in learning and in motivation.

Studying brain dysfunction in the neuroscience labs

To explore and comprehend the nature of brain dysfunction in schizophrenia also requires a broad approach in the basic (preclinical) sciences, ranging from molecular and cellular studies to the examination of normal and abnormal brain function in whole animals. The neuroscience program, which occupies about 18,000 square feet in the main MPRC building, consists of several independent laboratories, organized thematically, along with the Maryland Brain Collection. The primary investigators supervise up to forty neuroscience researchers (junior faculty, postdoctoral fellows, and graduate students) and support personnel.

Robert Schwarcz heads the MPRC neuroscience program and is also director of neuroscience research for the department. His laboratory was initially concerned with the molecular and cellular mechanisms that underlie nerve cell death in the central nervous system. This focus originated from his postdoctoral work in the 1970s, when he discovered that a direct injection of an amino acid derived from seaweed produces a faithful animal model for the neurodegenerative disorder Huntington's disease. As an offshoot of his subsequent work on excitotoxic processes, Schwarcz developed the concept that antagonists of excitatory amino acid (glutamate) receptors ought to prevent or arrest neurodegeneration and may thus hold promise as novel therapeutic agents for catastrophic brain diseases. This was verified in many relevant animal models and eventually led to the establishment of anti-excitotoxin-based drug discovery programs in many pharmaceutical houses around the world. Several of the resulting drugs are currently undergoing clinical trials.

A substance identified in the Schwarcz laboratory as a major determinant of cognitive processes is being used to develop entirely new cognition-enhancing medications.

Since the 1980s, most of the work in the Schwarcz laboratory has focused on the neurobiology of quinolinic acid (QUIN) and kynurenic acid (KYNA), two metabolites of tryptophan degradation with neuroexcitatory and neuroinhibitory properties, respectively. Using a combination of sophisticated techniques, Schwarcz and his coworkers have elaborated many of the characteristics and mechanisms that control the function of QUIN and KYNA in the brain. His most recent work, which is especially relevant for schizophrenia research, has identified KYNA as a major determinant of cognitive processes. This discovery is now being exploited in collaboration with pharmaceutical firms worldwide to develop entirely new cognition-enhancing medications.

Greg Elmer was hired in the late 1990s to launch a behavioral genetics lab, investigating potential causes for schizophenia's high rate of co-morbidity with substance abuse. Working with genetically engineered animals, Elmer's lab and collaborators elsewhere are investigating the potential common underlying mechanisms that might predispose individuals to both schizophrenia and substance abuse. Elmer and his team are particularly interested in issues of drug abuse and reward. These issues are inherently important in a center for schizophrenia research because drug use and abuse are highly prevalent in schizophrenia patients, and diminished capacity in natural reward processing is evident as well. Unfortunately, most currently available antipsychotic medications do little to improve the situation and may make matters worse. Unanswered so far is the basic question whether schizophrenia predisposes individuals to drug abuse, whether schizophrenia patients are self-medicating, or both. The relationships between schizophrenia, drug abuse, and aberrant reward processing are being investigated with behavioral genetic strategies that use studies of gene expression, genetically engineered animal models, brain stimulation, and other behavioral techniques. These studies are designed to lead eventually to novel interventions in co-morbid mental illness and drug abuse—interventions that are sorely needed to improve the quality of life in schizophrenia patients.

Greg Elmer's lab is investigating mechanisms that might predispose individuals to both schizophrenia and substance abuse. Are they related to diminished capacity in natural reward processing?

James Koenig, another independent investigator in the neuroscience program, investigates the impact of hormones and environmental factors on the brain, with a particular emphasis on the neurobiology of stress. Stress is known to contribute to most mental illnesses, but the exact mechanism through which it precipitates or exacerbates them remains unclear. Koenig employs experimental animal preparations to explore the mechanisms through which stress contributes to the development of diseases such as schizophrenia and depression. It is clear from various studies that stressful experiences, especially during critical periods of brain development, can reprogram a number of brain mechanisms, and human studies have revealed that fetal exposure to stressful experiences can promote the development of psychiatric diseases later in life.

Researchers in James Koenig's lab are exploring the exact mechanism through which stress precipitates or exacerbates mental illness.

In the Koenig laboratory, researchers manipulate the prenatal environment in rats to generate adult animals that exhibit an array of deficits associated with schizophrenia. These prenatal manipulations lead to alterations in several important chemical pathways in the brain that are integral to normal cognition and social functioning. These studies, which were initiated when MPRC had a contract with Novartis, are designed to identify novel therapeutic strategies to ameliorate the changes in brain programming induced by early exposure to stress. Possibly these new interventions will benefit not only individuals with schizophrenia but also patients suffering from other neurodevelopmental psychiatric disorders.

Paul Shepard was recruited to the MPRC faculty from Yale to establish a neurophysiology laboratory. He investigates the role of dopamine in the brain's elaborate reward signaling systems. Fundamentally, we learn by responding to rewards and avoiding punishments. There is some indication, however, that people with dopamine-related disorders, including Parkinson's disease and schizophrenia, do not respond to rewards or aversive events the same way healthy individuals do. Shepard (with MPRC's Jim Gold) organized and headed a team of eleven researchers at the University of Maryland at Baltimore, the Baltimore VA Medical Center, MPRC, and Princeton University around a project focusing on reward learning in schizophrenia—for which they received major funding from NIMH. This group of basic and clinical scientists is producing a significant body of research, has spun off several successful NIH applications, and is facilitating many more collaborations within the MPRC and with investigators in the university's program in neuroscience.

Michael Vogel, also recruited from Yale University, established a developmental neuroscience laboratory to investigate the mechanisms that regulate the normal or pathological development of cortical brain circuits. Part of his laboratory focuses on the mechanisms of nerve cell death. Studies using the lurcher mouse (which carries mutant genes for neurological defects or abnormalities) have revealed evidence of oxidative neuronal stress, accompanied by changes in a number of key enzymes and other proteins in the nerve cells. Those changes include a reduction in the activity of the sodium–potassium ATPase pump, which is critical for neuronal function. These studies may provide insight into a number of human neurodegenerative diseases that are linked to chronic oxidative stress, including several types of viral infections, Alzheimer's disease, and motor neuron degeneration in amyotrophic lateral sclerosis.

Vogel also developed a rat model for schizophrenia research in which he disrupted early brain development, based on the hypothesis that schizophrenia is caused by early developmental abnormalities that change synaptic connectivity. In the adult animals, he identified behavioral and functional impairments that are similar to deficits seen in patients with schizophrenia. Eliminating a select group of nerve cells toward the end of embryonic development, for example, causes distinct learning and memory deficits in adulthood, which can be traced to the early disruption of neuronal connections between the hippocampus and the frontal cortex. Vogel has become interested in determining how selective interference with neurogenesis (the generation of nerve cells) affects the development of the brain circuits assumed to be implicated in schizophrenia and other mental illnesses.

Major funding and collaborations

Will Carpenter has been the principal investigator for five NIMH centers: a Clinical Research Center, a Center for

One day a colleague from NIMH on a site visit to Spring Grove took Will Carpenter aside and said, "You've got a sleeping giant here. Why don't you apply to become a Clinical Research Center?" He went on to be principal investigator for five NIMH centers.

Neuroscience and Schizophrenia, an Intervention Research Center, an Advanced Center for Intervention and Services Research, and a Mental Health Center for Intervention Development and Applied Research (CIDAR).

One day a colleague from NIH on a site visit to Spring Grove took Carpenter aside and said, "You've got a sleeping giant here. Why don't you apply to become a Clinical Research Center?" Carpenter applied, and in 1986 the MPRC became one of two NIMH-designated Clinical Research Centers for the study of schizophrenia. Becoming a CRC was both prestigious and practical. With CRC status came an NIMH infrastructure grant to develop biostatistics systems and training. "Different programs were using different rating scales for the same things," says Carpenter. "This is the kind of thing that both forces you and enables you to harmonize things. We had to select instruments and train raters in all the programs, so that if, for example, Carol Tamminga wanted to do something, she just had to pick her instruments and tell her people to figure out how to use them."

The original CRC evolved into somewhat different models of support. On renewal of the CRC, the MPRC became an Intervention Research Center, or IRC, which meant that some basic science and animal models were not supported. (IRCs were oriented more toward clinical trials and services research). In 2003 the IRC evolved again, and the MPRC became an Advanced Center for Intervention and Services Research (ACISR), which eventually turned into an Advanced Center for Innovation in Services and Intervention Research (ACISIR). From the time of the original CRC funding through the IRC, the ACISR, and the ACISIR, the MPRC had twenty-two years of center funding. Initially, the grant had to be renewed after three years; its last application was for years 22 through 27.

In 1989 NIMH funded a second broad type of center grant, to establish the Center for Neuroscience Research in Schizophrenia. The University of Maryland at Baltimore became the only institution with both a basic and a clinical NIH center for the study of schizophrenia. In 2008, NIMH funded a third type of center grant, and MPRC became a Mental Health Center for Intervention Development and Applied Research (CIDAR).

With support from NIMH, in 1987 MPRC became the founding institution for the International Congress on Schizophrenia Research (ICOSR), the premier scientific meeting in the field. Carol Tamminga (for MPRC) and Charles Schultz (then at NIMH) founded and continue to lead the ICOSR. The MPRC was also one of three participating research centers in the first Patient Outcomes Research Team (PORT) study of evidence-based practices in schizophrenia, sponsored by the Agency for Health Care Policy and Research and the NIMH, for which the PI was Tony Lehman, now chair of the department.

MPRC researchers have tried particularly to understand and develop treatments for the impairments that antipsychotic medications do not address. Producing a dramatic impact on capacity in those areas would mean that a person might really be able to recover. For that reason, and partly because of the excellent Maryland Brain Collection, in 1999 the Swiss firm Novartis Pharma AG, one of the world's largest pharmaceutical companies, awarded the MPRC a grant of $24 million over six years to discover new treatments for schizophrenia. At the time, it was the largest grant in the history of the medical school. The partnership would investigate animal models of schizophrenia and apply proteomic and genomic methods for discovery with human postmortem brain tissue.

How did such a partnership begin? At a conference, Robbie Schwarcz ran into a Danish colleague whom he knew because they'd both studied Huntington's disease. The friend had become head of neuroscience at Novartis, and Schwarcz began telling him about the work MPRC was doing on schizophrenia. The friend's curiosity about MPRC's brain collection was piqued, so Schwarcz invited him over for a visit. Eventually twenty people from MPRC visited Novartis in Basel, Switzerland, twenty people from Basel visited the MPRC campus, and many friendships formed. Novartis was interested in doing something big. "Our investigators and their investigators were planning the science before there was any attempt to wrap a contractual arrangement around it," says Will Carpenter. "In that planning process, we laid down the principles that both sides had to adhere to. In that sense I think we put together what is probably a model academic–industry collaboration, particularly in this era in which there's so much concern that the commercialization of academic research is putting a bias on public science issues and curtailing whether the data generated is public."[10]

Under the Novartis grant, MPRC investigators established an animal model and human models for proof-of-concept testing for new compounds for cognition and negative symptoms. (The program they developed was later put forward by NIMH in the MATRICS[11] process.) Jim Koenig's rat model was developed and has become an influential model for the study of schizophrenia and an important element of the MPRC's CIDAR grant. Guni Thaker introduced new neurophysiological methods that made it possible to study core pathological mechanisms, rather than merely clinical symptoms, of schizophrenia phenotypes. These phenotypes provide novel targets for experimental drug evaluation.

Two years after discussions began, a contract was signed. Four years into the contract, after $16 million had been invested and an annex built onto the main MPRC building, Novartis decided that the company no longer wanted to study schizophrenia, so the arrangement was terminated, to the disappointment of investigators on both sides of the Atlantic.

MPRC's base budget, which was indexed at 1 percent of the state Mental Hygiene Administration budget in 1990, has not grown since then, so Carpenter had to close down MPRC's independently run inpatient unit in 2004. The center's treatment research program, of which Deanna Kelly is chief (replacing Robert Conley), is now conducted partly in two Spring Grove units. Without the independent units, research can no longer be done with patients who are off their medication.

In 2008, Conley accepted a senior scientist position at Eli Lilly and Company, after almost twenty years at the MPRC.

In 2007 the budget was shifted from the Department of Mental Hygiene into a special account for the university, so the MPRC's base funding and scientific administration are now fully based in the university. "Not shifting earlier was probably good because we were able to grow that budget in a way we couldn't have through the university, and the Mental Hygiene Administration was good at protecting us from cuts," says Carpenter. "But for years there was no growth potential, and we couldn't get cost-of-living increases or increases for inflation, although we had to pay them to our staff. Nelson Sabatini, as secretary of the state's Department of Health and Mental Hygiene (DHMH), was a strong supporter of MPRC and stated publicly that he closed Crownsville instead of Spring Grove because MPRC was here. But he thought it was best for us to shift us to the university. So for a couple of years we've gotten a little added to our budget for cost-of-living increases, and I don't have to go to Annapolis every year to fight for our budget when someone says, 'The DHMH does not have a research mission. Why is it funding research?'" On the whole, the MPRC has had strong support from state legislators and the DHMH, in part because of the unique clinical mission created by the research mission.

Of particular importance is the work the MPRC and the services research division downtown are doing with dual diagnosis. "For reasons we don't know, for example, there's very high co-morbidity with substance abuse: nicotine more than anything, alcohol next, but also marijuana and other illicit drugs," says Carpenter. "It may be that whatever is causing at least some forms of schizophrenia is also causing a liability for substance use—or maybe these are not mutually exclusive. They may be secondary phenomena. There's a lot of reason to think that a nicotinic receptor, particularly the $\alpha 7$ nicotinic receptor, is altered in schizophrenia. It's possible that people are intense nicotine consumers in relation to a deficit in stimulating the nicotinic cholinergic system. We don't know why there's so much alcohol abuse in people with schizophrenia. People can argue that it's related to feeling bored, or to feeling dysphoric, but who knows?"

The main focus of MPRC's efforts to develop treatments for co-occurring substance use disorders has been on nicotine dependence. MPRC researchers conducted a pilot study and clinical trial for the efficacy of the combination of bupropion and group therapy, documented the efficacy of group therapy, and showed that bupropion provides somewhat more benefit than a placebo in helping people with schizophrenia stop smoking cigarettes. By the end of the fourteen-week study, however, only 22 percent of the subjects had quit smoking—a cessation rate considerably lower than seen in studies with controls. A different approach may be required in people with schizophrenia, so Bob Buchanan's group has designed a study to examine the efficacy of varenicline, a partial agonist of the nicotinic receptor, which may be abnormal in schizophrenia.

Understanding these domains is important when it comes to treatment, says Carpenter, but "most mental health clinics don't do good substance abuse diagnosis and treatment. In fact, the treatment of schizophrenia and the treatment of substance abuse are studied in different institutes. And the ways states and insurance are organized, in principle this hospital shouldn't be taking anybody with substance abuse, but of course it's full of them. For a long time we tried to exclude substance abuse because we thought it would confound the research, but it's so common that we long ago quit trying to exclude people with a history of abuse. We wouldn't do an imaging study asking schizophrenia questions of somebody who is intoxicated, and we don't want to study the role of the dopamine system in schizophrenia in somebody who is in cocaine withdrawal, because we would get a strong signal that would turn out not to be schizophrenia."

Certain populations that seem particularly vulnerable to drug abuse also disproportionately develop schizophrenia. In 2005, the MPRC started a $25 million contractual collaboration with NIDA to study co-occurring disorders—with the participation also of investigators from the VA's Mental Illness Research Education and Clinical Center (MIRECC). As a result of this collaboration, NIDA moved its inpatient research program from east Baltimore to the Tawes Building, and the building underwent significant reconstruction to house investigators, laboratories, and patients. There volunteers can now participate in various clinical trials designed to study dual diagnosis. Understanding the connection between substance abuse and psychiatric disorders could have a profound effect on prevention and treatment, says Rob Conley, the original principal investigator on the NIDA grant. (Deanna Kelly is now PI on the residential research contract with NIDA.) NIDA provides $2 million a year in funding, which also covers some complementary basic science research focused on molecular biology, neurotransmitter systems, and the neural circuitry involved in both mental illness and substance abuse disorders.

There are three FDA-approved medications for treatment of alcohol use disorders: acamprosate, disulfiram, and naltrexone. There is reason to believe that acamprosate may provide a unique benefit to people with schizophrenia and co-occurring alcohol use disorders. It may enhance glutamatergic functioning when the system is understimulated and decrease glutamatergic functioning when it is overstimulated. Bob Buchanan's team plans to assess its safety and tolerability in people who have schizophrenia.[12]

Buchanan and Jim Gold played lead roles in consensus meetings for NIMH's Cognitive Neuroscience Treatment Research to Improve Cognition in Schizophrenia (CNTRICS) initiative. The MPRC was one of two sites in the country that participated in the two major NIMH initiatives on new therapeutic discovery, CNTRICS and MATRICS.

Along with other researchers around the country, the MPRC has explored new ways to measure various aspects of cognitive function and cognitive impairment, because quantifiable outcome measures are needed to develop and evaluate new treatments. For the FDA in particular, you must have a validated outcome to argue that the treatment is effective. You don't measure this kind of cognitive impairment with an IQ test. You are measuring a range of cognitive functions, including ability to pay attention and to register information.

The MPRC played a leading role in developing a set of standardized measures of cognitive function the FDA can now use. Those measures should make it possible for other investigators in both academia and pharmaceutical companies to more easily identify compounds that might safely improve cognitive function and therefore be marketable. Those measures may also help researchers identify genetic markers underlying variations in cognitive function, which in turn may lead to the development of targeted therapeutic interventions.

Moving beyond "me too" drugs

When Wayne Fenton opened the first public session on the FDA–NIMH MATRICS project in 2004, he told the assembled group that the basis for MATRICS was the paradigm shift Will Carpenter and John Strauss had introduced in 1974.[13] Negative symptoms and impaired cognition are the two unmet therapeutic needs identified in the NIMH MATRICS project; the paradigm shift has finally taken hold. Initially, their findings were considered both "surprising and very controversial," says Carpenter, "but as far as I can tell they are now so widely accepted that there's hardly any recognition of where they came from. We now know that the diagnostic class of schizophrenia is misleading. It is not a simple disease entity, but a heterogeneous syndrome comprising a number of pathological domains, with substantial variation between individual cases.

When Wayne Fenton opened the first public session on the FDA–NIMH MATRICS project in 2004, he told the assembled group that the basis for MATRICS was the paradigm shift Will Carpenter (shown here) and John Strauss had introduced in 1974. ""Now, even the FDA has come on board, agreeing that it should approve drugs not only for their antipsychotic properties but also for the treatment of negative symptoms and cognition impairments."

"Now, even the FDA has come on board, agreeing that it should approve drugs not only for their antipsychotic properties but also for the treatment of negative symptoms and cognition impairments. Fifty years of using psychosis to represent schizophrenia has given us fifty years of double-first-cousin drugs—'me too' drugs. Except for clozapine, none of them has documented superiority over the very first one."

Carpenter is now chairing the DSM-V psychosis working group as it develops a new approach and new criteria. "Part of that will be putting in the pathological dimensions that we've worked on for so many years. The field has really come around. There seems to be a growing consensus that we have to look at these different pathology domains rather than big heterogeneous syndromes."

Until there was differential pharmacology, it didn't matter much which box you put a patient in—only a few people would be interested in whether a patient was diagnosed with psychosis with depression or psychosis with schizophrenia, says Carpenter. Schizophrenia was still at a syndrome level the way mental retardation and dementia were at a syndrome level sixty or seventy years ago, before we knew there were forty or fifty discrete diagnoses for levels and types of impairment—before we knew how to separate Alzheimer's, with its tangled neurons, from other forms of dementia.

"In our view, the reality distortion turns out to have a very low correlation with dissociative thought process and a very low correlation with the negative symptoms. Everyone who gets a diagnosis of schizophrenia is very likely to have false beliefs (paranoid beliefs) and very likely to have hallucinations. John Nash (whose story is told in Sylvia Nasar's book, *A Beautiful Mind*) had the reality distortion, and there were times in the hospital when he had disorganized thought, but he didn't lose drive or emotion; he was absolutely engaged. That's why he was likely over time to do better than others—because the negative symptoms and impaired cognition cause so much social and occupational impairment.

"Contrast his case with that of a man who spends time alone but is not lonely, doesn't do anything that would strike you as engaging or interesting, but he feels fine about it. He'll have some false beliefs and hear voices and his thinking may be disorganized. He's very likely to be unemployed, to live in a supervised situation, to be unmarried. When you get his childhood history you learn he may have been sort of a loner growing up, started doing worse in school between the ages of eight and twelve, then got noticed later in life because paranoia came to public attention. This person could just be very, very different, except he would hear voices and share the paranoid delusions. In some patients the strongest component might be the negative symptoms: the lack of drive and emotion.

"Different people can present strikingly different clinical pictures. And of course people are very different when they're psychotic from when they're stabilized and in some form of remission. When you interview them, you're trying to find out if they hear voices, if they don't engage coherently with you. You may decide they're hearing voices because every now and again they quit talking and appear to be listening to something that you don't hear. They can also show gross disorganization of thought and behavior, be disheveled, not take care of themselves." Elements of the disease are present from birth, other aspects emerge during developmental years, and the illness becomes fully expressed in early adulthood, with long-lasting implications for most patients.

John Nash had the reality distortion, and there were times in the hospital when he had disorganized thought, but he didn't lose drive or emotion; he was absolutely engaged. That's why he was likely over time to do better than others—because the negative symptoms and impaired cognition cause so much social and occupational impairment.

"We went through probably fifteen years or so of neuroimaging studies where we'd look at what's going on in the brain for a number of patients with schizophrenia and a number of controls—looking for differences. But the schizophrenia population might be very heterogeneous: If we had two John Nashes and three disorganized and five predominantly negative, we might have very different findings and group differences. Sometimes people who reported negative symptoms didn't seem so different from normal controls. But in that group, maybe only a handful of people actually had this negative pathology. If you target these specific domains of study, you can start off saying 'I'm going to take subjects who meet criteria for schizophrenia but I'm also going to be sure if I'm testing a negative symptom hypothesis that they actually have the negative symptoms.'"

Carpenter thinks we have lost fifty years of drug discovery by measuring global symptoms of psychosis, time to discharge, time to relapse, relapse prevention. Everything has been related to reality, psychotic symptoms, or proxies for them. Only now are we recognizing the things that cause a poor outcome. "I think the industry, the FDA, and the field are now really lined up agreeing that these are unmet therapeutic needs and there needs to be discovery for them."

Elements of the disease are present from birth, other aspects emerge during developmental years, and the illness becomes fully expressed in early adulthood, with long-lasting implications for most patients.

MPRC assumes responsibility for *Schizophrenia Bulletin*

On November 9, 2004, the Maryland Psychiatric Research Center signed a memorandum of understanding with NIMH to assume responsibility for *Schizophrenia Bulletin*, a leading psychiatric journal, in January 2005. Paul Shepard and Gunvant Thaker led development of MPRC's proposal to assume responsibility for the *Bulletin*, selecting Oxford University Press as their publishing partner (making it the only jointly owned Oxford journal). Will Carpenter is editor-in-chief, Thaker is deputy editor, and Janet Smith is managing editor. The National Institute of Mental Health published *Schizophrenia Bulletin* from its inception in 1969, when an informal international complex of schizophrenia researchers had begun to form. Recent data confirm the growth in importance of the journal. Its impact factor rose from 2.871 (in 2005) to 6.592 (in 2008), and its rank moved from thirtieth to sixth, among 101 psychiatry journals, and to third among 85 social science journals. (Journal impact factor is a measure of the frequency with which the average article in a particular journal has been cited in recent years. This helps evaluate a journal's importance relative to others in the same field.)

Opposite: In 2002, the MPRC celebrated its twenty-fifth anniversary under Will Carpenter's leadership and as a joint operation with the University of Maryland School of Medicine and the Maryland Department of Health and Mental Hygiene. The crème de la crème of international neuroscience, including Nobel laureate Arvid Carlsson, participated in the celebration.

Of the many awards Carpenter and his colleagues have received, the following is a radically shortened list. Will Carpenter received the Stanley R. Dean Award for Psychiatric Research (in 1979), the William K. Warren Schizophrenia Research Award of the International Congress on Schizophrenia Research (in 1993), and the National Alliance on Mental Health (NAMI) Mind of America Scientific Research Award (2009). Will Carpenter and Carol Tamminga, both of whom also served as president of the American College of Neuropsychopharmacology, were elected to the Institute of Medicine of the National Academy of Sciences in 1998. In 2000, the National Alliance for Research on Schizophrenia and Depression (NARSAD) awarded Carpenter the Lieber Prize for Outstanding Research in Schizophrenia (shared with Nancy Andreasen). In 2007, Robert Schwarcz received the International League Against Epilepsy (ILAE) Epilepsy Award.

Below: The Tawes building.

SERVING *the* PEOPLE

years

of MARYLAND

MPRC

MARYLAND PSYCHIATRIC
RESEARCH CENTER

INFLUENCING *the*
WORLD *of* SCIENCE

8

Caring for Those Most in Need

Community Psychiatry

and Services Research

From early on, but particularly starting in the 1970s, the department has focused on treating patients with severe and persistent mental illness who could not afford private care. "That's probably a major theme in the identity of the department from its inception," says Tony Lehman, current chair of the department. In particular, many of the department's research programs began to focus on severe mental illness, especially schizophrenia, potentially one of the most disabling and persistent of illnesses—one that both the patient and the family must live with. There is also more emphasis now on recovery—on developing, evaluating, and disseminating new treatments—offering new hope for patients and their families.

Schizophrenia affects up to 1 percent of the world's population, including about 2.7 million Americans. The disease often manifests itself at about eighteen to twenty-two years of age, and it stays with you, and with your family, your whole life. Very few people with schizophrenia (maybe 10 to 22 percent) marry, and perhaps 15 to 25 percent join the workforce. Schizophrenia is the fourth leading cause of disability in the world.

Schizophrenia also adds significantly to the public health burden. Antipsychotic medications do not help all patients and often have unpleasant side effects. There is no established treatment for some core features of the illness. Creating opportunities for patients to get better is what motivates much of the research and patient care done in community psychiatry. Knowing how few opportunities some of the patients have had energizes faculty and staff often to work well beyond normal expectations.

Myths, stigma, and misinformation abound about mental illness—especially about schizophrenia—and homelessness. There is the myth that homeless people are patients with schizophrenia, released from state mental hospitals. "Many of the people who have schizophrenia live with their families," says Tony Lehman, addressing an audience likely to harbor myths about the mentally ill. "And most of the people who are homeless do not have schizophrenia."

Another popular myth, perpetuated in movies and other mass media, is that a person with schizophrenia has a "split personality." Split or multiple personalities are associated with a different mental illness: dissociative personality disorder.

Maybe 20 to 25 percent of people who are homeless have a severe mental illness like schizophrenia, says Lehman. "Substance abuse is probably the biggest problem. If you count substance abuse as the product of mental illness, perhaps the majority of people who are homeless are affected. Risk factors for ending up homeless include these: mental illness, being poor, being black, being male, being addicted to substances, having been raised in foster care. The more of those risk factors you have, the higher the risk you will end up homeless."

Schizophrenia combined with these other factors increases the chances people will end up homeless—basically because they don't have family, or their family can't accommodate them, and of course delusions may contribute to their decision to travel the country or live on the streets. Because of their thought disorders, people with schizophrenia are generally barely getting by, so they are more likely than other homeless people to become victims or to be exploited in various ways, just to get food or a place to stay. If they are paranoid they may also be afraid of treatments and medication, especially if they have had bad experiences with treatment or medication's side effects. Usually families can't manage someone who is very psychotic—who, if the family says, "You need to do treatment to stay here," may get paranoid, leave, and end up on the streets.

Moreover, many of the patients with severe mental illness (SMI) in West Baltimore have diabetes and metabolic syndrome and are on drugs and alcohol, says John Talbott. "Dual diagnosis is common. They have access to drugs and alcohol, overcrowding, poor living conditions, and all the other factors that make for bad outcomes. They are very sick. It's a different world."

When Russ Monroe resigned as chair of the department, Will Carpenter, whom he had recruited to revitalize the Maryland Psychiatric Research Center, urged the search committee to look at John Talbott, a well-known New York–based psychiatrist who had just been elected president of the American Psychiatric Association. Talbott was earnest about doing more to help people with serious, persistent mental illness.

Psychiatric Services

September 2009

PSYCHIATRIC SERVICES A Journal of the American Psychiatric Association

♦ Use of Intensive Services by 'Dual Eligibles' When Part D Plans Limit Access to Drugs   ♦ Extent of Off-Label Use of Antipsychotics in the VA: A National Analysis   ♦ Improving Quality of Care for First-Episode Psychosis: An Array of Existing Tools

John Talbott became editor of *Psychiatric Services* in 1981, when it was still called *Hospital and Community Psychiatry.** The journal, as Talbott saw it, "was intended for clinicians in the trenches. We wanted to retain its practicality but bring more research to bear on practice." Determined to bring more academic rigor to the publication, he instituted a system of peer review for manuscripts and began including columns on specific topics, such as psychiatry and the law. Former APA president Paul Appelbaum told Psychiatric News that in 1981 problems were surfacing at community mental health centers, the fallout from deinstitutionalization had been apparent for some time, and managed care was on the horizon. "John saw that the boundaries between the public and private sectors were blurring. He

knew it was necessary to focus on psychiatric services as a whole, not on the venue in which they were offered."

In 1981, the field of health services research was beginning to develop (just as the first desktop computers became available). An early proponent of health services research, Howard Goldman, was the lead author of a paper ("Defining and Counting the Chronically Mentally Ill") published in the first issue under Talbott's editorship. Goldman also played a role in bringing Talbott to the University of Maryland.

As editor of the journal and as APA's president, Talbott "brought the issues of public psychiatry to the forefront of the field—deinstitutionalization, care in the community, treatment of schizophrenia," said Steve Sharfstein in 2004, on Talbott's retirement as editor. "From science to public policy, the journal became the resource for the clinician and administrator in the fight for resources and attention."

"John offered the journal as a place to publish findings from the developing field of mental health services research and economics," said Goldman, who took over as editor of the journal in 2004. "He published special sections on prospective payment and DRGs,* the results of the evaluation of various service demonstration programs, co-occurring disorders, homelessness and mental illness, health care reform, and evidence-based practices."[1]

---

* The American Psychiatric Association first published the *A.P.A. Mental Hospital Service Bulletin* in January 1950. In the seventh issue of volume 2 it was renamed *Mental Hospitals*; in 1966, it became *Hospital and Community Psychiatry*, and in 1995 *Psychiatric Services*.

* Diagnosis-related groups (DRGs) are key units in a patient classification system designed to relate types of patients treated to the amount of hospital resources they consume, to facilitate calculating prices.

Stu Silver, then director of Maryland's Mental Hygiene Administration, John Talbott, and Will Carpenter, probably at MPRC's public conference on schizophrenia.

Talbott was pretty happy at Cornell, and as president of the American Psychiatric Association he was riding high. But Allen Frances, the director of outpatient care at Cornell, had returned from an interview for the Maryland chairmanship to say, "John, it's not the right job for me but it's perfect for you. It's schizophrenia, they do good teaching, they do good research, and it's just waiting to take off." Talbott decided to take a look.

Allen Frances later chaired both the DSM-IV Task Force and the department of psychiatry at Duke University School of Medicine.

Carpenter invited Talbott to Maryland to give a lecture and to stay in his home. "I had known Will Carpenter only very slightly, because I was in Vietnam when he was most active in New York, at Albert Einstein and then Columbia. But he was a very powerful person and we share an interest in schizophrenia." Talbott hit it off with Giuseppe Inessi, chair of the search committee, and Alp Karahasan, the state commissioner of mental health, who asked, "What would it take to get you here? How would you like the Carter Center?

Do you know where it is?" He was further wooed by John Dennis, the dean of the medical school, when they were negotiating his final package. Talbott said he would want things computerized and provided a laundry list of wishes. "Don't you want Alcoholism and Drug Abuse?" asked Dennis. Puzzled that it was not already part of the department, he was told that division had been given away in 1971, but he could have it back. As a further enticement, Veterans Affairs was building a VA hospital literally connected to University Hospital.

The department needed to strengthen its research base downtown. "Apart from John Lion, Denis Madden, and Will Carpenter, at the time Maryland didn't have much of a reputation. Not a bad reputation, just not a reputation"—except for the Maryland Plan, which Talbott had learned about when running for APA president in 1983. Maryland had been way ahead the rest of the country in providing training for psychiatrists to work in state hospitals.

Talbott accepted the chairmanship. Whether he recruited his first hires or they recruited him and each other is not entirely clear. He was interviewing at NIH at the same time he was interviewing at Maryland and met Howard Goldman, an up-and-coming health policy expert, in an NIH parking lot. Goldman had not previously considered going to the University of Maryland, but George Washington University and Georgetown University, near his D.C. home, were not interested in having a mental health services research center, which is what Goldman wanted to set up.

Goldman told Talbott, who already knew the quality of his work, that he could essentially come to Maryland bringing his own money. "I went there because Talbott was going to be a great leader and I thought we could build it," says Goldman. "Sometimes you go to a place that wants you when you need to do something

In 1986 Dennis moved the division of alcohol and drug abuse back from the dean's office to the department of psychiatry. In 1988, Talbott hired David R. McDuff, a retired army major and an expert in treating alcohol and drug abuse, to run the division. A superb teacher who still supervises fellows in the division, McDuff was admittedly not a researcher. While much of the department was growing by expanding its research, McDuff innovated by signing many service contracts (for clients ranging from sports teams and emergency rooms to companies' employee assistance programs). "His division's staff stabilized, its income grew sizably, and he was in the forefront of the department's efforts to stay ahead of the managed care curve," says Talbott.

Goldman's initial funding was from consulting for NIMH and for the American Psychiatric Association (through a contract with the Social Security Administration).

that's different. Talbott had the vision that he could build a modern, first-rate, twenty-first-century academic department of psychiatry and he hired us to do it, and to do it in a way that was not conventional, but that fit very much with the strengths of what Will Carpenter at the MPRC was doing. In one way or another, we were all intellectually committed to the sickest patients, who are often in the public sector. Talbott saw the connections and took advantage of our interest and our willingness to build something together."

"John was nationally known for his leadership in treatment, education, and research about people with severe mental illness," says Tony Lehman. "He was the guru of chronic mental illness, so he was a really logical person to head the department." Lehman had been running a long-term-care treatment and residency training program in Rochester when he first met Talbott, who had visited the school while campaigning for the APA presidency. "The main theme of his campaign was the lack of attention to people with severe mental illness. Howard and I were young guys who were also very interested in chronic mental illness and in the school's affiliation with the public mental health system." That Will Carpenter was at the MPRC gave Lehman confidence that the department would be able to support a research enterprise. It would be up to them to help build it.

Howard Goldman wanted to set up a mental health services research center and could bring his own funding. Talbott had a vision, saw connections, and took advantage of everyone's willingness to build something new together.

"It was a push–pull," says Talbott. "I came here because of Will Carpenter and because there were people here doing things with schizophrenia. I came here because Howard Goldman and Tony Lehman and Dave Mallott said, 'We'll come with you. We'll make this the best place in the world for schizophrenia research and treatment, for educating trainees, and for doing health services research on treating chronic mental illness.' So I was attracted to it and I came to it with my agenda."

"I knew both Howard and Tony," says Talbott. "I did not know Dave Mallott, but a friend of mine at Tulane called and asked, 'Are you looking to fill any inpatient slots, especially in the schizophrenia ward, because I've got this junior faculty guy who's really terrific and wants to move to Baltimore." When they met, Talbott learned that Mallott was interested in treating very sick people and teaching, but not necessarily in research. "To have a guy who loved teaching and whose primary commitment was to teaching about schizophrenia was a real gift, so it didn't take me long to make that decision. Dave headed up the acute psychosis (a/k/a schizophrenia) unit for seven years. He is quick, bright, talented, critical, and has a sharp wit and a wry sense of humor. The residents loved him."

After heading the acute psychosis unit from 1986 to 1993, Mallott worked for a while in the Carter Center.

Toward a hospital without walls

Both the university and the VA were moving from what had previously been a hospital-based system, emphasizing maintenance and containment of individuals with chronic mental illness, to a patient-centered recovery model for mental health, with an emphasis on hope and recovery. The department was an early participant in what became a national shift toward the recovery model—giving consumers a voice in their care, trying to empower consumers to have more control over their lives and health. In the recovery model, health care providers partner with health care consumers (no longer called patients) and help them identify goals, develop strategies, and move toward success in managing illness and recovering a life of meaning—with the aim of improving their quality of life and being integrated or reintegrated into the community. In the VA this orientation toward recovery is now mandated nationally through the Uniform Mental Health Services package.

In 2003, the President's New Freedom Commission on Mental Illness, under President George W. Bush, announced an official change in approaches toward helping people with mental illness—a switch from a disability model to a recovery model. "Successfully transforming the mental health service delivery system rests on two principles," reads the executive summary: "First, services and treatments must be consumer and family centered, geared to give consumers real and meaningful choices about treatment options and providers—not oriented to the requirements of bureaucracies. Second, care must focus on increasing consumers' ability to successfully cope with life's challenges, on facilitating recovery, and on building resilience, not just on managing symptoms."

The buzz words at first were "empowerment" and "patient-centered."

Recovery doesn't mean cure, says Lehman. "It's more a kind of philosophy. The recovery model focuses on people's strengths rather than weaknesses. Most of us feel and do better if we're focusing on things we do well rather than things we don't. So treatment and rehabilitation programs for people with schizophrenia now make more of an effort to identify people's strengths, figure out what they can do, what they want to do, and how to help them find a niche for themselves based on their strengths. The evidence-based programs tend to be aimed at promoting recovery." They place far less emphasis on the traditional patient hour and more on the kinds of psychosocial interventions that support people with mental illness, improve the quality of their lives, and keep them out of the hospital.

As Michael F. Hogan, chair of the President's New Freedom Commission on Mental Illness (2003), said, five years after its report was issued, "There is the reality now established in long-term studies. . . . Good outcomes are far more possible than we had imagined." Following people over decades, not just years, was what proved this point. Recovery is also the appreciation that it is possible to have a good life despite what can often be a crushing and catastrophic illness.[2]

Many people in the department joined in efforts to help the underserved Maryland population with severe mental illness—perhaps none more so than those who work at the Maryland Psychiatric Research Institute (on the Spring Grove campus) and in two divisions downtown: the Division of Services Research, which studies what services are most effective and worth doing, and the Division of Community Psychiatry, which provides those services. How the services research division came into being and thrived is an important part of the department's history of successful collaborations.

Under John Talbott, a department naturally receptive to community psychiatry had found a leader. He had a clear vision of what the department could do and immediately set about making that happen. "The research didn't really kick in here until acquisition of the Maryland Psychiatric Research Center," says Talbott, speaking about the development in 1977 that ultimately brought him to Maryland. "Some of the individuals were stars, but there was a silo mentality about research. Gene Brody was flying around the world talking about social psychiatry, Russ Monroe did research on episodic psychosis and violence, John Lion and Dennis Madden ran the widely respected violence program, Jonas Rappeport had a distinguished forensic program, but the department didn't come together as a department of psychiatry—or not as a premier department of psychiatry like Columbia, Cornell, Harvard, Pittsburgh, or San Diego. Washington University had a reputation because it had a focus: it pioneered in diagnostic criteria. Maryland's department didn't have a collective reputation. Maryland was viewed as a sort of sleepy, backwater place. It wasn't present at the chairmen's meeting, its people were not prominent at national meetings.

"At the time substance abuse was often not even assessed," says Lehman. "Now everybody knows that a high percentage of people coming to psychiatric hospitals have substance abuse problems."

"Will Carpenter was doing important work, but was a little isolated out at Spring Grove, where he wanted the MPRC to stay. The Carter Center was certainly focused on persons with chronic, severe mental illness, and University Hospital saw a lot of these people as well, including those who had problems with substance abuse. Walter Weintraub and his crew were very committed to producing psychiatrists for the public system. I had done research on schizophrenia. So the ingredients were all there."

Talbott had heard about the new field of health services research from Cornell's chair of public health, George Reader, who had come to his office there and said, "Do you realize how much money is out there for health services research?" Talbott hadn't known, but had formed a committee to investigate. Now, a year later, he was at Maryland with a mandate to expand the research downtown. "I was hampered by the lack of space. Without wet lab space, what are you going to do?" says Talbott. Remembering that funding was available for services research, he thought, *Let's go get it.* "It was easier to bring in people who needed just a computer than people who each needed fifty square feet of lab space. So the health services research was a no-brainer, as was epidemiology. Some things were serendipitously mutually beneficial."

Howard Goldman, his first new hire, joined the department in October 1985 and quickly began developing a mental health policy studies program. They hired Susan Ridgely to work on a project for the Alcohol, Drug Abuse, and Mental Health Administration (ADAMHA) on co-occurring mental disorders, also known as dual diagnosis (in particular, co-occurring severe mental illness and substance abuse disorder). In late 1985 the policy studies group also entered into a contract with the state Mental Hygiene Administration to study inpatient care in Maryland and develop a series of scenarios for the future use of state-operated inpatient facilities.

Goldman also worked part-time finishing and writing about some studies for NIMH and continued consulting with the American Psychiatric Association on a contract to evaluate a set of new mental impairment standards for the Social Security Administration. His involvement with SSA and its disability policies has remained a focus of his research and policy work.

Talbott's second hire, Tony Lehman, added clinical strength to the focus on community health care. "My specialty was health services research—studying healthcare delivery—and my

Howard Goldman was hired October 7, 1985; Tony Lehman and Dave Mallott were both hired July 1, 1986.

work had always focused on services for people with severe mental illness," says Lehman. "When I came here I was head of research for the Carter Center. Jose Arana, the clinical director, said, 'We've got two big problems associated with people who have schizophrenia or major mood disorders: homelessness and substance abuse.' We got a fair amount of research money to do this project on the mobile treatment program for homeless people (ACT) and then we did some work on treating substance abuse." Lehman ran a research project under a NIDA grant on patterns of prevalence for dual diagnosis.

"At the time substance abuse was often not even assessed in psychiatric settings," says Lehman. "Now it's a required point of assessment, because everybody knows that a high percentage of people coming to psychiatric hospitals have substance abuse problems. The more you look at the problem, the harder it is sometimes to tell which is cause and which effect, although we did a fair amount of work trying to figure that out."

With Harbor City Unlimited, a nonmedical psychiatric and residential rehabilitation program for mentally ill adults, Lehman also headed a group intervention program aimed to improve outcomes for persons with co-occurring severe mental illness and addiction. Such group programs are now commonplace, but at the time they were novel because of the chasm that existed between the addiction and mental health treatment systems. Lehman was also directing a state-funded training program for psychiatric rehabilitation.

Nine-city study for Robert Wood Johnson Foundation. Months after joining the department, Goldman and Lehman began the first of many productive collaborations. A disproportionate number of the homeless people in large cities had mental illness, and NIMH and the Robert Wood Johnson Foundation (RWJ) had been thinking about what to do about it and how to evaluate what they did. They were going to fund a nine-city demonstration project to find out whether creating local mental health authorities would improve care for those with chronic mental illness. The foundation invited the sixty largest U.S. cities around the country to submit

Tony Lehman, left, and Howard Goldman, discussing the Robert Wood Johnson Foundation project with Dee Roth, chief of the Office of Program Evaluation and Research, Ohio Department of Health.

proposals, offering them money to re-organize their service systems and providing them with housing subsidies from the Department of Housing and Urban Development (HUD). The foundation, together with the NIMH, invited ten research teams from around the country to submit proposals for the project's evaluation component.

Goldman and Lehman put together a team to compete against the other nine groups and, together with partners at Johns Hopkins and the University of North Carolina, wrote a proposal to evaluate the nine-city demonstration project. Their team won and was awarded a five-year evaluation grant, with Goldman as principal investigator. Lehman, an expert at assessing individual patient outcomes, was lead investigator on the more clinically oriented patient outcomes part of the evaluation, about the projects' effects on individual patients.

Among many other investigators on the project, Susan Ridgely, Cille Kennedy, and Sandy Newman (Johns Hopkins) headed the housing part of the study; Don Steinwachs (head of Johns Hopkins's department of health policy and management) worked on the bid; Richard Frank, from Steinwachs's department, headed the financing and economic aspects of the demonstration; sociologist Joseph P. Morrissey, an organizational sociologist in North Carolina, headed the part of the study about interorganizational network relationships, an area of research in which he pioneered.

"Linda Aiken (at RWJ) and medical sociologist David Mechanic of Rutgers (her consultant and then-husband) had urged the foundation to invest in a demonstration project to create local mental health authorities, to demonstrate that having an agency coordinate resources and care would improve things dramatically," says Goldman.

"The evaluation was originally set up to study whether the local authorities had been created and what their broad impact was," says Lehman. "From the policy standpoint, it was naive to think that the only thing needed was the integration and coordination of services. We had to argue pretty hard to have a patient-level outcome study done. I felt strongly, and Howard agreed, that it wasn't clear that coordination alone would improve patient outcomes, although that was the assumption."

The patient outcomes part of the study was important, so Lehman and Goldman began working to build infrastructure for the study. At the time this was a sizable project: RWJ had contributed two million dollars, which was the largest evaluation the foundation had done at that point, and NIMH matched that grant with another two million, which was unusual, because NIMH rarely provided matching funds for the foundation. NIMH eventually funded several additional studies related to specific aspects of the demonstration.

In 1986, the foundation launched its Program on Chronic Mental Illness, providing $29 million in grants, housing subsidies, and loans to nine large U.S. cities: Austin, Baltimore, Charlotte, Cincinnati, Columbus, Denver, Honolulu, Philadelphia, and Toledo. They were to create local mental health authorities to help organize and finance mental health services and to coordinate response to the needs—including housing needs—of those with chronic mental illness. The housing component was included to demonstrate that even individuals with the most disabling mental disorders could use rental subsidies (in this case, Section 8 housing certificates) to live in ordinary community housing, given the right services and supports.

"How could we do a study of this magnitude and not include New York? I was living there at the time, serving on the National Advisory Committee for the RWJ Program for Urban Systems of Care for the Chronically Mentally Ill," says John Talbott, "and their application was horrendous. Baltimore's, written by Marcella Schuyler, was right on." The local mental health authority created in Baltimore after this study—Baltimore Mental Health Systems—still exists, and the department works closely with them, says Tony Lehman.

HUD provided each city with 125 Section 8 certificates, permitting local mental health authorities to subsidize rents for people with severe mental illness.

The main point of the study was to find out if, in a local metropolitan area, having a central authority coordinate services for people with severe mental illness would improve services and outcomes. "The idea was that it would be more efficient," says Lehman, "but we learned that it wasn't. Not that the current system was so great, but that there were fewer effective services there to coordinate than one might assume. A case manager can't facilitate a patient's connection to services if the services aren't there or aren't very good. The analogy I used was that building a shopping mall doesn't get you a whole lot if it doesn't have any shops in it. It's hard to argue against better coordination, but coordination alone was not enough."

The systems change intervention focused on organizing and financing care rather than on providing resources for direct services. The cities never managed to provide the other things needed, says Lehman. They had central planning and central financial control, but they did not have adequate inpatient beds, community clinics, and supportive housing. "In the beginning, many of the program leaders at the foundation and on the evaluation team felt that "senior clinicians overvalued clinical work and did not really understand the service integration concepts at the heart of the demonstration. In the end, the importance of the quality of the clinical services became apparent."

Having concluded that changing the system—providing local mental health authorities—was not enough to produce good outcomes, the evaluators began to "focus on the content and quality of the services the clients received, speculating that many of the services delivered in the Program on Chronic Mental Illness cities were not the evidence-based services, such as assertive community treatment, whose effectiveness had been established through research."[3]

Other demonstration projects began coming to similar conclusions. During the early years of NIMH's Community Support Program, the emphasis had also been on changes in the system of care. By the 1990s, the Community Support Program began shifting its focus to the quality of services and evidence-based practices.[4]

> The ACCESS study Goldman led between 1996 and 2002 found that strategies to better integrate services for people with mental illness can help link organizations, but integration did not improve client outcomes beyond what can be achieved with good clinical services, such as assertive community treatment. Study investigators found that strategies to integrate systems are more likely to succeed within the mental health system than across human services agencies broadly or through their direct effects on clients. (Goldman and colleagues 2002.)

Assertive community treatment (ACT). One of the most enterprising programs the department launched was a mobile treatment program. Early in the Reagan years, the NIMH's Community Support Program had turned its attention to a new social problem that disproportionately affected individuals with mental illness: homelessness in the nation's urban areas. Newspapers and other media were also paying attention to the problem. The Robert Wood Johnson Foundation moved to fill the void created by the federal government's failure to address the problem of homelessness. Though its philanthropic programs had never dealt with mental health issues, the foundation decided it could not approach the problem of homelessness without addressing the issue of fragmented mental health services. Two of the three programs the foundation funded (the Mental Health Services Program for Youth and the Program on Chronic Mental

Illness, for which Baltimore was one site) focused on systems integration. The third program (The Mental Health Services Development Program) funded local service innovations. Leonard Stein, a professor of psychiatry at the University of Wisconsin, directed the third program.[5] Stein, an innovator in mental health services, had developed and shown the effectiveness of ACT.

In the late 1960s and early 1970s in Madison, Wisconsin, there was a morale problem in the unit at Mendota State Hospital that was in charge of helping *treatment failures*—patients with chronic schizophrenia—make the transition from the hospital to the community. Most of their patients were cycling in and out of the hospital—except for the patients a spirited social worker named Barb Lontz worked with. In addition to providing discharge planning, on her own initiative Lontz helped train them in the daily skills of living. She drove patients to their new residence in the community and gave them hours or days of hands-on support—helping them move in, get a phone installed, get sheets on the bed, learn how to use the coin laundry, and how to ride the bus to the medical center to get medications. She also gave them her home phone number to call in an emergency. Almost none of her patients were rehospitalized. Stein noticed.

In an experimental study, Stein, Mary Ann Test, and Arnold Marx randomly assigned patients into two groups: Those in the control group went into the hospital, got medication, and got regular inpatient care. Those in the experimental group remained in the community, where they were taught coping skills and provided with housing, jobs, and social support services. Ongoing monitoring was provided, including crisis intervention, and—where possible—family members were involved in the program. Stein had a staff enriched with a couple of workers who would pick up any patients who didn't get up in the morning, bring them to the day hospital, and make sure they took their the medication. That approach of sending a community team out to where the patients were was shown to be more effective than hospital care alone. Patients spent fewer days in the hospital, took fewer medications, were more satisfied with their lives, and had more friends and social contacts. Their care was even marginally less expensive, partly because of reduced costs for hospital beds. Hospitalization was no longer the main event; the community was the arena for therapy.

Led by Stein, Test, and Marx, the staff at Mendota changed its approach to one of "training in community living," later known as "assertive community training" (ACT). Their Training in Living project began providing intensive follow-up in the period immediately after a patient's discharge, helping patients learn to adapt to and cope with the stresses of living away from the hospital, providing most of their therapy in the patients' new neighborhood. In 1977 the NIMH undertook a related effort, launching the Community Support Program.[6]

With ACT, a multidisciplinary team with a small caseload provided intensive mental health services to individuals wherever they were, without requiring office appointments. An early evidence-based practice, ACT reduced hospitalizations and got its clients back to work more often than those in other community treatment settings with which it was compared. "At the time the program was viewed as more prosaic than the other two systems integration programs, but as time went on the content of care and evidence-based practices were of increasing interest and importance," wrote Grob and Goldman.

At Mendota State Hospital in Wisconsin, patients were cycling in and out of the hospital—except for the patients of a spirited social worker named Barb Lontz, who helped train her patients in the daily skills of living.

It was this model that Tony Lehman and Jose Arana had in mind when the division of community psychiatry introduced the Program for Assertive Community Treatment (PACT) in a grant-funded demonstration project[7] to improve services for homeless individuals with mental illness. They hired Lisa Dixon, who had worked briefly at MPRC, and who ended up playing a greater role in the research than anyone intended. Dixon showed up for her first day of work, in February 1991, just as word came from Peru that Jose Arana, who was to be clinical director on the project, had

Lehman and Arana hired Lisa Dixon to help on the program of assertive community training (ACT). Dixon showed up for her first day of work just as word came from Peru that Jose Arana had died quietly in his sleep on a visit home.

died quietly in his sleep on a visit home. "We really had to regroup," says Dixon. "Tony became my clinical supervisor, even though he was the PI. It was complicated, but I had worked with homeless people as a resident in New York. Most important, the program director, Nancy Krauss, had a huge amount of experience working with homeless adults in Baltimore and helped me learn quickly what was needed psychiatrically."

The model deemphasized traditional office psychiatry and the use of professional facilities, the central concern being to provide care to patients in the community and at their places of residence. "They took all the principles of hospital-based care—all the services in one package, access twenty-four hours a day seven days a week, and a team-based approach (with the whole health care team responsible for the whole panel of patients)," says Dixon. It evolved over time into a kind of "hospital without walls. You were it for those patients, and you saw them wherever they were, in hospital or not, and not by appointment only." The original model had been shown to reduce hospitalization rates and remains an evidence-based practice for that outcome. "The experiment we were a part of," says Dixon, "was testing to see whether this model, developed for heavy users of hospitals, would also be successful in reducing homelessness, and there were many reasons to think it would. By the time they wrote the grant, ACT was already ten years old, though it had not been used much. One of the innovations Tony and Jose introduced was to include consumer advocates on the team, individuals who had "been there"—who had prior personal experience with mental illness or homelessness or both. They also had the vision to include a family outreach worker named Bette Stewart

"We thought including consumer advocates would lend reality to the teams, translating between those served and those serving, an element lacking on a purely professional team," says Tony Lehman.

on that team. That was what made it so powerful for me. In this community-based approach, if you weren't getting the outcomes you thought you wanted, you had to regroup and ask, 'What does the consumer want? I can't impose my will.'

We spent a lot of time trying to understand how to connect what the consumer wanted to what we were charged to do, and our consumer providers were very helpful in that. We worked side by side with people who had mental disorders or who had once been homeless or marginally housed. That practice is widely accepted now but it was really new then. There was no literature on how to do this—on things like supervision and boundary issues and confidentiality—or even on what's the skill set? Not everybody who's been a mental health consumer can do this job. You need to have the right people to do it.

Members of the original PACT team were Lisa Dixon, Nancy Krauss, Calvin Smith, Leverne Williams, Jean Hyde, Gloristine Vines, consumer advocates Glenn Blanchard and Craig Lewis, plus the family outreach worker, Bette Stewart (a family member). Dedra Layne was an early worker.

"We were trying to get these folks off the streets," Dixon continues, "so we were trying to help them locate housing that would be acceptable to them and that they could be successful in—and it was not easy. Most of these folks had no interest in medications and often did not think they had a problem: It was we who had the problem, who had historically been patronizing. I'd only really had an office-based practice and came to realize what it's like to work with someone who is really quite ill, but on their terms, and in the community. Marty Bruce, a colleague who did a lot of home visits with geriatric patients, used to say, 'When you walk into a home, you walk into a life.' Recovery, at least in the professional community, was not something that anybody ever talked about at that point, but in many ways we were given license to think that way, and I just never went back. Once you have that kind of experience, you really can't do it any other way. It was a powerful experience for me professionally."

Family outreach worker Bette Stewart, a consumer advocate, was part of the original ACT team. At the time she was executive director of NAMI Metro Baltimore.

There were two systems in Baltimore: one for people who were homeless, and one for people who were mentally ill. Homeless people in Baltimore would show up for help with basic needs at shelters, food kitchens, and Healthcare for the Homeless, a loose network of providers of basic services for the homeless—many advocates for which were themselves homeless, or formerly homeless, people. There was also a network of providers for the mental health care system, which included the Carter Center and clinics that

"Recovery was not something anybody ever talked about at that point"

treated people who were willing to come to them. "We would come by the shelters and soup kitchens and Healthcare for the Homeless and identify people who everyone agreed might have schizophrenia," says Dixon.

PACT was staffed with a doctor, nurse, social worker, and nurse practitioner, as well as a case worker who had either been homeless or experienced mental illness. To gain credibility with consumers, the PACT team tried to help first with the needs felt most acutely—including food, shelter, and clothing. (At the time, they could get funding to put people up in a motel.) The idea was to gradually engage people and figure out what their medical problems were, says Lehman. A lot of homeless people have significant health problems, including diabetes and other conditions. Before creation of the mobile team, they were typically in and out of emergency rooms and inpatient settings in various kinds of crisis-oriented treatment—at a cost of tens of thousands of dollars a year for one individual. This treatment was not necessarily for psychiatric problems but for medical problems, because they didn't take care of themselves, got no preventive care, and had no other access to medical treatment.

"The majority of patients reported at least one medical problem," according to a study of the prevalence of medical co-morbidities done by the Schizophrenia PORT and reported in 1999. "Problems with eyesight, teeth, and high blood pressure were most common."[7]

Homeless people were randomly assigned either to get PACT services or not to get them. Those who got the services clearly did better. And the study found that the mobile treatment unit actually reduced long-term costs by providing ongoing treatment. Most cities have such teams now, says Lehman. ACT came out of the community mental health movement but was incorporated everywhere. Asked "Is that community psychiatry?" most psychiatrists would now say, "No, that's psychiatry."

In 2000, Richard Goldberg, Tony Lehman, Fred Osher, and others completed a demonstration project on supported employment, funded by the federal Center for Mental Health Services. This project brought to Baltimore an evolving evidence-based approach, developed by Deborah Becker and Robert Drake at Dartmouth, to help adults with severe mental disorders get mainstream employment. "Fred Osher, then director of community psychiatry, was the spark for this initiative," says Lehman. "Fred came to me and said this was an opportunity to enhance our vocational services that we couldn't pass up. Boy, was he right on the mark." Like many demonstration projects undertaken by Services Research, both PACT and supported employment programs (see pages 400 and 435) later became services offered in the division of community psychiatry, under Jill RachBeisel.

Schizophrenia PORT identifies evidence-based practices.
The Schizophrenia Patient Outcomes Research Team (PORT) Project, led by Tony Lehman, was one of the most important research efforts the department undertook. It began in 1992, when the notion of evidence-based practice had been introduced elsewhere in medicine but was still pretty new in psychiatry. In 1967, working with a regional medical program created with a grant under President Lyndon B. Johnson, a physician named John E. Wennberg began analyzing Medicare data to find out how well physicians and hospitals were performing—by researching local variations in medical practices for specific medical conditions. He started by examining variations in practice with prostatic hypertrophy in men. He found that what treatment a man got depended pretty much on which physician he went to, because patients were influenced by physician preferences. Some men got surgical intervention, some watchful waiting. Wennberg found compelling evidence that the kind of treatment one got for a particular problem had little to do with what worked and much more to do with where one happened to go for help. There were regional variations in treatment preferences, and few of them appeared to be based on scientific evidence that the preferred treatment was more effective than the others. What's more, regions that spent less and provided less care

There were two systems in Baltimore: one for people who were homeless and one for people who were mentally ill. PACT brought them together.

often showed better outcomes than those that spent and provided more. Wennberg and his associates began examining all studies of treatments for specific diseases and developing evidence-based guidelines for practice.

The broader PORT program funded research on many different conditions, aiming to publish national practice guidelines that were evidence based. A team of people would review the literature (study results on all the randomized clinical trials) for treatments for a given condition and develop an evidence base for effectiveness of treatments. Then, based on the evidence, they would develop practice guidelines. They could also study current practices and either generate more evidence or look at patterns of care that didn't fit the evidence. And they could do interventions to try to change medical practices.

The first PORT ruled out psychoanalytic psychotherapy as effective for people with schizophrenia. The second PORT ruled out second-generation antipsychotics as superior to first-generation drugs. Under Lehman, the PORT stood its ground, despite resistance on those issues.

"The whole movement was to try to bring medical practice more in line with science," says Lehman. "It ran into significant problems when they did the PORT on treatment for low back pain, which found basically that for routine low back pain, the less you do, the better—don't put people to bed, don't operate, and so on. The physicians groups didn't like this and I believe sued the federal government, so the Agency for Health Care Policy and Research (AHCPR, now called the Agency for Healthcare Research and Quality, AHRQ) stopped doing the guidelines. But we were funded to do the PORT on schizophrenia, so that's what we did."

Funded by both the AHCPR and NIMH, the Schizophrenia PORT was a major collaborative effort to identify evidence-based best practices for schizophrenia, carried out by the Hopkins–Maryland Center for Services Research as part of a large team, with investigators from the Hopkins School of Public Health, the Maryland Psychiatric Research Center, Maryland's community psychiatry division, and other countries. "The idea of evidence-based practice is widely accepted now, but it really wasn't something the medical field accepted or even understood at that time," says Dixon.

In 1995 and 1996, Lehman, Dixon, and others did literature reviews and wrote papers on practices for which there was a robust evidence base: case management, assertive community treatment and other psychosocial therapies, psychological therapies, family psycho-education interventions, medication therapies, and cognitive behavioral therapy (CBT). They wrote papers on patterns of usual care for schizophrenia, then compared standard care to the treatment recommendations they'd devised, to identify gaps between what works and what was actually being done.

Cognitive behavioral therapy became an evidence-based therapy, says Dave Mallott, because one could (and did) subject it to studies for effectiveness. And unlike psychoanalysis, which never measured results—which was in fact secretive and confidential—CBT never asks Why—just How and How not. It has been shown to be particularly effective for changing behaviors in patients with severe and persistent mental illness.

Lehman and his team announced results of the Schizophrenia PORT in a speech March 24, 1998, at the National Press Club in Washington, D.C. The team had assessed how well the treatment of 719 patients with schizophrenia conformed to twelve evidence-based treatment recommendations. Overall, said Lehman, less than half of treatments met the recommendations; conformance rates were higher for rural than for urban patients and higher for white patients than for minorities. Less than half of people with schizophrenia were receiving appropriate doses of antipsychotic medications. The team also found large gaps in the use and availability of psychosocial and vocational therapies and family interventions.[8] The team published its first guidelines in the late 1990s, doing an update in 2003 and again in early 2010.[9]

Looking back on the combined lessons of the RWJ nine-city study and the subsequent PORT schizophrenia study, Goldman reflects "that we spent twenty years pursuing systems integration strategies to improve care at the personal level and discovering that systems integration was only partly right—that it was necessary but not sufficient— in retrospect seems stupid, especially for somebody trained as a clinician. But that was how we thought about it in the 1980s and 1990s. Before it was too late, we shifted our attention to the quality of care. Tony's eye, and Lisa's after him, was always on the quality of care. I was more enamored of and involved in the social systems change part of things, but I learned from our studies that we didn't get the kind of results we wanted or expected. The system would change and the patients wouldn't get any better, or not as much better as we had hoped. What was missing was attention to the content and quality of care—and that's where the emergence of evidence-based medicine became so important. That's the intellectual lesson we learned. Our attention shifted from just better integration of services to improving the quality of the services themselves." After the Schizophrenia PORT study, the department and the state of Maryland began building their programs around evidence-based practices, and the department gained further strength in services research.

Some of the lessons learned made their way to the world through other channels. For example, Goldman was senior scientific editor of the Surgeon General's Report on Mental Health in 1999, the main message of which was that we now have lots of effective treatments; we just don't use them and we need to do something about using them.

Mental health services research

While Goldman was still at NIH, his mentor, Carl Taube, who had end-stage heart disease, "hatched the idea of a series of research centers to develop the field of services research and mental health economics." Taube had reached the point where it was reasonable for him to retire from the federal government, so he could work more autonomously and wait for a heart transplant. "Through an administrative stroke of genius," says Goldman, "he got his position abolished and was able to take early retirement from the federal government and retain his health insurance as a retiree. The question was, would he come to Maryland or go to Hopkins? He ended up going to Hopkins, but before leaving the federal government, he worked out these Mental Health Services Research Centers."

"When I met Carl," says Goldman, "he did not have an advanced degree, even though he was ten years my senior, but he knew more than any of us, and he slowly got himself a PhD. He taught us all so much. He had had a coronary at 38, he had developed arrhythmias and congestive heart failure, and he had an implanted defibrillator, one of the early ones." Taube died not long after retiring from NIMH and joining the Hopkins–Maryland Center for Services Research.

The University of Maryland and Johns Hopkins University partnered in a proposal and in 1987 established the first such center: the Johns Hopkins–University of Maryland Center for Research on Services for Severe Mental Illness (SMI Center). The SMI Center was established as a collaborative effort between Johns Hopkins (the medical school and the Bloomberg School of Public Health) and Maryland (Goldman's mental health policy studies program and the Carter Center's research program, under Lehman). The joint center, the first of its kind, was to work collaboratively with the Maryland Department of Health and Mental Hygiene and the National Alliance for Mental Illness (NAMI), as well as service providers and payers. To improve patient outcomes and the quality of care, the center would develop and refine ways to improve the match between patient needs and services, develop guidelines for financing and organizing care cost-effectively (reflecting variations in need and available resources), and test dissemination strategies to close the gap between research and practice. In an effective collaborative arrangement, organizations and people alternated in taking the lead.

Goldman had been principal investigator of record on research for the Robert Wood Johnson Foundation, so Don Steinwachs was made lead PI for the new center, based at Hopkins. The next huge project that came along, the Schizophrenia PORT, was based at Maryland (with Lehman as PI and Don Steinwachs as co-PI). A Lehman and Steinwachs paper would alternate with a Steinwachs and Lehman paper, and so on. They garnered the longest unbroken stretch of funding of any center under that grant program.

By 1990, a center for services research was developed within the department, representing a strong downtown services research presence to parallel and, over time, complement the strong program in neuroscience and schizophrenia at the MPRC. Goldman, a gifted executive producer on large studies, with particular strength and interest in health care policy, was instrumental in organizing teams of investigators to win contracts to evaluate demonstrations of services. These contracts often involved consulting firms (such as RAND, R.O.W. Sciences, and Westat). This contractual mechanism for funding research was somewhat foreign to universities, which were more accustomed to grants. At NIMH Taube had taught Goldman how to put together the best team of people to do a particular study and to be comfortable delegating responsibility to experts who knew about each of the component parts. An academic entrepreneur,

Goldman works mainly on policy issues, not clinical studies. Policy studies did not need to be tightly attached to a clinic or an inpatient unit. Goldman and Lehman realized, however, that if the department was going to keep doing big community-based services research studies, it needed to develop the infrastructure to support them.

They were organized by project and the budget was done by project, but once they got a significant number of projects, it became more useful to organize functionally—to have a data gathering unit, a data analysis unit, and an administrative unit, with each project contributing a portion of time to each of those functional units. Toward that end, in 1990 Goldman and Lehman merged their activities (the mental health policy studies program and the research program at the Carter Center) and established a new Center for Mental Health Services Research, geared to community-based services research.

"Tony was more interested in the specific interventions, and I was interested in the policies that would facilitate the financing and implementation of those interventions," says Goldman. "My work evolved into economics and finance, and Tony remained more clinically oriented. At that point it looked like we were growing a small business. I didn't want to be a small-business man, and I certainly didn't want to be a large-business man. I was happy to just do the science and executive produce the study: figure what's the best team, write the proposal, get it all situated and either run it, co-run it, or eventually just advise the people who run it. I was very happy to have someone else do all the rest, especially someone of Tony's ability and disposition. Tony clearly ran the operation."

Maryland's medical school was still accustomed to state support and unaccustomed to what Goldman describes as the new "you eat what you kill" world of contract and grant funding for research. Between them, Lehman and Goldman worked out an arrangement in which Lehman was administrative head of the research unit, with support from Goldman, who continued to develop contract research studies with multi-institutional teams of expert subcontractors to do the research and to support the work. Much of the subsequent research the department was able to do was the result of grants. Lehman focused on NIH grant funding. The university had more experience with these NIH grants than the contracts from foundations and other government agencies. This arrangement seems to work for everyone. After all, flexibility about formal arrangements had been what allowed Walter Weintraub and his young colleagues to make a success of the Maryland Plan, a decade earlier.

In the meantime, a great deal more was going on within the department. Many of these activities set the stage for the evolution of clinical services research Lehman and his local team of investigators would undertake. While Goldman continued to pursue policy studies and service evaluations all over the country, Lehman concentrated on investigating clinical assessment tools and clinical services in Baltimore.

In 2001, after Lehman became chair of the department, the Center for Mental Health Services Research was restructured and became part of the Division of Services Research (DSR), directed by Lisa Dixon. The services research division conducts applied research and policy studies on the delivery of services to adults with persistent and severe mental illnesses (and co-morbid somatic conditions) and to children with and at risk for serious emotional disturbances. It disseminates the results of this research, provides training on service delivery and policy implications, and offers technical assistance.

The total annual budget for the division's research portfolio is about $4.5 million, with a history of funding from various federal, state, and private sources, including (in alphabetical order) the Agency for Healthcare Research and Quality, the Center for Mental Health Services, the John A. Hartford Foundation, the Robert Wood Johnson Foundation, the MacArthur Foundation, the Maryland Department of Health and Mental Hygiene, the Maryland Systems Evaluation Center, the Maryland Training Collaborative, the National Association of State Mental Health Directors, NIDA, NIMH, and the Veterans Administration (now the Department of Veterans Affairs). The division also collaborates with the VA Capitol Network (VISN 5) Mental Illness Research Education Clinical Center (MIRECC), directed by Alan Bellack, and the Maryland Psychiatric Research Center, directed by Will Carpenter.

Within the division are three separate but interdependent research cores. The Mental Health Systems Improvement Collaborative (MHSIC), known as Center South, is directed by Eileen Hansen and Sandra Sundeen, under the overall direction of Howard Goldman. Center South disseminates the results of this division's research, provides training on service delivery and policy implications, and offers technical assistance. The Center for Mental Health Services Research (CMHSR), known as Center North, is directed by Lisa Dixon. Center

Di Seybolt, Eileen Hansen, and Sandra Sundeen are long-time staff at the Mental Health Systems Improvement Collaborative ("Center South").

North's portfolio of applied research interests includes the co-morbidity of somatic conditions (such as diabetes) with schizophrenia and affective disorders. The research in Center South tends to be more policy- and training-oriented, the research in Center North more patient- and family-centered. Laurel Kiser, whose work focuses on children and adolescents, heads a third group: the FITT Center and Children's Outcomes Management Center.

The terms Center North and Center South, substitutes for acronyms, designate general locations but do not designate two actual physical centers.

Center South

The creation of Center South is connected to the story of a brief period of disenchantment in the otherwise long and happy collaboration between the department and the state of Maryland. In 1988, when MHA director Adele Wilzack forced out Henry Harbin and his deputy, Ellen Anderson, after they tried expanding patient care using Medicaid resources, John Talbott offered Harbin and Anderson a spot in the department, working on a series of contracts the policy studies group had undertaken. In response, Wilzack had the MHA end all of Goldman's funding from the state. One of the two projects they cut was a project run by Barbara Burns, a leader in children's mental health services; seeing the writing on the wall, she left Maryland for a job at Duke. "That's it," said Goldman. "I'm not working with the state again." Some time went by before anyone from the state approached him again.

As part of the RWJ study, Baltimore had created a not-for-profit local mental health authority called Baltimore Mental Health Systems, Inc., to provide a single point of accountability for mental health, on the premise that with a single entity responsible for pulling together housing, employment, and other important services, mental health services would improve in urban areas and homelessness would decline. In 1991, as work on the nine-city demonstration project was winding down, Stuart Silver, the new MHA director, and his deputy director for policy, Jim Stockdill, asked Goldman to help them use some of the Baltimore Mental Health Authority's unspent money to set up a training center to improve the quality of mental health services in Maryland. They offered him a year's worth of funding.

"I wasn't terribly enamored of the idea," says Goldman, "but I liked Steve Baron, the CEO of Baltimore Mental Health Systems, and I liked the MHA leadership. I felt committed to improving care in Maryland, and it didn't feel right that I was doing things all around the country and not for Maryland. Also, they figured out how to get me money the state couldn't take away, so I didn't have to feel insecure about hiring someone. I couldn't say no anymore."

Goldman hired a succession of directors, including Stan Weinstein (shown here with Sandy Sundeen), to run the training. Sundeen pressed MHA to do more with the department than the training.

Goldman helped set up the infrastructure within the department for the Mental Health Services Training Center. He hired a succession of directors, including Stan Weinstein, who had been at MHA, to organize and run the training, and Goldman himself offered a series of symposia at which county leaders could ask about policies and practices of delivering mental health services. Initially the purpose was to provide technical assistance to the county mental health authorities (called core service agencies, modeled after Baltimore Mental Health Systems, Inc.), to learn from the experience of the RWJ program on chronic mental illness. The training center still provides training as needed throughout the year and puts on the annual MHA conference for 600 to 700 professional service providers.

After a few years, Sandy Sundeen, chief of nursing for the state and MHA project officer for the training center, began pressing for MHA to do more with the department than the training. Tony Lehman's team had finished the Schizophrenia PORT, which was getting a lot of attention, and people were asking, what were the right and wrong services to offer and the right and wrong ways to implement them? Oscar Morgan, the new MHA director, called Goldman, Lehman, and Don Steinwachs to a meeting and said, as Goldman recalls, "You've finished the PORT and Maryland has changed to a fee-for-service Medicaid-driven system. I now feel comfortable that I know how to organize and finance the system in Maryland, but I'm worried that the services we deliver may not be so good." Morgan and Sundeen asked Goldman to create two new centers to complement the training center. The Evidence-Based Practice Center (EBPC) and the Systems Evaluation Center (SEC) were created in 2001, and all three centers became an entity called the Mental Health Systems Improvement Collaborative (MHSIC).

Eileen Hansen heads both the training center and EBPC, located off campus in private space off Caton Avenue in Baltimore. A staff of about twenty (full- and part-time)—people more interested in improving services than in writing papers, says Goldman—can call upon child psychiatry faculty and division staff, including Deborah Medoff, the division statistician, Eric Slade, the division economist, and adult and child psychiatry faculty, as needed. Study coordination and biostatistical analysis units in MHSIC serve

Deborah Medoff, the division's statistician, provides statistical support for everyone in the division.

principal investigators and project managers for all center projects. These units maintain a well-trained staff of research assistants with bachelor's or master's degrees, with unit directors overseeing ongoing staff development, training, and supervision.

"We serve one client: the state," says Goldman, who oversees but by no means micromanages everything. "Our staff is all hired year to year, July to June, on a memorandum of understanding from the state. We participate with others in writing research grants and assist MHA with grant writing, but we are not dependent on most of these grants for our core support."

Also in 2001, Robert E. Drake (at Dartmouth) and Howard Goldman began heading up a national center at Dartmouth College medical school to lead an effort to disseminate information and provide training about evidence-based psychosocial practices, such as supported employment (to help people who are disabled move into the competitive workforce), family psycho-education, assertive community treatment, integrated treatment for individuals with severe mental illness and substance use disorders, and illness self-management (teaching people to be more responsible for their own health care). The work was sponsored by the Robert Wood Johnson Foundation, SAMHSA, and the West Family Foundation.

The EBPC became a node in the network established by the Dartmouth project. It also is using federal funds granted to the Mental Hygiene Administration to teach techniques designed to reduce the use of seclusion and restraint in child residential facilities and inpatient services as well as some adult services.

"We were early in this promotion of evidence-based practices for

"We spent twenty years pursuing systems integration strategies to improve care at the personal level and discovering that systems integration was necessary but not sufficient. Tony's eye, and Lisa's after him, were always on quality of care. Before it was too late, we shifted our attention to that."

people with severe mental illness, but we are lucky," says Lehman. "Most states want to promote evidenced-based practice but Maryland has done the most to promote it. Brian Hepburn, the state's current director of the Mental Hygiene Administration, has actually changed the reimbursement for services so that you get paid more if you provide an evidence-based practice that meets certain criteria. He is really invested in trying to get this to happen in Maryland."

A major national initiative in supported employment provides a good example of how the collaborative as a whole and the individual centers function. The supported employment initiative developed as part of two national projects in evidence-based practices. The MHA agreed to implement supported employment at three sites as part of the national evidence-based practices project cosponsored by SAMHSA and the Robert Wood Johnson Foundation and to add three more sites as a part of another initiative funded by the Johnson & Johnson family of companies. The ground had been broken for supported employment in Maryland a few years earlier, when Lehman and Goldberg conducted a local demonstration project (in collaboration with Drake and Becker at Dartmouth) under the multisite demonstration project funded by SAMHSA's Community Mental Health Services.

The collaborative began working with the initiative through the training center. Using the annual MHA conference in 2001 as a kickoff, it sponsored training by Drake and other experts in evidence-based practices. Training consultants from the EBPC taught organizational change and consensus building and provided onsite consultation at the six sites. The Systems Evaluation Center (SEC) monitored progress on implementation at each of the six sites and, with the training consultant for the EBPC, conducted monitoring activities every six months, to measure how well the model was being followed. Feedback from these evaluations provided the base for ongoing technical assistance. The EBPC and SEC provide continuous implementation and monitoring. The training center sponsors activities to promote the adoption of evidence-based practices throughout the state.

One of the supported employment sites in Maryland, at St. Luke's House, participated as one of twenty-three sites in a major demonstration program, the Mental Health Treatment Study, sponsored by the Social Security Administration. The Mental Health Treatment Study enrolled over two thousand participants in a supported employment and medication management effectiveness trial. Supported employment is an empowering alternative to sheltered workshops—the idea being that anyone can work, with some support. Instead of adults with severe mental illness being put in a sheltered workshop, doing simple, repetitive tasks (such as packaging plastic eating utensils in small bags), they were asked what work they might actually want to do, advised about finding such a job in the competitive marketplace, and provided training and support through a job coach. The analyses are not complete, but the participants—Social Security Administration beneficiaries with disability from mental disorders such as severe depression and schizophrenia—wanted to work and were able to engage in competitive employment.

William Frey of Westat, Bob Drake at Dartmouth, and Goldman put together the proposal to implement and evaluate the project. The project budget was more than fifty million dollars.

The SEC does evaluations for the state Mental Hygiene Administration. It does policy analyses and studies specific to Maryland, which may not generalize beyond Maryland. This is applied science for a single client, the MHA. The SEC looks at outcomes at the level of mental health service systems, to see if they are performing the way the state wants them to.

The SEC designed a statewide Outcomes Management System (to help the state figure out what measures to use in an ongoing system of assessing how people are doing in Maryland) and developed a survey tool to measure how patients perceive the cultural competence of the professionals who treat them. "They respond to requests from the legislature, which doesn't give them enough time to do the work," says Goldman. "These are people who care about improving services but not about publishing papers. We're more a research and development unit, facilitating what measures to use and testing them. Lisa Dixon's center does more rigorous studies, including experiments. She and several of her investigators happen to be especially interested in the medical problems of people with severe mental illness, for example—such as HIV/AIDS, hepatitis, and diabetes. She might do a study using the same measures we do but in addition collect her own set of measures from every patient to find out how well a new intervention works."

Center North

Located on campus, the Center for Mental Health Services (Center North, or CMHS) does real-world research in regular mental health settings with regular staff, to find ways to improve the quality of life of Baltimoreans who have serious mental illnesses. Dixon directs both Center North and the Division of Services Research, of which it is part, where she has recruited and nurtured a dedicated group of faculty and researchers. Others may search for the cure for schizophrenia. Center North focuses on interventions to promote recovery and improve the life experience of patients living with the disease.

Dixon, whose brother was diagnosed with schizophrenia when she was in medical school at Cornell, became deeply involved in services research while working on the Schizophrenia PORT with Tony Lehman. "The PORT study was looking for evidence-based practices," says Dixon, "but it also focused our attention on quality-of-care issues, among other things. It was formative for many of us, driving us into whole new lines of research."

One of those lines of research centered on general health and wellness in patients with schizophrenia. "The PORT data revealed high rates of diabetes in our sample, suggesting the possible importance of co-occurring medical disorders," says Dixon. "We sensed there was a problem and I got a NARSAD grant to study co-occurring disorders, which permitted us to look more carefully and systematically at a representative sample of individuals receiving services in various Baltimore treatment settings. We found high rates not just of diabetes but also of other medical problems, and associ-

A private, nonprofit public charity, the National Alliance for Research on Schizophrenia and Depression (NARSAD) supports research into the prevention and treatment of mental illnesses such as schizophrenia, depression, and bipolar disorder.

ations (if not direct causation) between co-occurring medical problems and other adversities. This seemed an important area for research in service delivery—one that had been under-researched."

After the NARSAD grant, Dixon got an R01 grant from NIMH to look more vigorously at the care of people with schizophrenia who also have diabetes.[10] Researchers interviewed, weighed, and tested blood glucose in 300 patients with diabetes (201 with severe mental illness and 99 without), in a study that "yielded some expected but also some unexpected findings." As anticipated, Dixon found that people with schizophrenia and major mood disorders do experience worse quality of care for their diabetes than other diabetes patients do. Richard Goldberg evaluated the medical charts of patients in the diabetes study for indicators of the quality of care established by the Diabetes Quality Improvement Project. Recommended services for patients with diabetes include a glycosylated hemoglobin examination, eye and foot examinations, blood pressure check, and urine and lipid profiles. Goldberg found that patients with severe mental illness (SMI) received fewer of the recommended services and less education about self-management of diabetes (including cues about the need for glucose monitoring) than patients without SMI.

On the other hand, Dixon and her colleagues found that people with SMI also showed better self-regulation of glucose (a major indicator for diabetes) than a control group of similarly impoverished people receiving services in primary care settings in the city of Baltimore. "This was initially a very difficult finding to explain," says Dixon. "We expected people with mental illnesses to do worse but in fact their diabetes management was better than we saw in the control group. That taught us a lot. Clinicians and researchers

Richard Goldberg found that patients with severe mental illness received fewer of the recommended services and less education about self-management of diabetes (including cues about the need for glucose monitoring) than patients with no mental illness.

tend to automatically assume that people with schizophrenia have no life skills and can't manage their illness. This study taught us that people who are in stable outpatient psychiatric treatment may in fact have some advanced skills in managing chronic illness." Such findings supported the division's hope and recovery approach to treatment, building on patients' strengths.

In the diabetes studies it also became apparent that certain of the antipsychotic drugs were very much associated with metabolic problems: olanzapine, for example, specifically predicted worse diabetes control, a fact that had not been widely reported. "Now, of course, it's well-established that olanzapine is problematic," says Dixon, but when Julie Kreyenbuhl, who had trained as a clinical pharmacist and health services researcher, presented this finding about metabolic problems in a poster session at a national meeting, she received some heat from pharmaceutical representatives. "Under Tony's leadership, we resisted the popular but not scientifically validated view that second-generation antipsychotics were superior to first-generation antipsychotics. Over time it became clear that at least some of the second-generation agents were associated with metabolic problems." Kreyenbuhl is currently testing a patient-centered approach to improving patients' knowledge of metabolic issues, to test whether, before patients go in to see a doctor, giving them specific information about their own metabolic measures (for example, blood pressure and glucose) and the recommended frequency of testing will change the dialogue they have with their doctors and the likelihood of appropriate monitoring.

Services research faculty sought ways to change behaviors that contribute to poor health. A range of unhealthy habits and health problems among adults with SMI—including obesity, diabetes, HIV/AIDS, substance abuse, and smoking-related medical problems—are of huge concern to families, who fear that poor physical health will kill their children before they reach old age. Families have long known about the poor health and high death rates for adults with SMI, but nobody was doing anything about it. Investigators at Center North have been researching how to empower people with

Julie Kreyenbuhl

SMI to deal with their own physical health problems, as part of having a good life in the community. The research staff is not sequestered in a rarefied research environment, but working in the community—exploring what works, or doesn't, in the real world.

For example, after describing the prevalence and pattern of smoking in people with schizophrenia, and recognizing that it was a major public health problem, Center North investigators began exploring interventions to help adults with SMI stop smoking. First they define the problem and estimate how serious it is (in adults with SMI, high rates of smoking lead to high rates of COPD and asthma, among other major health problems); then they find and test interventions to address the problem—in this case, finding effective smoking cessation strategies.

The simplest and most widely accepted evidence-based practice for smoking cessation is the five A's, says Dixon. "It takes thirty seconds for a physician to 'ask, advise, assess, assist, and arrange.' You ask patients if they smoke. If they do, you advise them that one of the best things they can do for their health is to quit. You ask, 'How ready are you to quit?' and say 'I can help you.'" Many studies showed that if primary care doctors do this in regular appointments with patients, smoking declines, so Dixon got an R01 grant to test whether implementing the five A's of smoking cessation in local mental health centers would reduce smoking. "It had never been tried in a community mental health center, even though 50 to 80 percent of our patients smoke," says Dixon. And the results were complicated. "We found that after six months there was no effect but after twelve months there was a suggestion that smoking was reduced. That's not a huge amount but any kind of small change can be big if the number of people who smoke is big. This was a minimal intervention—literally, the doctor taking thirty seconds to say something—and we didn't even get everybody to do it, yet we still found a modest reduction."

Smoking is not an easy habit to change under ordinary circumstances; it is even harder for adults with SMI. "If I have schizophrenia and I'm taking medication that makes me overweight," says Dixon, conveying the problem from the viewpoint of the adult with SMI, "I'm already worried about gaining weight, plus this illness of mine does something to my ability to pay sustained attention. How am I going to manage all these competing priorities?" The percentage of smokers among adults with SMI is two to three times that of the non-schizophrenia population. There is something unique about a disease that makes smoking more likely and probably makes quitting more difficult, says Dixon, and both patient and doctor have to deal with that reality. Such studies are often done in cooperation with the VA's MIRECC researchers, as so many veterans with SMI have a smoking problem and smoking-related diseases. Melanie Bennett, for example, is testing a behavioral treatment for smoking cessation.

There have been similar efforts to empower adults with SMI either to avoid developing certain conditions or diseases or to better manage them once they get them. Many adults with SMI who use IV drugs, for example, develop hepatitis C, a chronic but often fatal disease, sometimes acquired by sharing needles with someone who is infected. There was little indication that evidence-based practices recommended by the Centers for Disease Control and Prevention were being used. Under an NIMH-funded grant for the STIRR project, several Center North investigators are collaborating with a group at Dartmouth on a novel brief intervention at a Baltimore site to increase the use of evidence-based practices (screening, testing, immunization, and risk reduction) for patients at high risk for hepatitis C (adults diagnosed with both SMI and substance abuse). In an NIMH-funded study to improve illness self-management among adults with SMI and co-occurring medical problems, Richard Goldberg used mental health consumers as group facilitators. This study showed that peer support combined with wellness education and opportunities to learn and refine self-management skills led to better illness self-care and general health and resulted in less use of emergency rooms for routine medical care. Goldberg's research team is developing computer platforms to deliver the curriculum he

STIRR: to *Screen* for HIV and hepatitis C risk factors, *Test* for HIV and hepatitis C infection, *Immunize* against hepatitis A and B, *Reduce risk,* and (for those who test positive for HIV and hepatitis C) *Refer* for medical treatment.

designed for a recently completed trial of a weight management program for veterans with SMI.

Maximizing the medical and psychiatric treatment provided to adults likely to have more than one psychiatric or medical problem—and seeing them as a whole person, not just a diagnosis—is a priority in Center North. An important part of many patient-centered studies is figuring out why some things work and others don't—and often it's because of the complex nature of schizophrenia and the very high rate of co-occurring medical disorders. Whatever the specific medical problems, when an individual is coping with two illnesses and coordinating care for both of them, the issues are often similar in terms of personal economy, and both patients and doctors often have to set priorities in weighing alternatives. If patients feel better psychiatrically on olanzapine but it causes weight gain, for example, they may decide to live with the weight gain because it is so important to them to feel better mentally and emotionally.

Seth Himelhoch, a psychiatrist who originally worked primarily with people who had HIV and then developed a psychiatric problem, has also pursued novel interventions to treat psychiatric disorders in HIV medical settings, because doing so empowers better self-care in patients, improving both psychiatric outcomes and adherence to HIV treatment regimens. Psychiatric disorders are present in nearly half of HIV-infected people

In the department's HIV clinic, Seth Himelhoch has developed and tested novel interventions to treat depression, including telephone-based cognitive behavioral therapy for patients without transportation.

HAART (highly active antiretroviral therapy) is less likely to be prescribed to patients with serious mental illness., who are perceived as unreliable patients, because if patients don't comply daily, the virus can mutate and produce a drug-resistant strain that threatens public health. But those patients are then significantly more likely to use costly HIV-related medical inpatient services. Himelhoch showed that patients with depression are very compliant if mental health treatment is provided in the HIV clinic. And, surprisingly, patients with serious mental illness were significantly more likely to remain on HAART than were patients without psychiatric disorders.

In early studies of the prevalence of HIV and hepatitis C among adults with SMI, Himelhoch and colleagues at the University of Michigan found that in the absence of substance use, those with schizophrenia were significantly less likely to be infected with HIV than those without mental illness—in other words, that substance abuse plays a role in the risk of HIV and hepatitis C among those with SMI.

receiving HIV-related medical care, and psychiatric disorders (especially depression and substance abuse) are associated with worse adherence to HIV treatment and worse outcomes. In a pilot randomized trial, Himelhoch is comparing CONNECT, a telephone-based cognitive behavioral therapy intervention, with usual care for HIV-infected patients with major depression. The hope is that overcoming barriers that limit access to outpatient mental health care (such as problems with transportation), by decreasing depressive symptoms, will improve adherence to HAART.

Sometimes the goal of evidence-based practices conflicts with the goal of consumer choice, and then there is work to be done, finding an intervention that both works and is acceptable to consumers. On the original PORT project, Dixon reviewed the literature on programs for families and learned from many research studies that when families and consumers participated in family psycho-education (a nine-month intervention that provides support, education, crisis intervention, and skills training in problem solving), relapse rates were cut in half. As a structured approach to educating families—an intervention professionals delivered to groups of families—psycho-education was shown to be a powerful intervention over and above medication, effective in improving patient outcomes and reducing stress on families. But nationally, it did not catch on. "Our dissemination ultimately failed," says Dixon, "which required declaring defeat and asking, What's missing? What's wrong? Do we need a new practice?"

"Lisa then had the wisdom to look around the country," says Lehman, "and ask, 'What are people doing for families?'" The most widespread program available was a program called Family to Family (F2F), a self-help program developed in Vermont in 1991 by Joyce Burland as an education program for the National Alliance for Mental Illness (NAMI). Burland had developed the intervention partly out of frustration that professionals weren't offering families what they needed. Trained family-member volunteers teach a twelve-week program in weekly two-and-a-half-hour sessions, meeting evenings, when more family members are available. The course focuses on the family member, not the person who is ill, teaching family members the self-care they need to recover from trauma and manage the family burden. In addition to learning the causes, symptoms, and treatments for various mental illnesses (schizophrenia, major depression, bipolar disorder, borderline personality disorder, panic disorder, obsessive–compulsive disorder, and co-occurring addictive disorders), family members learn to manage their negative feelings—by expressing the anger and grief they feel at their sense of loss of the person their family member was before developing mental illness. Because the facilitators are family members, says Dixon, they can empathize and help each other let go of the anger and grief, reduce the amount of worry and displeasure they feel, increase the feeling of family empowerment, develop realistic expectations, and learn where to turn when they are feeling upset or having problems.

The Family to Family program does many of the same things the professionally run family psycho-education program does, but it has its own curriculum, it is run by families, and it is the service most widely available to families. "Through an impressive effort, Lisa persuaded Joyce Burland and NAMI that it was in NAMI's interest to do a randomized clinical trial—a trial they're just finishing—to determine if this was an evidence-based practice," says Lehman. "NAMI was worried that science getting involved would be the kiss of death, even if families liked it. In the evolution in family services, Lisa has led the transition, and I don't know anyone else who could have done that. She has the research credentials, she is committed to family education, and she is a family member herself. The underlying theme here is empowerment, in this case recognizing that families who are living with a problem often have the best idea of how to help someone else and can help each other. Even the professionally based interventions have adapted to the wisdom of families and the value of peer counseling. Dixon's greater involvement with family-based interventions led to a whole new level of psycho-education, says Lehman, and to the department's even greater involvement in identifying, using, and spreading the word about evidence-based practices.

Alicia Lucksted designed a study to find out why, although professionally led family psycho-education has been shown to be effective, it is rarely implemented successfully. She conducted interviews and focus groups with individuals with SMI, to come up with practical guidance for practitioners and researchers trying to strengthen family involvement in information, support, and caregiving interventions. She led a qualitative study of change processes in NAMI's Family to Family (F2F) program, to develop an explanatory model of how F2F comes to have its effects. NAMI has used that model to convey what potential participants may expect from the intervention; it has also informed outcome measurement for the current NIMH-funded randomized control trial of F2F, of which Lucksted is co-PI.

Through qualitative evaluation, Alicia Lucksted helped determine why family psycho-education, though shown to be effective, was less popular than NAMI's Family to Family program.

After using qualitative methods in her doctoral dissertation, "Turning Points in the Lives of People with Serious Mental Illness," Lucksted has used research and theoretically informed, applied problem-solving to help achieve grounded, consumer-oriented, positive outcomes, recovery-focused services, and consumer–community connections. "Quantitative methods can establish that an intervention has a significant effect," says Lucksted, but "qualitative examination of the *process* by which that effect occurs" is often needed to translate research into better practices. Many researchers depend on Lucksted for her expertise in qualitative methods of evaluation. Combining her knowledge of research methods with her observations about what erodes the lives of people with severe mental illness, she helps others develop novel interventions with potentially wide application.

The program Mental Health First Aid, for example, was developed in Australia to educate the community about mental illness so that members of the community could respond to a mental health emergency in much the same way people with basic training in CPR might respond to a person having a myocardial infarction. Many U.S. municipalities pursued the program after a college student's shooting spree at Virginia Tech. In a SAMHSA contract on Mental Health

First Aid, Lucksted is applying rigorous research methodology and concepts to an emerging community-based program that was created by people with no background in research or evaluation. She is balancing a collaborative working relationship with the MHFA-USA partners, rigorous evaluation methods, and objective analysis in a formative evaluation of Mental Health First Aid as it is implemented across the country. She also helped key MHFA-USA partners develop national certification standards. The prevailing new philosophy is that the failure of research to inform practices stems in part from the failure of research to understand and incorporate the views of the key stakeholders. Lucksted's SAMHSA project is part of a new commitment in the field to correct that problem.

Working with the other researchers, Eric Slade, the division's economist, calculates the probable and actual cost of testing interventions and disseminating them systemwide—analyzing if, on a large scale, they would be cost-effective, and for whom. Implementing evidence-based practices often elicits unintended consequences and, if criteria are too broad, evidence-based services tend to increase costs. Slade plays a crucial role in designing research both to work sustainably in the real world and to get realistic funding.

Eric Slade, the division's economist, calculates the probable and actual cost of testing interventions and disseminating them systemwide.

Some of the services research focuses more on how to improve the system, including medical practices. Goldberg was an investigator on Dixon's VA-based study of a brief critical-time intervention to improve continuity of care by bridging the gap between psychiatric hospitalization and community-based services. In this study, to promote post-discharge continuity of outpatient care, patients who were hospitalized and at risk for dropping out of treatment were assigned a case manager for three months after discharge.

The three-month intervention was markedly successful at promoting continuity of care. Much of Goldberg's work has focused on how to integrate psychiatric and somatic services and how to translate research into effective practice. His research has addressed such issues as how mental illness itself (including cognitive impairment) affects the ability of adults with SMI to manage their health, whether and how poverty limits their ability to access health care, and how the way they present may affect the medical care they get (especially from medical professionals who feel uncomfortable dealing with a patient who is psychotic).

Goldberg has also done research on vocational rehabilitation. Drawing on data gathered on the SAMHSA-funded supported employment study, he organized the supported employment studies for the 2003 update of the Schizophrenia PORT.

Kreyenbuhl studied why individuals with co-occurring psychiatric and substance use disorders, as well as those with early-onset psychosis (especially young men from ethnic minorities, with low social functioning), are at greater risk of dropping out of treatment. Engagement strategies to target high-risk groups and high-risk periods (for example, after an emergency room or hospital admission and during the initial period of treatment) range from appointment reminders to assertive community treatment and include more communication to promote the consumer's active involvement in treatment decisions (partly by explaining why it is important). Alicia Lucksted and Amy Drapalski are working on an intervention to end self-stigma among patients with SMI. Whatever the context—co-occurring addiction, co-occurring medical problems, supported employment, effective psycho-education with families, or intrapsychic work such as reducing self-stigma—researchers in Center North define the problem, find and test interventions to improve the quality of care, and create new practices to address any problems that unfold as the work proceeds.

The department is now participating in a major NIMH-funded research project that will integrate the work of faculty and staff at Centers North and South, MIRECC, and the MPRC. RAISE (Recovery After an Initial Schizophrenia Episode) is a study important to the field with which NIMH hopes to "fundamentally change the trajectory and prognosis of schizophrenia through coordinated and aggressive treatment in the earliest stages of illness."[11]

Most people who develop schizophrenia do not receive a diagnosis or treatment until months or years have elapsed after the initial symptoms appear. But research suggests that the longer treatment is delayed after a first episode of psychosis, the less likely the person will be to experience a significant degree of recovery. Left untreated, symptoms of schizophrenia can lead to a host of secondary problems, including disruptions in school and work, strained family relations, and estrangement from friends. The longer initial symptoms persist, the greater the risk for co-occurring problems such as substance abuse, incarceration, or homelessness. And negative changes in a person's life circumstances (unemployment, estrangement from the family, addiction to one or more substances, a police record, or medical problems) can make access to treatment, the likelihood of maintaining treatment, and the prospects of recovery both much more difficult and more expensive.

A federally funded demonstration project, RAISE is using a randomized clinical trial to learn which alternative interventions work better for young people who have experienced their first psychosis—especially to learn if certain early, proactive interventions produce better short-term outcomes. (Later, it is hoped, there will be studies of long-term outcomes.) RAISE researchers are combining medications and psychosocial treatments using evidence-based practices identified in the PORT project and Dixon's work with families.

Teams set up at four sites in New York (where Jeffrey A. Lieberman, of Columbia, is principal investigator) and four in Maryland (where Lisa Dixon is PI) will randomly assign patients to get a new intervention, a package intervention, or routine care. Many faculty members from Center North, MIRECC, and the MPRC are co-investigators, Howard Goldman is on the executive committee, and staff members at Center South are involved in program site recruitment, referrals, and assessments. This important project has the full support of the state Mental Hygiene Administration (including Brian Hepburn and Gayle Jordan-Randolph, who have strong connections to the department). The Division of Community Psychiatry will run one arm of the study, in the Carruthers clinic. "For the research protocol, we'll have two full-time staff, two half-time staff, and 20 percent of a physician to treat twenty patients," says Jill RachBeisel, director of community psychiatry. "That's exciting and it's bound to be successful. Trying to implement evidence-based practices in real life on a real-life budget, that's more of a struggle."

FITT Center and Children's Outcomes Management Center

Laurel Kiser, whose work focuses on children and adolescents, accepted a faculty position in the Division of Services Research in 2000. Supported by grants from NIMH and SAMHSA, she has spent twenty years addressing the high rates of exposure to trauma and the prevalence of trauma-related disorders in families living in urban poverty. Kiser is senior psychologist and principal investigator in the Family-Informed Trauma Treatment (FITT) Center—a Category II center authorized by SAMHSA as part of the National Child Traumatic Stress Network,[12] which is studying how to make available across various state agencies more effective treatments for underserved urban and military families experiencing chronic trauma and stress. The FITT Center at Maryland's medical school partners with the School of Social Work and the Kennedy Krieger Family Center. In 2007, the center received a four-year, $2.4 million award from SAMHSA. Kathleen "Kay" Connors is program director for both the FITT Center and Secure Starts, a program in the child psychiatry division. Connors and Kiser, both experts in trauma, bring that expertise to the team and help provide training and education about trauma. In addition to working in services research, Kiser teaches and provides supervision in child psychiatry.

Kiser and her husband, David Pruitt (director of the division of child and adolescent psychiatry) joined the department at the same time.

Families living in persistently harsh and impoverished conditions, with exposure to violence or physical and sexual abuse, find it difficult to attend to the daily tasks of living or to cope with daily stress. Multiple dangers and reminders of trauma can significantly disrupt emotional stability for everyone in the family. Families living in urban poverty report frequent exposure to community violence, illegal drug activities, residential and financial instability, safety concerns (such as house fires and rat infestations), difficulty finding a safe way to get children to and from school, and the many daily hassles associated with crowding and too little access to resources and opportunities. Parental distress makes positive parenting difficult and increases the risk that children will develop emotional or behavior problems.

The FITT Center puts such families together with treatments that are family-centered and trauma-specific. They develop, evaluate, disseminate, and put into practice family approaches that promote safety and recovery for all family members—using a model that builds on evidence-based trauma treatments. They offer three new family interventions to help families cope, recover, and gain resilience after either a complex family trauma or the multiple traumas associated with urban poverty.

Funded by a K Award, Laurel Kiser developed a multifamily group intervention, Strengthening Families' Coping Resources (SFCR, also in the FITT Center), which uses family rituals, routines, and traditions to help families cope, recover from trauma, and grow.

Laurel Kiser (shown here with her husband, David Pruitt, director of child and adolescent psychiatry) has spent twenty years addressing the high rates of exposure to trauma and the prevalence of trauma-related disorders in families living in urban poverty. She is principal investigator of the Family-Informed Trauma Treatment Center and the Children's Outcomes Management Center.

Some of the children have been traumatized by a one-time trauma, such as a murder or beating; many of them have what are called developmental trauma disorders, brought on by many traumas over an extended period. Studies have shown that many children who experience physical or sexual abuse react with symptoms of post-traumatic stress syndrome, and that repeated exposure to trauma creates even greater difficulties for the victim than single-event trauma does.

Research suggests that when families faced with stressors carry on with traditions, children grow up with much better outcomes than they would otherwise—the rituals and routines seem to serve a protective function. "Laurel has built this idea of traditions, rituals, and routines into a multifamily group where she brings three to five families together so they can support each other," says Barbara Baumgardner, a former lead group facilitator. "We build on that, teach them ways to manage stress, cope with change, and manage the traumatic experiences that they've gone through."

A group of five families meets two hours a week for fifteen weeks, starting with a "family meal." They are fed good food, especially vegetables and fresh fruit, served on tables set with tablecloths, centerpieces, and imprinted place cards. The staff models good behaviors, particularly loving voices and gentle touch, and parents are taught, for example, that if a child hits someone, not to respond by hitting the child. Parents and children play games together that build skills or teach a lesson—for example, to curtail the number of negative comments to the child, to praise the child's attempts, and to focus both their own and their child's attention on a particular task. They advise that if a child's birthday party is planned, it goes on as scheduled, even if one parent comes in drunk or behaves badly in some other way. They teach that families need to remember, rediscover, plan, and implement routines, rituals, and traditions that are comfortable, satisfying, and meaningful to all family members. Once the family has developed these new coping skills, the staff helps them talk about their family's traumas. The Secure Starts staff and Carol Norris-Shortle take a different version of the intervention to Early Head Start and to nurseries in domestic violence centers such as the House of Ruth.

The FITT Center is developing a toolkit to help child trauma clinicians develop the attitudes, knowledge, and skills necessary to effectively address complex family-level issues. The toolkit will support a family-centered approach to trauma treatment and help connect families to effective evidence-based trauma practices.

Kiser is also principal investigator of the Children's Outcomes Management Center (COMC),[13] which was formed in 2002 to help behavioral health providers and organizations manage accountability and quality improvement. COMC developed and operates KIDnet, an Internet-based outcomes monitoring system introduced in 2004 to meet the complex information technology needs of various stakeholders in children's behavioral health. Service providers can enter and store information on KIDnet about the level of services provided to each child or adolescent and keep track of the impact of those services as they are being provided rather than after the fact. Steven Herr is program director, over a staff that manages system development and maintenance, training and technical assistance, data storage and transmittal, management of data integrity and analysis, and reporting of results.

The services side of community psychiatry

Over the course of several phone conversations, Brian Hepburn, who was then an associate training director and is now head of the Maryland Mental Hygiene Administration, recruited Jill RachBeisel, now chief of the Division of Community Psychiatry, to do her psychiatric residency (1985–89) in the department. After she completed that residency, her first job in the department was inpatient attending, running a very active, thirty-bed, acute-care inpatient unit with Dave Mallott. Mallott, who had come from Tulane as a senior psychiatrist in 1986, when RachBeisel was a second year resident, was expert in running acute care and working with patients with severe mental illness. Each of them had two residents and two medical students to help care for fifteen patients—mostly acutely ill, psychiatrically unstable patients with schizophrenia.

"I learned a tremendous amount from Dave. He never got rattled and was able to meet with the staff and process things, so if a patient was particularly violent or inappropriate (sexually or otherwise), he was able to sit with the staff, think through the symptoms, develop a treatment plan, implement it, and get things under control. He was able to bring staff together, so our teams worked well together. This is important in acute care because things can be fine one hour and not, the next. Most of us appreciated his use of comic relief in difficult situations, and he gave me a sense of confidence."

In 1993 RachBeisel became director of inpatient psychiatry, and in 1998 she became both division director for adult and geriatric psychiatry and director of clinical services. In 1999, when Tony Lehman was acting chair of the department, he asked her to be acting head of the division of community psychiatry as well. For eighteen months she held three jobs—as director of adult and geriatric psychiatry, clinical services, and community psychiatry—and, she says, "I was about to lose my mind." Within a year Lehman had offered her a permanent job heading community psychiatry, but for some time she resisted, feeling she shouldn't abandon her home division of adult and geriatric psychiatry. She did, finally, because, she says, "I fell in love with community psychiatry: the people, the patients, the program. It was refreshing, it was exciting—it pierced my soul. It was what I wanted to be doing."

She resigned from adult and geriatric, which became two divisions, and became director of the division of community psychiatry in 2000. This was, among other things, a shift from acute care to longer-term care. In the adult and geriatric division, she'd been running acute-level services: inpatient units, the emergency room, and the day program. "People get very sick, they come to your program, you might know them for a couple weeks, and then they're gone. Inpatient care stabilizes patients and enables them to step out and embark on something, but community psychiatry is the *something* they can come to. There are people in our clinic we've been treating for fifteen or twenty years. We treat whole families—kids, Mom, Dad, Grandma, and Grandpa—although women are more likely to get treatment than men are. We develop relationships and we can develop programs that have a lasting impact on the quality of people's lives."

Community Psychiatry began as a complex of grant-funded outpatient mental health clinics in 1966, to provide community-based care for individuals previously treated in large state-operated psychiatric hospitals. As the financial and services landscape changed, the state gradually moved from a catchment-area system (under which where a person got care was determined by geographic boundaries, and the catchment area lived with a fixed budget) to a fee-for-service model operated by a network of private health care providers—often with reimbursement from Medicare, Medicaid, or other third-party payers.

Today there are four major programs in the division: the outpatient clinics (including a continuous care team), PACT, psychiatric and residential rehabilitation programs (Harbor City Unlimited, supported living, and supported employment) and targeted case management and benefits services (the Community Support Program, the SSI Outreach Project, and the Safe Haven shelter). The programs the division has launched over the years have mirrored (or piloted and tested) what was going on in services research—especially evidence-based practices. The Carter Center, for example, was the first program in the state to develop a PACT program with both child and adult arms.

PACT serves 170 adults and children, the residential rehabilitation program serves up to 52 homeless people with severe mental illness, and the community support program offers 626 services a year. Psychosocial rehabilitation provides 21,450 services a year.

"When I took over the division we focused on growing the program and bringing it into the twenty-first century," says RachBeisel, "so that it was more consumer-driven and more consumer- and recovery-focused. We worked with clients, not patients. We developed more integrated care— meaning we worked with the client, the family, and the support system. With a child, for example, our team works with the school, the teachers, the parents, the grandparents. They go into the home and try to engage the entire system an individual lives in. We know that the bigger the support system, the more family involved, the more likely clients will be to successfully manage their illness and do well."

Community psychiatry, which is regulated by the state of Maryland, is funded by the public sector, so the salaries are not high. A nurse, for example, can make more working in the hospital than in community psychiatry. "So if you're working in my division it's because you love the people and really want to do the work," says RachBeisel. "You have to get your gratification from doing the work. And I have never seen a more dedicated staff anywhere, with a level of energy and investment you don't often see. They have been here a long time and go above and beyond what they have to do. They each have a caseload of people who are their responsibility. Engaging the members often requires extended hours and a lot of creativity. This program gives them the right platform."

"The bigger the support system, the more family involved, the more likely clients will be to successfully manage their illness and do well," says Jill RachBeisel, director of community psychiatry. "You will never see a more dedicated staff anywhere."

Lisa Dixon and Alan Bellack in Services Research and the VA's Mental Illness Research Education and Clinical Center (MIRECC) run many of their studies in the community psychiatry program, which has huge numbers of target patients. Transferring their big studies to real life is never easy, says RachBeisel, because in real life the staff-to-patient ratio is less generous than it is in research projects. Everyone benefits from the extra staffing associated with a research project, which in a sense creates an artificial environment. Actualizing a model program on the regular budget of the clinical program is a challenge, but as a result of the partnership between community psychiatry and services research, the division is always on the leading edge in developing evidence-based practices.

In medical literature, they are patients, not clients.

Outpatient clinics. The division provides outpatient healthcare services to 1,500 to 2,000 patients a year. The outpatient clinics have been completely converted to a recovery model, in which the psychiatrist and therapists engage individuals around what they have determined their needs and goals to be. "We help them manage their illness and help them set small steps to achieve whatever goal they have identified," says RachBeisel. "It's not what we think they should be doing but what they want to do."

The clinic at the Carter Center has an active caseload of about 1,450 patients, of which about 400 are children or adolescents. From 65 to 70 percent of the adult patients served have serious and persistent mental illnesses. The clinic provides individual, group, and family therapies, as well as medication management, case management, and substance abuse services. At each clinic site teams also provide psychiatric services for children aged five to eighteen and their families. Services include individual, play, group, and family therapies, medication evaluation, socialization groups, and consultation with schools and other community agencies involved with a child. Substance abuse evaluations and treatment are also available.

In the complex system of comprehensive mental health services that has evolved, the majority of services are fee-for-service. People with Medicare, Medicaid, or no insurance are entitled to receive care in the publicly supported mental health system of the University of Maryland Medical Center. The department operates two outpatient clinics that provide comprehensive mental health treatment and case management services, mainly to residents of Baltimore City. Multidisciplinary mental health teams provide outpatient clinic services to children, adolescents, and adults at the Walter P. Carter Center (located on West Fayette Street until late 2009, when it relocated to 701 Pratt Street) and the Carruthers Clinic at the Inner Harbor. Eileen Hastings is the clinic program director and Jill RachBeisel is medical director. Brian Hastings is medical director for the continuous care team.

The continuous care team (CCT) is a specialized intensive psychiatric and case management service for adult patients who require services and coordinated community mental health care of intermediate intensity. By providing consistent outreach and coordination of care right after a patient is released from the hospital, this team works to reduce the incidence of psychiatric rehospitalization and to improve the patient's ability to function in the community. The CCT staff is on call by beeper, as needed, around the clock.

The Program of Assertive Community Treatment (PACT) evolved from the federally funded research PACT project that Tony Lehman and Lisa Dixon ran. In 1993 PACT became a freestanding treatment service in the division of community psychiatry, providing services to both adults and children who were homeless and mentally ill. The state accepted it as a reimbursable service in the mid-1990s and as an evidence-based mental health service in 2006. The interdisciplinary mobile

The state accepted ACT as a reimbursable service in the mid-1990s and as an evidence-based mental health service in 2006. The interdisciplinary mobile outreach treatment program is licensed, certified, and staffed by psychiatrists, nurses, social workers, counselors, and an employment specialist.

outreach treatment program is licensed, certified, and staffed by psychiatrists, nurses, social workers, counselors, and an employment specialist.

"We engage people who are homeless and mentally ill out in the community—connecting through shelters, the House of Ruth, My Sister's Place, Project Hope, and other community programs—and then get them to come in for treatment," says RachBeisel. "The child PACT team serves a cohort of very, very troubled children—from age six through seventeen (at eighteen they are considered adults)—who can't or won't come in for traditional care, or whose families refuse to bring them in. Many of our kids are from indigent, fragmented, inner-city families with poor role models: maybe Dad's in jail, Mom's using drugs, and they're being raised by Grandma or Aunt Sophie.

"When I first came, the child PACT was tiny and not very functional. We can now follow up to forty children at a time, with a staff of five. We engage the child around developmentally appropriate goals and behaviors, and help the family develop parenting skills, so they can better manage these children: give them incentive to do well, reward them for good behavior and good school performance, and help them find hope. We work with the teachers, the parents, and the children themselves. It is intensive work. We have had some significant success in helping to stabilize families, stabilize the kids, and help them do well in school."

PACT has summer programs through which the kids experience healthy recreational activity. "A lot of these kids are unsupervised, and, left to their own devices, they're running the streets selling drugs. The earlier you get them, the better chance you have of making a difference, although one kid who was referred to us at fourteen was into drugs, had been arrested and removed from the home, was in a residential setting, and was just a mess. He did so well that he finished school, is living at home with his mother, is working, and at nineteen graduated completely out of the system: he doesn't need mental health services anymore."

These mobile treatment teams are an important part of the department's community mental health program. There is a mobile treatment team for children who are homeless, and the department also runs housing and employment programs. "It is all part of therapy," says Lehman. "And the biggest champions of the program are legislators from the local community, because these are services for their constituents. The practitioners feel there is never enough money to do things, because of the magnitude of the need. It's like the school system: the need is endless. But there are lots of moving stories about dedicated staff doing good work with people who need help."

In 2010, Yolanda Jones is program director and Ann Hackman is medical director. Psychiatric services include crisis intervention, assessment and diagnosis, medication management, treatment for dual diagnosis, and twenty-four-hour, seven-day availability by phone. Case managers help clients locate and secure housing and work, apply for entitlements, find a representative payee (an individual or organization who accepts benefit payments on their behalf if they have trouble managing such benefits—if they have a drinking problem, for example), and get medical care and transportation to local medical providers. Staff also help children and adolescents by providing training in parenting, family support and education, and collaboration and advocacy in the school system.

Psychosocial services. In the 1980s, the department made its first foray into psychiatric rehabilitation, drawing on the experiences of pioneers elsewhere. Psychiatric rehab had begun in the 1960s as one of several grassroots movements to address communities' failure to provide adequate support and resources for the many patients being released from state mental hospitals in the period of deinstitutionalization. Psychiatry had been addressing people's needs for psychotherapy and medications but not such life problems as the need to find housing and work and to get along with others and in the community. People with severe psychiatric problems sometimes misinterpret social cues or don't know how to respond to them, face prejudice or bullying if they seem different, don't easily handle such daily hassles as bus travel or grocery shopping, and often have trouble concentrating and finding energy and motivation.

Rehab programs, when they first got going, were somewhat antiauthoritarian. One of the first important efforts, Fountain House, in New York (which is still going), was the original *clubhouse model*, a self-help program to empower people with disabilities to take care of themselves. Started by a group of people discharged from a New York psychiatric hospital, in the 1960s it evolved into an innovative community-based program to help people with mental illness reclaim their lives. Participants were called members, not patients, and efforts focused on their strengths and abilities, not their illness.

In the 1970s, Bill Anthony, at Boston University, who established the Center for Psychosocial Rehabilitation, developed a recovery model of rehabilitation. His work in personal growth and recovery focused on living, learning, working, and socializing—and had a major influence on community mental health care everywhere.

Anthony, who later developed multiple sclerosis, has also written a lot about napping.

In the early to mid-1970s, when, as John Talbott says, "all of the rest of us were riding around in police cars," UCLA psychiatrist Robert Paul "Bob" Liberman began developing *skills training modules*, a behavioral approach to training people with mental disabilities in social and independent living skills. He began adapting the principles of behavior therapy to what would be called *psychosocial rehabilitation*.

Talbott is referring to the period when social scientists were trying to change the way police officers related to members of the community.

"People who need to function in a society—as opposed to being locked up in an institution—have to acquire a lot of skills and learn to advocate for additional supports and services," he told interviewers. "Medication in no way can convey or generate those kinds of skills. Achieving this level of competency requires a partnership between patients and professionals, with a hefty input from the families."[14]

Liberman developed the training modules after he realized that "the only way to bring about improvement in the quality of life of people with severe mental disorders is to teach them how to do it all, from learning the skills they need to meet the expectations of society, to galvanizing the necessary supports and services that they need to function even if they don't have the skills. I was a resident physician training in psychiatry when the first translations of human learning theory and principles were being made to psychiatry and education. The students of the famous behavioral psychologist B.F. Skinner were beginning to publish striking benefits in mental patients who were seriously disabled from reinforcing or strengthening positive and functional behaviors while giving less attention to abnormal behaviors and symptoms. These reports were convincing because of the experimental methods that were used and the dramatic effects that were achieved. Principles and techniques of operant conditioning, now used in rehabilitation of all physical and mental disorders, made sense and were straightforward in their logic and simplicity. The same principles had been known for fifty years to be key influences on the development of normal children and the process of learning knowledge and skills in normal adults. . . . Coming from a different direction, behavior therapy offered me the relief from the frustrations and disenchantment I was experiencing in futile efforts to apply the prevailing psychoanalytic concepts to persons who lacked insight and couldn't even comprehend my verbal interpretations of their bizarre thinking and behavior."

"Changes in rehabilitation psychiatry have been dramatic. In the old days, psychiatry rehab was basket weaving. It was keeping patients occupied and diverted. Now it involves training patients in the practical activities of everyday living."

The social skills training modules Liberman developed involved role playing and modeling, prompting, feedback, and reinforcement by the therapist. Training in problem-solving skills helped participants develop strategies for dealing with various social situations and might cover such topics as conversational skills, friendship and intimacy, workplace fundamentals, good management of leisure time, medication and symptom self-management, and management of substance abuse. For patients who were withdrawn or highly distractible, an attention-focusing model was designed to teach skills through constant repetition of tasks, minimizing demand on cognitive abilities.

"Changes in rehabilitation psychiatry, which in a funny way paralleled changes in medical rehabilitation, have been dramatic," says John Talbott. "Both are way ahead of where they were in 1950. In the old days, psychiatry rehab was basket weaving. It was keeping patients occupied and diverted. Now it involves training patients in the practical activities of everyday living. It involves teaching the techniques of teaching to cadres of rehabilitation workers, who then work with patients. That has made life a lot easier for a lot of patients."

"When I went to my first rehab with something like a sprained ankle, they didn't know anything," says Talbott. "Now I go to a guy who knows all about bones, muscles, ligaments, counterbalance, and teaches me exercises they didn't know about forty years ago. The same thing happened in psychiatry."

In the early 1980s, the Maryland Association of Psychosocial Services (MAPS), advocated heavily for more state investment in psychosocial rehabilitation programs. "MAPs particularly wanted training dollars to help those programs develop," says Tony Lehman. "As director of the state Mental Hygiene Administration, Alp Karahasan set up a contract with the department to run a training program in psychosocial rehabilitation. In 1985 Alp began running that training program, in coordination with Ruth Hughes, MAPS's director."

Hughes later became director of MAPS's parent organization, the International Association of Psychosocial Rehabilitation Services (IAPSRS). In that position she wrote, "Mental illness is not the major barrier; it is poverty, lack of education, trained helplessness, the hopelessness people feel when they have been told, year in and year out, that you cannot be responsible for your own life. Psychosocial rehabilitation programs should work with people to change those things." Another major goal is to eliminate the stigma associated with mental illness and sometimes perpetuated by mental health professionals.

In 1986, when Lehman joined the faculty, he inherited the training program from Karahasan. "Ruth and I and Rosalie Rapoport, a social worker, worked together for a year or two doing statewide training for these rehab programs," says Lehman, "educating people about the different models of rehabilitation. Most of these rehab programs started as mom-and-pop operations run by people who were visionaries or advocates (often counter-psychiatry folks) who wanted to provide day services for local people with mental disabilities. They provided housing, but they often had very little training. Our desire

Rosalie Rapoport's spouse was Mort Rapoport, CEO of the university medical center.

was to train people in the clubhouse model, the Boston University model, the Liberman skills training model, and to give them basic information about mental illness: what is schizophrenia, what is bipolar disorder, what is depression, what are the medical treatments for them, and how to interface with psychiatry in the clinics. The idea was to give clients information and let them make their own decisions, but also to let them know the consequences if they made the wrong decisions.

"That program lasted for a while, but it was conceptually flawed. I think MAPS wanted to control the whole thing, but Alp had based it in the university with a psychiatrist— first him, then me—as head of it. I was supposed to manage it, but it was really unwieldy. Psychiatric rehab is pretty complicated, and things weren't working. The rehab programs weren't interacting with the clinics, the clinics didn't know much about the rehab programs and thought they had different philosophies about illness, and so on. The rehab view was antiauthoritarian, and the clinic view was fairly paternalistic and authoritarian. Henry Harbin, the MHA director who came after Alp, tried to break that down, but there wasn't a consensus even from the state on what the mission was, other than throwing money at these programs, so Henry eventually ended the program."

After several years, the state-supported training for psychiatric rehabilitation in Maryland was reinvigorated with a program Howard Goldman now runs, the Mental Health Systems Improvement Collaborative, which works with core service agencies to improve services throughout the state. In the meantime, the MHA replaced the grant-based financing of community services with a managed fee-for-service model funded by Medicaid. This arrangement led to the consolidation of providers into companies with several rehab programs, with community clinics working together more closely rather than as separate constituents competing for grants. The new arrangements also meant that all willing providers could offer services, which provided more consumer choice and led to the breakdown of strict catchment areas. And to be reimbursed, rehab programs were required to coordinate with the clinics' treatment plans.

In 1986 the division established Harbor City Unlimited, a nonmedical psychiatric and residential rehabilitation program for adults with severe mental illness, based on the recovery model. Harbor City operates both residential and employment programs and provides psychosocial rehabilitation services to adults with chronic mental illnesses. Services include skills training, leisure activities, and support for employment, housing, and substance abuse treatment.

The residential rehabilitation program helps individuals learn to live in the community, by providing a supportive home-like environment—the goal being that most clients advance to independent living. This program serves up to fifty-two people living in nineteen homes—with two or three people to a home, each in their own bedroom. This program provides varying levels of staff support, including a six-person transitional residency program for young men (ages sixteen to twenty-one) returning from out-of-state placements. Staff help adults manage their illness, establish an identity other than being mentally ill, and move forward with their life.

There is also day programming, which help residents meet such goals as getting a GED (classes are available onsite), getting a job, and living independently. Many people with mental illness do not know how to use their recreational time. More than a hundred people a day attend the psychiatric rehabilitation program, which teaches social and recreational skills. In a community atmosphere, people learn to reach their goals through various social and recreational opportunities designed to help them learn social skills.

In the fall of 2009 RachBeisel and her staff launched the Academy of Independent Living, a new program for all fifty-two members of residential housing. Structured in a college-like format, the academy teaches residential clients skills needed for independent living. They must register for the courses, which run nine to thirteen weeks, with both classroom and practicum work, with intensive skill development. At a final ceremony, those who complete the course get a certificate and demonstrate what they've accomplished.

The first academy, in December 2009, addressed hygiene and personal appearance. "Most of us take for granted that you dress differently if you're going to play basketball than you do if you are going for a job interview," says RachBeisel, "but dressing appropriately is a new skill for many of our clients. A lot of our folks are not socially aware and don't know how often you should wash your hair, take a bath, or brush your teeth. When we taught them the importance of cleaning their nails (showing them how many germs they may carry under their nails), they all got emery boards and orange sticks. They had fun smelling various shampoos, soaps, and body shower gels and were wildly enthusiastic learning about taking better care of themselves. A staff member took photographs in a professional studio of those who completed the course, and those portraits, matted and framed, hang on our wall of first impressions at Harbor City."

Clients in residential housing learn skills needed for independent living, such as how to cook a meal, sew a button, dress appropriately, manage their money, and manage their medications.

Nineteen members graduated from the course on nutrition and food preparation that was offered the second semester. People who said they couldn't cook learned how to plan meals, develop a grocery list, select and buy food at a grocery store, get the right proportions for the number they have to feed, then prepare, cook, and eat the food. They learned which foods, in which food groups, they should eat more or less of. They looked at cookbooks and learned things like how to measure and how to simmer or flash fry. Occupational therapy, which helped with the cooking, helped participants inventory and organize their kitchens. In groups of three, at semester's end they showed an audience how to prepare a favorite dish (including Fricking Fabulous French Toast) for a videotaped Julia Child–style cooking show, speaking with a microphone to a small audience. "Some were more nervous than others, but they were all smiling, and did a great job," says RachBeisel.

(*main text continues on page 434*)

John A. Talbott

"As I try to characterize the tenure of John Talbott as chairman of the department of psychiatry at the University of Maryland, I am reminded of the pundit's view of a dog riding a bicycle," wrote Dave Mallott on Talbott's retirement. "The amazing thing was not that the dog rode well, but that the dog could ride at all. In 1985, psychiatrists measured lengths of hospital stay in weeks, and often months, drafts of DSM-III-R worked their way through committees, SSRIs had not appeared in the clinical setting much less on the cover of *Newsweek*, and the second term of the Reagan administration promised little in terms of new social programs for psychiatric patients with severe and persistent mental illness. Computers did not grace every desk, the full impact of AIDS was still sinking into the minds of both medicine and society, and thoughtful people mused about the possible effect of a healthcare strategy known as the HMO.

Despite these turbulent times, the department of psychiatry not only survived but prospered. Much of this is a tribute to John Talbott.

"In 1985 John arrived with a national reputation as a prominent spokesperson for psychiatry and for those with chronic mental illness. As president of the APA, he articulated the need for more research, more care, and more creative approaches for our most vulnerable, stigmatized, and problematic patients. As chairman, he would preside over a department that made strides in all of these areas. He arrived wearing a clinician's white coat, providing the residents with an easy target for spoof, but conveying a message that psychiatry stood shoulder to shoulder with the other medical specialties."[*]

Talbott was born in 1935 in Cambridge, Massachusetts, the son of a nurse (a fine amateur pianist) and a prominent internist, John H. Talbott, who taught at Harvard Medical School.[†] During the war,

---

[*] David Mallott, "The Talbott Years (1985–1999)." *The Maryland Psychiatrist* (Fall/Winter 2000).

[†] As a youth, John A. accompanied his father, John H., to Massachusetts General Hospital, to McLean (where John H. tried to cool the patients enough that their schizophrenia would be "cured"), and to the Harvard Fatigue Laboratory, where he researched the physiological effects of exposure to high altitudes. John H. was an expert in extreme conditions—of cold, heat, rain, dehydration, or high altitudes, for example—in places such as Boulder Dam and the Andes. During World War II he ran the Army Climatic Research Laboratories, setting up conditions that mimicked wet tropical jungles or Arctic cold for testing equipment and clothing. He was later drafted to propose prevention and treatments for frostbite following the Chosin Reservoir disaster in Korea.

John A. began to cook, partly to help his mother. Food and cooking remained a lifelong passion.

After World War II, the Talbotts moved to Buffalo (where John H. became chair of medicine and editor of the *Green Journal*) and then Chicago (where John H. headed up *JAMA* and the publications of the AMA). "He was a fine writer and the best editor I've ever encountered," says John A., whose own career as an editor began in primary school. John A. was probably most influential as editor (1981–2004) of *Hospital and Community Psychiatry* (renamed *Psychiatric Services* in 1995).

Between prep school and college, Talbott went to France as part of the Experiment in International Living, living in a home where the father was a wine merchant and the owner of a small grocery chain and the mother an expert home cook. "This had a profound effect on me as it did on the other dozen participants, one of whom I eat with monthly in Paris." To this day he spends half his time in Baltimore and half in Paris.

He earned an AB at Harvard College (1957), where he worked at the Harvard Lampoon, "hanging out with the likes of John Updike, George Vaillant, and Larry Altman." He received his MD and psychoanalytic training at Columbia's College of Physicians and Surgeons, interned at Strong Memorial and Rochester Municipal Hospital (1961–62), and did his residency at New York State Psychiatric Institute–Presbyterian Hospital (1962–65). His Army experience, especially in Vietnam, increased his commitment to community psychiatry. There, as he told the National Alliance for Research on Schizophrenia and Depression (NARSAD), he experienced first hand "the addition of *community* (seeing the soldier–patient as part of a larger unit, the community)" to the principles espoused in World War I by Thomas Salmon: *immediacy* (treating soldier–patients immediately before symptoms can solidify), *proximity* (treating soldier–patients near the lines of battle), and *expectancy* (conveying to soldier–patients the expectation that they will recover from their acute stress disorders).

Later, directing a community psychiatry program in New York City, he was "appalled by the thoughtless, unplanned kind of deinstitutionalization going on in New York."[*] He left public service, hoping to use his energies more effectively on a national level. While serving on the faculty of Columbia College of Physicians and Surgeons (1963–80), he wrote his exposé of deinstitutionalization, *The Death of the Asylum* (1978), arguing for a balanced system of hospital and community care for patients with chronic and severe mental illness. He served ten years on the psychiatry faculty at Cornell University medical school (1975–85), served as president of the American Psychiatric Association (1984–85), and became a director of the American Board of Psychiatry and Neurology (1980–87) before moving south to chair the department at Maryland.

_____

[*] Anne B. Brown, ed., "An Advocate Who Doesn't Give Up: A Profile of John A. Talbott, MD," for NARSAD.

Talbott was nationally known for his leadership in public psychiatry—in treatment, education, and research about people with severe mental illness—so in 1985 he was a logical choice for this department. Under him, a department that had been psychoanalytically driven now focused on developing a model public psychiatry system. To complement the strong MPRC program in neuroscience and schizophrenia, he recruited strong talent to establish a better downtown research presence. "I saw an unprecedented opportunity to establish a model service system that could then be studied by the newly created cadre of mental health service researchers" he subsequently recruited. "I came to this department because there were going to be people like me," says Talbott. "Here I've got Will Carpenter, Tony Lehman, Howard Goldman, Lisa Dixon, Alan Bellack. We're the same, I can talk to them. At Cornell they were interested in psychoanalysis, they were interested in Woody Allens. (Now, of course, all of the psychiatric hospitals are treating psychotic poor people.)

"'The difference between psychosis and neurosis is that one gets better,' my old chairman used to say. Neurotics don't get better. Yes, you may have them in psychotherapy for ten years and they may not need social work and rehabilitation and day hospitals and emergency care and around-the-clock nurses, but they don't get better. With medication and rehab and cognitive behavioral therapy and so forth, we can help large numbers of seriously mentally ill people. It may be messier, it may be more complex, it may

need a different structure, but I would disagree that it's harder." This may seem like preaching to the choir now, but when he was running for president of the APA and his main theme was the lack of attention the medical profession gave people with severe mental illness, there was a fair amount of resistance to his message.

"If you develop schizophrenia at eighteen we're going to treat you right away," says Talbott, now talking about the changes that have come about since then. "We can't cure you with drugs or a stay in the hospital. Schizophrenia is a disease for which we haven't figured out the cure. But we can ameliorate some symptoms, and we can help you live better—partly through psychosocial interventions developed in the last twenty to thirty years. One of the problems with the public perception of psychiatry is that in 1955 we thought we had a miracle drug, so everyone overpromised on what was possible. Maybe it was wishful thinking—I don't think people really lied—but they testified before Congress that we were not going to need mental hospitals anymore because this miracle medication would treat mental illness. It's taken us fifty years to figure out that's not true. It was one thing to take patients out of mental hospitals in 1968 and put them into community facilities for treatment; it's quite another never to admit the mentally ill. The 'old chronically mentally ill' were the ones who developed a chronic mental illness, were treated, and were then pushed out of the hospitals. The 'new chronically mentally ill' are those who developed schizophrenia after 1955.

"But for many of these patients, things are a lot different today. They're not cured, they're not one hundred percent well, but they're a lot better. We always forget: We don't see the people who do well; they don't come back to the emergency room. When we do studies of who comes to the emergency room, we see our failures. We see relapse and people who don't take their medications. If you look at whole populations, going back to 1955 when medications first came in, 30 to 40 percent of people get better. They don't become the president of IBM, but they get better and they're okay. A third of them have bumpy careers and a third of them deteriorate; that's the nature of the disease or diseases. We've altered that somewhat. The NIH did a study during the Reagan years showing the recovery rate of patients in several specialties: gastrointestinal disease, cardiovascular disease, respiratory disease, mental disease. Mental illness had a higher success rate than most of the rest—maybe allergies and gastrointestinal disease were better—which is extraordinary." Talbott and his colleagues in the department helped move things along.

"John Talbott is a 'leader's leader,'" wrote Howard Goldman in a tribute edition of *Psychiatric Services*. "He was an early champion of those who most needed psychiatric services and a concerned observer of deinstitutionalization, who called for asylum, not asylums, and for assistance for those who were homeless, and who urged us to learn the lessons of our research. He organized committees and led the American Psychiatric Association as its president, all the while editing this journal to guide the field."

"He gave the department credibility that it hadn't had before, nationally and within the university," says another colleague. "He published and he brought in some good people. If you could get him in a room by himself for more than two minutes, he was great, but he didn't have regular meetings with his division heads, and I think he spent a good part of his time trying to get rid of me." At one of the faculty meetings soon after he arrived, Talbott asked for suggestions for new programs that the department might start. Someone (one of the incumbents, whom he undoubtedly saw as part of the deadwood) suggested sheltered workshops. "We already have that," said Talbott. "It's called the tenured faculty."

Talbott is an entrepreneur, not a manager. Leaving Tony Lehman in charge of the department as acting chairman in 1999, he put administration behind him. "I'm a builder, I love doing projects that get you somewhere, I've loved setting up the professionalism project in the medical school, I loved leading curriculum review (after the big reform), I've loved meeting a whole new set of people in medical school teaching, and I like teaching. I am bored stiff running a continuing operation. I can review spreadsheets and go over committee reports, but that doesn't interest me at all. I like new stuff. In Paris I'll review new restaurants; I don't want to go back to old places. I realized when I came here that I was going to have to be nice to people, to encourage and praise them. I'm not good at that either. I tend to see the glass as half empty. I'm impatient and I cannot understand why people cannot come in on time and do the things that they're supposed to do."

Talbott has a national and international collection of friends and colleagues, and even as department chairman he was often in the air, traveling to a conference or to give a speech. On issues about which there were varying opinions, he rarely adopted a neutral position. "A hearty laugh, a look of total disbelief, an angry shrug and wave of the hand, a wandering gaze during meetings, and an urgent clipped verbal message were all part of the repertoire," wrote Mallott in *The Maryland Psychiatrist*. "Whenever patient care suffered or our medical colleagues slighted psychiatry, the response was swift. His righteous anger and trademark beard combined to bring several Biblical prophets to mind. The listener might expect that fire and brimstone would shortly follow. He did what was necessary to preserve the core values of the department of psychiatry.

"What is John Talbott like as a person? He is a restless, uncompromising intellectual with a gentle soul. The combination of his high-octane education, his service in Vietnam, and his work with severely ill psychiatric patients have etched a sad wisdom around his eyes. John loves travel (especially to France), new ideas, and good food. He is a delightful dinner host. One finds good food and fine wine, and John holds court while his wife Susan provides commentary. Certainly John didn't know what he was going to face as our chairman. The department of psychiatry not only survived but thrived through these turbulent times. My words can hardly do justice to his efforts and to the department's successes."

(*continued from page 429*)
The third-semester topic is community mobility (how to get around town safely) and leisure activities (all the free things to do in the city, which they are unaware of). The fourth semester: laundry and clothing care—how to sew a button on, mend a tear, fix a zipper, launder and remove stains, and choose appropriate clothes that go together (dressing differently for different types of occasions). One semester will cover how to care for your dwelling: how to clean it, maintain it, keep it safe, change a light bulb, unplug a toilet, fix a garbage disposal, care for house plants, keep out germs, roaches, and mice—with basics on lighting, furniture, and products useful to people on a limited income. (They'll also learn how to care for house pets, as many of them want a pet but have no idea what it costs.) One semester will cover

how to manage their illnesses, medicines, and time (how to remember appointments and when to take medication). Another will cover money management (how to budget, save, plan for special activities, operate a checking or savings account, use an automatic teller machine).

RachBeisel is creating the curriculum, because she found nothing that met the needs of her clients. She also found too little behavior modification curriculum for clients with limited intelligence and began developing that, with the help of occupational therapists. She and Reggie Cunningham, the supervisor for residential, are teaching the first round of semesters; at the same time they are training the next round of trainers, the residential counselors. "It is labor intensive, but so rewarding," says RachBeisel. "We want the counselors to be competent. We want the members to benefit and be proud."

Training is rewarding. "We want the counselors to be competent. We want the members to be proud."

Supported employment. The division offers an individualized placement and support (IPS) model of a *supported employment program,* an extension of the demonstration project Tony Lehman ran in the 1990s. "You find out what the clients have done in the past that they're confident about, and what they would like to do," says RachBeisel. "They often mention the jobs they are comfortable with, such as housekeeping, maintenance, and dishwashing. We ask, 'But what would you really like to do?' Sometimes you get them a job they're comfortable doing, and a job coach helps them work toward something more challenging. We'll develop a relationship with the employer, and the employer will hire some of our folks. The employer is comfortable because they know we have job coaches. We'll show up on the job with our employee (semi-incognito so they won't stand out as a handicapped person) and work with them with their supervisor to make sure they can succeed on their jobs. We'll help teach them skills and make sure that they get to work on time, dress and behave appropriately, and understand how to do their job.

We have people working in the Orioles stadium, selling food or cleaning. One guy wanted so much to be a chef that we helped him get food prep work; he became a sous-chef, got a scholarship, and is now going to chef's school.

"Ultimately people want to be productive in the community," says RachBeisel. "They want to be able to work. They don't want to be dependent on a disability check. The $678 a month they get from SSI has to cover rent, food, utilities, and their bus pass; it runs out very quickly. There is a certain dollar amount they can earn a month without compromising their disability, so a lot of them work for supplementary income, so they can buy groceries or pay for their medication. The benefit of a supported employment program is that they get a taste of working and getting paid to work, feeling good about working, and coming home with money. You do the math with them and they see that even at minimum wage they would have more money and a better standard of living than they can get from their disability check. The staff tries to minimize the time between when members ask for a job and when they get one, but the recession has made things difficult and jobs are hard to find."

> *"The staff tries to minimize the time between when members ask for a job and when they get one, but the recession has made jobs hard to find."*

Targeted case management and benefits services. An important group of psychosocial services is provided in the division's Community Support Program, SSI Outreach Project, and Safe Haven. People with serious mental illness often lack the skills necessary to access and adequately manage desperately needed community resources. Problems with memory and attention make it difficult for them to remember to pay bills. Impaired social skills and maladaptive problem-solving abilities often result in their being taken advantage of by others—financially, sexually, and otherwise. Symptoms of mental illness can fluctuate greatly, depending on the level of psychosocial stress and support patients receive—leading to increased behavioral disorganization and failure to follow through on appointments or important day-to-day activities. Common ongoing problems for this population are drug abuse, homelessness, and failure to get proper medical care. All of these combined can lead to periodic crises that place these often marginalized patients on the verge of homelessness and even more dependent on the public welfare system and psychiatric hospitals.

The Community Support Program (CSP), with four staff members, is a targeted, intensive case management service for adults who are recovering from serious and persistent mental illness. There weren't enough case management programs in Baltimore, so Baltimore Mental Health Systems asked the division for its help, says Barbara Wahl, program director. The division took on this grant-funded community support project, launching CSP in 1993 in a windowless basement office in the main university hospital.

Baltimore Mental Health Systems, Inc., created at the time of the Robert Wood Johnson Foundation nine-city study, is the local mental health authority for Baltimore City.

The case management program helps maximize clients' independent living in the community by providing crisis management and rapid stabilization for people struggling with severe mental illness. All adults referred to the program are experiencing some type of crisis: acute loss of vital living supports, critically needed mental health treatment or medical care, and other social services and entitlements. They are at risk for declining into homelessness, unstable or dangerous housing situations, or psychiatric decompensation, which can often lead to lengthy hospitalizations, loss of employment, and destabilization of the family unit.

CSP offers help and support with housing; applying for income, disability, and other benefits (such as food stamps, pharmacy and medical assistance, and other public programs); applying for a bus pass; getting identification (from the Department of Social Services or the Motor Vehicle Administration); getting referrals to day programs and for educational, vocational, and legal services; connecting people with medical, mental health, and substance abuse treatment; getting them representative payee services (for those who cannot manage their own money); connecting them with other community programs (such as GED programs and parenting training and support); and helping coordinate things with the parole and probation staff. Wayne Wood is program coordinator and Keah Crosby and Angela Robinson are case management specialists.

"It was unusual to have these kinds of programs in the hospital," says Wahl. "These grant-based programs are not big moneymakers for the hospital. But we've got a pretty good track record in terms of doing what we say we're going to do for the clients. What happens is that somebody who is completely on the street, homeless, and hasn't had any contact with a care provider for a long time will start working with us (often on referral from an inpatient unit) through a particular program—say, SSI, to get their SSI benefits. When they get their SSI they also get their Medicaid benefits, so we can refer them to a clinic. Once they start getting physical and mental health care, they might end up doing vocational rehab over at Harbor City or use other services provided by the department."

Supplemental Security Income (SSI) is a federal income supplement program administered by the Social Security Administration but funded by general tax revenues (not Social Security taxes). It provides cash to meet basic needs for food, clothing, and shelter for aged, blind, and disabled people with little or no income. It is a welfare-based program, paying benefits based on financial need. Social Security Disability Insurance (SSDI) pays benefits only to people (or certain members of their family) who meet the criteria for disability, paid Social Security taxes, and worked long enough to be entitled to benefits.

The SSI Outreach Project, with four staff members, helps the same clients manage their Social Security benefits, SSI, and SSDI. This entitlement management program, which also began in that windowless basement in 1993, started as a one-year demonstration project for the Social Security Administration. Several people in the division were discussing what to do about helping the population of homeless people with mental illness—many of them with co-occurring disorders (often substance abuse)—get public benefits. The public benefits system is difficult to navigate, nobody was helping them, and if they couldn't get their benefits and were homeless, they could not succeed.

Yvonne Perret, the project director (1993–2002), put together a grant proposal and developed a way to streamline the process. Perret and Deborah Dennis created a training curriculum, *Stepping Stones to Recovery*,[15] for use by community clinicians and case managers working with homeless adults with serious mental illness. The guide captures all the strategies and interventions the project used, from initial engagement with homeless adults, through completion of paperwork and clinical assessment needed for benefits, to determining who to recommend for presumptive disability, submitting medical evidence, and creating a comprehensive report detailing eligibility criteria. A funded evaluation kept data on outcomes. For people whom the project director believed to be eligible and who obtained presumptive disability, the project achieved a 96 percent approval rate on applications from 1993 through 2002. (The national average approval rate is 37 percent.)

A staff of four serves a population of West Baltimore men and women, mostly African American, ages twenty-eight to forty-seven. Many have completed high school but are functionally illiterate. Most have never married, virtually all are unemployed, and most have no income at the time of initial referral. Receiving SSI or SSDI means they have access to better housing than an emergency shelter and can get Medicare or Medicaid insurance coverage for needed medical services and treatment. Funds for this kind of project are always short, but this project is now a model program for the SOAR initiative, now nationwide.[16] Both SSI Outreach and the Community Support Program moved to 701 Pratt Street in 2000.

The Safe Haven shelter. When more support for targeted case management came along, the division was able to get enough grant funding to start Safe Haven, a citywide shelter that provides transitional housing for individuals with a history of homelessness and mental illness who have not succeeded in residing in traditional shelters or engaging in treatment for their illness. They are not in treatment and they come to Safe Haven, says RachBeisel, "either because they are not tolerated in the other shelters or because they can't

The program started as a one-year demonstration project for the Social Security Administration. The public benefits system is difficult to navigate, and if they couldn't get their benefits and were homeless, they could not succeed.

tolerate those shelters. They are paranoid, mistrustful, disorganized, and disruptive, and they think a bath a month is okay. By the time they leave our shelter program they are in much better shape and we move them into more permanent housing."

Founded in 1995 and administered by the University of Maryland Medical Center, Safe Haven is funded by HUD, with a matching grant from the state. "Other shelters have been too restrictive, too difficult, with stringent rules that would be really hard on this population," says Barbara Wahl, Safe Haven's program director. "We consider ourselves a low-demand shelter, with no curfews or stringent rules, though alcohol and violence are not tolerated on the premises. Respect for each other is a fundamental principle of the shelter." In most city shelters, the homeless people come in at 6:30 p.m. and leave at 5 a.m. Those residing at the Safe Haven are provided twenty-four-hour, seven-day supervision and support, sleep two to a room (not on cots in a warehouse), receive three meals a day, laundry facilities, and health education. Above all, they are provided privacy, safety, support, and stability. The idea is to help them learn how to be integrated into the community. They stay for a matter of months, generally, and then move out into the community, into apartments (alone or shared), single-room occupancy rooms, group homes, or with board and care providers, or they are reconnected with their family or significant others.

This was the first Safe Haven in the city. It was so successful that the city started a second Safe Haven, which someone else runs.

Safe Haven rents space in an unused elementary school building on Old York Road. The building was rehabilitated and can now accommodate eleven men and nine women. "We're hoping some day to be able to get our own place, so we don't have to rent from someone else anymore," says Wahl. Safe Haven is moving toward introducing the recovery and illness-management model for residents. It has introduced a social skills group and substance abuse awareness groups as part of their weekly activities.

Applicants must be eighteen or over and homeless, must have a serious and persistent mental illness, and must agree to case management services. A staff of fifteen helps them with housing, income, medical care and mental health treatment, medication management, transportation and travel training, psychosocial support, and other social needs. Staff generally have bachelor's level training. Two case managers are completing their credentials to become social workers, but that's not required for their roles. Safe Haven has been identified as a community psychiatry placement for nursing students; one second year social work student did an internship there.

Early in 2010, during back-to-back blizzards, some staff stayed four days straight. Some of the shelter residents helped shovel out the front and everyone pulled together, despite getting a little stir crazy. "The residential counselors we have in the shelter are similar to the residential counselors who work in the residential rehabilitation program," says RachBeisel. "They are dedicated people who see themselves as making a difference in these people's lives. And they're working with people who may not understand that they have to take a bath once a week, if not more."

"In the shelter you start building relationships with people," says Wahl. "It's two-directional. You're cooking meals for the residents, helping them with their laundry, even bathing some of them. Sometimes someone will have hygiene issues and they just are not going to do it themselves. They may say they can't, or it might be they won't, and sometimes there are safety issues—they don't have good balance. It can be pretty intimate. Generally we don't do that, but it comes up pretty often."

"Everybody I know who does this work loves it," says Wahl. "They're being truly helpful and it's exciting work—it's not like a desk job. You meet these really colorful characters, you're running around day to day doing a hundred different things, and it's never boring."

"In an academic center," says RachBeisel, some people love their two-hundred-page CVs, their fifty million publications, their international talks. I could care less about those. The research is important and it has to be done, but what I care about is doing the work every day that makes a difference in people's lives and developing programs that will make their lives better."

Ribbon cutting ceremony for the Carter Center's reopening, January 5, 2010, at 701 West Pratt Street. Left to right, E. Albert Reece (dean, University of Maryland School of Medicine); Jeffrey Rivest (president and CEO, University of Maryland Medical Center, UMMC); David J. Ramsay (UMB president); Judith L. Cox (Walter P. Carter's daughter), Joy Richardson Carter (his wife), three other members of Carter's family, and Carter's other daughter, Maryland State Delegate Jill P. Carter; Larry Nunley (community outreach liaison for City Council's office); Tony Lehman (department chairman); Stephanie Rawlings-Blake (president, Baltimore City Council—who became mayor shortly thereafter); John M. Colmers (Maryland State Secretary of Health and Mental Hygiene); Robert Chrencik (president and CEO, University of Maryland Medical System); John H. Spearman (UMMC senior VP for external affairs and community relations); Eileen Hastings (director, community psychiatry clinics program); Jill A. RachBeisel (director, community psychiatry division).

9

Changing Times
Variations on Recurring Themes

The broad history of the department suggests a constantly upward trend, with bumps and spills along the way, some periods of stress, and enormous changes in the way psychiatry was practiced and taught. Early in the last century, when psychiatrists had very few techniques with which to help "the insane," as they were often called, there was a tendency toward long-term asylum and custodial care (often in state institutions) and toward biological and psychobiological interventions (or none at all, except isolation). Many patients were suffering from problems for which effective cures had not yet been developed but for which physical "remedies" were nevertheless fairly common. Psychoanalysis and psychodynamic psychotherapy, a form of talk therapy imported from Europe and adapted to American preferences, dominated psychiatric practice in the 1950s and 1960s, emphasizing the exploration of patients' dreams and memories to arrive at a better understanding of what fit the patient internally. However, psychoanalysis was not well suited to addressing problems with the major forms of chronic and persistent mental illness, although there was a period when psychiatrists explored its use with schizophrenia. Nor was it a practical therapy for the working class or the poor. But many new forms of therapeutic intervention were developed and adopted, and many new drugs came along that proved helpful.

The psychotropic drugs were slow in gaining acceptance, but when they did, psychiatry probably overpromised what they could deliver. Expecting a cure, and criticized for violating patients' civil rights, states all around the country began emptying their public psychiatric hospitals and cutting their mental health budgets, thinking medication would end the need for expensive state institutions. The community psychiatry that in the early 1960s raised hopes for a community-based alternative to hospitalization far from home failed to live up to expectations, partly because the funding to deliver it did not materialize and the approaches to making it work had not been developed. But Maryland did not empty all of its state hospitals, and in the mid- to late 1970s several idealistic members of the department stepped into positions of power in the state mental health authority, initiating a state–university collaboration called the Maryland Plan (chapter 6), which transformed training for psychiatric residents and state psychiatrists and replaced negative attitudes about working for the state with a sense that this was where the action was.

Changes within psychiatry often reflect what is going on in society itself, and the social consciousness that characterized the 1960s and 1970s was reflected in the social psychology that emerged then, focused somewhat more on the externals of a patient's life, helping to restructure or reposition that life in a social—including family—environment. In the last thirty years, that evolved into the department's strong emphasis on hope and recovery—on developing, evaluating, and disseminating treatments to improve the quality of life for people for whom decades ago there had been little hope.

The greatest change in the department in the last thirty years was probably a sharpening of focus during a period of rapid transitions. In the department's first official decades, the department tried to be both a mini-university and a place to develop sophisticated clinical skills. It was constantly exploring, testing new approaches, helping to invent and reinvent psychiatry—a new (and, some felt, too soft) science with a less than sterling reputation in the medical academy. In 1977 the state and the department together began the transformation of the Maryland Psychiatric Research Center (MPRC) into a world-class center for research in biological psychiatry, especially on schizophrenia and related severe and persistent mental disorders. From the mid-1980s on, the department made concerted efforts, through research into evidence-based services, to improve community psychiatry, so that individuals with severe mental illness could live in the community, receiving appropriate treatment and training in life skills to make that feasible. Those

The social consciousness that characterized the 1960s and 1970s evolved into the department's strong emphasis on hope and recovery—on improving the quality of life for people who had had little hope.

developments were described in some detail in the two chapters preceding this one.

In this final chapter, we bring the department's history and a few recurrent themes and storylines up to date.

New ways of doing business

John Talbott's tenure as chairman started off badly. While negotiating about his position with the medical school, he had asked Fred Raines, business manager at New York Hospital–Bloomingdale Division, to examine Maryland's books and tell him what he would be dealing with. Raines outlined the department's assets and problems, and Talbott had a good idea what to expect. His first day on the job was July 1, 1985. He arrived before the building opened and asked a security guard to let him into his office. At 8:30 his secretary knocked on his door and said three men with badges wanted to speak with him. They were from the Health & Human Services (HHS) Office of Inspector General and they were there to inform him, "You owe us a million dollars."

John Talbott's first day started badly. Three men from HHS came to inform him, "You owe us a million dollars."

"Surely there's been a mistake," said Talbott, but he was wrong. HHS was inspecting billing fraud. The audit at Maryland was one of the first in what became known as the PATH audits, investigating for Medicare fraud. "We were the first, then Colorado, and then everybody got caught in the same mess." The inspectors went through all the charts, matching the information there with what they found in the doctors' diaries, to find such irregularities as a doctor billing for surgery on a day when he was clearly at a conference in another town. HHS was particularly questioning payments to teaching physicians for services performed by residents or interns, especially if the attending did not sign or make a note in the chart. "In psychiatry it was largely that we had billed for weekend care when no attending physician had signed the chart," says Talbott, even though the requirement that

HHS launched the PATH audit initiative to "ensure that Medicare pays only once for the same medically necessary service, and that payment fairly reflects the level of service actually provided."

the attending must sign the chart "had never been enforced before."

Talbott was quickly immersed in finances. "I'm good at building," says Talbott. "I'm not good at handling day-to-day problems. I wanted to build this department, hire great people, and put it on the map, which we did. But here I had a million dollars to settle right off the bat and no money to pay for it." He hired a good lawyer and the department ended up paying something closer to $100,000. "A couple of teaching hospitals paid huge settlements—up to $32 million. We were small potatoes, but that used up my seed fund, an enormous amount of political capital, and a lot of my mental energy," says Talbott.

What happened next reflected major changes going on nationally: there was a shift back from federal to state funding. In 1978 the President's Commission on Mental Health (developed under President Carter) called for a national plan to care for the chronically mentally ill. The plan was completed and released in 1980, but the Reagan administration never adopted it as policy. President Reagan took steps to transform American health care from a not-for-profit business model to a for-profit model driven by the insurance industry.[1] With the Omnibus Budget Reconciliation Act of 1981, Reagan repealed the Mental Health Systems Act of 1980 (Public Law 96-398), which aimed to foster growth in community mental health centers and minimize hospitalization away from home, ending categorical grants to local communities. The community mental health center program was replaced with Alcohol, Drug Abuse, and Mental Health Services (ADAMHA). Under ADAMHA, funding for treatment and rehabilitation service programs was consolidated into a single block grant to each state, with the state administering its own allocated funds. The development of local services and service systems became the responsibility of the states, not the federal government. The federal role became one of providing technical assistance to increase the capacity of state and local providers of mental health services.[2]

Despite Reagan's approach of fiscal restraint and reduced federal role in providing human services, many of the Carter national plan's specific recommendations for changes in Supplemental Security Income, Social Security Disability Insurance, Medicaid, and Medicare were implemented.[3] When Ronald Reagan took office, "federal mental health policy debates went underground." While advocates worked with Congress to reshape the mainstream federal entitlement programs according to the recommendations of the national plan, the center of the action moved to the states— to state mental health authorities in particular. Carter's national plan was anathema to the new administration, which advocated, at least in theory, a sharp diminution in federal social, welfare, and medical responsibilities.[4]

In 1983, Congress introduced a payment scheme intended to control escalating Medicare costs. Under this scheme, hospitals were paid a fixed amount for each patient admission, no matter how much care was provided. Reimbursement was based on what were later called diagnosis-related groups (DRGs), "medically meaningful" categories of illness. All of the patients in the same DRG were expected, statistically, to display the same set of clinical responses, resulting in an equal use of hospital resources. This prospective payment system was expected to replace the fee-for-service model, in which payment is cost-based and determined after treatment (retrospectively).

John D. Thompson, of the Yale School of Medicine's Division of Health Services Administration, developed the DRG case classification system in 1975.

Under *capitation*, Medicare controlled costs by *limiting the time period covered*; DRGs were based on *episodes of care* and required hospitals to examine more rigorously the quality of patient care—especially for patients whose cases required extra reimbursement because their care exceeded the norm (such cases were *outliers*, because of their uniqueness or medical complexity, the complications of therapy, or inappropriate diagnoses or interventions).

"For this big experiment in funding, they funded eleven states, and the only state that continued rate control was Maryland," says Talbott. "If you talk to people in the hospital, they'll complain about rate control, but when I first came I said, 'What an enlightened system.' The downtown hospitals, Hopkins and Maryland, were taking all the poor patients, and the hospitals in the suburbs were getting all the rich patients. Under this system, someone uninsured in one hospital would be cross-subsidized from a hospital that could cover them. Maryland was the only state that stuck with the equity of this system. If you dumped all your uninsured patients on the University of Maryland, you'd have to pony up your share of revenues. It was imperfect, but it was a good idea."

Maryland is a funny state—a unique state, says Frank Calia. "We have a Medicare waiver, so it is called an all-payer state, which means that it doesn't matter whether the patient has Blue Cross Blue Shield, Aetna, United, Medicare, self pay, or no pay: the hospital gets paid. That's not true for the doctors. The doctors don't get paid if it's self pay or no pay, and Medicaid is a terrible payer, so that's an issue. But even the hospital doesn't do well with psychiatric patients. From the hospital's standpoint, the best patients are the ones who get surgery. So the method of payment shapes a lot of strategic decisions in the hospital."

Certainly state and university mental health budgets had to be cut. "The state had been funding the teaching program with hard money," says James Lynch, "but the period of largesse was over, and those who taught marginal programs (not essential to psychiatry) felt they got less support, except from George Balis, who devoted his life to the teaching program." During Talbott's tenure, there was no more money in the psychiatry department for the behavioral sciences and humanities. The rent had gone up, money was harder to come by, and priorities were going to change.

In the days of psychoanalysis, psychodynamic psychotherapy, and long-term treatment, the department provided services both to poor people and to those members of the middle class who carried health insurance or could afford to pay for mental health services. Starting in the late seventies and eighties, the department increasingly focused on providing treatment for people with serious mental illness—particularly inner-city poor (including homeless) people. Under Talbott the department kept its focus on serious mental illness but, downtown and at the MPRC, added significant basic science, clinical, and services research into chronic mental illness.

The culture of the department was changing. The old culture was a state-sponsored medical school with little extramural support, says Howard Goldman. "The only part of the department that had extramural support was the Maryland Psychiatric Research Center, which was on a

Psychiatry loses its exclusive franchise on psychoanalysis

Psychodynamic therapy and psychoanalysis in the last part of the century faced competition from such approaches as cognitive behavioral therapy, family therapy, systems therapy, supportive therapy, and medication therapy. In the 1960s, health insurance still provided good coverage for both analysis and intensive dynamic therapy; this declined precipitously beginning in the early 1980s. Health insurance now pays for diagnosis-based medication and some short-term therapy. It does not typically pay for analysis, and analysts don't usually take insurance, so patients must pay for it out of pocket, which relatively few can afford.

Although some young psychiatrists still have personal analyses (in part so their personal hangups won't interfere with their relationships with their patients), relatively few of them go into psychoanalytic training now. More nonphysicians do, however. Psychoanalysts in the United States are no longer required to have medical degrees; since 1988, psychoanalytic institutes in the United States have been permitted to train lay analysts. With fewer psychiatrists undertaking training in analysis, the institutes have had more incentive to broaden their outreach.* Analysis, which has been declared nearly dead more than once, has shown remarkable longevity, and arguments about psychological vs. organic causes and solutions for psychiatric problems have changed greatly in nature since the days when Jake Finesinger was setting up the Psychiatric Institute.

Psychiatric residents are now more constrained in seeing patients, seeing many of them mostly for brief sessions, to prescribe and monitor their medications—which gives them less opportunity to learn about psychology. This change reflects what is going on in the outside world, where psychiatrists increasingly monitor medications and the psychologists and social workers, who cost less to reimburse, are increasingly seeing patients for psychotherapy. One strength of Maryland's department of psychiatry has always been its willingness to keep an open mind about what works, to value both the mind and the brain, and to rule out particular schools of thought and approaches to diagnosis and treatment only when they have no logical or evidential basis.

---

* There had been a long-standing disagreement between the International Psychoanalytic Association (IPA) and its American constituency about the issue of lay analysis. Analysis had been a franchise of psychiatrists trained in medical schools for fifty years, but with the resolution of a three-and-a-half-year-long lawsuit against the American organization and the IPA, the agreement of the American Psychoanalytic Association was modified. The Americans gave up their exclusive franchise, allowing the IPA to recognize psychoanalytic groups in the United States organized outside the APA's framework, although APA retained full internal control over its own training and membership. All five training institutes in the area now accept candidates from a range of fields, including psychiatrists, psychologists, and social workers. Three of the local institutes (the original two plus the Washington Program of the New York Freudian Society) are accredited by the IPA. Training is also available at the International Institute of Object Relations Therapy (in Chevy Chase, Maryland) and the Institute of Contemporary Psychotherapy and Psychoanalysis of Washington (based on Heinz Kohut's self psychology).

separate campus, and even MPRC had started with a base allocation from the state. As a department of faculty who lived on state resources, the department was only as big as the availability of state money allowed. The department had no experience with large amounts of extramural support. But at Cornell, Talbott had seen the emergence of the soft-money academic department, where you hired talented faculty and gave them a hunting license. This new eat-what-you-kill world favored the entrepreneur, someone comfortable with the new way business was done."

"Under Brody and Monroe we were a *Journal of Nervous and Mental Disease* culture," says Herb Gross. "Under Talbott we were a *Hospital and Community Psychiatry* culture—more service-oriented. We were always service-oriented, but more for teaching and not for research dollars. We never did services research. That was Talbott's strength. He brought in Howard Goldman, Tony Lehman, and others more oriented to clinical services research. This was in keeping with

Gene Brody, John Talbott, and Russ Monroe, three department chairs, at dedication of the Finesinger Clinic, of which Michael Plaut (third from left) was director.

During a period of marked and sometimes controversial transitions, vice chair Stuart Keill was tasked with much of the administration of clinical and educational activities.

the mandate of NIMH, the state, and political and economic reality. The hospital saw us as a bunch of old war horses who had outlived our time. John Talbott's mission, which had to do with the economics of the times, seemed to be to get rid of us."

Under the old culture, people had been comfortable, even complacent, and many of them had been there a long time, says Lois Flaherty. "Certainly there was deadwood—people who hadn't taught or done anything else for a long time. I don't think that was true in child psychiatry, where we didn't have that many resources to begin with."

In 1986, Talbott brought in as vice chair Stuart Keill, who had been regional director of the New York State Department of Mental Hygiene, overseeing operations for ten state hospitals and a host of clinics and community mental health centers in New York City and Long Island. More recently he had been vice chair for clinical affairs at SUNY Buffalo and chief of psychiatry at the Buffalo VA Medical Center. "Stuart was a bright administrator with a huge job to do," says Talbott. "He could read someone quickly, and he was a witty guy, with nicknames for everybody." The two men worked together on the American

"I liked Stu," says Frank Calia. "He loved opera so much that he volunteered as spear carrier whenever the opera was in town." Says Keill: "I share with John Talbott an unbridled narcissism."

Psychiatric Association group that certified administrators in psychiatry, and they were co-editors, together with Robert Hales, of a *Textbook of Administrative Psychiatry*, to which other members of the faculty contributed.

During a period of marked and sometimes controversial transitions (1986–94), Keill was tasked with much of the administration of clinical and educational activities. "John was the external boss, a very public, nationally prominent guy, and I kept the store running while he was touring," says Keill, who received the APA's annual award in administrative psychiatry in 1990. Keill recalls, in his first days on the job, saying to Talbott, "Do you want to be the tough guy and I'll be the nice guy, or do you want me to be the tough guy and you can overrule me on decisions?" Talbott, puzzled by this conversation, said, "No, let's just be ourselves." And they pretty much agreed on most decisions—until the year Talbott was away.

"I didn't know how intimidating he was to junior people and how intolerant of mistakes," says Talbott, looking back. "He did so much for me, took so many headaches off my hands, that I was willing to look the other way." Talbott departed for a year's sabbatical, leaving Keill in charge of the department. He pointed out that Keill tended to "treat the secretaries like they're faculty and the faculty like they're secretaries," and he advised him not to constantly berate the junior faculty. He left Keill a plaque on which ten rules were listed, starting and ending with, "Be nice." In 1994, Talbott returned to a staff ready for mutiny and told Keill he was unhappy with the way Keill had reportedly treated the faculty—especially the junior faculty—while he was on sabbatical; he suggested Keill leave. Keill accepted a position as professor in New York University's department of psychiatry and still teaches a course there in health care administration. Talbott, impressed by Dave McDuff's administrative skills and zeal for growth as director of the division of alcohol and drug abuse, appointed him to replace Keill.

"You hired talented faculty and gave them a hunting license," says Goldman. *"This new eat-what-you-kill world favored the entrepreneur, someone comfortable with the new way business was done."*

Meanwhile, however it was to happen, the economics of psychiatry and the department had to change dramatically. "What worked and made sense in the fifties or the sixties had to change pretty drastically in the seventies and eighties," says Tony Lehman, the current chair. "Psychiatry had been a lucrative business: Reimbursement for mental health services had been generous, and there had been a lot of training money. In those days, there was also a lot of supported time for psychiatry faculty, so you could spend most of your time seeing patients or teaching. Psychiatrists weren't under such pressure to see volumes of patients or to get research grants—the money was easier to come by, and there weren't as many restrictions on private practice. Now we get very little state money for faculty, so people are under pressure to generate income through either research grants or clinical work. Teaching is an expected part of every faculty member's job, but few get paid explicitly for teaching, and the department relies heavily on volunteer faculty." All of the faculty experiences far more time pressure than it used to.

"In 1986, when I first came here, the whole faculty would come to the auditorium for grand rounds," says Lehman, "and we'd all have a leisurely lunch afterwards. People took a couple of hours in the middle of the day for education and lunch. Now it's very hard to get faculty to come to grand rounds, because everybody's doing work." It became harder to recruit volunteers to serve as small-group leaders, for example, because people had less time available.

"Reimbursement now is terrible and—as part of government oversight, out of concern about fraud—there is stricter accountability about how faculty spend their time," says Lehman. "We spend a lot of time on things like 'effort reports,' meticulously keeping track of how much effort we're putting into each research grant and how much into clinical work. This was unheard of in the fifties and sixties, when it would have been viewed as Big Brother."

"There was this demand to raise money, to be competitive with other medical schools, to be a top-tier institution," says Michael Plaut, "which changed the way a lot of things happened. Some of it, such as the medical service plan, has been good." The medical service plan placed stricter controls on faculty's clinical practice time, which helped keep faculty focused on the department's missions, not on a lucrative outside practice. "One thing that guides us all clinically is where our reimbursement comes from," says Plaut. "Very few of us now actually see private patients on a fee-for-service basis within the department; it's no longer cost-effective to do that, which is unfortunate. The amount taken off the top of patient-related income for overhead is so high that you'd have to see too many patients to make that part of your salary. It's easier to put together your salary through a contract with an outside agency or through getting paid by the hospital." Instead of taking income from seeing patients as salary, members of the department sometimes use that money to cover professional expenses such as travel or a new office computer, if their department can't fund that.

"The culture was different under Finesinger, Brody, and Monroe because the times were different," says Jay Phillips. "The expectations of an academic medical department evolved and were skewed more toward such products as research papers and presentations at scientific meetings. In Brody's time, all around the country there was much more emphasis on the clinical expertise, sophistication, and sensitivity of the trainees. Those values have been eclipsed, I think."

And yet, says Jonas Rappeport, "It is still a therapeutic department, as opposed to entirely research-oriented, as some departments are. The residents are still trained to be psychiatrists—to treat people, and not just to pass pills—and I think they're getting good training."

In academic medicine's current setting, says Tony Lehman, psychiatry has an image problem, for three reasons. "First, because of the complexity of mental illnesses, and our lack of tools to deal with that complexity, we're probably viewed by other areas of medicine as not very advanced," says Lehman. "The kinds of disorders we treat are difficult to understand, particularly from a medical standpoint. We're only now getting the tools we need to understand depression, schizophrenia, and manic–depressive illness. New tools allow us to study the genetics of the nervous system, to connect genetics to behavior and personality, and, with tools such as functional neuro-imaging, to look at the brain while it's working on things. Those tools are revolutionizing

"The brain was like a black box to Freud. If he had had tools like functional neuro-imaging, I don't think he would have developed his elaborate theories," says Lehman.

our capacity to understand these illnesses. If Freud had had these tools, I don't think he would have developed his elaborate theories. The brain was like a black box to Freud. He had to develop hypotheses and theories because there was no way to study the mind scientifically."

Second, there is the lingering stigma associated with mental illness and with psychiatry as a medical specialty. "Many physicians still view psychiatry as what they learned thirty years ago in medical school—when they had perhaps eight weeks of psychiatry and hated it because it was not very precise. Treatments for psychiatric conditions lagged decades behind those for other medical problems."

Third, money is a major driver, and mental health treatment is not a money maker for the medical center. "Most places that treat patients with mental illness lose money," says Lehman. "The medical centers have to provide comprehensive training and clinical programs—so that when mentally ill people come into the emergency rooms, they've got units to put them in—but they don't invest a lot in psychiatry. That's different from forty years ago, when psychiatry was a big money maker: Insurance then would pay for people to stay months—or years—in a hospital, which is why places like Sheppard Pratt and Chestnut Lodge did so well for so many years. When managed care came along, the cuts in mental health treatment were disproportionately severe in psychiatry. During the first ten to fifteen years of managed care, the net effect was about a 10 percent reduction in general medical spending and a 50 percent reduction in spending on psychiatric care (adjusted for inflation and medical care spending generally)."

Because of the inadequate science, the tradition of stigma, and the fact that psychiatry is not a moneymaker, "we're near the bottom of the pecking order," says Lehman. "I think that will change. It may take a while."

Nothing more concretely demonstrated the impact on mental health care of changing finances within the university than the demise of the Psychiatric Institute (the IPHB), the building which, decades earlier, had signaled the state's great expectations for psychiatry. The department had lost the physical building bit by bit, as the shock–trauma building went up around it. Feeling the pain of some losses (such as the auditorium) more than others, Russ Monroe had resigned in protest. Now, as part of the hospital's renewal program, the Harry and Jeanette Weinberg Building was going up, and psychiatry's faculty and administrative staff had to move out of what was left of the IPHB. Plans for the relocation were discussed and reviewed by the department's space committee for at least two years before the move took place. They had to coordinate and schedule the relocation of furniture and equipment, including IT and telephone lines and equipment, and the re-keying of office connections.

The department now moved in stages to a renovated building at 701 West Pratt. First to move was child psychiatry, whose faculty and administrative staff had occupied much of the flooded basement level, on the ground floor of the IPHB. Four years later, in July 1996, the department's executive offices moved, followed in 1997 by the rest of the adult faculty and administrative staff. In 2009 the administrative staff, human resources, and finance and payroll moved a few blocks away, to the fourth floor of 110 South Paca Street, leaving all of 701 Pratt devoted to outpatient care. After the closing of the Carter Center in 2009, all of the community psychiatry patients who had been seen at the Carter Center were also being seen at 701 Pratt.

Growth and stabilization in child and adolescent psychiatry

Maryland's residency program in child psychiatry doubled in the 1980s, when the division's training program merged with that of Sheppard Pratt. This came about as a byproduct of Dick Sarles's decision in 1983 to accept a position at the private hospital. Sheppard Pratt hadn't had a fellowship for some time, and its new medical director wanted

After accepting a position at Sheppard Pratt, Dick Sarles suggested a joint training program in child psychiatry.

(*main text continues on page 466*)

The department's indirect role in managed care

While Talbott, Lehman, and their colleagues were developing strong programs in community psychiatry and services research, and while Will Carpenter and his colleagues were exploring the science of severe and persistent mental illness, sweeping changes were taking place in the private sector—changes in which former leaders of the Maryland Plan played a major and interesting role.

The department has been good at training medical leaders and executives. In particular, it trained a core group of psychiatrists who were eager to do more than treat patients—who wanted to figure out how to bring social change to the psychiatry system. As children of the sixties, this group entered medical school enthusiastic about the social change that had already begun, including a push for community mental health and civil rights for the mentally ill. After being "let go" by the state, many of them became involved in managed care. A few critics have spoken of their "selling out" or "going over to the dark side." The real story of what happened is more interesting.

The leaders of the Maryland Plan were dealing with statewide issues—in particular how to correct the balance in what was clearly a two-tiered system of mental health care, says Jon Book (currently back serving as clinical director of Springfield Hospital, where the Maryland Plan was launched). People with health insurance had access to services in the private sector that were not available through the public sector, which served mostly low-income citizens, and in general everyone valued the private services more. "These issues became clear while we were still working in the public sector," says Book, "and we turned our attention to trying to close that gap—to make it possible for more patients from the public sector to be served in the private sector. To the extent that poor people had access only to the public mental health system when they required hospitalization, they tended to be hospitalized largely in state hospitals, because there were too few psych beds in general hospitals. We wanted to learn what resources for psychiatric hospitalization were available outside the public sector for the people who were the sickest and most in need of service. Should we have more beds for psychiatric hospitalization? Did poor people have access to those beds? In what ways could they be made available?"

The state also needed both state hospitals and general hospitals to take

Some private hospitals in Maryland refused to provide treatment for involuntary patients until mental health managed care companies began operating in Maryland.

more involuntary patients—especially those who were severely mentally ill. The resolution of a lawsuit in the seventies led to creation of due process procedures for civil commitment, to keep people from being indefinitely committed to a mental institution without good cause.[5] (Commitment now required two certificates and a hearing within ten days.) The rapidly escalating dehospitalization of patients with mental illness meant that the people psychiatrists were treating as outpatients were sicker and sicker. Struggling—and ill-equipped—to survive in the community, many of them were also self-medicating with drugs (including cigarettes) and alcohol.

Medicaid (public health insurance for the poor) would reimburse for services provided by the psychiatric units in general hospitals, but not for services provided by freestanding psychiatric hospitals. In the mid-1980s many units in general hospitals might take voluntary patients, but they were not taking involuntary patients. Some private hospitals in Maryland refused to provide treatment for involuntary patients until mental health managed care companies began operating in Maryland. "We needed them to welcome involuntary patients and those paid for through Medicaid," says Book. "We began to encourage the development and expansion of psychiatric units in general hospitals—especially psychiatric units that would take involuntary patients—and were successful. We were also looking at how crisis intervention and emergency services were provided for psychiatric patients in general hospital

After leaving his position as head of MHA—forced out after expanding Medicaid coverage for mental health care—Henry Harbin succeeded in another system of managed mental health care, like many of his colleagues from the Maryland Plan.

emergency rooms. And we were looking for ways to improve services to people in jail or coming out of jail."

The public sector and private sector operated under different principles, says Book. The private sector operated on a fee-for-service model. In the public sector many services were managed largely through *program design*: you identified a need, designed a program to meet it, got it funded through grants or the state, then provided oversight, to make sure the program did what it was intended to do. After population needs assessment and population service planning, the state provided funding for a population's service needs, not an individual's. The essentials in public sector mental health work were prevention, early intervention, and alternatives to hospitalization.

At this point in our story, economic reality and politics intersect. The national average turnover rate for directors or commissioners of mental health is typically one to two years, partly for systemic reasons. Typically the mental health director is running a large department and managing a large chunk of the state budget, covering operations at many hospitals, says Henry Harbin. In many states, including Maryland, the director of mental health services is buried in a large state agency, two or three layers from the top, with no direct access to the governor or the governor's chief of staff, so the nature of the job is often misunderstood. The citizen appointees who occupy the top layers of leadership often don't understand the nature of the mental health issues—which leads to finger pointing and scapegoating when there is a death, a problem in state hospitals, or inadequate community funding. The system is usually underfunded, which leads to inadequate care, at the same time that mental health care advocates, consumers, and providers are pushing for more and better care, so the situation gets politicized. With any changeover in government, a new health and human services secretary (or equivalent) is appointed, which creates instability; those running a large underfunded agency that is a magnet for complaints, as mental health agencies are, often get caught in the middle.

Compared with other states, Maryland has had a remarkable degree of stability. Gary Nyman served five years, Alp Karahasan four, and Henry T. Harbin three as state mental hygiene director. "All of us

were forced out," says Harbin. "We might technically have resigned, but we were pushed out the door, largely because we pushed for more resources. I was forced out after the mental health advocate, consumer, and provider groups pushed for expanding resources for mental health, especially through Medicaid. We succeeded in expanding Medicaid coverage, which irritated the secretary of health, who was responsible for Medicaid."

"My sense is that the secretary of health, Adele Wilzack, just didn't like Henry and didn't like the Maryland Mafia, as they called us," says Dennis Kutzer. John Talbott offered those who were fired in 1988 positions in the department, working on a series of contracts the policy studies group had signed in 1986. At this point, Harbin had been working for the state for ten years. Book, among others, interpreted Harbin's firing as a signal that MHA was no longer going to support the kind of work associated with the Maryland Plan, so he started looking for something else to do. One of the people he met with was Paul Shoffeitt, a PhD psychologist who was in charge of a project for the Columbia Medical Plan and Blue Cross Blue Shield of Maryland. "Paul was looking for a psychiatrist to talk to about how to manage inpatient care for an HMO, for patients admitted to a psychiatric hospital. I told him I wasn't interested in treating patients, but I was interested in the system-of-care issue they were wrestling with."

Blue Cross's health maintenance organizations (HMOs) and the state were both wrestling with how best (and most economically) to meet a patient's psychiatric needs. Like the state, HMOs are comfortable taking a population-based view of medical services, although they are much more focused on benefits contracts: Does a benefit contract provide for psychiatric service? How many days, with what providers? Whether a patient sees an MD, a PhD, or a social worker is very specific in an HMO contract, and HMOs are greatly concerned about flexibility or expansion of benefits. If they have a contract that covers mental health or substance abuse services, they want to be clear about which specific diagnoses are covered, which providers can legitimately provide services, and which specific services. When they know what they're covering, they can look at one year's cost to assess the expected cost of insuring against risk in the same population the next year.

HMOs and the state faced a common problem: Most of the money spent on mental health went to hospitals, although many patients need not go to a hospital if they have access to adequate outpatient alternatives. HMOs were trying to figure out how to wisely, efficiently, and competitively use hospitalization only when it is necessary, which meant there had to be adequate alternatives.

Shoffeitt was a successful PhD psychologist working in the mental health department of the Columbia Medical Plan when he became involved in the staff model HMO. When Blue Cross bought Columbia Medical Plan, they valued Shoffeitt as an administrator, noticed his interest in mental health, and gave him direct access to Charles "Ned" Vadakin, Blue Cross's vice president for operations. Both Vadakin and Blue Cross's president, Carl Sardegna, thought the concept Shoffeitt was proposing—mental health managed care—both innovative and important. To free the project from the constraints of a huge insurance company, they set up a separate, private, for-profit company, which was to start on July 1, 1988. Shoffeitt was on the Beltway, driving to dinner, when a lawyer from Blue Cross called to say they had to drop the name they'd planned to use and come up with a new one immediately. "He was on his way to see his fiancée, he had love in his heart, he saw the exit sign for Green Spring Avenue, and that was that," says Book. "The new mental health managed care company officially became Green Spring Mental Health Services, a subsidiary of Blue Cross and Blue Shield of Maryland."

Shoffeitt's first hire was Book, whom he hired to start a utilization review and utilization management project. "I had been working with systems of care in the public sector and now I would be looking at systems of care in the private sector. I was getting in on the ground floor of a project that could grow into something very interesting." Sardegna and Vadakin, with whom he met, "were concerned about costs but genuinely wanted good mental health care. They were worried that they were spending a lot for what wasn't necessarily good mental health and substance abuse care. In our first meetings they said, 'We're Blue Cross Blue Shield of Maryland, we're the biggest insurer here, we're not the cheapest guy in town and we don't want to be, but we do want to be the best. You need to tell us what that is.'"

Book found Green Spring's first problem interesting. Health care costs for mental health and substance abuse were rising faster than the general medical consumer price index and they couldn't understand why. There was another problem: Federal legislation from 1973 stipulated that a federally qualified HMO was required only to provide something like a minimum of twelve sessions for crisis intervention. It didn't have to provide for hospitalization and it didn't have to cover care for substance abuse, but the HMOs Book was now talking about commonly had a benefit limit of twenty or fifty outpatient therapy sessions a year and thirty days of inpatient care—a common package that was competitive in the marketplace. The common limit for treatment for substance abuse was up to seven days for inpatient detoxification, though people could buy a rider that allowed for twenty-eight or thirty days of inpatient rehabilitation for substance abuse.

If you had a chemical dependence problem in Maryland in 1988, says Book, there was no intensive outpatient program to go to. There was Alcoholics Anonymous and Narcotics Anonymous, there was some group treatment of chemical dependence, and individual therapy was available to people with addictions, but there was a big program gap. Folks who could make a lot of money on the inpatient side quickly filled up the gap. The HMOs thought they were protected by their benefit limit," says Book, "but it was common for firms in the private sector to design programs to use the maximum benefit, so more and more people nationally were using their full benefit."

Before insurance covered them, there had been few programs for residential treatment for addiction, and those that existed were mostly longer than twenty-eight days—people would often stay for months, though insurance didn't cover

"An addict on the street, if he had insurance, had access to the same care as a corporate vice president," says Book. "There were tremendous abuses, and the insurers were desperate to get out of the business of paying for care that was not medically necessary.

those long stays. Once insurance money was available, however, many private programs started up—designed not for twelve days or forty days but for twenty-eight days. There was an explosion of twenty-eight- and thirty-day programs for residential inpatient detox and rehab, because if they got you in the door they had you for the full benefit—valued at thousands of dollars. Firms were designing treatment programs to match the common benefit. Some programs—notoriously treatment centers opening in fancy spas and resorts in Arizona, California, and Florida—were twenty- or thirty-day inpatient addiction rehab programs that would advertise in Maryland with an 800 number: "Does your family member have an addiction problem?" They would pay airfare, pick you up in a limousine, and drive you from the airport to the treatment center. "An addict on the street, if he had insurance, had access to the same luxurious care as a corporate vice president," says Book. "There were tremendous abuses of this come one, come all advertising, and the insurers were desperate to get out of the business of paying for care that was not medically necessary."

"What's the science behind this?" asked Book. "Does everyone need twenty-eight days of inpatient treatment?" The Institute of Medicine asked the same question in a congressionally mandated study and, after reviewing the literature, issued a report in 1990 saying that the science did not support the twenty-eight-day model of treatment for alcoholism in the way it was being provided.[6] Alternative models were doing as well as the twenty-eight-day inpatient programs, reported the IOM, and the outcomes from the twenty-eight-day programs "for all comers" weren't as good as described. For one thing, many people returned from spa-type programs to a neighborhood where they still had to walk past the same old bars and drug dealers and addicted friends and were still subject to the same issues that brought them to addiction in the first place.

"When we started the utilization review and utilization management project for Blue Cross Blue Shield, we really thought that applying some public sector principles to the HMO world would be a major advantage," says Book. "Focused on a particular patient population, we would ask: What are their needs and how could prevention, early intervention, and crisis intervention prevent more intensive services later? How do we provide alternatives (either so many individual outpatient visits or so many days of inpatient care) that don't exist in the benefits package right now? What are the in-between models of service, such as day treatment, intensive outpatient therapy, or crisis intervention over a longer period of time (not just an extended one-shot intervention)? What other models of service not in the current benefit package might work—such as providing a sober residence from which to do outpatient treatment? We tried to apply a systems approach to managing care, studying everything from prevention, early intervention, crisis intervention, and alternative treatments to the most expensive, most intensive, approach to mental health and substance abuse in HMO settings.

"We also looked to see what was the best of Blue Cross's models. At the time, Blue Cross Blue Shield of Maryland had two different management and organization models for its healthcare maintenance organizations: a *staff model* (the

Columbia Medical Plan,* which Shoffeitt was in charge of—a multidisciplinary practice clinic that employed physicians, nurses, social workers, and psychologists) and a *preferred provider organization* (PPO) *model* (in which services are

> *"I give managed care credit for one thing,"* says Stan Weinstein. *"They started asking the hard questions that the field itself didn't ask."*

contracted out to service providers in the community who accept referrals and see the patients in their private offices, accepting reimbursement from Blue Cross on a fee-for-service basis). The leaders of Blue Cross Blue Shield were eager for us to review the various systems and to succeed, because they were very concerned about these skyrocketing costs in mental health."

---

* The Columbia Medical Plan was a staff model HMO that Blue Cross Blue Shield of Maryland bought and wholly owned.

In 1988 Book recruited Henry Harbin and Gary Nyman to work part time as managed care consultants for Green Spring. The former Maryland Plan psychiatrists rose quickly to leadership in the private, managed behavioral health company largely because of their experience managing a public mental health system. "The state mental health authority is actually a public specialty managed care company," says Harbin. "Both state and private managed behavioral care require living within a fixed budget, managing a system of care, developing clear treatment guidelines, allocating resources to those services with the best evidence base, and diverting patients from using inpatient settings as the first line of treatment to using an expanded array of outpatient settings. Both required being an effective steward in management of a complicated system."

Book, Harbin, and Nyman brought a public health management model to leadership of Green Spring. When they joined the firm, they were surprised to find that roughly 70 percent of treatment dollars for mental health and substance abuse were being spent on hospital treatment and only 30 percent on outpatient care. The public system had reversed those percentages by limiting inpatient care and expanding and creating a wide array of community-based treatment settings. They set out to reverse the percentages in the private system.

Between 1989 and 1998, Green Spring grew rapidly. By 1997, when it was sold in part to Charter Medical (renamed Magellan Health Services), it was the third largest managed behavioral healthcare organization (MBHO) in the nation. In 1998, as it was merged with a number of MBHOs, the name Green Spring was dropped, and it was renamed Magellan Behavioral Health. It was the largest MBHO in the country.

"There were managed care companies that just looked at the money," says Tom Krajewski,* who served as a senior consultant for Green Spring and later Magellan, "but Green Spring tried to manage the costs yet maintain the quality of care. Many psychiatrists don't believe that, but we put into place criteria that allowed patients who met the criteria to continue to receive inpatient services. Criteria for all levels of services were developed by representatives from the American Psychiatric Association, NAMI, and the Mental Health Association—these criteria were, in my mind, the national standard. Managed care primarily reduced the time patients were in the hospital. The problem is, Green Spring and Magellan were lumped together in everyone's eyes with the greedy managed care firms."

"I give managed care credit for one thing," says Stan Weinstein. "They started asking the hard questions that the field itself didn't ask." Managed care reimbursed for medication far more readily than for long-term talk therapy, which is one reason it seemed to many mental health professionals to be such a destructive force. "They were saying, 'Show me the evidence that this long-term therapy model works,' and the field didn't have a lot of data," says Weinstein. "I believe in the therapeutic relationship, and within the current limits it's harder to establish. And the data is weak, but that doesn't necessarily mean that it isn't right. The buzz word is *evidence-based* now, and for some things we don't have evidence, but we need to pursue them anyway."

Where Weinstein finds fault is with what happened when the length of hospital stays began to shorten significantly. "You could only be reimbursed for hospitalizing someone for x number of days, and I don't think patients suffered from the shorter stays, but some of the money saved on hospitalization was supposed to be shifted into outpatient dollars, and that often did not happen." The psychiatrist's role also changed. Social workers and clinical psychologists began to get proportionately more of the talk therapy with middle-class and wealthy patients. Psychiatrists, who could prescribe medication, tended to get proportionately more of the patients (private or public) who were more seriously mentally ill. Managed care pushed this change along, too, which some psychiatrists resented and some didn't. As one participant put it, managed care was an intrusion on a specialty that valued its autonomy and independence.

---

* Krajewski, a senior consultant who had worked for the state, did not consult on Maryland cases, but started up service centers in New Jersey, Pennsylvania, Montana, and Connecticut and reviewed tens of thousands of cases. Phyllis Greenwald, Dennis Kutzer, Sunday June Pickens, and Andy Rudo also went to work for Green Spring. "Quite a few other psychiatrists from the department of psychiatry worked with us on contract (for variable amounts of time) in roles as physician advisors, psychiatric consultants, appeals panelists, and members of the professional advisory board," says Jon Book.

(continued from page 457)

both a child psychiatry fellowship and "an infusion of modern-day psychiatry—more organic issues, more psychopharmacology, more research—on top of the hospital's strong tradition of long-term psychotherapy." With Sarles as head of Sheppard Pratt's child psychiatry program, the two departments developed a close working relationship. Sarles wanted to keep teaching child psychiatry and behavioral pediatrics one day a week at Maryland, and Sheppard Pratt wanted to restart a fellowship that had been discontinued. Enlarging an existing fellowship was easier than starting a new one, so Sarles suggested a joint program: instead of having four fellows each, the two hospitals would have eight fellows at two training sites, four funded by Sheppard Pratt and four by Maryland, with faculty from both organizations teaching and supervising.

Lois Flaherty, the department's training director for child psychiatry, became division director. It took Sarles and Flaherty about a year to work out a joint training program,

"The collaborative training that Maryland, a public university, developed with Sheppard Pratt, a private institution, was unusual, if not unheard of," says Lois Flaherty.

with trainees spending time at both sites. Sheppard Pratt's highly regarded school for children with special needs, which served both residential and day students, provided a valued training experience. This merging of child psychiatry fellowships worked for everyone, as the two programs were complementary and the sites are only eight miles apart. "The collaborative training that Maryland, a public university, developed with Sheppard Pratt, a private institution, was unusual, if not unheard of," says Flaherty.

The division always had a solid clinical and education program, says David Pruitt, the division's current director, and the "integrated training program in child and adolescent psychiatry that Sarles and Flaherty developed gave us one of the largest training programs in the country. It provided training experiences in the state mental health system, at Sheppard Pratt Hospital, and at the downtown University of Maryland Medical Center. It was the most varied smorgasbord of training opportunities any resident could possibly have—a microcosm of America. This richness of training opportunities forced the resident to understand children and families from diverse socioeconomic conditions, from different diagnostic categories, and in various treatment settings. And it produced excellent child psychiatrists for the region."

The division also worked with several special education programs. It had faculty and trainees at several sites where residents liked to train: the Regional Institute for Children and Adolescents (RICA), at the Rosewood Center (a residential treatment center for children with mental retardation), the Maryland School for the Deaf, and the Maryland School for the Blind. Kurt Glaser had started an inpatient adolescent program at Springfield Hospital (the only one in the state at the time) and later at the Carter Center, which provided training opportunities and stipends for residents.

In 2001, Sarles, who had retired as division director but had stayed on as training director, became a teaching fellow one day a week at the Frederick School for the Deaf. He had done similar consulting at a school for the blind in the early 1970s and liked working with special populations. One day a week he goes to Frederick and works with fellows on two-month rotations.

The 1990s were a decade of stable transition for the division of child and adolescent psychiatry. In 1992, Flaherty left Maryland for Pennsylvania, resigning as division head but continuing to teach part time and to work with the school mental health program (heading its advisory board from 1995 on). Sarles left Sheppard Pratt, which like many other long-term-care hospitals was shifting toward shorter-term treatment, with less emphasis on academic roles for psychiatrists, though it continued to support resident rotations and faculty. Sarles returned to Maryland as acting director of child and adolescent psychiatry in 1992, becoming director in 1993. The division had moved out of its old quarters in the Psychiatric Institute into the department's new base at 701 Pratt Street. In 1999, Sarles retired as chief of child and adolescent psychiatry and for roughly a year Hari Ghuman served as acting chief, while the department searched for a new leader. In August 2000 the medical school recruited

David Pruitt from the University of Tennessee, as he was coming off two years as president of the American Academy of Child and Adolescent Psychiatry. Pruitt agreed to be both chief of the division of child and adolescent psychiatry and director of the Center for Infant Study. Sarles, a remarkable child psychiatrist who is also a pediatrician, had been able for a number of years to have a full partnership with pediatrics. "That was an important phase in the development of the division and tradition here at Maryland," says Pruitt. "In recent years, we've added the research component, and I think the more academic types within the university probably view the division as being that much stronger. I would say, though, that the sort of research we are doing today is related to that solid foundation that was laid down by those clinical educators—especially in the way we always try to see the child in the context of the community and family." The respect psychiatrists, psychologists, and social workers in the division have for each other gives the division strength in providing interdisciplinary and transdisciplinary care.

At the downtown medical center, the division today offers inpatient services, a child day hospital program, and a variety of specialty outpatient clinics and programs, including programs for mood disorders, attention deficit hyperactivity disorder (ADHD), and trauma. The ADHD program evolved from the Maryland Center for Developmental Disorders, a clinical training and research effort developed and nurtured by Bruno Anthony and Laura Foster Anthony. Key faculty in 2010 includes Brenda Castells, Kay Connors, Dana Cunningham, Kevin Harrison, Laurel J. Kiser, Nancy Lever, Carole Norris-Shortle, Sheridan Phillips, David B. Pruitt, Gloria Reeves, Richard Sarles, Robert Schreter, Sharon Hoover Stephan, and Catharine Weiss. There are twelve residents in child and adolescent psychiatry, two postgraduate psychology trainees, three postdoctorate psychology trainees, and six to eight interns in social work.

"We probably have 5,500 visits a year in the outpatient and day hospital programs," says Pruitt. The division

David Pruitt, former president of the American Academy of Child and Adolescent Psychiatry, brought the Center for Infant Study back into the division. Pruitt is shown here with Kay Connors and Carole Norris-Shortle.

has grown rapidly, largely from state service contracts and federal grants. "We maintain strength in educational and clinical work and try to do more statewide evaluation and training through federal grants. We have grown the number of academic social workers in the division and are growing our research portfolio as rapidly as we can grow the pool of principal investigators." Pruitt encourages the "spinoff thinking from getting students and residents to look at both biologic and services components of research," and tries to integrate research, training, and clinical care. Most of those in the child division who do research also teach and see children clinically, which keeps the research relevant and makes the clinical care and teaching more effective. The division has always had good state support to develop model clinical service and training programs and is now expanding the federal research base.

The division's psychology internship program was accredited by the American Psychological Association in 1992, largely through the efforts of Sheridan Phillips. "Sheridan was devoted to the interns and was a strong advocate for getting the resources the program needed," says Flaherty. One requirement for accreditation was offices equipped to do child therapy, so Sheridan requested and got money to buy dollhouses, which are standard equipment for play therapy. (The psychology interns' offices ended up being better equipped than the psychiatry trainees' offices, engendering some envy.) The program attracted many applicants even before it was accredited, partly because both interns and postdoctoral fellows welcomed a chance to participate in the school mental health program.

The School Mental Health Program. School mental health and the Center for Infant Study (CIS) were two important programs that started before Pruitt came to Maryland and that have flourished under his leadership. In 1989, the Baltimore City Health Department asked if the division would put clinicians in the schools to work with the staff. "I couldn't believe it was happening," says Flaherty, "because we never were able to get any money from the regular Baltimore city schools to do that. They gave us a grant large enough to pay for a social worker to spend one day a week in each of four Baltimore schools, with some supervision from child psychiatry faculty and residents." The program grew from there. Baltimore was among the first cities to develop school-based mental health programs.

At one point, says John Talbott, when people thought medications would be almost curative, some believed that state hospitals would close and psychiatrists would become superconsultants, providing consultations to primary care physicians (who would do the work), to institutions, to the police, and to schools. In Maryland, this came true in only one case: the department's school-based mental health program.

Mark Weist, a clinical psychologist working in one of the schools, helped build and expand the school-based program. Helen Steck, a teacher in western Maryland, had died and left a $100,000 bequest to child psychiatry, and Flaherty budgeted the interest from that bequest as seed money for the program. "Mark used that $4,000, plus whatever we were paying him as base salary, to start, and built up from there," says Flaherty.

Research flourished because of Weist's ability to develop services-based research, which is difficult because it is "dirty research," says Flaherty. "You have so little control over the variables. If things improve, you don't know if it's because of a certain therapy intervention or something else that might have changed in the school. It's hard to tell if having a clinician in the school has an impact on the school above and beyond any other interventions that might be implemented."

Traditionally, the school nurse decided a child might have a mental health problem and referred the child and family to a clinic, to which the family often wouldn't go. Mark Weist developed a model for providing mental health services onsite, in the schools.

Many Baltimore city youth are exposed to greater than average violence and drug activity and may experience emotional and behavioral problems that interfere with learning. One of the program's first studies was to identify who did and didn't use school mental health services. They learned that adolescent boys who were often truant and had other risk factors—among the boys most in need of services—were unlikely to have been referred by teachers or nurses because they often didn't come to school. Traditionally, someone in the school sent a child to the nurse's office, the nurse decided the child might have a mental health problem and referred the child and family to a clinic, but the child and family often wouldn't go. "Mark developed a model for providing mental health services onsite, in the schools," says Flaherty. "He was an excellent clinician who was also able to attract, recruit, and train other people and develop research and funding." Today a close-knit interdisciplinary staff of psychologists, social workers, professional counselors, psychiatrists, and trainees provides comprehensive mental health evaluation and treatment services to students in over twenty-five Baltimore schools, from preschool through high school.

Weist was soon considered a national expert on the subject and a leader in the move toward comprehensive mental health care in schools. In 1995, the division received a federal grant from the Health Resources and Services Administration (HRSA) to establish one of two national Centers for School Mental Health Assistance to provide leadership, training, research, and technical assistance to advance school mental health. Under a three-year $1.2 million R01 grant from NIMH, Mark Weist, Nancy Lever, Sharon Stephan, and colleagues conducted the first experimental study of quality assessment and improvement (QAI) in school mental health. Under a grant from the National Institute of Justice they explored the impact of sexual assault and available services for victims. They helped the school mental health program grow in recognition regionally and nationally.

"We try to get to troubled children early, kids who wouldn't make it to center-based treatment, and to provide teachers with training and tools to intervene with children in the school setting," says Pruitt. "Evidence-based practices for prevention in children's mental health—especially school

The UCLA Center for Mental Health in Schools received the other one. The day he heard news of the grant, Weist's second son was born; he and his wife considered naming him Grant, but named him Nathan. The same year, Weist helped plan the first meeting of the National Assembly on School-Based Health Care. In 2000 HRSA re-funded its grant, with co-funding from SAMHSA. In 2005, HRSA funded it for another five years. In July 2010, Weist left Maryland to be a professor in the department of psychology at the University of South Carolina.

The Center for School Mental Health is headed by Nancy Lever (director of training and outreach), Sharon Stephan (director of research and analysis), Ellie Davis (managing director), Sylvia Huntley (training manager), and Christina Huntley (coordinator). The center's fifteen national conferences on Advancing School Mental Health (http://csmh.umaryland. edu) have drawn participants from all over the country. The center provides resources for clinicians, teachers, families, and students on child and adolescent and school mental health (www.schoolmentalhealth.org). Weist and colleagues also started the new international journal, *Advances in School Mental Health Promotion* (www.schoolmentalhealth.co.uk).

mental health—include providing a positive classroom climate and culture and a safe school environment, in which no bullying is allowed. You need adults who are attentive to kids in the classroom and on the playground, who identify bullying when it occurs and help kids learn to mediate their differences. What we see in Baltimore and across the country is more and more overt aggression toward peers, toward teachers, and toward other school staff. Out-of-control aggression is exhibited by many of the children admitted for inpatient care. It's a problem in schools and in the community as a whole."

In a study funded by the Maryland State AIDS Administration, Weist and Stephan developed an approach to trauma intervention and HIV prevention in the schools. Weist and colleagues also helped develop the International Alliance for Child and Adolescent Mental Health and Schools, which is promoting collaborative training and research across countries.

"From the kinds of kids we saw in the early seventies to the kinds we saw in the early nineties, there was a remarkable shift," says Sarles. "By the mid- to late eighties, child psychiatrists across the country were observing children getting much sicker much younger: sicker with depression, sicker with anxiety, sicker with psychotic-like illnesses, and then from the late eighties to the early nineties there was a surge of bipolar children. This was a trend that had nothing to do with insurance or managed care." There were a lot of theories about what was going on: that it was something in the environment; that if you keep the pool of kids and adults with mental illness well longer, with medication or otherwise, they're more likely to reproduce, and the gene pool changes. "Who knows?" says Sarles. "The absolute truth, though, is that kids were getting sicker younger, and that has been a dramatic change."

The Center for Infant Study (Secure Starts). In 1995, Taghi Modarressi's Center for Infant Study, which still operated independently of the division, had to move from its space at 645 Redwood to 408 West Lombard Street—the privately owned Marlboro Classic building—which, because it was officially off-campus, added to costs. When Modarressi had started out, says Pruitt, concerns about the needs of children from birth to five were being neglected. "Early childhood was still viewed as a blissful time, when children were happy and had no problems or concerns. Taghi, an extremely forceful individual, wanted to understand the rich inner life of these young children. He brought clarity and recognition to infant psychiatry." By the mid-1990s, however, Modarressi's health was failing and he decided to retire as director, although he still came to the center every day. His replacement as director of 4G, the inpatient child and adolescent psychiatry unit, and the Center for Infant Study, was Robinson "Robbie" Muñoz-Millan, who had originally been hired to work at the Carter Center. After Modarressi's death from lymphoma in 1997, Muñoz faced severe financial challenges as he struggled to keep the center going.

The center expanded the age range accepted to five years old, to accommodate more billable hours, but the fee-for-service model did not meet the center's needs. At the request of city officials, staff clinician Carole Norris-Shortle developed a Healthy Start program in well-chosen neighborhoods on Baltimore's east and west sides, working on attachment between very young children and their parents. The

Artist Robbie Muñoz-Millan took over as director of the Center for Infant Study when Taghi Modarressi became ill. Under trying circumstances, he kept the center going.

Out-of-control aggression is exhibited by many of the children admitted for inpatient care. It's a problem in schools across the country.

Baltimore Healthy Start program, one of thirteen demonstration projects around the country, ended when the national Healthy Start program went bankrupt, but the center kept working with parents and children on attachment issues.

In 2000, Muñoz retired as center director to pursue an art career. Despite the continued support of Modarressi's widow, novelist Anne Tyler, the center's future was in peril. Pruitt's arrival guaranteed the survival of the center, as he recognized its strengths and good working relationships with such partners as Baltimore Mental Health Systems and Early Head Start. Recognizing also the economic folly of maintaining operations at two sites, he brought the center back into the division, with everyone under the same roof. The division developed research in the birth-to-five-year-old program, and the Center for Infant Study (no longer working only with infants) got a new clinical name, Secure Starts, intended to more easily engage families.

Under program director Kay Connors, the center provides multidisciplinary outpatient treatment for infants, toddlers, and small children identified by pediatricians as having significant emotional or behavioral problems. Many of those problems are related to parenting issues, so the program treats the parent and child together. It offers a range of services: diagnostic assessment, psychological testing, urgent care services, consultation, and brief and

Tony Lehman, Al Zachik, Alma Troccoli, David Pruitt, and Kay Connors. All agree, Alma Troccoli was the main reason the center survived the financial landmines of its first fifteen years.

long-term psychotherapy—including individual, family, and group therapy, as well as parent–child counseling. "With her outstanding clinical skills and interdisciplinary beliefs, Kay Connors has been able to grow the center and the status of social work in the division," says Pruitt. The center is involved in several Head Start programs and in the Judy Centers—a model preschool program integrating all essential services for this young population.

CIS/Secure Starts now provides mental health services to newborns and children up to six years old who are at risk for or are already experiencing social, emotional, or behavioral challenges. Staff at Secure Starts try to understand how attachment or its lack is affecting the children they see. They try to help the parent, usually the mother, bond with her child. "The parent is the child's first and most important teacher," says Norris-Shortle. "We work on attachment because that's what we think builds resiliency in children. Early in life attachment is clearer and cleaner to work with. As the child gets older, some of those attachment difficulties become obscured in emotional and behavioral problems."

"It's not always easy for young mothers who live in the midst of violence, including domestic violence and abuse, drugs, and alcohol," says Pruitt. "But young children who don't have the opportunity to attach firmly often go on to have significant problems with emotional and behavioral regulation throughout their lives."

In child psychiatry, says Pruitt, a public health model is often more useful than a medical model (of a disease having a cause and effect). The public health model means thinking about prevention and population-based studies and understanding risk and protective factors, whereas the medical model means thinking only about intervention and

In child psychiatry, says Pruitt, a public health model means thinking about prevention and population-based studies and understanding risk and protective factors; the medical model means thinking only about intervention and patient-based knowledge.

patient-based knowledge. The division's public health work has moved steadily toward family-focused, strength-based interventions, of which the PACT therapeutic nursery (not to be confused with the PACT program in community psychiatry) is a prime example.

Norris-Shortle, in partnership with staff at the PACT therapeutic nurseries, a Kennedy Krieger Institute Program, developed an innovative, attachment-focused therapeutic childcare program for very young children and mothers living in emergency shelters. The nursery is located in the YWCA homeless shelter, to which parents (generally mothers) can come with their infants and young children. The parents come initially for the childcare, but the staff tries to help them form better attachment to their infants and toddlers. The nursery offers a weekly family-traditions breakfast, in which parents and children eat a healthy breakfast together, featuring fresh fruit (both fresh fruit and family meals eaten together are fairly uncommon in shelters). After breakfast, the staff leads circle time, encouraging parents to sit on the floor with their child in their lap. "We do a parent–child activity in which the parents are charged with following the children's lead (the parent imitating what the child does)," says Norris-Shortle. It's important for the parent to learn to follow the child's lead because this encourages the child's imaginative play, which correlates with later cognitive development. Together the parents and children learn relaxation techniques. After one session, the group was asked, "What do you do when somebody isn't feeling good?" The smallest boy in the room said, "You tell them to take a deep breath and let it out slow." This evidence-based clinical program serves high-risk families and provides a training laboratory for the center's trainees.[7]

Norris-Shortle uses the Nurse–Child Assessment Satellite Training (NCAST) system to help her staff help others improve their parent–child or caregiver–child interactions. She videotapes the mother and child playing together, studies the videotape, praises the parent and, on the videotape, points to strengths in her parenting, then suggests ways in which the parenting might be improved. With a depressed parent, it is often hard to engage the parent. "I find a spot on the videotape and say, 'Mom, look at your baby. Do you see how important you are to your child? Look at those eyes. The staff doesn't get that look.' That makes them pay attention, and we build on that. I always try to go through the child because they are much more powerful than anything I can say. Often, with a depressed parent, it's the child who will make the connection.

"As a group we look at *ghosts in the nursery*, the traumatic events that impinged on a person's life and are affecting their current parenting. Helping a mother begin to deal with the trauma of having had an abusive mother, for example, even if that mother is not there, can help her begin to deal with those negative influences. We also look for the *angels in the nursery*, those moments when someone did care, was supportive, and helped them get to the point where they are. Building on strengths is not Pollyannaish. I've learned over the years that it's the most effective, efficient way to work. And nothing is as effective as their own baby to help them get to their current strengths."

Engagement is essential in child psychiatry. Often parents of kids who live in the neighborhoods around the university are suspicious of mental health care. Their bad experiences have included substantial barriers to access to health care. The interdisciplinary team tries to make it easy for parents to connect and find the help they need. Social worker Page Hamby answers the phone in an engaging manner, knows what information to ask for so she can get the child and family to the right place, helps explain how to get to the

"As a group we look at *ghosts in the nursery*, the traumatic events that affect their current parenting," says Carole Norris-Shortle.

clinic, then meets the family when they come in. At their first meeting, the clinician taking the history asks what's most pressing on the parents' mind and lets them know that they are being heard. (They may think that Johnny going to school is the most important thing, where the staff may have another sense of what's most important.) The staff tries to provide continuity, so that patients keep seeing the same people. It considers: what are their problems, what are their strengths, how is the child doing at school and at home, how can we help the child be more successful at each place? Weekly therapy is done with the whole family or with a parent and child and, as the child gets older, one on one with the child. "We have the reputation of being cautious with the use of medications," says Pruitt. "We try to use them only when indicated and always together with other forms of therapy."

It is important to Pruitt that Maryland is "a public university, interested in community and in systems of care," focused on providing better access to mental health care for families living in disadvantaged conditions. He values understanding the inner life of a child but wanted to develop programs with greater impact on more children and families. He views problems and solutions through the lens of getting good treatment to kids in the organized mental health care system, the schools, the welfare system, and the juvenile justice system.

Pruitt interviewed for his position as John Talbott was resigning and Tony Lehman was negotiating for the chairmanship. "Tony called me one day and asked would it be all right if, in his chair package, he asked for two research positions in child psychiatry. I have worked under a number of chairmen and never had that question asked." Under Pruitt the division developed two new state partnerships: the Children's Mental Health Institute and the Innovations Institution.

The Children's Mental Health Institute, a partnership with Johns Hopkins's child psychiatry division and the Maryland Coalition for Families, is developing evidence-based practices across the state of Maryland and evaluating them to see if they work—often in partnership with researchers in the Division of Services Research. Among various projects, they are working to evaluate respite care, trauma-informed treatments, and rational psychopharmacology.

In 2005 the division launched the Innovations Institute to help the state agencies that serve children improve access, services, and outcomes for families of children with intensive needs.[8] With funding from the Governor's Office for Children on behalf of the Children's Cabinet, the institute, directed by Michelle Zabel, provides statewide technical assistance, training, and evaluation for children, youth, and families, helping to build the expertise needed. The institute's central agenda is to develop a model of care across the state called *wraparound services*.

Under a residential treatment center (RTC) waiver, a limited number of individuals with emotional disturbance or mental illness severe enough to require intensive care—at the level of a residential treatment center—instead remain in the community and receive intensive mental health care and medical services through a team-based approach. The team—including the youth, family members, care coordinators, and service providers—develops a plan of care that allows the youth to receive services and supports in the community rather than in a residential treatment center. Youth can receive services for up to two years. Because the services are specialized, the RTC waiver has a limited number of openings, or slots, each year.

The institute developed navigator training so that care coordinators and family support partners could become certified as wraparound practitioners.

Navigators help patients connect with financial, transportation, cultural, mental health, and substance abuse resources.

With wraparound services, many children with serious emotional or behavioral disorders who would otherwise be institutionalized have been able to live at home or in a home-like setting. By definition, wraparound is tailored to a child's specific needs and to building on the child's and family's strengths, so the exact services vary. Services are provided through teams that link children, families, and foster parents and their support networks with service providers (in health, mental health, education, child welfare, and juvenile

Wraparound services are reimbursable under Medicaid. Counseling and therapy, for example, can be covered as either clinic or rehabilitation services. Services to eliminate psychosocial barriers to developing or modifying the skills a child needs to function independently are rehabilitation services. The Medicaid Rehabilitation Option provides that services may be furnished in a variety of community locations, including the child's home, school, daycare program, or other natural setting. Formal wraparound services include diagnostic evaluations; behavioral support services; individual and family crisis planning and intervention services; parent coaching and education; medication monitoring; intensive in-home, individual, group, and family therapy; interactive psychotherapy using play equipment, physical devices, or other mechanisms of nonverbal communication; and rehabilitation services. In addition, therapeutic behavioral aides often work one-on-one with a child at home or in the community. These aides try to engage children in constructive activities or help them learn, improve, maintain, or restore problem-solving, anger management, or other social skills. Source: Judge Bazelon Center for Mental Health Law: www.bazelon .org/issues/children/wraparoundTFC.htm

justice) to develop and implement comprehensive service and support plans.

Juvenile justice is a major theme in the division. Ken Rogers, a child and adolescent psychiatrist and former training director for the child program, worked closely with the juvenile justice system, trying to identify kids with problems early on and help them get out of the juvenile justice system before they get into significant trouble. "It is tough work, because these are very troubled adolescents," says Tony Lehman. (In 2009 Rogers left to head the department of psychiatry for the Greenville, South Carolina, hospital system.) In the past, a child could come through the juvenile court and be labeled a delinquent or come through the mental health clinic with the same behavior and be labeled emotionally disturbed or mentally ill. This isn't unique to Maryland. Different agencies see problems differently and there are different government funding streams for education, mental health, child welfare, and juvenile justice.

Today, says child services expert Stan Weinstein, "there's much more focus on collaboration among disciplines and more involvement with state agencies. I can't speak for adult psychiatry, but I know in child psychiatry Dr. Pruitt and a lot of his faculty are looking at evidence-based practices for helping children in foster care." In dealing with the problems of foster children, the department tries to make sure that if a child is removed from the family home, it happens only once. The goal in foster care across the country is to try to support families so that reunification is possible. This is difficult, because it is hard to get the funds needed to provide integrated clinical programs for home, school, and outpatient support or treatment.

The Innovations faculty and staff also conduct research about better ways to implement systems of care—especially family-driven, youth-guided, culturally and linguistically competent, individualized wraparound care. The institute developed a Wraparound Fidelity Index to gather data and provide feedback to jurisdictions about implementation.

Pruitt meets regularly with Brian Hepburn (director of the state Mental Hygiene Administration), Gayle Jordan-Randolph (MHA's clinical director) and Al Zachik (state director of child and adolescent services). "To have three psychiatrists of their intellect and commitment is very unusual in a state department of mental health. Having that kind of leadership makes it much more productive to partner with the state. Maryland is a rich and progressive state. What we're now trying to do is expand that work from the Department of Mental Health to the Department of Social Services, the Department of Juvenile Justice, and the Department of Education. We're trying to develop evidence-based practices to help the child no matter where the child may reside. Under this administration, the state leadership seems truly committed to figuring out best practices—so we are trying to integrate how they look at these children across their different agencies."

Pruitt likes the fact that this department of psychiatry is so entrepreneurial. "If you're able to sell your ideas, you're able to gather resources," he says. "That has something to do with how money and resources allow you to develop and build the programs, which is exciting. When there are interpersonal conflicts, I think they are often about organizational structure and flow of resources. Nationally within divisions of child and adolescent psychiatry, there's a chronic, continuing argument, whether we should be a freestanding department, whether we should be under pediatrics, or whether we should continue to be under psychiatry. That relates a lot to where you are. I've got an outstanding chairman (Tony Lehman) and do not want to have that change."

Vital trends and partnerships in training and research
Training has changed radically in the six decades since the Psychiatric Institute opened. In the fifties the emphasis in psychiatric training was the acquisition of sophisticated clinical skills based on a largely theoretical knowledge base.

Much of the knowledge base from that time—including such dated explanations for psychiatric illness as the schizophrenogenic mother—has been replaced, revised, or discarded. A psychiatry once dominated by talk therapy now greatly values evidence-based medicine, in whatever form. The interventions valued decades ago were primarily psychotherapeutic; psychopharmacology is now important, supplemented by psychosocial approaches. Long-term isolation in state hospitals for patients with severe and persistent mental illness has given way to treatment in outpatient settings, with additional forms of social support and training to help recovering patients live in the community. Psychiatric educators have been challenged to incorporate new developments and a vastly increased knowledge base into training, and the resulting changes in psychiatry have been enormous.

Certainly the psychiatry department was well represented when the medical school overhauled its curriculum, shifting from discipline-based training (in surgery or cardiology, for example) to an emphasis on problem-based learning. Lecture time for first year medical students was cut back from eight hours a day to two. Students now met with a faculty member in small groups for two hours daily. The rest of the time, they worked on their own, preparing for the next day's discussion. "We set out to reduce rote memorization, foster self-directed study, and engage students in a lifelong commitment to learning," said Frank Calia, chair of medicine and vice dean of the medical school, in an interview in *JAMA*.[9] The school reorganized and renamed every course. "Anatomy," for example, became "Structure and Development." Basic sciences became multidisciplinary, with a basic scientist and a clinician together supervising a learning block, to emphasize the learning's clinical relevance. Cell biologists, surgeons, and radiologists taught Structure and Development together, for example, so students could see the material's relevance to clinical practice. "We introduced physical diagnosis in the first year to foster students' comfort in talking with patients about intimate topics from the start," said Calia, who led the reform effort, with help from psychiatrist Dave Mallott. They expanded students' training in ambulatory care and continuity of care and provided options for more research time. Students were no longer required to own microscopes, but the school built a computer lab and provided all students with a laptop. The incoming class of 1998 was the first required to start with training in informatics.

"Most people are committed to fellows and research," says Talbott. "Dave Mallott was committed to medical school education. Frank Calia realized that, brought him into the dean's office, and had him and a few others learn how to do problem-based learning. After seven years running the acute psychosis ward, Mallott needed a change. In medicine you can do a month or two of attending and then you don't have to do it again for a year. In psychiatry you are there every day, and it's a tough job. After two to five years, people typically burn out." Mallott had spent some time working for the VA and some time being clinical director for the Carter Center, all the while remaining actively involved in teaching first or second year medical students. Calia made Mallott chief of the problem-based learning group, and when the medical school introduced its revised curriculum it was Mallott who introduced it, rolling it out in the first two years heavily but not exclusively (half hog rather than whole hog), starting in 1994. The only person besides Talbott who understood the whole thing was Mallott. "He was the guy who constructed the schedules for the year. He knew that if you took one day out in November, everything cascaded. He had everything mapped out both in his head and on the computers. He understood the entire curriculum. He's the guts of the thing. He's Mr. Education." Talbott chairs the faculty committee on the curriculum and

The only person besides Talbott who understood the whole curriculum revision was Dave Mallott. "He constructed the schedules and knew that if you took one day out in November, everything cascaded. He had everything mapped out both in his head and on the computers. He's the guts of the thing. He's Mr. Education."

Dave Mallott was good at coming up with clinical pearls for the Yearbook of Psychiatry series— ways of being around really sick people, ways to identify this or that, says John Talbott. For eight years Talbott was in charge of the written exam that candidates take, along with a clinical exam, to qualify for the American Board of Psychiatry and Neurology. "Soon after I started chairing it, I put him on that committee, realizing that Dave had this dazzling, encyclopedic knowledge. He got along well with people, worked his way up the ladder of the boards, and is very involved in the American Psychiatric Association's committee on education."

if the committee decides to do something, Mallott implements it. "When the associate dean for medical education retired, Dave was appointed to that job. At Maryland, that's a huge job. He must have twenty people working for him."

In 2000, when Talbott stepped down as chair of the department of psychiatry, Frank Calia got him involved in another project. "We've done this curriculum revision," Calia told him, "but we've lost some things and we really need to reintroduce them." Talbott agreed to chair the medical school's professionalism project, which to begin with meant assessing the medical school's needs in terms of professionalism, medical humanism, and clinical bioethics. He sat in on classes and interviewed everyone who ran a course or a clerkship or was in any way involved in the educational enterprise. Small groups—typically seven students and four faculty members—met weekly for a couple of years to explore how to break bad news, address physical or sexual abuse, handle ethical problems, treat celebrity patients, maintain alertness, stay attuned to their own family's needs, and manage other sensitive topics.

Now similar small groups of students and faculty meet two hours a week for at least the first two years of school to discuss case vignettes that present intellectual and ethical quandaries. Students also meet with patients and families to gain insight into their perspective and appreciation for the value of narrative history. "We're trying to get medical students to keep journals and reflect on their experiences, to gain a deeper understanding of what they are doing and why they are doing it," says Talbott. He encourages them to write about what it is like to see their first dying patient, for example—to let it sink in rather than just go on to the next thing. "If they don't realize what mistakes they're making or don't see the impact they have on people, how can they improve?"

The psychiatry curriculum also changes constantly. In part, training was adapting to the increasing degree of subspecialization. "There was a time, probably from the late fifties to the early seventies," says Talbott, "when everyone was expected to be a triple threat: to teach, do research, and see patients—and, if you were the chair, to also be a good administrator, a good people person, and so on. Then, in both medicine and psychiatry, we began to subspecialize." The department today offers postgraduate fellowships in child and adolescent psychiatry, geriatric psychiatry, substance abuse, forensics, and consultation liaison psychiatry.

The list below shows which years the American Board of Psychiatry and Neurology (ABPN) first offered examinations for certification in various psychiatric subspecialties (some of them certified earlier by their own specialized professional organizations). For thirty-two years, child psychiatry was the only ABPN-certified subspecialty, and it was thirty years before child psychiatry became "child and adolescent psychiatry."[10] Then a series of new subspecialties became official.

1959   Child (and Adolescent) Psychiatry
1991   Geriatric Psychiatry
1992   Clinical Neurophysiology
1993   Addiction Psychiatry
1994   Forensic Psychiatry
2000   Pain Medicine
2001   Neurodevelopmental Disabilities
2005   Psychosomatic Medicine
2007   Sleep Medicine
2008   Neuromuscular Medicine
2008   Hospice and Palliative Medicine

"To find a general internist today is impossible," says Talbott. "You've got to diagnose what organ system is involved, then go see a gastroenterologist or a cardiologist or whatever, and our cardiovascular service has five different subdivisions: invasive, noninvasive, electrophysiology, and so on. And we're no different. Everyone's subspecialized: We've got people in addictions, in consultation liaison (doing consults in the main hospital), in child, in forensic, in psychopharmacology, in community. I've always maintained that you can't see yourself as just a forensic psychiatrist, handling court cases, or just a child psychiatrist. You may want to have a wrinkle that makes you different, but you also have to be able to do anything, if necessary. You have to be able to do general psychiatry."

Bill Regenold, head of geriatric psychiatry, forged relationships with neurology and medicine that didn't exist before.

Geriatric psychiatry is a good example of a new subspecialty. A geriatric population always comes with a lot of medical co-morbidities. Whoever is working on the department's geriatric inpatient unit has to be comfortable managing high blood pressure, heart failure, seizures, dementia, and delirium. The division offers electroconvulsive therapy for depression because it's safer for the elderly than most medications and acts pretty quickly. Brian Hepburn (now director of the state Mental Hygiene Administration) ran the geriatric unit for a while, Matt Wagner ran it for two years, then, after a series of attendings, the department hired Bill Regenold, who has managed the division for many years and does a lot of research. Says one colleague: "Bill forged relationships with neurology and medicine that had never existed before, so the division can take medically complicated patients back and forth. Bill handles those patients beautifully, so that unit has become almost a med–psych unit, taking both medically and psychiatrically complicated cases. That unit has a good reputation."

Another subspecialty that has experienced growth is consultation liaison (CL), which until the 1990s was limited to providing inpatient consultations to University Hospital and shock–trauma, with a faculty of 1.7 full time equivalents. Today the consultation liaison division has six FTE faculty, two full-time substance abuse counselors, and 1.5 FTE social work therapists. As other departments grow, so does CL. One of the first new CL programs was a multidisciplinary HIV psychiatry outpatient clinic, co-located with infectious disease (started in 1993, directed for several years by Charles Robinson and currently by Seth Himelhoch). As the medical center's transplant programs developed for kidney and liver (1993), lung (1996), and heart (1996), so did CL services integral to these programs: evaluating patients for transplant, evaluating potential donors, and serving on selection committees. The consultation service in the cancer center expanded to include services to the stem cell transplant program (1994). CL's medical crisis counseling center (1996) provides an outpatient service for patients and families affected by medical illness. CL also provides a consultation service for the state Department of Education's vocational rehabilitation program at the Workforce Technology Center; an outpatient consultation program within the Joslin Diabetes Center (2002); and, most recently, a consultation clinic within the University OB Clinic (started by Catherine Harrison-Restelli).

CL has had a training program for internal medicine residents since 1993 and serves as a training site for neurology residents. In 1995, when the division developed a fellowship program in consultation liaison psychiatry, its program was one of only nine approved by the Academy of Psychosomatic Medicine, the subspecialty society for CL psychiatry.

Noted faculty who taught CL in earlier years include Virginia Huffer, Paul McClelland, Susan Strahan, and Brian Hepburn. Neil Warres served as psychiatrist for shock–trauma and Montebello Rehabilitation Hospital for many years, and Kernan Hospital, when it merged with Montebello. And CL faculty (including Mark Ehrenreich, Ted Knowles, Charles "Chuck" Robinson, Joseph Sokal, and Cenk Tek) have won a number of resident teaching awards. Knowles, chief of CL psychiatry at the VA for many years, was known for his bedside manner and Lieutenant Columbo–like interviewing style, says Ehrenreich, the division's current director. Chuck Robinson's vocabulary is legendary, says Ehrenreich: Robinson has been likened to television's Dr. House, for his wit, intellect, and occasional cynicism. Seth Himelhoch, who does services research while also running the HIV clinic, is the best example of someone who bridges the clinical and research divide. David Glovinsky and Aderonke Falayi, currently on the faculty, also trained in internal medicine. David Loreck, current head of the VA CL service, is trained as a geriatric psychiatrist.

Many subspecialties were developing, but some were disappearing, too. When the department had a division of psychiatric social work, Smith College and the University of Pennsylvania, which had students training in the department, always differentiated between hospital social work and psychiatric social work. "When the hospital said, 'We're going to centralize things and end this privilege of you hiring (and paying) your own social work staff,' the hospital had to pay the staff," says Stu Tiegel. "The psychiatric social workers had been more psychotherapy oriented and also took on a training role. The hospital social workers played more of a service role, taking care of practical arrangements such as discharge planning—although even psychiatric social workers are doing more of that these days, now that the length of stay is so short."

When permission was granted for nonphysicians to get training in psychoanalysis, the psychiatric social workers were among the first to get psychoanalyzed.

"Medical school and residency curricula are funny beasts," says John Talbott. "They change to reflect what people need to know. Often changes in curriculum are driven by the residents. The psychiatric residents began to ask for things like group therapy, family therapy, and psychopharmacology before the faculty recognized that they needed to teach it. There was a strong family therapy group in Philadelphia, and Stuart Tiegel wanted to learn about that. There was a strong cognitive behavioral therapy group in Philadelphia, and Hinda Dubin wanted to learn about that and short-term therapy. Michael Plaut went to Cornell to train with someone on sexual therapy, and Harry Brandt went to NIH to learn more about eating disorders. What happens, I think, is a push–pull between the residents saying 'We need this, I'm reading about it, or everyone else in the country is doing it,' and a faculty member who becomes interested, gets training, comes back, and infuses others with interest. After the Institute of Medicine report on medical error and patient safety was released, I invited a guy from Hopkins to give a talk, and then an anesthesiologist upstairs began to work on patient safety, so we incorporated him into the curriculum. It's sort of an organic process, except it's a zero-sum game: If you are going to teach two hours on medical errors, what do you take out? You can't just add two hours: the curriculum for medical school and residency is bursting. What tends to get taken out is history and sometimes context."

CAPP remains popular with medical students. A sizable percentage of medical students are still invited to take advantage of CAPP, the accelerated track in psychiatry—the elective program that provides an advanced, enriched experience in the study of human behavior with a focus on the development of the doctor–patient relationship. "The CAPP program was one of the few positive memories I have of medical school, says Jeff Snow (class of 1987). "It helped

Eric, Walter, and Daniel Weintraub. Dan, a geriatric psychiatrist, specializes in work with Parkinson's and Alzheimer's patients. Phil Weintraub is a child and adolescent psychiatrist and Michelle Weintraub (not shown), trained as an analyst, does medication management in nursing homes.

me survive the rest of it—that and the unflappable kindness and warmth of Dr. Walter Weintraub, who looked a little like Henry Kissinger and was a definite father figure."

Walter Weintraub left his post as training director in 1990, when he developed a sarcoma of the arm. For a year or two, Beverly J. "Bonnie" Fauman served as director of both training and CAPP. Then Dave Mallott directed CAPP (1992–94), co-directing for a year or two with Eric Weintraub, who because he was Walter's son never applied for CAPP himself, but who then directed CAPP from 1995 until 2005. Gina Perez and Chris Welsh became co-directors in 2005. "Student interest in CAPP has always remained high," says Perez, "though it does vary from year to year." At least 10 percent of the 160 medical students apply.

"To this day I interview patients the way I learned to do it from Eric Weintraub in my first interview," says Leandrea Prosen Lamberton (CAPP class of 1997). Lamberton had not planned to be a psychiatrist, but her father, Melvin Prosen, who had loved being a psychiatrist at Sheppard Pratt, thought she would too. He died unexpectedly of a heart attack the

"To this day I interview patients the way I learned to do it from Eric Weintraub," says one CAPP student, echoing what others had said earlier about his father, Walter. Eric Weintraub directs the division of addiction psychiatry.

year she applied to medical school; in her grief, she was drawn to the CAPP program. Over the years there were many such examples of psychiatry as a family tradition.

In 1993, when Y. Pritham Raj was accepted to medical school, he was leaning toward a career in internal medicine. "A career in psychiatry was the farthest thing from my mind. That all changed even before I officially matriculated." During an orientation retreat in the mountains of Western Maryland, he met Dave Mallott, his assigned preceptor for small group discussions. Mallott described CAPP as "a longitudinal elective in psychiatry that would allow me the opportunity to gain early exposure to clinical medicine and help teach me valuable skills about interacting with and caring for patients. The idea sounded great—especially because I had no experience in psychiatry and was excited by the prospect of meeting live patients (not just reading about them in books). So I enrolled and was captured for life." As part of CAPP, Raj was given a small scholarship to complete an elective in forensic psychiatry at the Institute of Psychiatry at King's College, London. "I met and cared for some of England's most notorious criminally ill patients. This was a fascinating and life-altering experience."

Raj still loved internal medicine's "cerebral, comprehensive approach to the signs and symptoms of physical disease," but his "growing love of psychiatry, fostered by my experiences with the wonderfully supportive clinical teaching faculty at Maryland, left me in a bind. Then I discovered the combined training programs in internal medicine and psychiatry—affording me the best of both worlds. By learning to care for the adult patient holistically, treating both body and mind, I felt I would become a complete physician. After graduation, I spent the next five years at Duke University Medical Center, becoming the internist–psychiatrist I am today. I was the first Maryland graduate at Duke in medicine–psychiatry and helped recruit two more Maryland graduates to train there." After his residency and four years on the Duke faculty, Raj joined the faculty at Oregon Health & Science University (OHSU), where he does research on mild cognitive impairment and Alzheimer's dementia, while maintaining a busy clinical teaching practice. He is grateful to the department for "introducing me to the wonders of psychiatry and for helping me forge a career path that has been immensely rewarding."

CAPP influences many career decisions. On his first day in his favorite rotation, under Ruth Shaw Taylor and Constantine Sakles, Gavin Rose (class of 1988, residency class of 1992) "decided this is what I was going to do and this was where I was going to train. Brian Hepburn—cool guy, great approach to the whole business of psychiatry— told me if I wanted to train there, a position would be available." A rotation his fourth year of medical school with Jonas Rappeport and Christiane Telefson at the medical examiner's office piqued his interest in the criminal mind, and he became a forensic psychiatrist. Experiences with fellow residents and faculty helped "shape a global, fearless, not-always-linear approach to psychiatry that continues to serve me well. Tough as it may have seemed at the time, the training was first rate. I even got to feel what it was like to be in the midst of an adolescent riot on cell block C at Crownsville hospital before their adolescent unit closed." Today Rose is staff psychiatrist at two forensic short-term residential treatment units in Pembroke Pines, Florida.

CAPP also provided new opportunities early on in a medical student's career. After graduating from medical school in Chile and completing a research fellowship at Johns Hopkins, Marcela Horvitz-Lennon came to Maryland to do her residency in 1988, while Walter Weintraub was still in charge of training. Weintraub's illness and retirement halfway through her residency was a huge loss. "I was in analysis, was deeply enamored with psychoanalytic psychiatry, but I also was planning to go back to Chile, a country which, despite its economic growth and public health successes, has yet to eradicate extreme poverty or ensure widespread access to high-quality health care." Meeting Howard Goldman in her fourth year led her to a career in public psychiatry. Tony Lehman hired her as a psychiatrist on his study of assertive community treatment, working under Lisa Dixon. "Even the poverty and the crowding reminded me of my home town, Santiago. I learned a lot at Maryland and was grateful for the opportunity to treat needy, impoverished people and

Past and current CAPP students converged in the home of Tony Lehman to pay their respects to Walter Weintraub, seated at right end of couch. On the table is his book *Verbal Behavior in Everyday Life*.

meet wonderful psychoanalytical practitioners, people who helped me learn a valuable way of thinking about human emotions and behavior." She is a psychiatrist now with the Western Psychiatric Institute and Clinic at the University of Pittsburgh.

Training for CAPP students is provided on a volunteer basis. Key CAPP faculty in 2010 include psychiatrists Hinda Dubin, Ann Hackman, Gina Perez, Gloria Reeves, Donald Thompson, Chris Welsh, and Ikwunga Wonodi. In the old days, CAPP students were exempt from the normal psychiatry work other students did, says Michael Plaut, now retired, a faculty psychologist who became assistant dean for student affairs. "We can't do that anymore because the curriculum is structured differently. We don't have separate courses in different disciplines, such as anatomy and behavioral science. We tend to teach courses that are departmentally integrated, and we teach them in blocks. The first course they take, Structure and Development, includes gross anatomy, histology, and embryology. The second year students study Pathophysiology and Therapeutics, which includes pathology, pharmacology, and psychopathology. You can't exempt a student from a course like that; they go through it like everybody else does. CAPP students used to graduate half a year early. We can't do that anymore, because there are too many things they have to do now to prepare for a competitive residency. So they aren't as different as they used to be."

Today CAPP is more of an elective and less demanding, so the students get only two months of credit for completing all four CAPP years.

Any resident or any CAPP student, at least through the late 1980s, could see one of the local psychoanalysts who volunteered their time, accepting payment on a sliding scale—so that students could pay five or ten dollars a session. They were encouraged to go once or twice weekly. "For those of us who wanted to do it, this was an invaluable experience, crucial for our training, and they were allowing us to do it at a very early stage in our career," says Marguerite Pinard (CAPP class of 1990). "This is something you don't find in most medical schools."

The combined University of Maryland–Sheppard Pratt residency program

At one point there were three quite different psychiatric residency programs in Maryland: at Maryland, Hopkins, and Sheppard Pratt. Maryland traditionally provided training in the public sector, Hopkins's much smaller training program focused more on training academic psychiatrists, and Sheppard Pratt provided training for the private sector. In 1997 the University of Maryland and Sheppard Pratt merged their psychiatric residency training programs, in an arrangement for which the division of child psychiatry had led the way. The following account of this interesting merger and partnership is based on interviews and an article for *Academic Psychiatry* written by four participants in the negotiations and training program.[11]

Steven S. Sharfstein, past president of the American Psychiatric Association and a major player in state and national psychiatry, was CEO at Sheppard Pratt Hospital, one of the most prominent private, free-standing psychiatric institutions in the country. Under managed care, the hospital, which was known for valuing "a psychodynamic understanding of the patient and a prominent place for psychotherapy in the overall treatment," had lost millions of dollars in revenue and was facing the reality of far shorter patient stays, a greater mix of public and private sector patients, and

John Talbott and Steve Sharfstein, past presidents of the American Psychiatric Association, oversaw the merger of the Maryland and Sheppard Pratt psychiatric residency training programs.

the need to integrate hospital care with the right mix of outpatient services. It was increasingly difficult to support its sizable psychiatric resident training program.

The department of psychiatry at the university, known for its clinical care and research about patients with severe and persistent mental illness, faced different problems. "Because of demographic changes in the city, changes in reimbursement, and the loss of the contract to treat university students, the patient population at the University of Maryland outpatient clinic had become less diverse in terms of diagnostic entities encountered, with fewer 'higher functioning' patients."

After years of frustrated efforts trying to get Johns Hopkins to merge its residency program with his, Sharfstein welcomed the "responsiveness that he encountered at all levels within the University of Maryland Medical System to his proposal to merge the psychiatric residency training program at Sheppard Pratt with that at the University of Maryland."[12] Sharfstein and Talbott, and their respective training directors, Donald Ross and George Balis, recognized that combining the two training programs could significantly reduce administrative costs. Together the four men worked out a contract to combine training. Sharfstein has been quoted as saying that the University of Maryland was "content to collaborate—they didn't need to take over at Sheppard Pratt."[13]

In 1996, the University of Maryland had fifty-two residents and Sheppard Pratt twenty-four . They reduced the total number of trainees to sixty-six residents, but the joint program is still one of the largest training programs in the country. Unsurprisingly, there was resistance to the merger, particularly at Sheppard Pratt, where many residents experienced a sense of "profound loss" (apparently a common reaction for the smaller partner in any merger). Don Ross "argues that the grief for the lost program could be seen as mourning for what had in fact already been lost—i.e., the era of a predominantly psychoanalytic paradigm and of longer-term hospitalizations."[14]

Certainly the combined program provided variety in experience. Lisa Dixon, a community psychiatrist specializing in services research, became director of the combined program, and was succeeded by Phil Luber, an academic consultation liaison psychiatrist and a psychoanalyst, recruited from outside the state. Don Ross, a psychoanalyst at Sheppard Pratt, became associate director of the combined program and was succeeded by Neil Sandson, a psycho-pharmacologist. George Balis became ill not long after he helped launch the combined program, and he died at the end of 1997. Dixon, who had been active in training, replaced Balis as training director—thinking she could thereby influence practice and change doctors' behavior, not realizing how visible a leadership role it would be and how heavy the administrative responsibilities were. "It was a difficult time because, of course, George had been beloved, and the two training programs had just merged, but only on paper."

For a while, with so many experts on two campuses, the curriculum was rich but somewhat bloated, and was gradually "trimmed back." It also took a while to get the system running smoothly, in a way acceptable to the chief accrediting body. "The day I got the job was the day of our first site visit by the Accreditation Council in Graduate Medical Education (ACGME)," says Dixon. "This was the beginning of this era of a competency-based educational paradigm. Before it had been vague and general and no one was ever

Despite his thick Greek accent, George Balis, a master storyteller, won several teaching awards. Some of the residents called the beloved training director who succeeded Walter Weintraub "Pappa Bear." Balis was at times gruff, urging them to be competent, ethical physicians, but he cared for their well-being. Students and residents gathered at his home several times a year for Greek food and a "Plato Symposium."

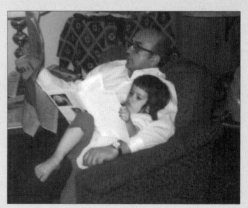

Tony Lehman, Lisa Dixon, Brian Hepburn, Mrs. George Balis and Theodora "Doris" Balis (also a psychiatrist), at the opening of the Dr. George Balis Library at 701 W Pratt Street. There is also a George Balis conference room in the Health Sciences and Human Services Library.

really accountable for what residents learned. Now the accrediting body was telling us we needed to detail specific skills to be learned on rotations in, say, consultation liaison, geriatric psychiatry, or substance use. Then we had to rate residents on those skills. The whole faculty participated, but we needed to be internally consistent and to comply with the requirements of our accrediting body. We didn't even have our combined program going yet. We had this complicated task of combining two programs at the same time that we were being pushed into the modern era, using modern technology." Dixon had to not only make the merger actually happen but also get all the paperwork associated with accreditation ready, showing they were accountable for the quality of training. One of the first things she did was hire a good administrator, Barbara Burns, who is still in the department.

"We had to write competencies for every single clinical rotation," says Dixon. "With the merger, the training program was so huge it had gotten out of control. I spent much of my time on discipline and competence issues and then on bringing the merged program into being. We had to let some people go. I remember preparing for the site visit, sitting outside on my porch with my computer, writing page after page, trying to describe the program and the specific skills we were trying to teach a psychiatrist. To be an accredited residency training program, we had to be able to demonstrate that our program met certain standards. There had always been requirements that they had to do three months of this and six months of that, but they could attend these things and not learn a darn thing. It wasn't enough to say they had a rotation in consultation liaison; we had to identify specific skills residents would be expected to learn within that rotation. And it couldn't be vague: Can they see a patient and figure out what to do? It had to be specific: Can they conduct an interview? Can they elicit important information? Can they make an accurate diagnosis? Can they draw up a treatment plan that makes sense? Can they implement the treatment plan? Do they know when something is unsafe? Do they understand cultural considerations, and can they apply them consistently? Can you understand their speech: Is their accent so heavy you can't understand them? Can they work effectively with other mental health personnel? No one had defined or listed those skills before. Over the last twenty or thirty years, in some ways for better and some ways for worse, all that has changed."

This all happened within three to five years. "You can imagine the pushback we got, because a lot of this does seem kind of made up," says Dixon. "It raised a million questions. Say you had a resident you did not think was competent. What did you do about it? What is competence anyway? What is the correct standard? There are many ways to elicit a history, for example; there is no one right way to do it. We try to give the residents tools, and if they can't get a history, you know it, because they end up with no information. But part of the challenge was turning these abstract concepts into something measurable. I am a believer that if you can't measure it you can't manage it, and medicine has been wrong a gazillion times, depending on everyone's gut knowledge, but there is also not only one way to measure something. We needed to organize things so there was a systematic way of evaluating the training. I learned administration and I learned risk management. I was on the phone with the lawyers not infrequently."

In 2002 Dixon stepped down and Phil Luber became training director. Thirteen years after it started, "the union is stable and the program is thriving," report the four participants. "The merger led to a stronger, richer program than either of its antecedents, and to a significant reduction in administrative costs."

One thing that makes the joint program attractive for residents and therefore excellent for recruitment is that residents in the joint program get clinical training in both an inner-city public-sector setting and a suburban private-insurance setting. Sheppard Pratt, which had had a fairly small apprentice-like training program, was increasingly treating more elderly (Medicare) and poor (Medicaid) patients, but their patient population was different from the university's. Under the merged residency program university residents now got exposure to a more suburban, private, middle-class population in the psychotherapy clinic at Sheppard Pratt, and a different patient mix, including more patients with mood disorders, with psychotic disorders without co-occurring substance abuse, and with problems related to job functioning.

Phil Luber, an academic consultation liaison psychiatrist and a psychoanalyst, was recruited from outside the state to run the combined training program.

Through other mergers and acquisitions, the Sheppard Pratt Health System is now Maryland's largest private mental health care system, with private psychiatric hospitals in the Baltimore suburbs, in Montgomery County, and in Ellicott City, as well as a self-pay, high-end treatment facility called The Retreat.

The larger University of Maryland program, which tended to attract residents looking for an academic setting, especially in community psychiatry, gave Sheppard Pratt residents more exposure to poor and working-class patients with serious and persistent mental illness, and to interventions ranging from medication and psychosocial counseling

Certificate ceremony for the combined training program, 2010. Back row, left to right: Will Keller, M. Philip Luber, Misty Borst, Trish Carlson, Joanna Galati. Front row: Anthony Lehman, Enrique Oviedo, Phillip Chung, Melanie Rowson, Maria Trent-Watson, Kiran Iqbal, Inna Taller, Francesca Staiti, Makesha Joyner, Natasha Thomas, Adam Glushakow, Marina Nikhinson, Pinar Miski, Steven Sharfstein.

to cognitive remediation and training in life skills. Moreover, they had a chance to rotate not only at University Hospital and the department's community psychiatric outpatient clinics but also at VA sites and state psychiatric hospitals (effectively giving Sheppard Pratt two new silent partners). The training programs were combined, but not the clinical services—so the two organizations maintained their special identities.

The department's partnership with the VA

The department of psychiatry has a long history with the VA, the abbreviation that conveniently remained suitable when, in 1989, the Veterans Administration became the Department of Veterans Affairs, achieving cabinet-level status under legislation signed by President Reagan. Jacob Finesinger recruited Walter Weintraub and Gerry Klee at the Perry Point VA, where he taught one day a week. "I came to both the VA and the University of Maryland at times when opportunities were expanding," says Weintraub, "and it hasn't always been that way in psychiatry. It was then (1956) and it is now. I tell people if you ever want to go to the VA, do it now because in terms of opportunities it's a

This section about the VA draws on one interview with four men who have been with the VA for some time (psychiatrists Joseph Liberto, Ted Knowles, and Paul Ruskin, and psychologist Stevan Levy), as well as interviews with Gary Nyman and Walter Weintraub.

little like after World War II"—when the GI Bill financed the medical education of many veterans.

The VA and the university have close ties for several reasons. First, the VA has long supported residency training with VA-based residency stipends. VA psychiatric residency training in Maryland was originally based at the VA's Perry Point hospital, a full-service medical center with sizable inpatient psychiatric capacity, fifty miles from downtown Washington. In the fifties, the VA residents at Perry Point came to Baltimore only for outpatient and child training. When university residents rotate through the VA, they occupy the VA stipends, which help support the university residency program. Residents and fellows benefit from exposure to the types of patients the VA has in its system, and the VA benefits from the training and research environment the university offers, which also helps the VA recruit medical personnel interested in cutting-edge programming. Some of the current VA staff were trained at the University of Maryland, and some psychiatric staff and faculty are jointly recruited and employed by the VA and the university.

The VA psychiatry service in Baltimore started in 1971 at the Baltimore Veterans Hospital at Loch Raven, says VA psychologist Stevan Levy. Loch Raven, which was built as a tuberculosis hospital in 1952, was redesignated a general medical and surgical hospital in 1967. What became the psychiatry service started as a substance abuse program. As the war in Vietnam wound down, many of the vets returning from Vietnam were addicted to opiates and alcohol, so the VA opened thirty-seven outpatient units to treat substance abuse. (Before the substance abuse program opened at Loch Raven, veterans were treated at a location downtown; this service continued until the new hospital opened downtown.) Both the university and the VA envisioned the substance abuse treatment programs later becoming full-fledged psychiatric units, says Levy.

Joe Liberto, current director of the VA's mental health services in Baltimore, was chief resident at the University of Maryland (1989–90) when the new Baltimore VA medical center was being built, across from and connecting to the University Medical Center. At the time, many University of

Joe Liberto, current director of the VA's mental health services in Baltimore, was chief resident at the University of Maryland (1989–90). "We are proud of our mental health assessment and referral clinic, which sees patients the day they present for treatment," says Liberto.

Charlie Savage, from the University of Maryland psychiatry faculty, did research at Spring Grove Hospital before leaving to head the VA's mental health services. Gary Nyman, who served for five years as director of Maryland's Mental Hygiene Administration, was instrumental in launching the Maryland Plan (see chapter six), before becoming chief of psychiatric services at the VA, a position he held for ten years.

"My best guess is that I was chief of psychiatry from March 1994 until the summer of 1998, when my responsibilities shifted toward research," says Peter Hauser. "There was this gray zone as we were consolidating the three facilities (Perry Point, Baltimore, and Fort Howard). John Lipkin at some point became the official chief of service, as his responsibilities shifted from chief of service at Perry Point to service line chief of the merged hospital system. He allowed me to keep the title of chief of psychiatry in Baltimore."

As part of these same negotiations over time, says Frank Calia, who was acting chief of medicine at Maryland (1981–84) at the same time that he was chief of medicine at the Baltimore VA (1977–87), the "arrangement between the deans was that Maryland would pull out of City Hospital and Hopkins would get the hospital in its entirety."

Maryland residents were doing a rotation through the VA's old Loch Raven campus, then the Baltimore Veterans Hospital. "You had to drive fifteen minutes to get to Loch Raven, and it was sort of a different world," says Liberto, "a smaller world, with a nurturing faculty providing a safe environment in which ideas could be exchanged and learning could happen."

Dan Johnston, from the University of Maryland faculty, was the first head of the Baltimore VA's psychiatry service (roughly 1971–75), when it was based at Loch Raven. Johnston had a private practice on Upshire Road, across from the Loch Raven campus, and could go back and forth easily. He was followed by Charlie Savage (roughly 1975–82), Gary Nyman (1982–91), Dave Barrett, acting (1991–94), Peter Hauser (1994–96), John Lipkin (1996–98), Christine LaGana (1998–2007), and Joe Liberto (2007 to the present). Under Lipkin, psychiatry, psychology, mental health social work, and mental health nursing were all consolidated into a single mental health unit. LaGana, a psychologist who had been deputy to Lipkin, became the first head of mental health who was not a psychiatrist.

In the late 1960s and early 1970s, the University of Maryland and Johns Hopkins medical schools both participated in the training of VA residents. By mutual agreement, Hopkins got all of the VA surgery and surgical specialties (except urology); Maryland got medicine, substance abuse (and later psychiatry), pathology, and urology; and the VA residency training was allocated accordingly. After January 1993, when the new Veterans Affairs Medical Center (VAMC) opened at 10 North Greene Street, across from the University of Maryland Medical Center, all of the VA services were consolidated there and Hopkins was no longer involved in VA training. The Baltimore VAMC boasted the world's first filmless radiology department.

The three main VA medical centers with which the department was associated before the new medical center opened were Perry Point, in Perryville; Fort Howard, in the eastern part of Baltimore (now only an outpatient unit); and Loch Raven. After the Baltimore VAMC opened on Greene Street, Loch Raven was rebuilt and became a "community living and rehabilitation center" with an outpatient clinic for aging veterans.

Until 1995, each VA medical center was independent, answering to the central VA office. "If a Baltimore and Perry Point doctor didn't know each other, trying to find out something about a patient was like speaking with somebody in a different universe with a different language," says Ted Knowles. "Understandably, I guess, one psychiatrist was trying to protect his turf and not wanting to feel like a dumping ground for referrals that were inappropriate."

That changed after 1995 when all of the VA hospitals were re-grouped into twenty-two Veterans Integrated Service Networks (VISNs), as part of VA health care reform. The same reform brought more population-based planning and decentralization, a shift to less inpatient and more outpatient care, and an attempt to measure health care performance based on patient outcomes. Primary care became available universally, more community-based outpatient clinics were established, and the VA developed the most advanced national electronic medical record system in the country.

"The thing that binds us together the most now is a system of care in which, wherever you are, the medical record is there and can be reviewed," says Paul Ruskin. The local network, VISN 5, includes Maryland (Veterans Affairs Maryland Health Care System, or VAMHCS), the District of

(*main text continues on page 506*)

Telemental health

There is growing evidence that psychotherapy can be delivered using teletechnology. Between 1997 and 2001, Paul Ruskin, Ted Knowles, and others at the VA participated in a landmark study of telemental health (telepsychiatry), comparing face-to-face treatment for depression with treatment using audiovisual telecommunication (usually a videotelephone). The treatment via telecommunication was as effective as the treatment in person.

The department of psychiatry has been trying to develop telemental services for a few years, with pilot funding from Statewide Health Network (funded by the Maryland Cigarette Restitution Fund). In the last two to three years, those efforts expanded significantly thanks to seed funding from the state's Department of Mental Health and Hygiene and VISN 5—funds that allowed the department and the VA to jointly hire Brian Grady, who leads the telemental health effort.

Cognitive behavioral therapy is being successfully delivered for patients with depression and HIV, who for various reasons find face-to-face therapy difficult.[15] Teletechnology has also facilitated specialty services for which there are professional shortages: child and adolescent services, geriatrics, substance abuse counseling, services for patients with hearing impairment, and bilingual counseling. The hands-on physical assessment required for other areas of medicine is not usually required for most aspects of psychiatric assessment and treatment. Up to 40 percent of patients receiving

Treatment by telemental health—using audiovisual telecommunication (typically a videotelephone)— was shown to be as effective for certain diagnoses as treatment in person, says Brian Grady, who leads the telemental health program. Doing psychiatric assessment and treatment with new technologies is especially important for remote and underserved populations.

medical care for HIV meet DSM-IV criteria for co-occurring depressive disorder, reports Seth Himelhoch (in the division of services research), and patients with the co-occurring problems "have been shown to have worse adherence to taking antiviral medication, increased HIV related morbidity, and among women a higher mortality." The advantages of telephone-based psychotherapy for these patients include more flexible scheduling and the use of patient-preferred locations (such as home), which offer more privacy, may alleviate concerns about stigma (felt when attending a mental health clinic), and are especially important for patients with financial or transportation problems. Patient adherence to antiviral medication regimens is normal when such mental health support is available.

Psychiatric assessment and treatment is important for remote and underserved populations, says Grady, especially in those parts of civilian Maryland with shortages of mental health specialists—including rural areas to the west and south and on the Eastern Shore. Telemental health has been shown to reduce the wait time for new appointments, provide access to specialty mental health care, and increase provider choice for residents in rural communities. Patients with some mental disorders, such as eating and trauma disorders, may actually benefit from the distance (in both senses of the word) of psychotherapy by videoteleconference as part of their overall treatment plan. And videoconferencing has met with some success in both individual and group psychotherapies (especially with small numbers of patients scattered in rural areas). Video consultations with specialists may be of particular value to geriatric patients in rural areas, whose complicated combinations of medical problems may require consultation with specialists, but who are unable (physically and financially) to travel to see those specialists.

Some adult and geriatric patients in Cambridge, on the Eastern Shore, for example, are being seen in their local clinic by VA providers in Baltimore. "It works pretty much like regular sessions, with a one-hour assessment and shorter follow-up assessments, depending on need, which for psychiatrists will probably be half an hour," says Liberto. "We're also using it for other sorts of therapy, like a social worker providing individual and group psychotherapy."

The university provides services to the Cambridge community through its child and adolescent telepsychiatry clinic at Mace's Lane Middle School. Child and adolescent fellows began to receive training in telepsychiatry in the 2009–10 academic year. Fellows then provide assessments and ongoing treatment via telepsychiatry during a second year elective rotation to several rural and suburban locations in Maryland.

Telecommunications may also be used increasingly in training and education. David Pruitt, chief of child and adolescent psychiatry, and Mark Riddle, his counterpart at Johns Hopkins, have been delivering a monthly seminar by videoconference to seven child and adolescent facility-based sites across Maryland, in a state-funded project called the Maryland Youth Practice Improvement Committee for Mental Health (MYPIC). In real time they discuss the latest advances in medications and treatment, with an emphasis on evidence-based practices. Psychoeducation in other specialties is also growing—including grand rounds and case presentations delivered to both mental health and non-mental-health providers. And teleconsultation to providers in rural practices has helped provide a sense of collegial support, reducing the sense of isolation rural providers sometimes feel.

(continued from page 503)

Columbia, and Martinsburg, West Virginia. "From a clinical point of view, it's a very integrated system of care, and pretty seamless for mental health," says Ruskin. "We're now one medical system, and information flows easily from one part of the system to the other."

The two main VA campuses now are Baltimore and Perry Point, but mental health services are also provided at five community-based outpatient clinics, in Glen Burnie, Fort Howard, Loch Raven, Cambridge (on the Eastern Shore), and Pocomoke (near Salisbury). The department's psychiatric residents may do rotations at these VA facilities. Brian Grady, a joint recruit of the VA and the University of Maryland, provides telemental health services to the Eastern shore from Baltimore.

The psychiatric patient population at the VA is slightly different from that of the university. The level of education is probably a little higher, says Liberto, and certain types of treatment are more common because the patients have been in military service and war-related activity. There is far more treatment for post-traumatic stress disorder, for example, and the addiction programs have been developed to meet the needs of returning veterans. In the past there were few women in the VA; now there are more, but it's still largely a male population, and there is now also a sizable geriatric population. Traditionally the VA has been a safety net for veterans who don't have other health care, providing excellent health care benefits and virtually all mental health services. This is fortunate for the substantial number of veterans with chronic and severe mental illness.

In 2009, in VAMHCS, there were about 33 psychiatrists (about 24 full-time equivalents), 55 psychologists, 65 social workers, 12 psychiatric nurse practitioners, 10 physician assistants (both the nurse practitioners and PAs can prescribe), and many psychiatric nurses. "The nurses run the inpatient units," says Levy. According to Liberto, "We have 12 acute psychiatric beds, 86 sub-acute psychiatric beds, 216 residential beds, and an extensive outpatient program. We also have funding for about 350 grant and per diem beds (capacity for different levels of care and lodgings in shelters and halfway houses), and vouchers for Section 8 housing subsidies for 105 people in Baltimore County and 70 in Cecil County (through the HUD housing authority structure for the counties).

"We are proud of our mental health assessment and referral clinic, MHARC, which sees patients the day they present for treatment. The person in charge—usually a social worker or psychologist, but sometimes a nurse practitioner—does an initial assessment the day they come in and makes a referral to the appropriate program within our system." The person doing intake decides whether to refer the patient for case management under a particular program and a particular type of case worker, depending on their needs. The case manager and the case team together determine what to do.

There has been some ebb and flow in the number of VA psychiatric residents in the VA–Maryland training program. From a low of four psychiatric residents the number increased substantially, as fellowships were added in addiction psychiatry, consultation liaison, and geriatric psychiatry. Over the past few years, the university has decreased the number of general psychiatry residents and there are currently about ten full-time equivalent psychiatry residents at the VA.

The psychology internship program, another Maryland–VA consortium, has also grown, to about twelve interns—on an increasing number of tracks, including geriatrics, neuropsychology, clinical psychology, and health psychology. Most of the psychology internship positions are VA-funded; some, such as child psychology, are funded by the university.

Alan S. Bellack and the MIRECC

The Baltimore VA has become an important partner in the department's mental health research and training. The VA itself is conducting research in substance abuse, neuropsychology, dementia, and post-traumatic stress disorder. The amount of research being done increased dramatically after 1995, when the university hired psychologist Alan S. Bellack to revitalize its psychology division and develop a research

Alan Bellack, co-director with Lisa Dixon of the VA's Mental Illness Research, Education, and Clinical Center (MIRECC), developed methods to validly and reliably assess behavioral skills. He also develops interventions to ameliorate social deficits associated with schizophrenia and to address the neuropsychological deficits that may play a role in poor social functioning.

program. Unhappy with the division of psychology, in 1993 John Talbott brought two PhD psychologists in as consultants, to advise him on how to improve the division. Bellack, a consultant suggested by Will Carpenter, recommended that the division develop a strong psychology research program and suggested they hire a senior clinical psychologist to run it. Talbott hired Bellack, under whom the psychology division began doing much more productive research.

Among other reasons for doing so, says Carpenter, PhD psychologists have better scientific training than most physicians do, and they cost less.

In particular, Bellack wrote a successful proposal to develop a Mental Illness Research, Education, and Clinical Center (MIRECC) for VISN 5, securing part of the major funding Congress had approved to establish ten MIRECCs to study the causes and treatments of mental disorders and to translate new knowledge of evidence-based practices into routine clinical practice in the VA medical centers. The strength of the basic and clinical mental health research being conducted at the Maryland Psychiatric Research Center and the solid services research going on downtown made the department a natural partner with the VA in the proposed MIRECC, especially with the new VA Medical Center on Greene Street literally connected to the university medical center. Research and treatment with evidence-based practices for severe mental illness and substance abuse are central to both departmental and VA research, and the department is doing considerable research on co-morbidity of medical problems common in VA patients, including diabetes, HIV/AIDS, and hepatitis C.

The VISN 5 MIRECC has become a close and important VA–University of Maryland partnership. The department gets funding through the VA, which gets strong research and training support from the department. Bellack is director of the MIRECC and runs psychology in the department. Lisa Dixon runs health services within MIRECC and is deputy director of MIRECC and associate director for MIRECC research (at the same time running services research in the department). The VA funds more than half their time. Within the department they are peers, at the VA Dixon reports to Bellack, but in practice they simply spend a lot of time problem-solving together. "It is a win–win situation," says Dixon, "particularly at a time when NIH funding is down and we don't get much money from the medical school."

When the VISN 5 MIRECC got funded, the amount of mental health research funded in the Baltimore VA jumped considerably (by one account, from about $150,000 a year to about $2 million). At the time, the Baltimore VA did not have a strong research base in mental health. With Tony Lehman assuming chairmanship of the department, Will Carpenter continuing as director of the MPRC, and Bellack directing the MIRECC, the department and VA headed into the twenty-first century with great strength and a united focus in research. Between MIRECC and services research, there's a substantial presence around schizophrenia and substance abuse in the department downtown, with the MPRC providing essential support in basic and clinical research. The combined strength of the various partners helps attract more bright young investigators, who in turn bring in further research projects and NIH and VA grant funding. And much is being learned.

The department encourages collaborations like that between Bellack and Dixon. Bellack has developed methods to validly and reliably assess behavioral skills, and in developing interventions to ameliorate the social deficits

"Alan developed a behavioral treatment for substance use, which was effective if he could get people there," says Lisa Dixon. "Getting people to come required arranging for transportation or working with the consumers' social support system, the kind of thing I'm comfortable with."

associated with schizophrenia and improve social functioning, he actively addresses the neuropsychological deficits in schizophrenia that may play a role in poor social functioning. His approach is strikingly different from Dixon's.

"Alan is a psychologist and a behaviorist and has a more traditional interventions research perspective," says Dixon. "I'm a psychiatrist and a health services researcher. I'm used to mess, to error, to not having tight controls, to looking at not just the behavior but also the environment. And we both can be pretty hardheaded. But I've learned from Alan how you can solve health services problems with behavioral approaches. Alan had developed a behavioral treatment for substance use, which was effective if he could get people there, but he had a big problem getting people to come for the intervention, which required arranging for transportation or working with the consumers' social support system, the kind of thing I'm comfortable with. We connected on this—we each had something the other didn't have—and it became mutually advantageous. We're really a part of the VA now, and the more we're in the VA, the more we contribute. MIRECC has a clinical core, an education core, and a research core, and I run a family intervention team.

"Alan creates manuals for behavioral interventions. He breaks behaviors down into little pieces and teaches people how to behave. I'm in the world of, 'Can someone afford to engage in this activity? Does someone have a ride? Are the parents helpful? What are people's attitudes? What effect is stigma having? How are things like payment, reimbursement, attitudes, and interactions influencing the care people get and how they benefit from it? I do experiments, but my experiments in many ways manipulate the system of care rather than the individual (whether they get a medication or a placebo). When you're manipulating systems of care, you can't control everything, and I'm comfortable with that. And my outcomes tend to be about quality of life or functional status."

In providing cognitive rehabilitation, Bellack is more likely to try to figure out how to teach an individual how to tackle a specific problem or improve a type of behavior associated with poor social skills. His approach is to focus on the behavior, because," says Dixon, "if we can change the behavior, maybe we can influence all the rest. When he figures out how to help an individual change a behavior, he puts it in a manual: 'When the person says A, you say B; when the person says X, you say Y.' It's like bounding the universe. I didn't really understand any of that when we first started working together, and I've learned a huge amount from him." It is in understanding the details that they have connected, and they have co-mentored many investigators.

The focus here is on Bellack's work on cognitive rehabilitation. Bellack also does considerable research on substance abuse, recovery, and rehabilitation.

"Schizophrenia is a severely impairing illness," says Bellack.[16] "The inability to perform social roles is probably more of a problem than the psychosis per se." The psychotic symptoms are relatively easy to treat with medication, but they only partially overlap with the primary cause of disability: cognitive impairment—the ability to reason, to process information, to do effortful processing (to think under pressure), to focus and sustain attention for a period of time. Significant problems with memory, especially working memory, are increasingly important to the fundamental impairment. Individuals with schizophrenia have pretty good memory stores but they have trouble pulling memories out of those stores and using them; they have slow processing speed. They also often have deficits in social skills: they're a little off-center, their voice and face may be inexpressive, they may seem not to be listening to you."

Clinicians and family members often think the patient doesn't care or isn't motivated, and that's often not the case, says Bellack. They may have problems with executive functioning, another critical dimension of the cognitive disability associated with schizophrenia. One area of executive function is to be able to see the continuity of experience over time and to integrate information you are hearing with information you already have. You may be working with the patient to help them solve a problem and they don't hear part of what you are saying. With impaired executive function, they may not be able to use or retain the information they're trying to take in well enough to use it to function well in the world. Whether they are on or off traditional medications for psychosis, they may still be neurocognitively impaired.

Those who inherit the illness seem to get a double hit, also getting a cognitive hit.

Ten or fifteen years ago, most interventions were directed at reducing symptoms, says Bellack. "We're now focusing more on neurocognitive impairments, improvements in which we can indirectly improve functional outcomes. Subtle markers of attentional impairment, which probably affect learning competence in social roles, may be detectable early, before college or early adulthood, when patients typically develop symptoms of psychosis. Medication is probably not adequate to correct neurodevelopmental dysfunction, which may show up early and is probably an anomaly in brain development that occurred before or during birth— a subtle set of effects that are distributed throughout the brain—not a single locus that develops later in life in a brain that otherwise develops normally. A simple chemical agent is unlikely to be able to affect this subtle impairment, which is a diffuse disruption of circuits, dependent on multiple neurotransmitter systems.

When people with schizophrenia are performing a task, they are often compensating—they are not using the brain the same way most other people do. That's why a pharmacological solution is unlikely to be able to repair the problem. What Bellack and his colleagues are doing is investigating whether psychosocial interventions can effectively improve performance on memory and attention, on problem-solving, and on learning complex strategies. With Wisconsin card sorting, a standard test of executive functioning, the subject's task is to figure out the rule for matching cards (the number, color, or shape of items on a card). People with normal executive functioning can figure the rule out pretty quickly; 80 percent of people with schizophrenia cannot. In another study, after fifteen weeks on clozapine was shown to have no effect on card sorting, "We gave them a one-session training program and there was a significant improvement, based solely on that session of training," says Bellack. "But there was no transfer from that skill to another type of category test. Generalization is not impossible, but you can't take it for granted."

Daniel Weinberg's work in the 1980s showed that with schizophrenia patients, the part of the prefrontal cortex where most people perform this task does not turn on.

The MIRECC researchers are investigating what works and what does not. Laboratory approaches are drill-oriented, with a focus on many types of single tests. Is a lot of drill training enough? Is a certain kind of training critical? Which works best: pen and pencil or computer tests? Should we use drill-oriented approaches (equivalent to learning musical scales but not playing melodies) or should we do the equivalent of learning language through total immersion (instead of just memorizing verbs)? Or should we use a hybrid approach? Is it essential to train both in the lab and in the community? Can we have a clinical impact? Can we manualize these tasks? And how can we get patients to come in and do this training?

Among researchers elsewhere working in the same area, "Morris Bell's work focuses on attention and memory," says Bellack. "Although most of the training is on memory, he gets only a little change on memory; most of the change is on executive function. Til Wykes in England focuses on executive function and produces most of the change on memory. Hans Brenner in Switzerland, replicated by Will Spaulding in Nebraska, did a six-month group intervention that integrated neurocognitive training with social skills training—focusing on social functioning. We know we can make something happen, in a variety of ways, but we're not sure what we need to do to make it work the way we want. You can make any number of things happen in a research program that you can't necessarily make happen in the community."

When people with schizophrenia are performing a task, they are often compensating—they are not using the brain the same way most other people do. That's why a pharmacological solution is unlikely to be able to repair the problem.

"We are learning that we need to do both top–down training (in executive function) and bottom–up training (improving memory and attention)," says Bellack. He's trying to develop multidimensional tasks that have a natural flavor and can be tested in a natural environment. "You learn best when you have both self-guided practice and active teaching; one without the other doesn't work. We have people come in for twenty-four one-hour sessions over twelve weeks. We can't get them to come in more than two times a week."

For cognitive remediation, commercially available software developed for children is very adaptable to adult patients with schizophrenia. "Adult patients love it for the same reasons kids love it. It's designed for people with minimal computer skills, and it provides positive feedback, praising you when you get a task right. Our patients are not used to having tasks at which they can succeed, so they enjoy it. But these are not pure measures of single domains (like memorizing a grocery list and going to the store). We don't know if they can take this out to the community."

"We are learning that we need to do both top–down training (in executive function) and bottom–up training (improving memory and attention)," says Bellack.

The field is trying to address key questions: How plastic is adult brain functioning? Can we do restorative and reparative training, or must we do compensatory interventions? The field is still struggling with the extent to which we can do one or the other. We seem to be teaching a compensatory strategy. Given that that is not as efficient, how will it translate into durable behavior change in the community?

Over the next few years, this field is going to significantly advance in answering these questions, says Bellack: What are the best ways to teach people to think? What are the critical dimensions for improving executive functioning? Do we focus on higher-level processes, do we do basic processes as building blocks to enable the higher processes to work, or do we focus on an integration of various approaches? Can we produce an effect? Assuming that we can, Bellack can imagine building on that effect in social skills training, vocational rehabilitation, or a life skills program. After developing their cognitive ability, people with schizophrenia may be able to learn to do tasks and assume roles important to more effective social functioning.

The Maryland Plan today

In the meantime, the Maryland Plan, Maryland's public system of training and managed care, is adapting to a changing national environment. John Talbott, whose agenda for the APA presidency had featured the kind of university–state collaboration the Maryland Plan represented, replaced Russ Monroe as department chair in 1985. Every year, Talbott's state-of-the-department talk included a rundown on how many psychiatrists had joined the state system and how many had left it. "People worked there for a while and then left, but we always had a constant supply, and still do," says Tony Lehman, who became chair in 2000. "But the state's public mental health system has changed. The psychiatric hospitals are much smaller than they were, and most public psychiatry is in the community. So several years ago the Maryland Plan went through a metamorphosis. Now the state funds training in our program for residents to work in community mental health centers and other kinds of community agencies. Meanwhile, Brian Hepburn, the current director of the Mental Hygiene Administration, is a graduate of our program; Jon Book, the medical director at Springfield Hospital, trained in our program; and we provided all the physicians for the Carter Center and sent residents there."

"Maryland did some things behind the curve and some ahead of the curve," says Jon Book. As populations in state hospitals shrank, many states just closed down their state hospitals. Maryland had the vision to see that state hospitals were still needed but should be smaller and closer to the community." The notion behind the community mental health center,

When NIMH developed grants for state–university collaboration, Talbott got funding for the department. "We went around the country providing training regionally for state heads of mental health and other organizations on the Maryland Plan and the Maryland model of state–university collaboration," says Lois Flaherty, who represented child psychiatry. "After I left, I became much more impressed with how unique Maryland is. Maryland had so much more interdisciplinary collaboration among state agencies. It has always been a fairly liberal state, so people support the idea of government activism. It's a small enough state that people can talk to each other fairly easily, and yet it's diverse: the Eastern Shore and western Maryland are different from the central part of the state. It has had gifted leaders in education, health, mental health, and juvenile justice, it has been able to develop many new programs, and it has always had faculty working in the community as well as doing private practice. You don't see the town–gown divisions in Maryland that you see elsewhere." Moreover, although faculty at Maryland and Johns Hopkins were competitive, they were also able to collaborate.

The Carter Center, which was only a couple of blocks away, was closed in 2009. Outpatient services were all moved to the building at 701 Pratt Street.

Maryland also invested state money in the transformation of the Maryland Psychiatric Research Center into a research center for the study of schizophrenia and other psychotic disorders.

introduced in the sixties, was that patients who were in the state mental hospitals would lead better lives in the community. This didn't work out nearly as well as expected for an awful lot of people, says Book. Many communities do not welcome people with severe and persistent mental illness and there are not enough resources to meet their needs in the community. So what happens? "More people with severe and persistent mental illness end up homeless or in jails and prisons. It's the swing of the pendulum back to when Dorothea Dix was urging that we create state mental asylums to take mentally ill poor people out of poor houses and alms houses and jails and off the street and give them safe asylum." The pendulum is swinging in the other direction now, says Book. "The good side of that movement is when the courts really look for appropriate mental health services to serve the needs of those who are ill. Not so good is when the courts look to the state hospitals to be detention centers for people who happen to have a mental illness diagnosis. The state hospitals do not have the funding to meet all needs. They never did and still don't."

State hospitals have undergone a remarkable shift in a short period, says Book. "In 2005, a quarter of Springfield's admissions were involved in the criminal justice system. Now about 80 percent of our admissions—higher some months—are. At the same time, there has been an expansion of alternative programs for those not involved in the forensic system." There was a shift under managed care toward more involuntary admissions of psychiatric patients in general hospitals, including private hospitals such as Sheppard Pratt, while the corresponding population in state hospitals declined. The Mental Hygiene Administration is purchasing care through private hospital stays for patients who would otherwise have been in the state hospital. So those who don't have health insurance, not even Medicaid, are not necessarily being squeezed out of getting psychiatric hospital care. But conditions under which patients are admitted involuntarily have changed drastically. More space is now controlled by the criminal justice system and there is far more forensic psychiatry, something over which the state hospitals do not have much control.

Reshuffling the deck

When Jon Book, who had been clinical director at Springfield Hospital, became superintendent, he hired Jonathan Chasen as clinical director and Paula Langmead as assistant superintendent (shown here with Chasen, left, and Book in 1985). After a sixteen-year career in managed care, Book longed for a return to his role as clinical director and in 2004 did so, working with Paula Langmead, who was by then the hospital's CEO.

"The system keeps changing," says Tony Lehman. "We reframe or retool the training program to make it more relevant to what's currently happening in the state. At first, the hospitals were most important; then community mental health came in and the Maryland Plan shifted to include training for community programs. Now more training is needed to deal with the courts' increasing involvement with the mental health system. More than ever, our residents who want to work in public mental health must be prepared to work at the boundaries between clinical practice and the legal system. Many of the patients are court-ordered—not involuntary, but court-ordered—because they've been arrested for a crime. Before the court puts them through a trial, it orders them into the state hospital for evaluation. Some of them need treatment and some of them don't, but the state hospitals are filling up with these kinds of cases. They are displacing the more traditional acute-care patients."

The state hospitals are also getting more and more patients with traumatic brain injury, in part as a result of the dramatic improvements in survival after severe trauma achieved by advanced trauma centers, such as the one at the University of Maryland. Many such trauma survivors have associated head injuries and develop severe psychiatric,

(*main text continues on page 522*)

Anthony F. Lehman

There are many parallels between playing the trombone and being a department chair, says Tony Lehman. You need a flexible but stiff upper lip. Deep breathing exercises help maintain endurance and relaxed control. Neither is a solo job: you are part of an ensemble. However, "I love playing the blues, and hope this will continue to be restricted to the trombone."

"Every so often nice guys finish first," wrote Lisa Dixon in 2000, when Donald Wilson, dean of the medical school, announced that Tony Lehman, who had been acting chairman, was to be the permanent new chair of the department. Lehman, wrote Dixon, "has received millions of dollars in research grants, published dozens of papers, won a long list of awards, and chaired myriad committees and task forces. But most important, he has won the deep respect and admiration of countless numbers of patients and colleagues. This respect and admiration comes from Dr. Lehman's ability to bring simple clarity to complex problems, to persuade forcefully without browbeating, and to do it all with a soft-spoken style and interpersonal warmth."[17]

Born in Utica, New York, in 1948, Lehman grew up the oldest of five children in a small town in the foothills of the Adirondacks. His father was a machinist, his mother, a homemaker. Graduating from a rural K-12 central school, he was valedictorian in a class of forty-eight. He had started playing trombone in fourth grade and considered a career in music, but his mother, who was intent on his becoming a doctor, died as he headed off to college. He became a doctor. After graduating summa cum laude from St. Lawrence University in Canton, New York, in 1970, he attended the University of Rochester School of Medicine.

He had never met a psychiatrist or considered a career in psychiatry and expected to be a surgeon, pediatrician, or family doctor, but Rochester's distinguished faculty in psychiatry captured his attention—especially, the first year, a gifted lecturer and psychoanalyst named Otto F. Thaler. Lehman rebelled against analysis but found the philosophical aspects of psychiatry fascinating. His role models at Rochester included the founding chair, John Romano (earlier a mentor to Will Carpenter), George Engel (the internist and analyst who formulated the biopsychosocial model in medicine), and John Strauss, a schizophrenia researcher with whom Lehman spent a year conducting research—the same Strauss who earlier had collaborated with Will Carpenter at NIMH. "These experiences solidified my commitment to a career in psychiatry."

After an internship at the University of Virginia, Lehman headed off to UCLA for his psychiatry residency. For a small-town guy used to small schools, going to California—as well as doing his residency in a big school in a great location with a diverse academic setting and a huge and fascinating psychiatry department—was "a fantastic experience." He stayed at UCLA to study health services research in the Robert Wood Johnson Clinical Scholars Program, earning a master of science in public health there.

"I returned to Rochester because the chairman of the department, Haroutun Babigian, wanted me to set up (from scratch) a training program for university residents at Rochester Psychiatric Center, a state hospital near the university, which I did," says Lehman.[*] As an assistant professor of psychiatry (1981–86), Lehman ran a large outpatient program at the university, where he trained many residents who went on to leadership positions. He also started and ran the training program at the state hospital, which focused on treating young adults with difficult-to-treat mental disorders and which eventually had fifty beds.

"Some people thought it was great and some thought it was a betrayal, a dumbing down," says Lehman. The department at Rochester, based in the university hospital, had been oriented to private practice. For many years the state hospital had a separate residency program, which the university viewed as second class and which ended shortly before Lehman returned. Babigian (with John Romano as a strong ally) was committed to changing the second-class status of treating patients with severe mental illnesses in the state hospital, partly because of the financial opportunities of collaborating with the state and partly because of his commitment to severely ill patients.

"Many faculty viewed the endeavor skeptically at first, but over time I think many were won over," says Lehman. "Remember, John Talbott was becoming a leading spokesperson nationally for providing better care for patients with severe mental illness, and there was much resistance to him as well. Today that focus is respected, and it is hard to imagine the snobbery about treating these patients that existed then in some academic and private sectors." While running the program at the state hospital, which in some ways was like a mini-Maryland Plan, Lehman met Talbott, who was running for APA president. Lehman was feeling bogged down with clinical and administrative duties and in need of a change. "I wanted to go somewhere where I could focus more on my research but maintain my commitment to persons with serious mental illnesses."

Talbott was considering whether to chair Maryland's department of psychiatry. Lehman offered to join him because of their shared interest in improving mental health services for people with severe and chronic mental illness. He was drawn to Maryland partly because of the opportunity, with colleagues like Talbott and Will Carpenter, to do research on severe mental illness, and partly because of the state–university partnership. "What was unusual about the Maryland Plan back

---

[*] As co-principal investigators, Babigian and Lehman did a study with a groundbreaking design, investigating the impact of capitation financing on services in Monroe County—an important early example of mental health services research, from the first wave of services research projects funded by the NIMH.

when it was developed was that much of the country's psychiatric training went on in private hospitals and universities and large private psychiatric institutions such as Chestnut Lodge, Sheppard Pratt, and the Institute for Living." He welcomed a chance to explore new ways of practicing public—especially community—psychiatry. It bothered him that the least-trained people were treating the most severely ill patients and the most-trained people were treating the patients with less serious problems.

He came to Maryland in 1986 as director of research at the Walter P. Carter Center. At the time, the Carter Center was a comprehensive community mental health center, whose director, Jose Arana, wanted to develop research programs on clinical issues related to the population the center served—largely inner-city poor people. "My job initially was to get a research program going there, which John and Jose were very supportive of.

"Most of the research when I began was about symptom reduction. Early on I became interested in studying and measuring—and seeing how treatments affect—quality of life and life experiences." He was especially interested in psychosocial interventions that improve quality of life—relying less on the traditional patient hour and more on providing the kind of support that keeps people with schizophrenia out of the hospital and enables them to lead a better life. "Lehman's Quality of Life Interview has become a standard research instrument," says Howard Goldman. "Tony's commitment to measuring quality of life reflects

"My style is to roll up my sleeves and lead by example," says Lehman, shown here discussing the budget for renovations in the building at 701 West Pratt Street.

his values and expectation about the goal of treatment and services."

Lehman and Arana applied successfully for a large NIMH grant to create a program in assertive community treatment (PACT), embracing an innovative approach of taking treatment directly into the community where the patients were, rather than expecting them to come to the office. (Lehman was the principal investigator and Arana was to be the clinical director, but Arana died just after the funding arrived.) This notion of working to keep patients in the community—by paying attention to things like housing and whether and how they got their medication—was radical at the time. His colleagues "admired Tony because he was in the trenches delivering care. Because of their illness, the people with schizophrenia couldn't or didn't find their way to the clinic, so he found ways to bring the clinic to them. He was very creative and seemed to have heart."

His specialty was and is health services research—studying healthcare delivery—with a focus on services for people with severe mental illness. For ten years he ran the Center for Health Services Research. He became internationally known as a researcher in evidence-based approaches to mental health services when he led the Schizophrenia PORT study, assessing outcomes for people with schizophrenia and developing treatments and strategies for improving their well-being. Colleagues praise him as a collaborator both for how easy he is to work with and how courageously he supports difficult findings. "Tony will not back down when he views his position as right," says Lisa Dixon. "He's nice, but he can be tough and tenacious and push back when needed." The first PORT took a stand against psychoanalytic psychotherapy for people with schizophrenia, says Bob Buchanan, and "Tony had to deal with a lot of people upset about the decision not to support that intervention as an evidence-based treatment." There was also a lot of flak on the second PORT, which did not support the commonly accepted belief (supported at the time by NIMH) that the second-generation antipsychotics were superior to the first-generation drugs. The PORT under Tony stood its ground, though some at NIMH were upset.

His strength is in research, but from a strong clinical perspective, and unlike many academicians, he is able to explain the results of that research in plain English. "He is approachable, down to earth, and smart at the same time," says Lois Flaherty, who, as a child and adolescent psychiatrist, was impressed that he was interested in the whole developmental perspective— was early in recognizing that an illness like schizophrenia begins early in life and in appreciating the role child psychiatry could play.

"He was my second recruit, my protégé to some extent, and I think the world of him," says John Talbott, who after retiring as chair remained in the department. "Tony took what I was trying to do and just moved it along. He didn't change it—there was no revolution, no blowback—he just moved it along." By improving its clinical and basic research, the department has contributed significant new knowledge to improving care for patients with mental disorders and improving training for those who will treat them.

As chair of the department since 2000, Lehman has substantially strengthened the department's research mission while maintaining and strengthening its strong training and clinical programs. He has managed to more fully integrate the major centers of research excellence on schizophrenia and other severe mental illness, including the Maryland Psychiatric Research Center (MPRC), the VA Mental Illness Research Education and Clinical Center (MIRECC), and the Center for Mental Health Services Research. He has also added research priorities in mood and anxiety disorders, addictions, child and adolescent disorders, and geriatric disorders. He is an effective advocate for the resources and support needed from strategic partners, and is particularly attentive to nurturing new ideas and the aspirations of faculty, trainees, and partners.

"Tony Lehman has probably done more than any chair to increase the stature of the place," said Gene Brody, the department's second chair, before his death in 2010. This is true inside the university as well as outside. In 2002 Dean Wilson named Lehman chair of the dean's fiscal affairs advisory committee (FAAC), overseeing the finances of his peer-led departments, and early in his tenure as chair he was named president of the organization of the UMMC medical staff, where he has earned a reputation as a fair and objective leader.

He still attends on inpatient units, which gives him a clear understanding of the population the department serves, and he does two half-days a week of outpatient work in the community psychiatry clinic. "He doesn't need to do it, but he remains committed to caring for severely mentally ill patients," says Tony Bibbo, department administrator. "In both his dedication and his behavior with patients he is an ideal role model." With Lehman, who is beloved within the department, patients feel heard and staff and faculty feel their opinions and suggestions really matter.

"He is clear, honest, transparent (what you see is what you get), and genuinely committed to the enterprise," says David Pruitt, director of child psychiatry. "The department he runs is complex, and Dr. Lehman's ability to manage and lead that diversity is remarkable." Among his other strengths: he's curious, he's a scholar. He is important both for the work he does and for the role model he exemplifies. He doesn't need to travel or do a lot nationally to get his satisfaction."

"Tony, why do you do this?" Pruitt asked once, at a particularly difficult moment. Lehman responded, "I just want to see if I can help make it work."

(*continued from page 517*)

emotional, or behavioral issues. Those patients who become aggressive as the result of a head injury may be managed in the community or may end up in a nursing home, but those considered unmanageable or severe enough to be potentially dangerous often end up in a state hospital. More and more of the people serving in the military, in Iraq and Afghanistan, also end up with serious head trauma. Those who don't end up in the VA often end up in the state system. So the people who need care for acute psychosis often go to the community hospitals, which is what the state wants to happen, but there is a shortage of beds in Maryland, as in other states.

Many of the facilities at Springfield—where bulletin boards list educational and creative programs patients may participate in, and where patient quarters are surrounded by rolling green hills of countryside—reflect the original and best sense of asylum, where tincture of time is part of the treatment plan for some patients. In 1980 Springfield developed a special unit for deaf people with mental illness—the only one of its kind in the state. Public advocacy lawyers from the Maryland Disability Law Center had brought suit on behalf of a deaf patient at Spring Grove—the lead suit in a class action to have Maryland's public health program provide more adequate services for patients who are both deaf and mentally ill. The case was settled with a consent decree that required the MHA to develop specific services for the mentally ill deaf—including a special inpatient unit at Springfield.

The Maryland Plan depends upon champions to survive, and it still has them. Moreover, says Lehman, "the Maryland Plan is closely woven into the fabric of the department now. Our residents interface with the public mental health system at many places, including but not only the state hospitals."

What often happens, says Brian Hepburn, is that high-energy people introduce a change that ends when they leave, because it was personality based. With the Maryland Plan, those high-energy people, working with Walter, started the ball rolling, and to everyone's credit subsequent leaders, such as George Balis, were able to build on the huge steps they took. The changes were institutionalized, not personality based. As a result, right now, between the University of Maryland, Hopkins, Sheppard Pratt, and the state, Maryland's public mental health system is regarded as one of the best in the country, if not the best. Walter was the linchpin and had a major influence on a lot of what happened. People like Carpenter and Talbott were attracted to Maryland because of its commitment to the public mental health system, and they attracted Lehman, Goldman, Dixon, and others who brought about changes that made the public

What often happens, says Brian Hepburn, current MHA director, is that high-energy people introduce a change that ends when they leave, because it was personality based. With the Maryland Plan, those changes were institutionalized, and they attracted new generations to the system.

system in Maryland both strong and credible.

"Look at the progression," says Hepburn. "As late as the early eighties, the emphasis in the department was on finding good training cases, and residents became psychiatrists who worked with a less severely ill population. By the mid- to late eighties and the early nineties, there was a real commitment to the consumer. Rather than think of consumers as a way of training the residents, the university became focused on what it could do to prepare residents and the university to do a better job with people who needed treatment for severe mental illness. That years-long commitment has really helped Maryland, because its residents are used to treating this population, and for many it becomes a life commitment. That has influenced Johns Hopkins and Sheppard Pratt, as well. In the late seventies, when I started, Sheppard Pratt didn't take care of people in the public mental health system. Now, through Walter's influence, the joint Maryland–Sheppard Pratt training program, and the commitment of Steve Sharfstein, it's a major player. Steve takes great pride in the fact that Sheppard Pratt takes care of the severely mentally ill."

"Many of us had and still have a lot of passion for trying to make a public system more functional and responsive to the needs of the patients we were trying to care for," says Gary Nyman, who helped get the Maryland Plan off the ground. One thing everyone agrees about is this: the current partnership between the department of psychiatry and the Mental Hygiene Administration is probably one of the strongest state–university partnerships in the country. "Most states want to promote evidenced-based practice," says Lehman, "but Maryland, especially Brian Hepburn, the current director of the state's Mental Hygiene Administration,

The Maryland Plan at Springfield Hospital Center, June 2010. Left to right: Sandra Johnson, (supervising psychiatrist), Lorriann Tran (resident, PGY1), Adam Glushakow (resident, PGY4), Andrew Barbera (CAPP student), Sarah Lynam (CAPP), Diane Stabler (attending psychiatrist), Eitan Kimchi (resident, PGY1), Paramjit Agrawal (program director, acute services), Katherine Heizer (attending psychiatrist), Michael Delano (attending psychiatrist), Jonathan Book (clinical director).

has really invested to make it happen. He is committed to getting evidence-based medicine practiced in Maryland."

The state of Maryland created the Psychiatric Institute to provide state-of-the-art psychiatric training, care, and research. Later it provided support for the Maryland Plan, for the Maryland Psychiatric Research Center, and for much of the community psychiatry practiced in the department. "This state–university collaboration was not unique to Maryland, but it was unusual," says Tony Lehman. "Other academic institutions around the country have had such an affiliation, but most academic medical schools have not. If anything there may have been some retrenchment in that area. Other hospitals and programs refer us the patients most in need of acute care (inpatient and emergency patients). They know that we will not turn them away and will provide comprehensive acute care."

Notes

Chapter 1: The First Round of Biological Psychiatry

1 Truitt, p. 2.
2 Weintraub P (2009).

Chapter 2: Child Guidance and Maryland's Shame

1 Letter from Riva Novey, MD, to John Rafferty, director of child psychiatry, January 17, 1962, with a second letter to Eugene Brody, June 6, 1966.
2 Ibid.
3 Menninger and Nemiah, pp. 1–2.
4 Oldham and Riba, p. 55.
5 Menninger and Nemiah, pp. 74ff; Katz, p.364.
6 Klee G (1998).
7 Ibid.
8 Interviews with Irving Taylor and Jonathan Tuerk.
9 This brief early history draws on an excellent history at the Spring Grove website: www.springgrove.com/history/HistoryPics/1822map.html
10 Maryland State Department of Mental Hygiene (1955).
11 Ibid.

Chapter 3: The Finesinger Years

1 Gerry Klee's interview with Bill Fitzpatrick.
2 Interview with Nate Schnaper.
3 Wallace (1957).
4 Ibid.
5 Poland (2006).
6 Walter Weintraub (1999).
7 A bibliography of his research papers can be found at www.finesinger.com/Finesinger%20publications.htm
8 Wallace (1957).
9 Walter Weintraub (1999), his book *Verbal Behavior*, and interviews.
10 Many of Gene Brody's comments were made in interviews and e-mail exchanges in the three years before his death in March 2010.

Chapter 4: The Sixties

1 Menninger and Nemiah, in the introduction.
2 Kotowicz, p. 492.
3 Hoffman.
4 Wallerstein.
5 Hale.
6 Flaherty and Brooks.
7 Weinstein.
8 Adapted from Klee, "Teaching Psychoanalytic Psychotherapy."
9 Klee, Scholl, and Wing; interview with Gerry Klee; and Klee (2004).
10 Sharfstein.
11 Grob and Goldman.
12 Interview with Jon Book, July 22, 2009.
13 Profile of Jonas Rappeport based on interviews with Rappeport and others; plus, see Janofsky and Tellefsen.
14 Rappeport and Hertzberg; interviews with Rappeport and Klee.

15 Quoted in Lee and Shlain, *Acid Dreams*, on which I relied for parts of the story about LSD research at Spring Grove.
16 Sidel and Goldwyn, Table 1, p. 144, as cited by Brecher.
17 Lee and Shlain, p. 40.
18 Savage and Stolaroff.
19 Treaser, among many other sources.
20 Lee and Shlain, pp. 39ff.; also DeBold and Leaf, as reprinted in chapter 47 ("LSD and Psychotherapy") of Brecher.

Chapter 5: From CAPP to the Maryland Plan

1   I am paraphrasing and borrowing from Lois Flaherty's remarks at Jose Arana's memorial service, March 11, 1991.
2   Pitrof and Foxwell, and correspondence with Frank Calia.
3   Balis, Weintraub, and Mackie.
4   Note the titles in this six-volume textbook produced by members of the department: *The Psychiatric Foundation of Medicine*, edited by Balis, Wurmser, McDaniel, Grenell. Vol. I: *Dimensions of Behavior*; Vol. II: *The Behavioral and Social Sciences and the Practice of Medicine*; Vol. III: *Basic Psychopathology*; Vol. IV: *Clinical Psychopathology*; Vol. V: *Psychiatric Clinical Skills in Medical Practice*; Vol. VI: *Psychiatric Problems in Medical Practice*. (Boston and London: Butterworths Publishers, Inc., 1978).
5   Ozarin. See also www.aupn.org/i4a/pages /index.cfm?pageid=3286
6   The distinction here is between clinical work (caring for human patients) and basic research (done in labs or with animals).
7   Imboden's article, "Questions, Questions, and More Questions." This story appeared in Rappeport and Hertzberg.
8   Sources: NIH Almanac, Brody (1976), and interview with Léon Wurmser.
9   Kim.
10 Troccoli and Norris-Shortle; interviews with several people in the department.
11 *Diagnostic and Statistical Manual of Mental Disorders*.
12 www.infed.org/thinkers/et-rogers.htm
13 Blazer, p. 93; Torrud (2006); Hornstein, pp. 383–390, Klerman.
14 Oldham and Riba, pp. 65–66.
15 Gross, Herbert et al.
16 Barzansky and Gevitz.
17 Plaut was interviewed before he retired.
18 Interview with James Lynch.
19 Pitrof and Foxwell.
20 Source: www.umms.org/overview/index.htm
21 Pitrof and Foxwell, p. 126; www.umms.org /overview/index.htm
22 Meyer and McLaughlin.
23 This story of R Adams Cowley and the Shock Trauma Center is drawn from Taylor; copy on the Shock Trauma Center website, www.umm .edu/shocktrauma/history.htm; Franklin and Doelp; and interviews with Bernadine Faw, Herb Gross, Tom Krajewski, Michael Plaut, Ronald Taylor, Walter Weintraub, and Léon Wurmser.
24 Franklin and Doelp.
25 Herb Gross, interview.

Chapter 6: The Maryland Plan

1   Talbott (1979). "Why psychiatrists leave the public sector."
2   Weintraub, Hepburn, Strahan, and Plaut.
3   Cheeks, as quoted in McGuire.
4   Katz.
5   Alp Karahasan, quoted in McGuire.
6   Russell.
7   Weintraub et al. (1984).
8   Miller.
9   Weintraub et al. (1984) and Weintraub et al. (1994).
10 Russell (1983) and interviews with Gary Nyman, Walter Weintraub, and others.
11 Weintraub et al. (1994).
12 Russell (1983).
13 Hausman.
14 McGuire.
15 Russell.
16 Interviewed in 2007.
17 Russell.
18 Weintraub et al. (1984).
19 Hausman.
20 Russell.
21 McGuire story, plus interviews with Krajewski and Book.
22 Weintraub et al. (1984).
23 Russell (1983).
24 Miller.
25 Quoted in Miller.
26 Russell.
27 This paragraph draws from McGuire and Russell stories and interviews with Jon Book.
28 Ebeling; NASW Foundation.
29 McGuire.
30 Weintraub et al. (1984); Hausman; Miller; McGuire; and Christine Russell.
31 Miller (1983) and Weintraub et al. (1984), p. 93.
32 McGuire.
33 Quoted in McGuire.
34 Hausman.
35 Christine Russell story
36 Stan Weinstein interview.
37 Am J Psychiatry 1984.
38 McGuire.
39 Weintraub et al. (1994).
40 Klee (1999).
41 Weintraub et al. (1984).
42 Ibid.
43 Russell.
44 Katz, p. 374.

Chapter 7: The MPRC Becomes a Center for Schizophrenia Research

1 Called the Bowman Gray School of Medicine of Wake Forest University at the time.
2 George Vaillant, Norm Garmezy, and Joe Stephens and Christian Astrup, had published prognostic scales.
3 "Diminished glutamatergic neurotransmission in hippocampal glutamate-mediated efferent pathways, and cerebral dysfunction in the hippocampus and its target areas, particularly the anterior cingulate cortex, may underlie some of the clinical manifestations of schizophrenia." Quote from Tamminga.
4 Organ donation in Maryland is regulated under the guidelines of the Anatomical Gift Act, which governs both live organ donations for medical transplantation and gifts of tissue to be used in medical research. More information is available at www.mprc.umaryland.edu/mbc_faq.asp
5 Institutional review boards became part of standard operating procedures in 1974, when Congress established the National Commission for the Protection of Human Subjects of Biomedical and Behavioral Research. Four years later, this commission issued the Belmont Report, the cornerstone of ethical principles guiding federal regulations for the protection of human subjects.
6 Carpenter and Koenig.
7 Buchanan.
8 Ibid. Researchers in the Division of Services Research (Center North) are also addressing problems of medical co-morbidity with schizophrenia.
9 Gold et al.
11 Measurement and Treatment Research to Improve Cognition in Schizophrenia.
12 Buchanan.
13 NIMH (2004).

Chapter 8: Caring for Those Most in Need

1 Mulligan.
2 Sederer.
3 Goldman, Morrissey, and Ridgely.
4 Grob and Goldman, p 156.
5 Ibid., pp 151–53.
6 Dixon (2000); Grob and Goldman, pp 99–100 (who draw on many sources).
7 The Baltimore McKinney Program for the Homeless Mentally Ill (Center for Mental Health Services, SAMHSA).
8 Eisenberg.
9 Agency for Healthcare Research and Quality (AHRQ).
10 Dixon et al. (2004). The findings were subsequently replicated in a larger sample.
11 NIMH (2010).
12 In the National Child Traumatic Stress Network (www.nctsnet.org) academic and community-based service centers are collaborating to raise the standard of care and increase access to services for traumatized children and their families in this country. Authorized by Congress in 2000 through the Donald J. Cohen National Child Traumatic Stress Initiative, it is funded by SAMHSA and the U.S. Department of Health and Human Services. A description of Maryland's FITT model can be found at http://fittcenter.umaryland.edu/TheModel.aspx
13 There is more information on COMC at www.comc.umaryland.edu/about.aspx
14 Cooper and Friedman interview with Dr Liberman.
15 Available online from SOAR, at www.prainc.com/SOAR/training/manual.asp
16 "SSI/SSDI Outreach, Access, and Recovery." The SOAR website (www.prainc.com/soar/) says, "The SOAR technical assistance initiative provides strategic planning and training to increase access to Social Security disability benefits. These benefits can increase access to housing, treatment, and other supports."

Chapter 9: Changing Times

1 Starr.
2 Grob and Goldman.
3 Koyanagi and Goldman.
4 Grob and Goldman, p 151.
5 Schmidt v. Lessard, 414 U.S. 473 (1974).
6 Institute of Medicine (1990).
7 Results from the program were published in the journal Zero to Three (2006).
8 You can learn more online at medschool .umaryland.edu/innovations/default.asp
9 Sources: Lynne Lamberg's article (2007); Pitrof and Krieger's history of the medical school (2006); and interviews with Frank Calia, Dave Mallott, and John Talbott.
10 Source: American Board of Psychiatry and Neurology, Inc. (www.abpn.com/mission .htm). ABPN added "and adolescent" to "child psychiatry" in 1989, three years after The American Academy of Child Psychiatry became The American Academy of Child and Adolescent Psychiatry.
11 Luber, Lehman, Talbott, and Sharfstein (in press). Quotations not attributed specifically to one person are from this article.
12 Meyer and McLaughlin, p. 225.
13 Ibid.
14 Luber, Lehman, Talbott, and Sharfstein.
15 Sources: Interview with Brian Grady; the Winter/Spring 2009 issue of In *Psych*, the department of psychiatry newsletter, an issue devoted entirely to telepsychiatry; and American Telemedicine Association (2009).
16 Bellack (2003).
17 Dixon (2001).

Bibliography

I referred to some of the works listed here in the course of writing this history, but many of them are included simply to show some of the subjects that were researched over the years.

Agency for Healthcare Research and Quality (AHRQ). The Schizophrenia Patient Outcomes Research Team (PORT) Treatment Recommendations. Available at www.ahrq.gov/clinic/schzrec.htm (Specific treatment recommendations based on exhaustive reviews of the treatment outcomes literature were published in *Schizophrenia Bulletin*, 21(4), in 1995, focusing on "treatments for which there is substantial evidence of efficacy."

American Telemedicine Association (2009). Evidence-Based Practice for Telemental Health. July 2009. Available at www.americantelemed.org/files/public/standards/EvidenceBasedTelementalHealth_WithCover.pdf (Telemental Health Standards and Guidelines Working Group).

Arango C, Buchanan RW, Kirkpatrick B, Carpenter WT (2004). The deficit syndrome in schizophrenia: Implications for the treatment of negative symptoms. *Eur Psychiatry* 19:21–26.

Asylum Projects Forum. Available at www.asylumprojects.org/tiki-index.php

Ayd FJ (1955). Treatment of psychiatric patients with thorazine. *South Med J* 48(2)177–186.

Ayd FJ, Taylor I (1978). *Mood Disorders: The world's major public health problem*. Tenth annual Taylor Manor Hospital scientific symposium. Baltimore: Ayd Medical Communications.

Balis GU, editor-in-chief. Wurmser L, McDaniel EG, eds. Grenell RG, consulting ed. [in neuropsychology] (1978). *The Psychiatric Foundations of Medicine*. (Vol. I: Dimensions of Behavior; Vol. II: The Behavioral and Social Sciences and the Practice of Medicine; Vol. III: Basic Psychopathology; Vol. IV: Clinical Psychopathology; Vol. V: Psychiatric Clinical Skills in Medical Practice; Vol. VI: Psychiatric Problems in Medical Practice.) Boston and London: Butterworths Publishers. (A textbook for medical students and physicians.)

Balis GU, Donaldson JY (1983). *Treatment of the DSM-III Psychiatric Disorders*.

Balis GU, Weintraub W, Mackie J. A Four-Year Behavioral Science-Psychiatry Track in Undergraduate Medical Education. *Journal of Medication Education* 1974; 49:1051–1056.

Baltimore Sun (1952). [No byline] "U.M. Medical School to Open Its New Psychiatric Institute," November 7, 1952. Facsimile at: www.finesinger.com/um%20medical%20school%20open%20new%20institute.htm

Barzansky BM, Gevitz N (1992). *Beyond Flexner: Medical Education in the Twentieth Century*. New York: Greenwood Press; p. 119.

Bellack AS (2003). Issues and Strategies for Cognitive Remediation in Schizophrenia, presented for MIRECC conference on psychosis, April 13, 2003. Video (embedded (.ram) format) available at www.desertpacific.mirecc.va.gov/conferences/treatment-and-rehab/bellack/bellack.shtml (with video of lecture)

Bellack AS (2006). Scientific and consumer models of recovery in schizophrenia: Concordance, contrasts, and implications. *Schizophrenia Bulletin* 32:432–442.

Bellack AS, Bennett ME, Gearon JS, Brown CH, Yang Y (2006). A randomized clinical trial of a new behavioral treatment for drug abuse in people with severe and persistent mental illness. *Archives of General Psychiatry* 63:426–432.

Bellack AS, Green MF, Cook JA, et al. (2007). Assessment of community functioning in people with schizophrenia and other severe mental illnesses: A white paper based on an NIMH-sponsored workshop. *Schizophrenia Bulletin*; 33:805–822.

Bellack AS, Mueser KT, Gingerich S, Agresta J (2004). *Social skills training for schizophrenia: A step-by-step guide*. Second edition. New York: Guilford Press.

Bierman JS (2000). An addition to the history of child psychiatry at the University of Maryland over the past 50 years. *Maryland Psychiatrist* 27(2):4.

Blazer DG (2005). *The Age of Melancholy: "Major Depression" and Its Social Origins*. New York: Routledge.

Bramucci N, Medicine in Maryland, 1752–1920. [Online history] Available at http://mdhistoryonline.net/mdmedicine/index.cfm

Brecher EM, the Editors of *Consumer Reports* Magazine (1972). "LSD and Psychotherapy." Chapter 47 of *The Consumers Union Report on Licit and Illicit Drugs*. Schaffer Library of Drug Policy. Available at www.druglibrary.org/Schaffer /Library/studies/cu/CU47.html

Brody EB. "University of Maryland Psychiatry 1957–1977: A Personal Reminiscence." Read from typescript.

Brody EB (November 1976). "Maryland Psychiatry in the Context of a Personal Career," *Bulletin,* University of Maryland School of Medicine; 4–14.

Brown, AB, ed. "An Advocate Who Doesn't Give Up: A Profile of John A. Talbott, MD," for NARSAD.

Buchanan RW (2007). "Recent Developments in the Treatment of People with Schizophrenia." *Maryland Psychiatrist* 34(1):4,10–11. Available at www.mdpsych.org/archive/07F_Buchanan.htm

Capp T. "Recent cloudburst causes extensive flooding in Psych Institute," *UMAB Happenings* 1975; 4:42. [University of Maryland at Baltimore; July 22, 1975]

Carpenter WT (2005). A View to the Future. *Schizophrenia Bulletin* 31(1):3–4. [doi:10.1093/ schbul/sbi023] Available at schizophreniabulletin .oxfordjournals.org/cgi/content/full/31/1/3 (explains the relaunch of *Schizophrenia Bulletin* under MPRC).

Carpenter WT (2006). The schizophrenia paradigm: A hundred-year challenge. Editorial. *Journal of Nervous and Mental Disease* 194:639–643.

Carpenter WT, Arango C, Buchanan RW, Kirkpatrick B. Deficit psychopathology and a paradigm shift in schizophrenia research. *Biological Psychiatry* 46(3):352–360.

Carpenter WT, Heinrichs DW, Wagman AMI (1988). Deficit and non-deficit forms of schizophrenia: the concept. *American Journal of Psychiatry* 145:578–583.

Carpenter WT, Koenig JI (2008). The Evolution of Drug Development in Schizophrenia: Past Issues and Future Opportunities. *Neuropsychopharmacology* 33(9):2061–2079.

Carpenter WT, Koenig JI, Bilbe G, Bischoff S (2004). At issue: A model for academic/industry collaboration, *Schizophrenia Bulletin* 30(4):997–1004.

Cooper C, Friedman G. "Dr. Liberman and Psychosocial Rehabilitation." *Ability Magazine* (the "Donny Osmond issue"). Available at www.abilitymagazine.com/dr_liberman.html (interview with Robert P. Liberman).

DeBold RC, Leaf RC (1967). *LSD, Man and Society*. Middletown CT: Wesleyan University, 1967), 23–24; cited in Brecher EM, the editors of *Consumer Reports* (1972) (see entry above).

Derbyshire R, Brody E, Schleifer C (1963). Family structure of young adult Negro male mental patients: Preliminary observations from urban Baltimore, *Journal of Nervous and Mental Disease* 136(3):245–251.

Deutsch A (1948). *The Shame of the States*. New York: Harcourt, Brace. (Published originally as ~50 articles in the New York newspaper *PM* in 1946–47.

Dixon L (2000). Assertive Community treatment: Twenty-five years of gold. *Psychiatric Services* 51:759–765. Available at psychservices .psychiatryonline.org/cgi/content/full/51/6/759

Dixon L (2001). Anthony F. Lehman, M.D., M.S.P.H., appointed chair of the University of Maryland Department of Psychiatry. *Maryland Psychiatrist* 27(3):1,12.

Dixon L (2009). Is family to family education an evidence-based practice? PowerPoint presentation. Available as PDF at http://dhs.wisconsin.gov /MH_BCMH/docs/confandtraining/2009 /062509lisaDixon.pdf

Dixon L, Adams C, Lucksted A (2000). Update on Family *Psychoeducation* for Schizophrenia. *Schizophrenia Bulletin* 26(1):5–19.

Dixon L, Friedman N, Lehman AF (1993). Housing patterns of homeless mentally ill persons receiving assertive treatment services. *Hosp Community Psychiatry* 44:286–288.

Dixon L, Goldberg R, Iannone V, et al. (2009). Use of a Critical Time Intervention to Promote Continuity of Care After Psychiatric Inpatient Hospitalization. *Psychiatric Services* 2009; 60(4):451–458.

Dixon L, Kreyenbuhl J, Dickerson F, Donner T, et al. (2004). A Comparison of Type 2 Diabetes Outcomes Among Individuals With and Without Severe Mental Illnesses. Psychiatric Services 55:892–900.

Dixon L, Postrado L, Delahanty J, Fischer PJ, Lehman A. The association of medical comorbidity in schizophrenia with poor physical and mental health. *Journal of Nervous and Mental Disease* 187(8):496–502.

Dixon L, Stewart B, Burland J, Delahanty J, Lucksted A, Hoffman M (2001). Pilot Study of the Effectiveness of the Family-to-Family Education Program. *Psychiatric Services* 52:965–967.

Ebeling B. A Brief History of Springfield Hospital Center. Available at www.dhmh.state.md.us/springfield/history.html

Eisenberg J (1998). "Schizophrenia PORT Results Provide Evidence-Based Treatment Information."

Speech given March 24, 1998 at The National Press Club. Available at www.ahrq.gov/news/spschiz.htm

ESI (2001). Schizophrenia: An interview with Will Carpenter. ESI Special Topics, December 2001. *Essential Science Indicators.* Available at www.esi-topics.com/schizophrenia/interviews/dr-william-t-carpenter.html

Finesinger JE (1948). Psychiatric Interviewing: 1. Some principles and procedures in insight therapy. *American Journal of Psychiatry* 105:187–195. Available at http://ajp.psychiatryonline.org/cgi/reprint/105/3/187

Flaherty LT (1991). State-university collaboration in child and adolescent psychiatry. *Hospital and Community Psychiatry* 42(1):56–59.

Flaherty LT (1991). Remarks at memorial service for Dr. Jose Arana, March 11, 1991.

Flaherty LT, Brooks BA. "The Evolution of Training in Child and Adolescent Psychiatry."

Foley HA, Sharfstein SS (1983). *Madness and government: Who cares for the mentally ill?* American Psychiatric Press.

Fountain H (1997). "Joseph Nospitz, 74, Expert in Children's Behavior, Dies." *New York Times*, 9 Feb 1997. Available at www.nytimes.com/1997/02/09/us/joseph-noshpitz-74-expert-in-children-s-behavior-dies.html

Franklin J (1972). "Electric Storms Deep in Brain Studied by Researcher. *Baltimore Sun*, 3 Aug 1972. (About Russ Monroe)

Franklin J, Doelp A (1980). *Shock-Trauma.* St. Martin's Press.

Geller J (2000). The Last Half-Century of Psychiatric Services as Reflected in Psychiatric Services. *Psychiatric Services* 51:41–67.

Gold JM, Hahn B, Zhang WW, Robinson BM et al. (2010). Reduced capacity but spared precision and maintenance of working memory representations in schizophrenia. *Archives of General Psychiatry* 67(6):570–577.

Goldberg RW, Kreyenbuhl J, Medoff DR, Dickerson F,Wohlheiter K, Fang LJ, Brown C, Dixon L (2007). Quality of diabetes care among adults with serious mental illness. *Psychiatric Services* 58:536–543.

Goldberg RW, Lucksted A, McNary S, Gold JM, Dixon L, Lehman A. (2001). Correlates of long-term unemployment among inner-city adults with serious and persistent mental illness. *Psychiatric Services*, 52, 101–103.

Goldman HH, Buck JA, Thompson KS (2009). *Transforming Mental Health Services: Implementing the Federal Agenda for Change.* American Psychiatric Association.

Goldman HH, Lehman AF, Morrissey JP, et al. (1990). Design for the national evaluation of the Robert Wood Johnson Foundation program on chronic mental illness. *Hospital and Community Psychiatry* 41:1217–1221.

Goldman HH, Morrissey JP (1985). The alchemy of mental health policy: Homelessness and the fourth cycle of reform. *Am J Public Health* 75(7):727–731.

Goldman HH, Morrissey JP, Ridgely MS (1994). Evaluating the Program on Chronic Mental Illness (RWJ PCMI). *Milbank Quarterly* 72(1):37–48.

Goldman HH, Morrissey JP, Rosenheck RA, et al. (2002). Lessons from the Evaluation of the ACCESS Program. *Psychiatric Services* 53:967–9.

Goldman HH, Rye P, Sirovatka P, Satcher D (2000). *Mental Health: A Report of the Surgeon General.*

Grob GN, Goldman HH (2006). *The Dilemma of Federal Mental Health Policy: Radical Reform or Incremental Change?* Rutgers University Press, 2006.

Grof S. List of publications (many about LSD studies). Available at www.stanislavgrof.com/pdf/Publications_List.pdf

Grof S, Halifax J (1977). Chapter 2 of *The Human Encounter with Death.* New York: E.P. Dutton. Available at www.psychedelic-library.org/dying.htm

Gross HS, Herbert MR, Knatterud GL, Donner L (1969). The Effect of Race and Sex on the Variation of Diagnosis and Disposition in a Psychiatric Emergency Room. *Journal of Nervous and Mental Disease* 148(6):638–642.

Gould JE. Ethical considerations in medication-free research with schizophrenia patients: An expert interview with William T. Carpenter, Jr., MD. Posted 25 Oct 2006 on *Medscape Today.* Available at www.medscape.com/viewarticle/546243

Hale NG. "American Psychoanalysis Since World War II." Chapter 4 of Menninger and Nemiah 2000. Washington DC: American Psychiatric Press; 77–102.

Hansen E, Sundeen S (2006). The Mental Health Services Improvement Collaborative. *Maryland Psychiatrist* 33(1):10. Available at www.mdpsych.org/archive/06F_Hansen.htm

Harbin HT [Chair] (2003). Mental Health Interface with General Medicine. An Outline for the Draft Report of the Subcommittee on Mental Health Interface with General Medicine (of the President's New Freedom Commission on Mental Health). 8 Jan 2003. Available at www.mentalhealthcommission.gov/subcommittee/MHInterface_010803.doc

Harbin HT, Weintraub W, Nyman GW, Karahasan A, Book J, Krajewski T (1982). Psychiatric Manpower and Public Mental Health: Maryland's Experience. *Hospital and Community Psychiatry* 33(4):277–281. Correction published: *Community Psychiatry* 33:488, June 1982. (The first sentence under "Results" on p. 280 should have read, "From July 1976 through December 1981, 67 psychiatrists who had completed university residency programs were recruited into Maryland's public mental health system.")

Hausman, K (1984). Cooperation needed between universities, state institutions. *Psychiatric News* 19(13):1,26.

Highton R (1959). "Psychiatrist Named By County Court," *Baltimore Evening Sun*, Oct 1959. (About Jonas R. Rappeport being named court psychiatrist)

Hoffman BH (1966 or 1977 [illegible]). "Dialogue in Maryland." SK&F *Psychiatric Reporter*, pp. 21–23. (SK&F was Smith Kline & French, is now GlaxoSmithKline)

Hornstein GA. *To Redeem One Person Is to Redeem the World: The Life of Frieda Fromm-Reichmann.* New York: Free Press, 2000.

Institute of Medicine (1990). Broadening the Base of Treatment for Alcohol Problems. National Academies Press. Available at www.nap.edu/openbook.php?record_id=1341

Janofsky JS and Tellefsen C (2007). Jonas R. Rappeport, MD: Founding father of the American Academy of Psychiatry and the Law. [Biography] *Journal of the American Academy of Psychiatry and Law* 35(3):290–293. Available at www.jaapl.org/cgi/content/full/35/3/290

Katz P. "Conflicts of Culture in a State Mental Hospital System." Chapter 14 of Gaines Atwood, ed. Ethnopsychiatry. Albany, New York: SUNY, 1992; 355–377. (Cites John Romano's keynote address, 1977)

Kim WJ (2003). Child and Adolescent Psychiatry Workforce: A Critical Shortage and National Challenge. The American Academy of Child and Adolescent Psychiatry Task Force on Workforce Needs. *Academic Psychiatry*. 2003 Winter;27(4):277–282. Available at http://ap.psychiatryonline.org/cgi/reprint/27/4/277

Kinnaman J, Slade E, Bennett M, Bellack A (2007). Examination of contingency payments to dually-diagnosed patients in a multi-faceted behavioral treatment. *Addictive Behaviors* 32, 1480–1485.

Kirkpatrick B, Buchanan RW, Ross DE, Carpenter WT (2001). A separate disease within the syndrome of schizophrenia. *Archives of General Psychiatry* 58:165–171.

Klee GD. "How I Got Into Public Health Psychiatry," Available at letreb.com/how_i_got_into_public_health_psy.htm

Klee GD. Jacob (Jake) Ellis Finesinger, MD, (1902–1959). (Website) Available at www.finesinger.com/

Klee GD (1967). The Limits of Social Psychiatry (talk at the Mental Hygiene Seminar, Johns Hopkins School of Public Health, May 1, 1967).

Klee GD (1998). Riots and Mental Illness. *Maryland Psychiatrist* 25(1).

Klee GD (1998). Teaching Psychoanalytic Psychotherapy, Then and Now: An interview with Walter Weintraub MD. *Maryland Psychiatrist* 25(2).

Klee GD, Gorwitz K (1970). Effects of the Baltimore Riots on Psychiatric Hospital Admissions. *Mental Hygiene* 54(3).

Klee GD, Scholl A, Wing W (1961). Public Health Psychiatry, Psychiatric Home Care, Experience in the Western Health District of Baltimore. Paper presented at the World Federation For Mental Health International Congress, Paris, France. August 1961.

Klerman GL (1990). The psychiatric patient's right to effective treatment: implications of Osheroff v. Chestnut Lodge. Am J Psychiatry 147:409–418.

Kotowicz Z (2008). Review of Nick Crossley's *Contesting Psychiatry: Social Movements in Mental Health. Bulletin of the History of Medicine* 82(2):492–493.

Koyanagi C, Goldman HH (1991). The quiet success of the national plan for the chronically mentally ill. *Hospital and Community Psychiatry* 42:899–905. http://psychservices.psychiatryonline.org/cgi/content/abstract/42/9/899

Krajewski TF, Bell C (1992). A System for Patients' Rights Advocacy in State Psychiatric Inpatient Facilities in Maryland. *Hospital and Community Psychiatry* 43:127–131.

Kreyenbuhl J, Nossel IR, Dixon LB (2009). Disengagement From Mental Health Treatment Among Individuals With Schizophrenia and Strategies for Facilitating Connections to Care: A Review of the Literature. *Schizophrenia Bulletin* 35(4):696–703 [doi:10.1093/schbul/sbp046]

Kurland AA (1985). LSD in the supportive care of the terminally ill cancer patients. *Journal of Psychoactive Drugs*, 17(4):279–290.

Kurland AA, Pahnke WN, Unger S, Savage C (1971). "Psychedelic LSD Research." In: Psychotropic drugs in the year 2000. Evans W, Kline NS. Springfield, Illinois: Charles C. Thomas; 86–108. Available at www.erowid.org/references/refs_view.php?A=ShowDoc1&ID=5328

Kurland AA, Shaffer J, Unger S (1966). Psychedelic psychotherapy (LSD) in the treatment of alcoholism: an approach to a controlled study. *Excerpta Medica International Congress Series*, No. 129. *Proceedings of the Fifth International Congress of the Collegium Internationale Neuropsychopharmacologicum,* Washington DC.

Kurland AA, Unger S, Shaffer J, Savage C (1967). Psychedelic therapy utilizing LSD in the treatment of the alcoholic patient: A preliminary report. *American Journal of Psychiatry* 123(10):1202–1209.

Lamberg L (2007). University of Maryland School of Medicine: 200 Years for Nation's First Public Medical School. *JAMA* 297:25–27.

Lee MA, Shlain B (1985) *Acid Dreams: The Complete Social History of LSD: The CIA, the Sixties, and Beyond.* Grove Press.

Lehman AF (1987). Capitation payment and mental health care: a review of the opportunities and risks. *Hospital and Community Psychiatry* 38:31–38.

Lehman AF (1988). A quality of life interview for the chronically mentally Ill. *Evaluation and Program Planning* 11(1):51–62.

Lehman AF, Goldberg RW, Dixon LB et al. (2002). Improving employment outcomes for persons with severe mental illness. *Archives of General Psychiatry* 59:165–172.

Lehman AF, Goldman HH, Dixon LB, Churchill R (2004). Evidence-Based Mental Health Treatments and Services: Examples to Inform Public Policy. New York: Milbank Memorial Fund. Available at www.milbank.org/order_form.html

Lehman AF, Kreyenbuhl J, Buchanan RW, Dickerson FB, Dixon LB, Goldberg R, Green-Paden L, Tenhula WN, Boerescu D, Tek C, Sandson N, Steinwachs DM (2004). The schizophrenia patient outcomes research team (PORT): Updated treatment recommendations 2003, *Schizophrenia Bulletin* 30(2):193–217.

Lehman AF, Steinwachs DS, PORT investigators (1998). At issue: Translating research into practice: the Schizophrenia PORT Treatment Recommendations. *Schizophrenia Bulletin* 24:1–10.

Lehman AF, Steinwachs DS, PORT investigators (1998). Patterns of usual care for schizophrenia: initial results from the Schizophrenia Patient Outcomes Research Team client survey. *Schizophrenia Bulletin* 24:11–20.

Linkage. Newsletter of The Mental Hygiene Administration, The Maryland Department of Health and Mental Hygiene 1998–2002.

Lion J, Madden D, eds (1976). *Rage·Hate·Assault and Other Forms of Violence.* New York: Spectrum Publications (distributed by Halsted Press).

Luber MP, Lehman AF, Talbott JA, Sharfstein SS (in press, 2010). Enhancing Quality and Reducing Costs in a Combined Training Program: The University of Maryland/Sheppard Pratt Experience. *American Psychiatry* (read in manuscript).

Maisel AQ (May 6, 1946). "Bedlam 1946: Most U.S. Mental Hospitals Are a Shame and a Disgrace," *Life.* (*Reader's Digest* published a short version of this exposé, July 1946).

Mallott D (2000). The Talbott Years (1985–1999). *Maryland Psychiatrist* 27(2):1–14.

Maryland State Archives. Department of Health & Mental Hygiene, Historical Evolution. Available at www.msa.md.gov/msa/mdmanual/16dhmh/html/dhmhh.html (requires authorization)

Maryland State Department of Mental Hygiene (1955). Catalog.

Maryland State Department of Mental Hygiene (1964). Maryland's Emotionally Disturbed Children. Release Vol. 6, Issue 1.

Maryland State Lunacy Commission State Care Campaign 1908–1910, traveling exhibit. Images and text available at www.msa.md.gov/msa/speccol/sc5400/sc5492/html/almshouse_image_introduction.html and www.msa.md.gov/msa/speccol/sc5400/sc5492/html/traveling_gallery.htm

McGuire P (1982). "Young idealistic psychiatrists win acclaim for state hospitals," and sidebar, "Old treatment practices give way to new approaches. *Baltimore Sun,* December 19, 1982.

Menninger RW and Nemiah JC, eds. (2000). American Psychiatry After World War II (1944–1994). Washington DC: American Psychiatric Press, Inc.

Meyer RE, McLaughlin CJ. *Between Mind, Brain, and Managed Care.* Association of Academic Health Centers.

Miller RH. Turnabout in Md. State Hospital Employment ("Chief Residents Vie for Jobs"). *Clinical Psychiatry News* Vol 11, No. 9, September, 1983.

Monroe RR. (1970). *Episodic Behavioral Disorders: A Psychodynamic and Neurophysiological Analysis.* Harvard University Press.

Monroe RR. (1978). *Brain Dysfunction in Aggressive Criminals.* Lexington MA: Lexington Books.

Monroe RR. (1981) Letter to T. Albert Farmer, Chancellor, University of Maryland, October 14, October 19, 1981, accompanying annual report by Herbert Gross, as associate director of the Institute for Psychiatry and Human Behavior.

Monroe RR. (1992). *Creative Brainstorms: The Relationship Between Madness and Genius.* NY: Irvington Publishers.

Morrissey JP, Goldman HH, Klerman LV. *The Enduring Asylum: Cycles of Institutional Reform at Worcester State Hospital.* NY: Grune and Stratton, 1980.

Mulligan K (June 4, 2004). "Talbott Retires After 23 Years as Editor of APA Journal," *Psychiatric News* 39(1):1–49 Available at http://pn.psychiatryonline.org/content/39/11/1.2.full

Narvaez AA (1990). "John H. Talbott, 88, Medical Researcher, Teacher and Author," obituary in the *New York Times,* October 13, 1990. Available at www.nytimes.com/1990/10/13/obituaries/john-h-talbott-88-medical-researcher-teacher-and-author.html

NASW Foundation (2004). "Henrietta DeWitt." Available at www.naswfoundation.org/pioneers/d/dewitt.htm (National Association of Social Workers)

NIMH (2004). Report from MATRICS conference. Available at www.matrics.ucla.edu/meetings/sept-2004/conf6-transcript-part2.htm

NIMH (2010). Recovery After an Initial Schizophrenia Episode (RAISE): A research project of the NIMH. Available at www.nimh.nih.gov/health/topics/schizophrenia/raise/index.shtml

Norris-Shortle CA, Melle AH, Leviton A, Cosgrove K, Kiser L (2006). Wee Cuddle and Grow: A model for parent-child intervention. *Zero to Three* 26(4):49–55.

Norton HM (1949). "Maryland's Shame." Series that ran January 9–19, 1949, in *Baltimore Sun.* (I worked from a photocopy of the series in book form.)

Noshpitz JD, editor-in-chief. *Basic handbook of Child Psychiatry.* In 4 volumes. Basic Books, 1979.

Novey R (November 1993). "Remembering: Ephraim T. Lisansky, M.D." *Maryland Psychiatrist* 20(5):5.

Oldham JM, Riba MB, eds., *Review of Psychiatry* Vol. 13. American Psychiatric Press, 1994.

Ozarin L (August 2, 2002). "APA and ABPN: The Beginnings," *Psychiatric News* 37(15):16.

Ozarin L, McMillan G, *The American Psychiatric Association: Historical Highlights.*

Pahnke W, Kurland A, Unger S, Savage C, Grof S (1970). The experimental use of psychedelic (LSD) psychotherapy. *JAMA* 212, 1856–1863.

Pitrof L and Krieger MM (2006). *University of Maryland School of Medicine: The First Two Centuries (1807–2007).* Baltimore: Medical Alumni Association of the University of Maryland.

Poland WS. "Clinician's Corner." His column in *American Imago,* a journal founded by Hanns Sachs (Jake Finesinger's analyst in Vienna).

Poland WS. "Struggling to Hear." *American Imago* (Volume 63, Number 2, Summer 2006, pp. 223–226). (Johns Hopkins University Press)

President's New Freedom Commission on Mental Illness. The final report, released in 2003, can be found at www.mentalhealthcommission.gov/ The executive summary is posted at www.mentalhealthcommission.gov/reports/FinalReport/FullReport.htm

Rappeport JR, Hertzberg LJ (1999). The MPS at 50! *Maryland Psychiatrist* 26(3):1,16–18.

Regenold WT, Hisley KC, Obuchowski A, Lefkowitz DM, Marano C, Hauser P (2005). Relationship of white matter hyperintensities to cerebrospinal fluid glucose polyol pathway metabolites—a pilot study in treatment-resistant affective disorder patients. *Journal of Affective Disorders* 85(3):341–350. [PMID 15780705]

Regenold WT, Prasad M (2001). Uses of intravenous valproate in geriatric psychiatry. *American Journal of Geriatric Psychiatry* 9(3):306–308. [PMID 11481141]

Regenold WT, Thapar RK, Marano C, Gavirneni S, Kondapavuluru PV (2002). Increased prevalence of type 2 diabetes mellitus among psychiatric inpatients with bipolar I affective and schizoaffective disorders independent of psychotropic drug use. *Journal of Affective Disorders* 70(1):19–26.

Rosenfarb IS, Bellack AS, Aziz N (2006). Family interactions and the course of schizophrenia in African-American and white patients. *Journal of Abnormal Psychology* 115(1):112–120.

Russell C (1983). "Young Psychiatrists Revolutionize Maryland Institutions," *Washington Post*, Metro section. June 26, 1983.

Sargeant M (1983). The Maryland Plan, Revolution in Mental Health Care. 9:1. June 24, 1983.

Savage C, Stolaroff MJ (1965). Clarifying the confusion regarding LSD-25, *Journal of Nervous and Mental Disease*, 140(3):218–221.

Scalia RA (2008). "Harvard Doctor Delivers Final Lisansky Lecture," *Voice*, Summer 2008. Available at www.oea.umaryland.edu/communications /voice/2008/2008-Summer-VOICE.pdf

Schleifer C, Derbyshire B, Martin J (1968). Clinical change in jail-referred mental patients. *Archives of General Psychiatry*.

Schleifer C, Derbyshire B, Martin J, Brody E (1963). A long-term follow-up study of neurotic phobic patients in a psychiatric clinic. *Journal of Nervous and Mental Disease*.

Sewick B (1997). "The Use of Psychedelics in Treating the Terminally Ill." Chapter 3 of Sewick B. *Psychedelic-Assisted Psychotherapy for the Terminally Ill*. A thesis for his MA in psychology. Submitted to Roosevelt University in Chicago (May 1997). Available at www.maps.org/research/sewick.html

Sharfstein SS (2000). Whatever happened to community mental health? *Psychiatric Services* 51:616–620.

Shechet B. Tribute to Ephraim Lisansky (unpublished script).

Schnaper N (2003). *I Pay You to Listen, Not to Talk: A Psychiatrist's 50-Year Odyssey*. Baltimore: Publish America.

Schowalter JE (2000). Child and Adolescent Psychiatry Comes of Age, 1944–1994. Chapter 19 of Menninger and Nemiah (2000); 461–480.

Sederer LI. Mental Health policy and services five years after the President's Commission Report: An interview with Michael F. Hogan. *Psychiatric Services* 59:1242–1244, November 2008. Available at http://psychservices.psychiatryonline.org /cgi/content/full/59/11/1242 [doi: 10.1176/appi. ps.59.11.1242]

Sidel VW, Goldwyn RM (1967). Chemical weapons, what they are, what they do. *Scientist and Citizen*, 9 (August–September issue).

Smith J (1999–2000). Looking Forward While Remembering the Past: A history of public mental health services in Maryland. *Linkage* 9(4). Available at www.dhmh.state.md.us/mha /Miscellaneous/historicals/linkagewinter00.pdf

SOAR. A Case Manager's Manual for Assisting Adults Who Are Homeless, with Social Security Disability and Supplemental Security Income Applications. Available at www.prainc.com/SOAR/training/manual.asp

Spring Grove Hospital. "Hospital Rules on the Use of Seclusion and Restraint, Spring Grove Hospital, 1951. www.springgrove.com/1951restraint.html

Spring Grove Hospital Center. A History of Spring Grove. (Includes a history of treatment of the mentally ill in Maryland) Available at www.springgrove.com/history.html

Starr P (1982). *The Social Transformation of American Medicine*. NY: Basic Books.

Strauss JS, Carpenter WT (1978). The Prognosis of Schizophrenia: Rationale for a Multidimensional Concept. *Schizophrenia Bulletin* 4(1):56–67. Available at http://schizophreniabulletin .oxfordjournals.org/cgi/reprint/4/1/56.pdf

Strauss JS, Carpenter WT, Bartko JJ (1974). The diagnosis and understanding of schizophrenia. Part III. Speculations on the processes that underlie schizophrenic symptoms and signs. *Schizophrenia Bulletin* 11:61–69.

Swingle AB, Grauer NA (April 2004). "A Dream of a Deal." *Dome* 55(3). Available at www .hopkinsmedicine.org/dome/0404/centerpiece.cfm

Talbott JA. John Talbott's Paris. [Blog] Available at http://johntalbottsparis.typepad.com/

Talbott JA (1978). Report to the President for the President's Commission of Mental Health (Stock No 040-000-00390-8) Washington DC, U.S. Government Printing Office.

Talbott JA (1978). *The Death of the Asylum: A Critical Study of State Hospital Management, Services, and Care*. New York: Grune and Stratton.

Talbott JA (1979). Deinstitutionalization: Avoiding the disasters of the past. *Hospital and Community Psychiatry* 30:621–624.

Talbott JA (1979). Why psychiatrists leave the public sector. *Hospital and Community Psychiatry* 30:778–782, 1979 as synthesized in Weintraub, et al., The Maryland Plan.

Talbott JA (1980). *State Mental Hospitals: Problems and Prospects*. New York: Human Sciences.

Talbott JA, ed (1981). *The Chronic Mentally Ill: Treatment, Programs, Systems*. New York: Human Sciences Press.

Talbott JA, Hales RE, Keill SL (1992). Textbook of Administrative Psychiatry. Washington DC: American Psychiatric Press.

Talbott JA, Sharfstein SS (1986). A proposal for future funding of chronic and episodic mental illness. *Hospital and Community Psychiatry* 37:1126–1130.

Tamminga C (1999). Glutamatergic aspects of schizophrenia. *British Journal of Psychiatry Supplement* (37):12–15.

Taylor B (June 1978). Close encounters of the Cowley kind: An exclusive Journal interview with R Adams Cowley, MD, Director of the Maryland Institute for Emergency Medical Services, State of Maryland. *Maryland State Medical Journal* 27(6):35–49.

Tessler R, Goldman H (1982). *The Chronically Mentally Ill: Assessing Community Support Programs*.

Test MA. The Origins of ACT and Freeman J. ACT History and Origins. On website of the Assertive Community Treatment Association (ACTA). Available at www.actassociation.org/origins/

Thaker GK, Ross DE, Cassady SL, Adami H, LaPorte D, Medoff DR, Lahti A (1998). Smooth Pursuit

Eye Movements to Extraretinal Motion Signals: Deficits in Relatives of Patients with Schizophrenia. *Archives of General Psychiatry* 55:830–836.

Thompson JW (1993). "Remembering: Ephraim T. Lisansky, M.D.," *Maryland Psychiatrist* 20(5):6.

Thompson JW, Checker A, Witkin MJ, Silverman MM, Goldman HH (1983). The Decline of State Mental Hospitals as Training Sites for Psychiatric Residents. *American Journal of Psychiatry* 140:704–707.

Tiegel SA (1998). Intervention as brief family therapy. In: White RK, Wright DG, eds. *Addiction Intervention: Strategies to motivated treatment seeking behavior.* New York: The Halworth Press.

Time (1973). "The Rediscovery of Nature," special section, April 2, 1973, Available at www.time .com/time/magazine/article/0,9171,907075-1,00 .html (On Stanislav Grof's use of LSD with dying patients)

Time (1975). "Battered Psychiatrists," June 9, 1975 ("In a new study, Drs. Denis Madden, John Lion and Manoel Penna of the University of Maryland School of Medicine conclude that psychiatrists may have a definite tendency to stir violence in their patients.") Available at www.time.com/time /magazine/article/0,9171,913137,00.html

Torrud J (2006). Unpublished dissertation.

Treaser JB (1976). "C.I.A.'s Files on LSD Death Found to be Contradictory." *New York Times Magazine,* Jan 11, 1976.

Troccoli A, Norris-Shortle C. *As It was, Is, and Will Be. A History of the Taghi Modarressi Center for Infant Study: Secure Starts 1982 to 2008.* Informally published by the Division of Child and Adolescent Psychiatry.

Truitt RP (1960). *Fifty Years of Psychiatry.* Unpublished manuscript. Courtesy of Virginia Sherr Truitt.

University of Maryland Medical Center. "R Adams Cowley Shock Trauma Center: A tribute to R Adams Cowley, M.D." Available at www.umm.edu /shocktrauma/history.htm

University of Maryland Medical Center, Department of Psychiatry (2009, Winter/Spring). *InPsych* (the department's newsletter). Devoted to Telepsychiatry Now.

Varms SC (1984). Problems in state hospitals versus university training. *American Journal of Psychiatry* 139:1036–1039.

Veterans Affairs, U.S. Dept. of, Training Manual: History and Organization. Available at www .cdva.ca.gov/vetservice/DocsAndImages /TrainingManual/MODULE%201D%2012-06.pdf

Wallace W (1949). "New U. of M. Psychiatry Head Likes 'To Work With People' *Baltimore Morning Sun,* Sept 25, 1949.

Wallace W (1957). Teacher, Pupil Are "Equals" in a Novel Psychiatry Course. *Baltimore Sun,* Dec 7, 1957.

Wallerstein RS (1998). The IPA and the American Psychoanalytic Association: A Perspective On the Regional Association Agreement. *International Journal of Psychoanalysis* 79:553–564. Available at www.pep-web.org/document .php?id=IJP.079.0553A

Warthen J, Gorwitz K, Bahn A, Klee GD (April 1967). Schizophrenia in America. American Psychiatric Association Research Report, "Epidemiology and Mental Health Planning," Number 22.

Weinstein SE (1974). Preadmission to a Children's Residential Program, *Child Care Quarterly* 3(1).

Weintraub P (2009). "When the doctor gets sick, the journey is double-edged. Only the doctor who has been a patient can really understand." Three-part series on the *Psychology Today* Emerging Diseases blog, January 9, 2009. Available at www.psychologytoday.com/blog/emerging -diseases/200901/when-the-doctor-gets-sick-the -journey-is-double-edged-part-i

Weintraub W (1989). *Verbal Behavior in Everyday Life.* New York: Springer Publishing Company.

Weintraub W (1997). Inpatient Therapy: Then and Now. *Maryland Psychiatrist* 24(4).

Weintraub W (1997). Recent Changes in Inpatient Psychiatric Residency Training. *Maryland Psychiatrist* 24(3).

Weintraub W (1999). Psychiatric Residency Training in the V.A.: Then and Now. *Maryland Psychiatrist* 26(1).

Weintraub W, Balis GU, Donner L (1982). Tracking: An Answer to Psychiatry's Recruitment Problem? *American Journal of Psychiatry* 139: 1036–1089.

Weintraub W, Balis GU, MacKie J (1974). The Combined Accelerated Program in Psychiatry: A Progress Report. *American Journal of Psychiatry* 131:1213–1216 [doi: 10.1176/appi.ajp.131.11.1213]

Weintraub W, Harbin HT, Book J, Nyman GW, Karahasan A, Krajewski T, Regan BL (1984). The Maryland Plan for Recruiting Psychiatrists into Public Service. *American Journal of Psychiatry* 141:91–94.

Weintraub W, Hepburn B, Strahan S, Plaut SM (1994). Inspirational Recruitment and the Maryland Plan: Overcoming the Stigma of Public Psychiatry. *Hospital and Community Psychiatry* 45(5):456–460.

Weintraub W, Nyman G, Harbin H (1991). The Maryland Plan: The Rest of the Story. *Hospital and Community Psychiatry* 42:52–55.

Weintraub W, Plaut SM, Weintraub E (1996). Medical School Electives and Recruitment Into Psychiatry: A 20-Year Experience. *Academic Psychiatry* 20:220–225.

Weintraub W, Plaut SM, Weintraub P (1991). The Role of Medical School Electives in the Choice of Child Psychiatry as a Subspecialty. *Academic Psychiatry* 15:132–136.

White BV (1984), assisted by Wolfe RJ and Taylor E. Stanley Cobb, *A builder of the modern neurosciences.* Boston: Countway Library. (Distributed by the University of Virginia Press, Charlottesville) (Gerry Klee quotes a story therein about Finesinger's falling asleep and provides biographic material, pp 168–170.)

White RK, McDuff DR, Schwartz RP, Tiegel SA, Judge C (1996). New Developments in Employee Assistance Programs. *Psychiatric Services* 43:387–391.

Wurmser L (1978, republished 1995). *The Hidden Dimension,* Jason Aronson, 1978.

Wurmser L (1981). *The Mask of Shame.* Baltimore/ London: Johns Hopkins.

to 1910—and one story kept leading to another. Instead of interviewing twenty people I interviewed eighty and corresponded with twenty more. I knew narrative was central to psychiatry, but I never expected so much humor and good storytelling from a department that takes its work so seriously."

McNees is president of the Association of Personal Historians, co-editor of *My Words Are Gonna Linger: The Art of Personal History*, and editor of *Dying: A Book of Comfort*, among other works. She teaches legacy and life story writing at the Writer's Center in Bethesda.

About the author

Science writer Pat McNees was a book editor (Harper & Row and Fawcett) and a freelance journalist before she began helping people and organizations write their stories. A commissioned biography of a Midwestern industrialist (*An American Biography*) led her to personal history work—helping ordinary people tell their life stories. Her approach is to base a strong, frank narrative on extensive interviewing, far more than on documents. She has written interview-based histories of a lift truck company, of the Young Presidents' Organization, and of the NIH Clinical Center. *Building Ten at Fifty: A History of Clinical Research at the NIH Clinical Center* won several awards.

"This history grew like Topsy," says McNees "because I unexpectedly discovered an unpublished memoir dating back

About the artist

Linda Carmella Sibio, whose painting, *Screwed,* is reproduced on the cover, had her first psychotic break at sixteen and was diagnosed with schizophrenia when she was in college, studying art. Drawing on her research into schizophrenia and other mental disorders, and her experiences teaching techniques of experimental art to mentally disabled people on Skid Row, she created a way of making art that helped each person understand and objectify their schizophrenia. Her work is represented by the Andrew Edlin Gallery, New York, NY (www.edlingallery.com).

Credits

Screwed, the artwork on the cover, is a painting, 48 × 96 inches, gouache and sumi ink on paper, copyright Linda Carmella Sibio. Courtesy Linda Carmella Sibio, who is represented by the Andrew Edlin Gallery, New York (www.edlingallery .com).

Note: Ownership of old photos is almost impossible to trace. The publisher has done its best, in the spirit of fair use, to properly attribute credit for photos used. In many cases this consists only in extending kind thanks to the people who so generously lent family treasures or went to the trouble of scanning them. Where the copyright owner is known, that information is noted. Photographers wishing to be credited in any future printing of this book or on the publisher's website are invited to contact the publisher.

In the list that follows, many of the photos furnished by the department of psychiatry were originally printed in its *Bulletin* (covering the years 1966–73). Others are unpublished photographs from the department's files.

Chapter 1, The First Round of Biological Psychiatry: 2, 5, 8, courtesy Alexandra Truitt; 10, courtesy Virginia Truitt Sherr.

Chapter 2, Child Guidance and Maryland's Shame: 14, © 1949 *Baltimore Morning and Evening Sun*, courtesy of *Baltimore Sun*, reprinted by permission; 16, courtesy Historical and Special Collections, Health Sciences & Human Services Library, the University of Maryland School of Medicine (hereinafter "Historical and Special Collections"); 21, courtesy Joseph Robert Cowen; 25, 28, 30, © 1949 *Baltimore Morning and Evening Sun*, courtesy of *Baltimore Sun*, reprinted by permission; 35, courtesy L. Guy Chelton; 38, courtesy University of Maryland School of Medicine Alumni Association; 39, courtesy Irving and Bruce Taylor; 41, courtesy department of psychiatry.

Chapter 3, The Finesinger Years: 42, reprinted from *Terra Mariae Medicus*, © University of Maryland School of Medicine, used by permission; 44, courtesy Gerald Klee; 50, courtesy department of psychiatry; 51 top, courtesy Historical and Special Collections; bottom, courtesy department of psychiatry; 52–53, reprinted from *Terra Mariae Medicus*, © University of Maryland School of Medicine, used by permission; 55, courtesy Historical and Special Collections; 58, courtesy department of psychiatry; 59, courtesy Nate Schnaper; 60, courtesy Gerald Klee; 66, courtesy department of psychiatry; 67, courtesy department of psychiatry; 68, courtesy Jonas Rappeport; 71, courtesy Gerald Klee; 73, courtesy Historical and Special Collections; 76, courtesy department of psychiatry; 78, courtesy Historical and Special Collections; 79, reprinted from *Terra Mariae Medicus*, © University of Maryland School of Medicine, used by permission.

Chapter 4, The Sixties: 80, 84, reprinted from *Terra Mariae Medicus*, © University of Maryland School of Medicine, used by permission; 86, 88, courtesy University of Maryland School of Medicine; 89, 90, courtesy Clif Lamb; 93, courtesy department of psychiatry; 94, 95, courtesy Kenneth Stern; 97, reprinted from *Terra Mariae Medicus*, © University of Maryland School of Medicine, used by permission; 98, courtesy Historical and Special Collections; 99, courtesy Bob Derbyshire; 104–108, courtesy Julie Anne Brody; 114, courtesy department of psychiatry; 117, courtesy Ulku Ulgur; 119, courtesy Marcio V. Pinheiro; 123, courtesy Bernadine Faw Arnold; 133, courtesy Jonathan Tuerk; 136, courtesy Gerald Klee; 141, courtesy department of psychiatry; 146, © Caudill Rowlett Scott, reprinted from the department of psychiatry *Bulletin*; 147 courtesy Jonas Rappeport; 149, 150, from scrapbook Gene Brody left with department of psychiatry; 151, courtesy Jonas Rappeport; 155, top, reprinted from *Terra Mariae Medicus*, © University of Maryland School of Medicine, used by permission; bottom, courtesy Nelson Goldberg; 160, courtesy Bob Derbyshire; 168, provided by Susan Hood, extracted from 1978 photo of VA psychiatry staff, courtesy U.S. Department of Veterans Affairs; 171, courtesy Hannah Kurland; 175, reprinted from *Terra Mariae Medicus*, © University of Maryland School of Medicine, used by permission.

Chapter 5, From CAPP to the Carter Center: 176, courtesy department of psychiatry; 179, courtesy Ron Taylor; 180, courtesy department of psychiatry; 181, courtesy Gary Bawtinhimer; 183, courtesy Bruce Rounsaville; 185, courtesy Robin Hatcher; 187, courtesy James Gamble; 190, reprinted from *Terra Mariae Medicus*, © University of Maryland School of Medicine, used by permission; 197, courtesy Léon Wurmser; 200, courtesy department of psychiatry; 203, © Nick Felkey, all rights reserved, used by permission; 208, courtesy Taghi Modarressi Center

for Infant Study, Division of Child and Adolescent Psychiatry; 210, courtesy Taghi Modarressi Center for Infant Study, Division of Child and Adolescent Psychiatry; 211, reprinted from *Terra Mariae Medicus*, © University of Maryland School of Medicine, used by permission; 216, courtesy Marianne Felice; 218, courtesy Denis Madden; 219, courtesy John Lion; 223, courtesy the Photo Archives of Sufism Reoriented; 224, courtesy Russell R. Monroe Jr.; 227, courtesy department of psychiatry; 229, courtesy Bob Derbyshire and department of psychiatry; 234, courtesy Frank Calia; 238, 239, courtesy Mike Plaut; 243, courtesy George Gallahorn; 247, courtesy the W. Horsley Gantt Collection, Alan Mason Chesney Medical Archives, Johns Hopkins Medical Institutions; 248, courtesy Sebastian Arana and Brian Hastings; 250, courtesy photographer Eve Morra; 255, courtesy Herb Gross; 263, courtesy Anthony Lehman and department of psychiatry; 264, courtesy Nate Schnaper; 265, 271, courtesy Anthony Lehman and department of psychiatry.

Chapter 6, The Maryland Plan: 272, courtesy Springfield Hospital Center; 276, courtesy department of psychiatry; 278, 286, courtesy Jonathan Book; 288, courtesy Springfield Hospital Center; 290, courtesy Stan Weinstein; 295, 302, 308, 309, courtesy Jonathan Book; 311, courtesy Dave Helsel; 315, courtesy Jonathan Book; 316, courtesy John Talbott; 317, courtesy Stan Weinstein; 325, left, courtesy Springfield Hospital Center; right, courtesy department of psychiatry.

Chapter 7, The MPRC Becomes a Center for Schizophrenia Research: 326, by Vito Seskunas, © Maryland Psychiatric Research Center; 329, courtesy Maryland Psychiatric Research Center; 337, courtesy Ann Summerfelt; 342, courtesy Carol Tamminga; 343, courtesy Robert Schwarcz; 344, 356, 362, courtesy Maryland Psychiatric Research Center; 366, by Vito Seskunas, © Maryland Psychiatric Research Center; 367, courtesy Maryland Psychiatric Research Center.

Chapter 8, Caring for Those Most in Need: 368, courtesy Jill RachBeisel, Division of Community Psychiatry; 372, courtesy Vertell Porter-Brown; 373, courtesy John Talbott; 375, courtesy Howard Goldman; 380, courtesy Anthony Lehman; 386, courtesy Division of Services Research; 387, courtesy Division of Community Psychiatry; 396, courtesy Division of Services Research; 397, courtesy Stan Weinstein; 398, 403, 404, 407, 410, 411, courtesy Division of Services Research; 415, courtesy David Pruitt; 419, courtesy Division of Community Psychiatry; 430, courtesy John Talbott.

Chapter 9, Changing Times: 442, 451, courtesy department of psychiatry; 452, courtesy Stuart Keill; 457, courtesy Dick Sarles; 459, courtesy Henry Harbin; 466, © Bachrach, courtesy Lois Flaherty; 468, courtesy David Pruitt; 470, courtesy Mark Weist; 473, courtesy Robbie Muñoz-Millan; 474, 477, courtesy David Pruitt; 483, by Tom Jemski, © University of Maryland School of Medicine; 486, courtesy Vertell Porter-Brown; 489, courtesy Eric Weintraub; 492, courtesy Anthony Lehman; 494, courtesy John Talbott; 496, 497, courtesy Theodora Balis; 499, courtesy Phil Luber; 500, courtesy department of psychiatry; 502, courtesy U.S. Department of Veterans Affairs; 504, courtesy Brian Grady; 508, courtesy Alan Bellack; 510, courtesy Lisa Dixon; 517, courtesy Jonathan Book; 518, 520, courtesy Anthony Lehman; 524, courtesy State of Maryland Mental Hygiene Administration; 525, courtesy Springfield Hospital Center.

Index

Alcohol and drug abuse programs, 196–197
alcohol use disorders, 360, 361
alcoholism, decriminalization of, 133–134
Alexander, Franz, 55
Alpert, Richard (Baba Ram Dass), 168
alpha chloralose, 225
alpha wave feedback machines, 170n
Alzheimer, Alois, 9n
Alzheimer's disease, 9n, 363
AMA (American Medical Association), 23n, 279
AMA Council on Medical Education, Millis Report, 193n
American Academy of Child and Adolescent Psychiatry, 115n, 205
American Academy of Psychiatry and the Law, see AAPL
American Board of Medical Specialties, 114
American Board of Pediatrics, 203
American Board of Psychiatry and Neurology, see ABPN
American College of Neuropsychopharmacology, 40n, 74
American Journal of Psychiatry, 148, 282
American Journal of Psychotherapy, 135
American Medical Association, 23n, 279
American Orthopsychiatric Association, 17n
American Psychiatric Association, see APA
American Psychoanalytic Association, 103, 450n
American Society of Hispanic Psychiatrists, 249
"An Advocate Who Doesn't Give Up" (Brown), 431n
Anderson, A. Russell, 92, 124
Anderson, Dave, 331
Anderson, Ellen, 396
angels in the nursery, 477
Anthony, Bill, 424, 424n
Anthony, Bruno, 468n
Anthony, E. James, *210*, 211
Anthony, Laura Foster, 468n
"The Anthropologist Looks at Contemporary Behavior" (Mead), 54
anti-anxiety medications, 74

anticonvulsant medications, 235
antidepressants, 74, 235
anti-psychiatry sentiment, 83, 84, 185n
antipsychotic medications, 74, 120, 347, 350–351, 404, 521
anti-war protests and medical students, 154–155
APA (American Psychiatric Association)
    administrative psychiatry, 293–294
    administrator certification, 452
    and internship requirements, 193–194
    task force recommendations, 279–280
A.P.A. Mental Hospital Service Bulletin, see *Psychiatric Services*
aphasia, 5
Appelbaum, Paul, 372
Arana, Jose, *248*
    clinical director, Carter Center, 247, 308, 520
    death of, 385–386
    director of inpatient services, 243
    profile, 248–249
    volunteer faculty with CAPP, 192
    writings of, 249n
aripiprazole, 343, 350
Arnold, Bernadine Faw, see Faw (Arnold), Bernadine
Aronson, Harriet, 92
Assertive Community Treatment, see ACT
Association of Psychiatric Clinics for Children., 17
Asylum and Training School for the Feeble-Minded, 30n
Atkins, Bob, 301
attachment difficulties, 475, see also bonding and nurturing
attachment-focused therapeutic childcare program, 476
Ayd, Frank, 39, 40n, 41
Azcarate, Carlos, 92

B

Babigian, Haroutun, 519, 519n
Bacillus Calmette-Guérin (or Bacille Calmette-Guérin, BCG), 85n
Bagley, Charles, 59, *60*, *71*, 113, 123
Bahn, Anita, *136*

Bailey, Ann, 244n
Balis, George, *496*
    and CAPP, 192
    division of alcoholism and drug abuse, 196–197
    as "giving a damn" about medical students, 160
    on student rebels, 157n
    and teaching program, 449
Balis, Mrs. George, *497*
Balis, Theodora "Doris," *497*
Baltimore City Health Department, 135
Baltimore Mental Health Systems, 437n
Baltimore Sun
    editorial, 313
    "Maryland's Shame," 22–23, 24–32
Baltimore VA medical center, see VAMC
Baltimore VA's psychiatry service, 502
Baltimore Veterans Hospital at Loch Raven, 501, 502, 503
Baltimore–Washington Institute for Psychoanalysis, 46, 110–111
Baltimore–Washington Psychoanalytic Institute, 38, 110–111
Band, Raymond, 75, 77, 92
Bankhead, Judy, 92, 244n
Barbera, Andrew, *525*
Barksdale, Wardell, 249n
Barnes, Carl, 93
Baron, Steve, 397
Barrett, Dave, 502
Basic Handbook of Child Psychiatry, 115n
Battle, William, 114
Baumgardner, Barbara, 415–416
Bawtinhimer, Gary G., *181*, 181–182
Bay View Asylum, 4, 4n, 5, 7
BCG (Bacillus Calmette-Guérin or Bacille Calmette-Guérin), 85
A Beautiful Mind (Nasar), 363
Beck, Aaron, 231
Becker, Deborah, 388–389
behavioral modification, 231
behavioral pediatrics
    and child psychiatry compared, 202–205
    fellows, 204n
    fellowship, 204
    and Modarressi, 207–209

Green Spring Mental Health Care, 461–465
Greenberg, Joanne, 112
Greenhill, Maurice, 36, 48–49, *60*
Greenspan, Stanley, *210*
Greenwald, Phyllis, 310, 465n
Greifinger, Bob, 158, 158n
Grenell, Robert, 44, *60, 70, 71,* 103, 128
Griffin, Rosalind, 93
Griffiths, R.R., 173n
Grob, Gerald, 139, 385
Grof, Stanislav, 170, 172, 173n
Gross, Alfred, 92, 105
Gross, Herb, 158n
Gross, Herbert S., *255*
  as "giving a damn" about medical students, 160
  and security system, 244n
  turf wars, 269
  volunteer faculty with CAPP, 192
group therapy, 228
Gruenwald, Frances, 148
guilt vs. shame, 112n
Guttmacher, Manfred S., 18, 34n, 147, 148, *149*

H

HAART (highly active antiretroviral therapy), 407n, 408
Hackman, Ann, 423, 492
Hafiz, Nasreen, *295*
Haggerty, John J. (Jack), 157n
Haley, Jay, 228–230
Hall, G. Stanley,, 7n
hallucinogenic agents, abuse of, 169
haloperidol, 350
Ham, Thomas Hale, 54
Hamby, Page, 477
Hansen, Eileen, 395, *396,* 398
Haran, Judy, 204
Harbin, Henry, *316, 459*
  and Green Spring, 459–465
  and Maryland Plan, 211n, 283, 286, 294, 297, 315, *316, 318*
  and MHA funding cut, 396
  Donaldson Brown weekends, 162
  research on violence, 220
  state mental hygiene director, 316, 396, 427–459
  state training director, 211n, 283, 308
Harbor City Unlimited, 380, 428

Harrison, Kevin, 468n
Harrison-Restelli, Catherine, 487
Harry and Jeanette Weinberg Building, 457
Hartmann, Heinz, 72
Hartmann, Peter, 87
"Harvard Doctor Delivers Final Lisansky Lecture" (Scalia), 87n
Hastings, Brian, 249n, 421
Hastings, Eileen, 247n, 421, *442*
Hatcher, Elizabeth (Robin), 63, *185,* 185–186
Hauser, Peter, 502, 502n
HDME (Human Dimensions in Medical Education), 237–241
Head Start Therapeutic Nursery Program, 212–213
Health & Human Services (HHS) Medicare fraud investigation, 446
health care funding, 139–140
  state vs. federal role in, 447–448
health maintenance organizations (HMOs), 460–465
Health Resources and Services Administration (HRSA), 471
health services research, 378–379, 521
Healthcare for the Homeless, 387–388
Heinrichs, Doug, 339
Heisler, Alice, 87, 189n, 204
Heizer, Katherine, *525*
Helsel, Dave, *309,* 309–311
hemodialysis as treatment for schizophrenia, 339
Hensala, John, 64
hepatitis C, 406, 406n
Hepburn, Brian, 221, 296, 481, *497, 524*
  and CL, 487
  current director MHA, 316, 328, 481
  Donaldson Brown weekends, 162
  encouraging CAPP student, 491
  and evidence-based practice, 400
  geriatric psychiatry, 486
  and Maryland Plan, 328, 515
  and RAISE, 413–414
Herman, Rochelle, *286*
Herr, Steven, 417
Herron, Eileen, 249n

Hickman catheter, 77
The Hidden Dimension (Wurmser), 197
Hildreth, Art, 190
Hill, Bill, 115
Himelhoch, Seth, *407,* 407–408, 407n, 487
hippocampus, focus on, 345
HIV/AIDS, 402, 404, 406n, 407–408, 472, 486, 504, 509
HMOs (health maintenance organizations), 460–465
Hobbins, Tom, *239*
Hodgson, Mary, 249n
Hofmann, Albert, 166, 166n
Hogan, Michael F., 377
Hohman, Leslie, 37
Holden, William "Bill," 63, *71,* 185, 192
Holder, Lewis, 116
homeless people and mental illness, nine-city study on, 380–383
homelessness, 370–371
Hopkins–Maryland Center for Services Research, 390
Hornick, Richard, 85n
Hornstein, Gail, 110n
Horvitz-Lennon, Marcela, 491
Hospital and Community Psychiatry, 372, 431, 451, see also *Psychiatric Services*
House of Ruth, 416
HUD (U. S. Department of Housing and Urban Development), 381, 382n
Huffer, Virginia "Ginny," *58, 60*
  consultation liaison service, 75, 126, 487
  outpatient psychiatric services, 58
  The Sweetness of the Fig: Aboriginal Women in Transition, 126
  volunteer faculty with CAPP, 192
Hughes, Harry, *316*
Hughes, Ruth, 426
Hulfish, Barbara, 130, 232, *286*
human connection, importance to healing, 41n
Human Dimensions in Medical Education (HDME), 237–241
The Human Mind (Menninger), 21
human sexuality course, 156n